SPORT AND FESTIVAL
IN THE
ANCIENT GREEK
WORLD

edited by
David J. Phillips
and
David Pritchard

Contributors:
Ben Brown, Nigel B. Crowther, Kate da Costa,
John Davidson, Paul Donnelly, Kevin Fewster,
Sarah Kenderdine, Helmut Kyrieleis, Stephen G. Miller,
Cliff Ogleby, Patrick O'Sullivan, David J. Phillips,
David Pritchard, John Ristevski, Carol Scott,
Tom Stevenson, Ian C. Storey, Harold Tarrant
and Peter Wilson

The Classical Press of Wales

Hardback edition first published in 2003 by
The Classical Press of Wales
15 Rosehill Terrace, Swansea SA1 6JN
Tel: +44 (0)1792 458397
www.classicalpressofwales.co.uk

Distributor
Oxbow Books,
10 Hythe Bridge Street,
Oxford OX1 2EW
Tel: +44 (0)1865 241249
Fax: +44 (0)1865 794449

Distributor in the United States of America
The David Brown Book Co.
PO Box 511, Oakville, CT 06779
Tel: +1 (860) 945–9329
Fax: +1 (860) 945–9468

ISBN 978–1–905125–52–4

A catalogue record for this book is available from the British Library.

Typeset by Ernest Buckley
Printed and bound in the UK by Gomer Press, Llandysul, Ceredigion, Wales

---

*The Classical Press of Wales, an independent venture, was founded in 1993, initially to support the work
of classicists and ancient historians in Wales and their collaborators from further afield. More recently it has
published work initiated by scholars internationally. While retaining a special loyalty to Wales and the Celtic
countries, the Press welcomes scholarly contributions from all parts of the world.*

The symbol of the Press is the Red Kite. This bird, once widespread in Britain, was reduced by
1905 to some five individuals confined to a small area known as 'The Desert of Wales' – the
upper Tywi valley. Geneticists report that the stock was saved from terminal inbreeding by the
arrival of one stray female bird from Germany. After much careful protection, the Red Kite now
thrives – in Wales and beyond.

SPORT AND FESTIVAL IN THE ANCIENT GREEK WORLD

Dedicated to the memory of Kevin Lee

CONTENTS

Contents

INTRODUCTION

David J. Phillips and *David Pritchard**

I. From ancient Greece to the Antipodes: a convergence of sporting and cultural traditions: Sydney 2000

> Australia is an island
> And whoever sets sail to her
> Easy it is to cross
> Difficult to return.[1]
> *Castellorizian folk song*

In 1766 an Englishman, William Chandler, rediscovered the site of ancient Olympia.[2] At about the same time other Englishmen, John Callendar (1766–68) and Alexander Dalrymple (1767, 1769), were urging their fellow countrymen in print to push for the discovery of *Terra Australis*, with Dalrymple pronouncing that the economy of its inhabitants 'would be sufficient to maintain the power, dominion, and sovereignty of *Britain*, by employing all its manufactures and ships'.[3] *Terra Australis* had been the subject of speculation since antiquity when the astronomer, mathematician and geographer of the second century AD, Ptolemy of Alexandria, coined the designation for a projected land mass 'connecting the east coast of Africa with China and converting the Indian Ocean into a great lake'.[4] In the sixteenth century several European naval powers, eager for trade and resources, began the quest to map and claim the uncharted territories of the Southern Hemisphere. The Portuguese who may have mapped part of the southern continent as early as 1542 were quickly followed by the Spanish and the Dutch who made many landfalls on the west and north of the continent in the early decades of the seventeenth century. However, it was the British, who had begun to explore the Pacific in the 1760s, who were to succeed. In Captain James Cook they had found not only a brilliant navigator but one who demonstrated the qualities of '*dauntless* and *perseverant* resolution' which Dalrymple had stated would be necessary for such success.[5] On 19 April 1770 Cook and his crew first sighted the east coast

---

* David Phillips has been responsible for sections I and II and David Pritchard for sections III and IV.

of what was later to be called Australia, reaching Botany Bay on 29 April and claiming New South Wales for the crown on 22 August. It was to take another sixteen years before a decision was made by the British Parliament, on 19 August 1786, to establish a penal colony in this new crown territory. On 26 January 1788 Captain Arthur Philip, leader of the First Fleet and Governor of the new colony, raised the British flag at Sydney Cove on Port Jackson.[6] On that day began the European chapter of Australian history. Sydney, the future host of the Modern Games of the XXVIIth Olympiad, had been born. Olympia itself was not to see excavations begin until 1829 – less than two years after the combined British, Russian and French fleets, under the command of the British Admiral Sir Edward Codrington had defeated the Ottoman navy at Navarino Bay on 20 October 1827, thereby paving the way for the birth of the modern Greek nation.[7]

In its infancy the new Greek state was to turn repeatedly to the glories and culture of its classical past and in 1859 Athens witnessed the first revival of games patterned after those held at the ancient festival of Zeus at Olympia. Further Olympic-style games were to be held in 1870, 1875 and 1889.[8] It was in 1869–70 that excavations of the Panathenaic stadium were begun, with a fully restored stadium being constructed in time to be used for the staging of the first modern Olympics in 1896.[9] Even then the first international Olympic Games – the inspiration and drive for which are credited to the Frenchman Baron Pierre de Coubertin – were still largely a Greek affair with 230 of the 311 athletes being Greek as were the majority of the spectators.[10] Australia was represented by a single athlete, Edwin Flack, a former Melbourne Grammar schoolboy and student of classical Greek, who won the gold medal for both the 800 and 1500 metre footraces.[11]

With the return of the Modern Games of the XXVIIIth Olympiad to Athens in 2004, Greece and Australia will continue to share not only the distinction of being two of the few nations to have participated in all Olympics of the modern era but also the honour of hosting them twice.[12] Both nations also share rich and ancient cultural traditions and a common heritage established by over a century and a half of Greek immigration to Australia that has drawn the country within the folds of the Greek diaspora.[13] According to ancient tradition, the first Olympics were celebrated in 776 BC.[14] By this time Greek speakers had been settled in Greece for more than a thousand years, building upon and integrating with the earlier neolithic and bronze age cultures of Greece and the Aegean.[15] However, the earliest evidence for human occupation in Epirus, in the north-west of Greece, goes back to the middle palaeolithic period, that is, about 40,000 BC.[16] In Australia human settlement also dates back at least 40,000 years, with some evidence even suggesting human occupation as early as 50,000 years ago.[17] There have been remarkable continuities in the traditions and beliefs of the aboriginal peoples of Australia who managed, in some regions, to survive the European occupation. The richness and diversity of Aboriginal culture was celebrated during the opening ceremony of the Sydney 2000 Olympics and is now a matter of pride for Australians.[18] In the modern Olympic Games two ancient cultures replete with myth and tradition have come together.

As well as bringing together the ancient and diverse cultures of two nations, the Sydney 2000 Olympics also combined two important traditions in Australian life, one widely recognized, the other much less so. Australia identifies itself as a sporting nation – a nation which competes successfully not only in the Olympics but on the international stage in a diverse range of non-Olympic sports from cricket, tennis, rugby and golf to netball, squash, motor sports and surfing.[19] Less well known is the Classical Tradition which has played and continues to play a modest but important part in the educational and cultural life of Australia. When the University of Sydney, Australia's first institution of higher education, began teaching in 1852, it began with a solitary Faculty of Arts in which all students took Greek, Latin, mathematics and science for a three-year bachelor degree.[20] The first Professor of Classics, John Woolley, was also the first Principal of the University.[21] Since then the teaching of one or more of Greek, Latin, Classical Archaeology, Classical Civilization and Ancient History has had a presence in most of the universities established in Australia up to and including the 1960s. Indeed this decade of university expansion saw the creation of a Department of Classical Studies at Monash University in 1965 and of Ancient History, now a Department in its own right, within the Department of History at Macquarie University in 1967. The same decade also saw the establishment in 1965–6 of the Australian Society for Classical Studies (ASCS), which commenced publishing its annual journal, *Antichthon*, in 1967. Classical art and Greek have since been established at La Trobe University and 2003 sees the appointment of the first ancient historian in the School of History at the University of New South Wales. Although Latin and especially Greek are taken by relatively small numbers at secondary school level, the number of high school students studying Ancient History is substantial with the total taking it for the Higher School Certificate in New South Wales very close to surpassing the numbers of students taking Modern History.[22]

Another enduring link with the Classical Tradition is that of specialist museums devoted to the ancient cultures of the Mediterranean and in particular those of Greece, Rome and Egypt which have been established at universities throughout Australia.[23] The oldest is the Nicholson Museum at the University of Sydney, which was founded in 1860. Of more recent establishments the Museum of Ancient Cultures at Macquarie University, established in 1974, has established an innovative schools programme. This museum holds the most extensive collection of papyri in Australia and displays some of the extensive coin holdings of the Australian Centre for Ancient Numismatic Study (ACANS). The Centre was established in 1999 and is home to the Gale Collection of over two and a half thousand coins from the Greek cities of southern Italy and Republican and Imperial Rome.[24] These, along with other university-based collections of antiquities, have full- or part-time curators, managers or directors and many casual employees. They play a significant role in community outreach and as educational resources not only for university departments but also for school groups who gain exposure to the cultures of the ancient world through visits to such collections. Given that little attention is paid to the cultures of the ancient Mediterranean world in major public museums and art galleries of Australia, this role is vital to the dissemination of the knowledge of such cultures to a wider public.[25]

Apart from the Olympic Games that were celebrated from 15 September to 1 October 2000, Sydney was home to two official events of the Sydney Olympic Arts Festival which drew upon the traditions of ancient Greece. The first of these was the Powerhouse Museum exhibition *1000 Years of the Olympic Games: Treasures of Ancient Greece* that was made possible by the generous loan of important artefacts by the Greek Ministry of Culture.[26] The second was the performance of *Mythologia* – a major work choreographed by Australia's leading choreographer, Graeme Murphy, and performed by his internationally acclaimed Sydney Dance Company and the Sydney Gay and Lesbian Choir. The score was by the Australian composer Carl Vine. The work drew on the myths associated with Herakles as the traditional founder of the Olympic Games and other mythical figures with whom this famous athlete interacted.[27] The choir sang texts, in classical Greek, ranging from Sappho (fr. 31 LP) and the *Homeric Hymn to Zeus* (23) to the Olympian victory songs of Pindar and the *Bacchai* by Euripides.[28] They were translated for the programme by Suzanne MacAlister of the Department of Classics at the University of Sydney, who also played an important role in development of Carl Vine's score.

It was at Sancta Sophia College, also at the University of Sydney, that the conference 'Olympia and the Olympics: Festival and Identity in the Ancient World' was held from 6 to 9 July 2000 as part of the cultural lead-up to the Sydney 2000 Olympic Games. The conference served as the genesis for this book.[29]

II. Sport and festival in the ancient Greek world

Although the summer festival for Zeus at Olympia in Elis in the western Peloponnesos – which served as the inspiration for the modern Olympic Games and has attracted the majority of scholarly and popular interest – was the first and the greatest of the ancient Panhellenic festivals, it was but one of four such festivals with the others being the Pythia, the Isthmia and the Nemea.[30] These made up the *periodos* or four-yearly cycle of games that was settled upon at some time during the first three decades of the sixth century BC.[31] These 'big four' Panhellenic festivals were also known as the crown games (*stephanitai*) after the vegetative crowns which were awarded to the victors: at Olympia a crown of wild olive from the sacred grove of Zeus in the Altis, at Delphi for the Pythia a crown from the leaves of the laurel sacred to Apollo, at Corinth for the Isthmia in honour of Poseidon a crown of pine, and at Nemea in the games for Nemean Zeus a crown of wild celery.[32] To win the same event at all four *stephanitai* was to earn the title of *periodonikēs*.[33] With the growth of Athenian power, during the fifth century BC, an unofficial 'fifth' Panhellenic agonistic festival could be said to have been added to the *periodos*: the Great Panathenaia at Athens (see TABLE 1 below).[34] Religious festivals, with or without *agōnes*, were characteristic of the *polis* (city-state) throughout the Greek world and were an integral and defining part of its public life.[35] In essence, a festival, for which the Greeks had several different terms, was a sequence of ritual acts which usually included a *pompē* (procession), prayers, libations, the singing of hymns and an animal sacrifice that was followed by the sharing

TABLE 1. The Four Panhellenic Agonistic Festivals + One[36]

Festival	*Location*	*Deity*	*Date*	*Frequency*
OLYMPIA	Olympia (Elis)	Olympian Zeus	776 BC (traditional foundation date)	Every four years in mid-summer (July–August)
PYTHIA	Delphi	Apollo Pythios	582 BC (re-organization)	Third year of each Olympiad in late summer (August–September)
ISTHMIA	Corinth	Poseidon	582–70 BC (re-organization)	Every second year of each Olympiad in spring (April–May *or* June–July)
NEMEA	Nemea	Nemean Zeus	573 BC (traditional foundation date)	Every second year of each Olympiad in late summer (September)
THE GREAT PANATHENAIA	Athens	Athena	566/5 BC (foundation date)	Third year of each Olympiad in summer (June–July)

and eating of food.[37] Festivals could take anything from a part or whole of a day to two or more days and some, perhaps many, also had *agōnes* or contests for prizes.[38]

The *agōn* or contest was a fundamental feature of Greek society and its social relations and was manifested not only in the multiplicity of *agōnes* linked with festivals but also in warfare, politics, law and oratory. It was also characteristic of the behaviour of the Greek gods and heroes.[39] At Athens it was to be seen in the assembly, lawcourts, dramatic competitions and even in the Athenian fondness for cockfighting, with a pair of fighting cocks serving as a symbol for *agōn* itself.[40] While having a number of local peculiarities, Spartan culture too was agonistic, as Stephen Hodkinson has recently demonstrated.[41] Greek festival *agōnes* included not just what we might today call sport – however that term is to be defined.[42] In addition to athletics (running, jumping and throwing the discus and the javelin), equestrian events (horse and especially chariot racing) and combat sports, such as boxing, wrestling and the 'no holds barred' *pankration*, there could also be contests in music; choral singing and dancing; poetry, including recitations of Homeric verse by trained rhapsodes; drama; painting (at the Isthmia) and even male 'beauty' contests like the *euandria* and the *euexia*.[43] However, one event, the marathon, which has been a feature of the modern Olympics since their inception in 1896, was never a part of any ancient agonistic festival, although trained long-distance runners, called *hēmerodromoi* or day-runners, who served as messengers, are well attested.[44] Nor is it likely that the first marathon was run by Pheidippides (or Philippides) who, according to tradition, died happily as he uttered the words, 'Be happy! We have won!', after running back from Marathon to Athens to report the Athenian victory over the Persians in 490 BC.[45] In the days before the battle he had actually run about two hundred and twenty kilometres to Sparta to request help in the defence against the Persians who had reached Eretria on the nearby island of Euboea. When help was not immediately forthcoming, he ran the same distance back to Athens (Herodotus 6.105–6).

Athletics or track and field events, which have remained the core of the modern Olympics, take their name from the ancient Greek term *athlos* meaning effort, contest, struggle or deed, and were, from the first Olympic Games, a central feature of festival *agōnes*.[46] Just as the key athletic events today are the men's and women's 100, 200 and 400 metre sprints, so at the ancient festivals the key event was the men's *stadion*: a sprint covering the length of the *stadion* or stadium. At Olympia the *stadion* was 192 m in length, those at Nemea and Delphi were around 178 m.[47] It was not the time taken or the distance thrown that was important, for the Greeks took little interest in such sporting records, it was winning that mattered and it was the victory that was recorded and remembered.[48] The winner of the *stadion* at Olympia, amongst other honours, became the *Olympionikos*: the victor by whose name the Olympiad would be known in perpetuity. Thus we read, for example, in Diodorus of Sicily (13.41.1) of '…the ninety-second Olympiad [in 412 BC] in which Exainetos of Akragas won the *stadion*'. Diodorus (13.82.7) also gives us some indication of the honours accorded Exainetos when he returned to his home city: '…he was conducted into the city in a chariot and in the procession there were, not to speak of other things, three-hundred chariots, each drawn by two white horses, all the chariots belonging to the citizens of Akragas'. But these were not the only honours and rewards that a victor in the *stephanitai* might expect to receive. At Athens, in a decree of the 430s BC, we read that 'for as many as have won at Olympia or Delphi or Isthmia or Nemea or may win hereafter, shall receive *sitēsis* (meals) in the Prytaneion and the other gifts in addition to *sitēsis*…' (*IG* I³ 131.11–18).[49] The decree continues to outline the same privilege of *sitēsis* for victors in the chariot race or the *kelēs* (horse race) at the same festivals. Other honours could include the setting up of statues with victory epigrams at either the sanctuary in which the victory was won or in the victor's home city and the commissioning of *epinikia* or victory songs.[50] The most complete set of *epinikia* are the Olympian, Pythian, Nemean and Isthmian odes of the Theban poet Pindar (518–438 BC).[51] It is through these and other *epinikia* by Bacchylides and Simonides that many of the aetiological and other myths associated with agonistic festivals have been transmitted.[52] Victors also frequently dedicated prizes, tripods, gold crowns, statues, figurines and items of athletic equipment, such as the discus, as thank offerings to the gods.[53] A victor might in some instances be heroized and so become the recipient of religious cult.[54] All of these *agōnes* and their associated activities and honours were almost exclusively for men and boys. Our evidence for the participation of women and girls in festival *agōnes* is very limited and has attracted relatively little scholarly attention.[55]

Greek festivals have received increasing scholarly attention over the past few decades, with an important theme of research being the roles of festivals in the formation of the Greek *polis* and the development and articulation of *polis* identity. Agonistic festivals in particular were an integral part of the *polis*, its discourses and its social relations, and Panhellenic festivals were fundamental to the notion of 'Greekness' – an identity based especially upon language and religion.[56] Although our extant literary and epigraphical evidence abounds with references to, and details about, Greek festivals, one passage in particular highlights the centrality of festival to *polis* identity and the reinforcement of community. Its context is the violent *stasis* (civil war or strife) between the democrats and oligarchs during the reign of the so-called Thirty Tyrants at Athens in 404 and 403 BC. Kleokritos, the herald of the famous Mysteries for Demeter and Persephone at Eleusis in Attica, is addressing the supporters of the Thirty Tyrants after a battle between their supporters and the democrats in the Piraeus:

> Fellow citizens, why are you driving us out of the city? Why do you want to kill us? We have never done you any harm. We have shared with you in the most holy religious services, in sacrifices and in splendid festivals (*heortai*); we have joined in dances with you, gone to school with you and fought in the army with you, braving together with you the dangers of land and sea in defence of our common safety and freedom. In the name of the gods of our fathers and mothers, of the bonds of kinship and marriage and friendship, which are shared by so many of us on both sides, I beg you to feel some shame in front of the gods and men and to give up this sin against your fatherland
>   (Xenophon *Hellenica* 2.4.20–1; transl. Warner).

Another revealing event from the period soon after the restoration of the democracy at Athens in 403 BC was the decision to build the Pompeion or assembly hall for the marshalling of festival processions (*pompai*) and in particular for the Panathenaia. Constructed just within the city walls between the Sacred and Dipylon gates in the north-west of the city, it was one of the first public buildings undertaken by the restored democracy and it demonstrates that reconciliation and community rebuilding through festival were major priorities for a *polis* which had just been through the destructive and disruptive experience of not only a prolonged war in which it had suffered defeat but also of nearly a decade of political turmoil at home in which the very survival of the democracy was at stake.[57]

III. *The Sydney Olympics book*

This edited book is a scholarly commemoration of the Sydney 2000 Olympic Games. Most of its chapters began as papers at the conference 'Olympia and the Olympics: Festival and Identity in the Ancient World' that was held in Sydney from 6 to 9 July 2000 in the lead-up to the city's hosting of the Modern Games of the XXVIIth Olympiad. The conference was conceived and convened by David Phillips and the late Kevin Lee and hosted by Macquarie University and the University of Sydney. Its chief aims were to explore the Graeco-Roman traditions behind the Olympic Movement and to reinforce the importance of the study of antiquity for understanding the modern world. The conference brought together scholars from Australia, New Zealand, North America and Europe and had as its keynote speaker Mark Golden of the University of Winnipeg.[58] The chapters by Stephen Miller, Helmut Kyrieleis, Nigel Crowther, Harold

Tarrant, Paul Donnelly and Kevin Fewster, and Carol Scott were commissioned after the conference to fill out the book's treatment of key topics and themes.

This book explores in detail the cultural, religious, political and social import of sport and festival in the Greek world of the archaic and classical periods. It investigates how athletics bore out and reinforced central aspects of ancient Greek culture such as *aretē* (manly excellence and bravery) and *agōn* (publicly adjudicated contest) and ideals like male beauty. The book also studies how the Greek *polis* (city-state) staged religious festivals not just to ensure the *kharis* (gratitude) of its city-protecting deities and heroes, but also as a way to articulate and broadcast civic ideology and the communal identity of its citizens and as a means to legitimate its political institutions and social structures. In particular it reveals how festivals and sporting and musical *agōnes* led the way, throughout the archaic period, in the crystallization and development of the *polis* and in the creation of its juridical and political practices. The book itself bears witness to the mainly positive relationship between the Olympic Movement and scholarship whereby successive games of the modern era have served as impetuses for research, exhibitions and publications on the ancient Olympics.[59] Yet it also illustrates how the changing agendas of the Olympic Movement have moulded and, at times, compromised historiography on ancient Greek sport and how research on the ancient Olympic Games has in the past been motivated by questionable political interests. The book contributes as well to important debates and practices of the New Museology.

Part I of the book focuses on Olympia and the Olympics. Stephen Miller gives a richly illustrated and well-documented reconstruction of the sporting and religious events of the Olympics of 300 BC, and considers the preparations that took place before the Games and the religious and political personnel responsible for their organization (ch. 1). Helmut Kyrieleis outlines the major phases and discoveries of the German excavations at Olympia, over the last century and a quarter, and the leading role these excavations have played in the development of Classical Archaeology and in the writing of the history of early Greek art (ch. 2). Nigel Crowther demonstrates that, in spite of their Panhellenic status, the Olympic Games were actually controlled by the local city-state of Elis which used this festival to consolidate its political institutions and regional standing and the sanctuary of Olympia as its main religious and civic centre (ch. 3).

Part II considers the poems athletes commissioned to broadcast their victories and mythology closely linked with the site of the ancient Olympics. Patrick O'Sullivan explains that Pindar belittled sculpture, the medium rivalling his sung poetry for commemorating athletic victory, by characterizing it as lifeless and static and his own victory songs as dynamic and analogous to the body of the athlete (ch. 4). O'Sullivan also illustrates how this poetical polemic reappears, outside athletics, in the writings of the new intellectuals and philosophers who likewise employed it to build up, at the expense of their rivals, the specific verbal medium or discipline they were marketing. John Davidson considers how the myth of Pelops and his winning of a bride in a chariot-race at Olympia was rendered in different literary and artistic contexts, and the ways in which its protagonists became linked with the sporting and religious structures of Olympia itself (ch. 5). He also explores how the different contexts in which the myth was rehearsed affected its treatment and development.

Part III concerns the origins of athletic and musical competitions. Ben Brown demonstrates that the sporting contests honouring the dead hero Patroklos in book 23 of Homer's *Iliad* constitute a resolution of the intra-elite crisis beginning in book 1 and are, along with the historically attested funerary games of the archaic period, the first manifestation of the evaluative practices and modes of thought of the archaic city (ch. 6). Peter Wilson suggests that dithyrambs were originally performed by choruses as an attempt to harness the religious power of Dionysos to combat *stasis* (civil war or strife) and that dithyrambic competitions were introduced to foster the solidarity of the civic community and to underwrite political reforms and structures.

Part IV studies Athens and its festivals. David Phillips turns our attention to correlations between milestones in the political history of sixth- and fifth-century Athens and celebrations of the Great Panathenaia (ch. 8). Phillips illustrates how an appreciation of festival context enriches our understanding of political events and how aspects of festivals were drawn upon to support the city and its institutions during times of military or political crisis. Tom Stevenson argues on the basis of detailed analysis that the Parthenon frieze represents an idealized celebration of the Great Panathenaia during the mid-fifth century (ch. 9). Ian Storey illustrates how the dismissive comments the poets of old comedy made about the plays of rivals in a dramatic competition constitute important clues for the programmes of specific dramatic festivals and the plots of non-extant plays (ch. 10).

Part V investigates the interconnections between athletics, education and philosophy in classical Athens. David Pritchard shows how classical Athenian athletics consisted of two closely integrated activities: competitions at festivals and the traditional classes of the athletics teacher (ch. 11). Pritchard also argues that these school classes provided the only opportunity for technical instruction in the standard events of track and field and that athletics remained, even in the most prosperous and demo-cratic city of classical Greece, an exclusive pursuit of the elite. Harold Tarrant explains that while new intellectuals and philosophers commended physical education and competition, they appropriated the language and values of athletics in the course of developing and promoting their own new disciplines (ch. 12).

Part VI discusses the Powerhouse Museum exhibition *1000 Years of the Olympic Games: Treasures of Ancient Greece*, which was an official event in the Sydney 2000 Olympic Arts Festival. Paul Donnelly and Kevin Fewster outline the negotiations and cultural considerations behind the Greek government's loan of a substantial collection of antiquities to the Museum and the curatorial and design decisions taken concerning their exhibition in an institution otherwise known for its showcasing of new technology, science and design (ch. 13). Kate da Costa, Sarah Kenderdine, Cliff Ogleby and John Ristevski detail the academic and technical challenges of making a three-dimensional digital model of ancient Olympia and an animated three-dimensional tour of the site based on the model and shown at the exhibition (ch. 14). Finally, Carol Scott analyses the audience evaluation of the exhibition and how it raises interesting questions for further research about the potential of museums to stimulate new learning (ch. 15).

IV. Acknowledgements

David Phillips came up with the idea to publish a work of classical studies as a more permanent legacy to the Sydney Olympics. He made the original approach to the Classical Press of Wales and gave scholarly and administra-tive advice throughout the production of the book. David Pritchard was employed as a research fellow by Macquarie University to co-edit the book and manage the Sydney Olympics Book Project and was responsible for bringing the book to fruition. He commissioned the extra chapters in the book, wrote the editorial reports on and edited each chapter, facilitated the applications for university grants and organized the other grants, donations and contributions needed to finalize the book. The editors together worked out the book's key themes and the final selection of chapters and were each responsible for two sections of the Introduction.

The publication of the book was greatly helped by the acuity of its anonymous referees and the careful and timely revisions its contribu-tors made to their chapters. Invaluable advice on academic and technical matters came from Mark Golden and Anton Powell, the general editor of the Classical Press of Wales. Three colleagues at Macquarie University should be singled out for their help: Ian Plant, who did much to ensure the smooth running of the conference and gave important scholarly advice on the book; Suzanne Binder, who translated the chapter of Helmut Kyrieleis; and Beth Lewis, who retyped all of the book's Greek.

The editors are grateful for two research grants that Macquarie University gave David Phillips for the Sydney Olympics Book Project. They are indicative of the University's unfaltering support, since its inception in 1967, of Ancient History. They are also indebted to the Department of Ancient History for its critical backing of the project. Many thanks are due to the International Olympic Committee for a generous grant from IOC Solidarity and to the Australian Olympic Committee for helping to secure this support. Critically important for finalizing the book were the donations and contributions of patriotic Greek-Australians and Sydney-siders who recognized its value as scholarship on ancient Greece and for the Olympic Movement. For their extraordinary support the editors would like to express their gratitude and sincere thanks to the following individuals and organizations: the Nicholas Anthony Aroney Trust; the Hellenic Club (Sydney), Chris Photakis and Nick Politis; Levendi Jewellers; Bank of Cyprus Australia, Brentnallsnsw Chartered Accountants, Angelo and Despina Hatsatouris, Laiki Bank (Australia), the National Bank of Greece (Australia), the Pan-Arcadian Association of N.S.W., Peters Crompton Worrall Solicitors and Tri-Anta Pty Ltd; and the Cyprus Hellene Club and Graeme H. Hill and Associates Chartered Accountants. The editors would also like to thank Manuel Aroney and Evangelos Damianakis, Consul General of Greece, for their advocacy in support of the Sydney Olympics Book Project. Final thanks go to the Faculty of Arts at the University of Sydney for a grant and the Australian Society of Classical Studies for a loan that enabled the organization of the Sydney Olympics conference.

There are several groups of people and individuals whom David Phillips personally wishes to thank for support and assistance through a two and a half year period that has seen him hampered by chronic illness and pain. Firstly, and most importantly, his wife, Fleur, his children, Stephen, Matthew, Meaghan and Jenny, and his parents, Joan and Lloyd, who together make up an extended family that has given love and support to each other for the past ten years at 6 and 6a Howard Avenue. Secondly his thanks go to his colleagues in the Department of Ancient History who have stepped in at short notice to cover teaching or have assumed many of his former administrative duties. In particular his thanks go to Alanna Nobbs who, as Head of Department, has insisted upon and found the funding for a lessening of his teaching load. Her care and compassion have been a source of much strength. Special thanks go to David Pritchard, his co-editor and former student, without whose input the book would never have seen the light of day. As ill health worsened David Pritchard assumed responsibility for all editorial correspondence and all stages of the editorial process and actively and successfully pursued the external funding and donations that were required to produce a longer and more complex work. Not only did David take the initiative to bring on board additional contributors, but it would be only fair to say that any coherence and quality that is to be detected in the book is largely due to his vigorous engagement with all contributors.

David Pritchard wishes to thank his partner, Christiana Köhler, for her support and understanding during a project which took considerably longer than expected and David Phillips for the opportunity to develop and help publish a substantial piece of scholarship on ancient Greece and an important commemoration of the Sydney 2000 Olympic Games.

The editors wish to pay a special tribute to the late Kevin Lee, Professor of Classics at the University of Sydney, who died on 28 May 2001 in his prime and at a time when he had become a public advocate for the contemporary relevance and study of the languages, literatures, cultures and histories of ancient Greece and Rome. While Kevin and David Phillips independently conceived of taking the Sydney Olympics as a chance to celebrate and explore the ancient roots of the Olympic Movement, Kevin did not hesitate, upon learning of David's plans for a conference, to propose that it should be jointly sponsored by the two universities in Sydney with departments of Classics and Ancient History. Kevin personally invited many of the participants at the conference and found a congenial venue for it at Sancta Sophia College. He was indefatigable in his commitment to the organization of the conference and meticulous as only a textual editor and critic can be in his attention to the details. His presence, participation and congeniality as a host contributed greatly to the relaxed, scholarly and friendly atmosphere of the conference upon which all commented. It is the unanimous wish of the contributors to this book that its dedication should be to his memory.

The contributors have used their own preferred spellings of Greek names and transliterations of Greek terms and have had a free choice in their use of Australian, British or American spellings of words. The abbreviations of journals and periodicals in the bibliographies of each chapter are those of *L'année philologique*.

13 January 2003

Notes

[1] Kanarakis 1987, vii.

[2] For the history of the modern discovery and excavation of Olympia, see the chapter by Helmut Kyrieleis in this book.

[3] Quoted by Frost 1987, 385

[4] *OCD*[2] s.v. Ptolemy (4).

[5] Quoted in Frost 1987, 369.

[6] Frost 1987, 389, 397, 408.

[7] Woodhouse 1986, 147–9.

[8] Young 1984, 28–43.

[9] On the excavation and reconstruction of the stadium, see Travlos 1971, 498.

[10] Young 1984, 69.

[11] Gordon 1994, 1–13.

[12] The Modern Games of the XVI Olympiad were held from 22 November to 8 December 1956 in Melbourne – a city with a significant Greek immigrant population (Gordon 1994, 193–225). The United Kingdom has also hosted the Games twice, in 1908, in London, and again in 1948. Only the USA has hosted the Olympics on more occasions: 1904 in St Louis, 1932 as part of the World Fair, 1984 in Los Angeles and 1996 in Atlanta. However, the USA boycotted the Games of the XXII Olympiad in 1980 in Moscow in protest over the 1979 invasion of Afghanistan by the Soviet Union and thus cannot claim a history of unbroken attendance (Bruce 1999).

[13] See Dimitreas 1987; Kapardis and Tamis 1988; Kanarakis 1987; Tamis 1997.

[14] The date was probably established by Hippias of Elis, for which see the chapter in this book by David Phillips with Morgan 1990 47–9 which argues that in terms of the archaeological record this was 'hardly a watershed in Olympic history'. There is evidence for cult activity in the form of terracotta and bronze votive figurines from as early as the tenth century BC (Morgan 1990, 57 and the chapter by Helmut Kyrieleis in this book).

[15] Pomeroy et al. 1999, 1–40; Drews 1988.

[16] Orrieux and Schmitt Pantel 1999, 5.

[17] White and Lampert 1987, 11–15.

[18] Brown 2000, 26–7. On the richness and culture of aboriginal culture, see the section 'Continuity and diversity: varieties of aboriginal life' in Mulvaney and White 1987 at pages 120–365. On aboriginal spirituality, see Cowan 2001. On the revival and success of aboriginal art not only in Australia but also internationally, see Caruana 1993; Kleinert and Kleinert 2000.

[19] Cashman 1995; 1997. Richard Cashman is the director of the Centre for Olympic Studies which was established in 1996 and focuses on the history of the modern Olympic Movement. It is the repository of the archives of the Sydney Organising Committee for the Olympic Games (SOCOG) and is responsible for a number of important publications on Australian involvement in the modern Olympics, the latest of which is Cashman and Toohey 2002 on the role of the

higher education sector in the Sydney 2000 Olympics. For further information, see its website at www.arts.unsw.edu.au/olympic/index.html.

[20] On the history of the University of Sydney and its Departments, see its website at www.usyd.edu.au/about/history.shtml.

[21] Separate chairs of Greek and Latin were created in 1891 and were not reunited until the appointment, in 1992, of Kevin Lee, who held the position until his untimely death on 28 May 2001. Kevin, who was a graduate of the University of NSW (Tighs Hill), later the University of Newcastle, held appointments as lecturer and senior lecturer at the University of New England, from 1968 and 1978, where he also completed his Ph.D. Before his appointment to the Chair at the University of Sydney he held the Chair of Classics at Canterbury University in Christchurch, New Zealand, from 1979 to 1991. Classical Archaeology was introduced at the University of Sydney in the 1930s and has a partially endowed chair, the Arthur and Renée George Chair in Classical Archaeology, currently held by Professor Richard Green. The University of Sydney is also the Australian base for the Australian Archaeological Institute at Athens which was established in 1981 and whose founding director, Professor Alexander Cambitoglou, preceded Richard Green as the Arthur and Renée George Professor of Classical Archaeology.

[22] For the state of classical studies in Australia at the end of the 1980s, see Sinclair 1990. For the current health and extent of its disciplines, see the ASCS website at www.arts.uwa.edu.au/classics/ascs/index.html and especially the online directory (the 'Blue Book') of staff and research students currently working in classical studies departments in Australia and their research interests and topics. Although Classics and Ancient History, like all Humanities disciplines in Australia, suffered through the 1990s, there are now encouraging signs of revival with posts having been advertised recently at the Australian National University, the University of New England and the University of Queensland.

[23] See the Australian Vice-Chancellors' Committee 1996, 93–132 for a complete list by state, and pages 135–6 for a listing of collections specializing in the cultures of the ancient Mediterranean world. To these should be added the Potter Gallery at the University of Melbourne which was opened in 2001. It contains a significant gallery of antiquities. Trendall 1990 gives an overview of such collections, while Kanowski 1990 reports on the history and function of one such museum established in 1963: the Antiquites Museum of the University of Queensland.

[24] For further information on ACANS, see its website at www.humanities.mq.edu.au/acans/ with links to the sites of the Department of Ancient History at Macquarie University, the Museum of Ancient Cultures and the Ancient History Documentary Research Centre. The latter is the largest of its kind in Australia and was a model for the Centre for the Study of Ancient Documents at Oxford University.

[25] Of public collections Trendall notes the significant collection of the antiquities, in particular the Greek vases, purchased through the Felton Bequest at the National Gallery of Victoria in Melbourne (1990, 14, 16).

[26] Measham, Spathari and Donnelly 2000. See also the last three chapters of this book.

[27] Graeme Murphy wrote in the programme notes: 'In *Mythologia* we have created our own Olympic Ode in the manner of Pindar, but with Heracles himself as both champion and main subject. Like Pindar, the amazing exploits of Herakles are sung by a choir, and like Pindar we digress into other myths and tales linked directly or indirectly to the hero.' *Mythologia* was performed at Sydney's Capitol Theatre from 19–26 August 2000.

[28] A CD recording of Carl Vine's score for *Mythologia* performed by the Sydney Gay and Lesbian Choir under the direction of Jonathan Welch and, as Carl Vine puts it in the liner notes, with music 'created entirely on my Macintosh computer', is available, with texts and translations by Suzanne MacAlister, on Tall Poppies Records (TP149; www.tallpoppies.au.nu).

[29] See section III of the Introduction below.

[30] Whilst monographs on the ancient Olympics, such as Finley and Pleket 1976, Yalouris 1979 and Swaddling 1980 (reprinted several times with a second edition appearing in 1999), are widely accessible and whilst there is an abundance of modern scholarship on Olympia and the ancient Olympics, we are lacking in monograph-length studies of the Pythia, Isthmia and Nemea, although publication of ongoing excavations, especially at the sites of the Isthmia near Corinth and at Nemea, continues. On the Pythia, see Fontenrose 1988. On the Isthmia, see Broneer 1958–62; 1961; 1962; 1971; 1973; Gebhardt 1987; 1992; 1993; Gebhardt and Hermans 1992. On Nemea, see Stephen Miller 1990; 1992; Stella Miller 1988. For additional bibliographies, see Crowther 1985a; Scanlon 1984; Østby 1993. Schoder 1974 and Sturzebecker 1986 provide 'bird's eye' views of several major sanctuary complexes.

[31] Golden 1998, 10–12. On the origin of Panhellenism (lit. 'all-Greek'), see Morgan 1993. On Panhellenic cults in general, see Bruit Zaidman and Schmitt Pantel 1992, 112–40; Raubitschek 1988.

[32] On the vegetative crowns, see Pausanias 8.48.3; Lucian *Anacharsis* 9. On other honours and prizes, see below note 48.

[33] Golden 1998, 11, 33.

[34] Like the Olympics, the Athenian Panathenaia has produced an abundance of publications (see in particular Neils 1992 and 1996) – two more being the chapters by David Phillips and Tom Stevenson in this book – as have the major Athenian dramatic festivals, the City Dionysia and the Lenaia, on which see Pickard-Cambridge 1988 and Csapo and Slater 1995 with extensive citation and translation of the relevant literary and epigraphical evidence. On an aspect of the Lenaia festival, see the chapter by Ian Storey in this book. See also Goldhill 1987; Osborne 1993; the chapter by Peter Wilson in this book with bibliography.

[35] We are not nearly as well served for 'local' festivals, agonistic or otherwise, held outside the main Panhellenic centres or Athens. In the absence of an up-to-date systematic survey and study, one must turn elsewhere. The only monograph-length study of festivals outside Athens is Nilsson 1906. For agonistic festivals in particular Ringwood 1927 is still useful together with the bibliography in Scanlon 1984, 71–3. See also Herrington 1985, 161–6 with table 1 on page 8 for *agōnes mousikoi* at religious festivals. For 'local' games, see the table at Stoneman 1997,

xlviii–liv. Østby 1993 provides an extensive bibliography, including site publications, on sanctuaries throughout the Greek world. Most of these, if not all, will have been the focus of festival with or without *agōnes*. On the footrace at the Athenian Oschophoria, see Kadletz 1980. On *agōnes* at Larisa, see Gallis 1988, although I would prefer the use of 'other agonistic festivals' to his 'Provincial Olympic Games'.

[36] Golden 1998, 10–14. For the date of the Pythia, held from 7–11 Buktaios (equivalent to the Athenian Anthesterion (February–March) see Fontenrose 1988, 125–8. The Great Panathenaia was held from 23 to 30 Hekatombaion with the procession (*pompē*) on 28 Hekatombaion: Athena's birthday. For these dates and the programme of the Panathenaia, see Neils 1992, 14–17.

[37] For a discussion of the various terms – *synodos, panēgyris, heortē, eranos* and *agōn* (pl. *agōnes*) – which the Greeks used to refer to festivals, see Cartledge 1985, 100–3. On *heortē*, 'holiday' or the lighter, carnival side of festival, see Mikalson 1982. On the 'play' element of cultures, see Huizinga's classic study of 1949.

[38] For good general introductions to the characteristics of Greek festivals, see Burkert 1985, 99–109; Cartledge 1985 which focuses on the Olympia and upon the City Dionysia at Athens; Bruit Zaidman and Schmitt Pantel 1992, 102–11 which focuses on the Athenian festival system.

[39] Raubitschek 1983; Scanlon 1983; Golden 1998, xi, 24–5.

[40] On cockfighting at Athens, see Csapo 1993. A facing pair of cocks, each upon a column flanking an armed Athena, appeared on the obverse of early Panathenaic prize amphoras. For illustrations, see, for example, Neils 1992, 43, 46, cat. nos. 13 and 18.

[41] Hodkinson 1999.

[42] For various attempts at a definition of ancient 'sport' by historians, see Kyle 1987, 2; Poliakoff 1987, 7; Golden 1998, xi, 17, 29.

[43] On drama, see above note 34. On painting, see Pliny *Natural History* 35.38. On musical *agōnes* and rhapsodic contests, see the fundamental study of Herrington 1985 with Shapiro 1992. On male beauty contests, see Crowther 1985b. On the full range of events, excluding drama but including acting, see Stephen Miller 1991, 21–62. On combat sports, see the definitive study of Poliakoff 1987.

[44] On *hēmerodromoi*, see Matthews 1974; Lee 1984.

[45] The words supposedly uttered by Pheidippides are first recorded in Lucian *A Slip of the Tongue in Greeting* 3, which was written around 170 AD. Pliny *Natural History* 7.20.84 catalogues famous *hēmerodromoi* and notes Pheidippides' (now called Philippides) run to Sparta but not his victory run from Marathon. Both sources are to be found as Stephen Miller 1991, nos. 8 and 9. Frost 1979 argues persuasively against the historicity of Pheidippides' marathon, whilst Badian 1979 argues against Frost and later traditions beginning with Pliny that the runner's name should be Pheidippides as found in the 'best manuscripts' of Herodotus and not Philippides which is found in the 'inferior manuscripts'. For the history of the modern marathon, see Lucas 1976 and Lovett 1997 which repeat, as do most accounts of the marathon and the tradition behind it, the myth of Pheidippides' marathon. See also Robert Browning's poem 'Pheidippides' from his *Dramatic*

Idyls (First Series, 1879).

[46] On *athlos*, see Scanlon 1983; Kyle 1987, 2. Many older and more general discussions of ancient sport and athletics, such as Gardiner 1910; 1930; Harris 1964; 1972 and Olivová 1984, while still useful for events and festival details, have been superseded by the directions now taken by modern studies of the history of ancient sport and festivals. In particular note the recent monographs by Golden (1998) and Scanlon (2002). An earlier study by Sansone (1988) contains an important set of anthropologically derived theories which focus *inter alia* on sport as the ritual sacrifice of energy in order to explain the origins of Greek athletics and sport. For critical comment on this explanation, see Golden 1998, 17–19, 23. For extensive bibliographies of scholarship until the 1980s, see Kyle 1983a; 1983b; Scanlon 1984; Crowther 1985; Kyle 1991. Golden 1998 and Scanlon 2002 give further updated bibliographies. See also *Nikephoros* – a journal established in 1988 and devoted specifically to scholarship on ancient sport. For recent directions in the study of Greek festivals, see below note 56.

[47] For the stadium length at Olympia, see Swaddling 1980, 25; for those of Nemea and Delphi, see Stephen Miller 1990, 176–7.

[48] Golden 1998, xi, 61, 139, 177. The standard work on Olympic victors is Moretti 1959 with a summary in Yalouris 1979, 478–85. For Athenian athletic victors, see Kyle 1987, 195–228.

[49] For a slightly freer translation, see Stephen Miller 1991, no. 161.

[50] On honours, privileges and rewards for victors, including victory dedications, see Stephen Miller 1991, nos. 81–5, 146–82. On the value of prizes, see Young 1984, 111–33; Golden 1998, 141–3. For a critique of the way Young uses ancient evidence to support his case for substantial non-elite participation in ancient Greece, see the chapter by David Pritchard in this book. On the representation of athletic victory in literature and art, see Golden 1998, 74–103 and the chapter by Patrick O'Sullivan in this book. For victory epigrams, see Ebert 1972.

[51] Stoneman 1997.

[52] For the discussion of many of these, see Burkert 1983. On myths associated with the Pythian Games and Apollo at Delphi, see Fontenrose 1959. On a key aetiological myth associated with Olympia and the Olympic Games, see the chapter by John Davidson in this book.

[53] For two examples of a discus dedicated by a victor, one at Kephallenia and the other at Olympia, see Swaddling 1980, 51; Measham, Spathari and Donnelly 2000, 50–1. The latter also illustrates an inscribed bas-relief dedicated by a victor in the four-horse chariot race, the *tethrippon*, at the Panathenaia (Cat. no. 10). For early dedications, by both victors and others, at Olympia, Delphi and Isthmia, see Morgan 1990, index s.v. 'dedications' and 'Isthmia'. See also Golden 1998, index s.v. 'dedications' and especially his page 85 where he raises the question of the elision of 'the distinction between a votive to honour a god and a monument to immortalize a victor'. Although raised in the context of the status of victors and their heroization, his comment also serves as a warning of the potential difficulties of the classification of some dedications.

[54] Golden, 1998, 18, 19, 86, 154.

[55] See Stephen Miller 1991, nos. 96–106 for some sources; note also Scanlon 1988; Golden 1998, 123–40.

[56] Note Herodotus 8.144.2. Seminal studies on festival now include Burkert 1983; Connor 1987; Goldhill 1987; Robertson 1992; Neils 1992; 1996; de Polignac 1995. See also some of the brief but important observations of Cartledge (2001, 29–31, 82) on festivals at Sparta and his earlier study on Greek festivals (1985).

[57] The passage from Xenophon is also cited and briefly discussed by Cartledge 1985, 117. Travlos 1971, 477 dates the Pompeion to 400 BC. For further discussion of the Pompeion and the Panathenaia, see the chapter by David Phillips in this book. See also the chapter by Peter Wilson in this book for the role of dithyrambic choruses in combating *stasis* (civil war or strife).

[58] His keynote address 'Slaves and Greek Sport' will be part of his forthcoming monograph '*Sport and Social Status in Ancient Greece*' which is to be published as the inaugural volume of the Fordyce Mitchel Memorial Lectures by the University of Wisconsin Press.

[59] This positive relationship is noted by Cartledge (1985, 224 n. 8; cf. 2000) and has existed for several decades. For example, the Berlin Olympics of 1936 had a major exhibition of Greek antiquities that included (amazingly) the Delphi Charioteer and the Zeus of Artemision (Blümel 1936). The Munich Games of 1972 occasioned Hermann 1972 and Mallwitz 1972 and also an important exhibition on a century of German excavations at Olympia (Fellman and Scheyhing 1972). The publication of Finley and Pleket 1976 and Swaddling 1980 coincided with the Olympic Games of Montreal and Moscow respectively. The Los Angeles Olympics of 1984 saw the publication of David Young's important book *The Olympic Myth of Greek Amateur Athletics* (1984) and a conference on the ancient Olympic Games and other ancient Greek festivals which generated the influential Raschke 1988. Interestingly, the international symposium on the Olympic Games which was held in Athens in 1988 and whose proceedings appeared as Coulson and Kyrieleis 1992 was conceived by the Mayor of Athens, Miltiades Evert, as part of the city's bid for the 1996 Olympic Games. Another part of this ultimately unsuccessful bid was the major exhibition of 1989 and 1990 on ancient Greek athletics at the National Archaeological Museum in Athens (Tzachou-Alexandri 1989). Finally, the Sydney Olympic Games of 2000 had the Powerhouse Museum exhibition *1000 Years of the Olympic Games: Treasures of Ancient Greece* (see Measham, Spathari and Donnelly 2000, and the last three chapters in this book).

Bibliography

Australian Vice-Chancellors' Committee
> 1996   *Cinderella Collections: University museums and collections in Australia: The report of the University Museums Review Committee*, Canberra.

Badian, E.
> 1979   'The name of the runner: a summary of the evidence', *AJAH* 4, 163–6.

Blümel, C.
1936   *Sport der Hellenen*, catalogue of the antiquities exhibition at the Berlin Olympic Games of 1936, Berlin.
Broneer, O.
1958–1962 'Excavations at Isthmia', *Hesperia* 27, 1–37; 28, 298–343; 31,1–25.
1961   'Isthmiaca: investigations at the site of the Isthmian Games', *Klio* 39, 249–70.
1962   'The Isthmian victory crown', *AJA* 66, 259–63.
1971   *Isthmia: Vol. 1: Temple of Poseidon*, Princeton.
1973   *Isthmia: Vol. 2: Topography and architecture*, Princeton.
Brown, M. (ed.)
2000   *Sydney 2000: The Games of the XXVII Olympiad: The official souvenir book*, Sydney.
Bruce, J. (ed.)
1999   *The Olympic Games*, special edition for the Sydney 2000 Olympic Games, London, New York, Sydney and Moscow.
Bruit Zaidman, L. and Schmitt Pantel, P.
1992   *Religion in the Ancient Greek City*, transl. P. Cartledge, Cambridge.
Burkert, W.
1983   *Homo Necans: The anthropology of ancient Greek sacrificial ritual and myth*, transl. P. Bing, Berkeley.
1985   *Greek Religion: Archaic and classical*, transl. J. Raffan, Oxford.
Callender, J.
1766–68 *Terra Australis Cognita or Voyages to Terra Australis*, 3 vols., Edinburgh.
Cartledge, P.A.
1985   'The Greek religious festivals', in P. Easterling and J.V. Muir (eds.) *Greek Religion and Society*, Cambridge, 98–127.
2000   'Olympic self-sacrifice', *History Today* 50.10, 10–15.
2001   *Spartan Reflections*, Berkeley.
Caruana, W.
1993   *Aboriginal Art*, London.
Cashman, R.
1995   *Paradise of Sport: The rise of organised sport in Australia*, Melbourne.
1997   *Australian Sport through Time: The history of sport in Australia*, Sydney.
Cashman, R. and Toohey, K.
2002   *The Contribution of the Higher Education Sector to the Sydney 2000 Olympic Games*, published by the Centre for Olympic Studies at the University of New South Wales, Sydney.
Connor, W.R.
1987   'Tribes, festivals and processions in ancient Greece', *JHS* 107, 40–50.
Coulson, W. and Kyrieleis, H. (eds.)
1992   *Proceedings of an International Symposium on the Olympic Games, 5–9 September 1988*, Athens.

Cowan, J.
  2001   *Mysteries of the Dreaming: The spiritual life of Australian aborigines*, rev. edn, Sydney.
Crowther, N.B.
  1985a 'Studies in Greek athletics: parts I and II', *CW* 78, 497–58; 79, 73–135.
  1985b 'Male beauty contests in Greece: The Euandria and Euexia', *AC* 54, 285–91.
  1990   'Recent trends in the study of Greek athletics (1982–1989)' *AC* 59, 246–55.
Csapo, E.
  1993   'Deep ambivalence: notes on a Greek cockfight', *Phoenix* 47, 1–28, 115–24.
Csapo, E. and Slater, W.J.
  1995   *The Context of Ancient Drama*, Ann Arbor.
Dalrymple, A.
  1767/69   *An Account of the Discoveries Made in the South Pacifick Ocean, Previous to 1764*, London.
De Polignac, F.
  1995   *Cults, Territory and the Origins of the Greek City-State*, transl. J. Lloyd, Chicago.
Dimitreas, Y.E.
  1998   *Transporting the Agora: Hellenic settlement in Australia*, Sydney.
Drews, R.
  1899   *The Coming of the Greeks: Indo-European conquests in the Aegean and the Near East*, Princeton.
Ebert, J.
  1972   *Griechische Epigramme auf Sieger an gymnischen und hippischen Agonen*, Berlin.
Fellmann, B. and Scheyhing, H. (eds.)
  1972   *100 Jahre deutsche Ausgrabung in Olympia*, catalogue of the exhibition of the Munich Olympic Games of 1972, Munich.
Finley, M.I. and Pleket, H.W.
  1976   *The Olympic Games: The first thousand years*, London.
Fontenrose, J.
  1959   *Python: A study of Delphic myth and its origins*, Berkeley.
  1988   'The cult of Apollo and the games at Delphi', in Raschke (ed.) *The Archaeology of the Olympics*, 121–39.
Frost, A.
  1987   'Toward Australia: the coming of the Europeans 1400 to 1788', in Mulvaney and White (eds.) *Australians*, 368–411.
Frost, F.J.
  1979   'The dubious origins of the Marathon', *AJAH* 4, 159–63.
Gallis, K.J.
  1988   'The games in ancient Larisa: an example of provincial Olympic Games', in Raschke (ed.) *The Archaeology of the Olympics*, 217–35.

Gardiner, E.N.
   1910   *Greek Athletic Sports and Festivals*, London.
   1930   *Athletics of the Ancient World*, Oxford.

Gebhard, E.R.
   1987   'The early sanctuary of Poseidon at Isthmia', *AJA* 91, 475–6.
   1992   'The early stadium at Isthmia and the founding of the Isthmian Games', in Coulson and Kyrieleis (eds.) *Proceedings...*, 73–9.
   1993   'The evolution of a Pan-hellenic sanctuary: from archaeology towards history at Isthmia', in Marinatos and Hägg (eds.) *Greek sanctuaries*, 154–77.

Gebhard, E.R and Hermans, F.P.
   1992   'University of Chicago excavations at Isthmia, 1989: Part I', *Hesperia* 61, 1–77.

Golden, M.
   1998   *Sport and Society in Ancient Greece*, Cambridge.

Goldhill, S.
   1987   'The Great Dionysia and civic ideology', *JHS* 107, 58–76. Repr. with revisions in J.J. Winkler and F.I. Zeitlin (eds.) 1990 *Nothing To Do with Dionysos? Athenian Drama in Its Social Context*, Princeton, 97–129.

Gordon, H.
   1994   *Australia and the Olympic Games*, Brisbane.

Harris, H.A.
   1964   *Greek Athletes and Athletics*, London.
   1972   *Sport in Greece and Rome*, London.

Hermann, H.V.
   1972   *Olympia, Heiligtum und Wettkampfstätte*, Munich.

Herrington, J.
   1985   *Poetry into Drama: Early Greek tragedy and the Greek poetic tradition*, Berkeley.

Hodkinson, S.
   1999   'An agonistic society? athletic competition in archaic and classical Spartan society', in S. Hodkinson and A. Powell (eds.) *Sparta: New Perspectives*, London and Swansea, 147–87.

Huizinga, E.H.
   1949   *Homo Ludens: A study of the play-element of culture*, London.

Kadletz, E.
   1980   'The race and procession of the Athenian *Oschophoroi*', *GRBS* 21, 363–71

Kanarakis, G.
   1987   *Greek Voices in Australia: A tradition of prose, poetry and drama*, Sydney.

Kanowski, M.
   1990   'Students, the public and potsherds', in Sinclair (ed.) *Past, Present and Future*, 17–22.

Kapardis, A. and Tamis, A.M. (eds.)
   1988   *Afstraliotes Hellenes: Greeks in Australia*, Melbourne.

Kleinert, S. and Kleinert, N.
   2000   *The Oxford Companion to Aboriginal Art and Culture*, Oxford.
Kyle, D.G.
   1983a 'The study of Greek sport: a survey', *EMC* 27, 46–67.
   1983b 'Directions in ancient sport history', *Journal of Sport History* 10, 7–34.
   1987   *Athletics in Ancient Athens*, Leiden.
   1991   'Athletes and archaeology: some recent work on the sites and significance of ancient Greek sport', *International Journal of the History of Sport* 8, 270–83.
Lee, H.M.
   1984   'Modern ultra-long distance running and Philippides' run from Athens to Sparta', *AncW* 9, 107–13.
Lovett, C.
   1997   *Olympic Marathon: A centennial history of the Games' most storied race*, Westport.
Lucas, J.A.
   1976   'A history of the Marathon race: 490 BC to 1975', *Journal of Sports History* 3, 120–38.
Mallwitz, A.
   1972   *Olympia und seine Bauten*, Munich.
Marinatos, N. and Hägg, R. (eds.)
   1993   *Greek Sanctuaries: New approaches*, London.
Matthews, V.J.
   1974   'The *Hemerodromoi*: ultra long-distance running in antiquity', *CW* 68, 161–9.
Measham, T., Spathari, E. and Donnelly, P.
   2000   *1000 Years of the Olympic Games: Treasures of Ancient Greece*, catalogue of the Powerhouse Museum exhibition, Sydney.
Mikalson, J.D.
   1975   *The Sacred and the Civil Calendar of the Athenian Year*, Princeton.
   1982   'The *heorte* of heortology', *GRBS* 23, 213–22.
Miller, Stella G.
   1988   'Excavations at the Panhellenic site of Nemea: cult, politics, and games', in Raschke (ed.) *The Archaeology of the Olympics*, 141–51.
Miller, Stephen G.
   1991   *Arete: Greek sports from ancient sources*, 2nd edn, Berkeley.
   1992   'The stadium at Nemea and the Nemean Games', in Coulson and Kyrieleis (eds.) *Proceedings...*, 81–6.
Miller, Stephen G. (ed.)
   1990   *Nemea: A guide to the site and museum*, Berkeley.
Morgan, C.
   1990   *Athletes and Oracles: The transformation of Olympia and Delphi in the eighth century BC*, Cambridge.
   1993   'The origins of Pan-hellenism', in Marinatos and Hägg (eds.) *Greek Sanctuaries*, 18–44.

Moretti, L.
   1959   *Olympionikai: i vincitori negli antichi agoni olimpici*, Rome.
Mulvaney, D.J. and White, J. (eds.)
   1987   *Australians: A Historical Library: Vol. 1: Australians to 1788*, Sydney.
Neils, J. (ed.)
   1992   *Goddess and Polis: The Panathenaic festival in ancient Athens*, Princeton.
   1996   *Worshipping Athena: Panathenaia and Parthenon*, Madison
Nilsson, M.P.
   1906   *Griechische Feste von religiöser Bedeutung mit Ausschluss der Attischen*,
           Berlin.
Østby, E.
   1993   'Twenty-five years of research on Greek sanctuaries: a bibliography', in
           Marinatos and Hägg (eds.) *Greek Sanctuaries*, 192–227.
Olivová, V.
   1984   *Sports and Games in the Ancient World*, London.
Orrieux, C. and Schmitt Pantel, P.
   1999   *A History of Ancient Greece*, transl. J. Lloyd, Oxford.
Osborne, R.
   1993   'Competitive festivals and the polis: a context for dramatic festivals at
           Athens', in A.H. Sommerstein et al. (eds.) *Tragedy, Comedy and the Polis*,
           Bari, 21–38.
Parke, H.W.
   1977   *The Festivals of the Athenians*, London.
Pickard-Cambridge, A.
   1988   *The Dramatic Festivals of Athens*, 2nd edn with addenda by J. Gould and
           D. Lewis, Oxford.
Poliakoff, M.B.
   1987   *Combat Sports in the Ancient World: Competition, violence and culture*,
           New Haven.
Pomeroy, S.B, Burstein, S.M., Donlan, W. and Roberts, J.T.
   1999   *Ancient Greece: A political, social and cultural history*, New York.
Raschke, W.J. (ed.)
   1988   *The Archaeology of the Olympics: The Olympics and other festivals in
           antiquity*, Madison.
Raubitschek, A.E.
   1983   'The agonistic spirit of Greek culture', *AncW* 7, 3–7.
   1988   'The Panhellenic idea and the Olympic games', in Raschke (ed.) *The
           Archaeology of the Olympics*, 35–7.
Ringwood, I.C.
   1927   'Agonistic features of local Greek festivals chiefly from inscriptional
           evidence', Ph.D. dissertation, Columbia University, New York.
Robertson, N.
   1992   *Festivals and Legends: The formation of Greek cities in the light of public
           ritual*, Toronto.
Sansone, D.
   1988   *Greek Athletics and the Genesis of Sport*, Berkeley.

Scanlon, T.F.
  1983   'The vocabulary of competition: *agon* and *aethlos*, Greek terms for contest', *Arete: The Journal of Sport Literature* 1, 147–62.
  1984   *Greek and Roman Athletics: A bibliography*, Chicago.
  1988   '*Virgineum Gymnasium*: Spartan females and early Greek athletics', in Raschke (ed.) *The Archaeology of the Olympics*, 185–216.
  2002   *Eros and Greek Athletics*, Oxford.
Schoder, R.V.
  1974   *Ancient Greece from the Air*, London.
Shapiro, H.A.
  1992   'Mousikoi agones: music and poetry at the Panathenaia', in Neils (ed.) *Goddess and Polis*, 53–75.
Simon, E.
  1983   *Festivals of Attica*, Madison.
Sinclair, R. (ed.)
  1990   *Past, Present and Future: Ancient world studies in Australia*, a commemorative volume of *Antichthon* published by the Australian Society for Classical Studies.
Stoneman, R. (ed.)
  1997   *Pindar: The odes and selected fragments*, a translation by G.S. Conway and R. Stoneman, London.
Sturzebecker, R.L.
  1986   *Photo Atlas of Athletic–Cultural Archaeological Sites in the Graeco-Roman World*, Madison.
Swaddling, J.
  1980   *The Ancient Olympic Games*, London.
Tamis, A.M.
  1997   *History of Greeks in Australia*/Ιστορία τῶν Ελλήνων τῆς Αυστραλίας, 2 vols., Melbourne and Thessalonike.
Trendall, A.D.
  1990   'The art and archaeology of the ancient Mediterranean world: progress and developments in its teaching and presentation', in Sinclair (ed.) *Past, Present and Future*, 8–16.
Travlos, J.
  1971   *Pictorial Dictionary of Athens*, London.
Tzachou-Alexandri, O. (ed.)
  1989   *Mind and Body: Athletic contests in ancient Greece*, Athens.
White, J.P. and Lampert, R.
  1987   'Creation and discovery', in Mulvaney and White (eds.) *Australians*, 2–22.
Woodhouse, C.M.
  1986   *Modern Greece: A short history*, 4th edn, London.
Yalouris, N. (ed.)
  1979   *The Eternal Olympics: The art and history of sport*, New Rochelle (New York).
Young, D.C.
  1984   *The Olympic Myth of Greek Amateur Athletics*, Chicago.

THE ORGANIZATION AND FUNCTIONING
OF THE OLYMPIC GAMES

Stephen G. Miller

Problems in reconstructing the organization of the Games begin with the sources available to us. Traditionally, these have consisted of the written sources that have survived, especially the author Pausanias whose description of Olympia is fundamental to our study. The visual documents are also basic, most notably Athenian vase painting and the physical remains at the site of Olympia itself, and at other sites in Greece. But immediately we encounter difficulties. The Games began in 776 BC and continued for more than 1,000 years.[1] Our written sources extend over this same time, but may we assume, for example, that practices described by Pausanias in the second century after Christ were already in use in the fifth century BC? We frequently combine sources of very different date even though we know that practices must have evolved over such a long period; as a student once asked, 'Did the rules never change?'

So, too, our best visual evidence comes from Athenian vase painting of the late sixth and fifth centuries BC (e.g. *Figs.* 3, 11, 13, 14, 17, 21), and from Panathenaic amphoras that extend into the fourth century and later (e.g. *Figs.* 6, 7, 8, 9). But may we assume that the athletic events portrayed on such vases remained the same through time? And since the Panathenaic amphora was a prize for the games at Athens, may we assume that Athenian customs and those at Olympia were the same? Again, we use this evidence even though we know that it may not be accurate for the Olympic Games.

The same difficulties exist in the physical remains at Olympia.[2] We may use the stadium as a single example. Excavations have revealed that the stadium which we see today at Olympia can be dated no earlier than about 350 BC.[3] How are we to understand the stadium of the fifth century? What we see today fits very well with the description of Pausanias at about AD 150, but did it stay the same for 500 years? This question becomes very important when we consider the vaulted entranceway to the Olympic stadium that the excavators have always called Roman, but which is surely original to the stadium of the second half of the fourth century BC.[4]

This re-dating of the tunnel emerges not so much from Olympia itself as when we bring into the equation the physical remains of other sites in Greece. These are, first and foremost, the other three Panhellenic athletic festival centers at Delphi, Isthmia, and Nemea. Given that the games at those sites were, in some sense, the equivalent of the Olympic Games, it should be legitimate to use evidence from them to supplement that from Olympia. Thus, the discovery at Nemea of a vaulted entrance tunnel to the stadium that must be dated no later than about 320 BC suggests that the vaulted tunnel at Olympia might be of a similar date.

But we must be careful in our use of comparisons with the other sites. Delphi, for example, offers us a fine example of a stone theater and Isthmia also had a theater although it is poorly preserved. Are we to expect, then, a theater at Olympia? Some scholars have sought one, but we must understand a fundamental difference between the Olympic Games and those at Delphi and at Isthmia where musical competitions – the *mousikoi agōnes* – were held. These competitions in flute-playing, in kithara-playing, and in singing with the accompaniment of the kithara, were never a part of the Games at Olympia – except for the aberration that occurred when the Emperor Nero visited Olympia in AD 67 – and so a theater was never needed and never constructed at Olympia.[5]

Finally, we now have a new kind of evidence that we may use in our reconstruction of the organization of the Olympic Games. This evidence admittedly does not fit the traditional types that scholars are wont to use. On 1 June 1996, and again on 4 June 2000, the Society for the Revival of the Nemean Games – an organization with 1810 members from 21 countries – brought the games back to life in the ancient stadium at Nemea (*Figs.* 15, 19, 20, 30). The experiences of those two days brought into sharp focus certain practical considerations that have increased my appreciation of the efforts involved with the organization of the ancient Olympic Games. I will use these experiences as we put together a reconstruction of the ancient Games. I believe that it will help to understand some of the details that were necessary to the success of the Games.

I propose to use the year 300 BC – the 120th Olympiad – as the date for the attempted reconstruction. There is no particular reason for this year as opposed to 308, 304 or 296 BC, for example, but a date within this period allows the Games to be set in a recognizable temporal and archaeological environment. By about 300 BC there was an architectural outline that simply did not exist in earlier times.[6] Indeed, it is one of the ironies of the archaeology of the Olympics that very little is preserved of the physical setting of the competitions from the heyday of Greek athletics in the sixth and fifth centuries BC.[7]

Preparation

By using 300 BC for our attempted reconstruction of the organization of the Olympic Games, we can assign specific dates within the year, for it is clear that the Olympic Games took place at the second full moon after the summer solstice or, in 300 BC, on August 9.[8]

We must begin our reconstruction at the city-state of Elis, however, and not at Olympia itself.[9] Elis is located about 36 km north-west of Olympia, although the distance by road was some 57 or 58 km.[10] This sleepy and conservative rural town was the political entity that controlled Olympia and that supervised the Games there, just as there were political entities in control of the other sites and games. Some excavations have taken place at the site where a small museum is located, but the ancient town as a whole is unknown. Nonetheless, the description by Pausanias is revealing, although difficult to reconcile with the reconstructed drawing which is based on the excavated remains (*Fig.* 1).[11]

The very first monument Pausanias mentions at Elis is: '…an old *gymnasion*. In this *gymnasion* the athletes go through all the customary training before they repair to Olympia'. He tells us that in this *gymnasion* was a race track, and a separate practice track for runners and pentathletes.

Fig. 1. Reconstruction of the center of the town of Elis based on excavated remains. From N. Papahatzis, Παυσανίου Ελλάδος Περιήγησις, 1979, Athens: Ekdotike Athenon S.A.

There was also a place in the *gymnasion* called 'Plethrium' (i.e. the 100-footer) 'where the *Hellanodikai* (Judges of the Hellenes) match the wrestlers by age and by abilities'.[12] Pausanias continues:

> ...there is another *gymnasion*, smaller in size, that adjoins the older. It is called Square because of its shape. Here the athletes practice wrestling and, when they are done, the boxers practice with soft gloves as protection from the blows.

He continues:

> there is a third *gymnasion*...which is reserved for the young men of the city (*ephēboi*) for the whole time of the Olympic festival... In this *gymnasion* is also the council house (*bouleutērion*) of the Eleans.

We next learn that one road from this *gymnasion* led to baths and another:

> ...to the market place (*agora*) and to what is called the Judges' Room (*Hellanodikaion*). This is the road the *Hellanodikai* take when they go to the *gymnasion*. They enter before sunrise to match the runners, and at midday to pair the pentathletes and the so-called heavy events (βαρέα ἆθλα).

In other words, from his entrance into Elis until he reaches the *agora*, Pausanias mentions only buildings that have to do with athletics in general, and training for the Olympic Games in particular. But the athletic orientation of the public spaces of Elis does not end there. Pausanias continues:

> The *agora* is now called the hippodrome (horse track) and the natives train their horses there... [I]n the portico on the southern side of the *agora*, the *Hellanodikai* generally spend their days... Parallel to the end of this portico is the *Hellanodikaion*.

Elis was, then, an athletic training town, the ancient predecessor to the modern Olympic Village.[13]

Obviously, the Olympic character of this village would have been dormant for three of the four years of each Olympiad, but nearly a year before the Games, Olympic activity began at Elis. Ten months before the actual Games the ten *Hellanodikai*, who were elected by the Eleans to supervise the Olympics, moved to and began to live in the *Hellanodikaion*. For our example, that means that the judges took up residence in this building in October 301 BC, and officials known as the 'guardians of the law' (*nomophylakes*) began to instruct the *Hellanodikai* about their duties at the Olympic Games.[14] We know nothing else about these 'guardians of the law', but we should probably imagine them as successful and long-term veterans of the Games who had frequently served as *Hellanodikai* themselves. We also do not know if the 'guardians of the law' were associated with the Olympic council (*Olympiakē boulē*), which was a fifty-member panel that exercised some sort of general supervision over the Games. It was to the Olympic council that an athlete might appeal a disputed judgement by the *Hellanodikai*.[15]

The number of *Hellanodikai* had varied in the early history of the Games, but it was stabilized in 348 BC as ten and remained at that number throughout the remainder of antiquity.[16] Although all ten were responsible for the smooth functioning of the competitions, it is clear that they also split into sub-committees which had specialized responsibilities.[17] One group was in charge of the horse races, another the foot races, and the third the heavy events of boxing and wrestling. The last two groups of *Hellanodikai* may have overlapped in the pentathlon, since that event contained both foot-racing and wrestling, as well as the specialized javelin, *diskos*, and jumping.

As the training of the judges progressed, preparations also had to be made for announcing the sacred truce, the *ekecheiria*, which covered the month before the Games or the period from July 10 to August 9 in 300 BC. This allowed for participants in the Games, whether as athletes or as spectators, to travel in safety to them. For the purpose of the announcement, there were groups of heralds – called sometimes *spondophoroi* (truce-bearers), sometimes *theōroi* (sacred envoys). We gain a notion of the highly developed and organized system which surely existed at Olympia by that which is documented at Nemea. A fragment of an inscription discovered at Nemea tells us that groups of six *theōroi* were to travel to specific parts of Greece.[18] In the preserved text we see repeatedly the word ἕξ (six) as well as references to the Peloponnesos, Ambrakia, and Akarnania which are mentioned as separate itineraries. Even more information comes from another inscription at Nemea where the name of a region is followed by the names of cities within the region, for each of which is listed one or two or three people.[19] For example, the cities of Salamis, Kourion, and Soloi are given for Cyprus with prominent local men listed for each. These men are the *theōrodokoi* (envoy-receivers), who facilitated the task of the *theōroi* (sacred envoys) when they came to their cities. These men – the *theōrodokoi* – are, in effect, the local representatives of the games and they constitute a highly organized support system for the games throughout the Greek world.

With the announcement of the sacred month for the Olympic Games (μεὺς Ὀλυμπικός) and of the truce throughout the Greek world, it was time for the athletes to gather at Elis.[20] They were to undergo a month of training under the watch of the *Hellanodikai*. An athlete who was late in arriving and who could not prove that illness, pirates or shipwreck had delayed him, was assessed a fine, and if he did not pay the fine, he was flogged.[21]

It should be noted at this point that the typical punishment for fouls at the Games was flogging and we see many examples of this in vase-painting (e.g. *Figs.* 22 and 25). There was a minor official called the *mastigophoros* (whip bearer) who apparently helped the judge with this responsibility.[22] The judges were, however, prohibited from hitting the head of the athlete.[23]

Although the athletes would take an oath before they competed that they had adhered strictly to their training for ten months, the judges could be sure that they had done so for the last month. During this month, the athletes were clearly training with and against one another, and there must have been attrition as the best athletes in different events became clear. This auto-selection process must explain the occasions when we hear that a given athlete was awarded the victory prize without having to compete against a rival.[24] While this training was going on at Elis, spectators began to trickle in. Each athlete had, of course, his friends and relatives and trainer with him, but we also hear of fans and casual tourists who arrived at Elis days and even weeks before the Games to watch the athletes practice and to follow this process of the selection of the best for the actual competition.[25] Although the final pairing of athletes, which was done by drawing lots from a vessel, may have occurred at this time, it is more likely that the final arrangements took place at Olympia itself.[26]

While all this preliminary training was going on at Elis, preparations were beginning at Olympia itself. We should not think of Olympia as abandoned, for pilgrims and tourists might visit at any time during the four-year span of an Olympiad, and there was a permanent staff of officials to take care of them. An inscription, although dating from 28 BC, probably reflects the situation already in 300 BC.[27] Many of the officials listed in this marble slab were on call to help the visitor make a sacrifice to Zeus; such was the 'on-call sacrificing priest' whose efforts were aided by a 'flutist', a 'libation-pourer', a three-man group of 'libation-dancers', a 'woodman' who provided the special fuel for the sacrifice, and a 'butcher-cook' whose task at the sacrifice is clear from his name. There were also five 'bailiffs' to keep order, and even an official 'guide' to satisfy the curiosity of the visitor. Each of these officials was paid with a part of the sacrificial animal, and items like the skins of the animals, as well as the monopoly on firewood for sacrifices, were a significant source of income for the Eleans.[28]

When the time came for the Games, special work and workmen were needed. The stadium, which might be rented out for grazing or even for growing crops into the early summer, as still happens at Olympia today (*Fig.* 2), had to be cleaned out and prepared for action.[29] Many of the other buildings at the site also needed repairs; fresh whitewash and paint were liberally applied to them and, if necessary, repairs to the water channel that

Fig. 2. The ancient stadium at Olympia during the hay harvest 1997, from the north-east. Photograph: the author.

surrounded the race track in the stadium.[30] Some sort of sanitary facilities must have been necessary, but there is no ancient evidence on this point. The next step was to dig up the surface of the track with handpicks. We hear of this process from inscriptions discovered at Delphi and at Delos.[31] The same excavation procedure is to be seen in many vase paintings as, for example, a red-figure skyphos of about 460–450 BC (*Fig.* 3).[32] The same skyphos shows us more details of the procedure – drawing water and then sprinkling it on the track. Then the surface must have been rolled and several vases show what appear to be rollers for such a job. The pits (*skammata*) for the jumpers were also dug up, although no trace of these

Fig. 3. Red-figure skyphos showing the digging of the surface of the track and the sprinkling of water on it. Ex-Hirschmann Collection. Photograph: Silvia Hertig / Archäologisches Institut der Universität Zürich.

pits has ever been discovered and their precise location within the stadium is unknown. Finally, the inscriptions tell us that white earth (λευκὴ γῆ) was applied to the stadium and this probably is white lime which we used in 1996 at Nemea to mark out the lanes on the running surface (*Fig.* 19).[33]

Now it was time to install the starting mechanism for the races.[34] The starting line (*balbis*) was made of stone and is preserved in many stadia (*Fig.* 4).

Fig. 4. Starting line (*balbis*) in stadium at Olympia with toes in the grooves. Photograph: the author.

But in addition to the starting line, there was a starting mechanism, called the *hysplēx*. It has recently been shown that the *hysplēx* utilized the technology of the recently invented catapult, and the stone bases added to the ends of the starting lines at Nemea have allowed a physical reconstruction of the mechanism (*Fig.* 5).[35] The starter (*aphetēs*) stands at the apex of a triangle the base of which is the starting line. At the signal, he pulls two cords that release the torsion-loaded arms at either end of the line. The arms, in turn, hurl vertical posts to the ground, and the posts carry with them horizontal barrier-cords the fall of which allows the runners to start.

Fig. 5. Nemea starting mechanism (*hysplēx*) reconstructed and in operation. Nemea Excavation Archives, University of California, Berkeley.

The day is 6 August 300 BC. At Olympia, the stadium and the hippodrome, which I have not mentioned because so little is known of it, are cleaned, cleared, and ready for action. And so is the crowd at Elis. They are about to go to Olympia, the Games are about to begin, the winners and the losers are about to be decided. But before departing Elis, the *Hellanodikai* assemble the athletes and deliver this charge:

> If you have worked so as to be worthy of going to Olympia, if you have done nothing indolent or ignoble, then take heart and march on; but those who have not so trained may leave and go wherever they like.[36]

With these words the procession (*pompē*) to Olympia begins. It is impossible to know precisely how many were in this march, although it surely included the ten *Hellanodikai*, probably the fifty-member Olympic council, perhaps two hundred athletes (although sometimes the total was clearly lower than two hundred), and perhaps one hundred equestrian units (whether single horses or four-horse or two-horse chariots).[37] In addition, there were large numbers of trainers, family members, and simple fans of the athletes; at least a few slaves or assistants to the *Hellanodikai*; and dozens (if not hundreds) of curious tourists. The members of the procession probably exceeded one thousand, and may have numbered several thousand.

The day and the night of August 6 were spent on the road. We have no details of what, if any, accommodations were provided for the marchers, but on the morning of August 7 they were nearly at Olympia when the march halted at a spring called Pieria and the *Hellanodikai* underwent a ritual purification during which they were sprinkled with the blood of a pig and the water of the spring provided for ablution.[38] Now cleansed, they could enter the sanctuary of Zeus, the *Altis*, as it was officially known. The Games were, at their core, a religious festival.

The Festival

A huge crowd awaited them, and the sacred grove of Olympia was surrounded by a tent city, peopled with thousands. Smoke from fires and sacrifices was thick overhead and the air filled with the cries of people of all types. One ancient author describes the scene at the Isthmian Games about fifty years before our Olympics, that is, about 359 BC:

> That was the time to hear crowds of wretched sophists around the temple of Poseidon as they shouted and heaped abuse on each other, and their so-called students as they fought with one another, and many historians reading out their dumb writings, and many poets reciting their poetry to the applause of other poets, and many magicians showing their tricks, many fortune-tellers telling fortunes, countless lawyers perverting justice, and not a few peddlars peddling whatever came to hand.[39]

Other sources relate that poets, painters and sculptors were at the Games to display their works and in hope of gaining a commission from a victorious athlete or a pious pilgrim.[40] Indeed, Herodotus publicized his history of the Persian Wars by going to the back end of the temple of Zeus and reading to the crowds at the Games from the manuscript he had just completed.[41] All of this hustle and bustle went on against a backdrop of discomfort which served to show just what one would put up with in order to be a part of the festival:

> There are unpleasant difficult things in life. But don't they happen at Olympia? Don't you suffer from the heat? Aren't you cramped for space? Don't you bathe badly? Don't you get soaked whenever it rains? Don't you get your fill of noise and shouting and other annoyances? But I suspect that you compare all this to the value of the show and endure it.[42]

But the *Hellanodikai* must go to the council house (*bouleutērion*) with the athletes to carry out their final examination and to administer the oath. The Olympic Games had no weight divisions; a man might have to wrestle an opponent who outweighed him by twenty kilograms and more. But there was an age division: the men (*andres*) who were 20 years of age or more, and the boys (*paides*) who were roughly of the years from 17 to 19.[43] Now, on the morning of August 7, a final determination was made, based at least in part on an examination of the athletes, their fathers, brothers, and trainers, in an attempt to discover the true age, and even then the *Hellanodikai* could decide that an athlete who was actually 18 or 19 years old was so well developed physically that he had to compete in the men's category. We hear of athletes who had nightmares because they feared that, although they had been allowed to march from Elis to Olympia with the boys, they would on this day be assigned to compete against the men.[44] The same certification of age was done for the horses, apparently at the same time and place as that for the athletes (see below). And the *Hellanodikai* were sworn not to take bribes in making their decisions. Clearly the age classification was important to the possibility of victory.

Now, too, in the *bouleutērion* the formal oath was administered in front of the statue of Zeus Horkios (Zeus of the Oath). Pausanias says:

> Of all the images of Zeus, the Zeus in the *bouleutērion* is the one most likely to strike terror into the hearts of sinners. This Zeus... holds a thunderbolt in each hand. Beside this statue it is established for the athletes, the fathers and brothers, and their trainers to swear an oath on slices of the flesh of wild boars that they will do nothing evil against the Olympic Games.[45]

Next came the first competitions, but not for the athletes. These contests were for the trumpeter (*salpinktēs*) and for the herald (*kēryx*); the

Fig. 6. Panathenaic amphora showing proclaimation (*anakēryxis*) of a victor who stands in the center holding a palm branch. To the right a herald (*kēryx*) shouts out the news, to the right of the herald the trumpeter (*salpinktēs*) watches with his trumpet in his right hand. At the far left another athlete runs off with his palm branch. Louvre, Paris, MN 706. Photograph : Herve Lewandowski. © Réunion des Musées Nationaux / Art Resource, N.Y.

competitions took place on an altar near the entrance to the stadium.[46] Together, the winners in these two events became the ancient equivalent of the public address system.

The trumpeter would blast on his trumpet when it was time to make an announcement (*Fig.* 6, right). Then the herald (*Fig.* 6, center right) would shout out the news: the next event, an introduction of the competitors, the name of the victor and so forth.[47] Clearly the winners in these competitions were chosen for the volume and clarity of their trumpet or voice. As we learned at Nemea in 1996, the system works, for the audience must be quiet if it wants to hear the announcement. The result is a more intimate participation by the spectators. On 7 August 300 BC, the winner of the trumpet contest was a man named Herodoros from Megara who was famous not only for his horn blowing and for the fact that he was only 160 cm tall, but also because he was accustomed, it is said, to eat five kilograms of bread and eight kilograms of whatever meat he could put his hands on while he drank six litres of wine. He also played two trumpets at the same time. 'His trumpet blast was very loud' and he was a ten-time Olympic victor, says our ancient source.[48]

The remainder of August 7 was taken up with sight-seeing, watching the crowd, and making sacrifices. Sacrifices were of particular interest to horse owners whose competitions would take place the next day and who wanted to appease the evil spirits (embodied in the Taraxippos – see below) that might operate against them in the hippodrome.

At dawn on August 8, a procession set out from the *prytaneion* (magistrates' house) – the building at the north-west corner of the Altis where the eternal fire burned on the hearth of Hestia.[49] This procession was led by the priests of Zeus and the *Hellanodikai* who were clad in purple, and it went to the sixty-three altars of many different gods located within the Altis.[50] That number does not include all the altars, for some were used for special purposes. Perhaps the most interesting was the altar of Zeus Apomyios, Zeus the Fly Averter. Given the crowds at the Olympics, with the sacrifices involving large quantities of blood and meat, fly control was clearly a concern.

After these sacrifices, the scene shifted to the hippodrome which was located outside the Altis and to the south-east in an area that has never been excavated.[51] The trumpeter blasted on his horn to summon the crowd, and the competitors and their horses passed in review. As each went by, the herald announced the name of the competitor, of his father, and of his native city-state. And this was the time when challenges might be voiced about the eligibility of the competitor: Is he under any charges of homicide or sacrilege? Is he a citizen in good standing of his city-state or is he an exile? Is he Greek? This opportunity for challenge was presented before every event for every competitor.

It may be noted here that one of the ironies of the ancient Olympics is still with us today. The Games brought together all the Greeks and, in some sense, promoted international (i.e. inter-polis) communication and understanding. At the same time, by the insistence upon the competitors being legitimately associated with a particular city-state, the Games promoted international competition. Who has won the most medals? Indeed, many cases are known from antiquity of an athlete being hired to represent another city to the dismay of his original hometown.[52]

The length, width, and other details about the hippodrome are unknown, although the actual track surface was perhaps about 600 m long and 64 m wide with a separate area for the start of the race at one end.[53] This area was equipped with an elaborate starting device, which included a bronze dolphin that fell down and a bronze eagle that flew up to signal the start of the race, and a series of gates that were released by some sort of mechanism.[54] The horses ran up and down the track and made turns around posts at either end. Unlike the Roman circus, there was no dividing barrier connecting the turning posts, since head-on wrecks, which could happen only in the absence of such a barrier, did occur.[55]

Another feature of the hippodrome was the Taraxippos – literally the 'Horse Frightener'.[56] This monument was located near the far turning post, and there was a long tradition of spin-outs and wrecks in front of it. There certainly was an altar dedicated to Taraxippos where horse owners and charioteers would sacrifice in the hope that this evil spirit would leave their horses alone. This sort of special hurdle for the horses existed elsewhere. At Nemea, there was a 'red rock' that caused crashes by means of the reflection from the sun into the horses' eyes.[57]

The first competition was also the most aristocratically oriented: the *tethrippon* or four-horse chariot race (*Fig.* 7). It consisted of twelve laps which may have been something like 14,000 m. This was the event where the wealthy would try to display their economic power. Hence Alkibiades entered seven different *tethrippa* in 416 BC, winning first, second and fourth places,[58] whereas several of the *tethrippa* entered by the unpopular Dionysios of Syracuse in 388 BC crashed.[59] The owners only rarely, if ever, actually drove the chariots. That was left to specialists, often slaves. This element of wealth in the equestrian competitions, rather than talent or training, was recognized in antiquity. In 396 BC, the king of Sparta, tired of hearing people brag about victories in the horse races, encouraged his sister, Kyniska, to enter a four-horse chariot. Although she could not be present at the Games, her horses won, and she was thus the first woman victor at the Olympic Games. As such, she set up a statue, and the base of that statue survives with Kyniska's proud claim to the first feminine victory.[60]

Fig. 7. Panathenaic amphora showing the four-horse chariot race (*tethrippon*); note the turning post (*kamptēr*) at the right. British Museum, London, B 606. © The British Museum.

The next race was the horseback race (*kelēs*), with small boys, frequently slaves, as jockeys (*Fig.* 8). It was only two laps or perhaps 2,600 m long. Since the ancients had neither saddle nor stirrups, the danger of the jockey falling off was real, and we even hear of a case when a horse – nicely named

Fig. 8. Panathenaic amphora showing the horse-back race (*kelēs*); note age of jockeys. British Museum, London, B 135. © The British Museum.

'Breeze' – finished the *kelēs* race even though her rider had fallen off.[61] Her owner was crowned victorious.

The two-horse chariot race (*synōris*) was a more recent addition to the program, but it was well-established already by the middle of the fourth century (*Fig.* 9). It was eight laps or perhaps 9,500 m in length. Finally, there had been added to the program a few years earlier than our Games in 300 BC a four-foal chariot race (*tethrippon pōlikon*) and this age category (*pōlos*) was again assigned by the *Hellanodikai* who examined and certified the horses as they did the athletes. Just as with the athletes, there were instances when horses were determined to be too old (or too developed) to belong to the younger category.[62] Its length was eight laps or perhaps 9,500 m. A few years into the future, races for this younger group of horses would be established in the *synōris* (in 268 BC) and the *kelēs* (in 256 BC).

Fig. 9. Panathenaic amphora showing the two-horse chariot race (*synōris*). Staatliche Museen zu Berlin – Preussischer Kulturbesitz Antikensammlung, V.I.4950.

Fig. 10. Panathenaic amphora showing three parts of the pentathlon: *halma, akōn* and *diskos.* British Museum, London, B 134. © The British Museum.

With the completion of the equestrian competitions, the scene shifted to the stadium, immediately north of the hippodrome, and to the competition in the pentathlon. This was the first of the *gymnikoi agōnes* or 'naked competitions'. The reason for the name is obvious (*Fig.* 10).

The pentathlon consisted of, in the order of competition: a *stadion* race which was exactly like the individual competition of that name – we will defer discussion of that until we come to the *stadion* event in its own place in the program – the *diskos*, the jump or *halma*, the javelin or *akōn*, and finally a wrestling bout or *palē*. This last event was, again, exactly like the independent wrestling competition, and we will defer discussion of it until the proper place for the *palē* in the program. But the three central events – discus, jump, and javelin – existed only as parts of the pentathlon and must be discussed here.

The *diskos* – a favorite of ancient artists – was very much like our modern event, although a lack of standardization of size and weight has troubled some modern critics. But characteristic examples that weigh about 2 kg and are about 20 cm in diameter are very similar to our modern examples if not quite so aerodynamically designed.[63] There were official discuses stored at Olympia so that, even if the discus might vary in size and weight from place to place, all the athletes would use the same discus on the same day in the same competition.[64] The throw was done with a pivoting motion that began in a crouch with the back toward the throwing field and ended with the previously coiled body extended in the direction of the throw. The throw had to land in bounds – the boundaries probably limited by the stone water channels down the side of the stadium track, and there is some evidence that each athlete had five opportunities to throw, the best (furthest) being the one that counted.[65]

Fig. 11. Red-figure kylix showing pentathlete jumping with the accompaniment of the flute. Antikenmuseum Basel und Sammlung Ludwig, KÄ 425.

The jump or *halma* was different from our modern long jump in two major respects. First, as can be seen in several vase-paintings (*Fig.* 11), it was done with the accompaniment of the flute. Indeed, we know that the flute-player for the Olympic Games was that person who had won the flute event at Delphi.[66] The second difference was that the jumper was aided by the use of weights – called *haltēres* – made of stone or of lead. Unlike the *diskos*, the *haltēres* were individualized, and there seems to have been no standard weight. Many of those that had been used in the competition, such as one from Olympia that weighs 4.6 kg, were dedicated to Zeus by happy victors. They had carried them to victory.[67]

A variety of vase paintings show the sequence of the jump. The athlete runs up to a point called a *batēr* carrying the weights with him. They gain speed as he does. At the *batēr* he leaps into the air, and throws the weights forward at the same time. At first the weights pull him forward, but as gravity begins to take effect and he begins to descend, he pulls the weights behind him and drops them as he lands in the pit or *skamma*. The whole sequence makes clear the need for careful co-ordination and rhythm, and why the flute player was important in assisting the athlete toward that rhythm.

The javelin or *akōn* was about two metres long and distinguished from the heavy hunting or military *dory* by its relatively thinner shaft and its bronze pyramidal point as opposed to a bladed head (*Fig.* 12).[68] It was also quite different from the modern javelin. This difference was with the leather strap or *ankylē* that was wrapped around the shaft of the javelin in such a way that a loop was left for the two first fingers of the throwing hand (*Fig.* 10). Many vase-paintings show the athlete forcing the strap tight against the throwing fingers by pushing back on the javelin with the left hand. As the javelin was thrown, the strap acted as a sort of sling in propelling the javelin, and as it unrolled, it caused the javelin to spiral like a rifle bullet. Limited but compelling evidence suggests that the actual throw was made with a run during which the thrower twisted his body backward in order to create a torsion that would propel the javelin further (*Fig.* 13).[69] This same technique has been used infrequently, but successfully, in modern times. The throws were marked, as in the discus and the jump, by pins, and the victor was determined by distance. Despite the assertions of some modern scholars, accuracy was not a criterion.[70]

Fig. 12. Bronze *akōn* head. Nemea Excavation Archive, University of California, Berkeley, inventory no. BR 1577.

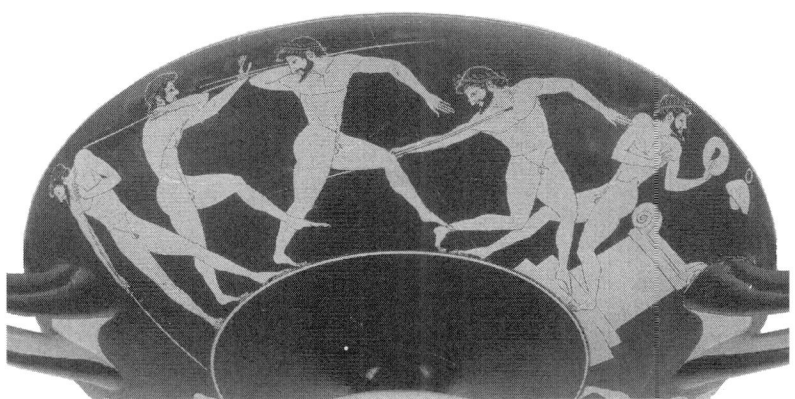

Fig. 13. Red-figure kylix showing sequence in throwing the *akōn*: (1) set *ankylē* on shaft with fingers through loop; (2) begin run toward throwing line; (3) twist torso 180 degrees; (4) bring arm forward and begin to untwist torso toward throw. The J. Paul Getty Museum, Malibu, California, 85.AE.25. © The J. Paul Getty Museum.

Although it is not known how the winner of the pentathlon was determined, it is clear that if a single athlete had won three events before the final wrestling, that event was not held. It also seems clear that the progress of the pentathlon allowed for some sort of elimination so that those who had no chance of winning were excluded from the final wrestling.[71] But however the victor was determined, his name was announced, and he received on the spot a ribbon tied around his head and a palm branch – as was the case for all the events.

With the conclusion of the competitions for the day, the victors celebrated and staged parties for their friends. We should imagine the tent city with isolated spots of light and great rejoicing and revelry, surrounded by silent darkness where losers bemoaned their luck, and athletes still to compete hoped to emulate the victory parties of this night.[72]

There is also evidence to suggest that the day of August 8 ended with sacrifices to Pelops, certainly at the shrine of this hero located between the temples of Zeus and of Hera. This seems the earliest cult center at Olympia, and we should understand the sacrifices late in the day on August 8 as being a preliminary to the great sacrifice to Zeus that would occur on the next day.[73]

The night of 8/9 August 300 BC, was the full moon, the *panselēnos*, that ushers in the religious highpoint of the Games: the great sacrifice to Zeus at his altar that was located roughly equidistant from the temples of Zeus and of Hera, and east of both. It was, at least in the second century after Christ, conically shaped, roughly 7 m high, and about 10 m in diameter.[74] But because it was created entirely from the ashes of previous sacrifices, it has disappeared today without a trace.[75] Its bulk was created in part by individual sacrifices at various times during the year, but especially on the day of the full moon every four years. In our year of 300 BC, August 9 is that day, although we should understand that the new day in ancient terms actually began with sunset on the eighth.

In the morning, the great procession came through the Altis led by the priests and the *Hellanodikai* with the athletes and the official ambassadors of the various city-states, eager to make a good impression for their home towns. We hear, for example, that the ambassadors would bring from home the finest table service in order to entertain guests at Olympia, and that these gold vessels and incense burners were especially on display during the procession of the *panselēnos*.[76] But the central element in the procession was the hundred oxen for the *hekatombē*, the sacrifice that the Eleans would offer to Zeus.[77] The animals were taken to the great altar and slaughtered. Then their thighs were taken to the top of the altar and burned for the gratification of Zeus, while the remainder of the animals was roasted and distributed to the crowd. This was the great banquet put on by the local hosts for their guests who, it can be imagined, supplemented the feast with food of their own. Anyone who has been in a rural Greek village on Easter Day will have a feeling for the scene.

Now we come to a problem that has yet to be solved. Many scholars have placed the competitions for the boys, the *paides*, on the afternoon of this day.[78] I must say that I wonder if anyone would pay much attention after the feast of the day, but perhaps this placement is correct. If so, and if we are correct in separating the competitions for the boys entirely from those for the men, then it will have been on the afternoon of August 9 that the *paides* competed in a 200-metre foot race (the *stadion*), wrestling, and boxing. Given the brevity of the program for the boys, perhaps it is correct to think that they competed late in this day, but I suspect they actually ran on the morning of the next day.

On August 10 the program is as clear as our sources can make it, for this was *the* day of the *gymnikoi agōnes* or the 'naked competitions' for the individual athletes. The path of the athletes can be traced here – the same path is to be understood for the pentathletes and the boy competitors of previous days. The *Hellanodikai* and the competitors approached the stadium from the Altis. Before arriving at the stadium, they passed twelve bronze statues of Zeus in two groups of six.[79] These were the Zanes – statues paid for by the fines levied against athletes who were caught giving and taking bribes to 'throw' a match. The first group of six had been set up in 388 BC, and the second in 332 BC; both warned our athletes in 300 BC that an Olympic victory was not to be bought or sold, and that the shame of their corruption would live beyond them tied forever to their names.[80]

Once past the Zanes, the *Hellanodikai* and the athletes entered the area behind the Echo Stoa which formed the eastern side of the Altis.[81] They went over the worn threshold just outside the tunnel entrance, and entered an area partially covered by a roof where they would disrobe. Now the athletes oiled their naked bodies which we know from many sources was the norm for athletic competition (*Fig.* 14).

Fig. 14. Red-figure krater showing athlete pouring oil from an *aryballos* in order to oil his body before competitions. Staatliche Museen zu Berlin – Preussischer Kulturbesitz Antikensammlung, F 2180.

In 1996 and 2000 athletes at Nemea were allowed to wear a *chiton* – an ancient tunic-like garment – rather than go nude. They were also provided with oil in the characteristic oil jar or *aryballos*. A long-standing question gained new evidence thereby. Moderns have been intrigued with the custom of oiling the body and the reasons for it. Some have suggested that it was done for aesthetic reasons – the gleaming body was particularly appealing – or for religious reasons, a ritual anointing.[82] Others have suggested that the rub-down with oil served to loosen muscles in preparation for exercise and competition. And others have thought of it as a kind of ancient sun-tan lotion. These solutions are not, of course, mutually exclusive and all may have contributed to the use of oil. But in the revival of the Nemean games several athletes commented that, because of the oil on their bodies, they did not lose as much body fluid as usual and therefore that their endurance had been increased.

The *Hellanodikai* now entered the stadium through the tunnel, or the 'hidden entrance' as Pausanias called it (*Fig.* 15).[83] At Olympia their robes were purple, but at the Nemean games the judges wore black robes, and they, too, were equipped with switches for flogging the athletes. The judges passed from the tunnel onto the track and across to the area of the judges' stand – the only permanent seating arrangement in the stadium. This was the base from which the *Hellanodikai* ran the Games. Even while the sub-committee responsible for the running events was supervising on the track, the other *Hellanodikai* were in these seats watching over the whole competition. They were surrounded by spectators, and those nearest were from Elis. A home-field advantage that was sometimes exploited, but not this year.[84]

Next the athletes entered

Fig. 15. Judges and heralds and trumpeter at the entrance tunnel of the Nemea stadium, 1996. Nemea Excavation Archives, University of California, Berkeley.

the tunnel where they waited for their names to be called. They passed from the light into the dark of the tunnel, and finally out onto the track to the light and noise of the actual competition. The tension, the heightened emotions and sensitivity, must have been enormous. As each athlete's name was announced and he ran out onto the stadium track, we can imagine that his friends and fans cheered and applauded, while those of his opponents jeered (*Fig.* 16). For the spectators the effect must have been dramatic, and for the athletes – as those who competed in the revived Nemean Games of 1996 and 2000 remarked – it would have been a magical moment. Athlete and spectator transcended their usual selves. For a few moments, everyday life was left behind.

The first race was the *dolichos* or long-distance race. The competitors approached the *balbis* (starting line, *Fig.* 4). It is characterized by two grooves for the receipt of the toes, and the location of those grooves accounts for the starting position of the runners that we see again and again in ancient depictions (*Fig.* 17): one foot slightly ahead of the other with the runner crouched in a position poised to run down the track as his arms extend out over the barrier cords of the starting mechanism

Fig. 16. Reconstructed drawing of the entrance to the Nemea stadium with athletes entering the track. Nemea Excavation Archives, University of California, Berkeley.

Fig. 17. Red-figure amphora showing a runner-in-armor (*hoplitodromos*) in the starting position. Louvre, Paris, G 214. Photograph: Hervé Lewandowski. © Réunion des Musées Nationaux / Art Resource, N.Y.

(*Fig.* 5). It is this position that accounts for the literary references to the commands given at the start of the race: 'Foot by foot' (πόδα παρὰ πόδα)! 'Ready' (ἕτοιμοι)! 'Take off' (ἄπιτε)! The first of these, 'foot by foot', must command the athlete to assume this position at the *balbis* or starting line.[85] With the command 'take off' the starter (*aphetēs*) pulls his cords that release the torsion mechanism, the barrier cords of the starting mechanism (*hysplēx*) fall, and the runners are off.

The evidence for the length of this *dolichos* race is not secure, but favors twenty-four laps up and down the track (distance at Olympia of about 4,200–4,500 m), with all the runners turning around a single turning post at each end of the track as can be seen in ancient vase-painting (*Fig.* 18).[86] And after the conclusion of the race, when the winner had a ribbon (μίτρα or ταινία) wrapped around his head and was handed a palm branch (κλάδος φοίνικος), his name was officially announced (ἀνακήρυξις) and he made a victory lap (περιαγερμός) while the crowd cheered and showered flowers on him in a tradition known as *phyllobolia.*[87] On one occasion in the fifth century BC, we hear of two brothers from Rhodes each of whom won a victory – one in boxing, the other in wrestling.[88] They took a joint lap and then ran into the crowd to pick up their father – himself an Olympic victor in his day. As the two sons paraded their father around the track, the crowd went wild and showered them with an extraordinary amount of flowers. At that point a Spartan shouted out to the father: 'Die now Diagoras! You will never be happier'.

Fig. 18. Panathenaic amphora showing *dolichos* with runners rounding a single post (*kamptēr*). Callimanopulos collection.

And now on the morning of 10 August 300 BC comes the premier and original event of the Olympics. This is the *stadion* race which took its name from the unit of measurement that was 600 feet in length. It was that unit of measurement that also gave its name to the track and the spectators' seats – the stadium. It is a straight sprint down the track which at Olympia is 192 m. Since the length of the ancient foot varied from place to place, other stadia were of other lengths. Nemea and Delphi, for example, were only 178 m in length, and this should remind us of a fundamental difference between our games and the ancient. Records were not kept about times or distances, but only about winners. Second place and last place were the same – losers' names are not recorded.

There is some evidence that in the *stadion* event there were so many competitors that it was normal to run two heats, followed by a run-off between the victors of each.[89] If there were two heats for the *stadion*, there may regularly have been up to forty-four competitors, since the *balbis* (starting line) at Olympia had twenty-two lanes. Indeed, on one occasion there were seven competitors from a single city-state.[90]

The victor of each contest was announced (ἀνακήρυξις) to the crowd by his name, name of his father, and the name of his city-state. But the victor in this, the *stadion* race, could expect even more. His name was attached to this Olympiad, which would forever be known as the Olympiad when Pythagoras of Magnesia (in Asia Minor) won the *stadion*.[91] Historians who wrote of events that occurred in the year 297 (by our reckoning) referred to them as happening in the fourth year of the Olympiad when Pythagoras won, and of events in 293 as in the fourth year of the Olympiad when Pythagoras won for the second time, for this athletic star will repeat his victory in four years. It is because of this custom of naming the Olympiad after the victor in the *stadion* that we know the names of more than two hundred and fifty ancient short-distance runners; that is, more than a millenium of *stadion* victors.

Once again runners take their places at the *balbis*, but now in alternate lanes for the *diaulos*, which is a double *stadion* in length (i.e. about 400 m) and in which the athletes run down the track in one lane, turn around their own posts, and run back to the line where they began (*Fig.* 19).[92]

After the *diaulos* race there may have been an intermission while the *skamma* was prepared for the heavy events. Like the pit into which the pentathletes jumped, the *skamma* seems to have been a simple area in the stadium which was dug up to serve as the 'ring' for these events. For these pairs of athletes had to be selected. This may have been done already at Elis, or in the *bouleutērion* here at Olympia, or at the last minute in the stadium. The last possibility might be the most likely for it would most diminish the possibility of 'fixing' the pairs. Whenever the pairing was done, the athletes were arranged in a circle around the *Hellanodikai* who had a silver vessel in which were small lots about the size of beans (*Fig.* 20).[93] These lots came in pairs: two with an *alpha*, two with a *beta*, two with a *gamma*, etc., depending on the number of competitors. Next to each athlete was a slave known as a *mastigophoros*, since he carried a whip for punishing fouls. It was the job of the *mastigophoros* to prevent his athlete from seeing the letter on his lot until all had drawn from the vase. Then one of the *Hellanodikai* went around the circle to inspect the lots and to announce which two athletes had drawn the *alpha*s, which the *beta*s, etc. In the case of an uneven number of

Fig. 19. Runners in a modern *diaulos* in alternate lanes on the ancient track at Nemea. Nemea Excavation Archives, University of California, Berkeley.

competitors, one would get a bye which was a great help to him. Those who won sometimes bragged that they had won without the help of a bye.

Fig. 20. Athletes in the Nemean Games of 1996 drawing lots (*kleroi*) from a bronze helmet held by a *Hellanodikēs*. Nemea Excavation Archives, University of California, Berkeley.

Fig. 21. Red-figure pelike showing the starting position (*systasis*) of the wrestling (*palē*). The State Hermitage Museum, St Petersburg, inventory no. B.2352.

The first of the heavy events was normally the wrestling or *palē*. But the sequence could be changed if an athlete was entered in two of the events and did not, for example, want to be cut up in the boxing before continuing.[94] In one case, the favorite to win the wrestling was so unpopular with the Eleans that they actually cancelled the event rather than allow him the chance to win an Olympic victory.[95] The wrestling began with a position called *systasis* (standing together) with foreheads pressing and bodies leaning in a position that Homer described as like the rafters on a tall building (*Fig.* 21).[96] The object was to throw the opponent to the ground without going down oneself, and many different holds were practiced that developed from the grappling begun from the starting position. Three throws were necessary for victory, and breaking the fingers of the opponent was not allowed.[97] On 10 August 300 BC, a famous strong man was victorious: Keras of Argos who, it is said, had such a tremendous grip that he once tore the hoof from a bull that was struggling to get away from him.[98]

Next came the boxing event, the *pyx* or the *pygmachia*. For this event, the competitors wore oxhide straps around their knuckles, wrists, and forearms (*Fig.* 22). These were called *himantes*, and originally they were simple strips the binding of which required some skill (*Fig.* 27). But by the time of our Games in 300 BC, those original 'soft' *himantes* had been replaced by the so-called 'hard' or 'sharp' *himantes* which consisted of a more formal arrangement with padding for the forearms and heavy projecting hard chucks of leather.[99] Clearly *himantes* were designed to protect the hands of the striker and inflict damage on his opponent. Such damage is to be seen over and over again in the ancient evidence as, for example, in the blood streaming down from the heads of both boxers on many vases (*Fig.* 23). It should be noted that while their heads are bloody, there are no cuts on

Fig. 22. Pseudo-Panathenaic amphora showing a boxing match (*pyx*) with the boxers flanked on the right by another boxer waiting his turn with the winner. He seems to be signaling to the judge that one of the boxers has been knocked out, and the judge prepares to flog the boxer who continues to hit the man who is down. Staatliche Museen zu Berlin – Preussischer Kulturbesitz Antikensammlung, F 1833.

Fig. 23. Black-figure amphora showing a boxing-match (*pyx*) with blood streaming from the faces of both boxers. Royal Museums of Art and History, Brussels, inventory no. R 336.

their bodies. This is because, as we also learn from written sources, body blows were virtually unknown.[100] This emphasis on head blows (i.e. knock-out punches) is because the winner was determined when his opponent either would not or could not continue in the bout. If the defeated boxer was beaten but still conscious, he would raise a finger to signal that he was giving up (*Fig.* 24).

One famous exception to the general practice of no blows to the body occurred at Nemea.[101] The two finalists in the boxing fought on and on but neither could defeat the other. Finally, they agreed to draw straws, the short straw to stand defenseless against the long straw holder. Kreugas of

Fig. 24. Red-figure amphoriskos showing boxers with soft *himantes*: one gives the sign of defeat. National Archaeological Museum, Athens, inventory no. 1689.

Epidamnos drew the long straw and gave his best punch to his opponent, but failed to knock him out. Then it was the turn of Damoxenos of Syracuse who told Kreugas to raise his arm. Damoxenos adjusted his *himantes* so that his fingers were extended straight out and then plunged his reinforced fingers with their sharp nails into the midriff of Kreugas, and pulled out his guts. But the Nemean *Hellanodikai* ruled that Damoxenos had broken the agreement because he had delivered four blows – one for each finger – rather than the single blow that had been agreed. They thus awarded the victory to the corpse of Kreugas.

The final event of the heavy competitions was the *pankration*, a combination of boxing and wrestling (*Fig.* 25). Again, as in the boxing, there were no rounds and no weight divisions and victory was awarded to the survivor.

Fig. 25. Red-figure kylix showing the *pankration*. The athlete who is gouging his opponent's eye is about to be flogged by the judge. British Museum, London, E 78 (1850.3–2.2). © The British Museum.

27

There were specialists in breaking fingers and in strangulation, and deaths did occur. The only restrictions were against biting and gouging, in which case the *Hellanodikēs* would flog the offending athlete.

The final event of the day, and of the Olympic Games, was probably the *hoplitodromos* or the race-in-armor (*Fig.* 17).[102] The armor worn by the competitors consisted of helmet and greaves or shin-guards on the lower legs, although this element had been omitted before the time of our Games in 300 BC (*Fig.* 26).[103] A shield carried on the left arm is always standard. It is not just the placing of this event in the program which is a bit of a mystery; so, too, is its inclusion in the program at all. It was a relatively late addition to the program, being added in 520 BC – a century after the remainder of the *gymnikoi agōnes* had been set. This late addition would seem to give the lie to the frequently repeated assertion that ancient athletics were a military preparation.[104] Of course, physical exertion was common to both, but the program of the Olympics has no element that can be called military. As Euripides asked, '…[D]o men drive the enemy out of their fatherland by waging war with *diskoi*?'[105] This *hoplitodromos* event even lacks fundamental necessities for the soldier: offensive weapons like spear and sword. Further, infantry maneuvers were predicated on team coordination not individual actions. If the Olympic event had anything in common with military practice, it was with running away from the battlefield. Whatever the reason for the race in armor being added to the Olympic program, and placed at the end of the program, it was clearly run by a distinct category of athlete. Although it was two stadia in length

Fig. 26. Panathenaic amphora showing the race-in-armor (*hoplitodromos*). Louvre, Paris, MN 704. Photograph: Hervé Lewandowski. © Réunion des Musées Nationaux / Art Resource, N.Y.

– the same as the *diaulos* – and must have been run in separate lanes, like the *diaulos*, it is rare to find an athlete who won in both the *diaulos* and the *hoplitodromos*. Special techniques must have been necessary that separated the athletes in the two different events.

Although the athletes must have returned to the *apodytērion* (undressing room) at the conclusion of their events, the losers to 'slink home to their mothers through the back alleyways',[106] all of them – winners and losers – shared in common a basic set of gear and the ways of using it. Every athlete carried in his kit, in addition to the *aryballos* filled with oil, a *stlengis* (scraper) and a *spongos* (sponge). The scraper – better known by its Latin name *strigil* – and the sponge can be seen frequently in vase-paintings (*Fig.* 27) and many real examples of strigils survive.[107] By the end of their exertions in the stadium, the athletes were covered with sweat, dirt and the oil they had applied beforehand, and so had now to clean up. Although the scraper can be seen in many vase-paintings (*Fig.* 28), the ultimate

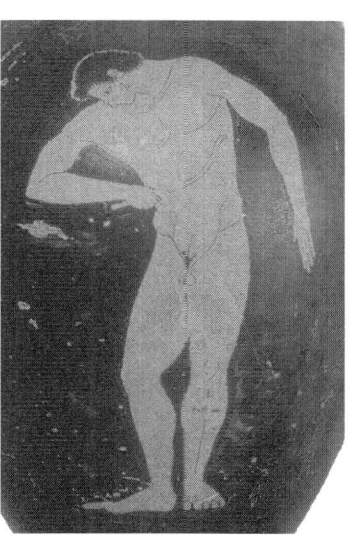

Fig. 27. Tondo of a red-figure kylix showing athlete with various pieces of athletic gear. He binds his hand with the *himas* while sitting next to a *diskos* and a pick symbolizing the *skamma*. Below him are two *haltēres*, and hanging on the wall two pieces of personal gear: his *spongos* and his *aryballos* filled with a daily ration of oil. The vase-painter has given us the athlete's name, Epidromos, and the adjective 'beautiful' (*kalos*) expressing his admiration. Hood Museum of Art, Dartmouth College, N.H.; gift of Mr and Mrs Ray Winfield Smith, class of 1918; C.970.35.

Fig. 28. Red-figure amphora showing athlete scraping body with a *stlengis* to remove the *gloios*. Kunsthistorisches Museum, Wien, inventory no. IV 3723.

destination of that which was scraped off is less frequently documented. This mixture of oil, sweat, dirt, and who knows what else, had a technical name – *gloios* – and we hear that it was collected and sold.[108] It was believed to have medicinal qualities, and that from Olympia must have been particularly valued – an unexpected source of income.

We should also imagine that now, in the evening of August 10 300 BC, as the last athletes clean up and leave the *apodytērion*, many have begun to depart from Olympia, hoping for a fast get-away. This must have been particularly true of the losers and their friends, but many more stayed behind, for there were still the final ceremonies.

On the next day, August 11 300 BC, in front of the Temple of Zeus, the final prize of victory was awarded. This was the crown of wild olive leaves that had been cut from trees probably located behind and to the west of the temple of Zeus. These branches had to be cut with a golden sickle by a boy whose parents were still alive.[109]

On this last day of the festival, the crowns were displayed on a special table made of gold and ivory (*Fig.* 29). This had been made by a certain Kolotes, a pupil of Pheidias, who had helped the master create the gold and ivory statue of Zeus housed in the temple of Zeus and counted as one of the Seven Wonders of the ancient world.[110] Now the victors, with their ribbons and their palms of victory passed before the *Hellanodikai* to receive their crowns of wild olive – the ultimate proof of victory that they will take home to share with their countrymen (*Fig.* 30). But this leafy crown of olive quickly wilts, dries, and disintegrates. It is ephemeral. The real reward lies beyond the token of victory. Fellow citizens will welcome them with an *eisēlasis* (triumphal entry into the city) and honor them with a free meal

Fig. 29. Bronze coin of Elis showing the awards table. Archaeological Museum, Olympia, inventory no. M 876.

Fig. 30. Victor at Nemean awards ceremony in 1996 with palm branch in hand and crown of wild celery over *tainia*. Nemea Excavation Archives, University of California, Berkeley.

every day for the rest of their lives.[111] Already they or their families may have commissioned a statue or an ode to commemorate the victory.[112] And their names are entered into the official register of victors.

Another reward comes in the form of a victory dinner party given by the Eleans to the newly crowned victors in the *prytaneion* where the ceremonies had begun on the morning of August 8. These new victors are now a part of a select few who enter the chapters of Olympic history. Meanwhile the crowds look for carriages, and the roads from Olympia are filled with pedestrians and horses, happy with their experiences, resolved to come again, but next time to find a way to beat the traffic. As one spectator said in AD 165:

> The end of the Olympic Games soon came – the best Olympics which I have seen, incidentally, of the four which I have attended. It was not easy to get a carriage since so many were leaving at the same time, and therefore I stayed on against my will.[113]

Acknowledgements

An earlier version of this chapter appeared as 'Organisation et fonctionnement des jeux olympiques' in *Olympie: Cycle de huit conférences organisé au musée du Louvre* (Paris 2001) 75–125.

This version has benefited greatly from the comments and suggestions of David Pritchard and an anonymous reviewer, and I am grateful to them. For the errors that remain despite their best efforts, I am responsible.

Notes

[1] The evidence for the date of the last Olympic Games is not certain. Modern scholars often regurgitate the date of AD 393 without critical examination (e.g. Ebert 1989, 106), but the assumption behind the use of such a date is that there was an official end to the Games. It is just as likely that they simply faded away. See the discussion by Drees 1968, 159. Note also that it was not until AD 435 that Theodosios II finally forbade all use of pagan shrines (Hunt 1993, 157).

[2] For an overview of the history of the excavations at Olympia, see the chapter by Helmut Kyrieleis in this book.

[3] See *Fig.* 1 in the chapter by Kate da Costa et al. in this book.

[4] The proof of this re-dating of the original Olympia tunnel is presented by Miller 2001, 190–210. For a reconstruction of this tunnel, see *Fig.* 2 in the chapter by Kate da Costa et al. in this book.

[5] Flute-singing (or *aulos*-singing) was held only at the first Pythian Games in 586 BC and dropped immediately thereafter (Pausanias 10.7.6 (Miller 2004, no. 75)). This event did continue in other local games as at Athens, as attested in inscriptions such as *IG* II² 2311 (Miller 2004, no. 120).

[6] See *Fig.* 1 in the chapter by Kate da Costa et al. in this book.

[7] A single exception is the starting mechanism in the early stadium at Isthmia from the second half of the fifth century BC. See Yalouris 1976, 158–9, for a reconstruction of the mechanism. We should note, however, that the excavator of this mechanism at Isthmia, Oscar Broneer, reported that the whole pavement and its mechanism were covered over deliberately with a layer of clay shortly after it had been constructed. Indeed, it may have been used – if ever – for only one competition. It was an idea that did not work in practice. See Broneer 1973, 50.

[8] Miller 1975, 223.

[9] For more detail about Elis and its relationship with Olympia, see the chapter by Nigel Crowther in this book.

[10] Swaddling 1999, 52.

[11] Pausanias 6.23–4 (Miller 2004, no. 83).

[12] It seems that the judge of the Olympic Games was originally called the *diaitatēr* and that the rather more grandiose *Hellanodikēs* was adopted after, and perhaps as a result of, the Greek successes in the Persian Wars (Siewert 1992, 115).

[13] We should also note that, although women were not allowed at the Olympic Games, there were competitions dedicated to Hera for maidens at Olympia (Pausanias 5.16.2–8 (Miller 2004, no. 158)). These games of Hera took place at some time distinct from the Olympics, and were supervised by a committee of Elean women called 'The Sixteen Women'. The Sixteen Women, like the male *Hellanodikai*, also had a special building on the *agora* of Elis so that the centralization of Olympic training at Elis – for men and for women – was complete. See Pausanias 6.24.10.

[14] Pausanias 6.24 (Miller 2004, no. 83).

[15] Note the example of Leon of Ambrakia who, in 396 BC, successfully appealed the split decision by the judges on the race track to the Olympic council (Pausanias

6.3.7 (Miller 2004, no. 108)).

[16] Pausanias 5.9.4–6 (Miller 2004, no. 109)

[17] For the sub-committee on foot racing, see Pausanias 6.3.7 (Miller 2004, no. 108). The tripartite division of the judges is implicit in the three basic training areas at Elis noted above.

[18] Nemea inventory no. I 73; Miller 1979, 77.

[19] Nemea inventory no. I 85; Miller 1988, 147–63.

[20] For documentation and discussion of the Olympic month, see Weniger 1904, 126.

[21] *IvO* 56 (Miller 2004, no. 199). For flogging in general and at the Games, see Crowther and Frass 1998, 51–82.

[22] Lucian *Hermotimos* 40 (Miller 2004, no. 106) and *IvO* 56 (Miller 2004, no. 199). The *mastigophoros* appears to be the same as the *rhabdouchos* (rod-bearer) of Thucydides 5.50 (Miller 2004, no. 238).

[23] Siewert 1992, 114–15; Ebert 1997, 205 (Miller 2004, no. 101).

[24] For example, Milo of Kroton (Moretti 1957, no. 122) was so feared that he was crowned victor without a fight on at least one occasion (*Anthologia Graeca* 11.316 (Miller 2004, no. 33)). This may also have been the case with a victory at Delphi by the boxer Dorieus of Rhodes (Moretti 1957, no. 322). Other cases of victory without a fight were due to the foolishness rather than the fear of the opponent as in the case when Theagenes of Thasos conceded the victory to Dromeus of Mantinea (Moretti 1957, no. 202; Miller 2004, no. 166).

[25] Lucian *Peregrinus* 3 and 32 (Miller 2004, no. 147).

[26] Lucian *Hermotimos* 40 (Miller 2004, no. 106).

[27] *IvO* 64 (Miller 2004, no. 133).

[28] For parts of sacrificial animals and skins, see Van Straten 1995, 154–5. For official 'sacrificial' poplar wood, see Pausanias 5.13.3 and 5.14.2.

[29] *BCH* 25 (1901) 368, side A, l. 21, records that the stadium and part of the hippodrome at Livadeia were rented out for pasturage; *BCH* 14 (1890) 390 l. 12 (= *IG* II/III 1638) records that the hippodrome and the starting area of the hippodrome at Delos were rented out for grazing.

[30] For a list of the contracts that were let in 246 BC in preparation for the Pythian games at Delphi, see *CID* 2.139 (Miller 2004, no. 81).

[31] At Delphi, op. cit. lines 23–4; at Delos, *IG* XI 203A.65; 233.3; 287A.133.

[32] See Lezzi-Hafter 1982, 80–1, no. 39.

[33] *CID* 2.139 (Miller 2004, no. 81), lines 25–6. See also Miller 1980, 159–66.

[34] See *IG* IV² 1.98 (Miller 2004, no. 82) for the fines assessed against Philon of Corinth for his failure to fulfill his contractual obligations to install the *hysplēx* in the stadium at Epidauros. For a consideration of the costs of installing the *hysplēx*, see Miller in Valavanis 1999, 172–3.

[35] Valavanis 1999, 31–49.

[36] Philostratos *VApoll.* 5.43 (Miller 2004, no. 84).

[37] Crowther 1993, 49.

[38] Pausanias 5.16.8 notes that the Sixteen Women underwent the same ritual

ablution. This probably indicates that the women who competed (at some other time) in the games of Hera also undertook the long march from Elis to Olympia.

[39] Dio Chrysostom 8.9–12 (Miller 2004, no. 145). For a similar view of the diversity of the crowd at the games, see Cicero *Tuscul. Disp.* 5.3.9 (Miller 2004, no. 128).

[40] Note, for example, the rivalry for such commissions between poets and sculptors which is discussed by Patrick O'Sullivan in this volume.

[41] Lucian *Herodotus* 1–4 and 7–8 (Miller 2004, no. 143). For a more detailed discussion of the use of the Games by sophists and philosophers, see the chapter by Harold Tarrant in this book.

[42] Epictetus, *Disc.* 1.6.26–8 (Miller 2004, no. 146).

[43] *IvO* 56.10–12 (Miller 2004, no. 199). The absolute ages of the boys' and men's categories varied from site to site. The best evidence for Olympia results in the ages given above. See further Pfeiffer 1998, 21–2 and especially n. 3.

[44] Artemidoros *Oneir.* 5.13 (Miller 2004, no. 93).

[45] Pausanias 5.24.9 (Miller 2004, no. 90).

[46] Pausanias 5.22.1 (Miller 2004, no. 73).

[47] Valavanis 1990, 325–59.

[48] Athenaios 10.414F (Miller 2004, no. 74).

[49] See *Fig.* 1 of the chapter by Kate da Costa et al. in this volume.

[50] Pausanias 5.14–15.

[51] I do not know the source of, or the evidence for, the frequently repeated statement that the river Alpheios had eroded the hippodrome away during the medieval period (e.g. Drees 1968, 96; Mallwitz 1972, 99; Ebert 1989, 89). To the best of my knowledge no excavations have ever verified this destruction. Recently Knauss (1998) indicates that there is reason to hope for the survival of significant parts of the Olympia hippodrome.

[52] One of the first examples is that of Astylos, double Olympic victor (*stadion* and *diaulos*) in three successive Olympiads (488, 484, and 480 BC). Astylos first competed as a citizen of his native Kroton, but subsequently ran for Syracuse. His former fellow citizens in Kroton pulled down his statue and turned his house into a prison. See Pausanias 6.13.1 (Miller 2004, no. 224).

[53] Ebert 1989, 93–6.

[54] Pausanias 6.20.10–19 (Miller 2004, no. 69).

[55] Sophokles *Electra* 681–756 (Miller 2004, no. 68).

[56] See note 54 above.

[57] Pausanias 6.20.19 (Miller 2004, no. 69).

[58] Thucydides 6.16.2 (Miller 2004, no. 219) and Isokrates 16.32–5 (Miller 2004, no. 67). The latter source is critically assessed by David Pritchard in his chapter in this book.

[59] Diodorus Siculus 14.109 (Miller 2004, no. 245).

[60] *IvO* 160 (Miller 2004, no. 151b)

[61] Pausanias 6.13.9 (Miller 2004, no. 71).

[62] Pausanias 6.2.2.

[63] Measham, et al. 2000, nos. 10 and 33 examples of discuses from Olympia. The first was a dedication by one Publius Asklepiades and its size, biconical shape, and weight take it outside the realm of actual competition; it should be understood as a trophy made for that purpose. The second discus (no. 33) could very well have been a competitive example. See the list compiled by Gardiner 1930, fig. 111.

[64] Pausanias 6.19.4 (Miller 2004, no. 56).

[65] *SEG* XV.501 (Miller 2004, no. 52).

[66] Pausanias 5.7.10 (Miller 2004, no. 59).

[67] Olympia Museum inventory no. L 189, dedicated by Akmatidas of Sparta. As an example of the considerable differences in weight, contrast the weight of this *haltēr* with that of the pair presented by Measham, et al. 2000, no. 34.

[68] Ammonios, *On similar and different words* 23 (Miller 2004, no. 62).

[69] Waddell 1991, 102–4, fig. 4. A second vase-painting seems to show the same sequence: Munich, Staatliche Antikensammlungen, inventory no. 2667; see Waddell, fig. 3.

[70] The possibility of accuracy as a criterion comes only from a tortured interpretation of Antiphon 3.2.1–8 (Miller 2004, no. 64). Distance, and not accuracy, is supported not only by common sense, but specifically by Pindar *Pythian* 1.43–5 (Miller 2004, no. 63). Accuracy did play a role in the local civic games which were a part of military training; see, for example, *IG* IX 2, 531 (Miller 2004, no. 124).

[71] The long history of scholarship on this question, which has not provided an answer, cannot be recounted here. The most recent additions to the list are Maróti and Maróti 1993, 53–60; Lee 1995, 41–55; and Kyle 1995, 60–5.

[72] Perhaps the best known of such victory parties is that celebrated by Alcibiades in 416 BC when he borrowed the official golden vessels of the Athenian delegation and passed them off as his own ([Andokides] 4.29 (Miller 2004, no. 116)).

[73] The evidence is not clear, but this does seem the most likely scenario, for it would be a reflection of the original cult at Olympia as derived from the worship of the hero Pelops to which the later Olympian deities were added. See Drees 1968, 18–19, 30–2, 77–8 and the chapter by Helmut Kyrieleis in this book.

[74] See *Fig.* 8 in the chapter by Kate da Costa et al. in this book.

[75] These dimensions rely upon the description of Pausanias 5.13.8–11.

[76] [Andokides] 4.29 (Miller 2004, no. 116).

[77] The 100-oxen sacrifice by the people of Elis is a standard feature of modern scholarship (e.g. Drees 1968, 78; Swaddling 1999, 16, 47, 53, 55). It is an obviously central feature of the reconstruction of the Olympic festival; the evidence for the size of the sacrifice derives from a single reference in Lucian, *bis acous.* 2, to his speaker's need to be present at the *hekatombē* at Olympia. Weniger (1904, 125–31) presents this and other oblique ancient references to the great sacrifice, and his interpretation has never been challenged to the best of my knowledge. I, too, accept it, but with a hope that stronger evidence will some day emerge.

[78] Most recently by Lee 1992, 108. It is clear that all the boys' competitions preceded the men's, rather than boys' and men's age groups alternating in the same event (Plutarch *Moralia* 639A). But the placement of the boys' competitions

on a separate day from the men's rests ultimately on a belief that it would not be possible to have all the competitions on a single day.

[79] See *Fig.* 2 in the chapter by Kate da Costa et al. in this book.

[80] Pausanias 5.21.2–4 (Miller 2004, no. 103).

[81] See *Fig.* 1 in the chapter by Kate da Costa et al. in this book.

[82] Ulf 1979.

[83] See Pausanias 6.20.8–9.

[84] For the cluster of locals around the judges, see Lucian *Hermotimos* 39 (Miller 2004, no. 106). Numismatic evidence from Nemea confirms the same situation in the stadium there; see Miller 2001, 233–4. Accusations of favoritism toward fellow Eleans were leveled from time to time (Pausanias 6.1.4–5 and 6.3.7 (Miller 2004, nos. 107 and 108 respectively)). The potential for problems – even the appearance of impropriety – can be seen as early as the sixth century BC in Herodotus 2.160 (Miller 2004, no. 105) and in the rules preserved on a bronze plaque recently published by Ebert 1997, 205 (Miller 2004, 101).

[85] See Valavanis 1999, 2 n. 8, 24, 168, for the sources and a discussion of these commands.

[86] Gardiner 1930, 136; Jüthner 1968, 108–9. Most recently Decker (1997, 733) opts for 20 laps as the length of the race.

[87] Borthwick 1989, 125–34; Kefalidou 1999, 96 and 110–18.

[88] Pausanias 6.7.2–3 (Miller 2004, no. 170); Pindar *Pythian* 10.22; Plutarch *Pelopidas* 34.4; Cicero *Tuscul. Disp.* 1.46.111.

[89] Pausanias 6.13.4 (Miller 2004, no. 99). Crowther 1993, 44–6 presents other evidence for heats, but uses twenty as the number of lanes. This may be correct, and there are twenty-one post sockets on the *balbis* that thus define twenty lanes. But the toe grooves continue beyond the post sockets at either end which suggests that there was, or could have been, a lane with a runner outside the last post on either end; that is, twenty-two lanes and runners.

[90] Strabo 6.1.12.

[91] Moretti 1957, nos. 500 and 511.

[92] Miller 1980.

[93] Lucian *Hermotimos* 40 (Miller 2004, no. 97).

[94] Pausanias 6.15.4 (Miller 2004, no. 95).

[95] Dio Cassius 80.10 (Miller 2004, no. 96).

[96] Homer, *Iliad* 23.710–13 (Miller 2004, no. 1). For another depiction of the *systasis* position, see the front relief from the base of the statue of a *kouros* in Measham, et. al. 2000, no. 24.

[97] This prohibition is clear from a fragmentary late sixth-century list of regulations even though Pausanias tells us of a wrestler, Leontiskos of Messene, who specialized in finger bending. See Ebert 1997, 205 and 210–11 (Miller 2004, no. 101) and Nigel Crowther's chapter in this book. *Contra* Pausanias 6.4.3 (Miller 2004, no. 34).

[98] Africanus Olympiad 120 (Moretti 1957, no. 502).

[99] Additional examples of the soft *himantes* and the hard *himantes* can be seen in Measham, et al. 2000, nos. 43–4, and nos. 40–1 respectively.

[100] See, for example, the bout between Amykos and Polydeukes described by Theokritos *Idylls* 22.27–135 (Miller 2004, no. 39).

[101] Pausanias 8.40.3–5 (Miller 2004, no. 38).

[102] It is not clear why this was the final event, especially since it is separated from the other running events and, therefore, from the facilities common to all the running competitions. But modern scholars have agreed that the race in armor comes at this point in the program. I have not been able to find ancient evidence to support this placement.

[103] Pausanias 6.10.4 (Miller 2004, no. 26).

[104] The interpretation of athletics as a preparation for war is as venerable as Plutarch *Moralia* 639D–640A, but it flies in the face of the clear ancient distinction between athletics of the Olympic type and those of the local, civic type. The athletics of the international games, like the Olympics, were for and by the individual which is not what the city-state needed in the training of its citizens. Hence local games have a decidedly military character not to be found at Olympia. See Miller 2000, 278–9. For the architectural manifestation of the distinction between the Panhellenic and the civic games, see Miller 2001, 222–4.

[105] Euripides, *Autolykos*, frag. 282 (Miller 2004, no. 230). For a different reading of this fragment and the relationship between athletics and military performance, see David Pritchard's chapter in this book.

[106] Pindar *Pythian* 8.79 (Miller 2004, no. 249).

[107] See, for example, Measham et al. 2000, nos. 21–3.

[108] *SEG* 27.261B97 (Miller 2004, no. 185); Pliny *N.H.* 15.4.19 (Miller 2004, no. 8); 28.50–2 (Miller 2004, glossary).

[109] Sch. Pindar. *Ol.* 3.60.

[110] Pliny *N.H.* 34.87 and 35.54.

[111] For the triumphal entry, see Aelian *V.H.* 12.58 and Pliny the Younger *Letters* 10.118 (Miller 2004, nos. 172b and 211 respectively). For free meals, see *IG* I³ 131 and Plato *Apology* 36d–e (Miller 2004, nos. 221 and 231 respectively).

[112] For the competition to receive such commissions, see the chapter by Patrick O'Sullivan in this book. Note also that the statues of victors at Olympia could not be over life-size, Lucian *Portraiture defended* 11 (Miller 2004, 117).

[113] Lucian *Peregrinus* 35 (Miller 2004, no. 147).

Bibliography

Alexandre, O. (ed.)
   1989   *Mind and Body: Athletic contests in Ancient Greece*, Athens.
Blech, M.
   1982   *Studien zum Kranz bei den Griechen*, Berlin and New York.
Borthwick, E.K.
   1989   'A phyllobolia in Aristophanes' *Clouds*?', *Nikephoros* 2, 125–34.
Broneer, O.
   1973   *Isthmia,* II: *Topography and architecture*, Princeton.

Coulson, W. and Kyrieleis, H. (eds.)
1992   *Proceedings of an International Symposium on the Olympic Games, 5–9 September 1988*, Athens.

Crowther, N.B.
1985a   'Studies in Greek athletics I', *CW* 78, 497–558.
1985b   'Studies in Greek athletics II', *CW* 79, 73–135.
1991   'The Olympic training period', *Nikephoros* 4, 161–6.
1993   'Numbers of contestants in Greek athletic contests', *Nikephoros* 6, 39–52.
1999a   'Athlete as warrior', *Nikephoros* 12, 129–30.
1999b   'The finish line in the Greek foot race', *Nikephoros* 12, 131–42.

Crowther, N.B. and Frass, M.
1998   'Flogging as a punishment in the Ancient Games', *Nikephoros* 11, 51–82.

Decker, W.
1997   'Dolichos', in *Der Neue Pauly 3*, 733.

Drees, L.
1968   *Olympia: Gods, artists, and athletes*, New York.

Ebert, J.
1989   'Neues zum Hippodrom und zu den hippischen Konkurrenzen in Olympia', *Nikephoros* 2, 89–107.
1997   *Agonismata*, Stuttgart and Leipzig.

Finley, M.I. and Pleket, H.W.
1976   *The Olympic Games: The first thousand years*, London.

Gardiner, E.N.
1930   *Athletics of the Ancient World*, Oxford.

Hunt, D.
1993   'Christianising the Roman Empire', in J. Harries and I. Wood (eds.) *The Theodosian Code*, Ithaca, 143–58.

Jüthner, J.
1968   *Die athletischen Leibesübungen der Griechen* II, Vienna.

Kefalidou, E.
1996   ΝΙΚΗΤΗΣ. Εικονογραφική μελέτητου αρχαίου ελληνικού αθλητισμού, Thessaloniki.
1999   'Ceremonies of athletic victory in ancient Greece', *Nikephoros* 12, 95–109.

Knauss, J.
1998   *Olympische Studien: Herakles und der Stall des Augias. Kladeosmauer und Alpheiosdamm, the Hochwasserfreilegung von Alt-Olympia*, Munich.

Kyle, D.G.
1995   'Philostratus, 'repêchage', running and wrestling: the Greek pentathlon again', *Journal of Sport History* 22, 60–5.

Lee, H.
1992   'Some changes in the ancient Olympic program and schedule', in Coulson and Kyrieleis, *Proceedings…*, 105–12.
1995   'Yet another scoring system for the ancient Pentathlon', *Nikephoros* 8 41–55.

Lezzi–Hafter, A.
  1982   'Skyphos des Zephyros-Malers, Herrichten des Sportplatzes', in
          H. Bloesch (ed.) *Griechische Vasen der Sammlung Hierschmann*, Zurich,
          80–1.
Mallwitz, A.
  1972   *Olympia und seine Bauten*, Munich.
Maróti, E. and Maróti, G.
  1993   'Zur Frage des Pentathlon-Sieges', *Nikephoros* 6, 53–60.
Measham, T., Spathari, E. and Donnelly, P.
  2000   *1000 Years of the Olympic Games: Treasures of Ancient Greece*, Sydney.
Miller, S.G.
  1975   'The date of Olympic festivals', *Ath. Mitt.* 90, 215–31.
  1979   'Excavations at Nemea, 1978', *Hesperia* 48, 73–103.
  1980   'Turns and lanes in the ancient stadium', *AJA* 84, 159–66.
  1988   'The theorodokoi of the Nemean games', *Hesperia* 57, 147–63.
  2000   'Naked democracy', in P. Flensted–Jensen, T.H. Nielsen, and L. Rubin-
          stein (eds.) *Polis and Politics: Studies in ancient Greek history: Presented
          to Mogens Herman Hansen on his sixtieth birthday, August 20, 2000*,
          Copenhagen, 277–96.
  2001   *Nemea II: The early Hellenistic stadium*, Berkeley and Los Angeles.
  2004   *Arete: Greek sports from ancient sources*, 3rd edn, Berkeley and Los
          Angeles.
Moretti, L.
  1957   *Olympionikai: I vincitori negli antichi agoni Olimpici*, Atti dell' Accademia
          Nazionale dei Lincei, Memorie, ser. 8, vol. 8, Rome.
Perlman, P.
  2000   *City and Sanctuary in Ancient Greece: The* theorodokia *in the Peloponnese*,
          Göttingen.
Pfeijffer, I.L.
  1998   'Athletic age categories in victory odes', *Nikephoros* 11, 21–38.
Scanlon, T.F.
  1984   *Greek and Roman Athletics, A bibliography*, Chicago.
  2002   *Eros and Greek Athletics*, Oxford.
Siewert, P.
  1992   'The Olympic Rules', in Coulson and Kyrieleis, *Proceedings…*, 113–17.
Swaddling, J.
  1999   *The Ancient Olympic Games*, Austin.
Ulf, C.
  1979   'Die Einreibung der griechischen Athleten mit Öl', *Stadion* 5, 220–38.
Valavanis, P.
  1990   'La proclamation des vainqueurs aux Panathénées', *BCH* 114, 325–59.
  1999   *Hysplex: The starting mechanism in ancient stadia*, Berkeley and Los
          Angeles.
Van Straten, F.T.
  1995   *Hierà kalá: Images of animal sacrifice in archaic and classical Greece*,
          Leiden.

Waddell, G.
    1991   'The Greek pentathlon', *Greek Vases in the J. Paul Getty Museum* 5, 99–106.

Weniger, L.
    1904   'Das Hochfest des Zeus in Olympia', *Klio* 4, 125–51.

Yalouris, N. (ed.)
    1976   *The Olympic Games*, Athens. Also published under the title *Athletics in Ancient Greece*.

2

THE GERMAN EXCAVATIONS AT OLYMPIA: AN INTRODUCTION

Helmut Kyrieleis

Today there is hardly any other name from ancient Greece as popular across the world as Olympia. This is undoubtedly due to the international importance of the modern Olympic Games. For most people Olympia is a synonym for sport and peaceful contest. However, while the modern Olympic ideal owes much of its impact to the archaeological discovery of Olympia, it is based in many ways on a misunderstanding of what Olympia stood for in the ancient world. Typically it is overlooked that Olympia was primarily a sanctuary that, as a result of its oracle, religiously motivated athletic competitions, and official state visitors, had an eminently cultic and political significance for the Greeks (*Fig.* 1).

The great importance Olympia had for the ancient Greek world has meant that the archaeological exploration of the site has been conducted from the beginning with high expectations. Johann Joachim Winckelmann, the founder of the modern archaeology of ancient art, already wanted to excavate there. Back in 1766 the site of ancient Olympia, which had disappeared in the Middle Ages under several metres of alluvial silt, had just been identified by the English explorer William Chandler. The first archaeological excavations were undertaken by the French Expédition scientifique de Morée in 1829.[1] At that time some sections of the temple of Zeus were superficially cleared and fragments of its early classical marble sculpture, today housed in the Louvre in Paris, were found.

But another half century had to pass and years of political and diplomatic negotiations take place before a thorough scientific investigation of Olympia could begin. In many ways the excavations conducted since 1875 have set the standard for classical archaeology in Greece. This was already the case with the contract for the excavations at Olympia that the Greek and German governments signed in 1874. For the first time in the history of modern archaeology this contract spelt out that all excavated finds would remain the property of Greece, while the German team would have the right to publish them and the results of the excavations scientifically. These principles remain the basis for the work of foreign archaeological institutes in Greece and around the Mediterranean to the present day.

Fig. 1. Olympia. View from the south-west to the hill of Kronos. The *Leonidaion* is in the foreground. Photograph: the author.

The German excavations at Olympia from 1875 to 1881 were the first large-scale excavation project of classical archaeology to be undertaken with scientific aims. In this nineteenth-century project there were developed and applied for the first time methods of observation and documentation as well as procedures for the recording of construction phases that, in principle, are still valid today. Nevertheless, the great influence the excavations and finds at Olympia had on the development of classical archaeology in the nineteenth century is due also to the excellent quality of the publication of the excavation results and the fact that this was done in a remarkably short period of time. Only sixteen years after the completion of the excavations, the complete scientific publication of the results was available in five volumes, which, to the present day, are regarded as foundational work in archaeological literature.[2]

The *spiritus rector* of the excavations at Olympia was Ernst Curtius who, together with the architect Friedrich Adler, directed the project from Berlin. The work on site was carried out by young archaeologists and architects whose names, in the cases of Gustav Hirschfeld, Adolf Bötticher, Georg Treu, Wilhelm Dörpfeld and Adolf Furtwängler, would later become famous. In six seasons the enormous area of the sanctuary was uncovered by removing a 3–4 metres-thick layer of alluvial sediment (*Fig.* 2). The volume of the work and the logistics of the enterprise are in themselves

Fig. 2. Excavations at Olympia in 1878. The uncovering of the *Heraion* and the *Philippeion*. Photograph: Archive of the German Archaeological Institute (DAI), Berlin.

remarkable. A cautious estimate is that around a quarter of a million metric tons of river sediment and soil were dug and removed by horse-drawn carts. At that time the modern town of Olympia did not exist – it only began to develop as a consequence of the ensuing tourism to ancient Olympia – and the area surrounding the ancient site was only thinly populated. Therefore, the hundreds of workmen required had to be recruited from farther afield and accommodated and provided for on site. Amongst other logistical challenges, equipment and tools had to be brought from Germany.

From the excavation reports and plans the progress of the work can easily be followed. First, the temple of Zeus, dating to the fifth century BC, and its immediate vicinity were uncovered. This was then taken as the centre for the laying down of a system of test trenches to explore and map the surrounding area of the excavation. In the northern part of the sanctuary, often called the 'Altis', the excavators uncovered the archaic temple of Hera, the small Doric temple of Rhea (*mētrōon*), the terrace of the treasuries at the foot of the hill of Kronos, the so-called *Philippeion* – the round temple begun by Philip II of Macedon and completed by his son Alexander the Great, parts of the *palaistra*, the *prytaneion* and the entrance to the stadium. In the south, they found, amongst other monuments, the *bouleutērion* and part of the *Leonidaion* – a guest-house of the fourth century BC (*Fig.* 3).

Fig. 3. Model of Olympia by A. and E. Mallwitz. Archaeological Museum, Olympia. In the foreground on the left hand side is the *Leonidaion*. Photograph: German Archaeological Institute (DAI), Athens.

A valuable guide for the excavators and the decisive source for naming individual buildings was Pausanias who, sometime between 160 and 180 AD, wrote a kind of compendium for travelling around Greece that describes extensively the monuments at Olympia. The excavators of this sanctuary literally went about their work with Pausanias in hand. Without the detailed descriptions and catalogues of this ancient Greek author, even today it would very likely be impossible to name and identify most of the buildings at Olympia.[3]

These excavations brought to light not only the architecture and topography of ancient Olympia but also a great abundance and variety of inscriptions, sculptures and votive objects that allowed totally new insights into the history and significance of Olympia and into hitherto unknown periods of the history of Greek art. Of the great bronze statues seen and described by Pausanias the excavations found only their inscribed bases and numerous base fragments, as the statues themselves had fallen prey to the plundering of artwork by the Romans or the recycling of metal during later periods. Nonetheless, the discovery of some isolated pieces such as the bronze head of a champion Olympic boxer,[4] the Nike by Paionios,[5] and the Hermes by Praxiteles did give an idea of the former artistic excellence and richness of classical sculpture at Olympia.[6] Unquestionably, the most significant group of finds from the nineteenth-century excavations are the sculptures from the pediments and metopes of the temple of Zeus, which had been known before their discovery by the description of them by Pausanias (*Fig.* 4). While the French expedition of 1829 had already found parts of the metopes, further pieces of them as well as the sculptures of the pediment only came to light during the thorough investigation of the temple between 1875 and 1877. Precise recording of the find spots in conjunction with the description by Pausanias made possible the almost complete reconstruction of the pedimental decoration. That this reconstruction was put on display in the museum and published only ten years after the discovery of the sculptural figures is one of the pioneering achievements of classical archaeology and is especially associated with the name of Georg Treu.[7]

Fig. 4. Apollo from the west pediment of the temple of Zeus, around 470–460 BC. Archaeological Museum, Olympia. Photograph: German Archaeological Institute (DAI), Athens

For historical reasons the sculptures of the pediment and the reliefs of the metopes of the temple of Zeus are to be dated to around 470–60 BC.[8] The massive pedimental decoration with its larger-than-lifesize figures depicts the myth of the chariot race between Pelops and Oinomaos and the battle between the Greeks and Centaurs at the wedding of Perithoos.[9] The twelve metopes along the front and back of the *cella* show the twelve exploits of Herakles. The rediscovery and publication of this most important ensemble of early classical art literally revolutionized the modern conception of classical sculpture, which, until that point, had been shaped by the Parthenon sculptures and Roman copies of Greek masterpieces. On account of their dramatic expression and monumentality, these figures are regarded as one of the absolute high points of Greek sculpture. Their heavy and energetic forms and serious, almost sombre, expressions encouraged the coining of the term 'severe style' to describe this phase in the history of Greek art.

The excavations at Olympia also opened a new chapter in research on the beginnings of Greek art. In the lowest levels of the excavations thousands of

Fig. 5. Geometric bronzes, eighth century BC. Archaeological Museum, Olympia. They are the contents of one of the many assemblage boxes in the bronze storeroom of the museum and give an idea of the abundance of geometric votives at Olympia. Photograph: Ingrid Geske / German Archaeological Institute (DAI), Berlin.

votive figurines of bronze and clay were found, which, with their simplified and abstract shape, were very different from any other examples of Greek art known up until that point. While most of these depict horses or cattle (*Fig.* 5), there are many human figures as well. Some of these figurines served as decorative elements on large bronze tripod cauldrons, numerous fragments of which were also found. The style of these figurines is marked by a reduction of natural forms to simplified basic shapes and an emphasis on a few characteristic features. The excavators at Olympia were surprised to find thousands of objects of this new type.

Today, after many years of scholarly debate and the discovery of such artefacts at necropolises and sanctuaries from all over Greece, we know these objects to be examples of the so-called geometric style of Greek art of the ninth and eighth centuries BC. Initially, opinion was divided on the dating and the significance of these finds. While Wilhelm Dörpfeld, for example, was convinced that they were prehistoric figurines, Adolf Furtwängler, who published the bronzes from the nineteenth-century excavations at Olympia, had correctly recognized their significance as the earliest examples of Greek sculpture and thus laid the foundation for the study of early Greek art.[10]

After this first extensive period of excavations, apart from a few small-scale re-investigations by Wilhelm Dörpfeld, no further work was conducted at Olympia for half a century. Essentially the site was considered excavated and further work did not seem worthwhile. Only in connection with the Berlin Olympic Games of 1936 did it occur to anyone to revive the German excavations at Olympia. The main idea was to excavate the ancient stadium and so recover the site of competition of the ancient

Olympic Games. The aim here was not so much to gain scientific insights but to influence public opinion. As a result, substantial financial support for this enterprise was successfully mobilized.[11] In keeping with this aim, a symbolic act was invented to emphasize the special connection of the modern Olympic Games with ancient Olympia. This act is still repeated every four years and has lost none of its popularity. The lighting of the Olympic flame and its relay to the site of each new Olympic Games took place for the first time in 1936. It has nothing to do with antiquity.

The new excavations began in 1937. What the politicians planned as a showcase project for the 'Third Reich' was understood and conducted by the archaeologists in charge as purely scientific research. However, the excavation of the stadium, which had played such an important role in the promotion of this expedition, was not the focus at first, because the opinion still prevailed among archaeologists that such a large-scale operation would yield few finds and next to no scientific results. This soon proved to be wrong. The excavations, under the directorship of Emil Kunze from the winter campaign of 1937/8, concentrated at the outset on the areas of the sanctuary in the south and south-west that had been untouched by previous expeditions. At that time, the only activity in the stadium was the excavation of a large trench across the stands for the spectators and the racetrack, which did allow preliminary insights into the structure and construction history of a monument that was built entirely of earth. This work had to stop in 1942, because of the war, and could only resume ten years later. As the aims and methods of the excavation as well as the directorship of Emil Kunze continued without change until 1966, the excavations stretching from 1937 to 1966 can be taken as the second major phase of excavations at Olympia. In this period, the site and its ruins expanded significantly. In the south-west the hitherto unexcavated part of the so-called *Leonidaion* was completely uncovered, a huge square guest-house of the fourth century BC which was altered in the Roman period. In the west most of the *gymnasion* was recovered and some columns of the *palaistra* were re-erected. The stadium was now completely excavated and reconstructed in line with its original form in the fourth century BC (*Fig. 6*). With the conclusion of this work in 1963, a grand monument of sporting history, impressive in its simplicity, had been recovered. Today, the stadium is so much taken for granted in the landscape of Olympia that it is hard to imagine that one of the most extensive archaeological excavations of the twentieth century was set in motion to restore it. Contrary to all expectations, the massive earthworks necessitated by this project yielded extremely interesting archaeological results. They revealed, for example, that the stadium was built in several

Fig. 6. The stadium of Olympia. Photograph: the author.

phases and that it was not until the late classical period that it had the location and form of its present reconstructed state.[12]

The abundance of finds, especially of bronze, that had been buried when the embankments for the spectators were constructed was quite overwhelming. These expand our knowledge of the variety and artistic quality of votive objects that were dedicated at Olympia from all over the Greek world between the seventh and fifth centuries BC (*Fig.* 7). Moreover, the finds from the stadium shed light on another historically significant aspect of ancient Olympia. In general, the excavations at Olympia have produced an extraordinary number of weapons, including helmets, greaves, shields, breast plates and spear- and arrow-heads. These, housed today in the site museum at Olympia, form the most extensive 'arsenal' of Greek weapons and allow for unique insights into the highly-developed production techniques, flourishing artistry and craftsmanship of the Greek armourers of the archaic and classical periods (*Fig.* 8).[13]

But why were there so many weapons at Olympia? The answer to this question is given in inscriptions engraved onto many of these objects. They are booty dedicated to Zeus of Olympia after victory in war.

Fig. 7 . Laconian bronze statuette of an old man, sixth century BC. Archaeological Museum, Olympia, inventory no. B 25. Photograph: German Archaeological Institute (DAI), Athens.

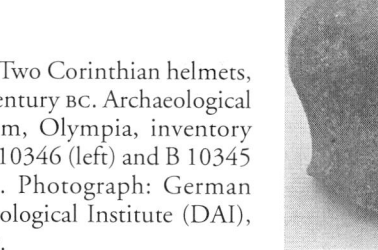

Fig. 8. Two Corinthian helmets, sixth century BC. Archaeological Museum, Olympia, inventory nos. B 10346 (left) and B 10345 (right). Photograph: German Archaeological Institute (DAI), Athens.

Often votive inscriptions name both the victors and the vanquished which allows the weapons on which they appear to be linked with historical events. Famous examples are an oriental helmet, which, according to the punched inscription, was seized by the Athenians from the Persians and so would have come from the battle of Marathon in 490 BC,[14] and a Greek helmet dedicated at Olympia in the name of Miltiades – the victorious commander of this battle.[15] But it was not just the victories of Greeks against foreigners that were celebrated in the inscriptions on these weapons. Far more frequent are the inscriptions mentioning the victories of Greek city-states over other Greeks that are so characteristic of the political history of ancient Greece. Indeed, these internal conflicts in Greece were the reason for the 'sacred truce' under which the Olympic Games took place every four years. It is particularly surprising that the majority of these weapons were found atop and within the embankments of the archaic and classical phases of the stadium. From the depositional circumstances of individual pieces and the existence of large postholes in various embankment surfaces, it can be inferred unambiguously that these captured weapons were originally exhibited as so-called *tropaia* which served as symbols of military victory. They would have been hung on wooden posts driven into the stadium embankment.[16] In view of the modern ideal that Olympic Games should be peaceful in character, it might come as a shock that the ancient Greeks used, of all places, a site of athletic competitions to display in front of tens of thousands of spectators such martial reminders of armed conflict. But these archaeological finds demonstrate that ancient Olympia cannot be understood from the perspective of the modern Olympic ideal. The dominant idea of ancient Olympia was not peace but victory, both in sport and armed conflict. This is borne out by many inscriptions and monuments at Olympia, and it is no coincidence that the cult image of Zeus in the main temple of the sanctuary represents the god holding in his right hand Nike – the goddess of victory (Pausanias 5.11.1).

The excavations directed by Emil Kunze are distinguished too by an unusually large number of significant finds made especially of bronze. This abundance is due to another remarkable feature of Olympia also discovered during the excavation of the stadium. It was revealed that there existed here, before the construction of the stadium of the classical period, numerous wells which, at first, only showed up as patches of discoloration during the excavation. These patches were the round shafts of wells that had been obviously dug during festivals to supply visitors with drinking water. Since they were only ever in use for a few days, they did not have to be lined with stone and were filled in again at the end of the festivities. Into these wells were thrown a great number of votive offerings which, while damaged or obsolete, had as the property of the god to remain within the sacred precinct. These earthen wells are a distinct characteristic of archaic and classical Olympia and were discovered in various areas around the periphery of the sanctuary. During their excavation many objects of ancient art, some still in excellent condition, were recovered.[17]

Of the numerous discoveries made during the directorship of Kunze I would like to draw attention to one other which was particularly sensational. The close examination of the early Byzantine basilica and its vicinity west of the temple of Zeus, between 1954 and 1958, reached the amazing conclusion that the original classical building, inside which this church had been set up in the sixth century AD, was nothing less than the workshop of the sculptor Pheidias and was where this famous Athenian had created the great gold and ivory cult image for the temple of Zeus.[18] Not a trace remains of this colossal statue of the enthroned Zeus that was counted as one of the Seven Wonders of the ancient world. Today, we can only visualize it on the basis of its description by Pausanias (5.11) and a highly simplified depiction of it on bronze coins from the reign of the emperor Hadrian.[19] The discovery of the workshop of Pheidias provides secure evidence – albeit a very modest amount – about how this famous work of art was manufactured. According to ancient descriptions, the statue must have been over twelve metres high and consisted most probably of an internal wooden structure and an outer cladding of gold and ivory. In the workshop – the size of which would have roughly corresponded to the room inside the *cella* of the temple of Zeus – the individual parts of the cult image were made and assembled. Since this statue, which was enormous in its completed state, could not have fitted between the columns of the temple or through its door, it was next taken apart, transported to the temple, and reassembled there. Interesting traces of the artistry and craftsmanship which went into the cult image were found in the debris outside the workshop: scraps of ivory and obsidian inlay, bone *spatulae*, a goldsmith's hammer, lead stencils for ornaments, remains of floral glass ornaments – along with the terracotta moulds for producing them – and terracotta matrices to make the glass coating of garments. These remains give a faint glimpse of the skilled craftsmanship that went into every detail of the colossus of Zeus and the ornamental splendour that once radiated from the image of this deity and his throne. However, amongst these workshop remnants the nicest find was a modest drinking vessel of black glazed clay with an inscription incised into its base: Φειδίου εἰμί ('I am the property of Pheidias').[20] Here is a direct and touching personal attestation of the great artist and possibly even an autograph of Pheidias himself.

After a break of ten years, which was spent mainly publishing results, the third major period of excavations at Olympia began under the directorship of Alfred Mallwitz. The main aim of this excavation was to clarify the topography of the southern area of the sanctuary. Metres of sterile sedimentary layers covering ancient Olympia were removed with bulldozers. In the course of this work, large structures, dating to the Roman empire and in most cases intact to the height of their vaulted ceilings, were exposed in the south-west of the sanctuary. Their size and fitting-out with valuable building materials, mosaics and marble facing that can be deduced from surviving fragments give a good impression of the significance Olympia still had during the Roman empire.

The most recent investigations at Olympia, conducted since 1985 under the directorship of the author, consist of two different research projects which, putting it simply, focus on the very latest and earliest periods of the history of the sanctuary.

The research project looking at Olympia during the Roman empire and late antiquity is led by Ulrich Sinn. This excavation has focused on the exploration of various structures of the Roman imperial age at the periphery of the site. It has also established secure stratigraphic sequences which, for the first time in the history of the excavations, allow the tracing of the later construction history of Olympia, its transformation from a sanctuary into an early Christian rural settlement, and the decline and covering over of that settlement in the early Middle Ages.[21] For example, there has been investigated in the area north of the *prytaneion* an early imperial complex with peristyle hall and adjoining baths whose individual buildings were altered several times until late antiquity when some were then used as storerooms and workshops.[22]

Further excavations have concentrated on the so-called 'South-West Building' to the south of the *Leonidaion* (*Fig.* 9). Its brick walls remained intact up to where the vaulting had begun. Before excavation they had been completely covered by alluvial sediment. This elaborately adorned

Fig. 9. The 'South-West Building' after excavation. Photograph: the author.

building was originally clad with marble architectural elements and had in front of it a swimming pool and a courtyard surrounded by columned halls. A dedicatory inscription on blocks subsequently reused indicates that this building was completed under the emperor Domitian.[23] Sinn interprets it as being the clubhouse of a society of professional athletes.[24]

The excavation programme investigating the earliest history of Olympia, conducted by the author since 1986, has focused on the origins and antiquity of what is the most significant sanctuary of Zeus in Greece. Scholars have long been concerned with these issues as different versions of the ancient mythological tradition appear to point to a very ancient origin for the cult of Zeus at Olympia.[25] Also, the quantity and quality of votive objects excavated at Olympia, especially the bronze geometric objects such as tripods, statuettes and jewellery, indicate that the sanctuary must have had interregional significance as early as the ninth and eighth centuries BC. However, these finds all came from later layers and not from their original contexts. In fact, no stratigraphic or structural feature securely attributable to an older phase of the sanctuary was found. The aim of our investigations was to determine the oldest traces of the cult of Zeus at Olympia and whether there was, as has been sometimes suggested, continuity from the Bronze Age into the early Iron Age.[26] In our search for stratigraphic clues to solve this problem, we concentrated mainly on the *Pelopion* – the *hērōon* (hero shrine) of Pelops that is situated at the centre of the sanctuary and where, according to ancient tradition (Pindar *Ol.* 10.24–5, 45–9), the cult festival at Olympia was founded (*Fig.* 10). As early as 1929 Wilhelm Dörpfeld had noticed in various sondages under this

Fig. 10. Excavation of the *Pelopion*. The *Heraion* is in the foreground. Photograph: the author.

hērōon – with its enclosure wall of the classical period – a stone circle which he interpreted as the border of a tumulus and so a structure predating the *Pelopion*.[27] In addition, to the north and east of the *hērōon*, he uncovered prehistoric houses with an apsidal ground plan, which, because of an error in his observations, he thought to be older than the tumulus itself. Yet the dating of the tumulus was not secure. Scholars later occasionally suggested a date in the Mycenean period,[28] or even denied the existence of the stone circle altogether.[29] When we re-excavated the area, Dörpfeld's observations proved to be correct in principle. However, we discovered that the prehistoric tumulus was not earlier but later than the apsidal houses. On the basis of the ceramic finds analysed by my colleague Jörg Rambach, the tumulus can be dated to the early Helladic II period, that is, the middle of the third millenium BC, while the apsidal houses were only built in the early Helladic III phase, towards the end of the third millenium BC.[30] The surface of the tumulus was originally paved with light-coloured limestone slabs and must still have been visible above ground in the early Iron Age.[31]

In the area immediately around the *Pelopion* the nineteenth-century excavators found substantial deposits of ash and soil mixed with charcoal that contained innumerable geometric votive objects. This so-called 'black layer', which also had many partly-burnt pieces of animal bone, fragments of iron spits and pot sherds, seems to have been waste from the cult and sacrificial rituals in the sanctuary. The ceramics found in these deposits enable the latest material to be securely dated well into the seventh century BC. In our re-investigation we were still able to analyse several cubic metres of this black layer from under the classical wall of the *Pelopion*. This showed that the layer was separated from the level of the early Bronze Age buildings by a sterile layer of sand. So, with respect to stratigraphy, there was no continuity with the much earlier buildings of the Bronze Age. The thorough analysis of this intact section also revealed that the black layer did not accumulate gradually but rather was a secondary deposit heaped up and levelled out at a later date. Obviously this again is the waste from one or several altars in the immediate vicinity of the *Pelopion*. As expected, a substantial number of geometric terracotta figurines and burnt animal bones, amongst other items, were also found here (*Figs.* 11, 12). No chronological differentiation based on stratigraphy is possible within this deposit. Nevertheless, the artefacts found in this area, such as numerous sherds of protogeometric pottery and fairly large parts of submycenean *kylikes* (drinking cups) datable to the late eleventh century BC, add considerably to our present knowledge about the sanctuary.[32]

Fig. 11. Geometric animal figurines of bronze, eighth century BC. Archaeological Museum, Olympia, inventory nos. (from left to right) B 11570, B 11562, B 11567, B 11575 and B 11577. Photograph: Ingrid Geske / German Archaeological Institute (DAI), Berlin.

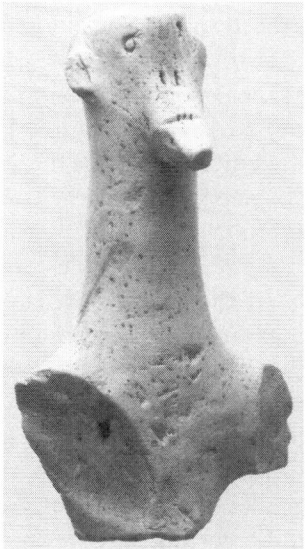

Fig. 12. Terracotta figurine of a male, eighth century BC. Archaeological Museum, Olympia, inventory no. T 1201. Photograph: Peter Grunwald / German Archaeological Institute (DAI), Berlin.

Therefore, what we are dealing with here is evidence pointing to cult activity of regional importance which, according to the archaeology, started in the late eleventh century BC and developed continuously from that point on. However, any continuity of cult at Olympia from the Mycenean period proper to the protogeometric period can be ruled out. Between the remains of the early Bronze Age and the beginnings of the Greek sanctuary there is a gaping hiatus of a thousand years.

What can be said as a preliminary result is that the cult of Zeus at Olympia was established in the late eleventh century BC, in direct association with the prehistoric tumulus still conspicuous at that time and that later would be considered the tomb of Pelops. Obviously, the early Iron Age cult at Olympia was a result of a conscious act to forge a connection with the venerable remains from prehistoric times. A faint memory of this event might even be preserved in a few lines of Pindar (*Ol.* 10.24 ff.) where Herakles founds the sanctuary of Zeus ἀρχαίῳ σάματι πὰρ Πέλοπος ('at the ancient monument of Pelops'). That the archaeological evidence and this version of the foundation myth should agree in principle is quite remarkable.

Notes

[1] See Blouet et al. 1831 and Pasquier 2000.

[2] Curtius and Adler 1890–7. Each of the five volumes of the publication of the nineteenth-century excavations was differently authored and has a separate listing in the bibliography. For reproductions of plates from these volumes, see *Figs.* 5 to 7 in the chapter by Kate da Costa et al. in this book.

[3] For further discussion of the value of Pausanias as a source for Olympia and the Olympic Games, see Stephen Miller's chapter in this book.

[4] National Archaeological Museum, Athens, inventory no. 6439; Furtwängler 1897, 10–11, pl. 2; Lullies and Hirmer 1960, 82, pls. 238–9; Bol 1978, 114 f., no. 159, pls. 30–2; Herrmann and Mallwitz 1980, 195 f., no. 137, pl. 137.

[5] Archaeological Museum, Olympia; Treu 1897, 182–93, pls. 46–8; Lullies and Hirmer 1960, 65, pl. 178; Herrmann and Mallwitz 1980, 189–91, no. 134, pls. 134 a–b.

[6] For the Hermes by Praxiteles, see Treu 1897, 194–205 pls. 49–53; Lullies and Hirmer 1960, 80 f. pls. 228–30; Herrmann and Mallwitz 1980, 192, no. 135, pls. 135 a–b.

[7] Treu 1897, 44–181, pls. 18–45. See also Buschor and Hamann 1924; Ashmole, Yalouris and Frantz 1967; Herrmann and Mallwitz 1980, 161–79, figs. 17–26, pls. 113–27. For an anthology of research works on the sculptures of the temple of Zeus, see Herrmann 1987.

[8] The building of the temple began sometime after the Persian Wars and most probably after the political re-organization of Elis in 472/1 BC. An approximate

date for its completion is given by the shield fixed to the top of its east pediment that the Spartans dedicated after their victory at Tanagra in 457 BC. (Pausanias 5.10.4). See also Mallwitz 1972, 211; Herrmann 1987, 2–3.

[9] For a detailed discussion of the history of the myth of Pelops and Oinomaos, including its treatment on the temple of Zeus, see John Davidson's chapter in this book.

[10] Furtwängler 1879 which is reprinted at Sieveking and Curtius 1912, 339–421. The controversy about the chronology is summarized in Dörpfeld 1935, 2–14.

[11] The high priority given to this project by the National Socialist Government is evident in the fact that the excavation funds came not from the budget of the Ministry of Education, their normal source, but from the Fuehrer's discretionary fund ('Dispositionsfonds des Führers'). See Juncker 1997, 70–1.

[12] For publications on the stadium excavations, see Kunze 1961a 17–24, figs. 10–16; 1967a; Mallwitz 1967.

[13] For publications and analyses of these weapons, see Baitinger 2001; Kunze 1937/8, 1967b, 1991, 1994, Schilbach 1992.

[14] Archaeological Museum, Olympia, inventory no. B 5100; Kunze 1961b; Herrmann and Mallwitz 1980, 96, no. 58, pl. 58.

[15] Archaeological Museum, Olympia, inventory no. B 2600; Kunze 1956; Herrmann and Mallwitz 1980, 95–6, no. 57, pl. 57.

[16] For a comprehensive discussion of the votive weapons and armour of Olympia, see Baitinger 2001, 80–92.

[17] For the wells under the embankments of the stadium, see Gauer 1975; Kunze 1967a, 4–6, figs. 4–5; Mallwitz 1977, 23, fig. 6, pl. 10,2. For the wells in Olympia in general, see Mallwitz 1999.

[18] For publications on this famous workshop, see Mallwitz and Schiering 1964; Schiering 1991. See also Mallwitz 1972, 255–66, figs. 202–19.

[19] See Franke 1984; Liegle 1952. Note also Herrmann 1972, 152 pls. 60 a–b.

[20] Archaeological Museum, Olympia, inventory no. P 3653; Kunze 1961a, 16, figs. 8–9; Mallwitz and Schiering 1974, 169, pl. 64; Herrmann 1972, 154, pl. 60 c–d.

[21] For preliminary reports, see Sinn 1992, 1993, 1997; Sinn et al. 1994, 1995, 1996. See also Sinn 1999, 2000.

[22] A final publication of this complex by Sinn and others is forthcoming in the *Olympische Forschungen* monograph series. For preliminary reports, see Touchais 1988, 632, fig. 38; 1989, 615–16, fig. 65; Pariente 1990, 746–7, figs. 56–7.

[23] See especially Wörrle 2000 and the short note 'Die Bauinschrift' by the same author at Sinn et al. 1995, 168.

[24] Sinn et al. 1994, 231–41; 1995, 162–8.

[25] The main source here is again Pausanias (5.7.6–8.5). See Ziehen 1937; Herrmann 1972, 37–4; Ulf 1997.

[26] e.g. Hermann 1962; 1972, 64–5.

[27] See Dörpfeld 1935, 73–102, 118–24, figs. 3–19, 21–4, Beilage 2–4, pls. 2–3, 5.

[28] e.g. Herrmann 1972, 55.

[29] e.g. Mallwitz 1972, 135–7.

[30] The results of the excavation of the prehistoric contexts at the *Pelopion* will be published by J. Rambach in the *Olympische Forschungen* monograph series. For preliminary reports, see Rambach 2001, 2002.

[31] The final publication by the author of the Iron Age deposits in the area of the *Pelopion* will appear in a forthcoming volume of the *Olympische Forschungen* series. For the present see the summary reports, Kyrieleis 1992, 1999.

[32] The full documentation and discussion of the Early Iron Age pottery from the *Pelopion* excavation by Birgitta Eder will appear in the final publication of the excavation. For a preliminary evaluation of this material, see Eder 2001.

Bibliography

Adler, F., Borrmann, R., Dörpfeld, W., Graeber, F. and Graef, P.
  1892   *Olympia II: Die Baudenkmäler von Olympia*, Berlin.
Adler, F., Curtius, E., Dörpfeld, W., Graef, P., Partsch, J. and Weil, R.
  1897   *Olympia I: Topographie und Geschichte*, Berlin.
Ashmole, B., Yalouris, N. and Frantz, A.
  1967   *The Sculptures of the Temple of Zeus*, London.
Baitinger, H.
  2001   *Die Angriffswaffen aus Olympia*, Olympische Forschungen XXIX, Berlin.
Blouet, A. et al.
  1831   *Expédition scientifique de Morée I*, Paris.
Bol, P.C.
  1978   *Grossplastik aus Bronze in Olympia*, Olympische Forschungen IX, Berlin.
Buschor, E. and Hamann, R.
  1924   *Die Skulpturen des Zeustempels von Olympia*, Marburg.
Coulson, W. and Kyrieleis, H. (eds.)
  1992   *Proceedings of an International Symposium on the Olympic Games, 5–9 September 1988*, Athens.
Curtius, E. and Adler, F. (eds.)
  1890–7   *Olympia: Die Ergebnisse der vom Deutschen Reich veranstalteten Ausgrabungen*, vols. 1–5, Berlin.
Dittenberger, W. and Purgold, K.
  1896   *Olympia V: Die Inschriften von Olympia*, Berlin.
Dörpfeld, W.
  1935   *Alt-Olympia*, Berlin.
Eder, B.
  2001   'Continuity of Bronze Age cult at Olympia? The evidence of the late Bronze Age and early Iron Age pottery', in R. Laffineur and R. Hägg (eds.) *Potnia: Deities and religion in the Aegean Bronze Age: Proceedings of the 8th International Aegean Conference, Göteborg, 12–15 April 2000*, Aegeum 22, Liège, 201–9, pls. LXIV–LXVI.

Franke, P.R.
   1984   'ΗΛΙΑΚΑ - ΟΛΥΜΠΙΑΚΑ', *MDAI(A)* 99, 325–33, pls. 50–2.
Furtwängler, A.
   1879   *Die Bronzefunde aus Olympia und deren kunstgeschichtliche Bedeutung*,
          Abhandlungen der Königlichen Akademie der Wissenschaften zu Berlin,
          phil.-hist. Klasse IV, Berlin.
   1897   *Olympia IV: Die Bronzen und die übrigen kleineren Funde von Olympia*,
          Berlin.
Gauer, W.
   1975   *Die Tongefässe aus den Brunnen unterm Stadion-Nordwall und im Südost-
          Gebiet*, Olympische Forschungen VIII, Berlin.
Herrmann, H.-V.
   1962   'Zur ältesten Geschichte Olympias', *MDAI(A)* 77, 4–34.
   1972   *Olympia: Heiligtum und Wettkampfstätte*, Munich.
Herrmann, H.-V. (ed.)
   1987   *Die Olympia-Skulpturen*, Darmstadt.
Herrmann, H.-V. and Mallwitz, A.
   1980   *Die Funde aus Olympia: Ergebnisse 100-jähriger Ausgrabungstätigkeit*,
          Athens.
Juncker, K.
   1997   *Das Archäologische Institut des Deutschen Reiches zwischen Forschung und
          Politik: Die Jahre 1929 bis 1945*, Mainz.
Kunze, E.
   1937/8 'Waffen-Funde', in *Olympiabericht II*, 66–103, figs. 42–64.
   1956   'Eine Weihung des Miltiades', in *Olympiabericht V*, 69–74, pls. 34–5.
   1961a 'Die Ausgrabungen in den Frühjahren 1956 bis 1958', in *Olympiabericht
          VII*, 1–28.
   1961b 'Ein Bronzehelm aus der Perserbeute', in *Olympiabericht VII*, 129–37,
          fig. 75, pls. 56–7.
   1967a 'Die Arbeiten vom Herbst 1958 bis zum Sommer 1962', in *Olympia-
          bericht VIII*, 1–15, figs. 1–11.
   1967b 'Waffenweihungen: Helme', in *Olympiabericht VIII*, 83–183, figs.
          28–67, pls. 30–95.
   1991   *Beinschienen*, Olympische Forschungen XXI, Berlin.
   1994   'Chalkidische Helme', in *Olympiabericht IX*, 27–100, figs. 40–77, pls.
          1–35.
Kyrieleis, H.
   1992   'Neue Ausgrabungen in Olympia', in Coulson and Kyrieleis (eds.)
          Proceedings…, 19–24, pls. I–VI.
   1999   'Neue Ausgrabungen in Olympia', *AW* 21, 181–8, figs. 6–15.
Liegle, J.
   1952   *Der Zeus des Phidias*, Berlin.
Lullies, R. and Hirmer, M.
   1960   *Griechische Plastik*, Munich.
Mallwitz, A.
   1967   'Das Stadion', in *Olympiabericht VIII*, 16–82, pls. 1–29.

1972   *Olympia und seine Bauten*, Munich.
1977   'Ein Jahrhundert deutsche Ausgrabungen in Olympia', *MDAI(A)* 92, 1–31.
1999   'Brunnen und Wettkampfplätze', in *Olympiabericht XI*, 186–99, figs. 110–11.
Mallwitz, A. and Schiering, W.
1964   *Die Werkstatt des Pheidias in Olympia, Teil 1*, Olympische Forschungen V, Berlin.
Pariente, A.
1990   'Chronique des fouilles', *BCH* 114, 703–850.
Pasquier, A.
2000   'Premières découvertes sur le site d'Olympie' in *Olympie: Cycle de huit conférences organisé au musée du Louvre 1999*, Paris, 15–43.
Rambach, J.
2001   'Bemerkungen zur Zeitstellung der Apsidenhäuser in der Altis von Olympia', in R.M. Boehmer and J. Maran (eds.) *Lux Orientis: Archäologie zwischen Asien und Europa: Festschrift für Harald Hauptmann*, Rahden, 330–3.
2002   (in press) 'Olympia: 2500 Jahre Vorgeschichte vor der Gründung des eisenzeitlichen griechischen Heiligtums', in H. Kyrieleis (ed.) *Olympia 1875–2000: 125 Jahre Deutsche Ausgrabungen: Internationales Symposion, Berlin, 9–11 November 2000*, Mainz.
Schiering, W.
1991   *Die Werkstatt des Pheidias in Olympia, Teil 2: Werkstattfunde*, Olympische Forschungen XVIII, Berlin.
Schilbach, J.
1992   'Olympia, die Entwicklungsphasen des Stadions', in Coulson and Kyrieleis (eds.) *Proceedings...*, 33–7, pls. 14–21.
Sieveking, J. and Curtius, L. (eds.)
1912   *Kleine Schriften von Adolf Furtwängler I*, Munich.
Sinn, U.
1992   'Bericht über das Forschungsprojekt 'Olympia während der römischen Kaiserzeit': I: Die Arbeiten von 1987–92', *Nikephoros* 5, 75–84.
1993   'Bericht über das Forschungsprojekt 'Olympia während der römischen Kaiserzeit': II: Die Arbeiten im Jahr 1993', *Nikephoros* 6, 153–8.
1997   'Bericht über das Forschungsprojekt 'Olympia während der römischen Kaiserzeit': VI: Die Arbeiten im Jahr 1996', *Nikephoros* 10, 215–16.
1999   'Olympia: pilgrims, athletes and christians: the development of the site in late antiquity', in R.F. Docter and E.M. Moormann (eds.) *Proceedings of the XVth International Congress of Classical Archaeology, Amsterdam July 12–17, 1998*, Amsterdam, 377–80.
2000   'Olympie, centre d'artisanat chrétien', in *Olympie: Cycle de huit conférences organisé au musée du Louvre 1999*, Paris, 217–37.
Sinn, U., Ladstätter, G., Martin, A., Völling, T.
1994   'Bericht über das Forschungsprojekt 'Olympia während der römischen Kaiserzeit': III: Die Arbeiten im Jahr 1994', *Nikephoros* 7, 229–50.

1995   'Bericht über das Forschungsprojekt 'Olympia während der römischen Kaiserzeit': IV: Die Arbeiten im Jahr 1995, Teil 1', *Nikephoros* 8, 161–82.

1996   'Bericht über das Forschungsprojekt 'Olympia während der römischen Kaiserzeit': V: Die Arbeiten im Jahr 1995, Teil 2', *Nikephoros* 9, 199–228.

Touchais, G.

1988   'Chronique des fouilles', *BCH* 112, 611–96.

1989   'Chronique des fouilles', *BCH* 113, 581–700.

Treu, G.

1897   *Olympia III: Die Bildwerke in Stein und Thon*, Berlin.

Ulf, Chr.

1997   'Die Mythen um Olympia: Politischer Gehalt und politische Intention', *Nikephoros* 10, 9–51.

Wörrle, M.

2000   'Des Kaisers neue Feste', in *Archäologische Entdeckungen: Die Forschungen des Deutschen Archäologischen Instituts im 20. Jahrhundert*, Mainz, 91–4, fig. 104.

Ziehen, L.

1937   'Olympia', in *Paulys Real-Encyclopädie der classischen Altertumswissenschaft*, XVII.2, Stuttgart, 2520–31.

3

ELIS AND OLYMPIA:
CITY, SANCTUARY AND POLITICS

Nigel B. Crowther

Today the remains of the city of ancient Elis, despite extensive excavations by Austrian and Greek archaeologists, are generally ignored by the hordes of tourists on their way to Olympia. Scholars too often underestimate the important role of Elis in relation to the Olympic Games, and especially the significance of Olympia for its civic identity and political organization. The role of this provincial city has been obscured by the undeniably Panhellenic features of the Olympic festival, such as the treasuries and sacred envoys (*theōroi*) of other cities. Yet despite these traits, the sanctuary and Games at Olympia were important to Elis in a similar way to 'local' games, which were organized by, and critical to, other city states. From the evidence of buildings in Elis and Olympia, and from inscriptional and other sources it is evident that the Eleans controlled the Olympic Games as if they belonged entirely to them.

Historical background to Elis and Olympia

The sources for the early history of the Olympic Games are problematic.[1] The exact period, therefore, when Elis had effective control over the festival at Olympia is far from clear, but Elis probably had authority over the sanctuary and Games for most of the first hundred years, as Strabo (8.3.30) suggests,[2] although we should temper this view with the statement of Xenophon (*Hell.* 7.4.28) that Pisa claimed to have been the first to have been in charge of the sanctuary.[3] For a time Elis had to contend with short takeovers of Olympia by the Pisatans, who administered the festival of 748 BC, according to Pausanias (6.22.2),[4] when Pheidon of Argos invaded Olympia and gave them control (Herodotus 6.127; Strabo 8.3.33, who cites Ephorus). The Pisatans also are said to have controlled the Games from the thirtieth to the fifty-second Olympiad, i.e. 660–572 BC (Julius Africanus). During this period it is known that Pantaleon, the King of Pisa, held by force the Games of 644 BC (Pausanias 6.22.2).[5] Mallwitz

(1988, 102) believes that this takeover by Pisa is supported by archaeological evidence, since the destruction of the black stratum in the Altis suggests a rearrangement by the invaders of the earlier altar area. It is clear, therefore, that Elis regained control in the sixth century BC, which can be supported by the so-called *leges sacrae* (below), the earliest inscriptional evidence for the Eleans at Olympia. In 364 BC the claim of Pisa to Olympia was revived by the Arcadians, who gained control of the sanctuary and celebrated the Games of that year together with the people of Pisa, despite a fierce battle against the Eleans in the Altis (Xenophon *Hell.* 7.4.28–32).

The control of Elis over Olympia was especially recognized in Greece after 471/70 BC, the time when the various small communities in the region were united into one institutional and political unit (Strabo 8.3.2, Diodorus Siculus 11.54.10). The political implications within Elis as a result of this synoecism are uncertain, since the oligarchy and democracy competed for power, but it is possible that the greater democratization of the city may have led to the democratization of the Games at Olympia.[6]

Conflict between two city states for the control of a Panhellenic festival was not unusual in Greece. Argos and Cleonae, for instance, strove to gain power over the Nemean Games.[7] The importance to a community of having authority over a major festival was that it brought prestige, perhaps even new or additional sources of revenue, increased leverage in disputed territory (an important factor for Elis), and much greater political influence in Greece.

Although Elis as a city did not become a major power in Greece, it did wield considerable political influence through Olympia, even though it was ostensibly known for its neutrality, according to Strabo (8.3.33).[8] Until 420 BC, Elis was a loyal ally of Sparta, but joined in an alliance with Athens and Argos, when Sparta championed Lepreon (Thucydides 5.49.1–50.4). At that time the Spartans were excluded from the Games and sanctuary at Olympia, since they had broken the Olympic truce, according to the Eleans, by attacking their territory, and had not paid the fine which was assessed against them according to Olympic law.[9] When the Spartans denied that they were in breach of the rules, the case was judged not by a neutral party, but by the Olympic court, which was composed entirely of Eleans, or at least was dominated by them.[10] The account of Thucydides shows that there was an established Olympic law, which the Eleans used, and perhaps at times abused, to control the Games and sanctuary. Elis seems to have exploited this incident involving the Olympic truce for its own political purposes, to enhance its claim to Lepreon.[11] Such was the accepted power of the truce and the control of the sanctuary that Sparta's response to the decision of the tribunal was not as severe as it otherwise might have been.[12]

Despite their occasional abuse of their control of Olympia, the Eleans were thought competent, even by their enemy, to administer the festival, as we can deduce from a second major incident involving Sparta. This is a notable point to bear in mind when assessing the impartiality of Elis in running the Games. In 399 BC the Spartans made war on the Eleans, since they were still angry at them for being excluded from the sanctuary a few years before, and for making the alliance with the Athenians and their allies (Xenophon *Hell.* 3.2.21–30). Hence Agis invaded Elean territory, but felt compelled to withdraw because of an earthquake. In the next year, however, he entered the city of Elis itself and damaged the outlying areas and the gymnasia, after first sacrificing without opposition in the sanctuary at Olympia. The Spartans forced the Eleans to swear a peace treaty, but significantly did not take away their control of Olympia, even though they had the power to do so. The Eleans were left in charge of the festival, not out of magnanimity, but for practical reasons, since, according to Xenophon (*Hell.* 3.2.31), the Spartans thought that their rivals (the Pisatans) were too unsophisticated and unfit for the task. This was a major concession to the Eleans by their adversary.

Elis and the Olympic sanctuary
A change in possession of Olympia and its festival was considered by the Greeks not to be detrimental to the sanctity of the place, nor did it disrespect the gods, since 'the ownership of sanctuaries was perceived as belonging to the human, not to the divine, sphere' (Sourvinou-Inwood 1990, 296). The city in charge of the sanctuary controlled all religious activity and participation. Even in Panhellenic sanctuaries, which were supposedly open to all the Greeks, one could participate only as a formal alien (*xenos*) of the controlling city. Hence visitors to Olympia were at the whim of the Eleans, who could decide which people could participate and sacrifice there, and in what ways religious rituals and the Games were to be performed (Sourvinou-Inwood 1990, 296–7). The Eleans did not allow, for example, Agis to pray there for a victory in battle in 399 BC, even though, as we have seen, they were unable to prevent him from doing so a year later (Xenophon *Hell.* 3.2.22). This domination over a sanctuary was an acceptable part of Greek life, so that relatively few complaints are recorded by other states against the Eleans. These states, however, could send *theōroi* to Olympia to act as sacred envoys in the name of the city, and erect treasuries in the Altis, which housed offerings and furnishings for the various cults and rituals (Sourvinou-Inwood 1990, 298).

The Eleans had official buildings at Olympia which were used not only for the administration of the sanctuary and the Games, but also for political and civic matters. One of these was the Council House (*bouleu-tērion*), where it is believed that political discussions took place among the Greek delegations.[13] This may have been the site of the Olympic Council, an institution about which little is known, although it probably consisted of fifty former judges (*Hellanodikai*) and other Olympic officials, who were perhaps elected on a permanent basis. Here no doubt the day-to-day administration of the festival took place (Drees 1968, 25).[14] It adjudicated on the Games and settled disputes, as in the case of Leon of Ambracia in the stade race in 396 BC (Pausanias 6.3.7).[15] It also arbitrated on civic matters, as when Xenophon was tried before it for accepting from the Spartans land in the area of Olympia (Pausanias 5.6.6). A second building, the Magistrates' House (*prytaneion*), was also multi-functional; it was the home for the Elean officials during the time of the Games, contained the eternal flame of Hestia and was associated with internal political affairs of the city of Elis (Sinn 1996, 79). Even though Olympia itself was not a *polis*, it seems that in such features as the *bouleutērion*, *prytaneion* and the flame of Hestia we have the standard political and religious elements of a city state.[16] Their presence probably points to Olympia being an important religious and political centre – if not *the* centre – for the Eleans.

The importance of Olympia as a religious centre for Elis is confirmed by the discovery of the *leges sacrae* in the area of the Altis, for in Greece it was the custom for cities to deposit laws in their major sanctuaries.[17] These laws are a critical corpus of evidence for understanding the relationship between Elis and Olympia. They date to the middle and late sixth century BC, and provide the first indisputable proof for the Eleans at Olympia. Some of these inscriptions relate to the Games, and show 'a remarkable separation of the agonistic sphere from the ritual sphere of the sanctuary' (Siewert 1992, 116). Most, however, are not primarily concerned with the Olympic festival (Siewert 1992, 114): there are, for instance, about forty laws (several of which are unpublished), referring to the state of Elis itself, which, according to Taeuber (1991, 111–13), deal with the use of land, treaties with other states, and official documents on the social structure of the Eleans.

One of these laws from the late sixth century contains part of the regulations for the Olympic Games, and significantly may represent a formal declaration of Elean control of Olympia. The first five lines of the fragments (B 6075 and B 6116) may be translated as follows:[18]

1 The wrestler shall not break any finger…
   the judge shall punish by striking except on the head…
   the wrong-doers shall bring and promise to him…
4 (he shall compete again at) the Olympic Games
   and start as being worthy of the victory…

Here we see that the judge (*diaitatēr*) could flog a wrestler who was going to break his opponent's finger during the course of the contest.[19] In the third and fourth lines, despite the lacunae, we can discern what appear to be regulations concerning penalties, compensation and competing at subsequent Olympics. The second part of the inscription (lines 6 to 9) – not translated here – is much more fragmentary and obscure, but contains such intriguing terms as 'alliance' (*symmachia*), 'woman', 'bribery', 'fine', 'sacred envoys' and 'war'. Unfortunately their context in this law remains conjectural.[20]

The city of Elis and the sanctuary were ritualistically linked at the time of the Games by the famous procession, which we can interpret as a kind of pilgrimage to Olympia, for after the training period was over, athletes, trainers, officials and others journeyed together from Elis to the festival (see Miller, this volume). We can deduce that this was a typical procession in Greece from the controlling city to what can be called 'a non-urban sanctuary'.[21] The distance, however, to Olympia – 36 km from Elis by a straight line, and probably much further for the procession, since the ancient road surely meandered[22] – made Olympia unusual, for most notable sanctuaries of this type in Greece are situated about 5 to 15 km away from their controlling cities.[23] To the people of the city of Elis as well as to the rest of the Greeks, the relative isolation of Olympia would make access difficult.

The *Hellanodikai*: their civic and political importance

One of the notable tasks of the *Hellanodikai,* or 'Judges of Greece', was to conduct the compulsory thirty-day training period in Elis (Philostratus *VA* 5.43), which was attended by boys as well as by adults (Pausanias 6.23.2).[24] The effect of this training period was that Elis had not only power over the sanctuary and Games at Olympia, but also unconditional control over the athletes even before the Games. Hence it could ensure high standards and add to the prestige of Olympia.[25] Yet the duties of the *Hellanodikai* extended beyond the Games, for these officials also had considerable civic and political responsibilities.

The *Hellanodikai* were selected by lot by the Elean Council (*bouleutērion*),[26] which was housed in one of the three gymnasia in Elis (Pausanias 6.23.7). This location of the Council symbolically linked sport and politics in the city. The number of the officials fluctuated according to the number of the tribes (*phylai*) of Elis, being fixed at ten in 348 BC (Pausanias 5.9.5–6).[27] We may infer from this last passage of Pausanias that the Eleans deliberately expanded their number to incorporate and solemnize the new regions that they had added to their city state.[28] The fact that there was a tribal basis for the *Hellanodikai* suggests that they were civic magistrates. Since it has been deduced that they ran and adjudicated the Olympic Games for only a ten-month period of one Olympiad,[29] their office would be a hiatus in their regular, and we presume, important duties as administrators in the city at other times. The *Hellanodikai*, for instance, had the power to punish the chief magistrate of Elis and others, if they abused their authority (*DGE* 409).[30] They themselves could be called to account by the Olympic Council and by the Board of Control (*mastroi*).[31]

The title, 'Judges of Greece', given to these officials is a significant one which reflects their important political duties outside Elis and Olympia. In the late sixth century BC they were known as *diaitētai* or 'umpires', as we have seen in the sacred agonistic law, which no doubt reflected their role in the Games. Yet in the early fifth century and thereafter they are referred to by the broader term of *Hellanodikai*.[32] It is conjectured that they adopted this new name after the Spartans granted them the power to monitor the Panhellenic truce throughout Greece, which they had organized in 481 BC in the face of the Persian invasion (Siewert 1992, 115).[33]

The impartiality of the Eleans and *Hellanodikai*

Elis excluded no *polis* in Greece from taking part in the Olympic festival, not even political adversaries, except when they were in breach of the rules. Although this may be considered an example of the high-mindedness of Elis in administering Olympia, the Eleans were not always so righteous in dealing with other festivals, for they attempted to interfere at Isthmia, where they asked the Corinthians to exclude the Argives (Pausanias 5.2.2). Elis itself was precluded for political reasons by the Corinthians from competing in the Games at Isthmia (Pausanias 5.2.2–5, 6.3.9, 16.2), although, as we have implied, Corinth was not excluded in turn by the Eleans from the Olympic Games. This illustrates well the power that a *polis* could wield in excluding another from its sanctuary.

The Eleans appear to have taken pride in the fairness and profession-alism of their officials at Olympia and may even have engaged in rivalry with other cities that ran their own games, both Panhellenic and 'local'. The judges administered the Games with honour; they considered them-selves to be on trial as much as the athletes and were anxious not to make any mistakes, or at least so states Apollonius of Tyana (Philostratus *VA* 4.29). One can indeed find other literary sources to support this view: it was, according to Pausanias (8.40.2), because of the fairness of the Elean judges that the pancratiast, Arrichion of Phigelia, was awarded victory at Olympia in 564 BC.[34] In the Games of 212 BC the officials at Olympia did not favour one of their own athletes in the pancration, but gave the advantage (at least in theory) to a non-Elean, by rescheduling the pancration before the boxing competition, even though it might have harmed the chances of victory of an Elean athlete (Pausanias 6.15.4–5). For advice on the running of the Games the Eleans are said to have visited Egypt in the sixth century BC, where they declared that they held the Games with as much fairness as possible.[35]

One wonders, however, why the Eleans really needed to consult the Egyptians, if they were as impartial as they claimed. The possibility remains that their handling of the Games had been questioned by their fellow Greeks. It seems that for every example of fairness of the Eleans one can find an example of unfairness or criticism, sometimes even in the same literary passage, as in Plutarch (*Lyc.* 20.3) and Athenaeus (8.350c), where apparent positive comments seem to be undercut by negative remarks. In the second or third century AD Philostratus (*VA* 3.30) criticizes the method of selecting the *Hellanodikai* by lot and suggests the possibility that on occasion there may not always be enough just men in Elis to make up the number of ten judges. This is strong censure indeed against the Eleans, if not against the officials. We may note that even the *Hellanodikai* themselves competed at Olympia until the fourth century BC, and ceased to participate only after one of their number won a chariot race in 368 BC (Pausanias 6.1.4, 6). It may, however, show some fairness on their part that he was the only judge known to have won in several hundred years![36] We should remember too that they were accountable for their actions, if only to their fellow Eleans.

That the decisions of the *Hellanodikai* at the Olympic Games were at least reasonably fair, we can infer from the number of Elean winners. In the men's events approximately 10.5% of the known victors came from the city of Elis itself,[37] not a huge advantage over other cities (see the TABLE overleaf).[38] Moreover this percentage of Elean victories at Olympia is not strikingly dissimilar from that at Delphi or Nemea, notwithstanding the even more scanty evidence available for those festivals: at Delphi Elis had 9.5% of the victories, and 10.0% at Nemea.[39]

In the events for boys Elis had a larger percentage (22.5%) of the victors. Assuming that we have a representative enough sample for comparison, this is still not outrageously high, given that more than half of the victors came from the Peloponnese. We should also take into consideration 'home-town' advantage, a phenomenon which can be seen in the modern Olympic Games, where a country usually wins more medals when it hosts the Games than when it does not. It would have been especially difficult for boys who did not live in Elis or close by to perform to their full capabilities, after travelling relatively great distances, and being

TABLE. Successful cities/areas at Olympia.

City/Area	Boy Victors	%	Men Victors	%	Total Victors	%
Elis	28	22.5	87	10.5	115	12.0
Sparta	5	4.0	75	9.0	80	8.5
Athens	3	2.5	40	5.0	43	4.5
Other cities	88	71.0	630	75.5	718	75.0
Total	124	100.0	832	100.0	956	100.0
Peloponnese	71	57.5	265	32.0	336	35.0
Non Peloponnese	53	42.5	567	68.0	620	65.0

separated from their home environment. Elis had a further 'home-town' advantage (for both boys and men) over other cities in Greece which hosted athletic festivals, in that it alone had an obligatory training period (above). The effect of a stay at Olympia for one month, in addition to lengthy and arduous travel, should not be underestimated, for this would be an expensive proposition for athletes, who were obliged to devote so much time to a single competition.

We may conclude that the Eleans in general were as impartial as could be expected in dealing with the Games (especially if we consider them in an ancient rather than in a modern context), but on occasion they were justly criticized for their lack of fairness, and with little or no accountability to the other Greeks they did at times abuse their power over the sanctuary, even shamefully.

Acknowledgements

I wish to thank the anonymous reviewers and especially the editors for their insightful suggestions and criticisms which have much improved this chapter. For the Games in general at Olympia, see Stephen Miller's chapter in this book, to whom specific references are given throughout.

Notes

[1] Although I follow in this chapter the traditional date of 776 BC for the first Olympics, the archaeological evidence points to a time of about 700 BC (perhaps 704). See Mallwitz 1988, 101 and Golden 1998, 63–5, who base this theory on the evidence of wells, on which see Helmut Kyrieleis in this volume.

[2] We should, however, be aware that Strabo's account of the Games may be political and perhaps inaccurate in places, since he was recording local Elean traditions justifying the city's control of Olympia (Morgan 1990, 64).

[3] Xenophon (*Hell.* 3.2.31) also states that Olympia originally did not belong to

the Eleans in 'ancient times'. Because of his pro-Spartan stance, this may also be considered in a way to be a 'political' claim.

⁴ Mallwitz 1988, 102 believes, *pace* Pausanias, that Pheidon re-organized the Games in 668 BC, since this fits better the archaeological evidence.

⁵ See also Swoboda 1905 and the contrasting views of Meyer 1950 for further details. Note also Pausanias 6.22.4 for Elis winning back the Games. For the possibility that an amphictyony controlled the early Games, perhaps led by Elis, see the comments in Roy 1998, 363–4 and n. 20 below.

⁶ Rashke 1988, 46–7. On Elis as a democracy, see O'Neil 1995, 32–3, 38–9, 79–81. See Kyle 1997 for the Olympics and democracy. This was also the time after the Persian Wars when Elis was allowed by Sparta to observe the Panhellenic truce (below).

⁷ See Miller 1982 for the ancient sources and discussion on the complex issue of the control of the festival at Nemea.

⁸ For the Eleans expressing political themes in art at Olympia, see Raschke 1988, 258.

⁹ See Krause 1838, 144–53 for more on the Olympic law.

¹⁰ Roy 1998, 362–4. One wonders, therefore, how an impartial judgement could be reached, especially since the Spartans were not present at the hearings, as Thucydides relates. The function of the court is obscure; it seems different from the Olympic Council (below).

¹¹ Roy 1998, 368. Roy 1998, 367–8, also considers a treaty of the Eleans preserved in an Olympic inscription (*IvO* 9) to be a further example of Elis' abuse of power against another city.

¹² Roy 1998, 366 suggests that Elis here was exploiting Olympian Zeus 'shabbily' for political reasons. Hornblower 2000 proposes that the Spartans were not banned from 420 to 400 BC, as is commonly believed, but were readmitted sometime before 416.

¹³ Sinn 1996, 78–9. For more on the *bouleutērion*, see Stephen Miller's chapter in this book.

¹⁴ For Eleans sitting on this Council, see Roy 1998, 363. Dyer (1908) believes that the *Hellanodikai* were the 'executive arm' of the Olympic Council.

¹⁵ See Crowther 1997 for more discussion on the Olympic Council and this dispute between Leon and the *Hellanodikai* who voted against him.

¹⁶ For the traditional location of the Hestia in the *prytaneion* in the centre of a city and its symbolizing of the community, see Bruit Zaidman and Schmitt Pantel 1992, 93.

¹⁷ We may note that the Athenians, for example, traditionally placed their inscriptions in their chief sanctuary on the Acropolis.

¹⁸ The translation is by Ebert and is found at Siewert 1992, 114. See Ebert and Siewert 1997 for further discussion.

¹⁹ Ebert and Siewert 1997 argue that the flogging occurred *after* the contest, but see the discussion in Crowther and Frass 1998. See there also for the physical and social reasons for not striking an athlete on the head. For the term *diaitētēr*, see below.

[20] For a possible translation in German, together with informed conjectures, see Ebert and Siewert 1997, 206. As an example of the difficulty of interpreting these lines, we may consider the word *symmachia*; Ebert and Siewert themselves (1997, 221 ff.) disagree on whether it refers to an alliance of Elis and smaller (independent) neighbouring cities (Siewert), or to Elis and the cities under its jurisdiction (Ebert). For a possible amphictyony controlling Olympia, see n. 5 above.

[21] On cities and non-urban sanctuaries, see the extensive discussion of de Polignac 1984, 31–92.

[22] Drees 1968, 45 conjectures that it may have been as far as 58 km. See Pausanias 6.22.8 for travelling from Elis to Olympia via Letrinoi (probably modern Pyrgos).

[23] De Polignac 1984, 33. Elis' rival for control of the sanctuary, Pisa, was of course much closer to Olympia.

[24] For a full discussion of the training period, see Crowther 1991. For its relevance to Elean victors, see below.

[25] This would be especially so, since the training period was unique among festivals until the Sebastan Games were founded in Naples in the first century AD (*IvO* 56).

[26] This consisted of 90 members within the oligarchy holding office for life; see Aristotle *Pol.* 1306a12 ff. which discusses a particular turning point in the constitutional history of Elis.

[27] We may compare here the Athenian practice of choosing officials, where each board of magistrates had a member from each of the Cleisthenic tribes.

[28] Similarly their number would be reduced when they lost territory. We may note also that the Council of Sixteen Women at Elis, who were in charge of the festival of Hera at Olympia, was established from the oldest, most noble and most honourable women from each of the sixteen cities of Eleia (Pausanias 5.16.5–6).

[29] See Oehler 1913, 156 which also lists their duties.

[30] See O'Neil 1995, 39.

[31] An inscription published at Mallwitz and Siewert 1981, 228–48 relates that a decision concerning the sacred Olympic truce made by the *Hellanodikai* in the fifth century BC was overruled by the *mastroi*.

[32] The term first appears in 476 BC in Pindar (*Ol.* 3.12), where it is used in the singular.

[33] For the Greek League which agreed to this ending of all wars among its members, see Herodotus 7.145. These allies called themselves 'Hellenes' and met in the Hellenium in Sparta (Pausanias 3.12.6), from which the judges may possibly have derived their name. At least we can assume that the title of *Hellanodikai* reflects their increasing importance in Greece as the Games grew in stature. Officials known as *Hellanodikai* were found elsewhere in Greece, as at the Games in Nemea (*IG* 4.578) and at the Asklepieia in Epidaurus (*IG* 4.946, 1508). The Olympic Games perhaps here served as a model for subsequent competitions, inasmuch as they were the oldest, if not the most revered, of festivals.

[34] Note also Dio Chrysostomus 31.111 on the judges attempting to remain

impartial. For further references and discussion on the fairness of the Elean judges, see Crowther 1997.

[35] See the accounts of Herodotus 2.160 and Diodorus 1.95. This visit is believed to be an unhistorical event by Lloyd (1988, 164–7), who considers it to be similar to other *logoi* in Book 2 of Herodotus. Contrast Decker 1974 who comments on the similarities and differences in Herodotus and Diodorus.

[36] For comments on many of these cases, see Crowther 1997.

[37] I refer here to those victors who are called Elean in the sources. See Crowther 1988. There are 12 further victors if we include the region controlled by Elis: Moretti 1953 lists 8 victors from Lepreon between 460 and 360 BC (with three boys' events), 2 from Disponton (772 and 672 BC), and one each from Lenos (588 BC) and Pisa (the inaugural diaulos of 724 BC).

[38] One should note too that this is an incomplete list of victors, since we have knowledge of fewer than one in seven of the total. For a fuller discussion on the winners at Olympia and the statistics, see Crowther 1988 and 1989. For the distribution of victors in the Roman period, see Scanlon 2002, 40–63. We should be aware also that much of the evidence for Olympic victors comes from Elean sources. See Golden 1998, 64 on the likelihood that some of the earliest victories assigned to Elis did not come from Elis, since it was then too small a state.

[39] All the known Elean victors at Delphi and Nemea were also victorious at Olympia. See Crowther 1988, 308–9. Elis was ineligible at Isthmia, as we have seen.

Bibliography

Bruit Zaidman, L. and Schmitt Pantel, P.
   1992   *Religion in the Ancient Greek City*, transl. Paul Cartledge, Cambridge.
Crowther, N.B.
   1988   'Elis and the Games', *AC* 57, 301–10.
   1989   'Boy victors at Olympia', *AC* 58, 206–10.
   1991   'The Olympic training period', *Nikephoros* 4, 161–6.
   1997   ' "Sed quis custodiet ipsos custodes?" ', *Nikephoros* 10, 149–60.
Crowther, N.B. and Frass, M.
   1998   'Flogging as a punishment in the ancient Games', *Nikephoros* 11, 51–82.
De Polignac, F.
   1984   *La naissance de la cité grecque: Cultes, espace et société VIIIᵉ–VIIᵉ avant J.-C.*, Paris.
Decker, W.
   1974   'La délégation des Éléens en Égypte sous la 26ᵉ dynastie', *CE* 49, 31–42.
   1997   'Zur Vorbereitung und Organisation griechischer Agone', *Nikephoros* 10, 77–102.
Delorme, J.
   1960   *Gymnasion*, Paris.

Drees, L.
1968   *Olympia: Gods, artists, athletes,* New York.
Dyer, L.
1908   'The Olympian council house and council', *HSCP* 19, 1–60.
Ebert, J.
1980   *Olympia von den Anfängen bis zu Coubertin,* Leipzig.
Ebert, J. and Siewert, P.
1997   'Eine archaische Bronzeurkunde aus Olympia mit Vorschriften für Ring-
        kämpfer und Kampfrichter', in M. Hillgruber, R. Jakobi and W. Luppe
        (eds.) *Agonismata,* Leipzig, 200–36.
Golden, M.
1998   *Sport and Society in Ancient Greece,* Cambridge.
Hornblower, S.
2000   'Thucydides, Xenophon, and Lichas: were the Spartans excluded from
        the Olympic Games from 420 to 400 BC?', *Phoenix* 54, 212–25.
Krause, J.H.
1838   *Olympia,* Vienna.
Kyle, D.G.
1997   'The first hundred Olympiads: a process of decline or democratization?',
        Nikephoros 10, 53–75.
Lämmer, M.
1982–3 'Der sogennante Olympischen Friede in der griechischen Antiken',
        Stadion 8–9, 47–83.
Lloyd A.B.
1988   *Herodotus Book II,* Leiden.
Mallwitz, A.
1988   'Cult and competition locations at Olympia', in Raschke (ed.) *The
        Archaeology of the Olympics,* 79–109.
Mallwitz, A. and Siewert, P. (eds.)
1981   *Bericht über die Ausgrabungen in Olympia* X, Berlin.
Meyer E.
1950   'Pisa', in *RE* 20.2, 1732–55.
Miller, S.G.
1982   'Kleonai, the Nemean Games, and the Lamian War', *Hesperia,* Suppl.
        20, 100–8.
Moretti, L.
1953   *Olympionikai, i vincitori negli antichi agoni olimpici,* Rome.
Morgan, C.
1990   *Athletes and Oracles: The transformation of Olympia and Delphi in the
        eighth century BC,* Cambridge.
Oehler, J.
1913   'Ἑλλανοδίκαι', in *RE* 8, 155–7.
O'Neil, J.L.
1995   *The Origins and Development of Ancient Greek Democracy,* Lanham.
Raschke, W.J.
1988   'Images of Victory', in Raschke (ed.) *The Archaeology of the Olympics,*
        38–54.

Raschke, W.J. (ed.)
  1988 *The Archaeology of the Olympics: The Olympics and other festivals in antiquity*, Madison and London.
Roy, R.
  1998 'Thucydides 5.49.1–50.4: the quarrel between Elis and Sparta in 420 BC, and Elis' exploitation of Olympia', *Klio* 80, 360–8.
  1999 'Les cités d'Élide', in *Le Péloponnèse. Archéologie et histoire*, textes rassemblés par Josette Renard, Rennes, 151–76.
Scanlon, T.F.
  2002 *Eros and Greek Athletics*, Oxford and New York.
Siewert, P.
  1992 'The Olympic rules', in W. Coulson and H. Kyrieleis (eds.) *Proceedings of an International Symposium on the Olympic Games 5–9 September 1988*, Athens, 113–17.
Sinn, U.
  1996 *Olympia: Kult, Sport und Fest in der Antike*, Munich.
Slowikowski, S.S.
  1989 'The symbolic *Hellanodikai*', *Aethlon* 7, 133–41
Sourvinou-Inwood, C.
  1990 'What is *polis* religion?', in O. Murray and S. Price (eds.) *The Greek City from Homer to Alexander*, Oxford, 295–322.
Swoboda, H.
  1905 'Elis', in *RE* 5.2, 2368–432.
Taeuber, H.
  1991 'Elische Inschriften in Olympia', in A.D. Rizakis (ed.) *Achaia und Elis in der Antike, Akten des 1. Internationalen Symposiums Athen, 19–21 Mai 1989, Meletemata* 13, Athens, 111–13.
Ziehen, L.
  1937 'Olympia', in *RE* 17.2, 2520–36.

4

VICTORY STATUE, VICTORY SONG:
PINDAR'S AGONISTIC POETICS AND ITS LEGACY

Patrick O'Sullivan

If a man enjoys good fortune in his actions, he provides the Muse with a sweet source for her streams of song; for great deeds of prowess lacking hymns of praise remain in deep obscurity. But for noble deeds we know a mirror in one way only – if by grace of Memory of the shining crown a reward for labours can be found in the illustrious songs of verse.

Pindar *Nemean* 7.11–16.

These days, in the aftermath of any major athletic event, successful competitors encounter public adulation in many forms. Among them are media saturation, ticker-tape parades, the new-found (if short-lived) companionship of politicians, and, if not Hollywood offers, then a good chance of endorsement money. The rewards of athletic success in the ancient Greek world could be similarly grandiose and go far beyond the ostensibly humble wreaths given to Panhellenic victors at the time of their triumphs.[1] The fruits of victory took a number of different forms, often publicly funded and lavished on the victor on his return to his *polis*. Victorious athletes in Panhellenic games could variously enjoy *sitesis*, or meals at public expense (*IG* I[3] 131.1–18; Plato *Apology* 36d–e), *prohedria*, or privileged seats at public festivals (Xenophanes B2.13 D-K), civic processions (Diodorus Siculus 13.82.7), heraldic announcements, as Euripides' victory song for Alcibiades shows (ap. Plutarch. *Alc.* 11), and gifts from the state, including money.[2] Plutarch (*Solon* 23.3) tells us that Solon imposed limits on financial rewards to successful Athenian athletes – five hundred drachmas to Olympic victors, one hundred to Isthmian victors – which suggests such gifts may have become extravagantly high if left unchecked. Indeed, celebrations of athletic performance and prestige accorded athletes were deemed excessive already by the time of Xenophanes (B2.1–22 D-K) in the sixth century BC, who set his own wisdom above physical strength.[3] Political mobility seems to have been another possible spin-off of athletic success, if Alcibiades' boasts of his chariot victories in the Olympic Games, when addressing the Athenian assembly, is anything to go by (Thuc. 6.16.1–2). The roles of song and visual monuments in commemorating athletic champions are yet further manifestations of the impact of athletics in archaic and classical Greece, and aspects of the interaction between them will concern us here.

Statues were made in honour of Olympic victors by the third quarter of the sixth century BC, a practice that continued into the fifth century.[4] The bronze Delphic charioteer, dedicated by the tyrant Polyzalos, is a famous, albeit rare, extant example, and is, of course, contemporaneous with the epinikian (victory) odes of Pindar and Bacchylides. Important aspects of the overall phenomenon of sport in the Greek world are to be found in these visual and verbal memorials which frequently aim to glorify not only the successful athlete, but also his family and place of birth.[5] As a result, these odes and images both testify and add to the prestige of Panhellenic sporting festivals, and show that the broader significance of such events embraces much more than acts of physical prowess in the stadium. Indeed, they may be understood as essential adjuncts to sport in archaic and classical Greece. For, as was known from Homer onwards, without recollection in song or visual monuments, great deeds – sporting and otherwise – would fall into oblivion.[6] Perhaps no-one was more acutely aware of this than Pindar, who makes this a *raison d'être* and a selling point for his own art (*Olympian* 11.1–6; *Nemean* 3.6–8; 7.11–16).

Recent scholarship on victory statues, agonistic monument inscriptions and poetic encomia by, for instance, Leslie Kurke and Deborah Steiner has emphasized the shared concerns between these visual and verbal media.[7] Kurke is primarily concerned with the links between epinikian odes and monuments regarding the bestowal of *kudos* on the athlete, observing that: '…both monuments and epinikion function to reanimate the victor's *kudos* by restaging the victory announcement and coronation'.[8] Steiner goes further to argue for a 'homology between the visual and poetic in the commemoration of athletes',[9] and to claim that Pindar's presentation of the *laudandus* parallels agonistic inscriptions on statue bases.[10] The valuable collection of these victory inscriptions by Ebert has facilitated such comparisons, and Steiner makes a number of interesting connections between Pindaric diction and the wording of certain epigrams.[11] Elsewhere she claims that the poet essentially endows his ode's subject with the same erotic and numinous allure evident in fifth-century images of athletes on red-figure pottery and in allusions to statues in some fifth-century literary texts.[12] Such approaches are right to draw attention to certain overlaps between agonistic inscriptions and Pindaric verse as another way of underlining the ostensible aims they have in common, at least from the patrons' view.

But some of Steiner's conclusions move into tendentious areas. More than once Steiner tells us that Pindar is 'no different from the sculptor' or 'statue-maker', thereby emphasizing the apparent assimilation between visual and verbal encomia.[13] This, however, leaves unexplained significant aspects of Pindar's conception of himself as poet in which he attempts to distinguish himself and his medium from sculptors and visual monuments. And it is these agonistic nuances of Pindar's poetics and their ramifications in later Greek writings that will be treated here. Why might Pindar be moved to criticize statues? He was not the first to do so, as is attested in the theological criticisms made by Xenophanes (B15 D–K) and Heraclitus (B5 D–K) of religious imagery. Yet more pertinent is the view of Simonides (*c.* 556–467 BC), an early exponent of epinikion and regarded as the first to practise his art as a money-making, secular profession, who jeered at an epigram by Cleobulus that promoted the durability of statues as monuments (fr. 581 *PMG*):[14]

> τίς κεν αἰνήσειε νόῳ πίσυνος Λίνδου ναέταν Κλεόβουλον,
> ἀεναοῖς ποταμοῖσ᾽ ἄνθεσι τ᾽ εἰαρινοῖς
> ἀελίου τε φλογὶ χρυσέας τε σελάνας
> καὶ θαλασσίαισι δίναισ᾽ ἀντία θέντα μένος στάλας;
> ἅπαντα γάρ ἐστι θεῶν ἥσσω · λίθον δὲ
> καὶ βρότεοι παλάμαι θραύοντι · μωροῦ
> φωτὸς ἅδε βούλα.

What man, trusting his wits, would approve of Cleobulus, dweller in Lindus, who against ever-lasting rivers, spring flowers, the light of the sun or of the golden moon or the whirling eddies of the sea pitted the strength of a statue? For all things are inferior to the gods. But even mortal hands break stone. This was the thought of a fool.

Simonides, jealous of his own medium, and keen to ensure a living from it, can be understood as attacking both a rival poet and a medium that could similarly rival his own services. Statuary here is reduced to its basic material of stone, and Simonides undercuts the idea that it has any durable μένος ('strength' or 'energy') at all. However, Simonides composed inscriptions for statue bases and even wrote captions to paintings by Polygnotus (Pausanias 10.27.4), so the view expressed in fr. 581 need not be considered the be-all and end-all of his thinking on visual images. But clearly here he did not refrain from running down a rival medium and poet, when the agonistic urge took him. This agonistic tendency can also be detected in Pindar, who likewise displays professional jealousy, and could also face competition from rival media. The scholiast's anecdote (Σ. 1a, III 89 Drachmann) on the proem of Pindar's *Nemean* 5 is of some interest, even if of doubtful veracity. We are told that the victor's parents decided to honour their son with a memorial statue instead of an ode when Pindar demanded three thousand drachmae for his services, but later changed their mind again and hired the poet. Whether we choose to believe this or not, the relevant point is not just that victory odes and statues have similar roles in the eyes of the patrons;[15] but a victory statue could also take the place of an epinikian ode, if the patrons so wished. Victory odes and statues could thus compete against, rather than simply complement, each other. This also underscores Pindar's awareness that he literally has to sing for his supper (*Isthmian* 2.6–11; *Pythian* 11.38–45; *Nemean* 1.19–24) and alerts us to something of the realities confronting a poet composing odes on a competitive basis for victors in other kinds of competitions.[16]

A palpable sense of competition between visual and verbal media is evident in Pindaric writings, which, while noticed by some commentators, does contain certain nuances worthy of more comment.[17] Agonistic features of Pindar's poetics comprise a significant strand of ideas within his own imagery as well as developing certain earlier poetic conceits. A key motif to be explored here is Pindar's presentation of his own medium as living and mobile, which is assimilated at times to an athlete's body in action, in contrast to the immobility of statuary. Much of this is connected to Pindar's habit of speaking of his medium in terms borrowed from visual monuments with the aim of promoting the superiority of his own song. As I will also argue, these Pindaric motifs are developed in a number of rhetorical and philosophical texts of the classical period more fully than has been recognized, and can thus be seen to leave a significant legacy in Greek thought. This may seem to take us away from the realm of sport, but we should bear in mind that athletics, poetic performance, rhetoric and philosophy were similarly competitive pursuits in the *polis* culture of Greece, and each could function as a metaphor for the other.[18] In fact, Panhellenic and other festivals, by the fifth century BC, began to include poetry competitions, rhetorical displays and prose recitations in addition to athletics. We have, for instance, fragments of Gorgias' Olympic speeches (B7, 8, 8a D–K), evidence of his speech in the Pythian Games (B9 D–K), and are told that Herodotus and sophists such as Prodicus and Hippias performed at Olympia.[19] Thus, public festival provides a unifying social backdrop to major aspects of athletics, poetry and rhetoric in classical Greece in terms of their performance and reception. All three activities could come under the rubric of ἄγων ('competition') – an element obviously essential to sport, but also significant for Pindar's conception of himself as poet, as well as later rhetorical concepts.

The agonism of Pindar and his poetry in motion

Pindar's most explicit reference to sculpture involves his famous denunciation of it as an immobile medium (*Nemean* 5.1–5), which will concern us presently; but his treatment of visual imagery works on a number of levels. Pindar, like other lyric poets, frequently refers to his own medium in craft-metaphors,[20] and at times compares his own song with sculpture and architecture (e.g. *Olympian* 6.1–4; *Pythian* 6.6–17; fr. 194).[21] The image of the poet-as-craftsman is used by Pindar when he calls the Muse to Aegina where μελιγαρύων τέκτονες | κώμων νεανίαι ('young men, builders of honey-sweet revels') long for her (*Nemean* 3.4–5). At *Pythian* 3.113–14 he sees the fame of Nestor and Sarpedon as arising ἐξ ἐπέων κελαδεννῶν τέκτονες οἷα σοφοί | ἅρμοσαν ('from the resounding words such as are fitted together by clever builders'). Elsewhere Pindar speaks of setting up a λίθον Μοισαῖον (memorial stone of the Muses) to the victor and his clan (*Nemean* 8.46–7). Also Pindar (*Nemean*. 3.13, 8.16) and Bacchylides (1.184; 5.4; 10.11; fr. 20B5 S–M) can speak of their song as an ἄγαλμα – a word for statuary, but often denoting a gift or ornament of a different kind.[22] The poet-as-craftsman motif and analogies between poetry and plastic art are not Pindaric inventions but commonplaces throughout the archaic and classical periods from Homer to Aristophanes and beyond.[23] Behind Pindar's craft analogies, then, is a long and living tradition, which he will use on various levels along with many other types of imagery.

But before inferring that Pindar is particularly keen to align his poetry with sculpture and the plastic arts, we should note that he often uses images, such as wine, nectar, wreaths and mixtures of honey and milk as analogies for song, for instance: *Olympian* 1.8–11, 7.1–10, *Nemean* 3.76–80 and *Nemean* 8.13–16. It has been plausibly suggested that imagery of wreaths and liquids are designed to recall, if not re-enact, the crowning of the athlete at his moment of victory (and return) and the pouring of libations.[24] Pindar, then, is by no means restricted to imagery from the plastic arts in depicting himself or his medium, and in these other images we may also detect further agonistic nuances. As Nisetich suggests in his discussion of Pindaric wreaths in *Olympian* 1, the poet ultimately claims that he 'produces a song that can do what the victor's coronation had done, only better'.[25]

Certain Pindaric craft analogies entail a more problematic relationship between visual and verbal media. In, for instance, *Nemean* 4 Pindar acknowledges the challenge to his song by memorial statues, yet still uses imagery from the visual arts to describe the efficacy of his own song to his patron (*Nemean* 4.79–85):

…εἰ δέ τοι
μάτρῳ μ' ἔτι Καλλικλεῖ κελεύεις

στάλαν θέμεν Παρίου λίθου λευκοτέραν·
ὁ χρυσὸς ἑψόμενος
αὐγὰς ἔδειξεν ἀπάσας, ὕμνος δὲ τῶν ἀγαθῶν
ἐργμάτων βασιλεῦσιν ἰσοδαίμονα τεύχει
φῶτα·

If indeed you bid me to set up also for your uncle Callicles a monument whiter than Parian marble – as gold when refined shows off in all radiance – so a hymn of noble deeds produces/fashions (τεύχει) a man to be equal in spirit to kings.

Willcock's bland gloss on this, 'Praise from a poet is like a public monument',[26] misses out the significance of the comparative λευκοτέραν (81). Pindar here is driven to surpass sculptural monuments, not just to reproduce their verbal equivalents in song. Indeed, this aim only has force if such monuments are prized already, and are likely to have been considered as fitting ways to celebrate athletic victories. Yet it is noteworthy that Pindar here still describes the work of his song in craft terminology. A man can be honoured in song and his status improved just as the smelting process improves the lustre of gold. So Pindar's hymn τεύχει ('fashions'/'produces') its subject to be the equal of kings (*Nemean* 4.83–5). Cognates of τεύχω, which Pindar uses elsewhere of his song (*Isthmian* 1.14, etc.), carry connotations from the plastic arts known from Homeric and Hesiodic epic where the word denotes the manufacturing of crafted objects, notably Achilles' shield and the woman-artefact, Pandora.[27] But this does not necessarily entail for Pindar a simple assimilation of visual and verbal artforms. Pindar's aim is to outshine visual monuments in more ways than one. Song, according to this claim, makes the man. Here song can explicitly recall his noble deeds (ἀγαθά ἐργμάτα), a claim made elsewhere by Pindar in calling his medium ἔργοις...καλοῖς ἔσοπτρον ('a mirror for noble deeds': *Nemean* 7.14). The narrative entailed by Pindar's words is thus more satisfying than what a visual monument can hope to convey – an idea given fuller treatment by Isocrates, as we shall see. To recast Nisetich's observation: by re-appropriating the language of craft here Pindar presents his medium as edifying its subject as do the plastic arts, only better.

Pindar, then, is at times willing to see himself as a purveyor of craft analogous to, but different from, that which produces visual plastic monuments. A key difference is the idea, reiterated often by Pindar, of song as medium of motion that makes it a 'living' art, better suited to celebrating its subject. The 'moving song' concept in Pindar takes a number of forms with song being likened to an eagle, a ship, chariot, or other vehicle that travels along paths or in streams.[28] Harriott rightly notes that such imagery is as old as Homer who speaks of ἔπεα πτερόεντα ('winged words': *Iliad*

1.201, etc.) and songs as οἴμαι (paths or ways: *Odyssey* 8.74, 481);[29] indeed, such imagery is developed in similes comparing Nestor's speech that flows sweeter than honey (*Iliad* 1.249) or Odysseus' words that fall as thickly as snow (*Il.* 3.221–2). Pindar's contemporaries, Parmenides (B1.1–28 D–K) and Empedocles (B3.1–5 D–K) similarly use the same metaphor of motion for song, as does Bacchylides (5.16–36). These concepts of the fluidity and mobility of song are, however, more than just traditional commonplaces repeated by Pindar, but are skilfully redeployed in his songs. As is fitting for epinikion, Pindar unites the realms of athletics and poetry, by using athletic imagery to describe the nature of his song, equating it with an arrow or javelin; elsewhere he will assimilate himself to an athlete, as we shall see more fully.[30] Moreover, he uses the idea of song as a medium of motion to make agonistic comparisons between visual and verbal media. At *Isthmian* 2.46, for instance, he tells us: οὐκ ἐλινύσοντας αὐτοὺς ἐργασάμην ('I did not craft them [my songs] to linger idly'). We may read this not only as a reiteration of Pindar's belief in the mobility of his song, but also as an aside aimed at other media like sculpture which he elsewhere calls ἐλινύσοντα ('immobile') and not the sort of thing he, as a poet, produces (*Nemean* 5.1–2). Yet even in *Isthmian* 2 Pindar uses the language of craft in ἐργασάμην by which he paradoxically underlines what separates him from other 'craftsmen'. What he produces by craft moves and lives; what artisans produce by craft is idle.[31]

Immobility and 'lifelessness' of statues are a major agonistic issue in the contrast between the work of a sculptor and the fluency of song at the beginning of the *Fifth Nemean*, which develops Simonides' denunciation of statues as inert matter (*Nemean* 5.1–5):

Οὐκ ἀνδριαντοποιός εἰμ᾽, ὥστ᾽ ἐλινύσοντα ἐργάζεσθαι
    ἀγάλματ᾽ ἐπ᾽ αὐτᾶς βαθμίδος
ἑσταότ᾽· ἀλλ᾽ ἐπὶ πάσας ὁλκάδος ἔν τ᾽ ἀκάτῳ, γλυκεῖ᾽ ἀοιδά,
στεῖχ᾽ ἀπ᾽ Αἰγίνας, διαγγέλλοισ᾽, ὅτι
Λάμπωνος υἱὸς Πυθέας εὐρυσθενής
νίκη Νεμείοις παγκρατίου στέφανον,

I am not a sculptor, so as to fashion stationary statues that stand on the same base. Rather, on board every ship and in every boat, sweet song, go forth from Aigina and spread the news that Lampon's mighty son, Pytheas, has won the crown for the pankration in the Nemean Games…

While much scholarship has understandably tended to focus on this striking proem, other features of the ode are important for understanding Pindar's treatment of visual and verbal art.[32] In the proem, the statue's inability to move renders it, for Pindar, inferior to his flowing song which can travel widely and announce itself. The contrast of place emphasizes the difference between the two media: Pindar's song travels 'in every boat' while the statues remain on 'the same base'. Because the ἀοιδά is διαγγέλλοισα Pindar implicitly touches on the silence of the statue as another one of its limitations. Here he may be understood as taking over for poetry the general claim of archaic statuary to speak or report, since inscriptions on archaic statue bases frequently addressed the onlooker in the first person.[33] At the same time the animated nature of his song is emphasized in his address to it as 'sweet song' to which he gives the command to announce its tidings everywhere. With such an apostrophe Pindar, in effect, presents his song as something personified.

Pindar's contrast with the rival visual medium is no casual one, but may refer to two areas particularly associated with Aigina: its sea-faring and statuary.[34] The latter appears most notably in the pediments of the temple to Aphaia (dated *c.* 500–490 BC). If this suggestion is correct, then the poet would be treading a fine line in exploiting one famous Aiginetan activity – the nautical imagery which frames the ode (2–3, 50–1) – at the expense of another. Also noteworthy is Pindar's invocation of a moving body as a metaphor for his own medium, which underlines its difference from sculpture in the opening of the ode (*Nemean* 5.19–21):

> εἰ δ᾽ ὄλβον ἢ χειρῶν βίαν ἢ σιδαρίταν ἐπαινῆσαι πόλεμον
>   δεδόκηται, μακρά μοι
> αὐτόθεν ἅλμαθ᾽ ὑποσκάπτοι τις· ἔχω γονάτων ὁρμὰν ἐλαφράν·
> καὶ πέραν πόντοιο πάλλοντ᾽ αἰετοί.

> But if it is decided to praise happiness, strength of hands, or steel-clad war, let someone dig for me a jumping pit far from this point, for I have a light spring in my knees, and eagles leap even beyond the sea.

The poet-as-eagle metaphor, found elsewhere in Pindar (*Olympian* 2.86–8; *Nemean* 3.80–2, etc.) and Bacchylides (5.16–30, etc.), is perhaps the culmination of the motion imagery here. But no less interesting is Pindar's use of the living body as an analogue for song and his assimilation of himself to an athlete in his role as poet in the expression as ἔχω γονάτων ὁρμὰν ἐλαφράν ('I have a light spring in my knees'). At this point Pindar has just alluded to, but announced he will not sing of, the fratricide committed by the Aeacidae; rather, he is on the verge of songs of a different subject. This motif occurs again when he elsewhere compares himself to an athlete about to race as he prepares to tell of the fall of Ajax (*Nemean* 8.19): ἵσταμαι δὴ ποσσὶ κούφοις, ἀμπνέων τε πρίν τι φάμεν ('here I stand on light feet and draw breath before uttering a word'). Both athletic images mark a pause in the song but immediately suggest ensuing athletic action that will serve as a metaphor for the song continuing on a different theme.

Steiner uses the athletic image at *Nemean* 5.19–20 to reinterpret Pindar's opening statement about sculpture, claiming that the 'agonistic metaphor retroactively gives a different meaning to the opening picture.'[35] For Steiner, ἐλινύσοντα does not mean 'idle' but 'resting like victors recovering from exertions' and she suggests that Pindar is evoking a visual motif used by sculptors of athletes at rest. But this is unconvincing. It ignores Pindar's essential contrast between the mobility of song and static nature of statues that is stressed at the ode's outset; and it is contradicted by the negative connotations of Pindar's use of ἐλινύσοντα at *Isthmian* 2.46, which, as Steiner admits, unequivocally means 'standing idle'.[36] It is hardly likely that the poet would attempt to align his song to the very medium he has already denounced. We are better off reading the latter image at *Nemean* 5.19–20 in the light of the opening eschewal of sculpture rather than vice versa. The image of the poet-as-athlete is better understood as another means by which Pindar stresses the mobility of his song; this is not only fitting for an ode in honour of athletic success, but is confirmed by the inclusion of the flying eagle motif, which Steiner does not discuss.[37] As has been suggested, the eagle image stands here for Pindar himself and facilitates the transition from the location of the ode's performance to the mythic world of Peleus: from Aigina to Thessaly. Again poetry is associated with movement and action, consistent with the athletic image that precedes it.

For Lefkowitz, analogies between athletics and poetic imagery show that Pindar wants to 'express his friendship' for the victor and 'appreciation of his sport'.[38] Whether or not Pindar's praise is as heartfelt as Lefkowitz suggests, there certainly is an agonistic tenor in the poet-as-athlete image in *Nemean* 5.19–21, which she underplays, but which emerges clearly when taken in conjunction with the denigration of statuary at the beginning of the ode. Thus, the mobility of the human body at *Nemean* 5.19–20 becomes a particularly pointed image, designed to stress the superiority of song over statuary as much as to ingratiate Pindar with his patron. Indeed, the connection between song and the moving body is already prefaced a few lines earlier by Pindar's use of στάσομαι (*Nemean* 5.16) as a way of saying he will not sing of the murder of Phocus by his half-brothers, the Aeacidae. Segal interestingly suggests that here 'I shall stand still' (στάσομαι) emphasizes the moral choices Pindar makes for the contents of his poem which has thus gained a greater complexity than the simple immobility of statues.[39] Also, the image assumes that the song has so far been moving, since it stops when its composer announces he will 'stand still'.[40] In this usage, στάσομαι works as a perfectly apt metaphor for bringing a song to a halt, and has as its corollary the image of the athlete primed for action, used a few lines later, to suggest a singer ready for songs on a different subject.

A further link between poetry and the living human body is evident in the ode. In paying tribute to Menander, the successful athlete's Athenian trainer (*Nemean* 5.49), Pindar indulges in deft word-play: χρὴ δ᾽ ἀπ᾽ Ἀθανᾶν τέκτον᾽ ἀεθληταῖσιν ἔμμεν ('it is fitting that a craftsman of athletes should be from Athens'). As a word for craftsman, τέκτων invites comparison with Pindar's opening disclaimer of eschewing the realm of sculpture, especially since τέκτων could mean sculptor, as, for instance, at Euripides' *Alcestis* (348). The trainer is seen as a sculptor not of the motionless statues left behind in the proem, but of living, vital athletes, whose bodies are used by Pindar as metaphors for his own song. Thus Pindar subtly reiterates the lifelessness of statuary with which he opens the ode. Also, the expression τέκτον᾽ ἀεθληταῖσιν echoes the image of the τέκτονες (craftsmen) of song Pindar uses elsewhere (*Nemean* 3.4–5; *Pythian* 3.113–14). It parallels his depiction of his song which 'produces/fashions' its subjects to be the equal of kings (*Nemean* 4.84) – a claim which, we saw, uses language for visual artworks in order to upstage them. Pindar, thus, adds the trainer to the list of those praised in the song, and in the process, equates him with his own poetic self, just as he attempts to identify himself with the successful athletes he praises.[41] Pindar presents both himself and the trainer in *Nemean* 5 in similar terms; their works are not the lifeless images on pedestals, and the physical bodies produced by one become metaphors for the living song produced by the other. We may thus see in this treatment of the trainer, as with the nautical imagery that frames the ode (2–3; cf. 50–1), a reprise of the earlier reference to sculpture, but with some polemical undertones.[42] If there is some irony in this use of τέκτων at *Nemean* 5.49, it should not surprise us, as it is part of a Pindaric technique of agonistic self-representation. As has been observed, Pindar's use of even ἐργάζομαι in *Isthmian* 2.46 uses craft-terminology, but to promote his own art.[43] Similarly, the use of τέκτων in *Nemean* 5 paradoxically serves to underscore how Pindar would differentiate between his medium and visual monuments.

In a number of odes, then, Pindar's subtle redeployment of craft-terminology comes with a keen agonistic edge. In *Nemean* 4, for instance, Pindar presents his song as more brilliant than marble and better at crafting and edifying its subject, and in *Nemean* 5 we find a sculptor of living bodies opposed to the famously static images that open the ode. Thus, he skilfully combines these metaphors from the plastic arts with the concept of poetry as a medium of motion, stipulated elsewhere in *Nemean* 5 with the image of the long-jumper and eagle, in addition to the famous opening conceit. These motifs are closely assimilated to the broader agonistic environment of his day, involving athletics and the means of celebrating athletic success.

They also parallel Pindar's habit of likening his medium to an athletic event and himself to an athlete (*Olympian* 13.93–5; *Nemean* 4.91–6, 7.71–3, 8.19, 10.54–5; *Isthmian* 2.35–7). Indeed, Pindar's odes sometimes appear scarcely less competitive in tone than the sporting events he celebrates.

Philosophical and rhetorical appropriations

The agonistic tendencies in much of Pindar's treatment of visual media form an interesting contrast to the ancient orthodoxy which tended to see such objects in animated terms.[44] It is now worth considering other ancient attitudes to artworks as lifeless matter for the way they parallel and extend certain Pindaric treatments of this medium. This indicates that Pindar's comments come in a context where the efficacy of visual media is open to dispute, as well as highlighting the significance of his contrast between songs and visual monuments. In the works of Plato, Isocrates and Alcidamas this contrast is notably redeployed; indeed it can be felt in the writings of much later periods too.[45]

An interesting parallel comes from Euripides' *Autolycus* (282N) and, like epinikian statues and odes, is part of a broader discourse on athletes. But, unlike the usual function of epinikian statues, the connection between athlete and monument here is not flattering. Rather, Euripides' reference to ἀγάλματα describes stupid athletes, in a passage which Athenaeus (10.413c) saw as an echo of Xenophanes' earlier attack (B2 D–K). The Euripidean piece focuses on athletes' gluttony, inability to endure poverty, add to their family's wealth, or look after themselves generally (282N especially 1–9); instead: λαμπροὶ δ᾽ ἐν ἥβῃ καὶ πόλεως ἀγάλματα | φοιτῶσι· ('in the prime of life they wander, radiant, as ornaments | statues of the city'). They may be splendid physical specimens in their prime, but are considered mere ἀγάλματα – a word that here carries connotations of shallowness and uselessness. Interestingly, this metaphorical link with statues does not preclude the idea of 'motion' for these figures, but rather involves the idea of good looks, but no intelligence or utility. This invective constitutes an apparent inversion of cultural practice whereby the *Autolycus*, which is probably satyric, here undermines the typically high regard of athletes in classical Athens.[46] Here the speaker stresses the worthlessness of athletes by paradoxically reducing them to the very kinds of monuments which would normally be expected to glorify them.[47]

Pindaric ideas re-emerge more palpably in some fourth-century texts, which address aspects of visual and verbal artforms in agonistic terms. Like Pindar, Isocrates in the *Evagoras* – a speech written for an Athenian ally and king of Cyprus late in the orator's life (*c.* 370–360 BC) – does not make comparisons between these media idly. Instead, he links them to his role as a professional speech-writer contending with rival media for commemorating aristocratic achievements. Thus, we find some striking parallels between Pindar's and Isocrates' presentations of their own media which are each born of similarly agonistic contexts. W. Race has offered a useful treatment of Isocrates' development of Pindaric encomia, and rightly stresses that he is deliberately promoting his own prose encomia in the face of poetic, clearly Pindaric, ones, and is thus engaged in polemics of sorts.[48] Race is correct in his comments on Pindar's and Isocrates' attitudes to visual monuments, but they are rather perfunctory. He restricts his focus to how poet and speech-writer present their own media as superior due to their mobility and powers of dissemination; and similar cursory treatment is found in Gentili's discussion of Pindar and Isocrates.[49] But more can certainly be added to these issues, so that we may see deeper parallels between Isocrates and Pindar.

Classical Athens and elsewhere witnessed the ascendancy of rhetorical prose over poetry as a vehicle for speculative thought, commemoration of individuals and shaping of public ideology at civic festivals. This cultural shift gained momentum with the sophists in their role as teachers of rhetoric and theorists about language. As a student of Gorgias, the Attic speech-writer Isocrates was obviously influenced by these developments, in which an *agōn* between rhetoric and traditional poetry is sometimes detectable. For instance, in Thucydides' account of Pericles' funeral speech the statesman makes a point of saying that commemoration of the war dead does not need the usual embellishments and falsehoods typical especially of Homeric poetry (Thuc. 2.41.4–5).[50] By implication, secular speeches can do the job better. Also noteworthy is Pericles' view that men's glory is not just restricted to the visual monuments where they lie, but endures as the ἄγραφος μνήμη ('unwritten memory') in the minds of Athenians and foreigners alike – part of his famous statement: ἀνδρῶν γὰρ ἐπιφανῶν πᾶσα γῆ τάφος ('all the world is a monument to famous men', Thuc. 2.43.2–3). Visual memorials and their inscriptions thus seem upstaged as a result. Pericles, then, appears to undercut the role of visual and poetic encomia in a way that anticipates Isocrates, albeit rather cursorily. A closer look at Isocrates' treatment of visual artworks in the *Evagoras* allows further insights into how he echoes Pindar and how he develops certain ideas not explicit in the poet.

The agonistic edge to the axe Isocrates grinds not only involves criticism of poetic encomia (9.8–11, etc.), but takes on visual memorials too (9.73–4):

> ἐγὼ δ᾽ ὦ Νικόκλεις, ἡγοῦμαι καλὰ μὲν εἶναι μνημεῖα καὶ τὰς τῶν
> σωμάτων εἰκόνας, πολὺ μέντοι πλείονας ἀξίας τὰς τῶν

πράξεων καὶ τῆς διανοίας, ἃς ἐν τοῖς λόγοις ἄν τις μόνον
τοῖς τεχνικῶς ἔχουσι θεωρήσειεν. προκρίνω δὲ ταύτας
πρῶτον μὲν εἰδὼς τοὺς καλοὺς κἀγαθοὺς τῶν ἀνδρῶν οὐχ
οὕτως ἐπὶ τῷ κάλλει τοῦ σώματος σεμνυνομένους ὡς ἐπὶ τοῖς
ἔργοις καὶ τῇ γνώμῃ φιλοτιμουμένους·

But, Nicocles, I think that while depictions of the body are fine memorials, nonetheless depictions of deeds and of character are of far greater value, and one may witness them only in speeches which have real skill. I prefer these (depictions) because I know, firstly, that noble and honourable men pride themselves not so much on physical beauty as they desire to be honoured for their achievements and intelligence.

Isocrates does acknowledge images as fine memorials (καλὰ μνημεῖα) in purely physical terms, but still sees these as inadequate compared to λόγος when commemorating an individual. He champions the medium of his own profession as offering a worthy likeness of a person's deeds and mind (πράξεις...διανοία) and claims that men who are noble and honourable (καλοί and ἀγαθοί) want to be noted more for their achievements and intelligence (ἔργα) and (γνώμη) rather than physical beauty. This claim plays up to his putative market, flattering his clients as men of real discernment, whom he also describes as εὖ φρονοῦντες ('right thinking'), whose approval is most to be desired (9.73–4). Like Pindar, Isocrates depended for his livelihood on a good client base.

Isocrates also suggests there is something less than human about the physical beauty of memorial statues and here parallels Democritus (B195 D–K) who speaks of images as devoid of inner life, however visually impressive they might be: εἴδωλα ἐσθῆτι καὶ κόσμῳ διαπρεπέα πρὸς θεωρίην, ἀλλὰ καρδίης κενεά ('images conspicuous for their dress and ornament, but empty of heart').[51] We may also note a similar comment from the *Hippocratic Corpus* (*Vict.* 21= 22C1.21 D–K): ἀνδριαντοποιοὶ μίμησιν σώματος ποιέουσιν πλὴν ψυχῆς γνώμην δ' ἔχοντα οὐ ποιέουσιν ('Sculptors make an imitation of the body without the soul, and do not make bodies that have intelligence').[52] This, too, is consistent with Isocrates here, whose λόγος alone, he claims, can do justice to a man's γνώμη and deeds. Such a claim is not far removed from the implications of Pindar's *Nemean* 4.79–85, discussed above. We recall Pindar's claim: 'a hymn of noble deeds (τῶν ἀγαθῶν ἐργμάτων) produces/fashions (τεύχει) a man to be equal in spirit to kings'. Not only does this use the language of craft to bolster his own song, but here Pindar emphasizes that his song can dwell on its subject's worthy achievements, thus making it a more shining tribute than visual monuments. Similarly, Isocrates stresses the ability of his λόγος to produce genuine likenesses of a man's deeds (πράξεις), which also recalls Pindar's idea of his song as 'a mirror for noble deeds' (*Nemean* 7.14).

Isocrates continues the idea from *Nemean* 5 that visual images are condemned to remain in the city where they were set up. On this reckoning they are inferior to his λόγος which can be broadly disseminated, just as Pindar's song was bidden to travel in every boat announcing its tidings:

> ἔπειθ᾽ ὅτι τοὺς μὲν τύπους ἀναγκαῖον παρὰ τούτοις εἶναι
> μόνοις, παρ᾽ οἷς ἂν σταθῶσι, τοὺς δε λόγους ἐξενεχθῆναι θ᾽
> οἷόν τ᾽ ἐστὶν εἰς τὴν Ἑλλάδα.

I know then that sculptures must necessarily remain only among those in whose cities they were set up, whereas speeches can be published throughout Greece (9.74).

There is something Periclean (or Thucydidean) about this, too. If the whole world is the monument to famous men, then Isocrates' encomium at least enables all Greece to resound with the praises of its subject, which static monuments do not allow. Isocrates goes on to claim that scope for real character-portrait resides only in words, since no-one can liken the nature of the body to sculptures and paintings:

> πρὸς δὲ τούτοις ὅτι τοῖς μὲν πεπλασμένοις καὶ τοῖς
> γεγραμμένοις οὐδεὶς ἂν τὴν τοῦ σώματος φύσιν ὁμοιώσειε,
> τοὺς δὲ τρόπους τοὺς ἀλλήλων καὶ τὰς διανοίας τὰς ἐν τοῖς
> λεγομένοις ἐνούσας ῥᾴδιόν ἐστι μιμεῖσθαι τοῖς μὴ ῥᾳθυμεῖν
> αἱρουμένοις, ἀλλὰ χρηστοῖς εἶναι βουλομένοις.

And in addition, I know that while no-one can make the nature of the body resemble moulded images and paintings, yet for those who choose not to be lazy, but desire to be good men, it is easy to imitate the characters of other men and their thoughts which are embodied in the spoken word (9.75).

Isocrates goes to some length in his attempts to constrict the realm of visual imagery to a superficial depiction of only physical beauty at best. This is an interesting, if specious, critique of contemporary developments in portrait sculpture (and, probably, painting if we had samples to judge by) which by the mid-fourth century was becoming more detailed and less obviously idealized than in earlier periods.[53] Again Isocrates makes accuracy of character-portrayal an issue and sees this as the domain of hard-working decent men for a similarly honourable clientele. Isocrates is marketing his services by defining his wares against visual media, as Pindar had done earlier. But Isocrates also takes the idea of the lifeless and static nature of visual memorials to another level in arguing that they cannot portray individual human character with any real penetration – an idea nowhere explicit in Pindar's work, but one we might expect would earn his approval.

Further parallels between elements of Pindar's concepts of poetry can be found in the writings of Plato and the sophist Alcidamas from Asia Minor – another student of Gorgias, who came to Athens and became a rival of Isocrates. Connections between Plato and Alcidamas have been noted before, but my aim here is to see an aspect of their literary criticism as an extension of Pindaric motifs.[54] It is not necessary to posit the direct influence of Pindar on the philosopher and rhetorician, but we may still see how he anticipates later developments in different but similarly agonistic contexts. Nor would this be the only example of a Pindaric precursor to literary ideas maintained by these two. For instance, that poetry or art is a 'mirror' occurs in Pindar (*Nemean* 7.14) and is used by Alcidamas to describe Homer's *Odyssey* (fr. 25 Muir) and by Plato to disparage the mimetic qualities of painting (*Republic* 10.596d).[55] A passage from the *Phaedrus* promotes dialectic over written discourse for its epistemological and philosophical value. And Alcidamas' *On the Sophists*, possibly datable to *c.* 390 BC, promotes extemporaneous speeches for their persuasive power.[56] His view is widely accepted as being directed at Isocrates, champion of the written style of speeches, and his works such as *Against the Sophists*.[57] Plato's aims seem rather lofty compared to Alcidamas' practical concerns as a teacher of rhetoric, yet both use an image predicated on the vitality of the oral word, contrasted with the deadness of the written word and visual arts.

Firstly, in Plato's *Phaedrus* (275d–e), during a discussion of the value of the oral over the written word, Socrates likens the silence of the latter to painting (ζωγραφία), and says of the painter's works: ἕστηκε μὲν ὡς ζῶντα, ἐὰν δ' ἀνέρῃ τι, σεμνῶς πάνυ σιγᾷ ('they stand as if alive, but if ever someone questions them on anything, they keep a majestic silence'). Painting here is silent and still, an inanimate graven image like the Pindaric statues in the proem to *Nemean* 5. We may also compare Pindar's description of the Rhodian sculptures in *Olympian* 7.52 as ζωοῖσιν ἐρπόντεσσι θ' ὁμοῖα ('like living creatures'), which paradoxically implies their immobility by stating they (merely) resemble creatures of motion.[58] Similarly, Socrates' expression ὡς ζῶντα ('*as if* alive') draws attention to the lifelessness of painted figures which is confirmed by their own silence: σεμνῶς πάνυ σιγᾷ. Moreover, Socrates' interlocutor, Phaedrus, gets the gist of this and sees the oral word as a living, conscious phenomenon, in contrast to the written word:

> Τὸν τοῦ εἰδότος λόγον λέγεις ζῶντα καὶ ἔμψυχον, οὗ ὁ γεγραμμένος εἴδωλον ἄν τι λέγοιτο δικαίως.

You are speaking of the logos (word) of the one who has knowledge, the word which is alive and imbued with a soul, of which the written word might be justly said to be some sort of image (*Phaedrus* 276a 8–9).

The visual image and written word are both contrasted with the liveliness of the oral word – a contrast which develops Pindar's propensity to see his song as a living medium opposed to static artworks. The Platonic idea here now makes written discourse part of the antithesis between living and dead media. This concept receives more extended treatment by Alcidamas, whose alignment of the living body with the oral word carries with it significant Pindaric resonances.

For the rhetorician in *On the Sophists* (27–8), written speeches are like visual artworks on the basis of their static nature, uselessness and inability to adapt to given situations. Oral speeches have the virtues of mobility, adaptability, vitality and are just like the living human body. Alcidamas considers written speeches to be like εἴδωλα καὶ σχήματα καὶ μιμήματα λόγων ('images, forms and representations of oral speeches'); he thinks it reasonable to equate them with 'bronze statues, stone sculptures and painted figures' which he calls μιμήματα τῶν ἀληθινῶν σωμάτων ('representations of real bodies', *Soph*. 27). But Alcidamas argues that a significant gulf separates real bodies from mere representations of them, as implicit in Pindar's reference to the Rhodian sculptures in *Olympian* 7.50–3; indeed the reference to 'real' bodies underlines the essentially unreal nature of representation in the first place. The sophist goes on to claim: ταῦτα μιμήματα...χρῆσιν δ᾽ οὐδεμίαν τῷ τῶν ἀνθρώπων βίῳ παραδίδωσι ('these representations...provide no use for the life of humans') and are thus unlike real bodies. But he does concede their ability to give τέρψιν...ἐπὶ τῆς θεωρίας ('pleasure to the sight', *Soph*. 27). For Alcidamas, then, visual artworks are like the written word since, while the sight of the written word can induce ἔκπληξις ('astonishment'), it, too, is useless because of its inability to move: ἐπὶ δὲ τῶν καιρῶν ἀκίνητος ὢν οὐδεμίαν ὠφελείαν τοῖς κεκτημένοις παραδίδωσιν ('it provides no use to those who possess it for a certain occasion, since it does not move', *Soph*. 28). In fact the uselessness of beautiful statues is not only a feature they share with written words, but parallels the presentation of the athletes in Euripides' *Autolycus* (282N) who were likened to statues precisely because they were fine-looking but equally useless.

Alcidamas' concluding remarks contain a strikingly similar image to that found in Plato's *Phaedrus*:

> ἀλλ᾽ ὥσπερ ἀνδριάντων καλῶν ἀληθινὰ σώματα πολὺ χείρους
> τὰς εὐπρεπείας ἔχοντα πολλαπλασίους ἐπὶ τῶν ἔργων τὰς
> ὠφελείας παραδίδωσιν, οὕτω καὶ λόγος ὁ μὲν ἀπ᾽ αὐτῆς τῆς
> διανοίας ἐν τῷ παραυτίκα λεγόμενος ἔμψυχός ἐστι καὶ ζῇ
> καὶ τοῖς πράγμασιν ἕπεται καὶ τοῖς ἀληθέσιν ἀφωμοίωται
> σώμασιν, ὁ δὲ γεγραμμένος εἰκόνι λόγου τὴν φύσιν ὁμοίαν
> ἔχων ἁπάσης ἐνεργείας ἄμοιρος καθέστηκεν.

And just as real bodies have a far less attractive appearance than beautiful statues, but for practical tasks provide more usefulness many times over, so too a speech spoken in the circumstances of the moment from one's own mind is imbued with soul and is alive and touches upon actual events, and resembles real bodies, but a written speech has a nature resembling (only) the image of a speech and is lacking in all power (*Soph.* 28).

Both εἰκών and εἴδωλον could denote visual artworks, and their appearances in the *Phaedrus* and here underline the static features being attributed to written discourse.[59] Alcidamas' antithesis between visual artworks and written λόγος ('speech') on the one hand and extemporaneous speech on the other develops Pindar's polemics in *Nemean* 5. His depiction of the former two as lifeless media recalls the proem (*Nemean* 5.1–2), and his equation between oral speech and the living body echoes Pindar's treatment of his own song as an athletic body in action or on the verge of it (*Nemean* 5.16, 19–21; 8.19).[60] Indeed, Alcidamas goes beyond Plato by emphasizing the oral word as like a living body, in addition to describing it as 'alive' or 'imbued with soul'.

Alcidamas' views are noteworthy on another level for using a broad aesthetic vocabulary similar to that of Gorgias, his master. He, too, speaks of artworks and visual objects as inducing τέρψις ('pleasure') and ἔκπληξις ('astonishment'), among other responses, and also uses σχῆμα to describe what painters and sculptors produce (*Hel.* 16–18). Alcidamas' use of specific terms such as εἴδωλον ('image'), σχῆμα ('form'), μίμημα ('representation') and εἰκών ('likeness') does not just show that he inherited his teacher's verbosity. It is also likely to refer to thinking about visual imagery in formal terms which was evidently widespread in the fifth and fourth centuries.[61] Democritus (B195 D–K), like Alcidamas (*Soph.* 27), speaks of visually impressive or pleasurable images (εἴδωλα) that are, however, essentially lifeless. Democritus (B194 D–K) also notes that viewing fine works can lead to great pleasures. So, too, Isocrates' belief in the *Evagoras* (73) that visual monuments can be fine, if limited, memorials is consistent with Alcidamas' acknowledgement of pleasant but ineffective statues. In fact, the focus on artworks here suggests a rising interest in speculation about aspects of visual artworks to such an extent that Alcidamas feels a need to address their role also. It is much more plausible to see a cultural discourse – traceable at least to Pindar – on aspects of visual and verbal media as Alcidamas' chief influence here, rather than Plato's Theory of Forms, as claimed by Muir.[62]

Alcidamas' critique of artworks entails a similar strand of ideas to that found in the *Evagoras* of Isocrates. Each rhetorician makes the idealized beauty or schematic form of visual artworks a problem for that medium.

For Isocrates, this leads to a gulf between image and subject in terms of accurate likeness and character portrayal. Alcidamas makes it an element of the uselessness of artworks, which parallel the uselessness of written words. Isocrates' *Evagoras* and Alcidamas' *On the Sophists* enjoy a perhaps unexpected connection through their discussion of the powers of verbal media. Isocrates refers to the capacity for broad dissemination through verbal encomia, as well as the ability to focus on their subject's deeds and character; Alcidamas uses a metaphor of the living body and applies it to extemporaneous rhetoric to illustrate its own vital nature. Underlying this paradoxical consistency between these two opponents is the development of ideas pithily expressed in Pindaric odes.

Conclusions

The agonistic strand of Pindar's poetics is just one of many in his array of conceits. However it does have considerable importance. When read in the context of other remarks on the lifelessness of visual images found in archaic and classical texts, the polemical tenor in Pindar's treatment of visual monuments becomes more palpable and wide-reaching. In a culture that so often treated images as efficacious and animate, Pindar's challenge to visual monuments is striking indeed. To some jaded modern eyes, claims undermining the animated status of artworks may be stating the obvious. But this would misread the situation in late archaic Greece in which the oral word and visual image were prime vehicles of cultural expression. In fact, we have only to think of the role of images in advertising, propaganda and pornography on billboards, the internet and elsewhere to realize that our own age is very much in the thrall of figurative imagery. For Pindar, the perceived power of visual imagery is a challenge to which he responds in kind on a number of levels.

Apparent unity of purpose shared by victory odes and statues should not blind us to the subtleties and brilliance of Pindar's polemical conception of himself and his art. Specifically, we have seen how Pindar exploits the idea of poetry as a medium of motion by likening it to an athletic body in action in contrast to static monuments. We have also seen how his use of terms from visual arts can imply the superiority of his songs to a medium which could rival his own for the favours of patrons. Like all great poets, Pindar breathes new life into old concepts. These he transforms largely by linking them to the experience of his audience, patrons and his professional persona. Much of his art, then, can be linked to a competitive milieu that was fostered by the rituals of festival, sport and aristocratic celebration within the Greek world.

The significance of this aspect of Pindaric poetics is borne out in the redeployment of his ideas in certain philosophical and rhetorical writings of Isocrates, Plato and Alcidamas, all operating in agonistic contexts. Self-aggrandizing claims made by these ancient writers tell us more about how they would like to be seen than about anything else. Yet a considerable amount can be gleaned from them, not least of which are insights into the ingenuity that each employed to promote himself and his medium. The fact that Pindar's polemical imagery found renewed treatment in the controversies of later writers testifies to its enduring utility in a culture where the *agōn* was one of the most conspicuous features of public life.

Notes

[1] We learn from Pausanias (8.48.2–3) and Lucian (*Anacharsis* 9) that olive, laurel, pine and celery wreaths were awarded at the Olympic, Pythian, Isthmian and Nemean Games respectively.

[2] For fuller discussions, see Harris 1964, 36–7, 41–2, 45–7; Buhmann 1972, 104–36; Kyle 1987, 145–54, 155–68; Golden 1998, 76–7, 141–3. See also the sources collected by Miller 1991, 75–8, 181–2.

[3] See Marcovich 1977, 13–26 and Kyle 1987, 126–8 for fuller discussion. Another early critic of athletes is the seventh-century elegist Tyrtaeus (fr. 12.1–4 West) who saw athletic ability as unworthy of mention compared to a man's military prowess.

[4] Pausanias tells us (6.18.7) that an athlete of the 59th Olympiad (=544 BC), Praxidamas, had the first epinikian statue made in his honour. For victor statues generally, see Hyde 1921 *passim*; Lattimore 1987, 245–56; Raschke 1988, 38–54. Bell 1995, 1–42 goes to great lengths to link the so-called 'Motya Charioteer' to Pindar's *Isthmian* 2, seeing it as a depiction of the charioteer Nicomachos, mentioned by the poet (cf. *Isthmian* 2.22); but such attempts must remain conjectural, however ingenious.

[5] For this feature of inscriptions on statue bases, see Ebert 1972, 18–20, and, for instance, Ebert no. 4, etc.; see also Steiner 1993, 167–72.

[6] Song as a vehicle of memory: e.g. *Iliad* 6.357–8; see also the discussion by Detienne 1996, 39–52 with notes. For Homeric visual monuments, see, for example, *Iliad* 7.84–91; *Odyssey* 24.80–4.

[7] Steiner 1993, 159–80; 1998, 123–49; cf. Kurke 1993, 131–63. The idea has had much currency amongst scholars; for instance, Jebb 1905, 37–8.

[8] Kurke 1993, 160 n.59.

[9] Steiner 1998, 124 and *passim*.

[10] Steiner 1993, 167–78.

[11] Ebert 1972; Steiner (1993, 177) compares, for instance, Pindar *Olympian* 10.1–2 and Ebert no. 62; *Isthmian* 8.62–4 and Ebert no. 48.1, etc.

[12] Steiner 1998, esp. 136–46.

[13] Steiner 1998, esp. 137, 139.

[14] Simonides was known to Xenophanes as 'skin-flint' (B21 D–K); see the

scholia to Aristophanes *Peace* 697b. Full discussion of Simonides' significance can be found in Detienne 1996, 107–16; Svenbro 1976, 141–72; Gentili 1988, esp. 68–71, 151–62; Rouveret 1989, 144–9; Carson 1992, 51–64. See also Campbell 1991, 346–9, for further ancient testimonia on Simonides' 'mercenary' attitude and mnemonics; note also Kurke 1991, 59–60.

[15] *Pace* Steiner 1993, 159.

[16] The mercenary tendencies behind much of Pindar's poetry are parodied already in Aristophanes' *Birds* (904–57, esp. 936–9). For the social position of the poet, see Svenbro 1976, 173–86; Gentili 1988, 155–76 with notes, and Kurke 1991, *passim*, esp. 240–56. My aim here is less to explore Pindar's social situation than to discuss agonistic features of his self-representation that are linked to it.

[17] Including Steiner 1994, 95–6. See also Webster 1939, 168; Holloway 1973, 198–9; Svenbro 1976, 190; Gentili 1988, 163; Kurke 1991, 251.

[18] As Kyle 1987, 137 n. 68 astutely observes, Plato makes many analogies between rhetoric, athletics and his political philosophy; see, *inter al.*, *Laws* 830a–b, *Sophist* 231e, *Republic* 403e (but criticizes athletic training, *Rep.* 404a), *Gorgias* 516e; cf. also *Gorgias* 456d–457b. For further references on and discussion of the relations between athletics, philosophy and the sophists, see the chapter by Harold Tarrant in this book.

[19] Philostratus (*VS* 1.11); Lucian (*Herod.* 1–3). Aelian (*VH* 12.32) tells us of sophists dressing in the purple robes of rhapsodes at public festivals; and we know of painting competitions by the fifth century (Pliny *HN* 35.58).

[20] On poetic craft analogies in general: Harriott 1969, 92–104; Svenbro 1976, 186–93 with references; Gentili 1988, esp. 50–3, 164–5 with notes; Shapiro 1988, 3 n. 16; Kurke 1991, 192–4.

[21] For Pindar's depiction of the architectural sculpture at Delphi, which Euripides (*Ion* 184 ff.) also describes, see Shapiro 1988, 1–5.

[22] See Kurke 1991, esp. 94–5, 104–5, 155–9; Steiner 1994, 91–9.

[23] e.g. Homer (*Odyssey* 17.383–6), Hesiod (*Works and Days* 25–6), Solon (fr. 13.49–52 West), Parmenides (B8.52 D–K), Democritus (B21 D–K), Aristophanes (*Peace* 749–50; *Frogs* 1004; cf. *Thesmophoriazousai* 52–7, where it is taken to extremes in the merciless parody of Agathon). Schmitt (1967, 296–8) and Nagy (1979, 297–300) both see such analogies as traceable to an Indo-European tradition in which poetry is compared to carpentry and craft.

[24] See Nisetich 1975, 59; Kurke 1993, 137–40; Steiner 1993, 165–6.

[25] Nisetich 1975, 68.

[26] Willcock 1995, ad loc.

[27] See, for instance: *Iliad* 6.314, 14.140, 18.373, 18.549; Hesiod *Theogony* 581; [Hesiod] *Shield of Heracles* 154, 219, etc.

[28] e.g. *Olympian* 2.84–95; 9.22 ff.; *Pythian* 1.43; 2.67; 4.299; 8.57; *Nemean* 1.1–7; 3.80–2; 5.19–21; 7.16; *Isthmian* 2.1–5; 4.1, etc.; cf. fr. 107a (S–M). For further references to this kind of imagery, see Harriott 1969, esp. 61–70, 88–90.

[29] Harriott 1969, 64–5; see also Walsh 1984, 3–36; Ritoók 1989 *passim*.

[30] *Olympian* 13.93–5; *Nemean* 4.91–6, 7.71–3, 8.19–21, 10.54–5; *Isthmian* 2.35; and on this, see Lefkowitz 1984, 5–12; 1991, 161–8.

[31] For fuller discussion of *Isthmian* 2 and the agonistic use of ἐργασάμην, see Kurke 1991, 240–56. For the connotations of the verb in producing works of artifice see LSJ s.v. ἐργάζομαι II.

[32] For instance, Webster 1939, 168; Holloway 1973, 198–9; Svenbro 1976, 190; Gentili 1988, 163; Kurke 1991, 251.

[33] See Svenbro 1988 *passim* for the role and function of reading statuary inscriptions in archaic Greece. Segal (1974, 399 n. 6) accepts the suggestion by Méautis that the proem also refers to the sheer physical difficulty of transporting a statue across the sea, as opposed to a song.

[34] As suggested by Mullen 1982, 145, 154.

[35] Steiner 1993, 162; cf. also Svenbro 1976, 190 n. 117.

[36] Steiner 1993, 162 n. 12.

[37] Pfeijffer 1999, 131–4.

[38] Lefkowitz 1984, *passim*, esp. 11.

[39] Segal 1974, 401–2.

[40] Conceivably this refers to a halt in the dancing of the chorus or solo singer in performance. Mullen 1982, *passim* argues for the choral nature of Pindaric epinikian performance, while the case for monody has been put by others (e.g. Heath 1988, 180–95 and, most fully, Lefkowitz 1991 *passim*). These controversies do not affect my reading.

[41] A parallel for this compliment is found at *Nemean* 4.93–6. Pfeijffer 1999, 81–3 sees Pindar's treatment of the trainer as 'extremely harsh', and suggests it has been influenced by Aigina's being at war with Athens at the time; but the nuances underlying the use of τέκτων here do not make it a hostile treatment.

[42] On Pindar's use of repeated imagery as a framing device for his odes, see Mullen 1982, 162, 250 n. 14.

[43] Svenbro 1976, 190; Gentili 1988, 287 n. 57; Kurke 1991, 251.

[44] e.g. the ecphrasis of Achilles' shield (*Il.* 18.483–607); for texts referring to animated Daedalic statues, see the collection at Overbeck 1868, 11–17. See also Delcourt 1957; Svenbro 1988 on first-person archaic inscriptions; Faraone 1992 on talismans; Morris 1992, 215–37; Spivey 1995, 442–59; Steiner 1998. Freedberg 1989 offers a rich overview of the ability of images throughout western culture to evoke powerful responses in the onlooker; see ibid. 65–78 for discussion of this and reactions to it in antiquity.

[45] Horace (*Ode* 3.30.1–9) owes something to Pindar, if not Simonides. Lessing's epoch-making *Laocoon, or the Limits of Poetry and Painting* of 1766 is largely built on the distinction posited by Pindar. It is beyond our scope to pursue these now, but for discussions and critiques of Lessing, see Mitchell 1986, esp. 102–15; Freedberg 1989, 372–5.

[46] On inverting cultural values as typical of satyric drama, see Lissarrague 1990; O'Sullivan 2000, 355, 358–9. For attitudes to athletes in classical Athens, see Kyle 1987, 124–54 and the chapter by David Pritchard in this book.

[47] Other texts alluding to artworks as lifeless or stupid matter include: Euripides *Trojan Women* 193–4; *Electra* 387–8; Antiphon B 15 D–K; Democritus B 195; Metagenes fr. 10 K–A; Demosthenes 18.129; *Hippocratic Corpus Vict.* 21

(=22C1.21 D–K). See also Aeschylus *Agamemnon* 240–2 and Aristophanes *Frogs* 537a–9a for the use of painting as a simile for silence or stillness. However, Xenophon (*Mem.* 3.10.1–8) and Aristotle (*Pol.* 1448a1–6, 1454b8 ff.; cf. *Pol.* 1340a34–40) suggest artworks may convey the ἦθος (character) or ψυχή (soul) of their subject; for further discussion of these two writers, see Lanata 1963, 288–99; Pollitt 1974, 184–9; Castriota 1994, 9–11.

⁴⁸ Race 1987 *passim*, esp. 136–7 on *Evagoras* 8–9.

⁴⁹ Race 1987, 131 n. 3 and *passim*; see esp., 149–50; 154–5; cf. Gentili 1988, 163.

⁵⁰ Thucydides is clearly aligning Pericles' view here with his own concerns regarding his historical method which he likewise presents as divesting itself of embellishments for the sake of accuracy (1.22.4; cf. 1.21.1. For full treatment of the role of the funeral speech in classical Athens, see Loraux 1986 *passim*, and esp. 15–76 for discussion of the epitaphios as a specifically democratic institution. See also the discussion by Lanata 1963, 248–51 of Pericles' critique of Homer. See Plato's *Menexenos* 236e.

⁵¹ Compare also Democritus (B105 D–K): σώματος κάλλος ζωιῶδες, ἢν μὴ νοῦς ὑπῇ ('beauty of the body is animal-like, unless intelligence underlies it'). In Euripides' *Electra* 387–8, Orestes speaks of statues as σάρκες αἱ κεναὶ φρενῶν ('physiques lacking brains'). Note the parallel with Democritus' καρδίης κενεά (B195 D–K). See Goldhill 1986 for a detailed defence of this disputed Euripidean passage.

⁵² Diels, following Wilamowitz, brackets πλὴν ψυχῆς.

⁵³ See Pollitt 1986, 20–37, 59–78. Lysistratus, brother of the famous sculptor Lysippus (both active *c.* 370–20), specialized in achieving realistic images of his subjects by working with plaster masks from his models (Pliny *HN* 35.153).

⁵⁴ By, for example, Guthrie (1975, 59) and Muir (2001, xiv, 59–62) who favours Platonic influence over Alcidamas, but no evidence prevents the opposite possibility. Richardson 1981, 8–9 interestingly suggests that Plato's *Republic* 10 is directed at Alcidamas' *Mouseion* (a literary miscellany), but overstates the case in claiming Alcidamas as Plato's prime target.

⁵⁵ As noted by Richardson 1981, 8 n. 31, who rightly observes that Aristotle's censure (*Rhet.* 1406b12 f.) of Alcidamas' description of the *Odyssey* suggests the metaphor was not a commonplace.

⁵⁶ The date is conjectural; see Muir 2001, xiv–xv.

⁵⁷ On their rivalry, see Brzoska 1894; Milne 1924, 21–53; Guthrie 1971, 312–3; Muir 2001, xiii–xv, xxvi n. 49 for bibliography on attempts to reconstruct the nature of the conflict between them.

⁵⁸ Considerations of space prevent a fuller discussion of *Olympian* 7.50–3 here; see Willcock 1995, 126–7 ad loc. In Aeschylus' *Theoroi* (7) the satyrs joke with their life-like portraits that 'lack only a voice'; for full discussion, see O'Sullivan 2000, 353–66.

⁵⁹ For εἰκών, s.v. LSJ I.1; for εἴδωλον, see Democritus B195.

⁶⁰ See also Pindar's athletic imagery for himself and his medium: for example *Olympian* 13.93–5; *Nemean* 4.91–6; 7.71–3; 10.54–5; *Isthmian* 2.35.

[61] For ancient treatises on the plastic arts, see Vitruvius (7 praef. 11) and Pliny, indices to books 34–6 of his *HN*; for fuller discussion, see Pollitt 1974, 12–31, and 1995, 19–24.

[62] Muir 2001, 60.

Bibliography

Bell, M.
  1995   'The Motya charioteer and Pindar's Isthmian 2', *Memoirs of the American Academy in Rome* 40, 1–42.
Brzoska, J.
  1894   *RE*, vol. 1, s.v. Alkidamas, coll. 1533–9.
Buhmann, H.
  1972   *Der Sieg in Olympia und in den anderen panhellenischen Spielen*, Munich.
Campbell, D. (ed. and trans.)
  1991   *Greek Lyric*, vol. 3, Cambridge, Mass.
Carson, A.
  1992   'Simonides Painter', in R. Hexter and D. Selden (eds.) *Innovations of Antiquity*, 51–64, New York and London.
Castriota, D.
  1992   *Myth, Ethos, Actuality: Official art in fifth-century BC Athens*, Madison.
Delcourt, M.
  1957   *Héphaistos ou la légende du magicien*, Paris.
Detienne, M.
  1996   *The Masters of Truth*, transl. J. Lloyd, New York.
Ebert, J.
  1972   *Griechische Epigramme auf Sieger an Gymnischen und Hippischen Agonen*, Berlin.
Faraone, C.A.
  1992   *Talismans and Trojan Horses: Guardian statues in ancient Greek myth and ritual*, Oxford.
Freedberg, D.
  1989   *The Power of Images*, Chicago.
Gentili, B.
  1988   *Poet and Public in Ancient Greece*, transl. T. Cole, Baltimore and London.
Golden, M.
  1998   *Sport and Society in Ancient Greece*, Cambridge.
Goldhill, S.
  1986   'Rhetoric and relevance: interpolation at Euripides *Electra* 367–400', *GRBS* 27, 157–71.
Guthrie, W.K.C.
  1971   *The Sophists*, Cambridge.
  1975   *A History of Greek Philosophy*, vol. 4, Cambridge.

Harriott, R.
  1969   *Poetry and Criticism before Plato*, London.
Harris, H.A.
  1964   *Greek Athletes and Athletics*, London.
Heath, M.
  1988   'Receiving the κῶμος: The context and performance of Epinician', *AJPh* 109, 180–95.
Holloway, R.R.
  1973   *A View of Greek Art*, New York.
Hyde, W.W.
  1921   *Olympic Victor Monuments and Greek Athletic Art*, Washington D.C.
Jebb, R.
  1905   *Bacchylides: Poems and fragments*, Cambridge.
Kurke, L.
  1991   *The Traffic in Praise: Pindar and the poetics of social economy*, Ithaca.
  1993   'The economy of kudos', in C. Dougherty and L. Kurke (eds.) *Cultural Poetics in Archaic Greece: Cult, performance, politics*, 131–63, Cambridge.
Kyle, D.
  1987   *Athletics in Ancient Athens*, Leiden.
Lanata, G.
  1963   *Poetica Pre-Platonica: Testimonianze e Frammenti*, Florence.
Lattimore, S.
  1987   'The nature of early Greek victor statues' in S.J. Bandy (ed.) *Coroebus Triumphs: The alliance of sports and the arts*, 245–56, San Diego.
Lefkowitz, M.
  1984   'The poet as athlete', *SIFC* 2, 5–12.
  1991   *First-Person Fictions: Pindar's poetic 'I'*, Oxford.
Lissarrague, F.
  1990   'Why satyrs are good to represent', in J. Winkler and F. Zeitlin (eds.) *Nothing to Do With Dionyos? Greek drama in its social context*, 228–36, Princeton.
Loraux, N.
  1986   *The Invention of Athens: The funeral oration in the classical city*, transl. A. Sheridan, Cambridge, Mass.
Marcovich, M.
  1977   'Xenophanes on drinking-parties and Olympic Games', *ICS* 2, 1–26.
Miller, S.
  1991   *Arete: Greek sport from ancient sources*, 2nd edn, Berkeley.
Milne, M.J.
  1924   'A study in Alcidamas and his relation to contemporary Sophistic', unpublished dissertation, Bryn Mawr.
Mitchell, W.J.T.
  1986   *Iconology: Image, text, ideology*, Chicago and London.
Morris, S.
  1992   *Daidalos and the Origins of Greek Art*, Princeton.

Muir, J.V. (ed.)

    2001   *Alcidamas: Works and fragments*, London.

Mullen, W.

    1982   *Choreia: Pindar and dance*, Princeton.

Nagy, G.

    1979   *The Best of the Achaeans*, Baltimore and London.

Nisetich, F.J.

    1975   'Olympian 1.8–11: an epinician metaphor', *HSPh* 79, 55–68.

O'Sullivan, P.

    2000   'Satyr and image in Aeschylus' *Theoroi'*, *CQ* 50, 353–66.

Overbeck, J.A.

    1868   *Die antiken Schriftquellen zur Geschichte der bildenden Künste bei den Griechen*, Leipzig.

Pfeijffer, I.L.

    1999   *Three Aeginetan Odes of Pindar: A commentary on Nemean V, Nemean III, and Pythian VIII*, Leiden.

Pollitt, J.J.

    1974   *The Ancient View of Greek Art*, New Haven and London.

    1986   *Art in the Hellenistic Age*, Cambridge.

    1995   'The canon of Polyclitus and other canons', in W.G. Moon (ed.) *Polykleitos, the Doryphoros and Tradition*, 19–24, Madison.

Race, W.

    1987   'Pindaric encomium and Isocrates' *Evagoras'*, *TAPhA* 117, 131–55.

Raschke, W.J.

    1988   'Images of victory: some new considerations of athletic monuments', in W.J. Raschke (ed.) *The Archaeology of the Olympics: The Olympics and other festivals in antiquity*, 38–54, Madison.

Richardson, N.J.

    1981   'The contest of Homer and Hesiod and Alcidamas' *Mouseion'*, *CQ* 31, 1–10.

Ritoók, Zs.

    1989   'The views of early Greek epic on poetry and art', *Mnemosyne* 42, 331–48.

Rouveret, A.

    1989   *Histoire et imaginaire de la peinture ancienne*, Paris.

Schmitt, R.

    1967   *Dichtung und Dichtersprache in indogermanischer Zeit*, Wiesbaden.

Segal, C.

    1974   'Arrest and movement: Pindar's fifth Nemean', *Hermes* 102, 397–411.

Shapiro, K.

    1988   Ὕμνων θησαυρός: Pindar's sixth Pythian ode and the treasury of the Siphnians at Delphi', *MH* 45, 1–5.

Spivey, N.

    1995   'Bionic statues', in A. Powell (ed.) *The Greek World*, 442–59, London.

Steiner, D.

    1993   'Pindar's "Oggetti Parlanti"', *HSPh* 95, 159–80.

1994   *The Tyrant's Writ: Myths and images of writing in ancient Greece*, Princeton.

1998   'Moving images: fifth-century victory monuments and the athlete's allure', *ClAnt* 17, 123–49.

Svenbro, J.

1976   *La parole et le marbre,* Paris.

1988   *Phrasikleia: Anthropologie de la lecture en Grèce ancienne*, Paris.

Walsh, G.B.

1984   *The Varieties of Enchantment*, Chapel Hill and London.

Webster, T.B.L.

1939   'Greek theories of art and literature down to 400 BC', *CQ* 33, 166–79.

Willcock, M.M.

1995   Pindar *Victory Odes: Olympians 2, 7 and 11, Nemean 4, Isthmians 3, 4 and 7*, Cambridge.

5

OLYMPIA AND THE CHARIOT-RACE OF PELOPS

John Davidson

Introduction

What has become perhaps the best-known myth associated with the region of Greece in which Olympia is situated tells how Pelops came from Asia Minor and won his bride and kingdom. A local king, Oinomaos, had set up a challenge for suitors of his daughter Hippodameia. They had to compete with him in a chariot-race, his daughter being the reward for victory, and death being the price of defeat. Following in the wake of a series of unsuccessful suitors, Pelops was able to outrace Oinomaos. In what emerged as the most popular version of the story, this was largely thanks to the activities of the king's charioteer, Myrtilos, who sabotaged his own master's chariot. Oinomaos' defeat led to his death, which opened the way for Pelops to establish his own dynasty with Hippodameia as his queen.

In its Greek context this story can be interpreted as reflecting the transfer of a woman from the control of her father to the control of her husband.[1] Hansen has recently identified three major versions of it and plausibly argued that these could not have developed in unilinear succession, but rather represent Greek variations of an early form of the international oral story AT 508, known as 'The Bride Won in a Tournament'.[2] An important implication of Hansen's thesis is that a significant detail found in Pindar's first Olympian ode (the earliest surviving Greek literary version), namely that it was help received from the god Poseidon which enabled Pelops to win the race,[3] could not have been invented by Pindar himself, as has often been supposed.[4] Accepting, then, that it is unsound to attempt an analysis of the story in terms of chronological development, we shall focus instead in this chapter on the main features of the story as they appear in various literary contexts from the fifth century BC onwards, and on the story's treatment by the vase painters of Athens and southern Italy, before considering its specific connections with Olympia and how its protagonists became linked with the religious and sporting structures of the site of the ancient Olympic Games. We shall also begin to explore how the different contexts in which the story was rehearsed affected its treatment and development.

Literary contexts for the story

Buxton (1994, 9–52) usefully surveys the wide range of verbal contexts, oral as well as literary, through which stories were transmitted in ancient Greece. In the case of Pelops and his chariot-race, as with all other stories, the picture which we can recover today is full of gaps, based as it is solely on a restricted selection of literary accounts, none of which pre-date the fifth century BC. Despite this, it is still possible to capture something of the story's different paths of development and shifting dynamics.[5]

In addition to Pindar's first Olympian ode, to which we will return later, there are a number of fifth-century literary sources for the story. The fragments of Sophokles' tragedy *Oinomaos*, though frustratingly meagre, nevertheless contain some useful information. Athenaios (9.410c), for example, attributes the colourful expression Σκυθιστὶ χειρόμακτρον ἐκκεκαρμένος ('scalped for a napkin in Scythian fashion') to this play, possibly a reference to the fate befalling defeated suitors.[6] More relevant for our purposes, however, is the other fragment from the play quoted by Athenaios (13.564 b–c), which begins (Hippodameia is speaking): τοίαν Πέλοψ ἴυγγα θηρατηρίαν | ἔρωτος, ἀστραπήν τιν' ὀμμάτων, ἔχει· | ἧι θάλπεται μὲν αὐτός, ἐξοπτᾶι δ' ἐμέ ('such a magic charm of love, a lightning of the eyes, Pelops has, by which he is warmed himself, and by which he inflames me').[7] This, of course, introduces an important dimension. Oinomaos is not only competing against Pelops. He is also competing against his own daughter, who has been won over by Pelops' sexual attractiveness. Thus the prize herself has in fact become part of the weaponry of one of the competitors. How Sophokles used this in his play we do not know, although we can make educated guesses based on what we find in other sources.[8]

In Sophokles' *Elektra*, the epode of the first stasimon (504–15) contains a reference to the story centring on the murder by Pelops of Myrtilos whom the chorus describe as being hurled into the sea from the golden chariot.[9] It can be assumed that further details of Myrtilos' role could have been filled in, at least by some of Sophokles' audience, since the scholiast on the passage quotes a fifth-century source, Pherekydes, by way of explanation. Even this, however, is far from complete. The scholiast merely comments (*FGrH* 3 F37b):

> Pherekydes says. After winning the contest and taking Hippodameia, Pelops ὑπέστρεφεν ('returned'?) to the Peloponnese with the winged horses and Myrtilos. On the way he caught Myrtilos making a pass at Hippodameia and hurled him into the sea.[10]

Further insight into Pherekydes' account and the role of Myrtilos in the story comes from the scholiast at Apollonios Rhodios 1.752 who observes (*FGrH* 3 F37a): 'Pherekydes says…that Myrtilos did not slot the lynch pin in the axle and so when the wheel rotated Oinomaos fell out.' This statement is actually inserted in the middle of the scholiast's potted account of the story, and offers an alternative version to his own explanation that Myrtilos made the lynch pin out of wax so that it would disintegrate during the race and Pelops could win and thus marry Hippodameia.

The fact that he gives Pherekydes' variant on one particular point quite possibly implies that the rest of the scholiast's account more or less agrees with Pherekydes. It is thus possible that other details of the story which he inserts in his account were already current in the fifth century.[11] These would include the point that Oinomaos had received an oracle that he would be killed by his own son-in-law, which is why he refused to give Hippodameia in marriage except to a suitor who had defeated him in a chariot-race (a seemingly impossible proposition). In addition, the starting point of the race was set at the river Kladeus and the finishing point was the Isthmus of Corinth.

A lacuna in the Apollonios Rhodios scholiast's report of Pherekydes has been reasonably filled in by Jacoby in the light of pseudo-Apollodoros (*Ep.* 2.7) who provides a motivation for Myrtilos to engage in his chariot sabotage. This is the point already confirmed for Pherekydes with regard to the *post-race* situation by the scholiast at Sophokles' *Elektra* 504, namely that Myrtilos had his own lustful eyes on Hippodameia. The Jacoby supplement, based on pseudo-Apollodoros, spells out that even before the race Myrtilos felt *erōs* for Hippodameia and agreed to her request that he should incapacitate Oinomaos' chariot (because she wanted to marry Pelops) to gratify her.

Other details in pseudo-Apollodoros (*Ep.* 2.3–9) in no way traceable to fifth-century sources include the point that Pelops' winged chariot, the gift of his former lover Poseidon, could travel over the sea without getting its axles wet. This raises an interesting point. The possession of a winged chariot (or winged horses, as in other accounts) might in itself seem enough to guarantee victory in a race. Pseudo-Apollodoros, however, as well as having a winged chariot, also has the Myrtilos chariot sabotage story. At first sight, then, this is a clear case of the over-determination of a motif.

The obvious explanation is that the pseudo-Apollodoros account carries simultaneously a supernatural reason for Pelops' victory (the winged chariot) and also a rationalizing explanation (the chariot sabotage).[12] This would be in line with the increasing tendency from the Hellenistic period, well characterized by Veyne (1988, 46), to pass off myth as history, or at least to present a blend of the two, in order to satisfy a new audience which though more educated still craved the wonderful.[13] At the same time, it is worth noting that the tradition records that Oinomaos was son of Ares,[14] and pseudo-Apollodoros actually says that Oinomaos had arms and horses given to him by Ares. So it could be said that Oinomaos' horses from Ares and Pelops' horses from Poseidon to some extent cancel each other out, and therefore that the chariot sabotage story was still felt to be needed to provide that crucial advantage. At all events, as Lacroix (1976, 335) puts it: 'A travers toute la tradition littéraire, le char magique garde sa célébrité…' ('Across the entire literary tradition, the magic chariot retains its noteworthiness').

Another important feature of the pseudo-Apollodoros account which is not traceable to fifth-century sources is the point, 'as some say', that Oinomaos lusted after his own daughter. This is offered as an alternative to the version that an oracle had told him he would be killed by his son-in-law. On either scenario, says pseudo-Apollodoros, Hippodameia was still a virgin, since she had in any case refused her father's advances. There is one other choice detail, namely that Oinomaos lopped off the heads of the defeated suitors and nailed them to his house. In this case, however, the same practice is ascribed already to the Oinomaos figure of Sophokles by the scholiast at Pindar *Isthmian Odes* 4.92a.[15]

It remains to mention some further elaborations, found only in other late sources, which concern the suborning of Myrtilos. As we have already seen, the explanation likely to have featured in Pherekydes was that Hippodameia herself had approached Myrtilos to cause Oinomaos to crash, because she fancied Pelops and wanted him to win. Myrtilos had then agreed, because he fancied her and wanted to do her a favour. But significant variations on this are found elsewhere. Diodoros (4.73.5), for example, has *Pelops* approach Myrtilos and bribe him, although there is no mention of how he bribed him or what the consequences were. Pausanias (8.14.11), on the other hand, states that Pelops promised Myrtilos a night with Hippodameia, and then reneged on the promise after his victory and threw Myrtilos 'out of the ship'.[16]

The variant details and emphases found in these literary sources are at least partly explicable in terms of the different genres involved and the different interests of their authors. Some questions, however, remain. In the case of Sophokles' *Oinomaos*, for example, it may be asked why such stress was apparently placed on the king's cruelty, as seen especially in his custom of nailing the heads of defeated suitors to his house. This would seem, at first sight anyway, to make Sophokles' task of creating a sympathetic tragic figure more difficult. Perhaps a mitigating factor was to be found in the role of a Hippodameia who, inflamed by love, was prepared to betray her own father. At all events, it does seem that the actual chariot-race may well have provided scope for the development of an exciting message narrative, and possibly also for the deployment of a chariot or chariots in the theatre. There is in any case no doubt that the evocation of Myrtilos' murder in lyric passages by both Sophokles (*El.* 504–15) and Euripides (*Or.* 990–4) enabled the troubles of the descendants of Pelops to be placed in a broader context.

It appears to have been the mythographers, however, from Pherekydes in the fifth century BC to pseudo-Apollodoros in the first or second century AD, who were the ones to highlight the overall role of Myrtilos. This was perhaps because treachery and the love triangle were motifs calculated to enhance narrative appeal. Mythographic contexts were also to become the forum for airing alternative versions of details in the story, such as Oinomaos' motivation in establishing the chariot-race contest in the first place. On occasion too, variant branches of the tradition could be accommodated together without being presented as alternatives at all. Interestingly, it seems to have been an easy matter to compromise the integrity of Pelops and even that of Hippodameia. An active role for the latter, which can perhaps be assumed already in Pherekydes, is manifest in pseudo-Apollodoros. However, the fact that both Diodoros and Pausanias make Pelops the one to bribe Myrtilos perhaps suggests some uneasiness about accepting a woman in this role. We can at all events conclude that the literary tradition strongly testifies to classical antiquity's ongoing engagement with the story, and its interest in exploring situations, characters and motivations involved in a context of competitive enterprise and sexual parade.

Vase-painting

At first sight it might appear that visual artistic representations of this story, as of all other stories, inasmuch as they would in many cases be monoscenic, would be more limited than their literary narrative counterparts.[17] In fact, even a monoscenic work, not to mention a synoptic one, can evoke dimensions of a story that go far beyond the confines of the primary subject. Indeed, a visual depiction can often 'tell the whole story' with greater economy and more concentrated tension than a diachronic narrative. In the case of the Pelops chariot-race story, we shall consider exactly which 'moments' vase-painting focuses on in particular and how further dimensions are evoked.

One of the rare pre-fourth-century depictions is preserved on an Attic red-figure lekythos of around 500 BC, now in Athens.[18] The basic moment captured here corresponds with one stage of the diachronic narrative as recorded by pseudo-Apollodoros. Pelops is seen to be preparing to mount his chariot, having been given a head start, while Oinomaos makes a sacrifice. The addition of wings to Pelops' horses implies at least that the lead opened up by Pelops during Oinomaos' sacrifice will prove decisive.

The proliferation of depictions on fourth-century South Italian vases gives the iconographic tradition an important boost.[19] Three discrete moments in the story predominate: first, Pelops meeting Myrtilos, usually with Hippodameia also present; second, the preliminaries to the race, involving Oinomaos and Pelops in particular, again usually with Hippodameia and sometimes with Myrtilos present; third, the actual chariot-race showing Pelops and Hippodameia being pursued by Oinomaos and Myrtilos.

A number of features of these depictions warrant closer attention, because they point beyond the immediate 'moment'. One such feature is the figure of Myrtilos. A Campanian squat lekythos, dated to the second half of the fourth century and now in Berlin, shows him thrown out of Pelops' chariot, the race by implication having already been won.[20] However, it is in scenes portraying earlier stages of the story that he appears most often. In depictions of the chariot-race itself, he is usually just shown in the pursuing chariot alongside Oinomaos. On one Apulian volute crater, however, dated to around 330 BC and now in Naples, his own disposition, allied with the fact that one of the horses has its head turned towards him, implies that something untoward is about to happen, this presumably being Myrtilos' own leap to avoid the collapse and crash of the chariot which he senses is imminent.[21] In the surviving literary accounts, there is no indication of how exactly Myrtilos escaped sharing his master's fate. This visual depiction attempts to address this issue, while at the same time capturing the excitement of the pursuit. In scenes of the preliminaries before the race, Myrtilos is sometimes shown already in position in Oinomaos' chariot, which evokes the actual race about to begin. In scenes where he is shown meeting with Pelops and Hippodameia, a chariot wheel or wheels may be associated with him. This iconography serves to identify him as a charioteer, but the very presence of wheels detached from their chariot may also perhaps be taken to imply the disintegration of Oinomaos' chariot in the race to come. The same effect may be implicit in the scene on the Apulian situla, dated to around 360 BC and now in Rome, which shows an even earlier stage in the story when Pelops arrives in Pisa to confront the enthroned Oinomaos, for also present in the scene are Hippodameia and Myrtilos with a wheel.[22]

Another important feature of South Italian vase-painting is the emphasis, through his Phrygian headdress in particular, on Pelops' non-Greek origin. In literary sources, this feature, even where initially mentioned, is soon lost sight of as the narrative progresses. The vase-paintings, however, can provide a permanent reminder of it. Similarly, the depiction of an Erinys figure in a number of the paintings, on occasion making a threatening gesture specifically against Oinomaos and even in scenes representing a stage in the story preceding the dénouement, serves as a constant pointer to the tragic implications and outcome. The inclusion of severed heads of previously defeated suitors also serves as a grim reminder, in this case of the enormity of the task facing Pelops and the formidable nature of his opponent. The vase-painting which perhaps casts its net widest, so to speak, is found on an Apulian volute crater, dated to around 330–320 BC and now in Naples.[23] Here, Pelops and Hippodameia are shown holding hands at an altar in the presence of Oinomaos, while a ram is being led in for the sacrifice. Included as well are an Erinys leaning on a spear, to the left, and, to the right, a Nike. The ramifications of the event are underlined by the portrayal in the background of both a severed head and a chariot wheel.

Other telling details include the prominence given in vase depictions of the race to Oinomaos' spear, which points both backwards to the king's previous victories and forwards to his anticipated strike against Pelops which is not in fact to eventuate. On one Apulian volute crater, dated to around 310 BC and now in London, there is shown behind the altar at which Oinomaos is preparing to sacrifice before the race a statue of Zeus thundering.[24] This perhaps indicates the overarching interest of Zeus in the situation, as also seen in the east pediment of the temple of Zeus at Olympia which we will shortly consider. Specific Olympian deities are otherwise not associated with the sacrifice scene.[25]

Of particular interest in the South Italian depictions is the prominence given to Hippodameia. Literary accounts naturally focus more on Pelops, since he is the one engaged in the life and death struggle with Oinomaos. In vase-paintings, however, Hippodameia shares the limelight. Alongside Pelops in the race scenes, she commands as much attention as her husband-to-be.[26] She is also often present even in scenes involving Pelops and Myrtilos and almost invariably in scenes of race preliminaries. In some of these scenes she is shown in tandem with another female figure who could be her mother Sterope or her bridesmaid. Either identification would fit the bridal appurtenances of the Hippodameia figure.[27] In some instances, she is shown holding hands with Pelops in the presence of her father, a detail which presumably not only indicates the promise of their future marriage should Pelops happen to win the contest, but also points to what the outcome of this contest will actually be.

It seems, then, that the fact that the outcome of the story was marriage between Pelops and Hippodameia often influenced the choice of both important details in these vase-paintings and also sometimes of the 'moment' to be depicted. It is even possible that the marriage factor lay at least partly behind the choice of the very story as a subject. In a discussion of nuptial iconography in a range of mythical scenes on Athenian vases whose central subject is not a wedding, Oakley notes the same phenomenon on South Italian red-figure vases connected, for example, with the figure of Andromeda. Hippodameia can easily be accommodated in this context.[28] As Oakley concludes:

> The most important aspect of this wedding iconography, however, is the way it is used as a pictorial language to deepen the meaning of a scene beyond its immediate action. Just as literary devices can be used in various ways, so can wedding iconography. It can produce irony, foreshadow a future event, enrich an image through metaphor or simile, or allude to a figure's psychological state. And just as imagery does in literature, it produces more than one level of meaning, so that in many cases several different aspects of a figure or scene can be implied by its use.[29]

Reinforcing this definite marriage slant given to the story in many of the South Italian vase-paintings is the frequent presence of Eros and/or Aphrodite. In literary accounts, the role of Eros can be brought into prominence at particular points in the narrative, whether associated primarily with Pelops, Hippodameia or Myrtilos. In the vase-paintings, however, this motivating force can be represented as a constant presence, drawing attention in particular to Hippodameia's desirability as a bride. She can thus be placed parallel with Helen, Atalanta, Thetis, and Andromeda, who are listed by Sabetai (1997, 319) as examples of female mythological figures in Athenian vase-painting 'whose nuptial guise makes them paradigmatic nubile maidens'. It is highly appropriate too that Hippodameia is either about to get into a chariot or is actually in one, given the close association of the chariot with wedding scenes.

To see a marriage interest, then, as the main reason for the popularity of the 'nuptial' pairing of Hippodameia and Pelops in the South Italian vase-painting seems a more fruitful approach than to detect, as has commonly been done, the major influence of Euripides' tragedy *Oinomaos*, whose date of production is unknown, but which has been dated by some scholars as late as 409 BC.[30] There is no doubting Euripides' general popularity in the fourth century, of course, and erotic emphases are not uncommon in his plays. Thus the possibility of at least some degree of associated Euripidean prompting cannot be altogether ruled out. At the same time, even if the erotic factor was prominent in this particular play, it would be misleading to present Euripides as taking the story in a totally new, erotic direction, as is also sometimes done, since the relevant Sophoklean fragment, already mentioned, testifies to the prominence of at least one manifestation of the love motif in drama perhaps as much as sixty years earlier.

Philostratos

The prominence accorded Hippodameia in vase-painting is also found in a work of the third century AD embracing literature and visual art, namely the written description of an arguably fictitious panel-painting in the *Eikones* of the elder Philostratos (1.17).[31] As Beall (1993, 351) emphasizes, Philostratos makes his readers imagine three distinctive stages of the story, these being the race, the death of Oinomaos, and the celebration following the victory. According to Philostratos, Oinomaos' chariot has disintegrated, but his horses still have plenty of running in them, horses which are, as Philostratos puts it, appropriately black for the sinister function for which they were harnessed. Pelops' horses, on the other hand, are white, obedient to the rein, and neighing gently. Oinomaos, as a stereotypical barbarian, lies there, while Pelops leaves the viewer in no doubt why Poseidon had once fallen in love with him. But here is Philostratos' climactic point:

> As for the race, Pelops and Hippodameia are the winners, standing together on the chariot and joining hands there; but they are so conquered by each other as to be on the point of embracing. He is decked out in the delicate Lydian manner, and is of such youth and beauty as you saw just before when he was entreating Poseidon for his horses; and she is decked out in the manner of a bride and has just unveiled her cheek, since she has won the right to a husband's kiss. Even the Alpheios leaps from his eddy plucking a crown of wild olive for Pelops as he drives along beside the river bank.

As Beall (1993, 355 with n. 23) puts it, while noting that Philostratos does not seek to make Hippodameia an active agent in her father's death:

> By juxtaposing Oenomaüs' ferocious challenge and Hippodameia's romantic 'victory lap', he adds emphasis to the comparison he is making between the king and his daughter. The point is that this race is a contest between natural love and unnatural hatred, and love wins (νενίκηκε). The entire painting can be reduced to the theme, 'amor vincit omnia'.

Oakley and Sinos (1993, 30), in a discussion of wedding iconography, also refer to the Philostratos passage, but focus more specifically on the detail of the bride's unveiling. What we are dealing with, then, several hundred years after the story's treatment by the vase-painters of Athens and southern Italy, is an interpretation of the myth as a celebration of the power of Eros leading to marriage.

The story at Olympia

As we saw earlier, one version of the story locates Oinomaos in Lesbos.[32] Whether or not this was the 'original' setting of the chariot-race, it was with the region around Olympia that the whole story became canonically linked.[33] In narrative contexts as a rule, however, very little was made of this setting, since the authors' main interest was centred on the universal human story of love, competition, betrayal, victory and defeat. In vase-painting too, it was the story that mattered. Thus no indication of a specific Greek locale was included, although the non-Greek origin of Pelops himself was clearly marked. It so happens, however, that the earliest surviving complete literary version of the story roots it strongly in the specific locale of Olympia.[34] This is hardly surprising, since the work in question is Pindar's first Olympian ode, written for Hieron of Syracuse, victor in the horse race at the Olympic Games of 476 BC.

Pindar treats the story allusively, working it into the overall fabric of the poem in his usual manner, but it is nonetheless inextricably linked with Olympia as the site of the Games. The focus is on Pelops himself, his coming to manhood, his desire for marriage, and his appeal for help to his former lover Poseidon in return for past favours. Noticeable too is his Homeric attitude that, given human mortality, there seems little point in ending up in the obscurity of old age. The formidable nature of the father having been stressed (Oinomaos has already disposed of thirteen suitors), Pindar needs to account for Pelops' success.[35] And so Pelops' prayer to Poseidon is answered, and he is given a golden chariot and winged horses that never tire. This is apparently sufficient to ensure his success, no mention at all being made of any corruption of Myrtilos in this literary treatment of the myth.

Pindar is also not interested in the behaviour and attitude of Hippodameia herself, who remains more or less unseen and just the prize of a contest, albeit a famous prize (she is given the epithet εὔδοξος). Nor is any attention paid to the reasoning behind Oinomaos' actions – actions which, on the face of it, are unusual, given that fathers normally co-operate with suitors, or at least wealthy ones, even against the express wishes of their daughters. Pindar's audience or readers, however, could presumably fill in these and other details for themselves, probably already having different versions to draw on, along the lines spelled out in other sources.[36] As far as the actual contest goes, Pindar disposes of it in one line (88): 'He (i.e. Pelops) defeated mighty Oinomaos and won the maiden as his wife.'[37] There is, however, perhaps a hint of how it was visualised as happening, when Pelops, in his prayer to Poseidon, is made to say (76): 'Hold back the bronze spear of Oinomaos.' This perhaps implies the situation found in later sources such as pseudo-Apollodoros (*Ep.* 2.5) where Oinomaos, until he is thwarted by Pelops, is made to give the suitor in his chariot with Hippodameia a head start, while he sacrifices a ram, and is then made to pursue him, catch up with him, and plunge a spear into his back.[38]

It is not the place here to attempt to probe all the complexities of Pindar's treatment of the wider Pelops myth. This involves, as well as the chariot-race, the story of how his father Tantalos cooked the young Pelops and tried to serve him as a meal to the gods, a story which Pindar 'rejects' in favour of a version in which Pelops is abducted by Poseidon, as Ganymede is by Zeus. The questions which this raises are compounded by further questions concerning the precise nature of the relationship between the myth and Pindar's celebration of Olympia and Hieron's victory.[39] At all events, Köhnken (1974, 205) seems right to stress that the chariot-race aspect of the myth is linked to Pindar's hope, expressed towards the end of the poem, that he may in future be able to celebrate a victory by Hieron in the Olympic chariot-race, a more prestigious event than the horse race.

At least within two decades of the performance of Pindar's poem, the east pediment of the temple of Zeus at Olympia was in place, containing the most famous iconographic depiction of the Pelops chariot-race story.[40] Reconstruction of the group and identification of the figures, on the basis of the surviving fragments and in the light of the description by Pausanias (5.10.6–7), has always been a contentious issue. As far as the basic compositional idea is concerned, the interpretation of Säflund (1970, 113–24) seems as convincing as any. We appear to be dealing with a proclamation scene before the race, with Oinomaos dictating the 'rules' and eliciting a range of responses from his various listeners.[41] The major players were certainly present,[42] Pelops with Hippodameia, Oinomaos with his wife Sterope, as Säflund reconstructs the group,[43] the two couples being divided by the central figure of Zeus. The dominating presence of the king of the gods himself is an especially striking feature of the composition. In a sense it is not surprising, given that the group is decorating Zeus' temple. However, as a version of the story, it casts into the shadow Pelops' special relationship with Poseidon, as this had been featured by Pindar.[44] Zeus is the presiding deity and ultimate arbiter of the outcome. Significant too is the presence of Oinomaos' wife Sterope. Even if the primary motivation for including her is as a balance for the other leading female player Hippodameia, her very presence sets up the nexus of relationships linking her not only with her husband and daughter but also with Pelops himself. An evocative ambiguity about her own emotional attachments is achieved, a feature entirely lacking in the literary accounts where she is simply the wife of Oinomaos and the mother of Hippodameia.

Identification of the other figures on the east pediment is more problematic. Pausanias (5.10.6–7) names the figures kneeling in front of the two teams of horses as Myrtilos and Pelops' charioteer respectively.[45] This seems unlikely, since the artist may well have been following the version of the race already depicted on the chest of Kypselos (Pausanias 5.17.7), by which Pelops has Hippodameia in his chariot and therefore does not require a charioteer. If so, Säflund (1970, 107) may well be correct in identifying the figure on Pelops' side of the group as Hippodameia's serving maid tying her sandals, with Myrtilos in fact being the figure beside the wheel of Oinomaos' chariot.

Modern scholarship most commonly interprets the elderly men towards the edges of the composition as seers, particular attention being paid to the one whose face is better preserved. Thus Woodford (1986, 94) speaks in terms of someone looking beyond the present to the disasters ahead and recoiling from them. Osborne (1998, 171–2) goes much further:

> Although the face is moulded with very simple forms, the attention devoted to eyes and to the slightly open mouth, along with the gesture of the right arm, afford to this one actor a single moment of vision that transforms the rather static tableau at the centre of the pediment by illuminating their past actions, present intentions, and future fates. Pelops and Oinomaos line up here, with their chariot teams alongside, as did competitors in the games; without the seer to tell their story the acts and intentions of those competitors remained inscrutable, but this story guarantees that no mask of innocence can prevent the malicious suffering in the end. The viewer is given the key here by which to read the results of this race, and is encouraged to pay equal attention to the possibility that those who compete in the games know more than they declare and that some may win by means more foul than fair.

This raises the question as to whether there could have been any overt indication of treachery on the part of the Myrtilos figure or whether such a figure was part of the composition at all. This has sometimes been denied on the grounds that it would send out a signal totally inappropriate to the ethos of the Olympic Games. After all, Pindar ignores Myrtilos, arguably because victory by cheating would have been an embarrassing mythical model for Hieron. Säflund (1970, 119), however, dismisses the problem. She accepts the presence of the Myrtilos figure, and argues that whether or not the charioteer was making any gesture indicating sabotage his very presence would be enough to imply such an action. She argues further that it is unlikely that the chariot-race story would have been regarded as referring to the origins of the games at Olympia, or that it would have been seen as the model for the chariot-racing event. She sees the pedimental composition as simply depicting 'a decisive moment in the sacred story of the foremost hero of Olympia and Altis', with Myrtilos being the tool through which Zeus is able to punish the wicked Oinomaos. This problem must, however, remain open.

Our most detailed information about the site of Olympia in general comes, of course, from the description of Pausanias where the connection made with the chariot-race story is striking.[46] Thus when seeking, for example, to establish a chronology for the early kings of the Eleans, Pausanias (5.1.6) refers to the story as a marker for the reign of Epeios. In that context, he makes no mention of the chariot-race as such, but it can be taken as a given, underlying Oinomaos' overthrow. This is clear from Pausanias' subsequent comment (5.1.7) that Pelops, having taken over Pisa and Olympia, was said to have established a temple of Hermes along with appeasing sacrifices for the death of Myrtilos, the role and fate of whom had clearly become a *sine qua non* of the story.

Pausanias also testifies to the close connection which had become established, at least among the Eleans, between Pelops himself and the actual site of Olympia. Thus in referring to the precinct dedicated to Pelops within the Altis at Olympia, he claims that the Eleans accorded Pelops the same pre-eminent status among heroes that they accorded Zeus among gods (5.13.1). He also notes the location and main features of the actual Pelopion (5.13.1), as well as remarking on its supposed foundation by Herakles and the fact that the annual magistrates still sacrificed a black ram to Pelops there in his own day (5.13.2–3). In addition, he refers (6.22.1) to the resting place of Pelops' bones (in a bronze chest inside a small building close to the sanctuary of Artemis Kordax), tells the story of the temporary removal and ultimate return of the hero's shoulder blade (5.13.4–6), mentions a statue of Pelops (5.24.7), and notes the presence of the hero's gold-hilted short sword in the treasury of the Sikyonians (6.19.6). In another context (5.8.2), he states that Pelops had celebrated the Games in honour of Olympian Zeus more strikingly than any of his predecessors had done.

Pausanias makes abundantly plain, too, how the characters linked with Pelops are also associated with the site of Olympia. Thus one of the pictures on the screen blocking access to the underpart of the great statue of Zeus is said by him to have been of Hippodameia with her mother (5.11.6). Hippodameia's supposed role in assembling the 'Sixteen Women' and with them inaugurating the Heraia is also noted (5.16.4), while one of the choral dances organized by the 'Sixteen Women' is called the dance 'of Hippodameia' (5.16.6). Her memory is also preserved through the presence, in the temple of Hera, of what is said to have been her play couch (5.20.1), and a Hippodameion, which is initially just mentioned in passing (5.22.3), but then described more fully, including allusions to the annual sacrifices to Hippodameia in this heroine shrine and to the fact that Olympia was the final resting place for her bones after she had spent the last years of her life in exile, having fallen out of favour with Pelops (6.20.7).

Pelops' defeated opponent Oinomaos is also said by Pausanias to have his permanent 'place' at Olympia. There are the foundations of his house which was destroyed by lightning (5.14.7) and the sole pillar to survive the catastrophe (5.20.6–8; 6.18.7), along with his actual grave adjacent to ruins said to be those of his stables (6.21.3). Even the memory of his mother Harpina is said to have been preserved through a statue (5.22.6), and through the ruins of the neighbouring city which he founded and named after her (6.21.8).

As far as the actual chariot-race story is concerned, its close connection with Olympia is most famously demonstrated in a physical sense, as we have seen, by the sculptures of the east pediment of the temple of Zeus. Pausanias not only describes this evocation of the story (5.10.6–7), but also mentions its depiction on the chest of Kypselos in the temple of Hera (5.17.7). In addition, he alludes to the presence, on one turning post of the race-course, of a bronze statue of Hippodameia about to crown the victorious Pelops with a ribbon (6.20.19). Moreover, in noting the altar of Hephaistos, he says that some Eleans called it rather the altar of Zeus Areios and said that it was here to this god that Oinomaos sacrificed before a race with one of his daughter's suitors (5.14.6). Other Olympian features preserving the memory of the story are, according to Pausanias, that point of the race-course called Taraxippos (6.20.17–18), the grave of the horses of the first unsuccessful suitor (6.21.7), and the monument raised by Pelops in honour of all the unsuccessful suitors (6.21.9–11). Reference is also made to Pelops' sacrifice before his race, in connection with the altar of Kydonian Athene (6.21.6), and to traces of the already mentioned sanctuary of Artemis given the title of 'Kordax' after the victory dance celebrated by Pelops' followers (6.22.1).

Final observations

By the time of Pausanias, then, the site of Olympia had become full of associations with Pelops and his famous race. Whether these associations went back to the earliest period of cultic activity at Olympia or even to the time of the original foundation of the Games, however, is quite another matter. Indeed, most modern scholarship is decidedly sceptical on this point. Thus Burkert (1983, 95–6) takes the view that the story only became significant for Olympia once chariot-racing had already been introduced as a new event in the twenty-fifth Olympiad.[47] Slightly more cautious is the approach taken by Weiler (1974, 217) that 'Die Beliebtheit der Wagen-rennen in Olympia und der Oinomaossage mag…Hand in Hand gehen' ('The popularity of the chariot-race at Olympia and the Oinomaos legend may…go hand in hand').

With regard to the period before the introduction of the chariot-race, it is, for Burkert at least, the story of the death, dismemberment, cooking and 'reintegration' of Pelops which provides the *aition* for the Olympic Games, specifically for the stadion or foot-race, the original event on the programme. Nagy (1990, 127–9), however, with particular reference to Pindar's first Olympian ode, finds significant connections between the dismemberment story on the one hand and, on the other, the story of Pelops' abduction by Poseidon with its sequel the incident involving Hippodameia and Oinomaos. He argues in effect that an older *aition* 'motivating' the foot-race is integrated with an expanded newer *aition* which 'motivates' both the foot-race and the chariot-race, and that Pindar's subordination of the first story to the second reflects the evolving aetiology of the Olympics.

This is an extremely complicated issue, as is the early history of the Pelops cult itself.[48] However, whatever the relative antiquity of the two stories, their interconnection or lack of it, or their associative relationship with the site of Olympia as such, and no matter what awareness of these issues Pindar might have had in his celebration of an Olympic victor in the single horse race of 476 BC, the fact remains that the chariot-race story found its way to the very heart of Olympic lore.[49] Indeed, as Krummen (1990, 160) stresses, the race was already 'anchored' in Olympia itself by the fifth century, with the sculptural group of the east pediment of the temple of Zeus actually facing in the direction of the stadion and hippodrome.

Notes

[1] This same transfer, with the emphasis placed rather on the separation of the woman from her mother, has been seen in the story of Demeter, Persephone, and Hades (e.g. Foley 1994, 80, 104–12). The story of Pelops and Hippodameia has also been seen, at another level, with specific reference to the arrangement by which Hippodameia rides in Pelops' chariot during the race (for which, see below), as reflecting the practice of 'rape marriage' or 'marriage by capture' (e.g. Devereux 1965, 10; *contra* Hansen 2000, 34–5).

[2] Hansen calls them the 'Poseidon Version', the 'Killos Version' and the 'Myrtilos Version' (2000). The first two of these are seen as subdivisions of the 'light' branch of the tradition (so called because the crucial help given to Pelops comes from a friendly supernatural source, namely Poseidon in the first case and the ghost of Killos in conjunction with Apollo in the second), while the third represents the

'dark' branch of the tradition. Least well known is the version involving Killos, the charioteer of Pelops, who dies before the race and is accorded funeral honours, as a result of which his master gains divine favour. The main source for this is Theopompos (*FGrH* 115 F350), as contained in a scholion at Hom. *Il.* 1.38, a further detail being added by another scholion at the same place.

³ This help, in the form of a golden chariot and tireless winged horses, was in return for earlier sexual favours.

⁴ See, for example, Kakridis 1928, 416–22; 1930, 177; Köhnken 1974, 203; Weiler 1974, 216; Krischer 1981.

⁵ For useful summaries of the sources, see Hansen 2000, 20–4; Gantz 1993, 540–3; Weiler 1974, 209–14; Frazer 1921, 157–63.

⁶ Fr. 473 (Radt, 1977).

⁷ Fr. 474 (Radt, 1977).

⁸ Sophokles' *Oinomaos* was almost certainly considerably earlier than his *Elektra* (Calder 1974, 205, who offers a plausible reconstruction of the *Oinomaos*, argues in fact for a date as early as 468 BC), so it seems highly likely that it anticipated the *Elektra* as far as the message narrative of a chariot-race is concerned. It may, in fact, have even featured a chariot or chariots on stage, as the start of the race, at least in a fourth-century revival. Demosthenes (18.242) twits Aiskhines for bad acting in the role of Oinomaos, and a series of anecdotes by later authors (for the testimonia, see Radt 1977, 381) tell of Aiskhines' actual fall from a chariot and injury in the role. This detail may, however, be no more than inventive elaboration. Perhaps Sophokles' original audience, or a subsequent fourth-century one, saw Oinomaos actually in his chariot, perhaps not.

⁹ Krummen 1990, 161 n. 15 argues for the likelihood that Myrtilos, being a trickster figure and therefore belonging to the 'logic' of the myth, is earlier in origin than the fifth century. The discussion of Sophokles' *Oinomaos* by Sutton (1984, 95–7) includes the strange assumption (97 n. 1) that Myrtilos is visualised in the *Elektra* context as having fallen asleep 'at the wheel'.

¹⁰ This raises a very difficult question. Kaibel 1896, 153 takes the view that in his *Elektra* Sophokles was assuming a version of the story by which Oinomaos was king, not of Elis, but of Lesbos, and that the ancient commentators signalled their understanding of this 'fact' by giving, as their explanation of the Sophoklean passage, Pherekydes' account which followed the same version. Crucial to Kaibel's interpretation is the word ὑπέστρεφεν which he takes as referring to Pelops' 'return' from Lesbos to the Peloponnese. He also thinks that the chariot-race, added later to the story when its setting was moved to Elis, has been interpolated into the original Pherekydean account from the later version. This seems over-complicated. Willink 1986, 249, in his note on Euripides' *Orestes* 988–94, which also contains a reference to the hurling of Myrtilos into the sea, supports the possibility that both Sophokles and Euripides had in mind a version of the Myrtilos story independent of the later canonical version involving a Peloponnesian chariot-race. It is this specifically Peloponnesian race which Willink assumes to have been attributed to Pherekydes by the Apollonian (see below) and Sophoklean scholiasts. Willink goes on to visualise an original scenario whereby Pelops 'will have come to Greece

with the blood of Myrtilus already on his hands', in support of which he points to the wording of *Elektra* 504–7: ὦ Πέλοπος ἁ πρόσθεν | πολύπονος ἱππεία, | ὡς ἔμολες αἰανὴς | τᾶιδε γᾶι. However, this by no means necessarily indicates that the tragic ἱππεία came to Greece as an already complete import, as it were. It is just as easy to interpret ἱππεία (which could even imply the chariot-race itself as well as the fatal ride subsequent to the race which ended with the ejection and death of Myrtilos) as an event which, by happening in Greece, has brought calamity to that country. For healthy scepticism in general towards the idea of an older version of the story originating in Lesbos and involving Myrtilos, see Stinton 1990, 246 n. 25; Lacroix 1976, 329–30.

[11] This cannot be regarded as more than a possibility, because the scholiast also cites Pindar as his source for the detail that Oinomaos had already defeated thirteen suitors before Pelops came along. He may thus also be drawing on other, unacknowledged sources, some of which may postdate the fifth century.

[12] The rationalizing approach to this story, as to many others, finds its most banal expression in Palaiphatos *Peri Apiston* 29:

They say that Pelops came to Pisa with winged horses to woo Hippodameia, the daughter of Oinomaos. I say the same as I do about Pegasos. If Oinomaos had known that Pelops' horses were winged, he would never have handed over his daughter to be put on Pelops' chariot. So we must say that Pelops came by ship, that the words 'Winged Horses' were written across the cabin, and that Pelops abducted the young woman and fled…

[13] This point is neatly picked up by Henrichs 1999, 227.

[14] See, for example, Hellanikos *FGrH* 4 F19a.

[15] The scholiast is commenting on what he says is Pindar's special slant in having Antaios crown Poseidon's temple with the skulls of his defeated adversaries. He goes on to say that this practice is generally attributed to Diomedes the Thracian, that Bakkhylides says it of Evenos and the suitors of Marpessa, and that Sophokles says it of Oinomaos. See, for example, Sophokles, Fr. 473a (Radt 1977). The story which became associated with Evenos and the suitors of Marpessa could on occasion be represented as a doublet of the Oinomaos and suitors of Hippodameia story. For a brief discussion of the sources, see Gantz 1993, 196.

[16] This version of the bribe is the one followed by the Vatican Mythographers (1.21; 2.169). The Latin sources also provide a number of variants. Hyginus (84) has Pelops promise Myrtilos half his kingdom, only to reflect after his victory that to honour this promise would involve him in shame. Hyginus also has the nice touch which makes Pelops get cold feet about his courtship of Hippodameia when he sees the heads of the defeated suitors above the doors of Oinomaos' house. This is clearly the inspiration for his rash promise to Myrtilos of half his kingdom. Also, there is the variant in Servius at *Georgics* III.7 that Hippodameia promised herself to Myrtilos in return for his help. In the Greek sources, yet another variant is found as an option in the scholiast at Euripides' *Orestes* 990 (where Oinomaos is also associated with Lesbos) and in the scholiast at *Iliad* 2.104. According to this, Hippodameia falsely accuses Myrtilos of rape.

[17] For a convenient summary of all the iconographical evidence, see Pipili

1990; Triantis 1992; 1994. The Etruscan and Roman material treated in these discussions, which is beyond the scope of the present study, includes depictions of versions of the story not found in any surviving Greek literary or pictorial source.

[18] Mus. Nat. 595 (CC 968). Shapiro 1994, 80–1 briefly discusses and illustrates an Attic black-figure lekythos of about the same date on which the actual race is depicted (Göttingen University, J 22).

[19] On South Italian depictions, see further in the various works of A.D. Trendall, for example, with regard to Apulia, Trendall and Cambitoglou 1978–1982.

[20] Staatl. Mus. F3072.

[21] Mus. Naz. 81394 (H3255).

[22] Villa Giulia 18003.

[23] Private Collection 370.

[24] Sir John Soane Museum 1014 (= V538).

[25] On an *Attic* red-figure bell krater, dated to around 380–370 BC and now in Naples (Mus. Naz. H 2200), however, both Poseidon and Athene are included in such a scene.

[26] There are a number of scenes showing Pelops and Hippodameia only, without the pursuing chariot. It is naturally difficult to tell whether these scenes are meant to indicate the race or the post-race situation. When either one or both of the figures are shown looking back, a race scenario is surely more likely. So argues Pipili (1990, 437), in connection with the Apulian red-figure loutrophoros in Boston, and also indeed with the *Attic* red-figure neck-amphora in Arezzo, Mus. Civ. 1460, of around 410 BC. *Contra* Triantis 1994, 286 who classifies the scenes under a 'Le Retour à Pisa' rubric. With regard to the Arezzo vase, on the basis in particular of the dolphin depicted under the horses, Lacroix 1976, 336–7 supports the interpretation that here the chariot is on the point of flying over the sea.

[27] A definite twist with regard to Sterope's own affections would be indicated if it is in fact she, rather than a bridesmaid, who is shown on the Apulian calyx crater, dated to around 350 BC and now in London (BM F271), in a depiction of a meeting between Myrtilos and Pelops, who is sitting on a rock, naked apart from his boots.

[28] Oakley 1995, 71.

[29] Oakley 1995, 72.

[30] The defective text of the Hypothesis by Aristophanes of Byzantium suggests that the play might have been presented along with the *Phoinissai* (which is probably to be dated to 409 BC). This is, however, by no means certain as the link identified between the plays possibly is thematic rather than related to performance date. Webster (1967, 102 and 117) guesses on (admittedly flimsy) metrical grounds that the play belongs to Euripides' early to middle period, a date in the 420s being favoured (on the basis of the few surviving fragments, he tentatively visualizes the Oinomaos figure as 'an unhappy father who is outwitted by the unscrupulous Pelops'). In any case, there seems to be insufficient evidence to justify confident statements such as that of Shapiro (1994, 80): 'Yet another reinterpretation occurred in 409, when Euripides staged his own *Oinomaos*.'

[31] Beall (1993, 350) presents the thesis that:

Philostratus communicates his interpretation of certain paintings indirectly through the structure and rhetorical ornamentation of his descriptions. In this way he imparts to his essays a charm akin to that of painting itself, which (in his view) uses color and form to convey a certain message to the beholder. Thus the εἰκόνες become 'pictures' in words.

[32] See notes 10 and 16 above.

[33] For some references to champions on both sides of this debate, see Hansen 2000, 21–2 n.7.

[34] As we know from Pausanias (6.21.10–11), the story certainly featured in the Hesiodic *Megalai Eoiai*, but the only surviving piece of text is the scanty Fr. 259 b (Merkelbach and West 1967). For discussion, see West 1985, 109–10. As it happens, we know of a relevant work of visual art which also pre-dates the first complete surviving literary account. However, the work in question, the depiction on the chest of Kypselos, is itself lost, so that we have to rely on the written description of Pausanias (5.17.7). This mentions the scenario implicit in Pindar's poetic account, and spelled out clearly in later literary sources, whereby Oinomaos chases Pelops who has Hippodameia in his chariot. Pausanias adds that the king and the suitor each have two horses, but that those of Pelops have wings, this last detail in the depiction, if not evoking the divine favour enjoyed by Pelops, at least pointing to his crucial speed advantage which anticipates the result of the contest.

[35] The question of the numbers and names of the defeated suitors is one of the main interests of the Pindaric scholiasts. Pausanias (6.21.10) tells us that this same aspect featured in the Hesiodic *Megalai Eoiai*.

[36] There has, of course, been endless debate about Pindar's choice of material for his version of the Pelops story. With regard to aspects of the race and its aftermath which Pindar omits, Graf 1993, 152 seems correct in saying: 'Obviously, Pindar had no use for any of this material.' Pindar's overall schema, with his stress on the relationship between Pelops and Poseidon, will have simply rendered redundant a detail such as, for example, the bribing of Myrtilos.

[37] Krummen 1990, 161 notes: 'dass...nicht der spannungsreiche Agon, sondern die Situation davor, thematisiert ist' ('that...not the tension-filled contest, but the situation prior to it, is made the theme').

[38] Whether or not one subscribes to the theory of an original 'rape marriage', Lacroix 1976, 340 is surely correct to emphasize that the very inseparability of the couple in the story is sufficient to explain Hippodameia's presence in Pelops' chariot in pictorial depictions of the 'race' from the chest of Kypselos onwards.

[39] For discussions, see, for example, Kakridis 1928; 1930; Köhnken 1974; Krischer 1981; Nagy 1990, 116–35.

[40] Some scholars (e.g. Calder 1974, 212–14) have suggested that this could have been inspired by the production of Sophokles' tragedy *Oinomaos*. This is, however, highly unlikely, not least because of the fact that Pindar, prior to the earliest possible date for Sophokles' play, so naturally associates the story with Olympia. For a general discussion of the excavation of the temple of Zeus and its

artwork, see Helmut Kyrieleis' chapter in this book.

[41] Alternatively perhaps Oinomaos and Pelops are swearing oaths before Zeus.

[42] Spivey 1997, 279 actually likens the figures to 'the actors taking a curtain call, or the cast assembling for their introduction to the audience'.

[43] Alternatively Oinomaos has been paired with Hippodameia, and Pelops with Sterope.

[44] Köhnken 1974, 204, however, with reference to the question of why it is to 'the house of Zeus' in Olympos that Pindar makes Poseidon convey Pelops, suggests that the poet is acknowledging the patron deity of Olympia in what is a celebration of an Olympic victory. 'Poseidon is responsible for the horses, but the victory is within the competence of Zeus.'

[45] He says that the Troizenians' name for Pelops' charioteer was Sphairos, but that the guide at Olympia called him Killas (a variation on the name Killos, for which see note 2 above).

[46] For discussion of Pausanias as a source for the Olympic Games, see Stephen Miller's chapter in this book.

[47] He follows Devereux 1965, *passim* in seeing the details of the Hippodameia 'abduction' as rather reflecting Elean animal-husbandry rites, arguing that the arrival of the story in Olympia demonstrates the increasing influence of Elis in the seventh century.

[48] Golden 1998, 14, for example, on grounds of the lack of early evidence for his cult, is sceptical about the common assumption that Pelops must have been accorded a significant role in the historical origins of Olympia. For the archaeology of the Pelopion and the early history of this structure, see Helmut Kyrieleis' chapter in this book.

[49] Krummen 1990, 161 with n. 14 suggests a possible connection between the approach taken to the treatment of the race in Pindar's account and that in the sculptures of the east pediment of the temple of Zeus, arguing that there is no decisive argument against dating the first Olympian ode to 472 rather than 476. She speculates that Pindar may himself have seen the sculptures as 'work in progress'. This seems unlikely and in any case, as she herself admits (n. 15), the temple of Zeus does not feature in Pindar's poem and his myth is intelligible without assuming any knowledge of the sculptures on his part.

Bibliography

Beall, S.M.
    1993   'Word-painting in the "Imagines" of the Elder Philostratus', *Hermes* 121, 350–63.
Burkert, W.
    1983   *Homo Necans*, Berkeley, Los Angeles and London.
Buxton, R.
    1994   *Imaginary Greece: The contexts of mythology*, Cambridge.
Buxton, R. (ed.)
    1999   *From Myth to Reason? Studies in the development of Greek thought*, Oxford.

Calder, W.M. III
  1974   'Sophocles, Oinomaos and the east pediment at Olympia', *Philologus* 118, 203–14.
Devereux, G.
  1965   'The abduction of Hippodameia as the "Aition" of a Greek animal husbandry rite', *SMSR* 36, 3–25.
Foley, H.P.
  1994   *The Homeric Hymn to Demeter*, Princeton.
Frazer, J.G.
  1921   *Apollodorus. The Library*, London and New York.
Gantz, T.
  1993   *Early Greek Myth*, Baltimore and London.
Golden, M.
  1998   *Sport and Society in Ancient Greece*, Cambridge.
Graf, F.
  1993   *Greek Mythology: An introduction*, Baltimore and London.
Hansen, W.
  2000   'The winning of Hippodameia', *TAPhA* 130, 19–40.
Henrichs, A.
  1999   'Demythologizing the past, mythicizing the present: myth, history, and the supernatural at the dawn of the Hellenistic period', in Buxton (ed.) *From Myth to Reason*, 223–48.
Kaibel, G.
  1896   *Sophokles Elektra*, Leipzig.
Kakridis, J.Th.
  1928   'Des Pelops und Iamos Gebet bei Pindar', *Hermes* 63, 415–29.
  1930   'Die Pelopssage bei Pindar', *Philologus* 85, 463–77.
Köhnken, A.
  1974   'Pindar as innovator: Poseidon Hippios and the relevance of the Pelops story in Olympian 1', *CQ* 24, 199–206.
Krischer, T.
  1981   'Die Pelopsgestalt in der ersten Olympischen Ode Pindars', *GB* 10, 69–75.
Krummen, E.
  1990   *Pyrsos Hymnon Festliche Gegenwart und Mythisch-Rituelle Tradition bei Pindar*, Berlin and New York.
Lacroix, L.
  1976   'La légende de Pélops et son iconographie', *BCH* 100, 327–41.
Merkelbach, R. and West, M.L.
  1967   *Fragmenta Hesiodea*, Oxford.
Nagy, G.
  1990   *Pindar's Homer*, Baltimore and London.
Oakley, J.H.
  1995   'Nuptial nuances: wedding images in non-wedding scenes of myth', in Reeder (ed.) *Pandora*, 63–73.

John Davidson

Oakley, J.H., Coulson, W.D.E., and Palagia, O. (eds.)
1997   *Athenian Potters and Painters*, Oxford.
Oakley, J.H. and Sinos, R.H.
1993   *The Wedding in Ancient Athens*, Madison.
Osborne, R.
1998   *Archaic and Classical Greek Art*, Oxford.
Pipili, M.
1990   In *Lexicon Iconographicum Mythologiae Classicae V1* and *V2* (pls.), s.v. 'Hippodameia I', Zurich and Munich.
Radt, S.
1977   *Tragicorum Graecorum Fragmenta*, vol. 4, Göttingen.
Reeder, E.D. (ed.)
1995   *Pandora: Women in classical Greece*, Baltimore and Princeton.
Sabetai, V.
1997   'Aspects of nuptial and genre imagery in fifth-century Athens: issues of interpretation and methodology', in Oakley, Coulson, and Palagia (eds.) *Athenian Potters and Painters*, 319–35.
Säflund, M.-L.
1970   *The East Pediment of the Temple of Zeus at Olympia: A reconstruction and interpretation of its composition*, Göteborg.
Shapiro, H.A.
1994   *Myth into Art*, London and New York.
Spivey, N.
1997   *Greek Art*, London.
Stinton, T.C.W.
1990   *Collected Papers on Greek Tragedy*, Oxford.
Sutton, D.F.
1984   *The Lost Sophocles*, Lanham, New York and London.
Trendall, A.D. and Cambitoglou, A.
1978–1982   *The Red-Figured Vases of Apulia*, 3 vols., Oxford and New York.
Triantis, I.
1992   In *Lexicon Iconographicum Mythologiae Classicae VI 1* and *VI 2* (pls.), s.v. 'Myrtilos', Zurich and Munich.
1994   In *Lexicon Iconographicum Mythologiae Classicae VII 1* and *VII 2* (pls.), s.v. 'Oinomaos' and 'Pelops', Zurich and Munich.
Veyne, P.
1988   *Did the Greeks Believe in Their Myths?*, Chicago. French original 1983.
Webster, T.B.L.
1967   *The Tragedies of Euripides*, London.
Weiler, I.
1974   *Der Agon im Mythos*, Darmstadt.
West, M.L.
1985   *The Hesiodic Catalogue of Women*, Oxford.
Willink, C.W.
1986   *Euripides Orestes*, Oxford.
Woodford, S.
1986   *An Introduction to Greek Art*, London.

6

HOMER, FUNERAL CONTESTS AND THE ORIGINS OF THE GREEK CITY

Ben Brown

In this chapter it will be argued that making sense of the athletic competition found in the *Iliad* – the funeral games for Patroklos (*Il.* 23.257–897) – cannot be disentangled from the broader social issues which this epic poem raises. The *Iliad* is more than simply a source for early athletic contests; the funeral contests in book 23 are crucial to the resolution of the social crisis sparked off in book 1. Making sense of the social function of funeral contests needs to develop alongside an understanding of how and why the *Iliad* situates the funeral contest at the heart of the resolution of conflict.

In the sections which follow, a path will be traced out through the *Iliad* with particular attention given to the way value is determined and established. Value is a powerful theme in the *Iliad*. An archaic notion pervades the poem that the social worth of great men is akin to the value of precious objects. Value is understood to be a magico-religious power that inheres in anything precious and it is in contexts of exchange that this power is released. The *Iliad* looks at the way exchanges of precious objects establish value in men and things and asks what ensues when the effectiveness of these exchanges is compromised. Is confidence in the value of the object at the heart of the exchange undermined as a result? If so, what of the social relations which are created and reinforced by such exchanges?

More specifically, the poet of the *Iliad* questions the effectiveness of those special exchanges by which a society of peers circulates honour and preserves a principle of equality. The value of the privileged share of the booty (*geras*) arises differently, but there is nevertheless an expectation that the receipt of a *geras* will authorize the claims of its possessor to inherent worth. The power of the relationship between the physical object and the claims which it supports cannot be overemphasized; when Achilles is forced to surrender his *geras* the effect is to negate his claim to be *aristos Akhaiōn* ('best of the Achaians'). In his exile – which is as much an intellectual

123

as a social exile – Achilles grapples with the failure of a public ritual to guarantee what he (like the audience) nevertheless knows to be a divinely sanctioned truth. The *Iliad* consequently places a question mark over value itself – if rituals can be perverted, thereby undermining confidence in the inherent value of things, how does one re-establish faith in one's own claims to *aretē* ('inherited excellence')?

The funeral contest represents a solution to this crisis. If a significant part of the *Iliad* unfolds as an unsettling of the institutions by which elites structure relations among themselves and accord each other rank and status, then we need to determine the strategies by which practices like funeral contests resolve the crisis and re-establish those relations. Funeral contests are understood as a quasi-juridical context at which competing claims to rank and prestige are 'sorted out' (*krisis*). The link between funerals and athletic competition can consequently be explained on this level: the function of the funeral contest for the heir who presides at the grave parallels the role of the contest in legitimating the victor's claims to *aretē*.

In this interpretation the idea of the prize represents a new and powerful response to the problem of the determination of social worth. The athletic prize acts like a certificate of authenticity. This authenticity no longer rests, however, upon the possession of a valuable object. Unlike the right to a privileged share of the distributed spoil (*geras*), the right to seize a prize is founded upon an explicit and formal determination of inherent worth in the *agōn* – the contest itself – and constitutes the *seal* of that public adjudication. The real value of the prize therefore exists beyond the object itself, in the practices which decide value in advance; a prize's value and that of the claims it supports are things determined elsewhere. The prize therefore constitutes a shift away from an archaic notion of value as a tangible essence toward a political one in which value is the product of consensus and public agreement, an abstract quality no longer considered part of the object itself. In the *Iliad* the prize replaces the *geras* as a more durable expression of a man's worth in a society of equals.

Two questions in particular will occupy us: what is the organic link between funerary ritual and athletic contests and what economic significance are we to ascribe to the emergence of the prize and its particular value in an early Greek system of objects? These questions can only be answered by restoring athletic competition to a world of pre-monetary economic structures, oral culture and specific social, mental and historical conditions.

The funeral of Patroklos and its famous contests take place in the second last book of the *Iliad* (*Il.* 23.257–897).[1] Two aspects of its athletic competition are initially striking. Firstly, it takes place in the context of funerary ritual; secondly, the contests are not part of an overarching sacred act – the festival framework for athletic competition to which we are accustomed from later practice is absent. By what logic, then, are these practices enacted? How are we to interpret the social ideology which manifests itself in these collective acts? What, moreover, is the value of its content for understanding the social and historical conditions under which athletic competition emerged in archaic and classical Greece?

To answer such questions the *Iliad* and its form and content – epic poetry and Homeric society – need to be investigated. Although to some degree there will always be problems in reading Homeric society as though it unproblematically reflected Greek social forms and practices of the late eighth century, there is nonetheless nothing to prevent us from treating the *Iliad* as a coherent social milieu.[2] Moreover, what we possess in this poem is a rich body of philological evidence with which to begin an assessment of the very language peculiar to the practices that interest us. The funeral of Patroklos cannot be disentangled from the complexities of the entire poem and even less from the themes of this work. The poet is a narrator and commentator who poses before his audience a familiar world of language and institutions and traces out the faultlines of a crisis in both. In the words of James Redfield, the *Iliad* is a 'structured problematic' produced in a manner that makes it particularly able to disclose the institutional anxieties of the early archaic period.[3] The poem focuses attention on the practices of a world which, as a reflex, will closely parallel that of the poet and his audience. The function and meaning of Patroklos' funeral contests are therefore not to be intuited or examined in isolation: we must recognize in them one dimension of a system of social economy in a poem whose theme itself is the crisis of social economy.[4]

The *Iliad* as an examination of elite practices of evaluation

The *Iliad* narrates the collapse of an *economy*. It presents us with an interrogation of the content of archaic value and evaluation as an important consequence of Achilles' rage. The breakdown of the mode by which elites acquire recognized social worth creates a crisis which is here presented as a problematization of archaic value via the authority of the poet. The destabilization of value (*Iliad* 1) undermines confidence in the exchanges which recognize and confirm *aretē* and in turn problematizes the practices which provide the framework for the public expression of worth (*Iliad* 9). A return to these practices can only take place as a reversal, a playing-back, of the crisis which ultimately proves unsatisfactory (*Iliad* 19). A different crisis, the death of Patroklos (*Iliad* 16–18), draws our attention to some of the roles played by Achilles' *hetairos* ('companion') and, in turn, following Seaford (1994) and Nagy (1979), we can see that grief for Patroklos, its consequences (*Iliad* 18–22) and his subsequent funeral (*Iliad* 23) provide Achilles with the opportunity to rearticulate the way social worth is measured. The funerary contest, presided over by Achilles, represents a wholly different social economy from that which dominates the first book.

Social evaluation in the *Iliad* is fundamentally an economic act. *Timē* as honour or esteem is semantically inseparable from *timē* as economic estimation and it is the content of the evaluative practices that generate social worth which the poet explores and lays bare.[5] *Social economy* will be used here to refer to the sum of practices and mental attitudes to those material objects whose circulation establishes and reinforces normative social relations. This view of the *Iliad* has been suggested in studies that touch on related themes even though the poem has never been analysed as a critique of social economy.[6] I wish, however, to stress the distance between this approach to economy, which draws upon theories of practice and object, particularly those developed by Pierre Bourdieu (Bourdieu, 1977, 1990 and 1998), and studies of the Homeric economy informed by Karl Polanyi, such as those by Finley (1978) and Donlan (1981). On the one hand, the assumption is made that a distinct sphere of economic thinking existed in archaic Greece which, although 'embedded', can be isolated and examined by the theorist as if it was a clearly differentiated field of human activity. In doing this, a system of practices is treated as though the rational mechanisms discerned and catalogued (e.g. generalized reciprocity, negative reciprocity, etc.) were a key part of the way agents were disposed toward themselves and objects. Bourdieu on the other hand outlines a theory of practice which can explain how, for example, the exchange of gifts provokes sincere responses via a complicity to misrecognize its role in an interested long-term economic system. Feelings of obligation arise when they are motivated by the *generous* act; in turn, a precondition of generosity is that it can only arise from a sincere belief in the fiction of the disinterested nature of the exchange. Therefore, for Bourdieu, a large part of the way the gift succeeds involves the misrecognition and denial in every-day life of that which the objective observer would make explicit in theory. The approach taken here prefers to treat the production of value as a total phenomenon – including speech, gesture and disposition – which both establishes and transforms human relations in often concealed and undeclared ways. In constructing a 'Homeric system of objects' one can begin to investigate the way in which value operates in objects like prizes in contests and to discern which gestures are appropriate to them and how they differ in key respects from other types of goods like gifts.[7] It is therefore important to include

126

a study of the prize as a particular type of object in any investigation of early athletic competition and ask what sort of value it possesses. This, in turn, requires that we briefly survey the nature of value in the *Iliad*.

Value and evaluation in the pre-monetary economy of early Greece

It is necessary first of all to consider the character of an economy which is *pre-monetary*. In the *Iliad*, all human relationships are mediated by precious objects in which a type of value resides, that type of value so well described by Louis Gernet in 1948 (Gernet 1981a). In fact, social relations are entirely circumscribed by the visible presence and exchange of these objects which is conveyed in a precise way by the language of epic. The milieu of Homeric society is therefore 'framed' by a whole 'system of objects' – the practical typology of human relations so clearly marked in the language itself.[8] That the economy is pre-monetary is of enormous significance: for in the absence of an explicit standardization of value such as coins, we must realize that economic value arises as a function of each unique exchange. Value is created in the performance of the exchange and is limited by the immediate dimensions of the transaction. The exchange value of an object can never be divorced from either its materiality or the exchange of which it forms the crucial part. If an object is valuable it is because the power to seal a relationship is conceived as part of the alchemical nature of the precious object. In the Homeric poems, the recitation of those past occasions when the same object has sealed a transaction is a way of illustrating its accumulated value.[9]

A useful example can be drawn from the complex meaning of a term for the precious item of value: *agalma*. This is a rare word in epic and yet one instance is suggestive. In the course of battle Menelaos is struck by an arrow and blood spurts from the cut. The poet, wishing to draw particular attention to the precious quality of the life-blood now pouring away, draws a fascinating analogy (*Il.* 4.141–7):

> Ὡς δ' ὅτε τίς τ' ἐλέφαντα γυνὴ φοίνικι μιήνη
> Μηονὶς ἠὲ Κάειρα, παρήϊον ἔμμεναι ἵππων·
> κεῖται δ' ἐν θαλάμῳ, πολέες τέ μιν ἠρήσαντο
> ἱππῆες φορέειν· βασιλῆϊ δὲ κεῖται ἄγαλμα,
> ἀμφότερον κόσμος θ' ἵππῳ ἐλατῆρί τε κῦδος·
> τοῖοί τοι, Μενέλαε, μιάνθην αἵματι μηροὶ
> εὐφυέες κνῆμαί τε ἰδὲ σφυρὰ κάλ' ὑπένερθε.

> Just as when a woman dyes ivory with purple,
> a Meionian or Karian, to be a cheek-piece for horses;
> it lies in a treasury and many riders long to possess it
> but it is stowed as an *agalma* for a *basileus*

> both an adornment for a horse and *kudos* for its rider;
> thus, Menelaos, were your shapely thighs stained with blood
> along with your legs and ankles below.

In a world where precious value could not be abstracted as a quality distinct from an object a man's blood could be compared to an *agalma* and without implying that it was being reduced to a crude material principle. Rather, when the poet thinks of precious drops of blood he thinks of a purple object of beauty whose loss would be painful and disastrous.[10] Blood, like the things which make up aristocratic wealth, is something precious – not for the value which has been accorded to it, but because value wells up from within it like light. Possession of the *agalma* by means of appropriate rituals of exchange in turn provides the possessor with *kudos* (*Il.* 4.145). *Kudos* especially is the *array* of the glorious man, the victor, and can itself even be conceived as an *agalma*.[11] Part of the significance of the analogy lies in its allusion to the way early Greek thought makes sense of value. There is an indissociable link between the social function and symbolic capital of the evoked object and the *presence* of the thing itself: the point of contact between Menelaos' blood and the precious object is its *visibility*, the fact of its appearing as an object worn, a *kosmos*, an adornment which simultaneously radiates the power of the object and evokes the social relations that it seals as the focus of exchange.[12] Value therefore arises as a public spectacle – the blood that adorns Menelaos' leg and trickles away into the dust is itself conceived as a dazzling purple object that when worn transforms the hero into a man to be marvelled at, as though *kudos* had been placed upon him by a god. To lose such a thing is comparable to the loss of the stuff of life itself.

What this example allows us to see is that both the precious object and the one who takes hold of it are evaluated as a social spectacle, perhaps even as a theatrical or dramatic event, since value itself is an appearance conferred and displayed.[13] The *kosmos*, the cunningly wrought object and artifice, reveals to the onlooker a quality that evokes the strangeness and wonder of the realm of the invisible gods at precisely the same time as it creates a spectacle out of the aristocratic exchange relations of which it has been, and will continue to be, the medium.[14]

Moreover, this suggests that the very uniqueness of the artefact inhibits the possibility of a standardized and transferable value. The transferability of the precious object will be a consequence of the transformations that it undergoes as it passes through new and different contexts of exchange and not because one can compare it to an interchangeable standard of value.[15] Exchange, before the advent of abstracted standards independent of the unique contexts of individual exchanges, created value by situating objects at the heart of social relations. The social worth of the individual (*timē*) was thought of as a function of one's relation to that precious object and its exchange.[16] It ought not to surprise us, then, that a man's life cannot be understood to be 'priceless' in and of itself, since the system of value against which his life is measured is a system of precious goods, physically tangible items which are value incarnate. This is an economy in which there is no alienable exchange value. Unlike the coin, the power of the precious object within the social economy is talismanic; feelings of obligation and generosity are part of the alchemical forces activated by these objects. Such items are not valuable because they are ranked according to an abstract system of equivalences but because the value of the precious object is magico-religious in nature.

Social evaluation among equals: the privileged share of *geras*

The crisis of social value in the *Iliad* is a crisis within the pre-monetary economy of *peer* relations. The *Iliad* focuses upon a society composed of many *basileis*, great warriors who find themselves outside of the comfortable hierarchies of home. This world of warrior peers – *homoioi* – is by no means stable.[17] The relations of equality and the claim to deserve recognition must be founded on each man's daily concern for his own *timē*, the complex of his social worth. Above all, this demands being involved in a continuous cycle of exchanges. It is nevertheless not gift-exchanges which give expression to the community of elite peers. The gift is an unequal exchange limited to two parties involved in an undeclared war of recurrent and unending transactions in which the socio-economic advantages are always covert, deferred and incomplete. The relations of a society of equals are founded not on the gift, but on the *geras*, the honorific share of any distribution, and its capacity to supply a social esteem that cannot be violated. The crisis of social value in the *Iliad* is a consequence of the failure of the *dasmos* (the formal division of spoil amongst the warrior group) to issue a publicly authorized and fixed token of a man's status among his social equals. It is a failure of the exchanges which underpin equality of status in a society of warriors to produce an irrevocable guarantee of *timē*.

In *Iliad* 1, Agamemnon's act is a personal violation of *timē* that simultaneously involves forceful entry into a dwelling (ἰὼν κλισίηνδε, 185; see also *Il.* 16.54), leading off animate property with impunity (Briseis, ἐγὼ δέ κ' ἄγω Βρισηΐδα, 184) and a potential threat to inanimate property (φέρω, 301). This is the inverse of the *dasmos* which structures and reinforces peer relations (cf. *Il.* 1.367–9, 391–2). All of these acts involve an attempt by Agamemnon to subvert the relations between peers based upon the *dasmos* '…so that he [Achilles] might well know by what degree I am greater than him and that even another man may well hesitate before declaring himself my equal and liken himself before me' (…ὄφρ᾽ ἐῢ εἰδῇς | ὅσσον φέρτερός εἰμι σέθεν, στυγέῃ δὲ καὶ ἄλλος | ἶσον ἐμοὶ φάσθαι καὶ ὁμοιωθήμεναι ἄντην [*Il.* 1.185–7]).

In the wake of this violent conflict (*neikos*) that erupts between Achilles and Agamemnon, value itself becomes *interrogated*: for Achilles, can the exchange and movement of precious objects truly express the value of a great man? Can he rely on the fact that the substance of his true worth as 'best of the Achaians' will be adequately expressed in the receipt of a precious object from his peers? Can this really measure his *aretē*, his innate value? And, in the end, if a more powerful man can take that object away by force, what of the security of his social status? That Achilles is 'best of the Achaians' is one of the preconditions of the poem, yet the public exchange upon which he is dependent for social acknowledgement of this fact is shown to be unstable and ineffective.

For Agamemnon, on the other hand, the problem lies with legitimacy: how does one assert personal sovereignty via a system of exchanges which functions to efface hierarchy, circumvent personal ascendancies and which, by definition, reinforces a principle of *isokratia*?[18] Like an archaic *tyrannos*, Agamemnon simply uses the threat of greater force to reinforce his claims to preeminence – the epitome of *hybris*. Even his attempt to make amends with *gifts* would replace relations of equality with those of obligation. It is worth adding that the voice of the poet articulates the situation more clearly and unequivocally than we hear even from Achilles himself: Briseis is called 'the girl whom they wrested away by force against his will' (τήν ῥα βίῃ ἀέκοντος ἀπηύρων, *Il.* 1.430). The phrase removes for us any ambiguity that might still surround Agamemnon's act. Not only has Agamemnon inappropriately *personalized* his supervision of the *dasmos*, blurring the sovereignty of the *laos* with his own (so Achilles will explain at *Il.* 9.328–36, especially at 334), but he seeks to transform independent relations into dependent ones,[19] transforming his *philoi* into *ekhthroi* in order to preserve his position (explicit at *Il.* 9. 378 and 16.76–7). Achilles' reply in *Iliad* 9 to Agamemnon's gesture (as reported to him by Odysseus) marks the point at which the social relations put into effect by the *dasmos* are shown to be beyond restoration, never to appear again in the course of the poem. It is into the gap left by the rejection of the evaluative practices of book 1 – the *dasmos* – and its corresponding physical expression (*geras*) that the poem will situate the athletic contest and prizes of book 23.

The way in which the *geras* is made valuable is nevertheless important, since it parallels the way in which the value of the athletic prize arises. The sources of the social value which the *geras* embodies are significant but still latent in the *Iliad*: public authorization and the formation of a public space – the *meson* ('middle') and the *agora* itself. Indeed, *agōn*, *agora* and *meson* are all rough synonyms for the same space: that of public speech (*agora*) and competitive activity (*agōn*) all understood to be 'in the middle' (ἐν μέσῳ). The unifying principle is that all practices and objects, including speech, located or undertaken there are neutral, unowned and belong to the group in common (ξυνεῖα, *Il.* 1.124). For Gernet (1955), the publicly vouch-safed ability to seize an object held in common in the middle constitutes one of the archaic precursors to a formal notion of private property and ownership.[20] This observation can be supported by the fact that the word *geras* is used with a limited field of verbs among which δίδωμι ('give') is conspicuously rare for an object often thought to belong to a system of reciprocities.[21] In fact, even when δίδωμι is used the subject of the verb is the entire *laos* whose very anonymity (*Il.* 2.488–90) precludes the formation of personal relations peculiar to the gift and denies the real force of the verb at the moment of its use. The 'gift' of the community is in fact an authorization and guarantee to act proprietorially: a comparison between *Od.* 9.159–60 and 9.548–51 reveals that Odysseus understands that his seizure (ἔξελον, *Od.* 9.160) of an extra portion (a tenth goat) can equally be conceived as the concession of the whole warrior band to his position: 'my companions gave to me alone a ram as the extra portion' (ἀρνειὸν δ᾽ ἐμοὶ οἴῳ...ἑταῖροι...δόσαν ἔξοχα, *Od.* 9.550–1).[22] There is therefore an antithesis between the personal gift and the object deposited in a public space (*res nullius*) that appears in the gestures appropriate to the object and the way in which the object and its location are described.[23]

When we turn to the public evaluation of individuals themselves we see the same antithesis. On the one hand, the social relations created by gift-exchange exist by being misrecognized and are therefore not just undeclared, but *undeclarable*.[24] In other words, since the exchange of gifts is never explicitly concluded (for to do so would be to annul the essence of obligation), its symbolic capital is always relative and ambiguous. On the other hand, communally owned and distributed objects possess a value which is declared and fixed by open public determination and recognition. Social worth (*timē*) embodied by the *geras* exists independently of the subject because 'it lies in a sort of virtual law of the group'.[25] The objectifying authority of the 'society of warriors' might be, as Gernet says, reduced throughout the *Iliad* to a passive presence, but it has nonetheless a binding authority. We have in this the beginnings of a process by which a man's esteem can be publicly adjudicated. The voice of the *laos* may be passive but its hostility to Agamemnon's use of force to undermine an exchange undertaken in its name and vouchsafed by its collective presence is palpable. To that extent, there is, as Gernet suggested (1955, 16), a 'quasi-legal effectiveness' to the witnessed distribution of spoil and honorific portions that begins to demonstrate that value need not be dependent upon the moment of exchange. Rather, it begins to suggest that value can be made subject to a political process of inquiry and be *determined* by the consensus of the group even if it cannot yet be made secure against the illegitimate use of violent force.

After Agamemnon's seizure of Briseis, Achilles' *geras*, there could be no return to the *dasmos* as a mode of evaluation. By his actions, the son of Atreus laid bare the stress points of an economy of equal social relations; moreover, this act activates Achilles' poetic critique: henceforth, what man's *geras* – that object which most articulates *timē* in a band of equal warriors – can truly claim to be a token of value independent of the arbitrary whims of superior violence?[26]

Even though the strife between Agamemnon and Achilles is temporarily allayed by the contrite *apoina* of book 19, the audience know only too well that Achilles' return to the battlefield is motivated by the loss of a thing of value which no precious object can express. Achilles' intimation in book 9 that no *kleos* is worth his life (*Il.* 9.400–20) – a fascinating declaration – becomes literally tangible in book 16: he must endure the death of his double. It is possible to see Patroklos as a representation of Achilles himself. In a characteristically Homeric way, reality and representation merge in the telling: the apparition of Achilles on the battlefield is destined to share the same cinerary urn as Achilles himself (*Il.* 23.91–2; 23.243–4).[27] To this extent, the later funeral of Patroklos is, like the presence of Achilles' simulacrum on the battlefield, simultaneously the premonition of Achilles' funeral and that very funeral itself.[28] The death of Patroklos allows the poet, through Achilles, to develop his critique of the social economy further, by reorienting the hero back toward his *philoi hetairoi* and the unqualified value of his own shining *kleos*, explicitly described as beyond articulation in the terms of the heroic economy (*Il.* 9.400–20); at the same time, it also allows the 'best of the Achaians' to preside at a vision of his *own* funeral,[29] a ritual context in which an institutional framework exists to express the social value of a man in a new way.

In the *Iliad* there is no return to the types of exchange revealed in books 1 and 9 to be incapable of representing the true value of a man's worth (*timē*) and innate virtue (*aretē*). This is clear even on the level of poetic diction: the language of booty distribution is used only once in the last four books of the poem (δάσονται, *Il.* 22.354) and then only in a perverted context. The word *geras* which is so crucial to the meaning of book 1 and the focal point of strife in the society of warriors is not employed by the poet after book 19. Books 20–22 constitute a period of social *aporia* where questions about the proper determination of *timē* are in stasis. On the path to resolution, Achilles must first descend into the hell of a second exile: the anguish of his own mortality, inseparable from his humiliation at the hands of Agamemnon which can itself be construed as a kind of death, and the violent grief for his *hetairos* and reflected self – all of this will manifest itself as an inversion of distributive exchange in the rage of the warrior. Such a representation can be read as the end point of a breakdown of the exchanges by which the community of heroes and its ideology is supported.

The language used is revealing. Instead of receiving a proper burial from kin, Hektor's body will become the spoil at a *dasmos* to which only birds and dogs are invited (ἀλλὰ κύνες τε καὶ οἰωνοὶ κατὰ πάντα δάσονται, *Il.* 22.354). By comparison, at *Od.* 24.290–6, Laertes contrasts the proper treatment of the dead ('dressing the body…as is right…for such is the *privileged share of the dead*,' περιστείλασα…ὡς ἐπεῴκει…τὸ γὰρ γέρας ἐστὶ θανόντων, 293–6) to the fate of the unattended corpse ('either the fishes eat him or he becomes *spoil* for beasts and birds', ἠε…φάγον ἰχθύες, ἢ…θηρσὶ καὶ οἰωνοῖσιν ἕλωρ γένετο, 291–2). It is noteworthy that these two polar opposites are nonetheless expressed by the same semantic field: ἕλωρ and γέρας are terms especially germane to war spoils. In this respect, then, even the spectrum of possibilities for disposal of the dead is expressed in terms of either positive or negative exchange; on the one hand, due burial is a man's death-right, his honorific allotment (γέρας); on the other, exposure and mutilation of the body is a consequence of the violent seizure of wild animals (αἱρέω). This reinforces the notion that the spectrum of possible positions in this society, even the dead, are expressed with reference to types of object-relation.

Book 22 marks one of the lowest points in the poem, the point at which only violence and disorder prevail. Achilles' return to civilization has been sketched by Richard Seaford: the reintegration of Achilles by means of death-ritual.[30] But any return to civilization must involve a real end to the strife between Achilles and Agamemnon which has left the economy of honour among all the warrior peers in ruins. The funeral which follows in book 23 provides the context within which the lines of a social economy of prestige are redrawn and this is not a coincidence: the convergence of two strands of thought here is deliberate and fundamental.

Funeral, contests, heirs and victors
Why should the funeral be so significant? As a context for the consolidation and restatement of the group the funeral is well-suited – ritual lament and

commensality around the tomb are powerful agents of group cohesion. Seaford's explanation for the presence of contests at a funeral is that they constituted 'a controlled outlet for aggressive anger at [the deceased's] death', which may 'serve to express the status, and reaffirm the strength, of a particular group owing loyalty to the dead man' (1994, 122). Like Nagy, for whom contests are 'the specific Greek variant of the general anthropological category of competition *in honor of the dead*' (1990,143, my italics), and other earlier studies of funeral competitions,[31] Seaford's view can ultimately be traced back to Erwin Rohde and his first anthropological discussion of funeral competition (Rohde 1925, 14–17). To a large degree it has been held that the relationship between the participants in the contest and the deceased is self-evident and can be simply explained in general terms as honouring the dead or giving cult to appease the dead, that is, as a kind of *Totenkult*. These explanations all appear to gloss the link between funerals and contests and can offer no reason why both institutions were regarded as particularly apposite.[32]

One solution might be found in the convergence of social practices and institutions. It may be possible to trace out a mode of thought in which the heir who succeeds a dead man at a funeral, the warrior who receives his share of spoil at a *dasmos*, and the victor at an athletic contest are all thought to be involved in the same kind of act. A clear linguistic and semantic homology exists between the lexicon of booty distribution and the sharing out of goods amongst inheritors at an intestate succession. The evidence of the *Iliad* indicates that the same vocabulary is employed in each context and can also be found in similar modes of expression in archaic law: the *Code of Gortyn* (*IC* 4.72) in particular uses the words *moira* ('portion', 'lot') and *timē* to indicate shares parcelled out to legitimate children.[33] The idea of the equivalent share – so crucial to Achilles in books 9 and 16 – is employed just as frequently to articulate familial relations after a man's death: the adopted son at Gortyn, for example, is declared to be *isomoiros* ('having the same portion') with legitimate daughters.[34] A man displays the objects he receives at an inheritance to demonstrate the authenticity of his relationship to the dead man; indeed, such a man can confirm his social relations in a way very similar to the member of the warrior band who receives a *moira* and a *geras* (cf. *Od*. 11.534). An equal share of the inheritance becomes the socio-economic definition of the *gnēsios*, one whose legitimacy is indicated by the public validation of his birth.

Legitimacy is also demonstrated by carrying out the *sacra* in relation to the body of the deceased: the *gnēsioi* properly 'dispose' of the body just as they dispose of the dead man's property.[35] But if legitimacy is challenged, what recourse is there? In early Greek legal thinking a challenge to one's legitimacy requires the intercession of a *dikē*, simultaneously a mode of proof and a ruling in the presence of witnesses.[36] This mode of proof must be authorized by the community itself; in the *Code of Gortyn*, the adopted son has recourse to the public declaration made by his adoptive father before the *polis* and *hetairia*; at Athens, the phratry plays the same role.[37] Indeed, at Gortyn the very verb for adoption is ἀμπαίνεθαι (= ἀναφαίνεσθαι), 'to show forth', 'proclaim', revealing that public recognition and demonstration before authorized witnesses is built into the very notion of legitimacy.[38] At Gortyn again, if heirs fall out over the division of their patrimony (δαῖσις), the city authorizes the intervention of an arbitrator (δικαστάς) whose function is twofold:[39] firstly, to enforce 'fair division' (δατέθθαι καλōς, *IC* 4.72 col. IV 38–9), which is laid down in the code as a *dikē*, that is, the right course of action; secondly, 'to decide under oath with reference to the pleas' (ὀμνύντα κρῖναι πορτὶ τὰ μολιόμενα, *IC* 4.72, col. V 43–4) in the event that an intractable dispute arises over how to divide. The final recourse of the judge is to sell all the property and before authorized witnesses to 'let each receive a share of the *timai*' (τᾶν τιμᾶν δι[λ]ακόντον τὰν ἐπαβολὰν Ϝέκαστος, *IC* 4.72, col. V 49–51).[40] In summary, at archaic Gortyn, the community decides legitimate succession through public adjudication – this manifests itself legally via the intercession of the sovereign community, the actions of an arbitrator, witnesses and finally by the use of an external standard of value. These elements parallel the key components of athletic competition in early Greece.

Though this formulation may be the case in archaic Crete, where are these elements in the world of epic? The elusive *polis* shows its hand in epic in the way the poet alludes to the very practices which resolve social crises. Achilles' new shield in *Iliad* 18 will carry as one of its heraldic devices the epitome of an intractable quarrel (*neikos*) brought under control by a panel of adjudicators sitting in public (*Il.* 18.497–508). This scene is in fact emblematic in the *Iliad* of the *polis* at peace. In that scene, the whole community guarantees the finality of the *dikē* to be pronounced and therefore explicitly denies the right of self-help to either party. In the shield scene, just as at Gortyn, an action of hubristic seizure, such as Agamemnon's violent appropriation of Briseis, would face a hostile community with the ability to deny it any kind of juridical legitimacy. Indeed, in a fascinating parallel, the Gortynian legislation makes Agamemnon's triple violation of Achilles – forcible entry into his dwelling (ἰὼν κλισίηνδε, *Il.* 1.185) and the leading and carrying off of property (ἄγω, *Il.* 1.184; φέρω, *Il.*1.301) – a punishable offence in the context of an inheritance distribution (δαῖσις): 'and after the *dikastas* has ruled, *should anyone enter with force or lead or carry anything off*, then he shall pay ten staters and double the value of the property' (αἰ δέ κα δικάσαντος τô δικαστᾶ <u>κάρτει ἐνσείει ἒ</u> <u>ἄγει ἒ πέρει</u>, δέκα στατêρανς καταστασεî καὶ τô κρέιος διπλεî, *IC* 4.72, col. V 35–9).

The funeral has the character of a proto-juridical context at which the public disposal of objects confirms new social relations both with respect to the community at large and with respect to the dead man. It is in this scenario that one can observe the settlement of disputes in a way that has greater recourse to concepts of proof and adjudication. To this extent, the funeral provides us with an institutional bridge between a crisis in one mode of social evaluation and the installation of another, between the allocation of a *geras* among a community of equals and the determination of the prize-winner in a funeral contest.

The relationship between funerals and contests held in funerary contexts is especially illustrated in the semantic field of the verb ἀναιρέω. In everyday speech this verb means 'pick up', but it also has a narrower sense of 'pick up in a special way' or 'pick up proprietorially'. Thus, ἀναιρέω can mean either 'take up, efface' (as in the annulment of a contract) or 'pick up' denoting the assertion of ownership and authoritative rights.[41] Significantly, the verb also refers to an act of oracular selection.[42] The semantic field of this word, however, points to the same range of attitudes throughout, that the object of the verb discards an old condition and is transformed into a new one, a process that Gernet described as a kind of *immersion*.[43]

Ἀναιρέω is also used idiomatically: firstly, of the heir who, in public, 'takes up' his inheritance legitimately; and secondly, of the victor who takes possession of his prize in an athletic competition. In the first situation it therefore can properly be translated as 'inherit';[44] whereas in the second translators have routinely translated the verb by 'won'.[45] The link is made clearer when we observe how prizes in early funeral contests appear to be taken specifically from out of those possessions which constitute the legacy of the dead man. It is likely that such prizes obtain a significant part of their value and identity from this fact. The victor enters into a legitimate ownership that is directly and literally analogous to that entered into by the successor of the dead man *at precisely the same moment and in the same manner*. In the same act both victor and heir, so to speak, 'take up' their special status.[46] Prize and inheritance each declare, reinforce and legitimate each other – both represent and embody the possessor's publicly confirmed legitimacy. In the setting down of prizes ἐπὶ τάφῳ, that is, literally 'upon the grave' of the deceased,[47] a son publicly proclaims his right to own and hence dispose of his father's objects. By participating, the athletes in the contest have also accepted that the heir's claims to set down such objects as prizes are valid and further confirm him by agreeing to his rules and adjudication. Finally, the victor who strides to his prize and proprietorially picks it up has his *aretē* and *timē* confirmed, simultaneously recognizing the heir as one whose right to make such a determination was authentic. The greater the attendance and participants, the more forceful the authentication of both claims.[48] In other words, the way a funeral functions for the successors of the deceased is homologous to, and reinforces, the functions of the funerary contest for the *agōnothetēs* and the participants. The fundamental connection, therefore, between funerary practices and athletic competition can be seen in the complementarity of gesture, language and material objects between the heir (*agōnothetēs*) and the victor, as well as between the inheritance (both symbolic and material) and the prize.

The grave also plays a key role in such rituals of legitimacy as the chief surviving physical point of contact – *sēma* – of the dead man. The heir is required to undertake almost all acts of succession either in the presence of, or literally on, the tomb itself. In Aeschylus' *Choephoroi*, the advent of Orestes is recognized by the placement of a lock of hair and footsteps on his father's grave site.[49] The presence of footsteps recalls the need for the heir to step upon the grave in order to claim the succession as well as, in the case of murder, to make the formal declaration to pursue the dead man's slayer.[50]

The funeral can thus be thought of as a turning point, not only in the existence of the dead man, but a critical *rite de passage* for those who will succeed to his name. It has been suggested that legitimacy demands modes of proof. These will not be objective proofs – as Odysseus illustrates (*Od.* 14.199–210), there is nothing to be gained by proclaiming a blood relation alone – but will rather be found in the demonstration of control over ritual and objects with the community as witness and a publicly enacted link with the deceased. In some key passages where we possess references to epic funeral contests other than those for Patroklos, competitions are very often offered by the son or sons of the dead man, where the language which expresses the act of holding contests has a strong formulary character. The main instances are as follows:

(1) *Il.* 23.630–1. Here Nestor recounts his prowess at a funeral in the north-west Peloponnesos: 'when once the Epeans buried mighty Amarygkeus | at Bouprasion and his sons set out the *basileus*' prizes' (ὡς ὁπότε κρείοντ' Ἀμαρυγκέα θάπτον Ἐπειοὶ | Βουπρασίῳ παῖδες δὲ θέσαν βασιλῆος ἄεθλα).

(2) *Il.* 22.163–4. During Achilles' duel with Hektor the simile of an equestrian contest is used: 'and a great prize is laid down when a man has died, | either a tripod or a woman' *or* 'and a great prize is laid down, | either

a tripod or a woman that belonged to the dead man' (τὸ δὲ μέγα κεῖται ἄεθλον, | ἢ τρίπος ἠὲ γυνή, ἀνδρὸς κατατεθνηῶτος).

(3) In *Works and Days*, 654–5, Hesiod boasts of his victory at Khalkis, when he travelled 'to the prizes of warlike Amphidamas…and many were the widely-announced prizes which his great-hearted sons set down' (ἐπ' ἄεθλα δαΐφρονος Ἀμφιδάμαντος…τὰ δὲ προπεφραδμένα πολλά | ἀέθλ' ἔθεσαν παῖδες μεγαλήτορες).

(4) Telemachos declares (*Od.* 21.116–17) that, should he meet the conditions of the bow contest, then 'I would be left here as one able to take up my father's beautiful prizes' (ἐγὼ κατόπισθε λιποίμην | οἷός τ' ἤδη πατρὸς ἀέθλια κάλ' ἀνελέσθαι).[51]

Taking the evidence altogether it is possible to discern a formulary pattern: ἆθλα τιθέναι + genitive of the deceased as the act of his successor(s). To these examples we can add a series of coins minted at Metapontion bearing the legend Αχελοιο αεθλον which may have been a special series of prizes for contests of the river god/hero Acheloos.[52] These constructions are paralleled by other formulae found inscribed on bronze prize vessels: παρά, ἐκ or ἀπό + genitive indicating the origin or source of the prize.[53] Such formulae form a complement to the more common usage involving ἐπί + dative of the deceased, insofar as all these formulae evoke the gestures of an heir in claiming to dispose of patrimony within the context of performing the *sacra* at a funeral. In these other formulae, the fact that these prizes originate from the property of the deceased is made explicit; in the latter (ἐπί + dative of the deceased), the emphasis is on the placement of prizes upon the tomb.[54]

Here we see expressions of ritual propriety in relation to legitimacy: in setting the terms under which the dead man's property can be seized as prizes a man demonstrates his legitimate succession. The receipt of such goods by the victor is a public declaration of his acceptance that the right to dispose of the inheritance was authentic. Henceforth, by being able to refer to a properly conducted funeral and a public event at which the successors were *athlothetai* – 'setters-down of prizes' – a man will have lasting proof of his authentic descent.[55] The nature of the relationship between Achilles and Patroklos suggested earlier is important in this respect – the funeral contest of Achilles' slain simulacrum serves as a context at which the still living 'best of the Achaians' (cf. *Il.* 17.689–90) can assert and proclaim his status afresh. This is perhaps hinted at when the hero proclaims that 'if we Achaians were now contending for the sake of some other hero, I myself should take the first prize away to my shelter' (*Il.* 23.274–5). It also should not surprise us that many of the prizes are in fact Achilles' own possessions (*Il.* 23.259).

In the funeral contest for Patroklos itself we find, then, the representation of a new way of marking out social value. A crisis in one mode of assigning worth to members of the group finds its resolution in a set of practices that weave together the juridical function of the funeral, at which succession is proclaimed, together with practices for the adjudication of social value which avoid arbitrary verdicts and prefer to rely on a publicly recognized demonstation of *aretē* with reference to rules. When Achilles awards second prize to Eumelos in the chariot race even though he has run last, Antilokhos can rightly object – the race itself has already decided the ranking and Achilles can no longer intervene. Achilles must instead resort to different exchanges in order to demonstrate Eumelos' relationship to him. Participation in funeral contests is therefore of critical importance both for adjudicator and athlete. The enormous capital of the moment of victory confers nothing less than eliteness itself and guarantees an honour that can exist independently from other aristocratic exchange relations such as gift-exchange and spoil-distribution which produce value that is unstable and contingent. It is funeral contests such as these which finally provide the institutional framework within which peers can pursue a more durable expression of their social worth.[56] By the public acknowledgement of Agamemnon as a man whose *aretē* is so self-evident he need not even compete (*Il.* 23.890–4), the *Iliad* displays the capacity of the formal contest to settle even the most intractable disputes about degrees of prestige. More generally, these conclusions perhaps enable us to recognize that the immense symbolic capital of an Olympic chariot victory, the possession of which allows a man like Kleisthenes of Sikyon the audacity to claim that he can judge the best man in Greece (Hdt. 6.126), arises out of practices central to the early Greek *polis* – rituals dealing with legitimacy and claims to authenticity.[57]

The invention of the prize (*aethlon*)

What enables this process to succeed is the evolution of a different type of precious object, a unique non-reciprocal exchange. This is the prize, the archetype of adjudicated value. In a recent article, Donald Kyle has, however, asserted without question that prizes were both regarded as gifts (*dōra*) and also that 'the ideology of early Greek prize giving was that of gift giving' (Kyle 1996, 107). With reference to the contests at Patroklos' funeral, Kyle states unequivocally that 'The formalized announcement and awarding of athletic prizes, so prominent in Homer's narrative of the games, derive from gift-giving rituals' (Kyle 1996, 110). This is a difficult position to maintain and the evidence seems to suggest that prizes evolved out of an entirely different system of thought. Only with an analysis of the function of the prize in the context of a particular poetic performance, with all its lexical specificity, can we avoid glossing over the importance of the prize as part a complex pre-monetary economy.[58]

That the prize is a fundamentally different type of object from the gift is strikingly illustrated by some uses of δίδωμι ('give') in the funeral contests of Patroklos. In each case the poet transposes gestures of gift exchange into the context of taking prizes and draws out the implications that arise. In the following, I hope to draw attention to some salient examples.

After all the champions on the plain of Troy have thundered past the *terma* in the chariot race, we encounter the sorry sight of Eumelos limping in and trailing the wreckage of his chariot, 'last of all' (πανύστατος ἄλλων, *Il.* 23.532). Standing up, Achilles announces his adjudication (ἀγόρευε):

> λοῖσθος ἀνὴρ ὤριστος ἐλαύνει μώνυχας ἵππους·
> ἀλλ᾽ ἄγε δή οἱ δῶμεν ἀέθλιον, ὡς ἐπιεικές,
> δεύτερ᾽· ἀτὰρ τὰ πρῶτα φερέσθω Τυδέος υἱός. (*Il.* 23.535–8)

> Last the best man drives his single-foot horses;
> but come let us give him a prize, as it is fitting,
> second prize; let Tydeus' son carry off the first.

The language here is clear. Diomedes' unambiguous victory automatically guarantees him the right to 'carry off' the first prize. φέρειν is the standard verb for expressing the proprietorial seizure of inanimate objects.[59] Achilles, however, declares that Eumelos is a man whose status (ἀνὴρ ὤριστος, *Il.* 23.536) would have been confirmed by the race had not a deity intervened; he had in fact been vying with Diomedes all the way. Nevertheless, since Eumelos does not possess the right to carry off any prize but fifth, Achilles summarily intervenes. To convey the special nature of this award, therefore, Achilles transposes the prize into the language of personal gift-exchange and consequently, into a relation of obligation (underlined by πόρεν, *Il.* 23.540). Eumelos cannot exercise a proprietorial right over the object and must accept it graciously from the magnanimity of Achilles. Like Agamemnon before him, Achilles here subverts the gestures and proper treatment of specific goods. The object is unambiguously a prize and the audience are only too aware by now of the specificity of this heroic economy: the words ὡς ἐπιεικές ('as it is fitting') will jar. The *laos*, the mass of spectators, significantly, roars its approval: πάντες ἐπήνεον ('they all cheered him', *Il.* 23.539–40). Under the circumstances, such a gesture seems to demonstrate Achilles' great generosity and he quickly wins the public authorization he needs. Antilochos, however, whose horses actually ran second, is seething and challenges the adjudication in the same language Achilles once used to describe Agamemnon's outrage: 'you mean to strip me of my prize (ἀφαιρήσεσθαι ἄεθλον, *Il.* 23.544 – the analogy with *geras* is decisive, cf. *Il.* 1.161; 16.54) and offer it to this man because he is noble and your friend' (ἐσθλός, *Il.* 23.546; φίλος, *Il.* 23.548). He was punished, Antilochos continues, for not having prayed to the immortals; however, should you, Achilles, wish to indicate your regard for the man then cast it in clear terms:

> ἔστι τοι ἐν κλισίη χρυσὸς πολύς, ἔστι δὲ χαλκὸς
> καὶ πρόβατ', εἰσὶ δέ τοι δμῳαὶ καὶ μώνυχες ἵπποι·
> <u>τῶν οἱ ἔπειτ' ἀνελὼν δόμεναι καὶ μεῖζον ἄεθλον,</u>
> ἠὲ καὶ αὐτίκα νῦν, ἵνα σ' αἰνήσωσινἈχαιοί.
> <u>τὴν δ' ἐγὼ οὐ δώσω· περὶ δ' αὐτῆς πειρηθήτω</u>
> ἀνδρῶν ὅς κ' ἐθέλησιν ἐμοὶ χείρεσσι μάχεσθαι. (*Il.* 23.549–54)

There is plenty of gold in your tent as well as bronze
and livestock and there are serving-girls and single-foot horses;
take up from these later and give him an even greater prize,
or even do so right now so that the Achaians might praise you.
But this (mare = second prize, *Il.* 23.265–6) *I will not give*; Let him
    contend for her
whosoever amongst men wishes to fight me with his hands.

Antilochos explicitly announces his proprietorial right over the second prize, negatively expressed as the right not to give. This further rejects Achilles' desire to give this prize away by differentiating the object from the domain of the gift. This is because the mare was a prize won and as such was configured in the middle (cf. 'for the defeated man he put a woman in the middle', ἀνδρὶ δὲ νικηθέντι γυναῖκ' ἐς μέσσον ἔθηκε, *Il.* 23.704), the polar opposite of the space of gifts, tied as they are to the personal space of the home (ἐν κλισίῃ, *Il.* 23.549; οἴκοθεν, *Il.* 23.558). Antilochos underlines his determination by his willingness to resort to self-help in order to defend his due.

That Achilles acknowledges his *faux pas* and the validity of Antilochos' grievance is clearly reflected in his acquiescence to the young man:

> Ἀντίλοχ', εἰ μὲν δή με κελεύεις <u>οἴκοθεν ἄλλο</u>
> <u>Εὐμήλῳ ἐπιδοῦναι,</u> ἐγὼ δέ κε καὶ τὸ τελέσσω.
> δώσω οἱ θώρηκα, τὸν Ἀστεροπαῖον ἀπηύρων,
> χάλκεον, ᾧ πέρι χεῦμα φαεινοῦ κασσιτέροιο
> ἀμφιδεδίνηται· πολέος δέ οἱ ἄξιος ἔσται. (*Il.* 23.558–62)

Antilochos, if you demand of me that *something else from out of my house should be given as a compensation instead to Eumelos*, then I will fulfil even
    this.
I will give him this corselet, the one I stripped from Asteropaios,
a bronze one, around which there is overlaid a plate of shining tin;
and it will be worth a lot to him.

In other words, Achilles readily agrees to act in a way more appropriate than the gesture he had originally tried to make. The expression underlined, οἴκοθεν ἄλλο...ἐπιδοῦναι (*Il.* 23.558–9), is an explicit acknowledgement that a public recognition of Achilles' *philia* for Eumelos must not be construed in the terms of a contest in which Eumelos has clearly lost. Since the exchange amounts to a personal assessment of Eumelos as a peer and a *philos*, the transaction must consequently be framed in the language of reciprocity.[60] The act is then completed as Automedon, Achilles' retainer, physically places the object into Eumelos' hands (ἐν χερσὶ τίθει, *Il.* 23.565) a gesture which is, as Gernet has argued, a precise analogue to διδόναι.[61] The episode therefore serves to illustrate the passivity and obligated condition of the gift-recipient in contrast to the unobligated proprietorial ownership which the victor asserts over the *res nullius* ἐν μέσῳ.

In the scene that follows immediately upon this we witness yet another play on the categorical difference between the prize and the gift. Antilochos runs second through the application of his father's (and his own) *mētis*.[62] He manipulates the course to his advantage and forces Menelaos to come in a close third and accept a lesser prize. Menelaos is furious since his horses were better and, in a way not dissimilar to Eumelos' case, publicly declares that he has a right to second prize:

ᾔσχυνας μὲν ἐμὴν ἀρετήν, βλάψας δέ μοι ἵππους,
τοὺς σοὺς πρόσθε βαλών, οἵ τοι πολὺ χείρονες ἦσαν. (*Il.* 23.571–2)

You have humiliated my *aretē,* and ruined my horses
by throwing your horses, which were far more inferior, in my way.

In a famous case of pre-law dispute settlement and via a skilful manoeuvre, Menelaos demands that Antilochos swear by Poseidon that he did not use a trick (δόλος, *Il.* 23.585) in order to claim the better prize. Antilochos is outwitted – or is he? Antilochos is contrite (*Il.* 23.587 f.): I defer to you lord Menelaos since you are my better; you know how impetuous and foolish young men can be;

               ...ἵππον δέ τοι αὐτὸς
δώσω, τὴν ἀρόμην. εἰ καί νύ κεν οἴκοθεν ἄλλο
μεῖζον ἐπαιτήσειας, ἄφαρ κέ τοι αὐτίκα δοῦναι
βουλοίμην ἢ σοί γε, διοτρεφές, ἤματα πάντα
ἐκ θυμοῦ πεσέειν καὶ δαίμοσιν εἶναι ἀλιτρός. (*Il.* 23.591–5)

        ...but, *I myself will give to you
the mare which I won.* If for something of greater worth from my house
you should also ask, I would immediately give it to you, beloved of Zeus,
rather than every day fall from your heart and be a wrong-doer in the eyes
    of the gods.

He then rounds off his speech with a formulaic public gesture of gift exchange, leading the mare to Menelaos and placing it, literally, in his hands (ἐν χείρεσσι τίθει Μενελάου, *Il.* 23.597 which parallels 565). Antilochos' speech-act is a masterpiece of practical strategy, again full of *mētis* ('cunning intelligence'), but nonetheless sincere for all that. In a bold stroke Antilochos carries off the object as a prize (ἀρόμην, *Il.* 23.593), solidifies his claim to the status that it signifies and, under the pressure of Menelaos' oath, relinquishes the object but under a different sign, that of the gift and its specific relations (εἰ καί νύ κεν οἴκοθεν ἄλλο | μεῖζον ἐπαιτήσειας [*Il.* 23.592–3], deliberately echoes οἴκοθεν ἄλλο…ἐπιδοῦναι [*Il.* 23.558–9] just as 596 parallels 565). Menelaos is therefore sundered from the symbolic capital of the prize at precisely the same moment at which he is woven into a relation of obligation to Antilochos. For Antilochos, the material loss is insignificant alongside the capital that arises from the conditions of this exchange: Menelaos cannot refuse since he has made a public claim to this particular object but to accept it *as a gift* involves conceding that Antilochos had in fact won it originally as second prize.

Menelaos can only respond by hasty deflection of the gesture back onto Antilochos:

τῷ τοι λισσομένῳ ἐπιπείσομαι, <u>ἠδὲ καὶ ἵππον</u>
<u>δώσω ἐμήν περ ἐοῦσαν</u>, ἵνα γνώωσι καὶ οἵδε
ὡς ἐμὸς οὔ ποτε θυμὸς ὑπερφίαλος καὶ ἀπηνής. (*Il.* 23.609–11)

I will therefore be ruled by your supplication, *and I will even*
give the mare to you though she is mine, so that these men may recognize
that my heart is never arrogant or stubborn.

It is all Menelaos can do to avoid the net of obligation with which Antilochos has enmeshed him. The aftermath is revealing: Noemon, Antilochos' retainer, leads off the mare in the opposite direction back to Antilochos' tent and Menelaos takes third prize, which all recognize as the only object over which he can lay any claim in spite of his weak ἐμήν περ ἐοῦσαν (*Il.* 23.610) to the contrary.

After Meriones carries off the prize to which he is entitled (fourth, *Il.* 23.614–15), we are reminded that the circumstances have left the fifth prize, a two-handled *phialē*, unclaimed. Again the language is subtle and precise:

…πέμπτον δ' ὑπελείπετ' ἄεθλον,
ἀμφίθετος φιάλη· <u>τὴν Νέστορι δῶκεν Ἀχιλλεὺς</u>
<u>Ἀργείων ἀν' ἀγῶνα φέρων</u>, καὶ ἔειπε παραστάς·
τῆ νῦν, καὶ σοὶ τοῦτο, γέρον, κειμήλιον ἔστω,
Πατρόκλοιο τάφου μνῆμ' ἔμμεναι· οὐ γὰρ ἔτ' αὐτὸν

ὄψῃ ἐνἈργείοισι· <u>δίδωμι δέ τοι τόδ᾽ ἄεθλον</u>
<u>αὔτως</u>· οὐ γὰρ πύξ γε μαχήσεαι, οὐδὲ παλαίσεις,
οὐδ᾽ ἔτ᾽ ἀκοντιστὺν ἐσδύσεαι, οὐδὲ πόδεσσι
θεύσεαι ἤδη γὰρ χαλεπὸν κατὰ γῆρας ἐπείγει. (*Il.* 23.615–23)

               ...and fifth prize was left behind,
a two-handled jar; *Achilles gave it to Nestor*
bearing it through the Argive assembly and standing by him spoke:
'There now, let this be for you, elder sir, as an heirloom,
to be a memorial of Patroklos' funeral; for you will no longer
see him among the Argives. *But I give this prize to you*
unclaimed as it is; for you will not fight with your fists, nor wrestle,
nor take part in javelin throwing, nor race with your feet ever again;
for already age sorely oppresses you.

Since the last prize remains unclaimed it is left for Achilles to decide its fate. He gives it to Nestor αὔτως – that is, 'as it stands', without a claimant and now a prize without a contest. This is a peculiar aberration, an object which straddles the fields both of gift-exchange and the prize and it is cast as such deliberately. Although a public gift from Achilles to Nestor, its function will always be to recall what it undoubtedly is – a keepsake, a memorial of the funeral for Patroklos, an un-won *aethlon* forever evoking its agonistic context. Nestor will keep the jar as a gift from Achilles and again we hear of it placed into the old man's hands (*Il.* 23.624); yet at the same time, Achilles presents it to a *victor* of old whose old age has diminished a once great *aretē*. Only standing alone without a victor could the jar have been treated in this way: a prize that is *simultaneously* a gift, the gift of a prize. The poet then is very much aware of the subtle difference between the prize and the gift and here, as indeed throughout the entire *Iliad*, weaves his story from these different social threads to great dramatic effect.[63]

    The prize, which draws its value from the adjudicatory practices of the contest and the public witnessing of the victory, can be thought of as a precursor to the emergence of coinage in the sixth century BC. In this context, a precious object can be situated in such a way that its value, once limited, as outlined above, to the context of its exchange, becomes transferable, that is, exchangeable without limit. For the victor's status to be universally fixed so must the value of the physical token of his victory and it is the public body who declare and certify it. Henceforth, the exchange value of the precious object can be expressed as something distinct from its physical material. Indeed, we can see a striking indication of this in the *Iliad*. Stimulated by a different context for adjudicating value, the poet now employs the verb τίω ('rate', 'value', 'assess') to make a proto-monetary estimation:[64]

Πηλεΐδης δ᾽ αἶψ᾽ ἄλλα κατὰ τρίτα θῆκεν ἄεθλα,

δεικνύμενος Δαναοῖσι, παλαισμοσύνης ἀλεγεινῆς,
τῷ μὲν νικήσαντι μέγαν τρίποδ᾽ ἐμπυριβήτην,
<u>τὸν δὲ δυωδεκάβοιον ἐνὶ σφίσι τῖον Ἀχαιοί·</u>
ἀνδρὶ δὲ νικηθέντι γυναῖκ᾽ ἐς μέσσον ἔθηκε,
πολλὰ δ᾽ ἐπίστατο ἔργα, <u>τῖον δέ ἑ τεσσσαράβοιον.</u> (*Il.* 23.700–5)

Now the son of Peleus set out the prizes for the third contest,
showing them before the Danaans, that of painful wrestling;
for the victor a great tripod to set over a fire,
which the Achaians valued among themselves at 12 oxen;
for the defeated man, he placed a woman in the middle,
and she knew the craft of many works, *and they valued her at 4 oxen.*

This verb (τίω), from which the concept of *timē* is derived, is here used in a way that implies a man's social value need not be dependent on a closed system of contingent exchanges, but rather find its expression through a political determination. What makes these precious things valuable now is not the waxing of some inherent value, or even the exchanges in which they have figured in the past, but rather their value is expressed as the consensus arrived at among a community of equal deliberators. Put differently, the expression of value '12 oxen' is an abstract equivalence that exists only 'among the Achaians'. Moreover, this example suggests that, unlike the *dasmos*, where a man's *geras* lacks the objective legitimacy of a strong authorizing body, the prize has its value, and, by extension, the social value of the victor, guaranteed by communal recognition of the *athlothetēs*, and the explicit *fiat* of the entire community (ἐνὶ σφίσι τῖον Ἀχαιοί, *Il.* 23.703).[65]

A significant part of the value of the prize lies, therefore, in its *reference* to victory: the object need only *refer* to the moment *kudos* graced the victor. A bronze tripod, once valuable for the role it might play as the medium of an aristocratic economy, now becomes a sign of value, precious as much for its signification of victory and authentic adjudicatory processes as for its inherent material value.[66] The value of the prize arises such that the physical object need not even be present – or, better still, need only be represented by a supplementary object which evokes the legitimate *source* of its value. Such is the nature of the crown or epinikian ode with its capacity to invoke again and again the moment of victory and the *kudos* of the victor.[67] The physical presence of precious material therefore becomes less important. The development of the idea of the prize in early Greek thought permits an object to be articulated as having a value that is distinct from its physical material – the worth of a thing can be construed in abstract terms and need only evoke the moment of original evaluation. Beyond the *Iliad* is the coin – a universal standard whose physical material value is guaranteed by the stamp which proclaims the *political* source of its authenticity, the civic body. Aristotle (*Politics* 1257a 41) was well aware that a coin's stamp (χάρακτηρ) also constituted its 'sign of value' (τοῦ ποσοῦ σημεῖον) which guaranteed the coin's metallic purity.

What must be recognized, however, is that *poleis*, in minting coins bearing both a symbol and a written seal of the issuing authority, declared a multiplicity of potentially conflicting claims as to the source of their coin's value. On the one hand, a mythical scene on a coin may evoke an original and unique talisman of value (e.g. the golden sheaf on Metapontian coins) which the city attempts to recall continually through reproduction of its image. The coin bears the sign of a source of value other than itself, while suppressing the fact that its own value is not unequivocal and universal. On the other hand, the collective citizen body declares itself the source of a coin's value as effective guarantors of metallic purity, misrecognizing the fact that the value of coins is political in nature and not objective. Like prizes, coins contrive to *refer* to a source of value other than the civic body or their metal, often the talismanic object stamped on the coin.[68]

By this stage the psychological foundations are laid for the distillation of personal and social value from out of the contexts of pre-monetary exchange. *Timē* can now refer to an abstract idea – 'honour' – and, furthermore, suggest that a man may have a value even if he possesses no property, does not appear noble and takes no part in aristocratic exchange. To this extent, it is possible to see that the appearance of citizenship as an abstract politico-legal concept is built upon foundations laid in contexts of evaluation such as funerary athletic contests; the determination of who is and who is not a valuable member of the political community evolves from institutions which decide and distribute prestige.

Sitta von Reden's remarks on the origins of coinage are fundamental in this regard (1997, 160):

> Less attention has been paid to the fact that such monies represent attempts to render value quantifiable and socially negotiable… The desire to assess value, to use standard units of value, and to render value comparable sprang from much wider concerns than trade and commercial exchange. If, then, coinage was the final stage of an increasing tendency to render value comparable, quantifiable and measureable, *we should seek the context of the development of coinage more generally in institutions where value needed to be measured, quantified and compared* (my italics).

Read from this perspective, the *Iliad* therefore illustrates a crucial historical moment in early Greek thinking about value and narrates a series of differentiations that emerge from an active inquiry undertaken through the figure of Achilles.

On this level, the prize is representative of a transformation of social relations among the elite and prefaces the transformation inaugurated by the increased use of coinage in the latter half of the sixth century BC. The resolution envisaged at the end of the funeral contests for Patroklos marks the triumph of transferable value, the end of a dialectical process at which a man's life and social worth ceases to be apposite to the great *agalma* and instead becomes 'priceless' – an expression which can only have meaning in a monetary economy.

From funeral to festival

We can conclude by suggesting how we might situate the emergence of formal athletic competition in the processes outlined above. In the absence of permanent and institutionalized mechanisms which would ground hierarchy and privilege in a guaranteed order, hundreds of communities in early Iron Age Greece grappled with questions about the legitimacy of eliteness and its expression through ritual spectacles. In the *Iliad* we see a system of exchanges, which function strategically to circulate and legitimate social value, interrogated in the poetic performance; this performance, whether a narrative voice or the *mēnis* of Achilles, is not simply inspired speech that is poetic and oracular, rather the performance enacts social possibilities through song. The funeral of Patroklos and its contests are an end point in this performance. Once it is reached, Achilles activates rituals wherein legitimacy and social value can be articulated afresh – the transformation of symbolic capital at the funeral.

For the audience of epic, the funeral contests of the great epic hero are a projection of the funeral contests for their local hero, which, as Nagy has explained, unlike those of epic, are re-enacted every year;[69] but the symbolic capital produced at each is fundamentally the same. In a public festival, the *polis* adjudicates an *agōn* and so casts itself as the inheritor of institutions originally set in place by its founder-heroes (*archagetai*), seizing and renewing the inheritance that is 'taken up' proprietorially by the entire community at the re-enacted funeral of the hero. It is important in this regard that some of the most well known athletic competitions of the archaic and classical periods were understood as funeral contests: 'all ancient contests were established in honour of the dead' (ἐτελοῦντο μὲν οἱ παλαιοὶ πάντες ἀγῶνες ἐπί τισι τετελευτηκόσιν, Schol. Pind. *Hypoth. Isth.* a, Drachmann iii, 192).[70] At this public festival, the athletes, by their very willingness to participate, confirm the institutional right of the host-*polis* to assess and rate their *aretē* and to seal that ranking with a prize. The victor, in turn, strides into the middle of the assembly and proprietorially 'takes up' the objectified capital of his own legitimate victory. By doing this the victor also publicly proclaims the effectiveness of those institutions over which the *polis* lays the claim of inheritance.[71]

This relationship between *polis* and victor is strikingly illustrated at the Panathenaia: here the relationship between heir (the Athenians) and Panathenaic victor is manifested in the prize-amphora itself. In a dramatic gesture, the most coveted prize at the Panathenaia is sacred olive oil which continues to flow from the original moment when Athens' autochthonous king-founder adjudicated between Poseidon and Athena and found in favour of the goddess.[72] The very token of Panathenaic victory is thus not only a materially valuable object for the victor, but the political capital for the Athenian *polis* of oil from the very trees which literally sprouted from Kekrops' judgment. In this way, a prize carries with it a *polis'* claims that its adjudications are effective and authentic, the inherited patrimony of founding heroes. As physical *sēmata* ('signs') these prize-amphoras are then carried and dispersed throughout the inter-*polis* community of the archaic Greek world, advertising the effectiveness and authority of a city's entire institutional framework.

It is possible, then, to see that in archaic Greece athletic competition emerges out of practices central to the origin of the *polis* itself – the changing structure of elite relations, the emergence of standardized value, the power of adjudication and, not least, the assuaging of disturbing fears about authenticity and legitimate claims. Athletic competition emerges in the *Iliad* not simply as part of a colourful episode but as an institution cut from the same cloth as the poet's speech. Like the *Iliad* itself, formal athletic and equestrian contests among an emerging aristocracy of birth belong to a mode of thought that is historically interstitial, oscillating at varying points between an archaic and mythical mode of thought and the dialectical rationality of the *polis*. On the one hand, the tomb at the heart of the funeral – the focal point around which early athletic and equestrian contests orbit – is situated among sites that according to one principle are, by definition, *oracular*: the site of a speech-act of legitimation and strategies of succession via the transmission of efficacious objects. The pronouncements and gestures made at such a nexus are ritualized, pre-legal and irrevocable. For the heir presiding over a contest as well as the victor, there is a performative magic in funeral and contest which confirms authenticity and legitimacy by 'making real' what is said and done, later inherited by the *Hellanodikas* at Olympia who, according to Pindar, 'puts into effect' the ordinances of Herakles in the act of placing the olive wreath upon the victor's head (κραίνων ἐφετμὰς Ἡρακλέος προτέρας, *Ol*. 3.11). But on the other hand, the contest can succeed only through practices of adjudication and investigation which cross-examine both heir and victor, demand *proof* of claims and possess the capacity to interrogate that proof. The contest itself is an ordeal and the eerie and oracular quality of the victor – *kudos* – will eventually be acknowledged as deriving from a juricical determination of victory and the verdict of civic judges appointed by the *polis*. The victor will owe his status to the city.

Notes

[1] For a general overview of Homeric athletics, see Richardson 1993, 201–3 with further literature. See also the excellent remarks of Macleod 1982, 29–32. For recent studies of Homeric 'sport', see Kyle 1984; Dickie 1984; and, in depth, Laser 1987. For a study of competition terminology, see Scarlon 1983. I will omit here what I believe is the special case of the athletic contests on Phaiakia in *Odyssey* 8. The themes at work in that episode are related to the present discussion but deserve a separate study.

[2] For the state of the debate on the historicity of 'Homeric society', see Raaflaub 1998; for the relationship between the world of the poet and the world of his poem, see Morris 1986.

[3] Redfield 1983, 219.

[4] I am here drawing on an approach to the poetics of the Homeric poems which is developing a sophisticated understanding of the interaction of the forms of thought and forms of society that occur within them; see in particular Nagy 1979; Martin 1989; Kurke 1991 (on Pindar); Seaford 1994; Detienne 1996; and, especially relevant here, Muellner 1996.

[5] That personal and social worth are not differentiated from economic and material estimation is clearest in the semantic field denoted by the verb τίω and its cognates τιμή, τιμήεις, τιμάω and their negatives, ἀτιμάω, ἄτιμος, ἀτίμητος and ἀτίζω. The lexica (Ebeling 1885, vol. 2, 336; Cunliffe 1963, 385, s.v. τίω (1) and (2); LSJ[9] s.v. τίω; Chantraine 1968–80, 1123) prefer to see a distinction between personal usage and purely economic statements (although note that German 'schätzen' preserves the ambiguity: Frisk 1970–3, vol. 2, 906 s.v. τίω). A survey of its use in the Homeric epics nevertheless reveals that τίω is a verb of general estimation and evaluation. As a result, it is preferable to translate τίω with an English word that preserves some of that ambiguity ('esteem', 'regard') before resorting to 'honour', which would give the impression that the ranking and evaluation of humans was something more abstract than that of inanimate things. The basic sense of 'rate', 'value', 'estimate' is clearest at *Il.* 23.703, 705 where one of the prizes at the funeral games for Patroklos is 'assessed' by public agreement at twelve oxen and another at four. In some isolated cases a sense of measurement is explicit. For instance, at *Il.* 9.378, Achilles says of Agamemnon that 'I regard him as worth nothing' (τίω δέ μιν ἐν καρὸς αἴση); *Il.* 9.608 echoes this statement: 'I know that I am held high in Zeus' calculation' (φρονέω δὲ τετιμῆσθαι Διὸς αἴση). The essential meaning is 'to ascribe a degree of value to'. In later usage this sense is still strong – compare Theognis' complaint (621) that 'everyone holds

a rich man in some esteem but the poor man is disregarded' (πᾶς τις πλούσιον ἄνδρα τίει, ἀτίει δὲ πενιχρόν).

⁶ See, for example, Gernet 1955, 1981a; Vernant 1991a; Seaford 1994; von Reden 1995, 1997.

⁷ In his *System of Objects*, Jean Baudrillard set out to ask: '…how objects are experienced, what needs other than functional ones they answer, what mental structures are interwoven with – and contradict – their functional structures, or what cultural, infracultural or transcultural system underpins their directly experienced everydayness…' (1996, 4). To some extent the questions asked here arise from a broader attempt to apply such a project to archaic Greece, especially Baudrillard's concern to discover 'the processes whereby people relate to [objects] and…the systems of human behaviour and relationships that result therefrom' (1996, 4).

⁸ On the idea of formulating a typology of man-made objects, see Baudrillard 1996, 3–11.

⁹ Space does not permit a fuller study of notions of price and measurement in the Homeric poems. It will suffice to say that it is not so much that the poems offer us evidence of a society in which rudimentary forms of value calculation exist; rather, the poems represent a society for which calculating value by means of a universal external measure is becoming more widespread and the impact of applying that measure to the socio-political sphere more apparent. The use of cattle as a measure of value (e.g. *Il.* 23.703, 705) is evidence for thinking about value as the product of a public consensus to use a common standard external to the precious object. The argument here however is that the *Iliad* consciously places this type of public evaluation of men and things as the resolution of a crisis about how to determine worth. For an example of the interplay in the *Iliad* between symbolic value and rationalized value, see 6.234–6; on similar themes, see recently Brown 1998. For precious objects whose genealogies consist of a catalogue of prior (or possible) exchanges in which the object figured as the medium, see Agamemnon's sceptre, *Il.* 2.101 ff.; Areïthoos' club and armour, *Il.* 7.138 ff.; Meriones' helmet, *Il.* 10.266–71; Apollo's aegis, *Il.* 15.309; Meges' corselet, *Il.* 15.530–4; Achilles' spear, *Il.* 16.143–4; Achilles' mixing-bowl, *Il.* 23.741–9; the *solos* (lump of iron) given as a prize, *Il.* 23.826–9; Menelaos' bowl, *Od.* 4.615–19; Odysseus' bow, *Od.* 21.13–38. In each case the value and power of the object waxes the more often it can recall the occasions of its prior exchanges.

¹⁰ It is possible that the double presence of μιαίνω tinges the simile with the negativity which this verb implies in different contexts (cf. *Il.* 16.795, 797; 17.439; 23.732; 24.420; as an epithet of Ares, see also μιαιφόνος: *Il.* 5.31, 455, 844; 21.402). In spite of this, however, the brilliance which this compared object evokes serves to highlight the 'shapeliness' of the wounded warrior's body. This comparison therefore undoubtedly positions the stain of blood as part of the beauty of the heroic death which instantly converts the horror of the wound into the radiance of *kudos*. The staining of the limbs is reconfigured as the staining of a precious ivory object at the moment when it might have implied pollution. I thank Dr Alan James for his comments on this passage.

[11] For *kudos* as a quality of the victor and of victory itself, see *Il.* 23.400 = 406, and more generally, Benveniste 1973, 346–56 and Kurke 1993. *Kudos* is conceived as a visible quality – the 'rayonnement de la force' (Chantraine 1968–80, 595 s.v. κῦδος) – that is, in effect, an objectification of *aretē* (excellence) in the fact of victory, either in war or athletics. It can be understood as the halo of the man touched or marked out by the divine as distinct. On this level, *kudos* is a manifestation of validity, the clothing of an authenticated hero – the crown of the victor. *Kudos*, therefore, derives its essence from the public spectacle of community recognition. In the example under discussion, *kudos* is more explicitly conceived as analogous to adornment even though it is already articulated throughout the *Iliad* as a type of precious artifact, a talisman, supplied by the gods and then *worn*: at *Il.* 23.400 = 406, to indicate that Diomedes is the chariot victor, Athena 'clothed him in *kudos*' (ἐπ᾽ αὐτῷ κῦδος ἔθηκεν). For examples of τίθημι in the sense of 'clothe', 'adorn', see Cunliffe 1963, s.v. τίθημι (3) and especially *Il.* 6.92, used of Athena's *peplos*.

[12] For the *agalma* as an object worn, see also *Od.* 18.300 and 19.256–7. At *Od.* 18.292–303 the poet dwells upon the visible power of a series of *agalmata* offered to Penelope by the suitors; Eurymachos offers a necklace which appears 'like the sun' (ἠέλιον ὥς, *Od.* 18.296), while a pair of earrings from Eurydamas 'shone forth with great beauty' (χάρις δ᾽ ἀπελάμπετο πολλή, *Od.* 18.298). This latter instance illustrates the way *charis*, a particular attitude or feeling produced by aristocratic exchange, is literally a physical and visible quality. In other words, exchanges produce concrete realities by literally embodying or incorporating them in the object itself. On this, see Bourdieu 1990, 66–79. On *charis*, see Carne-Ross 1985, 63 ff.; Nagy 1990, ch. 6; Kurke 1991, 103–7.

[13] Perhaps we can even discern the connection between the visible essence of the *agalma* and its later identity as the cult-object that allows the 'presentification of the invisible' as suggested by Vernant 1991, 153–6. *Agalma* occurs only once in the *Iliad* (4.144) and without the cult associations found in the *Odyssey* (3.274, 438, 8.509, 12.347; cf. however instances which recall an earlier meaning: *Od.* 4.602, 18.300, 19.257).

[14] 'We have to do with a sort of projection of the ideal notion in the other world on to the plane of human life: treasure is real enough socially – an institution indeed; but it is also real enough in myth. It is both a social reality and a mythic reality' (Gernet 1981a, 139). There is no question that objects exist in both planes simultaneously: on the one hand, the genealogy of an artifact invested with symbolic authority is a necessity if it is to continue to entitle its owner, while, on the other, the spectacle of its social identity will confirm the relationship between the practice and the object itself.

[15] See the list of objects in n. 9 above.

[16] See n. 9 above.

[17] For Achilles, relations between the Achaian elite should ideally be based on equal portions, typically of spoil at the *dasmos*; see especially *Il.* 16.52–9. For a similar articulation of the ideal through a depiction of its perversion, see *Il.* 9.318–19.

[18] Consider the terms by which Poseidon describes the nature of relations between Zeus and his brothers (*Il.* 15.186–99) and the homology between the *dasmos* of spoil amongst warriors (*Il.* 1.166) and the *dasmos* of an inheritance amongst heirs.

[19] The 'genealogy' of Briseis' movement as a precious object illustrates Agamemnon's attempt to subvert the symbolic capital of the *geras*. For Achilles, Briseis has been violently moved to the opposite pole of economic value: from (1) Briseis as *geras* [*Il.* 1] to (2) Briseis as *booty* [stripped from Achilles, ἀπηύρων, *Il.* 1.430, 9.131, etc.] and then (3) Briseis as *gift* [*Il.* 9.131–2]. Only at *Iliad* 19.249 does Briseis once more become Achilles' *geras* and go back into the *meson* in a way appropriate to her condition as a *geras*.

[20] Gernet 1955, 13–14.

[21] See, for instance, the treatment of the *geras* by Donlan in an article entitled 'Reciprocities in Homer' (1982, 160 ff.).

[22] If on occasion the vocabulary of gift-exchange is used to refer to communally owned objects, then they will be gifts 'sans maître, par le fait de celui qui les dépose et leur confère publiquement leur qualité de *res nullius*' (Gernet 1955, 13–14). Note Thersites' succinct description of the process, *Il.* 2.226–8. In general, exceptions arise when the *geras* and rights to confer or receive it are treated inappropriately (*Il.* 9.330–6, 365–9) as well as, say, in the context of the insult which deliberately seeks to diminish honour by casting the relations which underpin it as inferior or servile, such as at *Il.* 20.179–82 and *Od.* 20.296–7. On the semantic field of booty distribution practices, see, generally, Nowag 1983, 36–50.

[23] On this antithesis, see especially Gernet 1955, 14 and his concluding remarks on 18.

[24] For this idea, see especially Bourdieu 1998, 92–112.

[25] 'il réside dans une espèce de droit virtuel du groupe' (Gernet 1955, 16).

[26] See n. 17 above.

[27] At least three other instances deliberately blur the identities of Achilles and Patroklos. The first, at *Il.* 17.689–90, is Menelaos' message for Achilles: 'the best of the Achaians has fallen | *Patroklos*…' (πέφαται ὤριστος Ἀχαιῶν | Πάτροκλος…); the second, *Il.* 18.51 ff., is Thetis' lament for Achilles. Death here can be read on many levels: the death of Patroklos, the certain death of Achilles as a consequence, the imitation of death in grief, his social death at the hands of Agamemnon and so on. See also Seaford, 1994, 166–7. Thirdly, *Il.* 19.323–4, where Achilles compares the potential grief for the loss of his father or son with the grief he feels for the loss of Patroklos. In this instance Peleus is pictured weeping for the loss of 'such a son' (τοιοῦδ' υἷος). Lattimore, in his translation, adds 'such a son, *for me*' (my italics) in an attempt to efface an essential ambiguity. The point must surely be that Peleus would be weeping both for the simulated death of Achilles (Patroklos) and for the hero's real death inexorably activated by the actual death of Patroklos.

[28] The identification of Patroklos as Achilles' double has often been made (e.g. Loraux 1975) but I am here drawing in particular on G. Nagy's fundamental essay on Patroklos' thematic function in the *Iliad*, Nagy 1979, 94–117. For Nagy's discussion of the semantics of Patroklos' name, see Nagy 1979, 102 ff. For Nagy,

Patroklos' death can be read as a projection of Achilles' symbolic death should he accept a return (*nostos*) without *kleos*, that is, a world without Πάτροκλος ('ancestral *kleos*'). In other words, the death of Patroklos intimates Achilles' possible 'death' (i.e. forgotten in old age), but not his ultimate fate (*kleos*): it suggests and recalls the other types of death that arise from being deprived of the immortal glory of *song*. Henceforth, Achilles is activated to exchange *mēnis* over the loss of one type of *timē* for the *timē* of *kleos*. As Nagy shows, this idea operates on the level of ritual practice: cult, including ritual song, paid to a hero is the *timē* which prevents the *mēnis* of the dead man. Here we might suggest that Patroklos acts like a *kolossos*, a representation of the *psyche* (in this case the ritual substitute of Achilles own *psyche*), whose ritual immolation compels agents to fulfil oaths and undertakings; see Vernant 1983.

[29] A fascinating vase (Corinthian *olpē*, *c*. 570–550, Brussels A4) depicts Achilles alive (in mourning) and, at the same time, laid out dead at his own funeral.

[30] Seaford 1994, 159–80.

[31] On funeral contests in general see, Malten 1923–4; Malten 1925; Andronikos 1968, 34–7, 121–6; Roller 1981; Laser 1987, 21–5.

[32] For a general (and rather pessimistic) discussion of the various *Ursprungtheorien* for the Olympic Games and, by extension, athletic competition, see Ulf and Weiler 1980.

[33] A precise parallel is drawn between Achilles' dispute with Agamemnon over the *dasmos* of spoil and Poseidon's dispute with Zeus over the proper treatment of someone who is *homotimos*, 'equal in honour' (*Il.* 15.186); compare, for example, *Il.* 1.185–7 and 9.160–1 with 15.165–7; *Il.* 15.187–9 and 15.208–10 with 16.52–9. Note that Poseidon's *isomoiria* (*Il.* 15.209) with Zeus arises from the *dasmos* of their inheritance, *Il.* 15.187–9. This division is explicitly called a *dasmos* in the *Homeric Hymn to Demeter*, 85–6 (cf. also Hesiod's version: *Theogony*, 392–6, 881–5). For the division of an inheritance as *dasmos* generally, see Hesiod *Works and Days* 37. For the language of inheritance distribution in the *Code of Gortyn* (*IC* 4, 72), see col. IV 23–46 and V 9–54 *passim*; *moira* (IV 39–43); *timē* (V 49). It is interesting to note that the verb δατέομαι, which in the *Iliad* is so concerned with the non-reciprocal distribution of precious booty, survives at Athens in the title of magistrates (δατεταί) whose task was to oversee the distribution of common property, especially amongst relatives at an inheritance: *Ath. Pol.* 56.6. On this, see further in Rhodes 1981, 631 ad loc. with additional references.

[34] Col. X 53: Ϝισϝόμοιρος.

[35] The best evidence for the ritual strategies used by heirs are the speeches of Isaios: 'Since he (Chariades) neither took up (ἀνείλετο) the body of his adopted father, nor provided a pyre, nor gathered up the bones, but left everything to be done by those who had no relation to him, how is he not the most impious man in claiming to inherit the property of the dead man when he has fulfilled none of the sacred obligations (τὰ νομιζόμενα)?' (4.19); cf. also Isaios 2.10, 25, 36–7, 45–6; 4.26, 47; 6.40–1, 51, 63–5; 7.1, 19–22, 30, 32; 8.16–27, 38; 9.4–7, 19, 30, 32, 36; [Dem.] 43.11 f., 58, 65, 78 f.; 44.32 f.; 48.12. For the fulfilment of the *sacra* (τὰ νομιζόμενα) as part of demonstrating the legitimacy of an adoption at Athens,

see Rubenstein 1993, 68–76, and for legitimacy in general, Harrison 1968, 123 with n. 2. At Gortyn (*IC* 4, 72, col. X 42, 46; XI 1–2) these sacred obligations are a major priority for the adoptee, the fulfilment of which authorizes the rights of adoptive succession. The interwoven nature of legitimacy and sacred obligations to the dead is nicely illustrated in Euripides *Herakleidai*: 'O Children…you will see the *polis* of your father, set foot upon your estates and sacrifice to your ancestral gods' (…πόλιν πατρὸς | ὄψεσθε, κλήρους δ᾽ ἐμβατεύσετε χθονὸς | καὶ θεοῖς πατρῴοις θύσετε…, 875–7).

[36] In general, see Gernet 1981b; Thür 1970; and Sealey 1994, 91–111. On the archaic challenge and defence of a right to inherit in Athens (*diamartyria*), see Harrison 1968, 156 and 1971, 124–31. See 1971, 124 n. 2 for further literature.

[37] Gortyn: *IC* 4, 72, col. X 34–9 (note the same gestures in the act of renunciation, col. XI 10–14). On the function of the *hetairia* in Crete and its analogy with the Athenian phratry, see Willetts' commentary on this passage in his edition, Willetts 1967, 77, and his remarks: '[the *hetairia* was] a basis for the whole organization at Gortyn…since, as witnesses of the presentation of sons of their fellow citizens, the members of the *hetairia* guaranteed the legitimacy of their birth' (Willetts 1967, 11). For this as the key role of the Athenian phratry, see Lambert 1993, ch. 4 *passim*, esp. 161–89.

[38] *IC* 4, 72, coll. X 33–XI 23, *passim*.

[39] For the entire procedure, see *IC* 4, 72, col. V 28–54.

[40] Note that Hesiod's *Theogony* is conceived as the unfolding of the primordial distribution of an inheritance presided over by Zeus (112). The pattern of language closely parallels the Gortynian formulation (882–5): 'the blessed gods sorted out the Titans' dues by force…and [Zeus] distributed these honours to them well' (Τιτήνεσσι δὲ τιμάων κρίναντο βίηφι…ὃ δὲ τοῖσιν ἐὺ διεδάσσατο τιμάς).

[41] Or authoritative disavowal of legitimate rights: Solon fr. 36.6 (West).

[42] Cf. Hdt. 1.31.1–2; 2.52.3; 2.139.3; 6.34.2; 6.52.5; 6.69.3; 7.148.3; 9.33.2; see also Burkert 1985, 116.

[43] The transformation of the type of value that inheres in the precious object is represented as the traversing of special spaces – objects 'go down and come up', Gernet 1981a, 131. The resignifying space is usually the space of oracular legitimation. Consequently, legitimation always involves passing through spaces of reconfiguration. The quality of the space (which is never neutral or 'empty' space) leaves its mark by changing whatever moves through it, whether objects or humans, like an initiation. The case of Trophonios' cave is paradigmatic (see Detienne 1996, 53–67), but any space in which confirmation, authentication or legitimation takes place has an oracular quality. When the individual reacquires the object, its prior symbolic value has been altered. After Kleisthenes presented a list of one hundred Attic *archagetai* to the Pythia at Delphi, she 'picked out' ten (οὓς ἀνεῖλεν ἡ Πυθία δέκα, *Ath. Pol.* 21.6), those who, from that point on, would take on a new and different role as the eponymous heroes of the Athenian *polis*. Under the sign of the *polis*, it is the *agora* that possesses this authority. When the athlete 'picks up' his prize *from the middle* he confirms a claim and the herald speaks with *marked* speech. The use of marked speech carries with it

transformative power, the power to effect ritual alchemy (cf. the ease with which the herald's efficacious proclamation can be converted into a poetic utterance: Simonides ep. XXIX, XXXI Campbell/Page *FGE*; Timotheos fr. 802 Campbell). The ritual act achieves the same end, whether it is the initiate who slips into the cave of Trophonios, the son who places his foot upon the grave of his father or the athlete who 'goes down' into the *agōn* to have his *aretē* assessed (cf. Hdt. 5.22.2 where Alexander of Macedon 'proves' his Greekness (ἐκρίθη εἶναι Ἕλλην) in the context of the Olympic festival). For use of the linguistic concept of marked and unmarked, see Muellner 1976, 9–17 and Nagy 1990, 5–9.

[44] The best example is *Od.* 21.113–17 which deserves its own separate treatment since its imagery is complex but precise; *IC* 4, 20 l. 3 = *Nomima* II. 37 (Gortyn, *c.* 550); *Nomima* II 39 l. 4 (Phaistos, *c.* 500); *IC* 4, 72 (the code of Gortyn, *c.* 450), V 24, 25; VII 10; X 40–1, 44; XI 4, 34; the testament of Xouthias, *IPArk* 1 = *IG* V 2, 159, ll. 2, 11, 12, 15, 16, 18. Ἀναιρέω is used also of taking up the body or the bones of the deceased by heirs and relatives for the purposes cf burial: e.g. Eur. *Supp.* 471, 1167; Soph. *Elec.* 1140; Hdt. 4.14.2; 9.22.3; 9.23.2; Isaios 4.19, 26.

[45] Victors: *Il.* 23.551, 736, 823 (cf. *Il.* 1.301 for a parallel usage); Hdt. 5.102.3; 6.36.1; 6.70.3; 6.103.2–3; 6.122.1; 6.125.5; 9.33.2; 9.64.1.

[46] It is interesting to compare certain mythical and dramatic narratives in which the central hero occupies one or more of the main roles in a funeral contest. In Euripides' lost play *Alexandros*, summarized by Hyginus (*Fab.* 91), Priam holds funeral contests for Paris whom he believes to be dead. Paris, unaware of his identity and still very much alive, enters all the events and is victorious. In this version, Paris is simultaneously the deceased, the heir (the most authentic successor to oneself is oneself!) and victor. Another case where roles blur is at *Od.* 21.113 ff. In the contest for Penelope the patrimonial object (Odysseus' bow) in the hands of the rightful heir to Odysseus' household almost secures victory for Telemakhos (*Od.* 21.128–30). Both these examples draw their complexity and significance by drawing on different but analogous rituals concerning legitimacy.

[47] A case can be made, *pace* Nagy 1990, 120–1, for taking the use of ἐπί + dative literally (see LSJ[9] s.v. ἐπί B.1) rather than more abstractly. LSJ[9] s.v. ἐπί B.2 cites *Il.* 23.776 as an example for the sense 'in honour of', even though the narrative of the funeral ritual is explicit about where the oxen were slaughtered: around and upon Patroklos' pyre and corpse, *Il.* 23.166–9. Some grave markers bear this formula (Schwyzer 1923, nos. 348, 452, 455, 456) which is best understood as declaring over whom the stele has been placed. In the same way, the expression, ἆθλα ἐπί + name in the dative (e.g. Stesichoros' Ἆθλα ἐπὶ Πελίᾳ [frs. 178–80 Campbell]) needs to be taken literally: 'prizes (set) up over the dead man'. For a further parallel, see *Il.* 23.679–80, where Mekisteus 'once went to the grave (ἦλθε... | ἐς τάφον) of the fallen Oidipous at Thebes where he was victor over all the Kadmeians'; by extension, any *agōn* said to have taken place ἐπὶ τῷ δεῖνα (as for example, the *Epitaphia* in Athens, where the prizes are inscribed: ἆθλα ἐπὶ τοῖς τοῖ πολέμοι, *IG* I[3] 523–5; cf. also *Il.* 23.274 [ἐπὶ ἄλλῳ ἀεθλεύειν] and *Od.* 24.89–91) should be conceived as taking place on the grave of the deceased where his goods are offered as the prizes, literally set up on the tomb (cf. Hesych. s.v. ἐπ' Εὐρυγύη

ἀγών, where the formulation is ἐφ᾽ ᾧ τὸν ἀγῶνα τίθεναι ἐπιτάφιον Ἀθήνησιν ἐν τῷ Κεραμεικῷ). If a series of marble *diskoi* from the late sixth century BC (*IG* I³ 1394–5, 1397) were prizes at a funeral contest (as Roller argues, 1981, 3–5; a comparison with *IG* I³ 1396, Ὀέθεν ἆθλα could be suggested but would not be conclusive), then the inscribed phrase repeated on all three, ἐκ τῶν ἠρίων, 'from out of the grave-mound', is strongly reminiscent of Achilles' words to Nestor: 'let this [the unwon fifth prize of the chariot contest] be an object laid down | to be a memorial from out of Patroklos' grave' (κειμήλιον ἔστω, | Πατρόκλοιο τάφου μνῆμ᾽ ἔμμεναι, *Il*. 23.618–19). Given the nature of Patroklos' identification with Achilles, then all the prizes offered at Patroklos' funeral contests can be construed as 'issuing from the barrow' (cf. *Il*. 23.126) since they are all Achilles' possessions. On the other formulae for referring to prizes see above p. 138.

⁴⁸ Note Hesiod's emphasis: 'the widely-announced prizes' (τὰ προπεφραδμένα ἆθλα), *Works and Days* 655–6.

⁴⁹ ll. 165, 205 f.; note l. 200, where the lock of hair is described as 'this tomb's adornment and my father's honour' (ἄγαλμα τύμβου τοῦδε καὶ τιμὴν πατρός).

⁵⁰ For this complex of gestures, see especially Gernet 1981b, 177–81. For the proclamation of vengeance, see Harpokration s.vv. ἐπενεγκεῖν δόρυ and [Dem.] 47.69: 'If there is a relative, they are to make a proclamation upon the tomb' (προαγορεύειν ἐπὶ τῷ μνήματι, εἴ τις προσήκων ἐστί). To this example should be added Telemachos' gestures in the bow contest as a precise parallel, *Od*. 21.113–17.

⁵¹ In (1) it could be argued that the genitive is better put with παῖδες; it could equally be argued that in (2) ἀνδρὸς κατατεθνηῶτος makes just as much sense as a genitive absolute or even, as Richardson suggests (1993, 125, ad loc.), that it means 'in honour of a man who has died'; but comparison with other formulae points predominantly to a possessive sense.

⁵² Jeffery 1990, 260, no. 13. Note too that on a *dinos* by Sophilos (early sixth century BC, NAM 15499) is a depiction of the funeral contests for Patroklos identified by the words Πατροϙλυς ατλα, 'Patroklos' prizes', which is echoed at *Il*. 23.748.

⁵³ Amandry 1971, 615–18, nos. 2, 3, 3A–C, 6 (= *IG* XII 9, 272), 8; Jeffery 1990, 444, H; 476, C.

⁵⁴ One reason why the latter formula (ἐπί + dative of the deceased) became more common may have been that the appropriation of funeral contests by the *polis* in the context of hero-cult required less personal emphasis on the actual person of the *athlothetēs* as figurative heir and more emphasis on the hero's tomb as the site of legitimation. Indeed, the *polis* was only too aware of the tyrannical ambitions of those who instituted civic contests or claimed agonothetic rights over them: Pantaleon of Pisa (Olympia, Paus. 6.22.2), Pheidon of Argos (Olympia, Hdt. 6.127.3; Paus. 6.22.2), Kleisthenes of Sikyon (Pythia, *krisis* of the suitors, Hdt. 6.126); the Peisistratidai at Athens (Panathenaia, Dionysia). By immersing themselves in such effective ritual practices of legitimacy, tyrants could claim to be the inheritors of heroic privileges.

⁵⁵ Note that at least two archaic depictions of the funeral games for Pelias

named his son Akastos in the role of either *athlothetēs* (the chest of Kypselos, Paus. 5.17.10: τούτῳ δὲ νικῶντι ὀρέγει τὸν στέφανον ὁ Ἄκαστϛ) or adjudicator (Amphiaraos vase, now lost, Berlin F1655). In addition, the later tradition records Amphidamas' son, Ganyktor, in the role of adjudicator at his father's funeral contest: *Certamen Homeri et Hesiodi*, 63.

[56] In his study of *mēnis* (1996) Muellner develops the idea that in the *Iliad* the 'fulfilment of the word's meaning is the teleology of the story' (Nagy's words in the foreword, vii). Might not final words – such as ἄεθλον ('prize') at *Il.* 23.897, which brings the funeral and contests of Patroklos to an end – play a similar role, perhaps deactivating *mēnis* and closing the story? If so then the dénouement contained in such a final utterance gives the *Iliad* the character of an aetiology for the institutions of a particular type of social organization – the *polis*.

[57] Tyrants in the archaic period were particularly concerned to confer upon their claims to sovereignty an objective legitimacy. The *kudos* of victory therefore becomes powerful symbolic capital which is dangerous to the *polis*. On epinikian ode and other civic responses to the talismanic authority of athletic *kudos*, see Kurke 1991 and 1993. For the special place of an Olympic chariot victory in the repertoire of tyrants and aristocrats in the archaic period, see especially Hönle 1972, 45–66. On a somewhat different tack, see Lévêque 1982. It should be noted, however, that the currency of the Panhellenic victory first required that these contests achieve wider recognition outside their immediate locales; see the instructive example of Kylon at Athens. For an example of the talismanic properties of a Panhellenic victor at Sparta, see Plut. *Lyk.* 22.4.

[58] To a large extent, what will follow has been elucidated, with different emphasis, long ago in the seminal article by Louis Gernet (1955), a surprising omission in Kyle's study.

[59] Φέρειν does not, however, exhaust the semantic field, see Gernet 1955, 10.

[60] Ἐπιδοῦναι has the more precise meaning of 'give as a supplement' as well as 'to give a dowry'; cf. *Il.* 9.148 = 9.290.

[61] Gernet 1955, 11: 'it is a personal gift that he [Achilles] presents him [Eumelos] with, entirely different from the prize which he was going to award him and which Antilochos' opposition compels him to refuse' ('c'est un don personnel qu'il lui fait, tout différent du prix qu'il allait lui attribuer et que l'opposition d'Antilochos oblige à lui refuser').

[62] For a discussion of the cunning skill (*mētis*) at work in this episode, see Vernant and Detienne 1991, 11–26.

[63] One other instance of δίδωμι in a prize context occurs at *Il.* 23.807, but the object given is clearly differentiated from the actual prize itself, as Gernet demonstrates (Gernet 1955, 12 n. 1).

[64] On which, see n. 5 above.

[65] Note the explicit reference to community authorization at *Il.* 23.660–2 when Achilles sets down the prizes for boxing: 'let him to whom Apollo grants endurance and whom all the Achaians recognize go back to his tent leading a hardworking mule' (ᾧ δέ κ᾽ Ἀπόλλων | δώῃ καμμονίην, γνώωσι δὲ πάντες Ἀχαιοί, | ἡμίονον ταλαεργὸν ἄγων κλισίηνδε νεέσθω).

⁶⁶ This fact is illustrated particularly by the increasing artistic depiction of the archetypal prize, the tripod, in order to evoke this kind of adjudicated value. See Fittschen 1969, 29–30, section F, nos. 1–8, for a list of the earliest examples and, in general, Maass 1981. The best example is a tripod dedicated at Olympia in the eighth century BC (Olympia B 1730) which bears a formulaic image of two athletes themselves contending over a tripod (the so-called 'Dreifußkämpferbein': Fittschen 1969, 29, section F, no. 4; Maass 1978, 55–7). This is one reason why tripods and *lebētes* figure prominently among the first kinds of identifiable standard, particularly in Crete of the early sixth century BC: *IC* 4, 1, l. 1(f), 3(a); *IC* 4, 5, l. 2; *IC* 4, 8 i+a–f ; *IC* 4, 14 (g–p); *IC* 4, 21, l. 8; *SEG* 35. 991. See also von Reden, 1997, 157–61. Von Reden also draws attention to Syracusan coins which are struck with the legend, AΘΛA, 'prizes' (1997, 165). To this observation one might add coins which bear as their stamp well-known prize signifiers such as early Athenian coins with a vase device, which may depict the Panathenaic amphora (e.g. Neils 1992, 190, no. 67). As von Reden rightly observes (1997, 168), it would seem that for some time one expression of value evoked the other and *vice versa*, prize-objects as currency, coins as prizes.

⁶⁷ The crown, perhaps a funeral garland (see n. 70), may have been originally an accessory to the prize as the particular sign of the victor in early funeral contests, as it is in one early representation of the games for Pelias (Paus. 5.17.10–11). The absence, however, of victor crowns in *Iliad* 23 prevents generalization.

⁶⁸ On this see Gernet 1981a, 138 ff. and now generally Kurke 1999. For Aristotle's theory of coin value, see *Politics* 1257a 31–41 (intrinsic metal value) and 1257b 10–14 (conventional value).

⁶⁹ Nagy 1979, 116–17.

⁷⁰ For the strong evidence that athletic crowns had funerary associations, see Rohde 1925, 141 n. 22. The statement of the Pindar scholion is supported by Clement of Alexandria to the same effect: *Protr.* II 34. The funereal garland set up at the funeral or on the tomb itself makes a strong visible chain of relations, victor – deceased – heir, which throws attention back on to the effective adjudication – a sign of authenticity – of the agonothetic heir. That hero-cult is essentially funerary in character and extends rituals of solidarity and legitimacy to a broader group conceived of as descendents of the dead hero, has been established on solid ground by Seaford 1994, chs. 3–5. For the entire *polis* represented as adjudicators, it is enough to note that athletic judges at Elis (Olympia) and Athens were drawn proportionally to the tribal organization of the city: *Hellanodikai*, Harpokration s.v. Ἑλλανοδίκαι = Aristotle *Eleiōn Politeia*, fr. 492 Rose; Hellanikos *FGrHist* 4 fr. 113; Aristodemos *FGrHist* 414 fr. 2; *Athlothetai, Ath. Pol.* 60. Note also Plutarch's story of the ease with which the ten *stratēgoi* at Athens could be made *ad hoc* judges of the tragic contest at the Dionysia (*Kimon* 8.7).

⁷¹ Note the anxious claims by the Elean *polis* to superlative institutional competence, Hdt. 2.160: we are the best athletic adjudicators in the world, aren't we?

⁷² Kekrops adjudicates, see Parker 1987, 198 with 210 n. 48 for references. Pindar, however, may be drawing on associations between Erechtheus and the Athenians in their capacity as *agōnothetai* of the Panathenaia at *Isth.* 2.19–20:

'...and when at shining Athens [Xenokrates of Akragas] was fitted out with the glorious favour of the sons of Erechtheus...' (καὶ τόθι κλεινιαῖς <τ'>Ἐρεχθειδᾶν χαρίτεσσιν ἀραρώς | ταῖς λιπαραῖς ἐν Ἀθάναις); cf. also Ἐρεχθέος ἀστοί, *Pyth.* 7.10. Although the use of Erechtheidai here need not be more than a poetic gloss for Athenians, it nevertheless tells us that the Athenians enjoyed being referred to collectively (and considered themselves) as the descendants of one of their most important cult heroes.

Bibliography

Amandry, P.
   1971   'Collection Paul Cannellopoulos (I): lébès de bronze', *BCH* 95, 585–626
Andronikos, M.
   1968   *Totenkult*, Archaeologica Homerica III, W, Göttingen.
Baudrillard, J.
   1996   *A System of Objects*, transl. J. Benedict, London and New York.
Benveniste, E.
   1973   *Indo-European Language and Society*, transl. E. Palmer, London.
Bourdieu, P.
   1977   *Outline of a Theory of Practice*, transl. R. Nice, Cambridge.
   1990   *The Logic of Practice*, trans. R. Nice, Oxford.
   1998   *Practical Reason: On the theory of action*, Cambridge.
Brown, A.
   1998   'Homeric talents and the ethics of exchange', *JHS* 118, 165–72.
Burkert, W.
   1985   *Greek Religion*, transl. J. Raffan, Harvard.
Carne-Ross, D.S.
   1985   *Pindar*, Yale.
Chantraine, P.
   1968–80   *Dictionnaire étymologique de la langue grecque*, Paris.
Cunliffe, R.J.
   1963   *Lexicon of the Homeric Dialect*, Norman, Okla.
Detienne, M.
   1996   *The Masters of Truth in Archaic Greece*, transl. J. Lloyd, New York.
Dickie, M.W.
   1984   'Fair and foul play in the funeral games in the *Iliad*', *Journal of Sport History* 11, 8–17.
Donlan, W.
   1981   'Scale, value, and function in the Homeric economy', *AJAH* 6, 101–17.
   1982   'Reciprocities in Homer', *CW* 75, 137–75.
Ebeling, H.
   1885   *Lexicon Homericum*. Reprinted 1963 by Hildesheim, Leipzig.

Finley, M.I.
1978   *The World of Odysseus*, 2nd edn, Harmondsworth.
Fittschen, K.
1969   *Untersuchungen zum Beginn der Sagendarstellungen bei den Griechen*, Berlin.
Frisk, H.
1970–3 *Griechisches etymologisches Wörterbuch*, Heidelberg.
Gernet, L.
1955   'Jeux et droit (remarques sur le XXIIIᶜ chant de l'*Iliade*)', in L. Gernet *Droit et société dans la Grèce ancienne*, Paris, 9–18.
1981a   '"Value" in Greek myth', in R.L. Gordon (ed.) *Myth, Religion and Society*, Cambridge, 111–46.
1981b   'Law and pre-law in ancient Greece', in L. Gernet, *The Anthropology in Ancient Greece*, transl. J. Hamilton, S.J. and B. Nagy, Baltimore, 143–215.
Harrison, A.R.W.
1968   *Law of Athens*, vol. 1, Oxford.
1971   *Law of Athens*, vol. 2, Oxford.
Hönle, A.
1972   *Olympia in der Politik der griechischen Staatenwelt*, Bebenhausen.
Jeffery, L.
1990   *The Local Scripts of Archaic Greece*, 2nd edn, Oxford.
Kurke, L.
1991   *The Traffic in Praise: Pindar and the poetics of social economy*, Princeton.
1993   'The economy of *kudos*', in L. Kurke and C. Dougherty (eds.) *Cultural Poetics in Archaic Greece: Cult, performance, politics*, Cambridge, 131–63.
1999   *Coins, Bodies, Games and Gold: The politics of meaning in archaic Greece*, Princeton.
Kyle, D.G.
1984   'Non-competition in Homeric sport: spectatorship and status' *Stadion* 10, 1–19.
1996   'Gifts and Glory: Panathenaic and other Greek athletic prizes', in J. Neils (ed.) *Worshipping Athena: Panathenaia and Parthenon*, Madison, 106–36.
Lambert, S.D.
1993   *The Phratries of Attica*, Ann Arbor.
Laser, S.
1987   *Sport und Spiel*, Archaeologica Homerica III, T, Göttingen.
Lévêque, P.
1982   'Approche ethno-historique des concours grecs', *Klio* 64, 5–20.
Loraux, N.
1975   '*Hebe* et *andreia* : deux versions de la mort du combattant athénien', *AncSoc* 6, 1–31.

Maass, M.
   1978   *Die geometrischen Dreifüsse von Olympia*, Olympische Forschungen 10, Berlin.
   1981   'Die Geometrischen Dreifüsse von Olympia', *AK* 24, 6–20.
Macleod, C.W.
   1982   *Homer, Iliad XXIV*, Cambridge.
Malten, L.
   1923–4   'Leichenspiele und Totenkult', *MDAI (R)* 38/39, 300–40.
   1925   'Leichenagon', *RE* 12, 1859–61.
Martin, R.
   1989   *The Language of Heroes*, Ithaca.
Muellner, L.
   1976   *The Meaning of Homeric* εὔχομαι *through its Formulas*, Innsbruck.
   1996   *The Anger of Achilles*, Ithaca.
Nagy, G.
   1979   *Best of the Achaeans*, Baltimore.
   1990   *Pindar's Homer*, Baltimore.
Neils, J.
   1992   'Catalogue of the Exhibition', in J. Neils (ed.) *Goddess and Polis: The Panathenaic festival in ancient Athens*, Princeton, 143–91.
Nowag, W.
   1983   *Raub und Beute in der archaischen Zeit der Griechen*, Frankfurt.
Parker, R.
   1987   'Myths of early Athens', in J. Bremmer (ed.) *Interpretations of Greek Mythology*, London, 187–214.
Raaflaub, K.
   1998   'A historian's headache: how to read "Homeric society"', in N. Fisher and H. van Wees (eds.) *Archaic Greece: New approaches and new evidence*, London, 169–93.
Redfield, J.
   1983   'The economic man', in C.A. Rubino and C.W. Shelmerdine (eds.) *Approaches to Homer*, Austin, 218–47.
Rhodes, P.J.
   1981   *A Commentary on the Aristotelian* Athenaion Politeia, Oxford.
Richardson, N.
   1993   *The* Iliad: *A commentary: Vol. VI: Books 21–24*, Cambridge.
Rohde, E.
   1925   *Psyche: The cult of souls and belief in immortality among the Greeks*, trans. W.B. Hillis, London.
Roller, L.
   1981   'Funeral games for historical persons', *Stadion* 7, 1–18.
Rubenstein, L.
   1993   *Adoption in IV Century Athens*, Copenhagen.
Scanlon, T.F.
   1983   'The vocabulary of competition: *agōn* and *aethlos*, Greek terms for contest', *Arete: The Journal of Sport Literature* 1, 147–62.

Schwyzer, E.
  1923   *Dialectorum Graecarum exempla epigraphica potiora*. Reprinted in 1960 by Hildesheim, Leipzig.
Seaford, R.
  1994   *Reciprocity and Ritual*, Oxford.
Sealey, R.
  1994   *The Justice of the Greeks*, Ann Arbor.
Thür, G.
  1970   'Zum *dikazein* bei Homer', *Zeitschrift der Savigny-Stiftung für Rechtsgeschichte, romanistische Abteilung* 87, 426–44.
Ulf, C. and Weiler, I.
  1980   'Der Ursprung der antiken Olympischen Spiele in der Forschung', *Stadion* 6, 1–38.
Vernant, J.-P.
  1983   'The representation of the invisible and the psychological category of the double: the Kolossos', in J.-P. Vernant *Myth and Thought among the Greeks*, London and Boston, 305–20.
  1991a 'A "beautiful death" and the disfigured corpse in Homeric epic', in J.-P. Vernant *Mortals and Immortals: Collected Essays*, Princeton, 50–74.
  1991b 'From the 'presentification' of the invisible to the imitation of images', in J.-P. Vernant *Mortals and Immortals*, Princeton, 151–63.
Vernant, J.-P. and Detienne, M.
  1991   *Cunning Intelligence in Greek Culture and Society*, transl. J. Lloyd, Chicago.
Von Reden, S.
  1995   *Exchange in Ancient Greece*, London.
  1997   'Money, law and exchange: coinage in the Greek *polis*', *JHS* 117, 154–76.
West, M.L.
  1978   *Hesiod: Works and Days*, Oxford.
Willetts, R.F.
  1967   *The Law Code of Gortyn*, Berlin.

7

THE POLITICS OF DANCE: DITHYRAMBIC CONTEST AND SOCIAL ORDER IN ANCIENT GREECE

Peter Wilson

Agōn, *stasis* and 'the labour of choruses'

When our predecessor in the study of ancient festivals – Hadrian's freed slave, Phlegon of Tralles – turned his attention to the greatest of all ancient *agōnes*, his stab at scholarly fame was to try to popularize a revisionist chronology of the earliest days of the Olympics. He wanted to accommodate the venerable foundation stories centred around Pelops and Herakles with the influential body of learning in favour of Koroibos and 776. Phlegon bridged the gap between myth and history with a story of ritual neglect that led to social discord (*FGrH* 257 F1):

> After the Peloponnesians had abandoned the observance of the *panēgyris* for a period…and neglected the *agōn*, *stasis* broke out throughout the Peloponnese. In a desire to establish peace and *homonoia* among the people once more, Lykourgos the Lakedaimonian…and Iphitos…and Kleosthenes decided to revive the Olympic *panēgyris* to its ancient practices and reinstate the gymnic *agōn*.

Few historians turn to Phlegon to bolster their attempts to raise the date of the first Olympiad. But his explanatory impulse is extremely illuminating for a different reason – for the clarity with which it relates the *agōn* and *stasis*, formal festival competition and uncontrolled social violence within the community. It struck Phlegon as the most plausible way of explaining the intermission and later reappearance of the Olympics to posit the outbreak of *stasis* in the broad region hosting the Games after they had been allowed to fall into neglect. And the *agōn* was the antidote to *stasis* naturally prescribed by the leading men of Sparta, Elis and Pisa – what we might see as a controlled version of the same thing.

Though it was never part of the *Olympic* formula, the *khoros* is a prime (and neglected) instrument in the armoury of Greek festival culture to perform this kind of social 'work'. The cogent sociological interpretation of competition which views it as a form of displaced violence is generally applied only to Greek sport;[1] the competitive *khoros* should be placed in the same perspective. It is also important to see at a more general level how the *khoros* occupies a position in a spectrum of collective activities that leads, at one extreme, to war – passing on its way through more manifestly athletic activities of a kind found in the Olympics, such as the race in armour and the javelin throwing of the pentathlon. Sokrates was credited with the statement that 'Whoever honours the gods best with *khoroi* are the best in war' (Athenaios 628e), and this expresses a proximity rather more than a distinction: the most widespread form of military dance found across Greece – the *pyrrhikhē* – was a strictly choral activity showing some affinities with the dithyramb.[2] It is sometimes remarked that the Greeks had little in the way of team sports, and that war came closest to the mark; but the *khoros*, particularly the agonistic *khoros*, is perhaps a better candidate.

As a means for the displacement of violence, the *khoros* is a much more sophisticated mechanism than, say, the *pankration*, involving as it does the complexity of verbal narrative, music and movement from a highly trained collective with a distinct and shared social identity. Consider the account given by Pausanias of the election of the famous Sixteen Women of Elis: the eldest, the most pre-eminent in worth and repute of women from each of the sixteen cities in Elis, were chosen 'to put an end to the issues that divided [the Eleans and Pisatans]' after the fall of the tyranny of Damophon (5.16.5). Among their tasks were the organization of the *agōnes* of the Heraia, the weaving of the *peplos* for Hera and the establishment of two *khoroi* (5.16.6). We cannot say whether these *khoroi* competed against one another, but it is certainly clear that they formed some part of the 'solution' to the problems of discord dividing the northern Peloponnese in the archaic period. And it is also clear that Dionysos loomed large in their performance: theirs is the ancient cletic hymn to Dionysos that invokes the hero-god in the form of a bull (*PMG* 871).[3] This hymn may have been a dithyramb, or at least a precursor to the form. And in this chapter I shall argue that in certain of its manifestations, Dionysos' dithyramb – probably the most widespread and long-lived form of *khoreia* in the Greek world – served this important function of socio-political *katharsis* through dance and song.

The neglected genre
Dithyramb is the ugly sister of the Dionysian family. While the last thirty years have seen an explosion of fruitful approaches to her dramatic siblings, dithyramb has not enjoyed the sort of interest expressed in them. Part of the problem is the lack of surviving texts. But at least as far as Athens is concerned, we have better evidence for the context of

dithyrambic performance than we do for drama.[4] One feature of the problem is dithyramb's apparent (Dionysian?) ability to change its shape so readily. Literary histories of the genre tend to plot its move from a primitive cult song to a hypersophisticated artistic spectacle watched by thousands in the theatres of Athens alongside the equally sophisticated performances of drama. Pickard-Cambridge's epigrammatic judgment is fairly typical: 'Thus the history of the dithyramb proves to be a somewhat puzzling and disappointing affair.'[5] Put more positively, dithyramb offers itself as an intriguing litmus of the changing character of Greek *mousikē* over a span of more than half a millennium, and so of the changing character of Greek culture itself. The scope of this chapter will permit only limited exploration of some less-travelled paths that may point to new directions in the larger picture.

To begin near the end: the importance of dithyramb in the Hellenistic period and beyond scarcely registers in the scholarly literature. But contrary to rumour, the *khoros* did not wither away at the close of the classical period. It remained for centuries a major cultural institution for social re-creation and reflection, particularly for reflection on issues of social cohesion. In the second century *of the common era*, his gaze fixed (imaginatively at least) on the prize tripods erected in the Rhodian Dionysion, Aelius Aristeides called the Rhodians away from *stasis* to *homonoia* (concord) by means of a comparison with a very ancient pedigree (Oration 24.52):

> Look at these tripods... do you think that these ever would have been erected if the members of each *khoros* fought among themselves? Or is it not quite clear that even if they did not sing in opposite ways or each member something different, but all sang the same text, yet not in the same way, all that would be left for them would be to flee the stage? Indeed, no *khoros* out of harmony is so unpleasant a spectacle as the people of Rhodes in disagreement.

The analogy between a single, unified and euphonous *khoros* and a well-ordered community is indeed ancient (e.g. Xen. *Oec.* 8.3), but it could only be effective here because the practices and mentalities on which it is based persist into Aristeides' own age. Pausanias confirms the fact with a complaint, made in an editorial aside, that 'there are many and false traditions current among the mass of mankind, since they are ignorant of history and consider trustworthy whatever they heard from childhood in *khoroi*...' (1.3.3).

By the closing decades of the *fourth* century BC, the *kyklios khoros*, the circular *khoros* of dithyramb,[6] was widely established as an event of major significance in which the festival community – and that, as far as we can tell, is equivalent to the political community[7] – performed choral songs, usually at a Dionysia and usually in a competitive format. They surface in Kyrene as early as 330, where in their annual accounts the *dēmiourgoi* (civic magistrates) reckon the expense of providing their leaders with a bull, the traditional beast of dithyramb.[8] Later in the century Antiokhos son of Seleukos was diplomatically honoured with an invitation to front-row seats 'at the *kyklioi agōnes*' of the Milesian Dionysia as well as the Didymeia for Apollo.[9] We can trace a tradition of boys dancing competitively for Dionysos on the island of Khios stretching over a period of some five hundred years.[10] They were an integral part of the Eretrian Dionysia by the fourth century, and it was at this particular event that the citizens of Eretria chose to announce honours for their benefactors.[11] This last feature is also reproduced elsewhere. And it casts an important light on the wider socio-political role of the event, evidently seen by these cities as the prime moment of collective display and civic self-presentation. It was, for instance, just before *khoroi* of Arkesinian boys danced for Dionysos in their island home on Amorgos that that city honoured its benefactors.[12] While at Athens the *tragic agōn* had long been the preferred event for such action,[13] it is the *dithyrambic khoros* that attracts this attention elsewhere. The reason is surely that, in the Hellenistic age, these *khoroi* had a tenaciously epichoric character, and were certainly filled by citizens, or by citizens-in-training in the case of the *paides* (boys). In these cities in this age tragedy was, by contrast, increasingly a product provided by travelling, trans-*polis* professionals.

This long Hellenistic chapter in the history of dithyramb is for us a chapter more or less entirely without poetry. By a lucky chance we do know that works of the arch innovators of late-fifth-century dithyramb, Timotheos and Philoxenos, had become sufficiently 'mainstream' to be central to the programme of state education of youths in Arkadia, who probably sang these in the theatre at their massive new post-synoecism centre of Megalopolis from the fourth century, and in the new tribes that were to be the basis for their interaction as a state.[14] This tribal configuration is another important and revealing phenomenon: the reflex to pattern a community's *khoreia* according to this major ethnic or territorial articulation of the citizenry was very widespread. Among the cases just cited tribal configuration is certain or likely in Megalopolis, Kyrene and Eretria. *Khoroi* drawn from the Dorian tribes danced competitively on third-century Kos in a fascinating event described as the *kyklios khoros tai pyrrhikhai*, – 'dithyramb à la *pyrrhikhē*', evidently a special kind of dithyramb with a marked militaristic aspect.[15] On Rhodes, after the massive island-wide synoecism of 408, the three old major cities became the local focal points of new tribes, and these provided patterning for a wide range of agonistic interaction. That the *kyklioi khoroi* of men and boys were the most important of them all is suggested again by the fact that it was here that crowns were awarded to benefactors of the new Rhodian state.[16]

When this tradition of tribally-affiliated *khoroi* became formally agonistic is difficult to determine, and in any case it may be misguided to look for a simple pattern of linear progression. Tantalizing scraps of Alkman hint at young women dancing – perhaps for Dionysos – in *khoroi* drawn from the tribes of early Sparta: the girls affiliated with the Dorian tribe Dymanes, the 'curl-loving Dymainai', are explicitly so named in one fragment of their songs, suggesting a sense of performed tribal identity that is hard to find in the better-documented world of Athenian tribal *khoreia*.[17] An ancient commentator may tell us that these '[D]ymain[ai] often came to Pitane to join in [? *khoroi*] with the girls of Pitane'.[18] The fact that the crucial word 'join in *khoroi*' (συγ[χορεύσουσαι]) is largely a supplement does not help us much in our search for the earliest signs of formal choral competition.[19]

The ends were many and varied to which the tribal systems of the Greeks were put. They were a supple means for rethinking and reshaping communities on a global scale and in response to change. It is common to find major tribal re-organizations following the downfall of tyrannies and the military and political crises that resulted, to glimpse them strategically deployed against neighbours in territorial or cultural rivalry, and as a means of firming up internal stability in communities divided against themselves.[20] The habit of making choral performance one of the principal activities of tribes points to its perceived value in all these areas of enormous social and political importance. I shall return in my conclusion to the most famous tribal re-organization of all, that of Kleisthenes the Athenian – and to the way dithyrambic *khoroi* played their part in this vastly influential reshaping of Attike.

Athenian dithyramb

First I want to glance at the broader picture of dithyramb in classical Athens, because although not its first historical home, only from Athens do we have a (relative) density of information as to the place and organization of dithyramb in a city's festival scene. The material is well known, so I adopt a selective approach.

The crudest indicator that the Athenians did not share modern scholars' distaste for the genre is the fact that they filled their festival calendar with dozens of dithyrambs. There were in the region of fifty *khoroi* dancing each year by the time Lykourgos added 'no fewer than three *kyklioi khoroi*' ([Plu.] *Mor.* 842a) to the Peiraieus Dionysia around 330. Well before that time it had firm grounding not only at the City Dionysia, but also at Apollo's

Thargelia; at that most urban of festivals, the Panathenaia; and probably also at the city festivals for Prometheus and Hephaistos. This pre-eminently *urban* siting of Athenian dithyramb is worth noting: there are *very* few indications that it had much of a life in the demes – unlike drama.[21]

To frequency we must add scale of material support and social estimation. At the most prestigious occasion, the City Dionysia, there were two categories – men's and boys' dithyramb – with ten *khoroi* in each, for almost two hundred years. The *khoroi* were fifty-strong, their members drawn representatively from the tribes of Kleisthenes. In an important sense this was clearly the most prestigious and magnificent of *all* festival performances contested between Athenians (something students of drama systematically underestimate). These *agōnes* were a major focus of the attention of the city, and vast resources of wealth were diverted to them: by my rough estimation, the city, through its élite of wealth, spent in the region of a *hundred* talents on their training and presentation in the course of a single decade.[22]

For Athenian boys, such dancing for Dionysos could be construed as a vital act of early political or pre-political participation.[23] Training for an extended period with fellow-boys from one's tribe, drawn from geographically diverse regions of Attike, will have helped develop the early stages of a sense of tribal solidarity that would be important to later socio-political and military life.[24] Consistent with this 'parapolitical' character, the constituencies of the *men's khoroi* show a clear analogy with that of the democratic Council, similarly constituted by fifties across the tribes.[25] Conversely, participation in the Council was also an agonistic business: its internal proceedings were conducted as a *competition* between the tribes, for the title of 'winning' *prytaneis*. The language used of this is very like that used of choral contests – a nice illustration of the parallels that existed between political and cultural performance in Athenian society. A formal judgment (*krisis*) was passed on the tribes' performance in the Council, and individual tribes praised and honoured members who had 'vanquished' their fellows in the Council.[26]

A word on the songs these Athenian boys and men were singing. The City Dionysia alone required twenty dithyrambs each year, and there is every indication that new compositions were the rule in the classical period. The almost total loss of the hundreds of dithyrambs created for Athenian festivals leaves us incapable of making secure pronouncements about possible forms of self-representation adopted by the *khoroi*, and by the tribes. There is little sign that they sang and danced as Pandionidai or Erekhtheidai, in the way that those Spartan girls of the Dymanes (or from Dyma) apparently had sung as Dymainai; or that their songs explored the traditions, myths and cults associated with their Eponyms. We can point to the part of Aigeus in Bakkhylides' dithyramb for the Athenians (18) that may have suited some prominent man and skilful singer of the tribe Aigeis, but still, the *khoros* does not obviously sing in a manner that foregrounds their status *as* Aigeidai.[27] Perhaps there was an active mythopoetics at work here that brought the Eponyms to life. In the early days, when they were new to their tasks, this could have been an important way of rooting the Eponyms in an Attic past suitable to their new careers, and of forging a sense of tribal identification with them – perhaps especially important for those heroes who already had an established local home in a particular Attic deme. It was clearly within the *urban* environment that a man normally expressed and most acutely felt his relation with his Eponym: most of their sanctuaries were in or near central Athens, and joining in *khoroi* that told of their actions in Athenian myth – or supporting one's team in the theatre as it did so – will have been a highly participatory and pleasurable means of making a *phylētēs* of the *dēmotēs*.[28]

From the hypothetical to the reasonably probable: in addition to the markers of Dionysiac cult-song we should expect to find that a strain of *polis-*encomium characterised at least some of this poetry. And this is certainly relevant to the way in which a vision of a unified city – over and above its individual tribes – may have been promulgated in Athenian dithyramb, for all its competitive character. The indications point to praise of Athens' military prowess and role within the wider Greek world – hardly surprising for *khoroi* of men whose principal mode of interaction was in their military units. One of the surviving 'Athenian' fragments of Pindar is the famous passage (it opened the song) that sounds as much like a hymn to the city as to the god: 'O shining and violet-crowned and celebrated in song, bulwark of Hellas, famous Athens, divine citadel!' (fr. 76 M).[29] Fr. 77 M probably comes from the same poem, and describes Artemision as the place 'where the sons of the Athenians laid the bright foundation of freedom'.

Another of Pindar's Athenian dithyrambs (fr. 75 M) weaves praise of the city into its religious agenda. It begins with a summoning of the Olympian gods to join in the *khoros*, to shower it in 'glorious grace' as they come to the 'city's crowded, incense-rich navel in holy Athens', and its 'famous agora which shows on all sides the products of artists.' This summoning of the gods to enter the mortal *khoros* at the heart of Athens is no mere metaphor. It expresses a desired fusion of god and mortal in Dionysiac dance that is common to early dithyramb, and that is indeed a principal modality of Dionysiac religion. Only Dionysos could achieve such a mixing of men and gods. What seems to distinguish this from other instances is the way it 'begins from Zeus' (Διόθεν 8) and moves on 'with splendour of songs secondly to that ivy-knowing god', and so places the worship of Dionysos and his mother firmly in the wider context of the civic pantheon. The emphasis on the *agora* as a flourishing and famous religious and commercial centre is more than a choreographic deictic. It reflects the degree to which, in Athens, Dionysiac dance and song is an event that brings all together at the centre of the populous and prosperous city – those very qualities being guaranteed by the performance of dithyramb.[30]

Apollo's Thargelia is the second most important home of tribal dithyramb in Athens. It is perhaps a little odd to find the devotion of scores of dithyrambs to Apollo in a city where we listen in vain to hear the sound of his more familiar hymn, the paian.[31] The issue is complex, but there are good reasons why Pythian Apollo might be willing to share ritual practices with Dionysos: he certainly shared his sanctuary at Delphi with Dionysos, a situation possibly replicated in the Attic deme of Ikarion.[32] The Thargelia was a festival of civic 'purification' – and those ritually expelled appear to have had the curiously Dionysiac name of 'pig- (or is it fig-?) bakkhants' (Hellad. in Photios *Bibl.* p. 534b). When at Delphi, Dionysos received 'winter dithyrambs', and his cult there had major eschatological associations – both facts which might make this sharing of dithyramb more intelligible and which will be relevant to my subsequent discussion of Pindaric dithyramb. For Dionysos' dance-song had powerful associations with ideas of cleansing and renewal, particularly of civic renewal.

Much of the accepted wisdom about the development of dithyramb in the later fifth century must be at least approximately right: under the impetus of an increasingly competitive and professional musical culture of spectators and performers, the form was transferred to the worship of gods whose cultic ties to it were more tenuous. It is rarely remarked that the notorious complaint of 'Nothing to do with Dionysos' was levelled against dithyramb as much as tragedy (Zenobios 5.40). We *could* think of this in terms of the fashioning of new and relevant forms of religious and perform-ance experience. However, the usual interpretation comes with a lapsarian spin, derived as it is from conservative critics whose attacks were couched in moral and aesthetic terms but were driven largely by ideological distaste. As Eric Csapo has recently emphasised, the music industry of the age had given a new and powerful independence to a broad group of performers from non-élite backgrounds.[33] All the same, we can point to *some* kind of continuity, even at the baroque heights of the 'New Music', of traditional Dionysian themes: Timotheos himself composed a famous '*Birthpangs of Semele*' (*PMG* 792), and if the musical and physical *mimēsis* employed in its execution offended Aristotle and his type (cf. *Poet.* 1461b), that need not mean that it was empty of all religious meaning for its broader audience.

Pindaric dithyramb

From this snapshot of the place of dithyrambic dance-song in classical Athens, I turn to some important evidence for its operation beyond Athens in the early classical period. In the scraps of Pindaric dithyramb it is possible to trace elements of a wider pattern. This has at its heart the god who sometimes shares with his mortal worshippers the experience of death, yet who also transcends it. I would suggest that dithyramb brings this god – normally seen as the preserve of devotees initiated into a specific 'mystery' cult – into the most public religious arena, and so harnesses to the benefit of the city as such the resources of cleansing and regeneration that lay in his mythic store. The political sickness of a community divided against itself in *stasis* is prominent among the ills to which this choral cure is applied; and it is here that we return to the powerful socio-political pragmatics of dance.[34]

Pindar's 'Korinthian' dithyramb (fr. 70c) will form the focus of my discussion:[35]

```
                         ]ναλ[
                         ]
                         ]ϱιτο μὲν στάσις·
                         ]πόδα
          5      ] ατε[. . . . . ]ον κυανοχίτων
                         ]τεὰν τε[λετ]ὰν μελίζοι
                         ]πλόκον σ[τεφά]νων κισσίνων
                         ]κρόταφον[ ]
                         ]εωγ ἐλθὲ φίλαν δὴ πόληα
          10     ]ιόν τε σκόπελον γείτονα πρύτανιγ[
                         ]αμα· καὶ στρατιά
                         ]τ᾽ ἀκναμπτεὶ κρέμασον
                         ]ς τε χάρμας
                         ]π [ . . . .] γτος αὐχὴν ῥύοιτο πα[
          15             ]ωγ πέλοι
                         ]λαν πόνοι χορῶν [
                         ]εες τ᾽ ἀοιδαί·
                         ]οιο φῦλον ϙ[
          19     ]ϙ πετάλοις ἠρ[ινοῖς
                         desunt 2 vv.
          22     ]μιον ἰπ[π
                         ]τι ταμίας[
                         ]ν στολο[
          25     ]λθε[
                         ]. ν[. . .
```

3: παύσ]αιτο (Schroeder) καταλύ]οιτο (van der
Weiden) μὴ γέν]οιτο (Zimmermann)
13 Σ: τὰς ἐπιδορατίδας

...may *stasis* [be resolved/cease]
...foot
5   ...with a dark blue tunic
...may [. .] sing of your festival
...wreath of ivy crowns
...temple
...come to the city that is dear indeed
10   ...and to the neighbouring rock that is lord[36]
...and the army
...inflexibly hang up
...and spear-heads
...may the neck rescue
15   ...may there be
...labours of *khoroi*.
...and songs;
...tribe of . .
19   ...leaves of spring.

22   ...?of horses . .
...steward . . .

I dub the piece 'Korinthian' because Korinth is the least bad guess as the commissioning city and place of performance. Bury thought that the expression 'the neighbouring rock that is lord' (10) was especially appropriate for the geography of the Akrokorinth, while the 'neck' (14) to which the singers look for protection later in the poem could be a reference to the natural military defence provided by the Isthmos.[37] This was moreover a city that made energetic claims on the paternity of dithyramb itself: 'Korinth' is the answer to Pindar's own rhetorical question at *Olympian* 13.18–19 as to 'Whence came the delights of Dionysos, with the ox-driving dithyramb?'

In what may have been the opening lines of their song,[38] the *khoros* seem to express a wish that bears on the immediate context of their performance – a wish that *stasis* should no longer engulf their city. 'May *stasis* end' or 'May *stasis* be resolved' are the best suggestions for making sense of the remains of line 3.[39] Someone – maybe the *khoros* itself – is then called upon to 'sing of your festival' (6), where 'you' is certainly Dionysos and the singer (or Dionysos himself) is wearing a dark tunic (5). If worn by the *khoros*, the dark tunic may suggest grief or mourning, and so suit a situation of real civil disaster in action or recently passed. But if sported by a god, it is very likely to be Demeter (cf. *Hymn. Hom.* 2.319, 360, 374). And there are good reasons for thinking that Demeter is involved: Korinth is one of the few places where she and Dionysos shared mystery-cults (Lerna is the most prominent other). Indeed, archaeology has revealed something that Pausanias failed to mention – that Dionysos received worship under the Akrokorinth itself in the great sanctuary of Demeter and Kore. Perhaps in this song Demeter was being asked to serve as the welcoming deity to the god whose position in her sanctuary was evidently that of a special visitor. Perhaps it was performed in the intimate, rock-cut theatral area now known to have formed part of the goddess' complex, where a terracotta mask and name-plate of Dionysos have also been found.[40]

There follow references to a wreath of ivy crowns on the temples of someone's head. Then comes the distinctive summoning of the god: '...come to the city that is dear indeed...and the neighbouring rock that is lord' (9–10). This intense cletic appeal is much more than a necessary formal element of the dithyramb. It is, in an important sense, the pragmatic religious heart of the performance, inducing the active involvement of this god of epiphanies in his own choral performance and to the benefit of his sedulous worshippers. The prayer articulates a divine itinerary with some clarity: he is, it seems, asked to appear in his shrine in the city centre and (?) then ascend to the heights of the Akrokorinth.[41]

It is more than likely that this epiphany is meant to *give effect* to the *khoros*' earlier prayer, the wish that *stasis* should end. This would also make sense of the following references to an army; of the order to hang up [shields?] and spear-heads; and, perhaps, of the curious hope in line 14: 'may the neck rescue'. Zimmermann makes the bold but attractive suggestion that in this salvational neck we should see a reference to 'der ekstatische Taumel': the ecstatic frenzy of Dionysiac dance with its characteristic head-flinging might well be depicted in this way as an active agent in bringing an end to military aggression.[42] Such a reading would be consistent with the familiar motif that with the end of military violence comes the return of Dionysiac pleasures, especially the pleasures of the seasonal life of agriculture – a return symbolized by the putting under the yoke of the bull's αὐχήν at Hesiod *Works and Days* 815–16, an action perhaps also anticipated hopefully in the 'rescuing neck' here.[43] It at least seems clear that a close and causal relation is established between the appearance of Dionysos among his performing choral worshippers in the festival and an end to *stasis*.[44]

We do not have much more: a shipwrecked reference to the 'labours of *khoroi*', to 'songs', to 'a tribe' and to 'spring leaves'. It is a fair guess that these 'choral toils' and 'songs' self-referentially describe the *khoros*' own performance of this springtime dithyramb, and expound on the idea of its social *work*.[45] And the evidence, archaeological and textual, points to a cult of Dionysos with a distinctly mystic or 'teletic' (cf. line 6 τε[λετ]ὰν) character as the religious and performative environment for this piece.[46] The special powers of such a cult are being summoned to the aid of the *polis* by means of the performance of a major dance-song for (and with) the god. This is the 'sweet toil, the weariness happily unwearying' in which the mainads are engaged as they enter in Euripides' *Bakkhai* (66–7) – a choral entrance-song that is effectively a dithyramb on the tragic stage.[47]

Vestiges of Dionysiac mystery cult have long been divined in the language of extant Attic drama; the importance of aspects of mystic initiation in Euripides' *Bakkhai* is now generally acknowledged.[48] There are also clear hints in what is perhaps our oldest testimony to the dithyramb, the boast of Arkhilokhos – or rather of his projected and performed persona as dithyrambic *exarkhōn* – that 'I know how to lead the fair song of lord Dionysos, the dithyramb, when my wits are blasted with wine' (fr. 120 W: ὡς Διονύσου ἄνακτος καλὸν ἐξάρξαι μέλος οἶδα διθύραμβον οἴνωι συγκεραυνωθεὶς φρένας). The extremely rare word συγκεραυνῶ fuses the fate of Dionysos' mother, blasted by Zeus' lightning – an event central to the mystic aspects of Dionysiac theology – with the experience of the dithyrambic *khoros*-leader and poet under the effect of wine. And this shared experience of cosmic incineration may have had a parallel for the bakkhic initiand in the use of a stunning 'epiphanic' light.[49] One of the core mythic stories of dithyramb was that of the god's birth: and this was always a *second* birth – that, indeed, is the most popular among the ancient etymologies of the term 'dithyramb' itself.[50] Inextricably connected to the story of the god's (re)birth is that of the death and rescue of his mother Semele from Hades. Semele herself is virtually a co-recipient with her son of the dithyramb.

Only very recently, however, have the mystic associations of a number of other Pindaric dithyrambs been revealed, at the same time as archaeology has been rolling back the date by which we can confidently claim that Greeks in some numbers turned to Dionysos the 'Liberator' (*Lysios*), Dionysos 'god of ecstatic *bakkhoi*' (*Bakkhios*) in the hope of liberation from ills in and after this life.[51] Two of Pindar's dithyrambs that survive in scraps from Oxyrhynkhos were very probably commissioned by the Argives (frs. 70a, 70d M). The Argive hero Perseus, who came into conflict with Dionysos, figures prominently in both. Those who have given the issue any thought consider the Argive Agr[i]ania as the most likely performance-context for these dithyrambs – a 'festival of the dead' (νεκύσια: Hesykh. s.v.) for one of the daughters of Proitos, who had been driven mad for refusing to accept the τελεταί of Dionysos (Hesiod fr. 131 M-W).[52] However, there is another candidate, the event held around a famous watery entrance to the underworld, the stagnant, bottomless lake Alkyone at Lerna, about ten kilometres south of the city.[53] The cult of Dionysos in this mysterious region clearly had a mystic dimension.[54] And the festival in some sense served a *kathartic* role for the city of Argos; as much is implied by the proverbial status of 'Lerna' in antiquity as a kind of rubbish-dump of ritual refuse and evils. It was here for instance that the embarrassing remains of the forty-nine severed heads of the Aigyptids were discarded (Hesykh. s.v. Λέρνη κακῶν; cf. Strabo 8.6.8).

Dionysos shared the place with Demeter. He was known there by the name *Saōtēs*, the Saviour.[55] Pausanias says that it was not religiously permissible for him to write 'for everyone' about the nocturnal *drōmena* for the god that took place there (2.37.5–6), but what can be salvaged from Pausanias' reticence and other evidence reveals a story of how Dionysos leapt into the murky depths to rescue his mother. This tale of maternal salvation became intertwined with a characteristic resistance myth, though one with a very distinctive twist: Perseus vigorously opposed the arrival of the god, and Dionysos appears – extraordinarily – to have been defeated, perhaps even killed in the conflict that followed. Perseus cast Dionysos into the 'Lernaian lake'.[56] Death was certainly the fate met by the mainads, collectively called the *Haliai*, who came together across the sea from the Aigean islands to assist their god. Pausanias points out the tomb of their leader to the north of the agora in the city, the aptly-named *Khoreia* (2.20.4; 2.37.7–8; cf. 2.22.1). At the culminating point of the orgiastic *drōmena*, Dionysos was summoned from the Underworld by the Argives – perhaps from death – by musical means, with trumpets concealed in *thyrsoi*.[57] The commissioning and execution of a prestigious Pindaric dithyramb, at the heart of which the god is summoned to make such an epiphany, may well have been the analogue, at the grand end of the performative scale, of this musical evocation of the god from Hades that was the central story of the mystic god's 'passion'. And, just as '*Khoreia*' – the mainad 'Dance-song' herself – had been destroyed along with her god, she too is emphatically 'reborn' in the choral dance-and-song that enacts the summoning of Dionysos from the Underworld.[58] Indeed, the dithyrambic *khoreia* of ritual restores the mythic *khoreia* of the god's original advent, forever correcting the scene of conflict and disorder that surrounded its first appearance in the city.

The mystic associations of another Pindaric dithyramb, this one composed for the god's and poet's own city of Thebes, were to some extent clear already from its principal fragment and title, the *Herakles* or *Kerberos*. But in the 1960s they took on an altogether new dimension with the reinstatement to the song of an orphaned fragment that tells among other things of the establishment of a teletic ritual for (?) the townsfolk in honour of 'Phersephona…and the gold-throned mother, *from Eleusis*'. These are the principal fragments:

Fr. 70b M[59]

Πρὶν μὲν εἷρπε σχοινοτένειά τ᾽ ἀοιδὰ
     διθυράμβων
καὶ τὸ σὰν κίβδηλον ἀνθρώποισιν ἀπὸ στομάτων,
διαπέπ[τ]α̣[νται δὲ νὺν εὐο]μφάλ[οις κύ]-
5   κλοισι νεαγ[ίαι, εὖ ε]ἰδότες
οἵαν Βρομίου [τελε]τάν
καὶ παρὰ σκᾶπτον Διὸς Οὐρανίδαι
ἐν μεγάροις ἵσταντι. σεμνᾶι μὲν κατάρχει
Ματέρι πὰρ μεγάλαι ῥόμβοι τυπάνων,
10 ἐν δὲ κέχλαδ[εν] κρόταλ᾽ αἰθομένα τε
     δαὶς ὑπὸ ξανθαῖσι πεύκαις·
ἐν δὲ Ναΐδων ἐρίγδουποι στοναχαί
μανίαι τ᾽ ἀλαλαί τ᾽ ὀρίνεται ῥιψαύχενι
σὺν κλόνωι.
15 ἐν δ᾽ ὁ παγκρατὴς κεραυνὸς ἀμπνέων
πῦρ κεκίγη[ται τό τ᾽]Ἐγυαλίου
ἔγχος, ἀλκάεσσά [τ]ε̣ Παλλάδο[ς] αἰγίς
μυρίων φθογγάζεται κλαγγαῖς δρακόντων.

ῥίμφα δ᾽ εἶσιν Ἄρτεμις οἰοπολὰς ζεύ-
20   ξαισ᾽ ἐν ὀργαῖς
Βακχίαις φῦλον λεόντων α[
ὁ δὲ κηλεῖται χορευοίσαισι κα[ὶ θη-
     ρῶν ἀγέλαις. ἐμὲ δ᾽ ἐξαίρετο[ν
κάρυκα σοφῶν ἐπέων
25 Μοῖσ᾽ ἀνέστασ᾽ Ἑλλάδι κα[λ]λ̣[ιχόρωι
εὐχόμενον βρισαρμάτοις ο[?? Θήβαις,
ἔνθα ποθ᾽ Ἁρμονίαν [φ]ά̣μα γα̣[μετάν
Κάδμον ὑψη[λαῖ]ς πραπίδεσ[σι λαχεῖν κεδ-
    νάν· Δ[ιὸ]ς δ᾽ ἄκ[ουσεν ὀ]μφάν,
30 καὶ τέκ᾽ εὔδοξο[ν παρ᾽] ἀνθρώπο[ις γενεάν.
Διόνυσ[.] . θ . [. . . . . . .] . τ̣[.]γ[
ματέ[ρ
πε̣ι .[

In the past the song of dithyrambs proceeded
    stretched long-drawn-out
and the *san* came out falsely to men from their mouths;
but [now] the young [men] have been spread out
5   in [well-c]ent[red cir]cles, knowing well
what kind of Bromios-revel
the Ouranidai hold also beside the sceptre of Zeus

in their halls. In the presence of the venerable
Great Mother the whirlings of tambourines lead off,
10 there too the castanets ring, and the blazing torch
        beneath the yellow pines;
there too the loud-sounding groans of the Naiads
and the ecstatic cries are aroused
in the agitation of tossing necks.
15 There too the all-powerful, fire-breathing thunderbolt
is shaken, as is Enyalios'
spear, and the intrepid aegis of Pallas
rings out with the hisses of countless snakes.

And lightly comes solitary Artemis,
20   having yoked the race of lions
    in bakkhic frenzy ...
and he is charmed by the herds of wild animals
        dancing in *khoroi*. And the Muse has appointed me
as her chosen herald of wise verses
25 for Hellas with its beautiful *khoroi*
boasting for Thebes, powerful in chariots,
where, the story goes, Kadmos once won
Harmonia as his cherished bride with his lofty mind.
        [?] She heeded the voice of Zeus
and gave birth to a child famous among men.
Dionysos
mother...

Fr. 346[60]

[ἐν και]ρῶι κτεάν[ων
[   ]αμοοσύνας[
[   ] τα λατερπεῖ φιλοφ[
    Ep.?
[. . .]Ἐλευσίνοθε〟 Φερσεφόναι Ματρί 〟τε χρυσοθρόνωι
θῆ[κεν ἀστ]οῖσι〟ν τελετάν, ἵν᾽ ἐς ἐν [
    [   ]διδύμαις εἶδον Εὐμο[λπ
    [   ]αραι
    [   ]πορεν Ἡρακλέι πρώτω[ι

[in due me]asure, of his possessions
        [?? of Mn]emosyne
        pleasing the people kindly

...from Eleusis established for the townsfolk
the rite for Persephone and the gold-
        throned Mother, so that to .../ to the pair

177

> saw Eumo[lpos . . .
> gave to Herakles for the first time

This dithyramb evidently included an account of – perhaps '*enacted*' is the better word – a transference of the Eleusinian mystery cult from Eleusis to Thebes. And it did so in a song which opened with a history of the hymns to Dionysos that seems to proclaim the novelty of the great circular *khoros* performed by young men ('In the past…but [now] the young [men] have been spread out in [well-c]ent[red cir]cles'). A distinctly orgiastic dithyramb for Dionysos of Thebes was evidently an appropriate home for the narration of Herakles' transference of mystery-cult from Eleusis – an Eleusis, presumably, firmly under Attic control – to Thebes, a city in which Demeter was effectively the poliadic deity.[61] One minimal implication is that the Theban cult of Dionysos was likely to have had marked teletic associations of its own. Perhaps Pindar linked the novelty of the circular dithyramb heralded in the opening of this work – a performance modelled on the orgiastic *teleta* held for Bromios in heaven – to the novelty of the cult that Herakles brought to Thebes from Eleusis. Λύσιοι τελεταί which we hear of in Thebes for Dionysos Lysios are probably the most attractive candidate for the original performance-context of such a song. One of the few things we know about them is that they were held in a sanctuary that also had a statue of Semele.[62]

Further exploration of the cultic, political and literary ramifications of this discovery are awaited. We have little way of securing a date for the work, but it seems to fit a context of 'cult skirmishing' between Boiotia and Attike early in the fifth century, whose best-known expression is the 'struggle' over a Dionysos whose future was to be spectacular, the god from Eleutherai.[63] Just how the 'transference' of the Eleusinian cult was presented in the poem we cannot say. Could it have implied that after Herakles' mythic action it was practised exclusively in Thebes, and so represent a kind of cultic 'theft' that would in effect de-authorise the long-standing Athenian claim over the centre;[64] or simply that its practice was no longer exclusive to Eleusis (and so represent a kind of familiar cultic duplication)?[65] In either case if, as is now clear, a dithyramb performed for Dionysos in Thebes helped engineer or affirm this transference, what are we to make of its opening claim, *à propos* of dithyramb itself, that 'now' such song is no longer (?) processional, but 'the young men are stretched out in well-centred *kykloi*' (διαπέπτανται δὲ νῦν εὐομφάλοις κύκλοισι νεανίαι)? Does this claim for performative novelty equally represent an assertion that the *kyklios khoros*, the great new format of Dionysiac song, is a *Theban* phenomenon, in competitive ripost to the (perhaps) recent appearance of massive new circular choral performances in the city that had 'stolen' Eleuthereus?[66]

To return to our 'Korinthian' song, in which I argued that Dionysiac dance in a mystic milieu may have been harnessed to the social goal of working against *stasis*. This complex of elements – a city threatened by *stasis* and an emotional choral invocation of a mystic Dionysos – finds a striking parallel on the tragic stage, in the doomed prayer of the Theban elders in the *Antigone*'s last choral song (1136–52). In language drenched with mystic associations the old men call on the 'many-named one…with the lightning-struck mother' to make an epiphany in, and so save, a sick and *stasis*-ridden Thebes, 'with a purifying foot' (καθαρσίωι ποδί) – clearly a reference to the powers of kathartic Dionysiac dance (1144), to be executed by this '*khoragos* of the stars' in company with his *khoros* of Thyiads – and notice again the isolated 'foot' in line four of the 'Korinthian' dithyramb, just after the reference to *stasis* and just before the *khoros* initiate the song of their god's *teleta*.[67] Antigone's Thebes will not be cleansed by Dionysiac dance: as ever, such tragic *khoreia* is bound to fail.[68] But those 'real' Thebans who commissioned the 'chosen herald of wise words for beautiful Hellas' to compose a dithyramb to do the same for their city will doubtless have been more hopeful of ritual efficacy.[69]

What I want to suggest is that the kind of dithyrambic performance exemplified by the 'Korinthian' poem represents a politicization of the mystic, choral powers of Dionysos: such dithyramb called upon the powers of the god for the benefit of the *polis* as such, especially in enacting and establishing a sense of solidarity, of cohesion, often in the face of the real aggressive internal divisions endemic to Greek *polis*-life. Cults of Dionysos which had a mystic character were evidently most suitable for this purpose. These offered to the worshipper a resource of ideas to do with cleansing, release and salvation after ordeals, that were readily translatable to the broader political context. This form of dithyramb would be the most 'public face' of the god's mystic cult, a politicized version of his choral song harnessed to the needs of a civic community, and harnessed in so grand a form as a Pindaric commission presumably on an occasion of particular importance, perhaps of particular urgency.[70]

In a fascinating passage of the long and learned essay in which he tries to bring some sort of order into the 'incoherent and often monstrous *mythologoumena* circulating among the Greeks concerning Dionysos', Diodorus Siculus points to this association of ideas around the god and the practices of his worshippers. Diodorus leaves to the last place in his account a sketch of the 'third' Dionysos – and this is the familiar Theban son of Zeus and Semele. He dwells on the god's double birth, his rearing among nymphs in *khoroi* and *thiasoi* of women. This is the god who 'demonstrated the matters relating to *teletai*' to the world and shared his *mystēria* with the pious; who set up festivals and *mousikoi agōnes* everywhere 'and who, in short, dissolves the quarrels between peoples and cities, creating concord and deep peace in place of *stasis* and war' (3.64.7).

The identifying features of the Theban god which persist in this digested form are very illuminating: habitué from childhood of *khoroi*, a god of teletic revelation, of *mystēria*, as well as of public festival and musical contest. In closing and capping this sketch with the god's powers to dissolve *stasis*, Diodorus draws on a meaningful nexus of attributes that is both ancient and persistent.

Dionysiac festival and political salvation

To suggest something of that persistence I return briefly to those Hellenistic Dionysia with which I began, and whose *civic* significance I established. Some fascinating features of their historical and political placement suggest that ideas of cleansing and salvation attached themselves to these performances, just as they evidently did to dithyramb of the earlier period. For we frequently find Hellenistic cities using their Dionysia to signal major moments of socio-political 'liberation' or 'purification'. At the close of the fourth century the Athenians famously honoured one Demetrios, the Besieger of Cities, for liberating their city from another, Demetrios of Phaleron and his narrow oligarchical régime, or tyranny as some saw it: they renamed the Dionysia the 'Dionysia and Demetrieia' in his honour; he and his father were worshipped as *Sōtēres* (Saviours); and his visits to the city were to be celebrated like those of Demeter and Dionysos.[71]

In the same period, an epigraphic find from Eretria on the island of Euboia provides us with an instance of beautiful clarity (*LSCGSuppl.* no. 46):

ὁ ἱερεὺς τοῦ Διονύσου Θεόδοτος
Θεοδώρου καὶ οἱ πολέμαρχοι Σ[ω]σί-
στρατος Πρωτομένου, Αἰσχύλος Ἀν-
τανδρίδου, Ἰθαιγένης Αἰσχύλου
εἶπα(ν)· ἐπειδὴ τῆι πομπῆι τῆι Διονύσου ἥ τε φρου[ρ]ὰ ἀπῆλθεν, ὅ τε δῆμος
4 ἠλευθερώθη κ[αὶ] μετὰ τοὺς ὕμνους καὶ
τὴν δημοκρατίαν ἐκομίσατο, ὅπως
ὑπόμνημα τῆς ἡμέρας ταύτης ἦι, ἔ-
δοξεν τῆι βουλῆι καὶ τῶι δήμωι στε-
φανηφορεῖν Ἐρετριεῖς πάντας
καὶ τοὺς ἐνοικοῦντας κιττοῦ στέφανον τῆι πομπῆι τοῦ Διονύσου.

8   τοὺς δὲ πολίτας [
       ἀπομι<σ>θοῦν τε [
       αν [τ]οὺς σ[τεφ]άνους· ἐπάρχεσθαι δὲ
       καὶ τοὺς χορούς [- - - - - - - - χορ-]
       είας τὰς τῶι τῶι Διονύσωι [
       οἶνον καταπεμπο. . .

4: Sokolowski. Boeckh: κατὰ τοὺς ὕμνους.
(Cf. Hesykhios s.v. ὕμνος· χρησμός.)

Theodotos son of Theodoros priest of Dionysos and the *polemarkhoi*
Sosistratos son of Protomenos, Aiskhylos son of Antandrides, Ithaigenes
son of Aiskhylos proposed: since at the procession of Dionysos the garrison
departed, and the *dēmos* (4) was liberated [?] after the hymns and reintro-
duced democracy, so that there might be a memorial of this day, the *boulē*
and *dēmos* decided: all the Eretrians, even the (foreign) residents, are to
wear ivy crowns at the procession of Dionysos.
(8) And the citizens…
and to hire…
the crowns. And also to consecrate
the *khoroi*…
[?choral performances] for Dionysos…
send for (?) wine…

The Macedonian garrison which had been occupying the city departed –
with an air of the miraculous it seems – just as the procession for Dionysos
was taking place, and perhaps more precisely, just after the performance of
hymns for the god (efficacious *hymnoi* these).[72] The liberation of the *dēmos*
and the restoration of democracy that followed were solemnized by the state
provision for all of ivy crowns, to be worn at the Dionysiac *pompē* in the
future. The Eretrians seem also to have devoted a number of special *khoroi*
– very probably *dithyrambic* – as a memorial (ὑπόμνημα) for these events
but frustratingly the inscription gives up at the crucial point.[73]
    A final example: very soon after the restoration of democracy in Athens,
we find Philippides the comic poet and statesman serving as agonothete
of the Great Dionysia of 288. Among the many special features of his
tenure of the office, Philippides 'was the first to arrange an extra *agōn* for
Demeter and the Kore as a reminder of the (?) liberation of the *dēmos*'
(*IG* II² 657.43–6). The invitation of the Eleusinian goddesses to the city's
Dionysia in this way points to a divine familiarity that had long existed.
The three most prestigious divinities of 'salvation' come together in a new
configuration at the level of the major *polis* festival. Changing civic history
continues to pattern itself in the contours of Dionysiac festivals.

Kleisthenes' *kyklioi khoroi* and the shape of Attic society

The last movement in this somewhat manic dance is back to Athens, and to the turbulent closing decade of the *sixth* century. The city had for some time been under the threat of overwhelming *stasis*. The entire programme of Kleisthenes was in an important sense a strategy designed to avoid its endemic recurrence. I want to suggest that the *choral* re-organization of the Dionysia – often regarded as little more than a matter of faintly antiquarian literary history – should be seen as an absolutely *integral* part of that plan.[74] And if my interpretation of Pindaric dithyramb has any validity, we can see here a further degree of continuity in the promotion of the dithyramb for such social objectives, whether or not it drew some special strength in Athens as elsewhere in this period from its roots in mystery cult, to serve as a form of major public civic purification or renewal through song.[75]

But the Kleisthenic case is, as far as we can tell, strikingly different from any before it for its pervasively *agonistic* pattern. The festival brought to the centre of Athens representatives of the great new tribes for major choral competition, and intense and aggressive competition between them was a defining character of their performance in the historical period. The 'new', late-sixth-century Athenian Dionysia may well be the *first certain* case in the historical record of a *choral agōn* of any kind. The lack of precise localization in the tradition (*Souda* s.v. Λάσος) that Lasos 'introduced dithyramb to a contest' (πρῶτος δὲ οὗτος…διθύραμβον εἰς ἀγῶνα εἰσήγαγε) has often troubled, and 'in Athens' is widely assumed. But the passage may be most readily intelligible as intending to stress the novelty of Lasos' introduction of the agonistic to dithyramb *tout court*. *Mousikoi agōnes* had existed since at least the seventh century, but these tested the instrumental and vocal skills of *individuals*. Formal, prize-winning competition between collective *khoroi* on the other hand is, as noted already, difficult to detect.[76]

One way to understand this development is through the logic of the *agōn*'s relation to *stasis* with which I began. On this view the great new Attic choral contests are a special form of '*stasis*-management': the Kleisthenic tribes were newly created precisely so as to cut across older attachments that had become aggressively entrenched, to break up the factional divisions into which Peisistratid Athens had fallen and to 'make everyone as much as possible intermingled with one another' (Aristot. *Pol.* 1319b26–7).[77] What is more, these great tribal *khoroi* appeared at the *very* time of the Kleisthenic reforms. In fact, a case can be made that the dithyrambic *khoros* was the very *first* form of collective action in the new tribal system. Although we cannot confidently ascribe a (re)organization of the Dionysia directly to Kleisthenes' hand, Herodotos (5.67–9) thought the Athenian was imitating (ἐμιμέετο, ἐμιμήσατο 67, 69) his homonymous maternal uncle in Sikyon, who had made interventions in the choral and cultic realms that favoured Thebans (the god Dionysos and the hero Melanippos), in addition to tampering with the existing tribes. We could then see the massive dithyrambic contests as forms of ritualized internal conflict, designed to promote 'healthy rivalry' rather than 'unholy *stasis*', according to precisely the same cultural logic that led Phlegon to his interpretation of the origin of the Olympic *agōn*. And so dancing for Dionysos perhaps *led the way* in introducing and shaping this new social identity, and in forging a new mechanism for regulating internal civic equilibrium.[78]

I have aired the hypothesis elsewhere that the three-way tragic *agōn* – which, in the absence of comedy, will presumably have been the only other event in the *agōnes* of a 'Kleisthenic' Dionysia – may at some level have been patterned in accordance with the tripartite geopolitical shape of Attike in the late sixth century. That is to say, the format of the tragic choral *agōn* – which we should expect in any case to reflect some kind of socio-political or religious grouping – may relate to those three stasiotic divisions of the men of the Coast, the men of the Plain and the men 'beyond the Hills' which were deemed by later writers to have reflected the struggles of the three great aristocratic factions contesting power in sixth-century Athens, and a memory of which was perhaps preserved in transmuted form in the Kleisthenic *trittyes*.[79] If there is anything in this, we would be faced with a fascinating double deployment of the Dionysiac choral solution: in the tragic *agōn*, the ritual of the choral contest which preserves a memory of that internal conflict establishes forever a performance which reflects profoundly on social violence, in particular on violence within the community. While, in the huge dithyrambic *agōnes*, citizens were engaged in 'healthy' internal rivalry, in *khoroi* representative of the very social units designed to do away with the horrors of *stasis*.

That *khoreia* should serve such *primary* political and social functions would not have come as a shock to Plato, whose *Laws* envisages a city effectively danced into existence.[80] Nor did *khoreia* in Athens entirely lose this character as the years wore on, change though it inevitably did with the wider currents of social and political change. A final vignette to demonstrate some of the force of this continuity: it is a passing but telling image from a full century after the Kleisthenic reforms, at one of the most critical moments of classical Athenian history, when the democracy itself was under assault. In fact, it comes from the midst of the real and terrible *stasis* that shook Athens in 404, when the social accord in some sense worked out in the Kleisthenic reforms had fallen apart for the second time in ten years.

The scene is the ford at the Kephisos river, where the democratic party had just won a bloody victory over the oligarchs (Xen *Hell.* 2.4.19–20).

Kleokritos, the clear-voiced Herald of the Initiates, called across the line of civil war that had divided Athens geographically and politically between the Peiraieus and the City, to make a speech attempting reconciliation. That the task was given to the Hierokerux of the Mysteries is owed to more, I would suggest, than his fine and powerful voice (μάλ᾽ εὔφωνος). And he opened that speech – the first step towards rebuilding the social unity of Attike after the divisions of bloody *stasis* – with an address to the partisans of the Thirty which emphasised the things both sides shared as citizens:

> Fellow citizens, why do you drive us out of the city? Why do you want to kill us? For we never did you any harm, but we have shared with you in the most solemn rites and sacrifices and the finest festivals; we have been fellow *khoros*-members and schoolmates and comrades in arms (καὶ συγχορευταὶ καὶ συμφοιτηταὶ γεγενήμεθα καὶ συστρατιῶται)...

Shared participation in *khoroi* continues to stand readily beside participation in the ranks of the city's army as a means for actively instantiating citizenship, and for expressing solidarity as citizens. Surely the great tribal *khoroi* of dithyramb that cut across the divisions of wealth and political affiliation are among those we are meant to think of here. We might not even be entirely deluding ourselves if we were to divine here a distant refraction of that great 'choral' solution to *stasis* adopted over a century before.

Acknowledgments

I am much indebted to Barbara Kowalzig for productive discussions of things dithyrambic. Thanks too to Simon Goldhill, Scott Scullion, the editors and their referees, all who participated at the Olympics Conference in Sydney, and audiences in Oxford, Birmingham and at the Harvard Department of Classics and Humanities Center.

Notes

[1] Poliakoff 1987.

[2] Ceccarelli 1998.

[3] Note its emphasis on the foot, with p. 179 above: ἐλθεῖν ... τῶι βοέωι πόδι δύων. The Sixteen Women, and perhaps the *khoroi*, were later affiliated to the eight-tribe system of Elis. See Mitsopoulos-Leon 1984.

[4] There are signs that things are changing: Zimmerman 1992 is an introductory survey; Ieranò 1997 an extremely useful collection of, and commentary on, the testimonia; and see now Zimmermann 2000. The recent commentary of Lavecchia (2000) represents a major advance, attempting to see the form as part of the lived reality of Dionysiac cult. Van der Weiden 1991 is still useful: see d'Alessio 1995. A new text and commentary by d'Alessio are eagerly awaited, as is the interpreta-

tive work of Barbara Kowalzig. Recent work on Bakkhylides: Pfeijffer and Slings 1999; Bagordo and Zimmermann 2000.

[5] Pickard-Cambridge 1962, 58.

[6] '*Kyklios khoros*' may not always be a simple synonym for 'dithyrambic *khoros*': the most explicit ancient equation is Σ MQ in Aiskhin. *Tim.* 10. The issue deserves closer analysis, but at a minimum, I would suggest that the widespread adoption (late in the fifth century; but note d'Angour 1997) of such a bland choreographic term for the cult song of Dionysos points to the generic malleability so prominent in its history, some features of which Plato found so disturbing: see esp. *Laws* 700 with Wilson 1999–2000; note also Käppel 2000.

[7] Metics could dance in dramatic *khoroi* at the Athenian Lenaia (where there were no dithyrambic *khoroi*) but not in dithyramb at other Dionysia; see Wilson 2000, 28–31.

[8] Wilson 2000, 389 n. 120.

[9] *OGI* 213, *c.* 299.

[10] Wilson 2000, 309; comparable evidence exists for Delos, Orkhomenos, Khaironeia, Kos, Samos, Tenos, Halikarnassos, Rhodes, Priene, Kolophon, Teos, Nisyros, among others.

[11] Wilson 2000, 283.

[12] Wilson 2000, 391 n. 147.

[13] Goldhill 1987; Perrin 1997, 205–6.

[14] Polybios 4.20–1. Wiles 1997, 36–8, 53.

[15] Ceccarelli 1995.

[16] Wilson 2000, 290. The same can be said of Kos, since *kyklioi khoroi* were the only event regularly presented each year.

[17] Alkman fr. 61 (Calame):] . ων Δυμαί[ναις...φιλοπλ]οκάμοις χα[

[18] π[ολ]λάκις δ(ὲ) [Δ]υμαιν[ῶν παρθένοι ἀφί]κοντο ε[ἰς] τὴν Πιτά[ν]ην συγ[χορεύσουσαι τ]αις Πιταγάτισι: Alkman 24 (Calame), part of a commentary on a highly fragmentary passage that includes 'παρσεν[ ]', reference to '?winged words' and a second-person plural injunction to sing 'κάμᾶ πα[ίγνια πα]ρσένω[ν]'. See Calame 1983, 388–9; Harvey 1967.

[19] There are also insoluble problems here concerning the social organization of archaic Sparta. Pitanatides look like girls from the *region* (*obe*) of Pitane, while Dymainai look like girls from the (non-regional) *tribe* of the Dymanes; joint performance of, or competition between, girls drawn from such formally different constituencies seems unlikely. However, limited evidence supports the existence of a place (*obe*) called Dyme (Hesykhios s.v.), which might suggest two local *khoroi*. On the other hand Hesykhios also records a notice that Pitane was the name of a tribe as well as a locality (s.v. Πιτανάτης στρατός). The extremely tentative connection with Dionysos is provided by the further notice of Hesykhios (s.v. Δύ[σ]μαιναι) that 'Dy[s]mainai' are female bakkhic khoreuts in Sparta: αἱ ἐν Σπάρτηι χορίτιδες Βάκχαι. But if the choral name refers to Dionysiac association it cannot also refer to membership in a local or tribal group.

[20] Jones 1987; Roussel 1976. See also p. 164 above (Pisa) and note 77 below (Miletos). Tribal re-organization could also serve the ends of social stability by

redistributing the wealthy across the citizen body, to circumvent their tendency to form a coherent group pursuing their own interests: see Ain. Tact. 11.8–10 (Argos, probably after Leuktra); and 11.10a–11 (Herakleia-on-Pontos.)

[21] Wilson 2000, 305–7.

[22] Based on: 20 *khoroi* (@ 3,500 dr. spent on the men, 2,500 dr. on the boys) x ten years = 600,000 dr.

[23] See esp. Demosthenes 39.

[24] Golden 1990, 67. Roussel 1976, 284 describes the Kleisthenic tribes as 'des écoles de civisme et de sociabilité'. For further consideration of participation in the dithyrambic choruses of classical Athens, see Pritchard 2001 and forthcoming.

[25] Representation on the Council was also based on the demes as well as the tribes, however (Traill 1986, 123–40), and there is no sign that this was so with dithyrambic *khoroi*. Members of the Council had to be thirty years old; presumably *khoreutai* did not.

[26] See especially the fascinating tribal decree (early fourth-century) *IG* II² 1142.

[27] That the part of Aigeus was taken by a soloist is no more than a deduction from the text. Maehler 1997, 211–14 for proposed performance-contexts.

[28] Perhaps the Eponyms' links to Dionysos were played up, although some would have a clear head-start in this. The Oineidai are encouraged elsewhere ([Dem.] 60.30) to think of themselves as the offspring of Oineus, son of Dionysos; and the Pandionidai could boast that it was in the reign of their hero that Demeter and Dionysos came to Attike; see Kearns 1989, 192.

[29] Dated by Wilamowitz (1922, 273) to *c.* 475–460. Note also the emphasis on the military prowess of Athens expressed in Bakkhylidean dithyramb: e.g. 18, esp. 12–15, but implicit throughout.

[30] A striking feature of the action envisaged is what virtually amounts to the worship of Dionysos by other gods. In this it has a parallel in the way the dithyramb for the Thebans (fr. 70b M) shows us a festival of Bromios held by the Olympians 'beside the sceptre of Zeus in their halls' (7–8) at which the Great Mother Kybele, Naiads, Enyalios, Athena and Artemis are present. Their actions are in turn the model for the performance of the dithyramb itself by mortal νεαγ[ίαι] (5 cf. 1–6).

[31] Cf. Rutherford 2001, 32–3, 86–9.

[32] Ieranò 1992b; the doubts of the editor of *IG* I³ 1015 weaken the epigraphic basis for his discussion.

[33] Csapo forthcoming, in the context of a brilliant analysis of the 'New Music'.

[34] The aversion of *stasis* might be a cause for the performance of a paian: cf. Pindar fr. 52k with Rutherford 2001, 193–200. Much archaic poetry could be said to serve the ends of social stability, but this is especially true of choral poetry: note Kurke's (1991) thesis concerning the integrative function of the epinikion. The relation between choral song and *stasis* can also be seen in a shared vocabulary: the word στάσις, and related forms of ἴστημι, are used both of the 'internal divisions' of civil discord, of a community divided against itself, *and* of the 'setting up' of

a *khoros*, of a *khoros* itself, or of a position within a choral group. Hesykh. s.v. στάσις includes the gloss χορός. See Suda s.v. χοροδέκτης; Nagy 1990, 366–7.

[35] I cite the text of Lavecchia 2000, except at line 10 and 12: see the next note.

[36] Lavecchia 2000, 42 punctuates so as to read: 'and to the neighbouring rock, O lord of...'

[37] Bury in *P.Oxy.* 13 (1919) 45. On the other hand, 'le milieu isthmique était autant que poseidonique, dionisique' (Will 1955, 218). The Boiotian divinity Melikeretes/Palaimon (son of Ino and Athamas), carried by a dolphin to the Isthmos, maintained his Dionysiac attachments when he was celebrated (with *teletai* and *orgiasmos*) there, where there was also a temple of Dionysos: Plu. *Thes.* 25.5–7; Paus. 2.1.6; Philostr. *Im.* 2.16 ff.; cf. Ieranò 1992a. But while 'the neighbouring rock that is lord' might still suit the Akrokorinth as described from the Isthmos, it is less likely that a *khoros* performing at the Isthmos would summon the god 'to the city that is dear indeed'.

[38] Zimmermann 1992, 50.

[39] See van der Weiden 1991, 113 for παύσ]αιτο (Schroeder) or καταλύ]οιτο (van der Weiden) in preference to μὴ γέν]οιτο (Zimmermann), since κρέμασον in 12 implies that weapons have already been taken up. I much prefer a compound of λύω (διαλύοιτο might also be possible), given their prevalence as the verbs for the 'releasing' [=ending] of *stasis* (cf. Loraux 1987) and their appropriateness to the god known as Λύσιος in Korinth (Paus. 2.2.6). Bury (in Grenfell and Hunt 1919, 44) wanted to connect this στάσις with the idea of the establishment of *khoroi* κατάστασις (χορῶν) – or as a term for a choral 'division', pointing to the 'foot' in the next line as a potentially 'choral' foot. Zimmermann 1988 *contra* argues for an instance of the topos which sets the pleasures of festival against the horrors of civil war. On πόδα, however, he writes: 'Vielleicht... vom Tanz die Rede', and I would certainly wish to entertain the possibility of a Dionysian or/and choral 'foot' here.

[40] Pausanias 2.2.6–7 only mentions two statues of Dionysos in the Korinthian agora, which he regards as ancient. On this cult and its connections with that of Dionysos in Thebes see Casadio 1999 which, however, makes no mention of the presence of Dionysos on the Akrokorinth. Ure 1969 presents the evidence, which includes a plaque with διονύσου, a terracotta mask and numerous fragments of a terracotta youth who may be him. The many *likna* found also point to a *Liknites*; see Will 1955, 216–18. On the 'theatral' area, with seating for some forty spectators, see Stroud 1968, 300, cf. 305–7; Stroud also suggests that 'Dionysos shared somehow in the activity that went on in the theatral area' (1968, 329).

[41] See Cole 1994, 207.

[42] Zimmermann 1992, 50; cf. fr. 70b 13. Kevin Lee reminded me that αὐχήν is sometimes used in tragic poetry to refer to the head more generally rather than simply the neck; see Lavecchia 2000, 154–5. In fr. 70b the violent agitation of mystic *orgia* is itself described in terms suitable to military aggression: Lavecchia 2000, 152–3, 157–9. The followers of Dionysos are frequently assimilated to an army (cf. 70c.11?): opposition to Dionysos is a kind of war – or a kind of *stasis*.

[43] My thanks to Richard Thomas for this suggestion.

[44] The dithyramb of which Pindar fr. 70d M formed part gives indications of an Argive performance-context: van der Weiden 1991, esp. 157. Fr. 3* + fr. 210* is probably from the same poem: 'most dangerous are those men in cities bent on excessive ambition (ἄγαν φιλοτιμίαν μνώμενοι); they establish manifest grief (ἱστᾶσιν ἄλγος ἐμφανές)'. This grief within cities from over-ambitious men is *stasis*: in fact, most manuscripts of fr. 210 have ἢ στάσιν rather than ἱστᾶσιν. A story of *stasis* (between Akrisios and Proitos) may also lie behind the Argive dithyramb from which fr. 70a derives; see van der Weiden 1991, 39–40.

[45] Of the further traces, there is a striking reference to a φῦλον immediately after the 'songs' and just before reference to the Dionysiac season (19). van der Weiden 1991, 119 supposes it may be a reference to the (people of the) city for which the dithyramb was composed – more likely than a 'tribal' division of performers within a city; see further n. 69 below.

[46] The term *teleta* is unusually prominent in the remains of Pindaric dithyramb: fr. 70a.33; fr. 70b.6, fr. 346.5 with *PSI* 14, 1391 fr. B, col. 1.28; fr. 70c.6. Some claim that the word means no more than 'festival' in Pindar (e.g. Hamilton 1990, 218), but its concentration in Dionysiac contexts where there are other reasons for postulating a properly 'teletic' character is very striking: see Lavecchia 1994, 49 and 2000, 11–13, 135–6; Versnel 1990, 153; Morand 2001, 140–2; Graf 2000, 67 ff. Elsewhere in Bakkhic contexts: Eur. *Bakkh.* 22, 238; Aristoph. *Frogs* 342, 368; cf. Hes. fr. 131 M-W; Alk. fr. 19 Cal. The collocation of the 'technical term' of mystery-cult *olbios* with the noun in the important fragment of a Pindaric *thrēnos* is also significant: fr. 59.1 Cannatà Fera; see Cannatà Fera 1990, 187–90.

[47] Seaford 1996, 156, cf. 195–7. The very earliest institution of dithyrambic performance in Korinth (under the influence of Periander? Hdt. 1.23) may have been related to the violent political upheaval that saw the overthrow of the Bakkhiadai: Ieranò 1992a has an intriguing discussion.

[48] After Seaford 1981.

[49] Mendelsohnn 1992.

[50] Ieranò 1997, 18–23, 159–67.

[51] Graf 1993; Burkert 1993; Cole 1993. See most recently the various contributions in Cosmopoulos 2003. There is much in the account of Plutarch at *de E* 9–10 = *Mor.* 389 to support the mystic associations of the dithyramb.

[52] Van der Weiden 1991, 26–7; Lavecchia 2000, 94.

[53] A full case for Lerna as the performance-site for these fragmentary poems will soon be made by Barbara Kowalzig. Lavecchia 2000, 94–5 considers and rejects Lerna, but *inter alia*, the fact that its mythology includes a story of the death of Dionysos (Σ Townl. *Il.* 14.319) suits his own interpretation of dithyramb extremely well. That this was the Argives' principal, perhaps only Dionysia, is suggested by Plu. *Quaest. Conv.* 4.6 (= *Mor.* 671e); cf. *de Is. Os.* 35 (= *Mor.* 364e). On Lerna: Casadio 1994; Arrigoni 1999.

[54] Apart from the many suggestions in Pausanias' account, dedications of the Imperial period are made by initiates to 'Bakkhos and Prosymnaia' in the sanctuary of Demeter; see Casadio 1994, 316–19, 324–5. Piérart 1996 argues against any

connection between the worship of Dionysos and Demeter at Lerna.

[55] *Bougenes* is the other epithet associated with Argive Dionysos: Plu. *de Is. Os.* 35: cf. Arrigoni 1999; Casadio 1994, 232.

[56] Σ Townl. *Il.* 14.319. Arrigoni 1999 emphasizes the importance of this tradition, which stresses that Perseus killed (the hero) Dionysos *by throwing him in* the lake (not that he simply discarded his dead body there). See Casadio 1994, 252–60 on the co-presence of themes of divine death and maternal rescue in this cult.

[57] Plu. *de Is. Os.* 35, on authority of Sokrates of Argos (3rd cent.? 310 F2 Jac.), see Casadio 1994, 237–41. On ἀνακαλεῖσθαι as the word for summoning the dead with the aid of magic see Arrigoni 1999, 41–4.

[58] It is tempting to see in this group of mainads the aetiological prototype of the dithyrambic *khoros* of cult, which may suggest a female *khoros*: see Calame 1997, 136; Privitera 1970, 16. See also Nonnos *Dionys.* 25.35–147; 47.496–741 with Casadio 1994, 255–6.

[59] The text is basically that of Maehler, although I have not marked every supplement. At 4–5 I adopt the important new reading of d'Angour 1997. I omit fr. 81 (an address to Geryon), certainly from the same dithyramb.

[60] I have cited only the first eight lines of the fragment. The text is basically that of Lavecchia 2000, whose full apparatus and commentary should be consulted. Note Lloyd-Jones 1967. Lavecchia (1994, 1996 and 2000) secures the reinstatement of this fragment to the dithyramb on (slender) metrical grounds, by virtue of his new reading at line 3 (]τα for]ια). See also Suárez de la Torre 1992.

[61] In the fifth century the Eleusinian cult had the degree of independence implied by the fact that its principal officers and administrators were provided by the *genē* of the Eumolpidai and Kerykes; and Athenian control over its finances was partially circumscribed; see Clinton 1974, 8.

[62] Souda, Photios s.v. Λύσιοι τελεταί; Pausanias 9.16.6; cf. 2.7.5. This despite Pausanias' anachronistic aetiology for their institution, on which see Casadio 1999, 124–6. Previous commentators have tended to opt for the Agrionia, in honour of Dionysos Kadmeios: van der Weiden 1991, 27. Lavecchia 2000, 124 airs the attractive hypothesis that the Agrionia provided the context for the Lysios cult, celebrating Dionysos as a god of rebirth and liberation. See Lavecchia's full discussion (2000, 109–25); Lloyd-Jones 1967. Further on Dionysos and Demeter in Thebes, see Moreaux 1970.

[63] Paus. 1.38.8–9 for the pro-Athenian aetiology. The stories of the combat between Melanthos and Xanthos are part of the same general background; see Seaford 1994, 245 with bibliography.

[64] It is worth noting that the Argives also claimed to be founders of the Eleusinian mysteries (Paus. 1.14.2).

[65] Thus Lavecchia 2000, 118: 'molto probabilmente...la τελετά *importata* veniva presentata come *Abbild* dei Misteri eleusini'. Lavecchia 2000, 117–19 also draws attention to evidence for the diffusion of the Eleusinian cult in Boiotia and elsewhere, where Demeter held the epithet Eleusinia.

[66] *Kyklioi khoroi* performed in Athens at least from *c.* 500; *Marm. Par.* Ep. 46

sets [?] 509/8 as the year of the first victory in the men's contest: Wilson 2000, 17, 216–18. Hard evidence for the category of *paides* is rather later (Wilson 2000, 214), but *paides* are unlikely to represent the same age-class as *neaniai*.

[67] Griffith 1999, 313–14. Scullion 1998 is an important discussion of the idea of cathartic, Dionysiac dance curing the city's ills in this passage.

[68] Stehle forthcoming. Amid all the death at the end of the *Antigone*, some hope may rest in the eschatalogical elements of this specifically *Dionysiac* tragic *khoreia*.

[69] Fr. 70b.23–5. Note possible Eleusinian echoes in this use of κᾶρυξ of the poetic-choral voice; perhaps even of καλλίχορος, used of Hellas: Richardson 1974, Index s.v. dancing in mystery cults; Hardie forthcoming. The last complete word in the 'Korinthian' dithyramb is ταμίας, a term used of Iakkhos at *Antigone* 1154 and shared by those 'dispensers' of death and blessings, Dionysos and Demeter, in the context of mystery cult; see Griffith 1999, 322; cf. also Lavecchia 2000, 228 for the possibility that στό]μιον in the previous line refers to the entrance to an underground *adyton* connected to the cult of Melikertes.

[70] It might be objected that the public character would conflict with the elements of secrecy in such a cult. No ritually restricted information need be exposed, however, and the linguistic and mythic material of dithyramb, with their prominent use of riddle and allegory, may well have served to send a clear message to the συνετοί while not distancing – indeed, doubtless enticing – the πολλοί: Lavecchia 2000, 121. See Hardie 2000, 169 on etymological punning in the opening of the Theban dithyramb: in the comparison between the old dithyramb and the new, '[t]he *khoros* acquires new knowledge (εὖ ε]ἰδότες, 5) about Dionysiac revels in heaven, thereby implying earlier ignorance, which may be inherent in the dispraise of the early ἀοιδὰ διθυράμβων (1)' (since an etymology of ἀοιδά from οἶδ- and privative alpha was available). Hardie goes on to note that this would fit with the 'revelatory force of the Muse's choice of Pindar as κάρυκα σοφῶν ἐπέων, 24'.

[71] Parker 1996, 258–63. The hymn for Demetrios Poliorketes' entry to the city, welcomed by the Eleusinian deities, includes the detail: οἱ φίλοι πάντες κύκλωι, | ἐν μέσοισι δ᾽ αὐτός, ὅμοιον ὥσπερ οἱ φίλοι μὲν ἀστέρες | ἥλιος δ᾽ ἐκεῖνος (Duris *FGH* 76, 13). Had a *kyklios khoros* been devoted to Demetrios?

[72] Lewis 1990 attempts to rearrange the traditional lineation (in which little trust can be placed, based as it is on Cyriacus' notes made in the fifteenth century, the stone being lost). Lewis 1990, 199 follows Reinach's interpretation of Boeckh's text at 4: ὅ τε δῆμος ἠλευθερώθη κ[ατ]ὰ τοὺς ὕμνους and understands: 'according to the oracles' (Hesykh. s.v. ὕμνος. χρησμός). He rejects Sokolowski's καὶ μετὰ τοὺς ὕμνους as syntactically unsatisfactory (true, though perhaps not an improbable epigraphical error). If one way the Eretrians readjusted their Dionysia so as to make its programme serve as an effective ὑπόμνημα of this event was to consecrate (ἐπάρχεσθαι) special *khoroi*, a reference earlier in the inscription to the role of 'hymns' in the events that gave rise to this would certainly be appropriate.

[73] Cf. Jacottet 1980, 151. *Kyklioi khoroi* formed an important part of the Eretrian Dionysia in the fourth century (see page 166 above) and into the third, the age

of *Tekhnitai* (*IG* XII 9.207). There were probably three *khoroi*, each representing two tribes: Knoepfler 1997, 391. A recently published law of Eretria against tyranny and oligarchy of *c.* 340 stipulates that violators are to be solemnly cursed at the city's Dionysia, as well as at the Artemisia, thereby demonstrating further the relation between Eretria's Dionysia and notions of civic liberty; see Knoepfler 2001, esp. 229–34.

[74] Connor 1989 attempts to give due historical weight to the re-organization of the Dionysia. His case for its institution by the young democracy as something of a 'liberationist' festival would be entirely consistent with my discussion of dithyramb and its new competitive format.

[75] The evidence for Dionysiac mystery-cult in Athens is scattered and slender: at Agrai: Steph. Byz. s.v. Ἄγρα with Parker 1989; Casadio 1994, 292–3; at the Anthesteria? Casadio 1994, 237–9 is cautious; cf. Bravo 1997; at Eleusis: Dionysos clearly had an important role in the goddesses' mystery-cult: Soph. *Ant.* 1119–52; Σ Aristoph. *Frogs* 330; Clinton 1992, 123–5. At his own Dionysia in the deme he could share with Demeter and Kore the honour of two special *khoroi* (one of boys, one of men) given by a Theban, Damasias and his 'students': *IG* II² 1186. Were these *khoroi* offered by a Theban exile to a community that had granted him salvation after the annihilation of his own city, and that of the god? Note also the tradition that Diagoras of Melos τὰ ἐν Ἐλευσῖνι μυστήρια ἐξορχησάμενος καὶ ἐξειπὼν ἀσεβέστατος ἐκρίθη (Σ Aristoph. *Clouds* 830c, with 'Aristagoras the Melian' as subject). However 'it is virtually certain…this "Aristagoras" is a phantom' (Sutton 1989, 42). This sounds like a reference to a public choral performance conducted by Diagoras as a dithyrambic *didaskalos*.

[76] See also above p. 167. Note too Bremer 2000.

[77] Comparison can be made with Miletos, where the musico-religious ritual of the *molpoi* was established as a civic ceremony after, and clearly as part of the 'solution' to, a period of extended *stasis*; see *LSAM* 50; *SEG* 37, no. 981; Milet I.3, no. 133; *SEG* 36, no. 1050.

[78] 508/7 may have been the year of the first dithyrambic *agōn* for men at the Dionysia, at least under some new arrangement: *Marm. Par.* Ep. 46. However one resolves the chronological difficulties, it is clear at a minimum that the change in the dithyrambic organization of the Dionysia stood in some *very* immediate relation to this massive upheaval in Athenian socio-political life.

[79] Wilson 2000, 19.

[80] This suggestion goes beyond the idea, articulated with subtlety and force by Stehle 1997, 69–70, that the image of unity (re)created and evoked by *khoreia* existed only at the level of ideology: 'Communal performance is not prepolitical.'

Bibliography
Arrigoni, G.
   1999   'Perseo contro Dioniso a Lerna', in *Ricordando Raffaele Cantarella (Quaderni di Acme 36)*, 9–70.

Bagordo, A. and Zimmermann, B.
2000   *Bakchylides: hundert Jahre nach seiner Wiederentdeckung*, Munich.

Bravo, B.
1997   *'Pannychis' e Simposio: feste private notturne di donne e uomini*, Pisa and Rome.

Bremer, J.M.
2000   'Der dithyrambische Agon: ein Kompetitiver Gottesdienst oder gar keiner?', in A. Bagordo and B. Zimmermann (eds.) *Bakchylides: hundert Jahre nach seiner Wiederentdeckung*, 259–75, Munich.

Burkert, W.
1993   'Bacchic *Teletai* in the Hellenistic Age', in T. Carpenter and C. Faraone (eds.) *Masks of Dionysus*, Cornell, 259–75.

Bury, J.
1890   *Pindar: Nemean Odes*, London.

Calame, C.
1983   *Alcman*, Rome.
1997   *Choruses of Young Women in Ancient Greece*, Lanham. First edn 1977.

Cannatà Fera, M.
1990   *Pindarus Threnorum Fragmenta*, Rome.

Casadio, G.
1994   *Storia del culto di Dioniso in Argolide*, Rome.
1999   *Il vino dell'anima: storia del culto di Dioniso a Corinto, Sicione, Trezene*, Rome.

Ceccarelli, P.
1995   'Le dithyrambe et la pyrrhique: à propos de la nouvelle liste de vainqueurs aux Dionysies de Cos (Segre, ED 234)', *ZPE* 108, 287–305.
1998   *La Pirrica nell'Antichità greco-romana: studi sulla danza armata*, Pisa and Rome.

Clinton, K.
1974   *The Sacred Officials of the Eleusinian Mysteries*, Philadelphia.
1992   *Myth and Cult: The iconography of the Eleusinian Mysteries*, Stockholm.

Cole, S.
1994   'Demeter in the ancient Greek city and its countryside', in S. Alcock and R. Osborne (eds.) *Placing the Gods: Sanctuaries and sacred space in ancient Greece*, 199–216, Oxford.

Connor, W.
1989   'City Dionysia and Athenian democracy', *C&M* 40, 7–32.

Cosmopoulos, M. (ed.)
2003   *Greek Mysteries: The archaeology and ritual of ancient Greek secret cults*, London and New York.

Csapo, E.
Forthcoming   'The politics of the New Music', in P. Murray and P. Wilson (eds.) *Music and the Muses: The culture of 'mousike' in the classical Athenian city*, Oxford.

D'Alessio, G.
1995   Review of van der Weiden 1991, *JEA* 81, 270–3.

D'Angour, A.
1997   'How the dithyramb got its shape', *CQ* 47, 331–51.
Golden, M.
1990   *Children and Childhood in Classical Athens*, Baltimore and London.
Goldhill, S.
1987   'The Great Dionysia and civic ideology', *JHS* 107, 58–76.
Graf, F.
1993   'Dionysian and Orphic eschatology: new texts and old questions', in T. Carpenter and C. Faraone (eds.) *Masks of Dionysus*, 239–58, Cornell.
2000   'Text and ritual: the Corpus Eschatologicum of the Orphics', *AION(ling)* 22, 59–78.
Grenfell, B. and Hunt, A.
1919   *The Oxyrhynchus Papyri: Part XIII*, London.
Griffith, M.
1999   *Sophocles 'Antigone'*, Cambridge.
Hamilton, R.
1990   'The Pindaric dithyramb', *HSPh* 93, 211–22.
Hardie, A.
2000   'The ancient 'etymology' of ἀοιδός', *Philologus* 144, 163–75.
Forthcoming   'Muses and mysteries', in P. Murray and P. Wilson (eds.) *Music and the Muses*, Oxford.
Harvey, D.
1967   'Oxy. P. 2390 and early Spartan history', *JHS* 87, 62–73.
Ieranò, G.
1992a   'Arione e Corinto', *QUCC* 41, 39–52.
1992b   'Dioniso Ikarios e Apollo Pizio: aspetti dei culti religiosi nell'Atene dei Peisistratidi', *QS* 36, 171–80.
1997   *Il Ditirambo di Dioniso: le testimonianze antiche*, Pisa and Rome.
Jacottet, A.
1990   'Le lierre de la liberté', *ZPE* 80, 150–6.
Jones, N.
1987   *Public Organization in Ancient Greece*, Philadelphia.
Käppel, L.
2000   'Bakchylides und das System der chorlyrischen Gattungen im 5. Jh. v. Chr.', in A. Bagordo and B. Zimmermann (eds.) *Bakchylides: hundert Jahre nach seiner Wiederentdeckung*, 11–27, Munich.
Kearns, E.
1989   *The Heroes of Attica*, Institute of Classical Studies Bulletin Suppl. 57, London.
Knoepfler, D.
1997   'Le territoire d'Erétrie et l'organisation politique de la cité (*dēmoi, chōroi, phylai*)', in M. Hansen (ed.) *The Polis as an Urban Centre and Political Community: Acts of the Copenhagen Polis Centre*, vol. 4, Copenhagen, 352–449.

2001   'Loi d'Érétrie contre la tyrannie et l'oligarchie (première partie)', *BCH* 125, 195–238.

Kowalzig, B.

Forthcoming   'From drama to ritual: performance of, by, and for Dionysos'.

Kurke, L.

1991   *The Traffic in Praise: Pindar and the poetics of social economy*, Ithaca and London.

Lavecchia, S.

1994   'Il "Secondo" Ditirambo di Pindaro e i Culti Tebani', *SCO* 44, 33–93.

1996   '*P.Oxy. XXXII 2622* e il "Secondo Ditirambo" di Pindaro', *ZPE* 110, 1–26.

2000   *Pindari Dithyramborum Fragmenta*, Rome and Pisa.

Lewis, N.

1990   'The "Ivy of Liberation" inscription', *GRBS* 31, 197–202.

Lloyd-Jones, H.

1967   'Heracles at Eleusis: P. Oxy. 2622 and PSI 3891 [=Pindar fr. 346 S.-M.]', *Maia* 19, 206–29.

Longoni, F.

1976   'Nota sulla storia del ditirambo : ancora a proposito di *P.Berol.* 9571 verso', *Acme* 29, 305–8.

Loraux, N.

1987   'Le lien de la division', *Le cahier du collège international de philosophie* 4, 101–24.

Maehler, H.

1997   *Die Lieder des Bakchylides*, Leiden and New York.

Mendelsohnn, D.

1992   'Συγκεραυνόω: dithyrambic language and the Dionysiac cult', *CJ* 87, 105–24.

Mitsopoulos-Leon, V.

1984   'Zur Verehrung des Dionysos in Elis nochmals: ΑΞΙΕ ΤΑΥΡΕ und die sechzehn heiligen Frauen', *MDAI(A)* 99, 275–90.

Morand, A.-F.

2001   *Études sur les 'Hymnes Orphiques'*, Leiden, Boston and Cologne.

Moreaux, B.

1970   'Déméter et Dionysos dans la septième *Isthmique* de Pindare' *REG* 83, 1–14.

Nagy, G.

1990   *Pindar's Homer*, Baltimore and London.

Parker, R.

1989   'Dionysos at Agrai', *LCM* Dec., 154–5.

1996   *Athenian Religion: A history*, Oxford.

Perrin, E.

1997   'Propagande et culture théâtrale à Athènes à l'époque hellénistique', in B. le Guen (ed.) *De la scène aux gradins: théâtre et représentations dramatiques après Alexandre le grand*, Pallas 47, 201–18, Toulouse.

Pfeijffer, I. and Slings, S.
  1999   *One Hundred Years of Bacchylides*, Amsterdam.
Pickard-Cambridge, A.
  1962   *Dithyramb, Tragedy, Comedy*, Oxford.
Piérart, M.
  1996   'La mort de Dionysos à Argos', in R. Hägg (ed.) *The Role of Religion in the Early Greek Polis: Proceedings of the Third International Seminar on Ancient Greek Cult organized by the Swedish Institute at Athens, 16–18 October 1992*, 141–51, Stockholm.
Poliakoff, M.
  1987   *Combat Sports in the Ancient World: Competition, violence, and culture*, New Haven and London.
Pritchard, D.M.
  2001   'Dancing for Dionysos', *Classicum* 27, 6–13.
  Forthcoming   'Participation in the tribally organized dithyrambic contests of late archaic and classical Athens.'
Privitera, G.
  1970   *Dioniso in Omero e nella Poesia Greca Arcaica*, Rome.
  1977   'Il ditirambo: da canto cultuale a spettacolo musicale', in C. Calame (ed.) *Rito e Poesia Corale in Grecia*, 27–37, Rome and Bari.
Richardson, N.
  1974   *The Homeric Hymn to Demeter*, Oxford.
Robertson, N.
  1987   'Government and society at Miletus', *Phoenix* 41, 359–78.
Romero, F.G.
  2000   'The Dithyrambs of Bacchylides: their position in the evolution of the genre', in A. Bagordo and B. Zimmermann (eds.) *Bakchylides: hundert Jahre nach seiner Wiederentdeckung*, 47–57, Munich.
Roussel, D.
  1976   *Tribu et Cité*, Paris.
Rutherford, I.
  2001   *Pindar's paeans: a reading of the fragments with a survey of the genre*, Oxford.
Schachter, A.
  1981   *Cults of Boiotia I*, London.
Scullion, S.
  1998   'Dionysos and katharsis in *Antigone*', *ClAnt* 17, 96–122.
Seaford, R.
  1981   'Dionysiac drama and the Dionysiac Mysteries', *CQ* 31, 252–75.
  1994   *Reciprocity and Ritual: Homer and tragedy in the developing city-state*, Oxford.
  1996   *Euripides: 'Bacchae'*, Warminster.
Stehle, E.
  1997   *Performance and Gender in Ancient Greece*, Princeton.
  Forthcoming   'Choral prayer in Greek tragedy: euphemia or aischrologia?', in P. Murray and P. Wilson (eds.) *Music and the Muses*, Oxford.

Stroud, R.
1968   'The sanctuary of Demeter and Kore on Acrocorinth: Preliminary Report II, 1964–1965', *Hesperia* 37, 299–330.

Suárez de la Torre, E.
1992   'Expérience orgiastique et composition poétique: Le *dithyrambe* II de Pindare (Fr. 70b Snell-Maehler)', *Kernos* 5, 183–207.

Sutton, D.
1989   *Dithyrambographi Graeci*, Munich and Zurich.

Traill, J.
1986   *Demos and Trittys*, Toronto.

Ure, A.
1969   'Demeter and Dionysos on Acrocorinth', *JHS* 89, 120–1.

Van der Weiden, M.
1991   *The Dithyrambs of Pindar*, Amsterdam.

Versnel, H.
1990   *Ter Unus: Isis, Dionysos, Hermes: three studies in henotheism*, Leiden.

Wilamowitz, U. von
1922   *Pindaros*, Berlin.

Wiles, D.
1997   *Tragedy in Athens*, Cambridge.

Will, E.
1955   *Korinthiakà*, Paris.

Wilson, P.
2000   *The Athenian Institution of the* Khoregia: *The chorus, the city and the stage*, Cambridge.

Wilson, P.
1999–2000   'Euripides' Tragic Muse', *ICS* 24–25, 427–50.

Zimmermann, B.
1988   'Pindar, Dithyrambus III 3 (Fr. 70c Snell – Maehler)', *ZPE* 72, 22.
1992   *Dithyrambos: Geschichte einer Gattung*, Göttingen.
2000   'Eroi nel ditirambo', in V. Pirenne-Delforge and E. Suárez de la Torre (eds.) *Héros et héroïnes dans les mythes et les cultes grecs : Actes du Colloque organisé à l'Université de Valladolid du 26 au 29 mai 1999*, Kernos supplement 10, 15–20, Liège.

8

ATHENIAN POLITICAL HISTORY:
A PANATHENAIC PERSPECTIVE

David J. Phillips

This chapter is a preliminary study of some of the ways in which historians interested in the writing of narratives of Athenian political history may better nuance their interpretation of events or add new elements to their narratives by drawing more fully upon recent scholarship on Greek society and especially on Greek religion and its central *polis* expression – festival. Section I briefly surveys some of the challenges facing event-based political history (*histoire événementielle*) in the light of developments in the new social history which now dominate the study of ancient Greece. Section II outlines the importance of the Athenian festival calendar for establishing an alternative framework for viewing and dating events. Section III focuses on the Panathenaia which is one of the best attested Athenian festivals and one which has been the subject of much recent scholarship. Sections IV and V explore the relationship between the Panathenaia and political crises and change in archaic Athens. Section VI provides a brief examination of some ways in which a closer consideration of the Panathenaia may add to our understanding of selected events in fifth-century Athenian history. Section VII argues that the first performance of Timotheos' *The Persians* at a Panathenaic kitharodic contest was an event of some political importance in late fifth-century Athens. Section VIII briefly argues that the decision to construct the Pompeion made by the restored democracy in about 403/2 BC was an event of political and symbolic importance. Finally, three short appendices examine participation in Athenian festivals, Athenian politics and festivals other than the Panathenaia, and politics and festivals outside Athens.

I. Political history and the new social history
The approaches advocated in this chapter arise, in part, out of what has been perceived in some quarters as a decline of interest in event-based political history, and, more importantly, out of a concern that political

history is not always as fully informed as it could be by the advances in social history which have characterized the study of the Graeco-Roman world over the past few decades.[1] The two, social history and political history, are not mutually exclusive. Rather what we should be seeking, especially in any study of the history of the Greek *polis* where the social, economic, political and religious aspects of *polis* life are inextricably inter-woven, is a more integrated approach, one which views the history of a *polis* holistically. An agenda for such an approach was set over a decade ago by Robert Connor in his essay 'The new classical humanities and the old'.[2] Connor argued that the political history of the Greek *polis* should 'become political in precisely the sense that Aristotle said that man was a political being – a creature of the *polis* (*Politics* 1353a3)'. He also pointed to the work of anthropologists such as Clifford Geertz as providing a guide to a reconceptualization of political history which would focus on 'the struc-tures of meaning through which men give shape to their experience' and in which 'politics is not coups and constitutions, but one of the principal arenas in which such structures publicly unfold'.[3] However, the difficulty of such political history should not be underestimated:

> It means taking the history of mentalities seriously and attempting to study from the ground up the structures of meaning within the culture, from the organization of space and time, the perception of kinship, and the forms and practices that the Greeks saw as central to and distinctive of their forms of civic life – the *agōn*, especially athletic and dramatic competition, antilogistic debate, supplication rituals, the symposium, the Greek forms of sacrifice, the importance of kinship structures, the organization of time through festival and civic calendars, the organization of civic space through sacred ways, agoras, and sanctuary preserves – not to mention once again the dividing line between public and private (Connor, 1989a, 36–7).

In a series of important studies which began in 1985 Connor set about tackling his own agenda.[4] But they, like this present chapter, are but a prolegomenon to attempts to write new narrative histories of Greece or of a *polis* such as Athens.[5]

The approaches outlined also attempt to draw upon the increasing sophistication of our study of Greek religion and of Athenian festival and constitute a call for a greater use in the writing of political history of the insights to be gained from late twentieth-century studies of major Athenian *polis* festivals such as the City Dionysia, the Panathenaia, the Eleusinian Mysteries and the Anthesteria.[6] For the purposes of this chapter, my examples will focus on the Panathenaia.[7] The approach is not completely new but it has not been deployed as frequently or as effectively as perhaps it could be.[8] By way of contrast, in the study of Greek poetry and drama the reading of texts both in their social, festival and performative contexts and in the light of what is known of their political and historical background is well established. The reading of political events in a similar manner has a long way to go to catch up with the work of the literary and cultural critics.[9]

II. Festivals and the dating of events in Athenian history

In viewing Athenian history most historians adopt the filter of the Julian calendar (i.e., for example, 451 BC) overlaid, where the evidence exists, upon the Athenian civil/bouleutic year or archon year (i.e. 451/0 BC or more precisely 45_1_/0 BC for the second half of 451 and 451/_0_ for the first half of 450).[10] As Rhodes reminds us, the bouleutic year and the archon year, which was linked to the festival calendar and lunar months, were not identical. This discrepancy gave rise to extensive mid-twentieth-century scholarly debate about synchronisms between the two with Meritt and Pritchett as the protagonists.[11]

Towards the end of the fifth century BC Hippias of Elis,[12] drawing on lists of victors (*Olympionikai*) already kept at Olympia,[13] produced a list of Olympic victors upon which he is also credited with writing a treatise. Hippias thereby created a dating scheme which potentially could accommodate the numerous differing *polis* calendars.[14] Dating by Olympiads, however, does not appear to have been first used for the temporal structuring of a narrative by an historian until its adoption by Timaeus of Sicily for his universal history in the third century BC.[15] Faced with the same problem of incompatible *polis* calendars, Thucydides (5.20; 26.1) adopted a dating scheme of summers and winters and only made use of Olympiads for time-reckoning twice.[16] Both instances (3.8 = 428 BC and 5.48.1 = 420 BC) use the formula 'when x was victorious at Olympia'. This always referred to the victor in the foot race – the *stadion*.

Although Olympiad dating was not adopted by historians until the Hellenistic period, several facts indicate that this key Olympic festival and its victors in the *stadion* played an important role in the recollection of past events and in the reckoning of time for contemporary events. These facts include firstly, the status which was afforded to victors in the Olympic and other Panhellenic festivals (cf. *IG* I[3] 131); secondly, the evidence which indicates that Olympic victories figured in the recounting of events in popular tradition (cf. Thuc. 1.126.3; 3.8.1; 5.50.5);[17] and thirdly, the use of the Olympic Games as a means of setting dates for *poleis* with differing local calendars. An example of the latter is to be found in Thucydides 5.47.10, which records the renewal of oaths for the treaty between Athens, Argos, Mantinea and Elis agreed to in the summer of 420 BC.[18] These serve as a reminder that for Athenians and other Greeks the festival calendar, whether Panhellenic or local, was an important means of reckoning the passage of time. Indeed at Athens, despite some scholarly controversies over details, we can go a step further and state that the Panathenaic year, and especially the quadrennial period from the celebration of one Great Panathenaia to the next, the so-called *pentetēris*, was of particular importance as it was used to determine the duration of office of some magistrates including sacred treasurers, the *athlothetai* and probably the *Hellēnotamiai* who served as treasurers for the Delian League.[19]

Although the bouleutic calendar at Athens was used for official purposes such as dating decrees of the *ekklēsia* and the *boulē*, this civil calendar, based upon prytanies and the solar year, did not replace the festival or archontic calendar. This religious calendar, identified by its eponymous archon and divided into 12 (or 13) lunar months, 'remained the calendar by which all festivals were fixed'.[20] It also remained the 'natural' calendar by which the ordinary citizen instinctively dated.[21] Furthermore, it was this calendar which more than any other marked out the passage of time and created the backdrop against which events were played out.

In his 1975 study Jon Mikalson reached a number of important conclusions which reinforce the significance of this fact.[22] Firstly, based on available evidence, both epigraphical and literary, the Athenians celebrated at least 144 festival days each year. These included festivals celebrated each month as well as those only celebrated once a year.[23] Such evidence clearly substantiates the claim of the 'Old Oligarch' ([Xen.] *Ath. Pol.* 3.2; cf. Thuc. 2.38.1) that the Athenians celebrated more festivals than any other Greek city. Strabo 6.280 states that Tarentum had more public festival days per year than non-festival days and, but for the fragmentary nature of our evidence, the same may have been the case at Athens as well. Mikalson also notes, secondly, that 'with very few exceptions meetings of the ekklesia did not occur on monthly or annual festival days' and, thirdly, that 'likewise meetings of the boule did not occur on annual festival days'.[24] Fourthly, despite slightly less than half of all the days of each year being (on surviving evidence) designated as festival days, 'every day established as a festival day was not a day of vacation for all Athenians'.[25] Although the 'Old Oligarch' might rightly protest that during Athenian festivals it was impossible for anyone to transact state business (3.2), the life of the *polis* did not come to a complete standstill on festival days.[26] On monthly or lunar festival days the *boulē* continued to transact business. Eleven of the thirty-eight financial transactions made by the treasurers of Athena and recorded on the Choiseul marble (*IG* I[2] 304B = I[3] 377) occurred on festival days, nine on monthly festival days and two on annual festival days.[27] Finally, 'sacred and civil were…tightly interwoven in ancient Athenian life', with the

Athenian calendar being 'a unity of interrelated sacred and civil elements'. For Mikalson this last conclusion has specific implications for the restoration of epigraphic texts, but collectively his accumulated evidence adds weight to the conclusions of a generation of scholars that religion and festival were inextricably woven into the fabric of *polis* life. Festival not only framed public life, it underpinned it.[28]

Despite this evidence and these conclusions one gets very little idea from either ancient sources or modern scholarship of the relationship between festivals and political events. In the former they are likely to be an unspoken 'given' as much as they are deliberate omissions. Thucydides, for example, has been criticized for his omission of religious matters, especially as explanations of events.[29] However, although Thucydides may have lacked the acknowledgement of the 'priority of the divine' to be found in the works of Xenophon and other writers,[30] his work, despite his scepticism about oracles, is not without reference to religious matters.[31] The Panathenaia, for example, is referred to at 1.20.2, 5.47.10, 6.56.2 and 6.57.1. Three of these references occur in relation to his account of the assassination of Hippias in 514/13 and the other occurs in the terms of the quadruple alliance between Athens, Argos, Mantinea and Elis agreed to in the summer of 420. Important details on festivals are also to be found at 2.15.2 on the Synoikia and at 3.104 on the purification of Delos and the re-organization of the Delia.[32] On the whole, however, the normal course of events is not considered, either by Thucydides or most modern authors, against the backdrop of festival activity at Athens. In the case of modern scholars this is despite the abundant scholarship that now exists on Attic festivals and their significance and the fact that *inter alia* festival participation was seen as central to the recognition of who was a citizen and who was not (Isaios 8.15–16).[33]

III. The Panathenaia[34]

The Athenians took pride in, and were widely known for, the number of festivals which they celebrated each year, with Perikles proclaiming in his funeral speech: 'We celebrate games (*agōnes*) and sacrifices (*thusiai*) all the year round' (Thuc. 2.38.1).[35] Of these the Panathenaia, which was celebrated in honour of Athena, the city's patron deity, was one of the most important. This is not the place to give a detailed account of the Panathenaia but, given my focus upon it, there are a few points that need to be made and several recent developments in the study of the Panathenaia that need to be noted.[36] It was held in the summer month of Hekatombaion (about July) each year and included contests in poetry, music, beauty and athletics. Once every four years, in the third year of each Olympiad, it was celebrated as the Great Panathenaia with ceremonies spread out over eight days.[37] In each of the other three years it may have spanned as few as two days and was known as the Lesser Panathenaia. Each year the focal point of the festival was the procession held on 28th Hekatombaion to mark Athena's birthday. Hekatombaion takes its name from the *hekatombē*, the one-hundred-cattle sacrifice which was the central cult act on the 28th after the conclusion of the *pompē*.[38] From its re-organization during the archonship of Hippokleides in 566/5 BC (Pherykydes *FGrHist* 3 F2) the Great Panathenaia was clearly promoted by the Athenians as a Panhellenic festival to rival the 'Big Four' celebrated at Olympia, Delphi, Nemea and the Isthmus/Korinth and, like those festivals, it was a key element in the reinforcement of *polis* identity and community values.[39]

The Panathenaia has been variously characterized. Robin Osborne, for example, writes of it as:

> ...a great carnival, a religious procession of sacrificial cattle combined with a display of military and civic might which included a parade of cavalry and the trundling along of a warship. This was a festival which highlighted the actions of the Athenians as a political body and exhibited their preparations to face the outside world (1987, 172).

Jennifer Neils, who has edited two major collections of essays on the Pana-thenaia, has characterized the Panathenaia in the following terms:

> In its inclusiveness, it exemplified the city's participatory democracy; in its contests it demonstrated the competitive spirit of its people; with its prizes it displayed the skills of its artisans and the wealth of its produce; and above all it celebrated Athena as the divine protectress of a glorious city.[40]

In her 1998 article 'The Panathenaic procession: Athens' participatory democracy on display?' Lisa Maurizio queries the extent to which the Panathenaia with its *pompē* which gave prominence to the wealthy, both citizen and metic, and in particular to the cavalry, did in fact embody the ideals of the direct participatory democracy as has often been claimed. For example, the thetes, who as rowers and as the majority in meetings of the *ekklēsia*, played a major role in the power and defence of the fifth-century democracy, did not have a separate formal presence in the Pana-thenaic procession other than as 'demesmen' at its rear. It could be argued, however, that the wheeled ship gave some recognition of the importance of the 'naval mob' (*nautikos ochlos*; Thuc. 8.72.2) to the military and political power of fifth-century Athens.[41] This was after all a festival which predated the democracy and which, in its origins, harked back to the very formation of the Athenian *polis* in an age dominated by the aristocracy. That it underwent changes and was adapted to the needs of the evolving *polis*, and ultimately to those of the Athenian democracy and its empire, are not denied, but Maurizio argues that it also served to problematize and confront the democracy and its notions of political citizenship, by presenting an image of Athens and the Athenians which was more focussed on what she calls 'religious citizenship'.[42] As she puts it:

> From before the democracy, in the seventh and sixth centuries, and during the democracy in the fifth and the fourth centuries...the Panathenaic procession persisted as a form of ritual that defined the Athenian community as a collection of individuals who dwelt in the same land and worshipped the same goddess. In other words, it realized religious citizenship, and this religious citizenship did not change as the political definition of citizenship in democratic Athens evolved. (1998, 316)

Part of Maurizio's aim was to review both the literary and iconographic evidence, in order to establish more securely the composition and order of the Panathenaic procession at the height of its formalization during the fifth and fourth centuries BC. Her final order serves to highlight the significance of the Panathenaia as a truly all-Athenian festival with the incorporation of both citizen and non-citizen elements in the procession. The extent of non-citizen participation is highlighted by the following elements which are listed in the order assigned to them by Maurizio: (2) metic girl parasol-bearers (*skiadēphoroi*), (3) metic girl stool-bearers (*diphrophoroi*), (7) metic men tray-bearers (*skaphēphoroi*), (8) metic girl water-bearers (*hydriaphoroi*), (13) representatives of other cities who, in the case of tributary allies of the Delian League, brought offerings of 'a cow and a panoply' of hoplite armour[43] and, at the 'end of the procession proper', following the citizens (demesmen), (20) non-citizens and freed slaves (with oak branches).[44]

IV. The Panathenaia and political crises in archaic Athens

A significant example of the ways in which political events can be read in the context of both religious *mentalité* and of festival was given by Robert Connor in his study 'Tribes, festivals and processions in archaic Greece' (1987).[45] Drawing upon the study of ritual and ceremonial in civic life, especially as influenced by cultural and symbolic anthropology in the writings of anthropologists such as Clifford Geertz (1973), Connor investigated 'the possibility of applying such approaches to archaic Greece and thereby of exploring the nature of political life and leadership, the role of propaganda, manipulation...[of popular religious sentiments], and the significance of ritual festivals and ceremonial in [the] civic life' of the archaic *polis*.[46]

Connor's exploration of the relationship between civic ceremony or festivals and politics was begun by an examination of two episodes from archaic Athenian history. The first was Peisistratos' return to power in the 550s with which is associated the tradition of his entry into Athens in a chariot accompanied by a statuesque young woman (*parthenos*), Phye, dressed as Athena (Hdt. 1.60.2–5). Connor dismisses Herodotus' incredulity and offers a plausible explanation based upon the shared religious *mentalité* of Peisistratos and the Athenians and the involvement of the populace in a 'shared drama' which, *inter alia,* was familiar with the traditions of Athena riding in the chariots of her favoured heroes and mortals.[47] The second episode was the establishment by Solon of a census system based on agricultural production and wealth expressed in *medimnoi* (*pentakosiomedimnoi, hippeis, zeugitai* and *thētes*, Aristotle *Ath. Pol.* 7.4) from which Connor argued that one of the roles of festival processions was to provide a means for both the display, and perhaps the determination, of the wealth of its citizens, especially its rich citizens.[48]

In his preamble to these two explorations Connor drew attention to 'an apparent convergence between festivals and political disturbances'. This he illustrated with two further examples from archaic Athens, one from the late seventh century and the other from the sixth century. The first was Kylon's attempted coup (*c.* 630s or 620s BC), purportedly in response to his misinterpretation of an oracle from Delphi that foretold that he should seize the Acropolis at the time of 'the greatest festival of Zeus' (Thuc. 1.126.4). In view of his prior Olympic victory Kylon took this to be the summer festival of Zeus at Olympia (1.126.5). Unfortunately for the success of his planned coup he should have looked closer to home to the Athenian spring festival, the Diasia (23 Anthesterion). This festival, which was held in honour of Zeus Meilichios, 'the friendly', and which was characterized by bloodless offerings, was celebrated outside the city, which would have facilitated the seizure of the Akropolis (Thuc. 1.126.6).[49] Connor's second example was the assassination of the Peisistratid Hipparchos at the time of the Great Panathenaia of 514 (on which see section V below). In addition to these two episodes Connor also refers to an earlier study by Thomas Figueira (1984) in which it was suggested that 'the principal periods of instability in the early sixth century in Athens coincided with the years of the Great Panathenaia'.[50] These are illustrated and taken further in TABLE 1 below where the conjunction of events with either the Great Panathenaia itself, or with Great Panathenaic years, can be seen to continue beyond the periods of *anarchia* early in the sixth century through to the end of the rule of the Peisistratids. It can be no mere coincidence that Hippias, and later his son Peisistratos the Younger, both held the office of eponymous archon in years which commenced with the celebration of the Great Panathenaia.[51]

TABLE 1. Great Panathenaic years: sixth century BC.[52] (Great Panathenaic years in bold)

Archon Year	Olympiad	Athenian Archon	Develin 1989 (page)	Ancient Evidence and Events
594/3	Ol. 46.3	Solon	37	
590/89	Ol. 47.3	*anarchia*	39	*Ath. Pol.* 13.1
586/5	Ol. 48.3	*anarchia*	39	*Ath. Pol.* 13.1
582/1	Ol. 49.3	Damasias	40	Damasias was archon for 26 months (*Ath. Pol.* 13.2)
579/8	Ol. 50.2	10 Archons		Restoration of annual archons after 2 months (?) (cf. *Ath. Pol.* 13.2 with Rhodes 1981, 182–3 and Figueira 1984)
578/7	Ol. 50.3	?	40	
574/3	Ol. 51.3	?		
570/69	Ol. 52.3	Aristomenes	40	
566/5	Ol. 53.3	Hippokleides Teisandrou	41	Re-organization of the Great Panathenaia (*IG* I³ 507) by Peisistratos (?) (Scholia Aelius Aristeides XIII.189.4–5; Aristotle fr. 637 Rose)
562/1	Ol. 54.3	?	41	Peisistratos *stratēgos*: war against Megara (?) (Hdt. 1.59.4; *Ath. Pol.* 14.1)
561/60	Ol. 55.4	?		First attempt at tyranny by Peisistratos (*Ath. Pol.* 14.1; Plut. *Solon* 29; cf. Hdt. 1.59.3–6)
558/7	Ol. 55.3	?		
557/6	Ol. 55.4	Polemarchos	43	Second attempt at tyranny by Peisistratos: Phye as Athena (Hdt. 1.59.3–6; *Ath. Pol.* 14.4; Develin 1989, xi n. 3 following Rhodes 1981, 191–9 with tables 1 and 2)
554/3	Ol. 56.3	?		
550/49	Ol. 57.3	Pha[....]	44	
546/5	Ol. 58.3	Phor[mion]	45	Third, successful, attempt at tyranny by Peisistratos (Hdt. 1.63–64; *Ath. Pol.* 15.3–16.1)
542/1	Ol. 59.3	?		
538/7	Ol. 60.3	?		
534/3	Ol. 61.3	?		
530/29	Ol. 62.3	?		
529/8	Ol. 62.4	?		
528/7	Ol. 63.1	?		Death of Peisistratos
527/6	Ol. 63.2	[On]eto[rides]	46	Fragment of archon list (*IG* I³ 1031 = *ML* 11 = Fornara 1985, no. 23C)
526/5	Ol. 63.3	[H]ippia[s]	47	*IG* I³ 1031
525/4	Ol. 63.4	[K]leisthen[es]	47	*IG* I³ 1031
524/3	Ol. 64.1	[M]iltiad[es]	47	*IG* I³ 1031; Dion. Hal. *Ant. Rom.* 7.3.1
523/2	Ol. 64.2	[Ka]lliades	47	*IG* I³ 1031
522/1	Ol. 64.3	[Peisi]strat[os]	47	*IG* I³ 1031; Thuc. 6.54.6
518/17	Ol. 65.3	Habron ??	48	
514/3	Ol. 66.3	??		Assassination of Hipparchos (Thuc. 6.53–59; *Ath. Pol.* 18)

511/10	Ol. 67.2	Harpaktides	48	Expulsion of Hippias and the Peisistratids (Hdt. 5.64–65.2; Thuc. 6.59; *Ath. Pol.* 19.6)
510/09	Ol. 67.3	Skamandrios	51	First Great Panathenaia after the tyranny. Statues set up for Harmodios and Aristogeiton (Pliny *Natural History* 34.17) Great Panathenaia becomes linked to anti-tyrant sentiments (?)
508/7	Ol. 68.1	Isagoras	51	Kleisthenes' tribal reforms (Hdt. 5.69; *Ath. Pol.* 21)
506/5	Ol. 68.3	?		First Great Panathenaia after tribal reforms
502/1	Ol. 69.3	?		

Major *polis* festivals with their focus on the political and religious centre of a *polis* may be assumed to have resulted in the presence within the *asty* (the urban centre or city) of larger numbers of citizens than at non-festival periods. As a result it would seem that they were perceived by some as opportune moments, both in terms of the numbers present and in terms of the manipulation of a shared religious *mentalité*, to promote political changes or to stage coups. Their celebration may also have provided the opportunity to introduce new elements into a festival. Such would appear to have been the case with changes made to the Panathenaia by the Peisistratids, who closely identified themselves with it as an all-Athenian festival, and with its honorand, Athena.[53] This known association of the Peisistratids with the Panathenaia also helps to explain the timing of the attempted coup against the Peisistratid tyrant Hippias which resulted in the death of his brother Hipparchos.

V. The murder of Hipparchos, the Panathenaia and the Leokoreion[54]

Alan Shapiro, in a general set of observations, draws our attention to the symbolic importance of the location of the murder of Hipparchos. What was, in both intention and effect, a political assassination, took place near the Leokoreion which 'was sacred to the daughters of Leos, who had given *their* lives to save Athens from plague and famine in primitive times, just as Harmodios and Aristogeiton sacrificed themselves to save the city from tyranny'. However, Shapiro neither comments on the 'problem' of the Leokoreion nor elaborates on the daughters of Leos.[55] Thucydides at 1.20.2 writes that Harmodios and Aristogeiton 'did not attack Hippias [that is 'the' tyrant, cf. 6.55], but not liking to risk their lives and be apprehended for nothing, they fell upon Hipparchos near the Leokoreion and slew him while he was arranging the Panathenaic procession' (trans. Crawley, modified). In the surviving traditions there is confusion about the location of Hippias and Hipparchos at the time of the assassination and uncertainty about the location of the Leokoreion, the sanctuary for the daughters of

Leos, with at least one scholar doubting both the myth and the existence of a sanctuary for them in the agora.[56] Thucydides at 6.57.1 has Hippias and his bodyguard outside the city in the Kerameikos organizing the order of the *pompē*. However, the Aristotelian *Athenaion Politieia* disagrees over the location of Hippias:

> When they [Harmodios and Aristogeiton] were waiting to catch Hippias on the Acropolis at the Panathenaia (it was his function to receive the procession, and Hipparchos's to despatch it), they saw one of the men involved in the plot meeting Hippias in a friendly manner,[57] and thought he was turning informer. Wanting to achieve something before they were arrested, they went down from the Acropolis, and acted without waiting for the others: they killed Hipparchos as he was organizing the procession by the Leokoreion. This ruined the whole plot. (*Ath. Pol.* 18.3, trans. Rhodes, modified spelling)

The logical conclusion, as Rhodes notes, would be to place Hipparchos near the Leokoreion despatching the procession, or soon after its despatch, with Hippias on the Acropolis. This is consistent with Thucydides' location of Hipparchos in 1.20.2.[58] Both Demosthenes in his funeral speech (60.29) and Diodorus Siculus (17.15.2) briefly recount the myth of the daughters of Leos saving the city by the willing sacrifice of their lives. Details are not given but myths of young women or heroines willingly dying to save the city at a time of crisis are well attested for Athens.[59] The myth of the daughters of Leos and its antiquity need not be doubted, nor that they received cult at the Leokoreion near which Harmodios and Aristogeiton assassinated Hipparchos.[60] The location of the Leokoreion is another matter. Travlos originally associated the Leokoreion with a small round building 18 m in diameter in the north-west of the agora, but it proved to be too late (fifth century AD); however, it remained his belief that the Leokoreion must have been in the north-west of the agora near the Altar of the Twelve Gods.[61] Wycherley identified it with a small enclosure 3 m square in the north-west of the agora in front of the Stoa Basileus, but Camp considers this no more than a possibility.[62] Few have any doubt that the Leokoreion existed in the Peisistratid period or that it was located in the north-west corner of the agora near the point where the Panathenaic way enters from the Kerameikos before cutting diagonally through the agora on its way to the ramp at the west end of the Acropolis. If the points made by Connor and others about the shared symbolism and significance of festival processions are accepted, we can, without causing any serious offence in the use of our sources, infer that as the Panathenaic procession, marshalled by and including Hipparchos, made its way into the agora and reached a point opposite the Leokoreion, his assassins, later to become the recipients of hero cult as 'The Tyrannicides' and have their statues set up in the agora, made their symbolic, if unsuccessful, attempt to 'save the city'.[63] A political assassination had been deliberately staged on a date, the occasion of the Panathenaic procession, and at a place, near the Leokoreion, which would carry the clearest of messages to those in attendance about Peisistratid usurpation of the traditional freedoms and magisterial roles of the aristocracy.

VI. Great Panathenaic years and selected political events in fifth-century Athens

TABLE 2. Great Panathenaic years: fifth century BC. (Great Panathenaic years in bold)

Archon Year	Olympiad	Athenian Archon	Develin 1989 (page)	Ancient Evidence and Events
498/7	Ol. 70.3			
496/5	Ol. 71.1	Hipparchos	54	(Hipparchos was a Peisistratid: *Ath. Pol.* 22.4)
494/3	Ol. 71.3	Pithokritos	55	
490/89	Ol. 72.3	Phainippos	55	Battle of Marathon: Metageitnion (August 12? Burn 1962, 257) which was the month which came immediately after Hekatombaion. The Great Panathenaia would have been celebrated in the shadow of the Persian advance.
486/5	Ol. 73.3	?		
482/1	Ol. 74.3	?		
478/7	Ol. 75.3	Timosthenes	66	
474/3	Ol. 76.3	Akestorides	69	
470/69	Ol. 77.3	Demotion	70	
466/5	Ol. 78.3	Lysanias	70	
462/1	Ol. 79.3	Konon	72	The reforms of Ephialtes (*Ath. Pol.* 35.2)
458/7	Ol. 80.3	Habron	74	Battle of Tanagra and anti-democratic conspiracy at Athens (?) (Thuc. 1.107.6; cf. Aeschylus *Eumenides* 858–66)
454/3	Ol. 81.3	Ariston	77	Transfer of the Delian League treasury to Athens (*IG* I³ 259 = Fornara 1985 no. 85)
450/49	Ol. 82.3	Euthynos	80	Second tribute assessment period
446/5	Ol. 83.3	Kallimachos	84	
442/1	Ol. 84.3	Diphilos	88	
438/7	Ol. 85.3	Theodoros	93	Completion and dedication of Pheidias' statue of Athena Parthenos at the Great Panathenaia (*IG* I³ 453–60; Fornara 1985 no. 114; Hurwit 1999, 310, 314, 323)
434/3	Ol. 86.3	Krates	97	
432/1	Ol. 87.1	Pythodoros	101	Outbreak of the Peloponnesian War
430/29	Ol. 87.3	Apollodoros	118	Plague at Athens (Thuc. 2.52.3–4; 53.4)
426/5	Ol. 88.3	Euthynos	126	
422/1	Ol. 89.3	Alkaios	137	Peace of Nikias: 24 Elaphebolion (Feb./March) 422/1
420/19	Ol. 90.1	Astyphilos	142	Quadruple Alliance – decree to be set up on

				the Acropolis before the Lesser Panathenaia (?) (*IG* I³ 83; Thuc. 5.47.11, at the time of 'the Olympic Games now in hand' = mid-summer)
418/17	Ol. 90.3	Antiphon	144	
414/13	Ol. 91.3	Teisandros	152	
410/09	Ol. 92.3	Glaukippos	165	The first Great Panathenaia of the restored democracy; the first performance of *The Persians* by Timotheos (?) (see below section VII)
406/5	Ol. 93.3	Kallias	178	Preparations for the relief force which fought at Arginousai (Xen. *Hell.* 1.6.24, 'within 30 days') during Hekatombaion. Battle of Arginousai *c.* August (Metageitnion). Trial of the generals at the Apatouria (Pyanepsion = Sept./Oct.; over 4 days, dates uncertain)
404/3	Ol. 94.1	Pythodoros + *anarchia*	183	Thirty at Athens
403/2	Ol. 94.2	Eukleides	199	Restoration of democracy at Athens
402/1	Ol. 94.3	Mikon	201	First Great Panathenaia of the restored democracy. Pompeion constructed and/or inaugurated? (or 398/7; see below section VIII)

TABLE 2 is only meant to be indicative of some events that fall in Great Panathenaic years and does not attempt to list all events that may be placed in such years, whether proximate to 28 Hekatombaion or not. Nor is it to be taken as implying a causal connection between the Great Panathenaia and the events listed. Rather it is intended to suggest possibilities and raise questions for the further exploration of the relationship, either symbolic or more general, between festival, in this case the Panathenaia, and politics at Athens.[64] Thus, for example, it is worthy of note that the political mood at Athens prior to the battle of Marathon, which saw its commanders divided as to whether to avoid battle with the Persians or to stand and fight (Hdt. 6.100–10), may have been influenced not merely by the kind of civic pride which is revealed, however anachronistically, in Miltiades' address before the battle (Hdt. 6.109–10). It may also have been given impetus by the celebration of the Great Panathenaia just a couple of weeks before the battle and at a time when the attack of the Persians was imminent. Nor may it have been without significance that the democratic reforms of Ephialtes in 462/1 belong to a Great Panathenaic year. Similarly, assuming, as some do, that the battle of Tanagra took place in the summer of 458, a suspected anti-democratic coup at the time of the battle (Thuc.1.107.6) may have been planned to take advantage of the larger than usual gathering of citizens in Athens for the Great Panathenaia.[65] In both of these last two examples we may be seeing a continuation into the fifth century of significant political changes or crises associated with the four-yearly Panathenaia that Figueira noted for the sixth century.

Another issue raised by TABLE 2 is the entry for the Great Panathenaia of 430/29 which places it in the middle of the plague at Athens. Given that Thucydides' observations at 2.52.3 imply that festivals were not observed, or not properly observed, during the worst ravages of the plague, are we to assume that the Athenians would have run the risk of not observing, or not correctly observing, a major festival such as the Great Panathenaia, especially one the central day of which honoured their patron deity? As a final example, the timing of the transfer of the treasury of the Delian League from Delos to Athens in 454/3 may have had more to do with its being a Great Panathenaic year than with any supposed crisis in the Alliance. It should be remembered that the reassessment of tribute took place in association with the Great Panathenaia and that the *Hellenotamiai* served a quadrennial term from one Great Panathenaia to the next.[66] At the very least it is hoped that TABLE 2, or similar tables for years which correlate known events with the celebration of key festivals in the Athenian religious calendar, may assist in the viewing of events with an eye to what was going on as part of the regular community life and religious observances of the Athenian *polis* and not just with an eye to the happenings of the *ekklēsia*, the lawcourts or the battlefield.

Finally, in considering the possible relationships between political events and the Panathenaia one should not forget the annual or Lesser Panathenaia which, although lacking the extensive *agōnes* that characterized the Great Panathenaia, was still an important event in the Athenian religious and civil year. During the period of the Athenian empire (477–404 BC) the Lesser Panathenaia would still have seen the annual offering of a cow and panoply from allies which would have made the Panathenaic procession, with its metic and non-Athenian participants, a regular and impressive testament to Athenian power. A set of regulations for the Lesser Panathenaia from 336/5 BC (*IG* II² 334) indicates that Athena's birthday on 28 Hekatombaion was still celebrated on a lavish scale.

Two events, which do not appear at first glance to be of particular significance, must serve as a final pair of examples of the ways in which details and events may be enhanced by reading them in the light of their festival associations. The first example illustrates the way a festival event, the contest for kitharodes, may be seen as politically significant by viewing it in its wider political context. The final example accords a politically significant status to a decision of the Athenian *ekklēsia* to construct a marshalling hall for festival processions.

VII. The first performance of *The Persians* of Timotheos of Miletos

This event does not make its way into historical narratives of the late fifth century nor perhaps as fully as it should into the work of historians of Greek literature.[67] However, if, as I argue below, the first performance of *The Persians* of Timotheos, which took as its story the defeat of the Persians at Salamis in 480 BC, belongs to the Great Panathenaia of 410/09, then it may have had no less an impact upon morale than the performance of Aeschylus' *Persians* at the City Dionysia of 472 (*IG* II² 2318.9–11) is believed to have had.[68]

Satyrus in his *Life of Euripides* (*P.Oxy.* 1176 fr. 39 col. xxii = Campbell 1993, 74–5 T6) writes that 'when Timotheos (was despised?) among the Greeks for his musical innovation' and in depression contemplated suicide he was encouraged by Euripides, himself a composer of 'new music', to continue with his work. Satyrus continues, stating that Euripides 'even composed the prelude to *The Persians* with the result that Timotheos won the prize and was despised no longer'. The prize must have been in the musical *agōnes* held in the Periklean Odeion as part of the Panathenaic festival.[69] Timotheos is also known to have competed at the Karneia at Sparta (Plut. *Inst. Lak.* 17. 238c = Campbell 1993, 76–7 T7).[70] Herrington has argued that *The Persians* is the only Greek poem the performance of which can be 'reconstructed with any degree of assurance'.[71] He follows Bassett (1931), for whom the connection between Timotheos and Euripides who died in 406 is decisive, in dating the performance to between 412 and 408 BC. Neither, however, assigns a more specific date. Others, misled by Plutarch's quotation in *Agesilaos* 14 of a line from *The Persians*, 'Ares is king [*tyrannos*]; Greece fears no gold' (Ἄρης τύραννος· χρυσὸν Ἑλλάς οὐ δέδοικε), in the context of Agesilaos' campaigns in Asia Minor in 395, propose a date for composition between 400 and 395.[72] But by then these words had already achieved the status of a proverb. Indeed, such was the success of the poem that it was still being performed two centuries later (Plutarch *Philopoemen* 11; cf. Pausanias 8.50.3). Both Plutarch and Pausanias also repeat the opening line of the poem: 'Fashioning for Greece the great and glorious ornament of freedom' (Campbell 1993, 92–3, fr. 788). Indeed Xenobius in his *Proverbs* says that 'Ares is king…' was 'a phrase from *The Persians*, which, owing to the success the poem met with at Athens, spread and survived as a proverb'.[73]

Apart from a few fragments (Campbell 1993, 90–3, frs. 788–99) the beginning of *The Persians* is lost. Podlecki, following Bassett, has argued that the poem may have begun with a speech by Themistokles with Timotheos drawing on traditions concerning a speech which Themistokles gave to the Greeks before Salamis (Hdt. 8.83.1).[74] If this was the case, then the expression, 'Ares is king (*tyrannos*)', may also derive from Themistokles and not be original to Timotheos. Such a hypothesis could help to resolve the potential difficulty caused by the use of the word *tyrannos* for 'king' rather than the more acceptable *basileus*. During the period of the direct participatory democracy at Athens the term *tyrannos*, in the sense of 'tyrant' rather than 'king', had acquired negative connotations in Athenian democratic ideology and was seen as the very antithesis of democracy. Thucydides and others critical of the Athenian empire of the second half of the fifth century BC also applied the term *tyrannos* to the Athenians themselves. *Tyrannos* is included by Thucydides in speeches for both Perikles (2.63.2) and Kleon (3.37.2). The ambiguity of *tyrannos* is clearly exemplified in the title of Sophocles' tragedy, *Oidipous Tyrannos*, of the 420s which some still prefer to Latinize as *Oedipus Rex* or translate as *Oedipus the King*.[75] Whether the expression, 'Ares is *tyrannos*', was original to Themistokles or to Timotheos it is also worth noting that *tyrannos* is here applied to a god, the Greek god of war, Ares, whose power was chaotic and disruptive, and not to an individual ruler or to imperial rule.[76]

Our only significant fragment of *The Persians* is from the Berlin papyrus (*P.Berol.* 9875) which preserves 240 lines. As noted, the poem may have begun with a speech by Themistokles. It certainly included a vivid narration of the battle of Salamis and 'ended with a series of four quoted speeches by defeated Persians, ranging from the fractured Greek of a common Phrygian soldier to the following solemn lament of the Great King':[77]

> …and when the King had looked on his army rushing in confusion in backward-travelling flight, fallen to his knees he maltreated his body and said as he tossed in the billows of his misfortune, 'Oh, the ruination of my house! Oh, you scorching Greek ships (ναες Ἑλλανίδες) that destroyed the young men of my ships, a great throng of my contemporaries, so that the ships will not carry them away backward-travelling, but fire's smoky strength will burn them with its savage body, and lamentable sufferings will befall the Persian land!' (ll. 173–86 trans. Campbell 1993, 107–9).

At any time between 412 and 408 when the Athenians and their allies were engaged either in trying to foil a Spartan alliance with Persia or in naval warfare with the Persian-backed Spartan fleet (Thuc. 8; Xen. *Hell.* 1.1–3),[78] these words, together with those about Greek freedom in the opening line and the defiant proclamation, 'Ares is king; Greece fears no gold', would have struck a resonant chord in the hearts of those Athenians, their allies and friends, who listened to the career-changing song of Timotheos in the Odeion.[79] So too Timotheos' emphasis at line 179 on 'Greek ships' at Salamis, and not on Athenian ships, could be seen as reflecting the current joint effort of Athens *and* her allies during the Ionian War. In seeking to date the first performance of *The Persians* more specifically there are two details which would seem to point to the Great Panathenaia of 410/09. Firstly it was the first Great Panathenaia celebrated by the restored democracy and, secondly, it would have been celebrated in the full knowledge of the recent conclusion of the Persian alliance with Sparta (Thuc. 8.57–8).[80] In the context of the alliance between Sparta and Persia, with its promise of Persian funding for the Spartan fleet, the significance of the line, 'Ares is king; Greece fears no gold', takes on a new meaning: a united alliance of Greeks did not fear the gold of Persia. If these lines are also a recollection of Themistokles' exhortation, 'Ares is king', as Podlecki and Campbell conjecture, then there may have been yet a further parallel and lesson to be drawn between Salamis and the situation in 411–410: the Athenians and their allies would rely on the Greek god of war, together with the destruction he could bring to his enemies and the valour which he inspired, and they did not need to depend upon Persian gold as the Spartans were now doing. They would not medize in the face of threats to their freedom. In the words of the opening line of *The Persians*, they would fashion 'for Greece the great and glorious ornament of freedom' (fr. 788, Campbell).[81]

So significant was the impact of this one song at the Panathenaia that Timotheos' reputation, which was at a low ebb because of his 'new music', was turned around almost overnight with one line: 'Ares is king; Greece fears no gold.' This line became a proverbial battle cry for the continued struggle against the Persians *and* the Spartans, victory for whom would mean, indeed all too soon came to mean, defeat for democracy. This was a unified rallying cry which recalled Salamis not as an Athenian victory but as a victory of the Greeks against the Persians. The same unified effort was required once more, but this time with even greater urgency because the Spartans were no longer allies but in league with the mortal enemy, the Persians![82]

VIII. The construction of the Pompeion at Athens[83]

Another event missing from the historical record and from historical narratives, this time from the years immediately after the end of the Peloponnesian War, is the decision taken by the Athenians to construct the Pompeion within the walls between the Sacred and Dipylon Gates as a marshalling hall for key participants in festival processions, especially for those of the Panathenaia.[84] Archaeologists place its construction and completion about 400 BC.[85] The decision to build the Pompeion must have been a significant one not only because of the importance placed by Athenians on shared cult and festival (Xen. *Hell.* 2.4.20–1) but also because of its likely role in the process of reconciliation after the defeat of the Thirty and the restoration of the democracy. Given the difficulties in dating the Pompeion on purely archaeological grounds it is perhaps not unreasonable to assume that it was inaugurated for first use at a Great Panathenaia. The decision itself could have been one of the first acts of the restored democracy (cf. *Ath. Pol.* 40–41.1), but, unless the construction was completed in about a year, the first Great Panathenaia (402/1) celebrated by the restored democracy may have been too soon. Unless inaugurated at a celebration of the Lesser Panathenaia the building may not have been ready until the next Great Panathenaia of 398/7.[86]

Appendix 1: Mikalson on festival participation

In his study of the Athenian sacred and civil calendar Mikalson draws our attention to *IG* II[2] 1672, ll. 32–3 (329/8 bc) which indicate that workers at the sanctuary of Demeter and Kore at Eleusis were paid for 40 successive days of work from 4 Hekatombaion through to early Metageitnion, thereby missing the opportunity to attend not only the Kronia (12 Hekatombaion) and the Synoikia (16 Hekatombaion) but also the Panathenaia (28 Hekatombaion). From this he draws a conclusion that could have important ramifications for our understanding of festival participation and the role of festival in the formation and reinforcement of civic identity: 'those of the lower economic strata would be less able to enjoy festival days as non-working days' (Mikalson 1975, 203). However, we should also note the likelihood that those resident or working in demes outside the city of Athens and the central Attic plain may have been less likely to attend city-based *polis* festivals, because their activities were governed instead by local deme calendars.[87] For Eleusis we only have fragments of its sacred calendar relating to the months of Pyanepsion and Skirophorion (*IG* II[2] 1363 = *SEG* 23.80). We are lacking any information about monthly or annual festivals that might have been celebrated at Eleusis during the months of Hekatombaion and Metageitnion and hence cannot determine whether the workers at Eleusis were missing any key local festivals. Our evidence for festivals during these two months does not enable us to cast much further light on the matter, as, apart from key attested *polis* festivals, we only have evidence for minor monthly festival days at Athens and local festivals at Erchia.[88] The date of the one festival which was celebrated during Metageitnion which would have impacted upon Eleusis, the biennial and quadrennial agonistic Eleusinia associated with the harvest, is disputed. Mikalson places it within the period 13–20 Metageitnion[89] which, in all probability, would place it *after* the 40 consecutive days commencing on 4 Hekatombaion which were worked by the workmen at Eleusis (*IG* II[2] 1672, ll. 32–3: ἀπὸ τῆς τετράδος ἱσταμένου τοῦ Ἑκατομβαιῶνο). As the fortieth day would have fallen on 13 Hekatombaion, perhaps that date can be ruled out as well given that 329/8, the fourth year of an Olympiad (Ol.112.4), is attested as a year in which the Eleusinia was celebrated (*IG* II² 1028, l.16). It is unlikely that any work would have been carried out during the Eleusinia ἐν τῶι ἱερῶι and especially during a festival that was not only an Eleusinian festival but one which became a *polis* festival at some stage during the sixth century. Indeed, we might conjecture that the 40 consecutive days of work were the result of having to complete whatever had to be done within the sanctuary prior to the celebration of the quadrennial Eleusinia which, although largely celebrated outside the sanctuary, required the perform-ance of sacrifices within the *temenos*.

The Eleusinia was once thought to have been celebrated biennially in the first and third years of an Olympiad and quadrennially during the second year of an Olympiad.[90] On the basis of annual payments made to the Eleusinian 'priests and priestesses' in *IG* II² 1672, Simms argued that the Eleusinia was held each year in association with the annual harvest and the celebration of Triptolemos as the hero entrusted by Demeter with the teaching of the arts of agriculture.[91] Clinton, however, has since argued against Mikalson, Simms and earlier scholars proposing that there was only one 'trieteric' Eleusinia – there being a two-year gap between what we might call a 'lesser' and 'greater' Eleusinia.[92] These were held respectively in the second and the fourth year of each Olympiad. If Clinton is correct, less weight can be given to Mikalson's conclusion, based on *IG* II² 1672, ll. 32–3, about the participation in festivals of those from lower socio-economic strata.

Appendix 2:
Athenian politics and festivals other than the Panathenaia

I note here some other documented instances where festival contexts can further enhance our understanding of political events at Athens. Not all have gone without notice but each offers the scope to take our current analyses further.[93] At the very least the festival associations can sometimes give us either exact or closely approximate dates in terms of the Athenian lunar and festival calendar, details which may enhance the precision of our historical narratives.

1. Kleisthenes and the City Dionysia (508/7 BC, 10–13 Elaphebolion). Connor 1989b has argued that the status of the City Dionysia as a key democratic festival is to be credited to the reform programme of Kleisthenes.[94]

2. The trial of the Arginousai generals in 407/<u>6</u> and the Apatouria (19–21 *or* 26–28 Pyanepsion).[95]

3. The return of Alkibiades to Athens and the Plynteria in 408/<u>7</u> (25 Thargelion).[96]

4. Alkibiades and the *pompē* of the Eleusinian Mysteries in 40<u>7</u>/6 (19 Boedromion).[97]

5. Festivals and the Thirty (404–403 BC). The important study of Green (1991) has, I believe, resolved a number of chronological conundrums about the dates of the Thirty at Athens. Green's solutions make it possible to explore the issue of festival continuity and participation under the Thirty more fully than has been done.[98]

APPENDIX 3: POLITICS AND FESTIVALS OUTSIDE ATHENS

Several brief examples of the interaction of politics and festival in *poleis* other than Athens may be noted. A significant Spartan example was the celebration of the Karneia for Apollo Karneios which delayed the Spartans' arrival at Marathon in 490 BC (Hdt. 6.106–107.1). Burkert (1985, 234–6) gives references to other occasions when the Karneia, an agonistic festival at Sparta and elsewhere, had consequences for the military actions of both Sparta and Argos. The latter, like Sparta, celebrated a Karneia during the month Karneios, named after its main festival.[99] Similarly, in 412, the Corinthians delayed their departure to assist the Peloponnesian fleet in fomenting revolt at Chios until they had celebrated the Isthmia (Thuc. 8.9.1–2). Finally, Gebbard (1993, 167–8) notes the political disputes between Sparta and Argos, each with the backing of a different Corinthian faction, which resulted in the double celebration of the Isthmia in 390 BC (Xen. *Hell.* 4.5.4).

Notes

[1] For a brief conspectus of approaches to, and trends in, the study of ancient history, see the two recent introductions by Morley (1999, 2000). For the current dominance of social history and some excellent examples of its use in the study of classical antiquity, see the series *Key Themes in Ancient History* edited by Paul Cartledge and Peter Garnsey and published by Cambridge University Press. None of the titles thus far published could be said to deal with traditional political or event-based history. For a recent title see Golden 1998.

[2] Connor 1989a. See also Morris 1993.

[3] Geertz 1973, 312; Connor 1989b, 35–7.

[4] See Connor 1985, 1987, 1988a, 1988b, 1988c, 1989a, 1991, 1996. Independently Shapiro, without reference to Connor's studies, has produced

a series of important studies, 1989, 1990, 1992, 1993, and especially 1994, which integrate the evidence of cult, myth and festival into readings of key events or periods of Athenian history. However, these are done primarily from his art-historical perspective and, whilst providing valuable and perceptive insights into the visual record of Athens' past, do not of themselves constitute narrative studies of events. Note also the promising multidisciplinary project commenced in 2001 and based in the Faculty of Classics at the University of Cambridge directed by Robin Osborne: 'The Anatomy of Cultural Revolution: Athenian art, literature, language, philosophy and politics 430–380 BC'.

[5] The most recent significant historical narratives of Athenian history to the end of the fifth century BC, Kagan 1969–87 and Ostwald 1986, were both conceived at what may be termed the 'dawn' of the new social history. Meier 1993 is a general narrative and Munn 2000 is a detailed intellectual and political history which concentrates on the period 415–395 BC.

[6] For the purposes of this chapter late-twentieth-century studies of Athenian festival will be taken as commencing with the German edition of Burkert's *Homo Necans* (1972; English translation 1985; cf. Burkert 1992), Mikalson's 1975 study of the Athenian sacred and civil calendar and Parke's month-by-month survey of Athenian festivals (Parke 1978). Parke, and indeed Mikalson, could be said to have been writing in an older tradition of the study of both Greek religion and of Athenian festivals dating back to Mommsen (1898) and to Deubner (1932), but each was significant in its own way. Mikalson, drawing upon nearly half a century of new epigraphical findings and research, gave greater precision and clarification to the placing of festivals throughout the Athenian sacred and civil year. Parke synthe-sized the 'state-of-play' on Athenian festivals at a point when the work of scholars like Burkert and members of what has been dubbed by some as 'the Parisian school' – Vernant, Vidal-Naquet, Detienne and Loraux *inter alia* – were in the process of producing studies which were to lead to a radical rethinking of the ways in which ancient historians and classicists approached the study and interpretation of Greek religion and its central cult sequences, festivals. The scholarly output in the field of Greek religion since the 1970s has been prodigious and shows no signs of abating. Useful bibliographical starting points can be found in Bruit-Zaidman and Schmitt Pantel 1992, 247–67, which also provides a good example of the approach of 'the Parisian School' (see especially xiii–xvi, 3–15, 20–3), and in Price 1999, 186–209. Loraux, Nagy and Slatkin 2001 provides an excellent selection of post-war French scholarship on both Greek religion, society and *mentalité*. Morris 1993 provides a useful survey of the history of the interpretation of ritual action in archaic Greece from 1863, whilst Buxton 2000 has collected together and reprinted fifteen key articles on Greek religion from the past three decades. His introduction (1–10) also provides a concise discussion of the many scholarly approaches to the study of Greek religion that are currently in use.

[7] For the Panathenaia, see below section III. For studies of other Athenian festivals, see Burkert 1972 (English translation 1983); 1992; Connor 1989b; 1996; Goldhill 1987; Hamilton 1992; Robertson 1992; 1996; Simon 1983; Whitehead 1986, 176–222.

⁸ For example, neither Ostwald, despite the promise of the subtitle of his 1986 volume, *Law, Society and Politics in Fifth-Century Athens*, an important chapter on 'Popular Sovereignty and the Control of Religion' and two appendices on Athenian impiety trials, nor Munn 2000 who, like Ostwald, explores similar themes and events with a particular focus on the world of ideas and public debate carried on through oratory and publicly performed literature, pays much attention to the interaction between events and festival. Indeed, the tendency has been to write about the 'history' of religion separately (so for example, Parker 1996) and not to integrate it into a narrative or analysis of events, that is, into 'political' history. Garland 1992, subtitled *The Politics of Athenian Religion*, provides a set of important case studies which more successfully integrate events with their religious contexts. See also Shapiro above, n. 4. As Hornblower 1993 reminds us, the precedent for the separation of the religious from the political and from the general narrative of events was established by Thucydides. Hornblower provides a telling set of 'omissions' of religious matters by Thucydides which, when considered, can cast events in a rather different light. For important early exceptions to this lack of consideration of the religious dimension of political events, see Powell 1979a; 1979b; 1988, 383–414. See also McCowan 1999, 128–49 on 'Priest(esse)s and Politics'.

⁹ For the interpretation of Greek drama in its social, festival and performative contexts, see the seminal article by Goldhill 1987. See also Winkler and Zeitlin 1990; Goldhill and Osborne 1999, both with earlier bibliography. The political interpretation of tragedy in particular has a much longer history for which see Castellani 1998; Pelling 1997; 2000; Saïd 1998.

¹⁰ See Rhodes 1972, 224–9; cf. Develin 1989 whose entries are arranged by archon years. The name of the eponymous archon appears on Panathenaic *amphorai* from 379–312 BC (Beazley 1986, 81–92) but these are of no assistance for anything other than dating the vases themselves.

¹¹ On the Athenian calendar, see also Woodhead 1981, 117–22, and 140 n. 17 for a bibliography which includes key publications by Meritt and Pritchett.

¹² Hippias of Elis *FGrHist* 6 F2 = Plutarch *Numa* 1.4; Hippias' dates: *c.* 485–415 BC (*OCD*² s.v. Hippias of Elis) or mid-fifth to early-fourth century (Golden 1998, 43, 63).

¹³ Pausanias 3.21.1, referring to 'the Eleian records of the *Olympionikai*', and 6.22.3.

¹⁴ See Samuel 1972.

¹⁵ *OCD*² s.v. Hippias of Elis. For the adoption of Olympiads for dating by Timaeus, see Diodorus 5.1.3; Polybius 12.11.1. See also *P.Oxy.* 12 (*FGrHist* 255) and Samuel 1972, 189–90 for another early example of dating by Olympiads. For problems with the list of the *Olympionikai* see Jacoby 1955, 221–8, 233–6.

¹⁶ See Gomme,1956, 699–715; Pritchett 1965; 1986.

¹⁷ See Thomas 1989, 287–8, on the mnemonic value of lists of officials or victors such as those at Olympia.

¹⁸ As well as being sworn by the Athenians going to Elis, Mantinea and Argos thirty days before the next Olympic Games (416/15, Ol. 91.1), the alliance was to

be renewed by being sworn at Athens by the Argives, Mantineans and Eleans ten days before the next Great Panathenaia (i.e., that of 41<u>8</u>/17, Ol. 90.3). A bronze pillar was to be set up by all treaty parties at Olympia during the games of 42<u>0</u>/19 (Ol. 90.1; Thuc. 5.47.11). The renewal of the treaty never eventuated because of the breakdown of the alliance before its first year was completed. See also Gomme, Andrewes and Dover 1970, 61.

[19] Rhodes 1972, 227–8. See also Develin 1984 which argues that for the purposes of the Athenian constitution the phrase ἐκ Παναθηναίων ἐς Παναθήναια meant a Panathenaic quadrennium, i.e. from one celebration of the Great Panathenaia, held every four years during the third year of each Olympiad, to the next.

[20] Rhodes 1972, 228.

[21] Rhodes 1972, 228.

[22] Mikalson 1975, 182–204.

[23] Mikalson 1975, 210.

[24] Mikalson 1975, 203.

[25] Mikalson 1975, 201.

[26] See also my Appendix 1.

[27] Mikalson 1975, 207–14. Mikalson (208) has inverted Pritchett's dates for *IG* I² 304B. Pritchett 1970, 25–6 dates the records from Mounychion 408/7 to Boedromion 407/6.

[28] Mikalson 1975, 201.

[29] Hornblower 1992.

[30] Wall 1998. 'The priority of the divine' is Mikalson's useful turn of phrase (Mikalson 1983, 13–17).

[31] On Thucydides and religion, see Marinatos 1981; Jordan 1986; Hornblower 1992. On oracles in Thucydides see, for example, 2.17.2; cf. 5.26.3 and Dover 1988; Powell 1979a; 1979b.

[32] See Thucydides 1.8.1; 2.8.2; 5.1.1; 32.1; 8.108.4 with Plutarch *Nikias* 3; Hornblower 1991, 517–31.

[33] See also Jameson 1998 on participation in festival under the democracy at Athens and Peter Wilson's chapter in this book. When metics and *xenoi* (foreign visitors, ambassadors or *theōroi*) were in attendance at such major civic festivals as the City Dionysia and the Panathenaia they also served as a meeting place for the wider Attic and Greek community. The correlation between meeting days of the assembly and festival days which Mikalson tabulates (1975, 188; cf. also meeting days of the *boulē* and festivals at 1975, 194–5) will have served to enhance opportunities for combining attendance at Athens for festivals with participation in the political life of the *polis*.

[34] For the characteristics of, and recent scholarship on, Greek agonistic festivals such as the Panathenaia, see Phillips in section II of the introduction to this book.

[35] Note also [Xen.] *Ath. Pol.* 3.2; Mikalson 1975.

[36] For the Panathenaia see the studies edited by Neils (1992; 1996) and note in particular Neils 1992a; Kyle 1992; 1996; Shapiro 1992. Both volumes by Neils contain excellent bibliographies of both older and more recent scholarship. Among

earlier scholarship, Davison 1958 with its 1962 addenda remains important. On the origins of the Panathenaia, see Robertson 1985; 1992, 90–119; Mikalson 1976; Shapiro 1989, 40–7. Ancient sources for the Panathenaia are listed at Harris 1995, 261–2. For recent studies of the distinctive Panathenaic prize amphorae, see Neils 1992b; Tiverios 1996; Hamilton 1996. Hamilton 1992, 231–40, gives an extensive listing of Panathenaic amphorae with provenance and publication details, whilst Neils 1992 contains many superb colour and black and white photographs of these vases. Bérard captures the 'holiday' character of the Panathenaia, observing that of Athenian festivals it most directly engaged the entire community (1989, 109). Recent studies which explore aspects of participation in the Panathenaia or examine it as a reflection of Athenian civic ideology or of the ideology of empire include Kavoulaki 1999; Jameson 1998; Lefkowitz 1996; Maurizio 1998; Neils 1994; Osborne 1994; Wohl 1996.

[37] Both the duration of the Lesser Panathenaia and the nature and extent of any associated *agōnes* are far from clear. I will be pursuing these matters in a separate publication.

[38] Mikalson 1975, 34; Parke 1977, 33–50; Neils 1992a, 13–17, Harris 1995, 285.

[39] See Morgan 1993, 18 and my Table 1 in section II of the introduction to this book.

[40] Neils 1992, 27. Note also Shapiro who states that the Panathenaia 'commemorated many of the events of the distant past associated with Athena: the unification of Attica by her protégé Theseus; the kingship of her stepchild Erechtheus; her victory, together with the other Olympians, over the Giants; and her birth from the head of Zeus' (1994, 128). Noting subsequent events that took place in Panathenaic years Shapiro believes that 'the Panathenaia had evolved into a kind of recapitulation of the history of democratic Athens' (1994, 128). For other festivals for Athena at Athens, see Robertson 1996.

[41] Maurizio 1998, 297, 301, 303.

[42] Maurizio 1998, 315–7. See also Jameson 1998, 176–9 on the expansion of festival participation under the fifth-century democracy and its empire.

[43] On the cow and the panoply, see *IG* I³ 34.41–2 (448/7, 430s or 426/5 BC, Kleinias decree = Fornara 1985 no. 98 = *ML* 46); *IG* I³ 46.11–12 (447/6, *c.* 445, 439/8 or 426/5 BC, foundation of the colony at Brea = Fornara 1985 no. 100 = *ML* 49); *IG* I³ 71.57–9 (425/4 BC, reassessment of tribute = Fornara 1985 no. 136 = *ML* 69). See Parker 1996, 142 with n. 80 for further sources and discussion and 221–2 for post-empire, fourth-century contributions to the Panathenaia from Paros and some of the cities of Asia Minor such as Priene and Kolophon.

[44] Maurizio 1998, 302. See also Kavoulaki 1999. The dates and the circumstances for the inclusion of the various elements of the Panathenaic procession are far from clear. For example, see Stevenson's chapter in this book on the inclusion of the cavalry in their tribal units. On the complexities of the social mix of citizen and non-citizen at Athens see now the important study of Cohen 2000 who argues that in many ways Athens was not only an atypical *polis* but also that there are good grounds for using the term *ethnos* rather than *polis* to characterize the

Athenian state.

[45] Connor 1987 has now been reprinted in Buxton 2000, 56–75.

[46] Connor 1987, 41.

[47] Connor 1987, 44–5. On Herodotus' credulity, see also Lavelle 1993, 106 n. 62 which, although having virtually nothing to say on the Panathenaia *per se*, does suggest that Herodotus' comment on the credulity of the Athenian *dēmos* may be explained by 'the refusal of his sources to say more about it or their inability (through the silence of their forebears) to know and say more'.

[48] Connor 1987, 47–9.

[49] On the date of the Diasia, see Mikalson 1983, 117. The key sources are Herodotus 5.71; Thucydides 1.126; Herakleides Lembus *Epitome of the Athenaion Politeia* F4, Plutarch *Solon* 12.1; Eusebius *Chronica* 92 ed. Kaerst; scholiast on Aristophanes' *Knights* 445. For a full discussion and commentary, including the dating of the coup and further references, see Hornblower 1991, 202–10 on Thuc. 1.126. Morris notes that 'Thucydides links the coup with religious festival at all stages' (1993, 36).

[50] Connor 1987, 41 with n. 8: 'Note, however, that the events of 579/8 come in a year of preparation for the Panathenaia, rather than in the year of its celebration.' Connor's note and Figueira's study raise a question which neither addresses, namely the evidence for the 'foundation', or rather the re-organization, of the Great Panathenaia in 566/5 BC – a re-organization which is in line with traditions about the institution and/or re-organization of the Panhellenic festivals at Delphi (582), Nemea (573) and the Isthmus (582–570), for which see TABLE 1 in section II of the introduction to this book. However, for all that the Panathenaia aspired to be a Panhellenic festival which promoted Athens to the wider Greek world and affirmed her status within it, it never became recognized as part of the *periodos* of great Panhellenic festivals.

[51] Shapiro 1994, 128 notes the coincidence of key events of the late sixth and early fifth centuries with celebrations of the Great Panathenaia, but does so without apparent awareness of either Connor 1987 or Figueira 1984.

[52] Great Panathenaic years in TABLES 1 and 2 are printed in bold type. Despite the evidence for a re-organization of the Panathenaia in 566/5 which, it is widely assumed, created a four-yearly Great Panathenaia after the manner of the 'big four' Panhellenic crown games, it is not known whether a cycle of more elaborate celebration of the Panathenaia every fourth year already existed in some form or another before 566/5. Figueira observes that 'from the late 590s, significant events seem to be taking place at 4-year intervals' and, after a discussion of the evidence for the origins and early history of the Panathenaia, he concludes that 'for all the conflicting data on the Panathenaia, there is nothing to deny the existence of quadrennial festivals in the early 6th century' (1984, 466–8). Following Figueira, Connor (1987, 41 with n. 8) would also seem to assume a four-yearly pattern of some kind for the early sixth century.

[53] On the Peisistratids and the Panathenaia, see Shapiro 1989, 18–47, with Morris 1993, 35, 37. On the likelihood of Peisistratos' re-organization of the Panathenaia as an agonistic festival, see Kyle 1987, 28–9.

[54] On Harmodios and Aristogeiton as tyrannicides and as recipients of hero cult at Athens and on the subsequent traditions about them, see *Ath. Pol.* 58.1; Kearns 1989, 55, 150; Thomas 1989, 238–82; Lavelle 1993, 27–58; Shapiro 1994, 123–4.

[55] Shapiro 1994, 124.

[56] Robertson 1992, 98–105. Robertson not only dismisses the myth of the daughters of Leos, the eponymous hero of the Kleisthenic tribe Leontis, but also any evidence for the existence of either cult or a sanctuary for them. In an ingenious discussion he argues that Λεωκόρειον means 'the place for marshalling the host' (1992,104–5). Kearns appears to have no difficulty with such heroines, their myth or their cult (Kearns 1989, 181 s.v. Λεώς, the eponymous, and Λέω κόραι with source references).

[57] *Ath. Pol.* 18.3 tells us that Harmodios and Aristogeiton had 'many supporters'. Again Thucydides disagrees, choosing to see the whole affair as a private matter involving few conspirators (6.54, 60; cf. 1.20.2).

[58] See Rhodes 1981, 231–2 for commentary.

[59] On virgin self-sacrifice, see Kearns 1989, 57–63 with the entry for Aglauros at 139–40. The myth of the sacrifice of Erechtheus' daughters is retold in Euripides' fragmentary *Erechtheus*. See also Kearns 1990.

[60] Leos was one of the 100 potential eponymous heroes for the ten new tribes submitted by Kleisthenes to the oracle at Delphi (*Ath. Pol.* 21.6) and clearly was the recipient of existing cult and associated myth. Neither the late sources for his daughters, cited by Kearns 1989, 181, nor the confusion over their names, should be cause for much concern given the frequently late, contradictory and all too brief evidence for so many of the Attic heroes and heroines.

[61] Travlos 1971, 3, 5, 578 with fig. 5 no. 22.

[62] Wycherley 1978, 63–4, with reference to a brawl that took place near the Leokoreion in the mid-fourth century BC (Demosthenes 54.7–8); Camp 1986, 47–8.

[63] On the hero cult, see *Ath. Pol.* 58.1 with commentary by Rhodes 1981, 651–2. For the statues set up in 510/09, the year of the first Great Panathenaia after the liberation of Athens from the tyranny, see Pliny *Natural History* 34.17. Note also the honour of *sitēsis* in the prytaneion accorded to the direct descendants of Harmodios and Aristogeiton in the 430s if not before (*IG* I³ 131.5–8).

[64] Where evidence exists, the approaches which I have been outlining should have applicability beyond the Panathenaia at Athens not only to other Athenian festivals but also to the politics and festivals of other *poleis*. See Appendices 2 and 3.

[65] Kagan 1969, 85–93 places Tanagra and the suspicions of a plot to overthrow the democracy in the summer of 458. Hornblower 1991, 167–71 places these events in 458/7.

[66] For the date of the transfer of the treasury, see *IG* I³ 259 l. 3. Thucydides fails to make any mention of it. On the terms of office of the *Hellēnotamiai*, see above section II with n.19.

[67] For example, it is not to be found in either Kagan 1987 or Ostwald 1986 and receives but a passing mention by Munn 2000 (438 n.89). It is, however, fully

treated and accorded the significance it deserves in Herrington 1985, 151–60. For a discussion of the lost beginning of the poem which argues, following but developing upon Bassett 1931, 154–6, that it drew on traditions concerning Themistokles' speech before the battle of Salamis (Hdt. 8.83.1), see Podlecki 1975, 62–5.

68 See the introduction to Hall 1996.

69 Shapiro 1992, 202 n. 99; Herrington 1985, 151–2.

70 Timotheos' time at Sparta belongs more properly to the time of Spartan activities in Asia Minor and the campaigns of Agesilaos in the early 390s on which see below.

71 Herrington 1985, 151. For testimonia on Timotheos, see Campbell 1993, 70–81 nos. 1–14. For *The Persians* see also the fragments in Campbell 1993, 90–111, frs. 788–91. Most of what we have of the poem comes from the fourth-century BC papyrus, *P.Berol.* 9875 = Campbell fr. 791. For a new edition with commentary on the fragments of Timotheos see Horden 2002 (not seen) with the cautious review by S. Douglas Olson in *BMCR* January 2003.

72 For example, Munn (2000, 438 n. 89, without references) adopts a date in the early 390s. Bassett gives a full discussion of the dating issues opting for the period 412–408 (1931, 159). On the basis of conjectures about Timotheos' age Podlecki 1975, 64 adopts 415 as 'a rough *terminus post quem*' for the first performance.

73 Miller *Mélanges* 363 cited in Edmonds 1940, 309.

74 Podlecki 1975, 62; Bassett 1931, 155.

75 For the ambiguity of *tyrannos*, see Connor 1979; Hornblower 1991, 337–8, 422–3.

76 On Ares' chaotic and disruptive power, see Burkert 1985, 169–70. The description of Ares as *tyrannos* is echoed in what West and others consider to be the decisively late *Homeric Hymn* 8: *To Ares*, probably to be attributed to the fifth-century AD writer Proclus (West 1970). There we find that Ares is characterized as 'tyrant to enemies and leader of truly just men' (line 5, ἀντιβίοισι τύραννε, δικαιοτάτων ἀγὲ φωτῶν). With φωτῶν Ares is being identified as the leader of men, not gods (LSJ⁹ s.v. φῶς III). Although other elements of this hymn are late, the identification of Ares as *tyrannos* and, given the historical circumstances of both 480 and 410, his characterization as leader of just men, can be traced back to at least the fifth century BC and to the period of the Persian and/or the Peloponnesian wars.

77 Kurke 2000, 67–8. Note the parallels between the speech of the Phrygian soldier and the character of the Phrygian slave in Euripides' play *Orestes* of 408 BC. See especially *Orestes* 1367 ff. which includes the so-called 'Phrygian aria' (1369–1502) and the 'Dialogue of Orestes and the Phrygian' (1503–36). On these lines, see West 1987, 276–85. Festival performance, including reperformance such as that of *The Persians* of Timotheos before Philopoemen at the Nemea in 207 BC (Plutarch *Philopoemen* 11), was the major means of 'publication' for such poetry.

78 Kagan 1987, 1–273 notes that the Athenians did not 'need to believe that the bond between Sparta and Persia was unbreakable' (251).

[79] Timotheos' native *polis*, Miletos, had revolted in 412 BC (Thuc. 8.17.1–3) and was presumably still in oligarchic and enemy hands in 409 (cf. Xen. *Hell.* 1.2.2–3 with commentary by Krentz 1989, 110–12; Kagan 1987, 265–70; Krentz 1988). However, there was a democratic faction at Miletos; see Plutarch *Lysander* 8, 19, referring to the democrats who were executed as a result of Lysander's intervention in 406/5 BC. Presumably Timotheos was not identified with the Milesian oligarchs while at Athens.

[80] Absolute certainty in the matter of dating *The Persians* cannot be achieved. If it was not performed first at the Great Panathenaia of 410/09 as I have attempted to argue, it is, in my view, still most probable that its anti-Persian theme and its apparent success best fit the period 410 to 408. If one accepts a *terminus ante quem* of 408 on the basis of the assistance given to Timotheos by Euripides, the relationship of *The Persians* to Euripides' *Orestes* and the departure of Euripides from Athens, then the only other possibility is the Lesser Panathenaia of 409/8.

[81] Podlecki 1975, 62; Campbell 1993, 93 on frs. 788 to 790. As a proverbial catch-cry, 'Ares is king; Greece fears no gold' would have taken on further resonances for Agesilaos' campaigns against the Persians in Asia Minor in the 390s just as did the slogan, 'the freedom of the Greeks of Asia', on which see Seager and Tuplin 1980.

[82] If my analysis of the significance of *The Persians* of Timotheos has some validity, then it provides us with a rare example of the use of a non-dramatic festival to promote Athenian democratic and imperial 'propaganda' to an audience of Athenians and allies. This is more often found associated with plays performed at the City Dionysia. The justification of Athenian rule to be found in the concluding speech by Athena in Euripides' *Ion* at lines 1553–1605 and dated to about 413 BC, although not with certainty to the City Dionysia, is a clear example of the reinforcement of Athenian imperial ideology whether intended for Athenians alone, as at the Lenaia, or for an audience including allies.

[83] See also Phillips in section II of the introduction to this book.

[84] For example, the full discussion of these years by Strauss 1986 makes no reference to the Pompeion or a decree ordering its construction. That there would have been such a decree is an inference, but a necessary one, from the existence of the building itself. As an inference, however, it could not find its way into the entries for decrees based on extant evidence to be found in the annual entries of Develin 1989.

[85] Travlos 1971, 477–81; Pausanias 1.2.4.

[86] For the close association between the Panathenaia and the Parthenon, see Harris 1995, 1–39 which also notes that the inventories of the 'Parthenon treasures' were undertaken by the treasurers of Athena 'during the annual Panathenaic procession perhaps just after the procession when the gold and silver trays and *hydriai* (water-jars), the furniture and the cult items were distributed to the worshippers for the Panathenaic procession' (1995, 10). For a chronological list of the extant inventories see Harris 1995, 253–7.

[87] On deme calendars, see Whitehead 1986, 185–208.

[88] Mikalson 1975, 25–46.

89 Mikalson 1975, 46.

90 On the Eleusinia, see *IG* I² 5 = *IG* I³ 5 and *Hesperia* 4 (1935) 21 fr. C (back) cols. 2 and 3, ll. 60–76 together with Simms 1975 and K. Clinton 1979 with its endnote on 'The Trieteric and Penteteric Festival'.

91 Simms 1975, 274–7. On Triptolemos, see Kearns 1989, 201.

92 Clinton 1979, 9–12; cf. Mikalson 1975, 46; Simms 1975.

93 See also McCowan 1999, 128–49 on 'Priest(esse)s and Politics'.

94 For the date, see Mikalson 1975, 125–8, which notes, with references, that earlier scholars such as Mommsen, Deubner and Pickard-Cambridge placed the City Dionysia from 9–12 Elaphebolion. On Kleisthenes and religion, see also Kearns 1985.

95 For the date, see Mikalson 1975, 79. Of three recent treatments of the trial of the Arginousai generals – Ostwald 1986, 442; Kagan 1987, 368–9; and Munn 2000, 185 – only that of Kagan gives reasonable attention to the significance of the Apatouria.

96 For the date, see Mikalson 1975, 163–4 with Fornara 1985 no. 159; Xen. *Hell.* 1.4.8–21, and especially 1.2.12; Plut. *Alk.* 33; scholiast on Aristophanes *Frogs* 1422–3. For modern accounts, see Ostwald 1986, 428; Kagan 1987, 290; Ellis 1989, 89; Munn 2000, 167. Again only Kagan pays much attention to the significance of the Plynteria.

97 For the date, see Mikalson 1975, 58–9. Xenophon's *Hellenika* 1.4.20 is our only source. For modern accounts, see Ostwald 1986, 429; Kagan 1987, 290–2; Ellis 1989, 89; Munn 2000, 169. Only Kagan explores the significance of Alkibiades' leadership of the *pompē* of the Mysteries to Eleusis.

98 I intend to pursue the political and festival implications of Green's chronology and interpretation elsewhere. Krentz 1982 pays no attention to such matters. A similar exercise could be conducted for the Four Hundred, beginning with Thucydides' statement that upon entering office the Four Hundred, who had just staged a coup that had been precipitated by intimidation, violence and assassination, made the usual 'prayers and sacrifices to the gods upon entering office' (Thuc. 8.70.1).

99 Samuel 1972, 90–1, 93.

Bibliography

Bassett, S.E.

   1931   'The place and date of the first performance of the *Persians* of Timotheus', *CPh* 26, 153–65.

Beazley, J.D.

   1986   *The Development of Attic Black-Figure*, revised edn, Berkeley.

Bérard, C.

   1989   'Festivals and Mysteries: the city on holiday: the Panathenaia', in C. Bérard et al. *A City of Images: Iconography and society in ancient Greece*, transl. D. Lyons, Princeton, 109–20.

Boedeker, D. and Raaflaub, K.A. (eds.)
1998   *Democracy, Empire, and the Arts in Fifth-Century Athens*, Cambridge, Mass.

Bruit-Zaidman, L. and Schmitt Pantel, P.
1992   *Religion in the Ancient Greek City*, transl. P. Cartledge, Cambridge.

Burkert, W.
1972   *Homo Necans: Interpretationen algriechischer Opferriten und Mythen*, Berlin.
1983   *Homo Necans: The anthropology of ancient Greek sacrificial ritual and myth*, transl. P. Bing, Berkeley.
1985   *Greek Religion Archaic and Classical,* transl. J. Raffan, Oxford.
1992   'Athenian cults and festivals', in D.M. Lewis, J. Boardman, J.K. Davies and M. Ostwald (eds.) *The Cambridge Ancient History*, Vol. 5, 2nd edn, Cambridge, 245–67.

Burn, A.R.
1962   *Persia and the Greeks: The defence of the West, c. 546–478 BC*, London.

Buxton, R. (ed.)
2000   *Oxford Readings in Greek Religion*, Oxford.

Camp, J.M.
1986   *The Athenian Agora: Excavations in the heart of classical Athens*, London.

Campbell, D.A. (ed. and trans.)
1993   *Greek Lyric V: The New School of poetry and anonymous songs and hymns*, (Loeb), Cambridge, Mass.

Castellani, V.
1998   'Athenian politics and tragedy of the later fifth century', in T. Hillard et al. (eds.) *Ancient History in a Modern University*, Grand Rapids, Vol. I, 139–47.

Clinton, K.
1979   '*IG* I² 5, The Eleusinia and the Eleusinians', *AJPh* 100, 1–12.

Cohen, E.E.
2000   *The Athenian Nation*, Princeton.

Connor, W.R.
1977   'Tyrannis Polis', in J. D'Arms and J.W. Eadie (eds.) *Ancient and Modern Essays in Honor of Gerald F. Else*, Ann Arbor, 95–109.
1985   'The razing of the house in Greek society', *TAPhA* 115, 79–102.
1987   'Tribes, festivals and processions in ancient Greece', *JHS* 107, 40–50. Reprinted in Buxton 2000, 56–75.
1988a   ' "Sacred" and "Secular": Ἱερὰ καὶ ὅσια and the classical Athenian concept of the state', *AncSoc* 19, 161–88.
1988b   'Seized by nymphs: nympholepsy and symbolic expression in classical Greece', *ClAnt* 7, 155–89.
1988c   'Early Greek warfare as symbolic expression', *Past & Present* 119, 3–29.
1989a   'The new classical humanities and the old', in P. Cullham, L. Edmunds and A. Smith (eds.) *Classics: A discipline and profession in crisis?*, Lanham, 25–38.

1989b 'City Dionysia and Athenian democracy', *C&M* 40, 7–32. Reprinted in W.R. Connor, M.H. Hansen, K.H. Raaflaub and B.S. Strauss 1990, *Aspects of Athenian Democracy*, Copenhagen, 7–32.

1991 'The other 399: religion and the trial of Socrates', in M.A. Flower and M. Toher (eds.) *Georgica: Greek studies in honour of George Cawkwell*, *BICS* Supplement 58, London, 49–56.

1996 'Festivals and democracy', in M.B. Sakellariou (ed.) *Colloque international: démocratie athénienne et culture*, Athens, 79–89.

Coulson, W. et al. (eds.)
1994 *The Archaeology of Athens and Attica Under the Democracy*, Oxford.

Davison, J.
1958 'Notes on the Panathenaia', *JHS* 78, 23–42.
1962 'Addenda to "Notes on the Panathenaia"', *JHS* 82, 141–2.

Deubner, L.
1932 *Attische Feste*, Berlin.

Develin, R.
1984 'From Panathenaia to Panathenaia', *ZPE* 57, 133–8.
1989 *Athenian Officials, 681–321 BC,* Cambridge.

Dougherty, C. and Kurke, L. (eds.)
1993 *Cultural Poetics in Archaic Greece: Cult, performance, politics*, Princeton.

Dover, K.J.
1988 'Thucydides and oracles', in *The Greeks and Their Legacy: Collected papers*, Oxford, Vol. II, 65–73.

Edmonds, J.M. (ed.)
1940 *Lyra Graeca*, Vol. III, Loeb, revised edn, Cambridge, Mass.

Ellis, W.M.
1989 *Alcibiades*, London.

Figueira, T.J.
1984 'The ten archontes of 579/8 at Athens', *Hesperia* 53, 447–73.

Fornara, C.W.
1985 *Translated Documents of Greece and Rome: Vol. I: Archaic times to the end of the Peloponnesian War*, 2nd edn, Cambridge.

Garland, R.S.J.
1992 *Introducing New Gods: The politics of Athenian religion*, London.

Gebhard, E.R.
1993 'The evolution of a Panhellenic sanctuary: from archaeology towards history at Isthmia', in Marinatos and Hägg (eds.) *Greek Sanctuaries*, 154–77.

Geertz, C.
1973 *The Intepretation of Cultures*, New York.

Golden, M.
1998 *Sport and Society in Ancient Greece*, Cambridge.

Goldhill, S.
1987 'The Great Dionysia and civic ideology', *JHS* 107, 58–76. Reprinted in Winkler and Zeitlin 1990, 97–129.

Goldhill, S. and Osborne, R. (eds.)
  1999   *Performance Culture and Athenian Democracy*, Cambridge.
Gomme, A.W.
  1956   *A Historical Commentary on Thucydides*, Vol. III, Oxford.
Gomme, A.W., Andrewes, A. and Dover, K.J.
  1970   *A Historical Commentary on Thucydides*, Vol. IV, Oxford.
Green, P.
  1991   'Rebooking the flute-girls: a fresh look at the chronological evidence for the fall of Athens and the ὀκτάμηνος ἀρχή of the Thirty,' *AHB* 5, 1–16.
Hall, E.
  1996   *Aeschylus: Persians*, edited with an introduction, translation and commentary, Warminster.
Hamilton, R.
  1992   *Choes and Anthesteria: Athenian iconography and ritual*, Ann Arbor.
  1996   'Panathenaic amphoras: the other side', in Neils (ed.) *Worshipping Athena*, 137–62.
Harris, D.
  1995   *The Treasures of the Parthenon and Erechtheion*, Oxford.
Herrington, J.
  1985   *Poetry Into Drama: Early Greek tragedy and the Greek poetic tradition*, Berkeley.
Horden, J.H. (ed.)
  2002   *The Fragments of Timotheus of Miletus*, Oxford.
Hornblower, S.
  1991   *A Commentary on Thucydides: Vol. I: Books I–III*, Oxford.
  1992   'The religious dimension of the Peloponnesian War, or what Thucydides does not tell us', *HSCPh* 94,160–97.
  1996   *A Commentary on Thucydides: Vol. II: Books IV–V.24*, Oxford.
Hurwit, J.M.
  1999   *The Athenian Acropolis: History, mythology, and archaeology from the Neolithic era to the present*, Cambridge.
Jacoby, F.
  1955   *Die Fragmente der Griechischen Historiker IIIb. Kommentar zu Nr. 297–607 (Text)*, Berlin.
Jameson, M.H.
  1998   'Religion in the Athenian democracy', in I. Morris and K.A. Raaflaub (eds.) *Democracy 2500: Questions and challenges*, Dubuque, 171–95.
Jordan, B.
  1986   'Religion in Thucydides', *TAPhA* 116, 119–47.
Kagan, D.
  1969   *The Outbreak of the Peloponnesian War*, Ithaca.
  1974   *The Archidamian War*, Ithaca.
  1981   *The Peace of Nicias and the Sicilian Expedition*, Ithaca.
  1987   *The Fall of the Athenian Empire*, Ithaca.

Kavoulaki, A.
  1999   'Processional performance and the democratic polis', in Goldhill and
         Osborne (eds.) *Performance Culture...*, 293–320.
Kearns, E.
  1985   'Change and continuity in religious structures after Kleisthenes', in P.A.
         Cartledge and F.D. Harvey (eds.) *CRUX: Essays in Greek history presented
         to G.E.M. de Ste Croix on his 75th birthday*, London, 189–207.
  1989   *The Heroes of Attica*, BICS Supplement 57, London.
  1990   'Saving the city', in O. Murray and S. Price (eds.) *The Greek City from
         Homer to Alexander*, Oxford, 323–44.
Krentz, P.
  1983   *The Thirty at Athens*, Ithaca.
  1988   'Athenian politics and strategy after Kyzikos', *CJ* 84, 206–15.
  1989   *Xenophon, Hellenika I–II.3.10*, edited with an introduction, translation
         and commentary, Warminster.
Kurke, L.
  2000   'The strangeness of song culture: archaic Greek poetry', in O.Taplin (ed.)
         Literature in the Greek World, Oxford, 40–69.
Kyle, D.G.
  1987   *Athletics in Ancient Athens*, Leiden.
  1992   'The Panathenaic Games: sacred and civic athletes', in Neils (ed.) *Goddess
         and Polis*, 77–101.
  1996   'Gifts and glory: Panathenaic and other Greek athletic prizes', in Neils
         (ed.) *Worshipping Athena*, 106–36.
Lavelle, B.
  1993   *The Sorrow and the Pity: A prolegomenon to a history of Athens under the
         Peisistratids c. 560–510 BC*, Historia Einzelschriften Heft 80, Stuttgart.
Lefkowitz, M.
  1996   'Women in the Panathenaic and other festivals', in Neils (ed.) *Worshipping
         Athena*, 78–91.
Loraux, N., Nagy, G. and Slatkin, L. (eds.)
  2001   *Postwar French Thought, Vol. III: Antiquities*, transl. A. Goldhammer et
         al., New York.
McCowan, J.E.
  1999   'Athenian Priests and Priestesses: their qualifications, responsibilities,
         and perquisites from 508–c.300 BC', Ph.D. dissertation, Macquarie
         University, Sydney.
Marinatos, N.
  1981a *Thucydides and Religion*, Koenigstein.
  1981b 'Thucydides and oracles', *JHS* 101, 138–40.
Marinatos, N. and Hägg, R. (eds.)
  1993   *Greek Sanctuaries: New approaches*, London.
Maurizio, L.
  1998   'The Panathenaic procession: Athens' participatory democracy on
         display', in Boedeker and Raaflaub (eds.) *Democracy...*, 297–317.

Meier, C.
1993   *Athen: Ein Neubeginn der Weltgeschichte*, Berlin
Mikalson, J.D.
1975   *The Sacred and the Civil Calendar of the Athenian Year*, Princeton.
1976   'Erechtheus and the Panathenaia', *AJP* 97, 141–53.
1983   *Athenian Popular Religion*, Chapel Hill.
Mommsen, A.
1898   *Feste der Stadt Athen im Altertum, geordnet nach attischem Kalender*, Leipzig.
Morgan, C.
1993   'The origins of Pan-Hellenism', in Marinatos and Hägg (eds.) *Greek Sanctuaries*, 18–44.
Morley, N.
1999   *Writing Ancient History*, London.
2000   *Ancient History: Key themes and approaches*, London.
Morris, I.
1993   'Poetics of power: the interpretation of ritual action in archaic Greece', in Dougherty and Kurke (eds.) *Cultural Poetics*, 15–45.
Munn, M.
2000   *The School of History: Athens in the age of Socrates*, Berkeley.
Neils, J.
1992a   'The Panathenaia: an introduction', in Neils (ed.) *Goddess and Polis*, 13–27.
1992b   'Panathenaic amphoras: their meaning, makers, and markets', in Neils (ed.) *Goddess and Polis*, 29–51.
1994   'The Panathenaia and Kleisthenic ideology', in Coulson et al. (eds.) *The Archaeology of Athens*, 151–160
2001   *The Parthenon Frieze*, Cambridge.
Neils, J. (ed.)
1992   *Goddess and Polis: The Panathenaic festival in ancient Athens*, Princeton.
1996   *Worshipping Athena: Panathenaia and Parthenon*, Madison.
Osborne, R.
1987   *Classical Landscape with Figures: The ancient Greek city and its countryside*, London.
1994   'Democracy and imperialism in the Panathenaic Procession: the Parthenon Frieze in its context', in Coulson et al. (eds.) *The Archeology of Athens*, 143–50.
Ostwald, M.
1986   *From Popular Sovereignty to Sovereignty of the Law: Law, society and politics in fifth-century Athens*, Berkeley.
Parke, H.W.
1977   *Festivals of the Athenians*, London.
Parker, R.
1996   *Athenian Religion: A history*, Oxford.
Pelling, C.B.R.
2000   *Literary Texts and the Greek Historian*, London.

Pelling, C.B.R. (ed.)
  1997   *Greek Tragedy and the Historian*, Oxford.
Podlecki, A.J.
  1975   *The Life of Themistocles: A critical survey of the literary and archaeological record*, Montreal
Powell, A.
  1979a   'Thucydides and divination', *BICS* 26, 45–50.
  1979b   'Religion and the Sicilian expedition', *Historia* 28, 15–31.
  1988   *Athens and Sparta*, London.
Price, S.
  1999   *Religions of the Ancient Greeks*, Cambridge.
Pritchett, W.K.
  1965   'The Thucydidean summer of 411 BC', *CPh* 60, 259–61.
  1970   *The Choiseul Marble*, Berkeley.
  1986   'Thucydides' statement on his chronology', *ZPE* 62, 205–11.
Rhodes, P.J.
  1972   *The Athenian Boule*, Oxford.
  1981   *A Commentary on the Aristotelian* Athenaion Politeia, Oxford.
Robertson, N.
  1985   'The origin of the Panathenaia', *RhM* 128, 231–95.
  1992   *Festivals and Legends: The formation of Greek cities in the light of public ritual*, Toronto.
  1996   'Athena's shrines and festivals', in Neils (ed.) *Worshipping Athena*, 27–77.
Saïd, S.
  1998   'Tragedy and politics', in Boedeker and Raaflaub (eds.) *Democracy...*, 275–95.
Samuel, A.E.
  1972   *Greek and Roman Chronology*, Munich.
Seager, R. and Tuplin, C.
  1980   'The freedom of the Greeks of Asia: on the origins of a concept and the creation of a slogan', *JHS* 100, 141–54.
Shapiro, H.A.
  1989   *Art and Cult under the Tyrants in Athens*, Mainz.
  1990   'Oracle mongers in Peisistratid Athens', *Kernos* 3, 335–45.
  1992   '*Mousikoi Agones*: music and poetry at the Panathenaia', in Neils (ed.) *Goddess and Polis*, 53–75.
  1993   'Hipparchos and the rhapsodes', in Dougherty and Kurke (eds.) *Cultural Poetics...*, 92–107.
  1994   'Religion and politics in democratic Athens', in Coulson et al. (eds.) *The Archaeology of Athens*,123–9.
Simon, E.
  1983   *Festivals of Attica: An archaeological commentary*, Madison.
Simms, R.M.
  1975   'The Eleusinia in the sixth to fourth centuries BC', *GRBS* 16, 269–79.

Strauss, B.S.
1986   *Athens after the Peloponnesian War: Class, faction and policy 403–386 BC*,
        London.
Thomas, R.
1989   *Oral Tradition and Written Record in Classical Athens*, Cambridge.
Tiverios, M.
1996   'Shield devices and column-mounted statues on Panathenaic amphoras:
        some remarks on iconography', in Neils (ed.) *Worshipping Athena*,
        163–74.
Travlos, J.
1971   *Pictorial Dictionary of Athens*, London.
Wall, B.
1998   'Evidence for popular religion in Xenophon', in *Ancient History: Resources
        for teachers* 28,136–53.
West, M.L.
1970   'The Eighth Homeric Hymn and Proclus', *CQ* 20, 300–4.
1987   *Euripides: Orestes*, edited with an introduction, translation and commen-
        tary, Warminster.
Whitehead, D.
1986   *The Demes of Attica 508/7 to c. 250 BC*, Princeton.
Winkler, J.J. and Zeitlin, F.I. (eds.)
1990   *Nothing To Do With Dionysos? Athenian drama in its social context*,
        Princeton.
Wohl, V.
1996   '*Eusebeias heneka kai philotimias*: hegemony and democracy at the
        Panathenaia', *C&M* 47, 25–88.
Woodhead, A.G.
1981   *The Study of Greek Inscriptions*, 2nd edn, Cambridge.
Wycherley, R.E.
1978   *The Stones of Athens*, Princeton.

9

THE PARTHENON FRIEZE AS AN IDEALIZED, CONTEMPORARY PANATHENAIC FESTIVAL

Tom Stevenson

The Parthenon continues to generate enormous interest, and no part of this magnificent building has received more attention recently than the Ionic frieze.[1] Ancient writers overlook it, including the second-century AD traveller Pausanias, who commented upon the pediments (1.24.5). Consequently, modern scholars have been able to range far and wide in their search for meaning. There was for a long time a general consensus that the frieze represented an idealized Panathenaic procession in the time of Perikles. However, in the last quarter-century or so, this orthodox view has been challenged strongly. It would be wrong to deny that there are good reasons for this reaction, but to my mind the orthodoxy, in slightly modified form, still provides our best interpretation. The main aim of this chapter, therefore, is to argue through detailed analysis that the best interpretation of the frieze is that it represents an idealized, contemporary Panathenaic festival – 'festival' rather than 'procession', for some figures evoke sporting competition more immediately than religious procession, and 'idealized' in the sense of a de-personalized, ennobling, often calm and youthful depiction. I accept that we are dealing with an evocative, polyvalent monument but would argue that it did have a primary subject.

The Parthenon was built over the foundations of an unfinished temple of Athena (the 'old Parthenon') that was begun soon after the battle of Marathon (490 BC) but destroyed in the Persian sacks of 480/79.[2] Planning for the 'new' Parthenon probably began *c.* 448, construction work commenced *c.* 447,[3] the temple was dedicated in 438,[4] and it is generally agreed that the frieze was sculpted *c.* 442–438.[5] As with its predecessor, it is likely that the Parthenon was meant to honour Athena and Athenian victories over the Persians, especially the victory at Marathon.[6] Yet if the pediments with their scenes of Athena's birth (east) and triumph over Poseidon (west), and the metopes with their depictions of struggles against centaurs (south), giants (east), Amazons (west) and Trojans (north) may seem to accord with this aim reasonably well, the frieze is less easy to align with it and points to a monument whose messages are more complex, even flexible. Lewis understands the building programme of the Periklean age from various perspectives: a group of dedications to the gods for past achievements, symbols of the triumph of civilization over barbarism, the Parthenon as victory dedication, the creation of a new goddess, self-worship, political and economic motives.[7] Stewart has wondered whether the frieze was included on the building as part of a morale-boosting programme following the reverses of 449–446.[8] A contractual element should be contemplated: the frieze praises Athena and the Athenians but also calls upon each party to live up to the ideal depicted. Perhaps the assumption of an underlying unity to the sculptural programme should be questioned more seriously than it has been to date.[9]

Problems of reconstruction on the south side should not be minimized,[10] but from the available remains, including fragments and drawings, we have a fairly good idea about most of the figures on the frieze, which was 1 metre high and 160 metres (524 feet) in length. It was richly provided with metal accessories, now lost, and certain details may have been painted rather than carved. Several distinct groups of figures have been identified: horsemen, chariot groups, marshals and ceremonial functionaries, sacrificial animals and attendants, groups of women, Athenian heroes or officials, the Olympian gods, and a group of figures who seem to be handling Athena's new robe or *peplos* (*Fig.* 1).[11] Surprise has been expressed at the position of the frieze.[12] Situated within the colonnade, at the top of the *cella* wall and *c.* 12 metres (40 feet) above ground level, it occupied a relatively inconspicuous spot – which might explain the lack of attention it receives from our literary sources. The view from within the colonnade is certainly too oblique to make it easily intelligible (*Fig.* 2). Understandably perhaps, given the frieze's survival and impact in modern times, scholars have been reluctant to accept the implications of its position. Many have thought that its upper part was cut in higher relief, that the slabs were tilted slightly forward, and that the indirect light on it was probably quite strong. Osborne was prompted to argue that the best view would have been obtained from outside the colonnade, at least 20 m from the frieze. Intermittently framed by the columns in the manner of a cartoon strip, the frieze would both compel and accompany movement by the viewer. The position of the frieze, he thought, required a procession by the viewer, who both created and reproduced the frieze procession; the subject and the presentation were intimately linked.[13] However, it now seems that there were no optical corrections to allow for the low viewpoint or for any particular view through the columns, and the slabs were not tilted

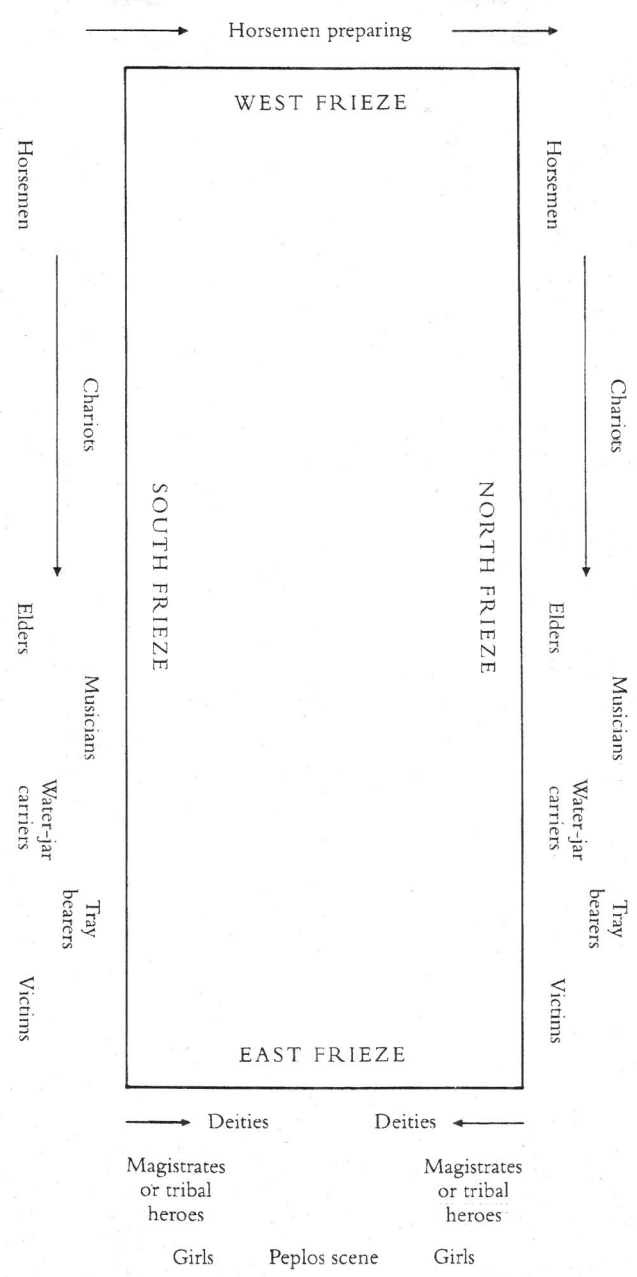

Fig. 1. Plan of the Parthenon frieze (from I. Jenkins *The Parthenon Frieze*, London 1994, 23 fig. 12b, drawn by Sue Bird). © The British Museum.

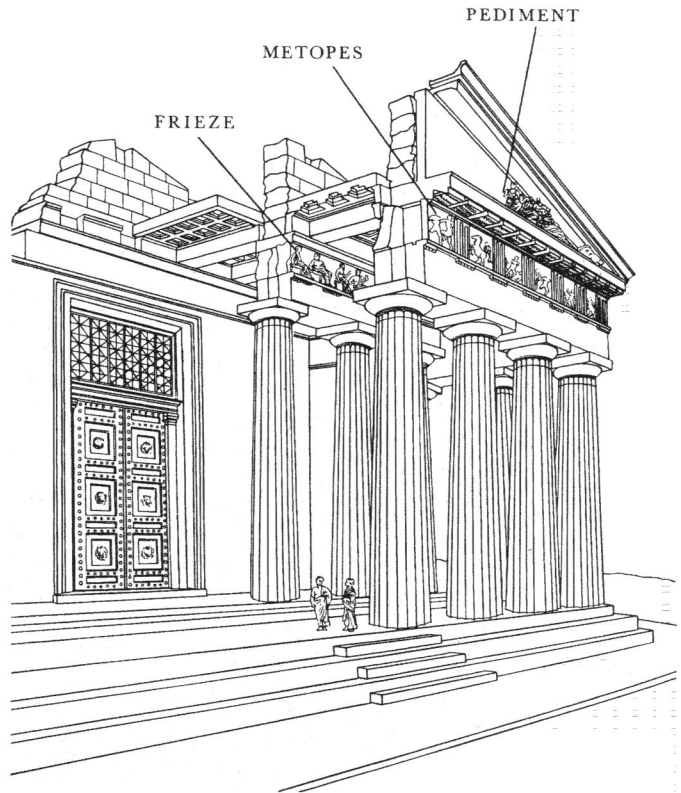

Fig. 2 . Cut-away diagram of the east side of the Parthenon, showing the position of the frieze, metopes and pediment (from I. Jenkins *The Parthenon Frieze*, London 1994, 9 fig. 1, after G. Niemann). © The British Museum.

forward. Korres has shown that the front plane of the frieze is vertical and the background is slightly tilted back, allowing greater depth for the torsos and overlapping figures at higher levels.[14] Thus, thinks Boardman, although the frieze was neither invisible nor insignificant, the designer cared little about visibility: 'at best the viewer was aware of something shadowy behind the larger and far more imposing metopes', 'in antiquity there was only the slightest reflected light', and the frieze's significance did not depend on its visibility but 'on it simply being there and being known to be there'.[15] We should think of the intentions of the designer and what we presume a contemporary viewer could have understood.[16] In the fifth century, a visitor to the Acropolis approached the Parthenon from the west through the Propylaia (*Fig.* 3). The path leading to the front (east side) of

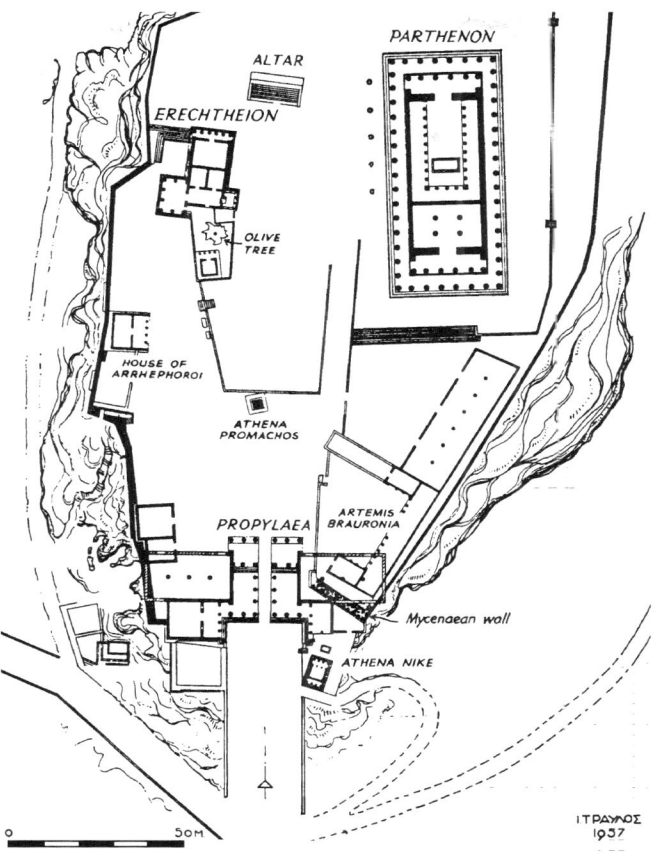

Fig. 3. Plan of the Acropolis around 400 BC (from I. Jenkins *The Parthenon Frieze*, London 1994, 19 fig. 8, after J. Travlos). © The British Museum.

the temple took the visitor by the northern side of the building.[17] It has been thought in consequence that the north side was more important than the south.[18] Perhaps more people did see the north than the south, but most attention would have been focused upon the east, the front of the temple, from where the marvellous gold and ivory statue of Athena within the Parthenon would have been visible.[19]

The basic subject was probably clear to fifth-century Athenians.[20] Knowledge of it faded, however, during later ages. Since the eighteenth century, the most popular theory has been that the frieze represents an idealized Panathenaic procession, celebrated with special pomp every four years at the Great Panathenaia, on the date assigned to Athena's birthday (28 Hekatombaion, roughly July/August).[21] This traditional interpretation stems ultimately from a conjecture published by two British travellers, the artist James Stuart and the architect Nicholas Revett, members of the Society of Dilettanti in London, who returned from a visit to the Acropolis with comprehensive drawings and descriptions.[22] However, scholars have seen 'problems' with the conjecture of Stuart and Revett for some time now.[23] Why, it is asked, would the Parthenon frieze record a mortal event? Greek temple decoration seems to demand scenes from myth. Would it not be impious arrogance to depict a contemporary Panathenaia? If it is the Panathenaia, where is the wheeled ship that literary sources indicate was drawn to the temple bearing the sacred *peplos* of Athena? Where are the hoplites? The frieze shows horsemen who are apparently unarmed,[24] but no foot-soldiers. Where are the Athenian allies? Where are the maiden basket-bearers and water-carriers? There are males carrying *hydriai* (vases commonly but not exclusively used for carrying water) (N VI 16–19; S XXXIX 115–118 conjectured),[25] and there are chariots, which were not used in combat by classical armies. Horsemen and chariots would not have been allowed onto the Acropolis. What of the fact that the central scene on the east side includes two widely-spaced female figures carrying what appear to be cushioned trays or stools on their heads (E V 31–32) (*Fig. 9*)? Did those responsible for the design or carving slightly miscalculate the space available, and how could they deliberately allot so much of the central scene to minor temple servants?

Numerous attempts have been made to solve these 'problems'. Some commentators have chosen to keep the Panathenaic context; others have not. Some see a specific mythical or historical occasion; others see a contemporary or generalized one. The Panathenaic elements are most clearly emphasized by Robertson, Parke, and Simon.[26] Kardara has seen the very first Panathenaia, while Holloway describes the restoration of the archaic treasures of the Acropolis that had been plundered by the Persians, with elements like the women and the cavalry standing in for *korai* and equestrian statues.[27] Boardman has argued for the Panathenaic procession immediately preceding the battle of Marathon, marked by heroic depiction of the 192 Athenians who would soon die in that struggle.[28] Simon and Harrison have detected a number of different processions within the frieze, so that time and place become variable factors.[29] Lawrence and Root have written of influence from the monuments of Persepolis; Castriota feels that Ionian models in particular have been employed to express the anti-Persian, anti-tyrannical style of Athenian imperialism.[30] Younger and Stewart find homoerotic undertones and a monument both laudatory and program-matic, calling on Athenians to live up to their responsibilities during a period of danger.[31] Osborne would emphasize function over subject: the frieze is a way of conveying someone in procession to the eastern door of the temple, so that they can catch sight of the magnificent statue inside.[32] Connelly discovers a 'foundation' event, glorified in Euripides' *Erechtheus*, of which only fragments remain: the sacrifice of the daughters of Erechtheus, which enabled Athens to withstand an invasion by Eumolpos, the king of Thrace.[33] Jenkins is inclined to stress ambiguity.[34] A final group of scholars might even hold the field at the present time. Pollitt, supported lately by Hurwit, though anticipated in the basic thesis by Ridgway and Beschi, has sought to demonstrate that the frieze evokes the general idea of festival at Athens and thus does not relate to any one particular festival, though the Panathenaia is not excluded from its range of associations.[35]

Many alternatives, therefore, exist to the Stuart/Revett idea that the frieze represents an idealized, contemporary Panathenaic procession. This situation has resulted from sophisticated readings of the frieze which pay close attention to iconographical details. The scholarship is often exemplary. I wonder, however, whether the forest is being missed somewhat in all the close attention that has been given to the trees. The notion that the Stuart/Revett idea is beset by problems is misleading, and it would seem to be time to reassert the fundamental inspiration provided by the Great Panathenaia – the festival in general, not merely the procession. This should be the base from which other interpretations, such as the idea of festival itself, flow. I would like to argue that, with due allowance for conventions of the medium and the day, each of the groups of figures on the frieze makes sense as participants in a contemporary celebration of the Great Panathenaia, Athens' premier showpiece event. The 'problems' – points made against the frieze's being an idealized, contemporary depiction – can be answered satisfactorily in detail as well as in general.

Some preliminary points should be made. We have a frieze depicting a procession which ends with the *peplos* (see below) being handed over. The frieze is located on a temple of Athena that is in turn located on the Acropolis at Athens. There were other festivals, processions and sacrifices at Athens, but how many of them involved all these elements: Athena, Acropolis, *peplos*? How many specifically celebrated Athena's birth, and apparently also her role in the defeat of the giants, as depicted in the pediment and metopes at the front of the Parthenon?[36] And what of the lavish scale of the event depicted? The Great Panathenaia was the greatest of the Athenian festivals. Our literary sources may mention details which cannot be traced in the frieze, but this is hardly surprising, for the frieze is not a comprehensive record. Nor, for that matter, are our literary sources, which turn out to be snippets of information preserved here and there in scholia and late lexica.[37] There is no warrant in this case for implying that the literary sources form a control against which to measure the art. No extant author attempted to give a detailed description of the procession. The two types of sources are not complementary. In fact, the limitations of all our classes of evidence are such that no amount of combining them can permit full appreciation. Their respective degrees of incompleteness especially prevent any decent impression of changes in the ritual over time.

We have episodes rather than a complete overview, so that time and place are not unified throughout the frieze.[38] As for the 'impious' presence of a mortal procession on a divine building, it certainly does appear that the depiction is without good precedent. The idea of votive forerunners has been floated, but there are massive differences of scale and spirit. In particular, the Olympians do not dwarf the mortals as do the deities on votives, and they are not the object of the sacrifice or *peplos*.[39] Votives, moreover, focus upon individual divinities, or upon pairs and triads of deities united by cult practice.[40] What is appealing, nonetheless, about the idea of a votive is that the frieze similarly wants to imply perpetual devotion which deserves ongoing benefits in reply; both the goddess and her people are constrained by a contract for extraordinary worship and patronage. It is as though the Great Panathenaia, Athenian worship at its ultimate, is going on all the time. For Osborne, anyone who appreciates the frieze may join in;[41] but such a person would probably benefit regardless. Fragments of a sixth-century marble architectural frieze from the Acropolis, possibly belonging to the old temple of Athena, show a draped figure climbing into a chariot.[42] Because additional fragments seem to depict seated figures, Brommer and Ridgway wonder whether the frieze of the Peisistratid temple depicted an archaic precursor to the Parthenon frieze, which would make the latter less exceptional than it otherwise seems.[43] Boardman accepts the fragments as an architectural frieze, but opposes attempts to assign them to the Peisistratid temple because he regards the style as too late.[44] We can agree with Castriota that there is simply too little of the frieze remaining to permit the identification of its subject or its attribution to a specific monument.[45] In addition, whereas Brommer finds mortals in temple sculpture of the archaic period, Ridgway argues cogently that these are not real precedents, for the human element serves merely as an accessory to the main mythological scenes.[46] Yet even if, as it seems, a mortal procession was unprecedented in temple sculpture, Neils has demonstrated that fifth-century Athenians were probably quite used to seeing painted representations of the Panathenaic procession on pots. She also reminds us that the distinction between mythical and historical times is a modern one.[47] The Athenian distinction between a 'generation of heroes' (Hdt 3.122) and the later age of men has by no means the same connotations; Athenians took their descent from figures like Erechtheus seriously.[48] Boedeker stresses the innovativeness of fifth-century Athens and in particular the developing practice of employing events from the recent past in public visual and verbal art. The Stoa Poikile, constructed *c.* 460, juxtaposes an Amazonomachy and Trojanomachy against wall paintings of the battle of Marathon and the battle of Oinoe, the latter a very recent event that probably took place in the 460s. Living Athenians were being compared favourably with the glorious heroes of a time long ago.[49] Modern commentators have probably worried far more about the presence of mortals in the frieze, especially ones ennobled, than did the Greeks themselves.

Another basic point is that the frieze is an idealizing monument. There is not always much awareness of what is at stake when scholars criticize it for not showing elements that were present in reality. To a great degree the criticism is unfair or misguided.[50] Artistic conventions,[51] notions of aesthetic balance, and the limitations imposed by the medium would have been in the designer's mind, as would preconceptions about gender and sexuality. It need hardly be pointed out that the horses are too small in relation to their riders.[52] Numbers (e.g. groups of four on the north and ten on the south) will have been as subject to these kinds of considerations as to others. We might be misinterpreting the significance of some of these numbers gravely in our readiness to see things historical or political. These and other factors militate against a realistic depiction, if ever there can be such a thing. Moreover, the designer's capacity for innovation should not be underestimated.[53] It was an extraordinarily energetic time, and a time to expect pride, even arrogance, rather than modesty.[54] I would accept unity in the frieze with regard to subject matter, and that any overall view of its subject affects the identification of all its parts, and vice versa,[55] but it seems that omissions and modifications are natural products of the situation.[56]

Finally, a few remarks about ambiguity. There can be little doubt that much Greek art is evocative or metaphorical in character.[57] The Parthenon metopes, pediments, and Athena's statue were covered with symbols of conflict which can justifiably be interpreted to cover Athens' recent history as well as its mythical past. It is not too hard, for instance, to read Athenians and Persians into battles between gods and giants, or Greeks and Trojans, and so on.[58] The difficulty for interpreters comes with setting limits and providing foundations (Troy, for instance, was Athena's city too). It does not seem right to think that the Greeks merely accepted multiplicity, even inconsistency, or that they intended no precise definition, believing that the message is often 'paradox itself and the irreconcilability of the forces that govern human destiny'.[59] Some degree of precision should be present.[60]

Meanings can be constructed on top of meanings, and this is probably intrinsic to the process of creating meaning, but there needs to be a base.[61] It is, for instance, hard to believe that 'ambiguous' or 'evocative' images were confusing or difficult for contemporary viewers to understand. The designer of the Parthenon frieze, with a hypothetical viewer of the Periklean age in mind, was trying to impress and stimulate rather than make uneasy or uncertain. Surely evocations were to be constructed on the foundation of a rather solid idea.

The frieze procession runs in two streams down the long sides of the Parthenon (i.e. the north and the south sides). It begins at the south-west corner (i.e. not the centre-west), but culminates at the centre-east, over the main door of the temple (*Fig.* 1). Sixty-eight per cent of its length (more than two thirds) is devoted to the cavalcade of horsemen and chariots. The horsemen form the largest single component of the frieze, taking up about forty-seven per cent of its length. All the west side is occupied by the cavalcade, and most of the north and south sides. The action starts on the west (*Fig.* 4), with handsome youths mounting feisty steeds and beginning to fall into formation. Nakedness is more apparent on this side than elsewhere in the frieze, as though to attract attention and engender excitement by enlisting desire at a considerable pitch. Only one figure on the whole frieze is completely naked, and he is a young groom on the west side (W III 6).[62] In line with a development of precisely this period, only beardless youths appear with genitals exposed; bearded men on the frieze are either clothed or otherwise have their genitals obscured.[63] Some youths are still donning equipment and preparing to mount. The action is regulated at intervals by marshals. Two of the youths on the west side (W VI 12; W XV 29) make use of low rocks to assist in tying their sandals. Such rocks appear intermittently throughout the frieze, though it is doubtful that they indicate changes of setting. To Ridgway, they are merely 'props in a bare landscape'.[64]

Meanwhile, fellow cavalrymen stream along the north and south sides (*Figs.* 5 and 6). A number of the youths on the north are also largely naked, whereas others are clothed in a variety of garments, topped at times by sun-hats, helmets or wreaths. The impression made by the riders on the north is quite different to that made on the south. It is partly a matter of dress: long-sleeved *chitōn*s appear at times on the north, and combinations that include crested helmets with body armour (e.g. N XLIII 118). These do not appear on the south. More noticeable, however, is the irregularity and variety of the north versus the regularity and uniformity of the south. The sixty horsemen appear to be divided into ten groups on the north,[65] though the numbers vary within each group, dress varies within each group, and the number ten can only be arrived at if you accept that there are two separate groups, slightly overlapping, on slabs XLVI and XLVII (*Fig.* 7). On the south, however, there is far greater orderliness: sixty riders are divided into ten groups of six each, with each group marked by its own distinctive dress, the individual horsemen overlapping one on another. The faces of all the figures on the frieze are serious, calm and introverted, even when they are moving or exerting themselves. In general one is struck by the uniformity of facial type in contrast to the great diversity of pose and garb. This tends to convey notions of both the individual and the group.

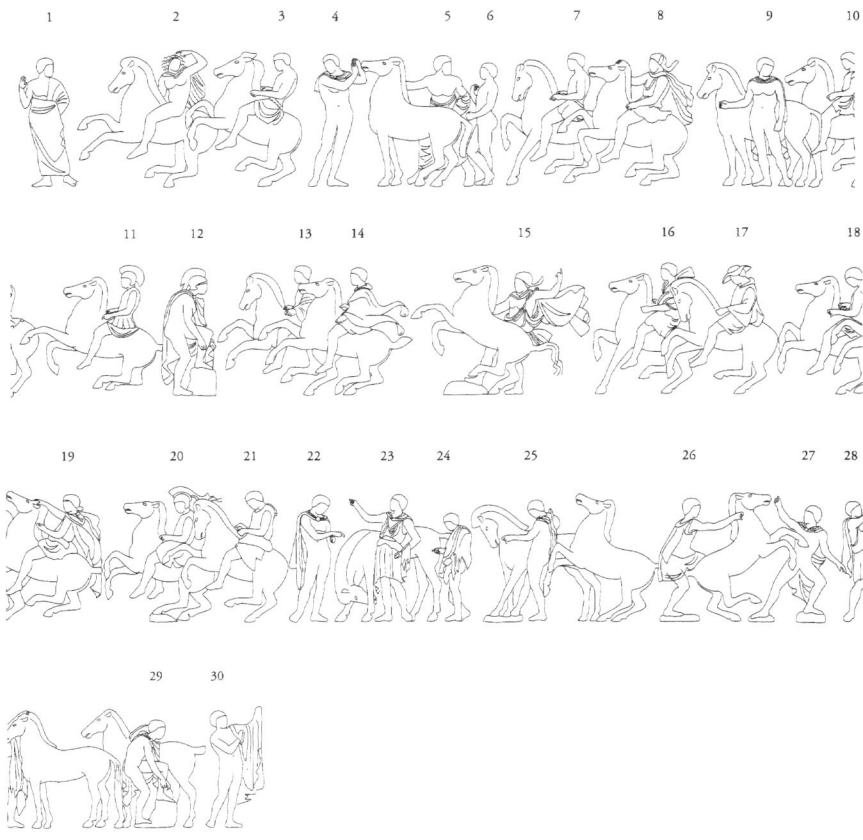

Fig. 4. The west frieze of the Parthenon (from J. Neils *The Parthenon Frieze*, Cambridge 2001, drawn by Rachel Rosenzweig). © Cambridge University Press.

243

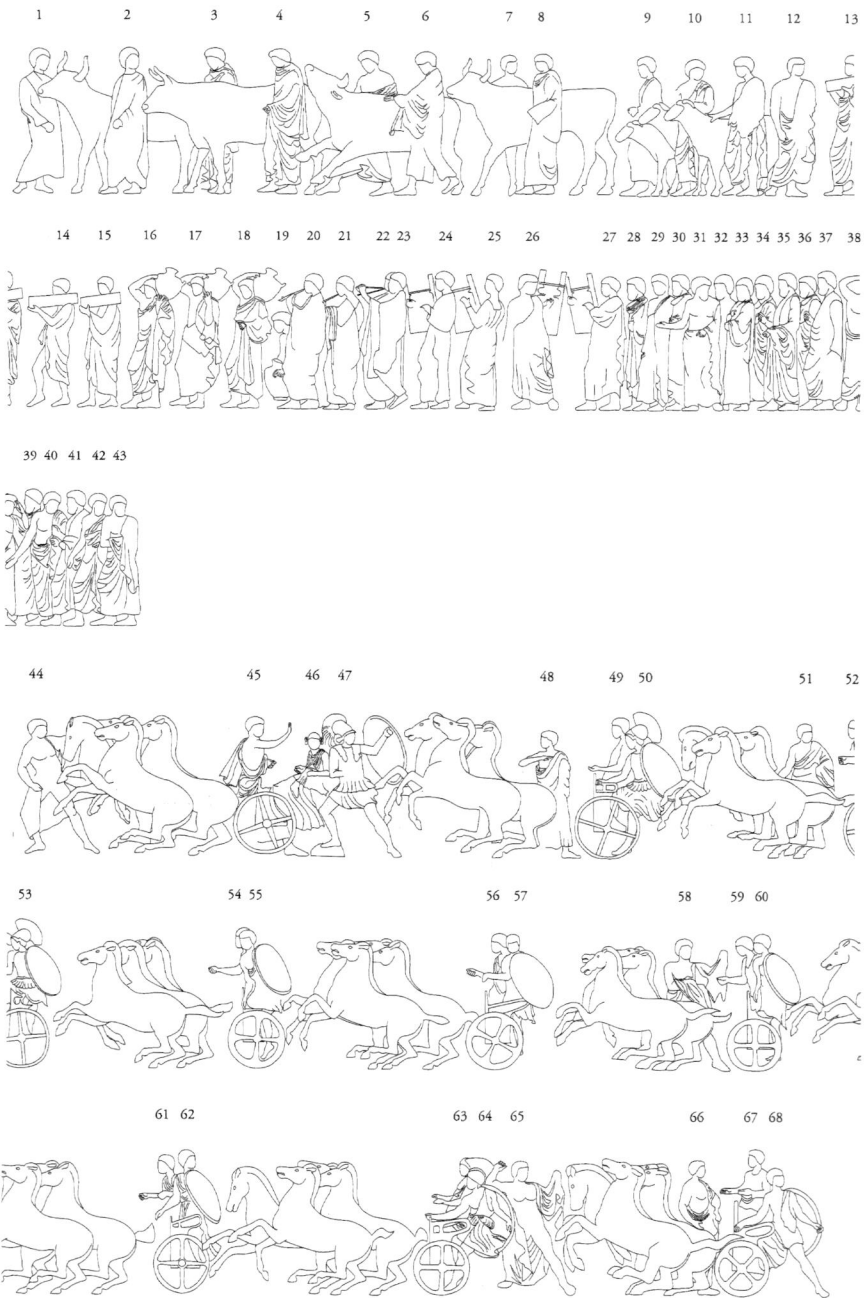

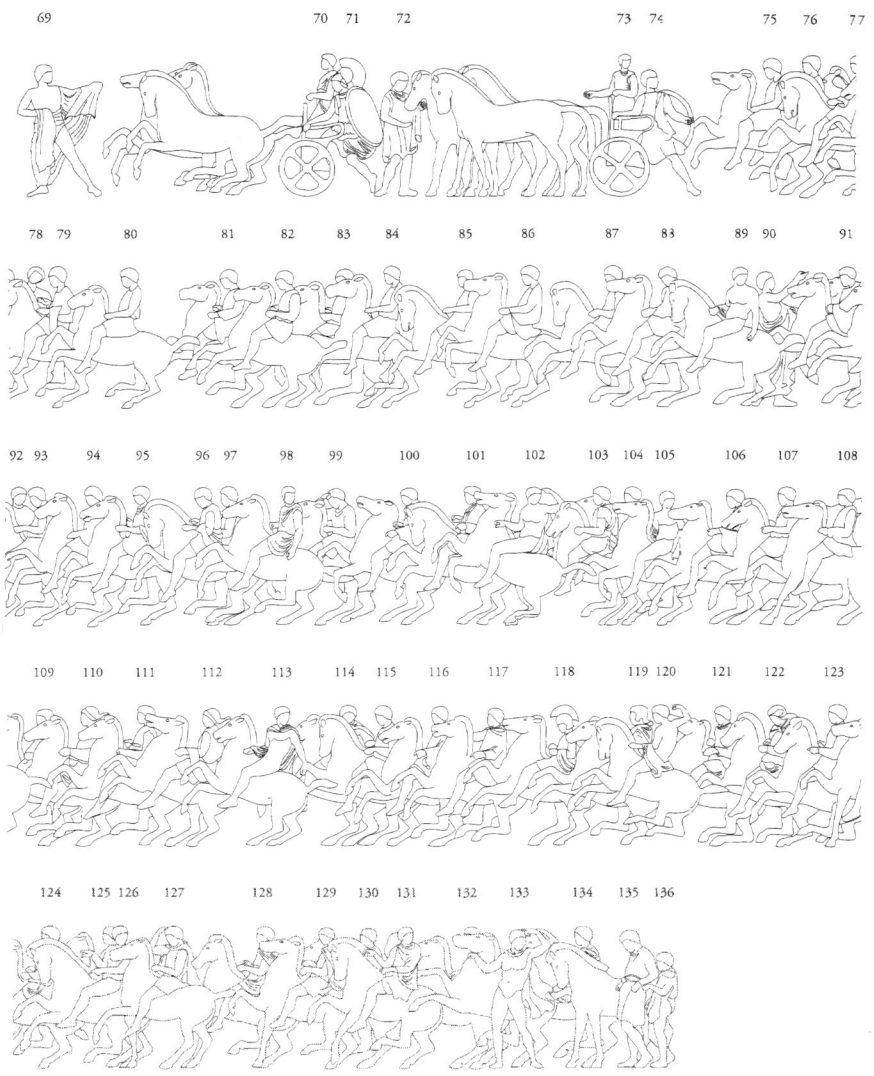

Fig. 5. The north frieze of the Parthenon (from J. Neils *The Parthenon Frieze*, Cambridge 2001, drawn by Rachel Rosenzweig). © Cambridge University Press.

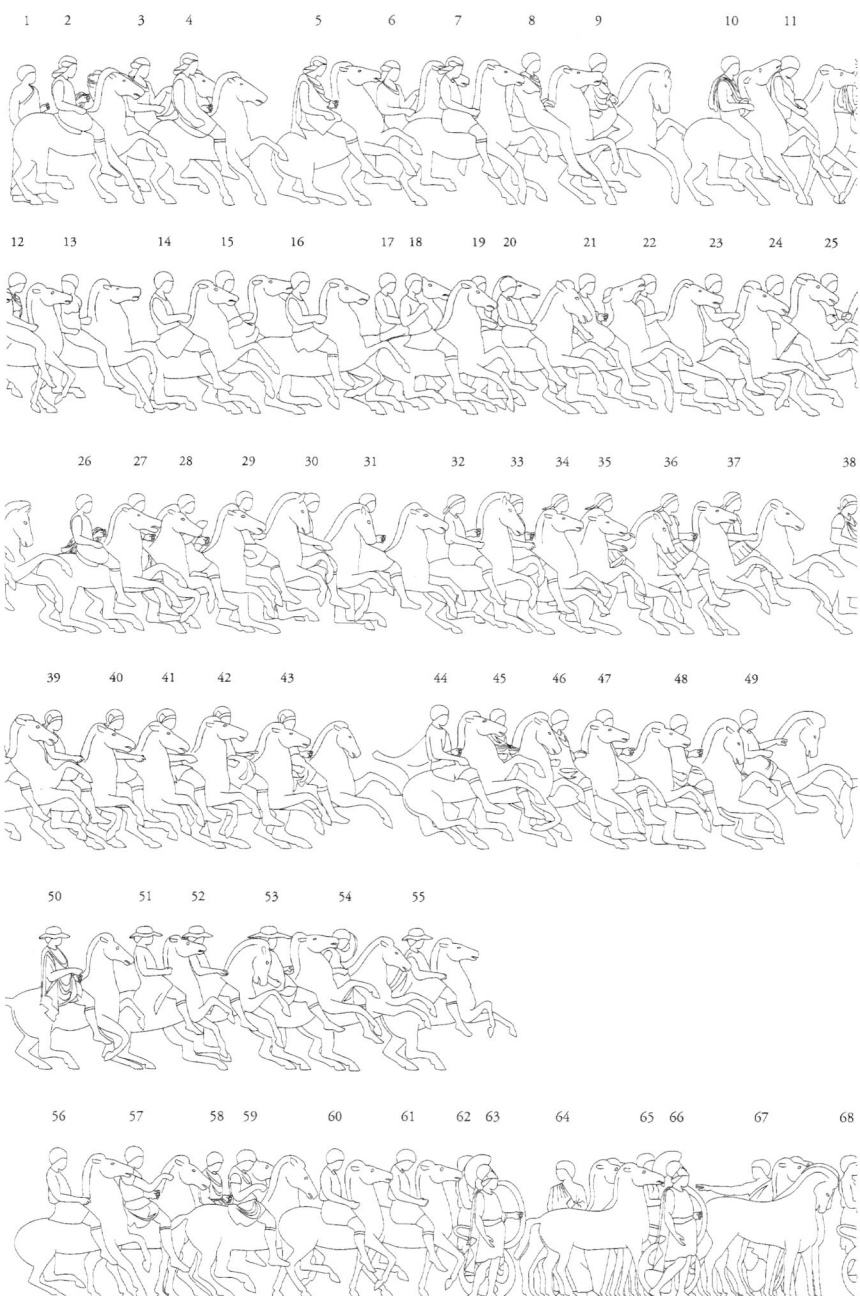

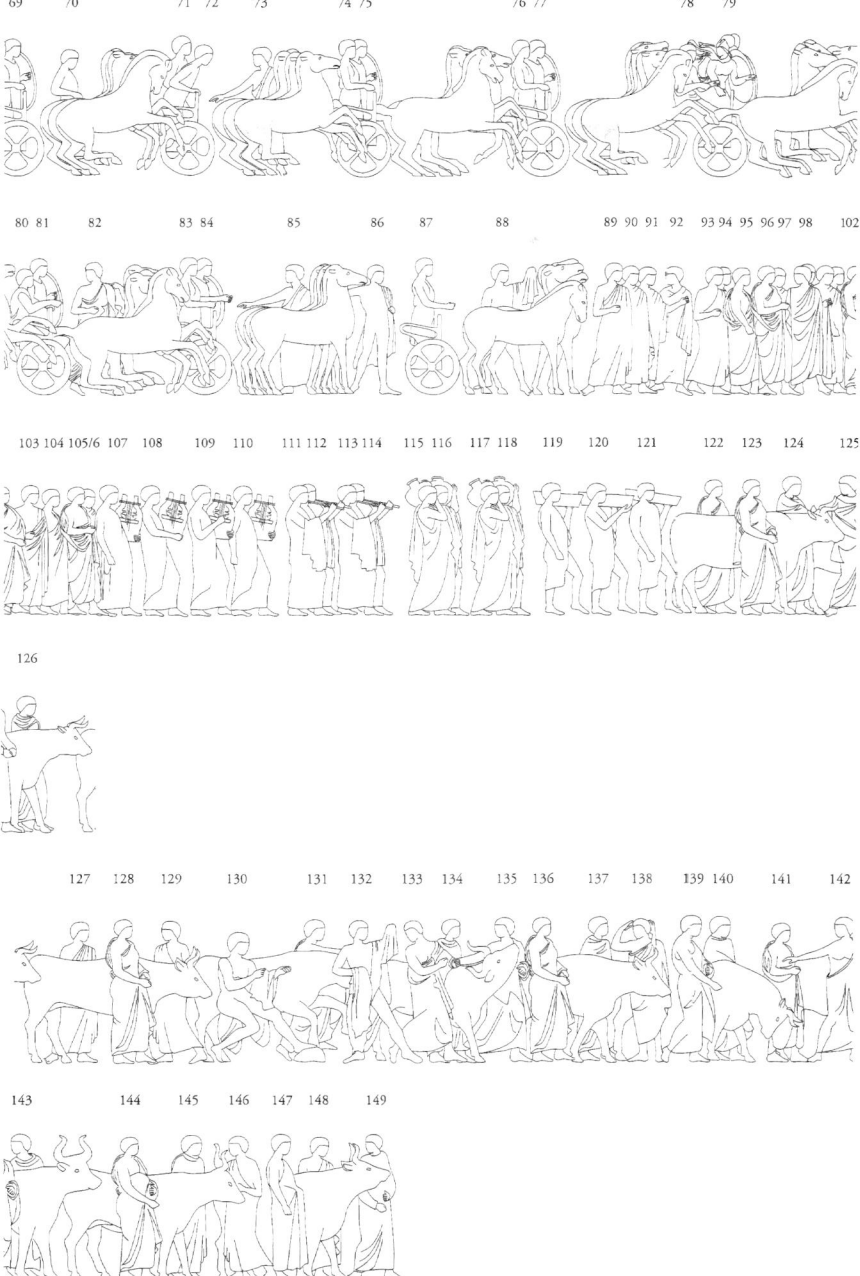

Fig. 6. The south frieze of the Parthenon (from J. Neils *The Parthenon Frieze*, Cambridge 2001, drawn by Rachel Rosenzweig). © Cambridge University Press.

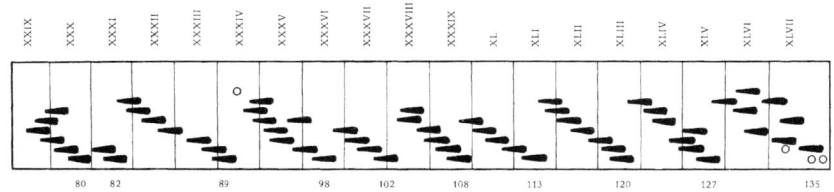

Fig. 7. Diagram of the ranks of horsemen on the north frieze of the Parthenon (from I. Jenkins *The Parthenon Frieze*, London 1994, 99). © Trustees of the British Museum.

Why are the cavalry such a prominent part of the frieze?[66] It need not be doubted that formations of hoplites could have been rendered successfully. Parke expresses concern that they might have been too monotonous, but rows of cavalry are potentially subject to the same problem.[67] An Attic black-figure band cup from a private collection in London effectively shows hoplites participating in a religious procession to Athena, and despite the fact that differences of scale and setting render the frieze a very different proposition, it does seem that a conscious choice has been made to exclude hoplites in favour of horsemen.[68] It cannot have been from fear that the hoplites would have lent a misleadingly martial rather than processional quality to the frieze in its early stages. The vase noted above, admittedly very different in scale, does not support this idea, and it could as easily apply to the horsemen. Precedents in architectural sculpture must provide some part of the answer. Castriota in particular has shown that even though the frieze as a total conception is without good precedent, the individual elements are readily apparent in earlier work. Rows of cavalry and chariots would have been familiar from buildings like the Siphnian Treasury at Delphi, as well as from a decent corpus of East Greek monuments.[69] They bespoke a heroic context and proximity to the gods. On the Siphnian Treasury, for example, the cavalry and chariots on the west and south friezes moved toward assembled, enthroned Olympians on the east.[70] Equestrian imagery, therefore, acts to elevate the atmosphere; it is a prime way of ennobling the citizens, their democracy, and their participation in the Great Panathenaia.[71] Osborne points out that there are rampant horses in the pediment, metopes, and frieze on the west.[72] Horsemen also serve as standard space-fillers in earlier work.[73] It would be wrong to deny that their prominence is at least partly related to the fact that there was a large amount of space to be filled.[74]

Of special importance, however, is the image of the Athenian cavalry as a brilliant and youthful élite in the Periklean age. There are strong indications that the contemporary Athenian cavalry is being represented, and it seems reasonable to think that Athenians would have appreciated this depiction – with elements equestrian, heroic and youthful – as a way of ennobling the citizenry in general. Cavalry reforms, probably sponsored by Perikles himself, have been dated to the period after the invasion of 446.[75] Although state subsidization enabled expansion of the corps, service remained essentially a matter for the élite. Nevertheless, literary references indicate that the cavalry became a focus of pride for all Athenian citizens,[76] and the corps was viewed favourably until the time of its association with the Thirty Tyrants at the end of the fifth century.[77] The chorus in Sophokles' *Oidipous at Kolonos* (706–19) praises the cavalry corps in striking terms, putting it on a par with the olive tree and the navy. Even Aristophanes is by and large positive. In *Knights*, he does have old man Demos cast aspersions on horsemen's bravery (1369–71); but in the same play the chorus of cavalrymen are ἄνδρες ἀγαθοί (excellent men) who help to free old man Demos from the political con artist Paphlagon (222–6), and they are permitted to assert in glowing terms the military contribution they and their forebears have made to the city (565–73, 595–610). Aristocrats who were victorious in equestrian contests were admired and honoured (e.g. Thuc. 6.16.1–2), and at festival time Athenians were filled with awe at the sight of their cavalry, especially when prancing and also when galloping in groups.[78] This is, of course, the effect intended by the frieze, and it nicely calls up the festival context that becomes clearer as the frieze unfolds. The ten groupings of horsemen on both the north and south sides point strongly to the ten Kleisthenic tribes,[79] and it is natural to think first of Periklean Athens, where Perikles' own sons were said to be the finest cavalrymen (Pl. *Meno* 94b). The number 60 was probably determined by the dimensions and design of the frieze rather than by its being the number of riders in a tribal regiment out of a total force of 600. Worley has conjectured (mainly using the frieze) that this was the number of horsemen established by recent reforms before that number was quickly raised to 1000 'in the last decade before the Peloponnesian War'.[80]

There is nothing, on present knowledge, that categorically rules out a contemporary Panathenaic festival as the setting. All but one of the young horsemen have short hair; all but two are shown as unbearded youths. Although some fifth-century vases show horsemen with long hair, in general this depiction accords well with images of cavalrymen and their (bearded) commanders in other art of the period.[81] The Olympians on the east side have short hair too,[82] which tends to intensify the link between gods and mortals. The degree of nakedness is surely not realistic. Neils emphasizes the theme of undressing and dressing-up which permeates the festival and its rituals,[83] but in this case it seems more connected to established conventions for awakening a homoerotic response.[84] Considerations of the latter type might similarly govern depictions of boy jockeys racing in the nude.[85] Members of the Athenian cavalry certainly participated in equestrian events at the Panathenaic festival. Some of these events, like the javelin throw from horseback, were not held at Olympia and were probably restricted to Athenians at the Panathenaia.[86] Pollitt has doubted the cavalry's participation in the Panathenaic procession, pointing out that Demosthenes *Against Meidias* 171 and *First Philippic* 26, and Xenophon *Hipparchikos* 3, the texts most commonly used in support of this contention, make mention only of 'processions' in general. This is true, but is it likely that the cavalry did not participate in the most important of these processions?[87] Xenophon (*Hipparchikos* 3.2) writes of the cavalry riding around the Agora during festival processions, saluting the various shrines of all the gods. He also indicates that the hipparchs and phylarchs were instrumental in organizing their men so that an awe-inspiring performance would result on public occasions.[88]

Pollitt has also argued that the varied dress of the cavalrymen on the frieze indicates the different attire they wore for the different festivals and displays of the Athenian calendar;[89] on balance, this seems unlikely. The degree of nakedness alone is a reminder about the hazards of searching for an accurate reflection of reality. Yet if this must be done, I do not see why it is assumed that varied items of dress could not have been in evidence during the Panathenaia itself. The state apparently helped with the buying and feeding of a cavalryman's horse, but the cavalrymen themselves seem to have been responsible for what they wore, and so variety of attire was the result.[90] This applied particularly in the fifth century, while for the fourth century Spence has shown that more cavalrymen were opting for boots and breastplates.[91] There may have been a certain limited uniformity at festival time. Xenophon describes how a phylarch, mindful of his own reputation as well as that of his tribe, could be pressed by a hipparch to ensure an awe-inspiring display from his men (*Hipparchikos* 1.21–2). It is likely that such a phylarch would have commanded his men to dress impressively, and possibly distinctively.[92] In the second century BC, at the Theseia festival, there was a contest for the tribal contingent with the best equipment.[93] Consequently, at times during a festival the cavalry regiments might have paraded in distinctly-dressed units, as on the south frieze. At other times, with the north frieze in mind, they might have been more mingled, as when competing, processing or performing complicated manoeuvres of the kind that Xenophon also writes about (*Hipparchikos* 3.9). Therefore, the horsemen might at times within the same festival have appeared in distinctly-dressed units and in more mingled formations. Both the north and south friezes might have some grounding in reality. However, this is all highly tentative. It is probably wiser to concentrate upon artistic and aesthetic concerns. The more mixed appearance of the north side might simply be one way of calling to mind the variously dressed individuals of the Athenian cavalry. Boardman sees the different dress on the south as an artistic device employed simply to differentiate the ranks.[94] All the items of dress on the frieze were employed by cavalrymen in the Periklean age.[95] Osborne argues that a viewer would appreciate the frieze by measuring its elements in terms of conformity and difference.[96] Such a viewer, one imagines, would notice the variety of dress on the north side; this would help to keep his attention as he processed along it. On the south side, for the same viewer, the same arrangement would not work as well, especially given the similarity in facial features. So perhaps the frieze opts for ten groups of uniformly dressed riders as its way of keeping the viewer's attention; it is representation according to a different conceptual order. Ridgway emphasizes that we can find semi-nude figures next to a youth entirely muffled in his mantle (cf. W VII 14, W IX 17, and the figures around them), in spite of the fact that the Panathenaia took place at the height of summer. This marks the composition as a product of 'artistic selection for variety's sake',[97] and acts as a salutary reminder that there are clear limits to any search for realism in the frieze.

The absence of cavalry weapons is puzzling. If they were not actually painted on, it would seem to be another artistic device, a preliminary cue that this is a procession rather than a battle, or perhaps a way of avoiding awkward positioning problems. It is hard to believe that cavalry weapons were deemed too dangerous in the city at this time. During the Peisistratid tyranny the Panathenaic procession was the only event at which Athenians could bear arms without arousing suspicion (Thuc. 6.56). When Xenophon recommends performing manoeuvres in the city carrying weapons, he is careful to stress a performance both safe and beautiful (*Hipparchikos* 3.14), and he takes care to advise where the riders should position their spears during a gallop.[98] But this might not mean that the carrying of weapons was a new practice; instead he seems chiefly concerned with the carrying of weapons in the exercise known as the Anthippasia, a mock battle in which two lines, each composed of five tribal units, charged full tilt at one another. While not attested until the third century, it is usually thought to have been included in the Panathenaia earlier, possibly at the end of the fifth century.[99]

It has been thought that the bearded male restraining the rearing horse on the west side (W VIII 15) is Theseus and that the theme is the *synoikismos* or unification of Attica, with the setting being Eleusis at the south end of the west frieze.[100] Ashmole notes his position on the central slab of the west frieze, the counterpart to the *peplos* scene on the east side, and asks whether this might be an allegorical reference to the art of government, calling to mind Perikles' relationship with the *dēmos*.[101] In the absence of distinctive attributes, however, the bearded figures are better identified as hipparchs.[102] Scholars have seen that they are identically dressed. Spence sees Thracian cap (*alōpekis*), tunic (*chitōn*), cloak (*chlamys*), and boots; Stewart sees 'Theseus' wearing the same Thracian cap, tunic (*exōmis*), and cloak as the second bearded horseman seven figures to his left. His head is now missing but an old cast certifies the cap.[103] The action of the west side would seem to be set in the vicinity of the Dipylon Gate, from where the procession began.[104] Subsequently, on the north and south sides, we move into the Agora.[105] One cavalryman (W XII 23) has been interpreted as lifting his arm in protest, possibly at being excluded from the procession.[106] It is hard, however, to see deficiency being commemorated on the Parthenon. Ashmole thinks he might have been holding reins, which have since perished, and that the action of his horse in lowering its head is what now makes his arm seem elevated in a gesture of address.[107]

Preceding the horsemen are four-horse chariots. The consensus now seems to be that there are eleven chariots on the north, and ten on the south.[108] Of the ten chariots on the south, each carrying a charioteer in a long saffron robe,[109] and a hoplite in armour and having an attendant close by, two are standing (S XXV–XXVI 62–67), six are running (S XXVII–XXXII 68–82), and the remaining two are standing (S XXXIII–XXXV 83–88). Chariots on the north are similarly composed but most are more active, showing the hoplite *apobatēs* (dismounter) leaping on or off the moving chariot as occurred during competition (e.g. N XII 47, N XXVII 71).[110] How can we understand the presence of the chariots, and in particular the *apobatai*? For a start, there are precursors to both the chariots and the *apobatai* in architectural sculpture.[111] They might also commemorate Erechtheus' introduction of the chariot and the use made of it by the Athenian army of heroic times.[112] More immediately compelling, however, are associations with the Panathenaic festival. There is direct evidence that *apobatai* competed in the Panathenaic games.[113] Simon and Neils, employing the priceless inscription *IG* II² 2311, feel that the dismounter contests took place on Day 7 of the festival, i.e. the day after the procession day.[114] There is not, it might be added, explicit evidence that the *apobatai* competed in other festivals at Athens beyond the Panathenaia, though it would be unwise to surmise that they did not. Certainly, they did not mount the Acropolis any more than the cavalry did. Both the chariots and the horses raced along the *dromos* or raceway in the Agora,[115] and it does seem, from the action of the hoplites jumping on and off the chariots, that the frieze alludes as much to competing as to processing. It is possible that some place was found for these chariots in the procession, but the main point to stress is that the frieze is evoking the dismounter contests and maintaining the excitement engendered by the preceding groups of prancing horses and youthful riders. The depiction of the *apobatai* makes it clear that the frieze evokes the Great Panathenaic festival in its entirety. Several days of competition, procession and religious ceremony, conducted in varying degrees of exuberance and solemnity, are described.[116] Before races or displays could be conducted, the course had to be cleared of spectators or loiterers (Xen. *Hipparchikos* 3.10). Some echo of this, or at least of the excitement and danger of the competition,[117] is conveyed by the marshal who leaps out of the way of a speeding chariot in such a fashion that his cloak blows away from his otherwise naked body (N XXIII 65). Stewart might indeed be right about wit and erotic teasing on the frieze.[118] Another marshal (N XI 44), who brings the racing chariots to a screeching halt, signals the transition between the chariots and the next phase of the procession, between one time and place and another, even one mood and another. This part of the frieze in particular speaks eloquently of the relationship between sport and festival in ancient Athens: sporting competition reflected the power of the city, the city's power reflected Athena's patronage, Athena is reflected in the level of competition. Thus sport and festival are appropriate subjects for inclusion on the Parthenon.

In front of the chariots on the north and south sides, and culminating on the east, is a sacrificial procession, which appears to move imperceptibly from the Agora to the Acropolis.[119] At the east end of the north and south sides, reading from west to east, a line of figures, including elders, musicians, and those charged with carrying the varied paraphernalia of sacrifice, or with leading sacrificial animals, go ahead of the chariots. The elders (N VIII–X 28–43; S XXXV–XXXVII 89–106), a group of bearded men, are endowed with that idealized calm and noble bearing that pervades all the figures on the frieze from this point onwards. They are commonly identified as *thallophoroi* (branch-bearers), men who had been successful in a Panathenaic beauty contest.[120] Yet none of them carries the olive branch that symbolizes their victory and there are no holes in their hands for metal attachments. Brommer thought the branches might have been painted on,[121] but it appears unlikely that leaves would have been painted across the sculptured folds of the garments. With fists empty, however, is exactly the manner in which men in votive reliefs approach a deity. Boardman questions the beauty of the few heads that remain and prefers to see them as the gnarled veterans of Marathon.[122] Certainly they are respected old men, quietly dignified, possibly officials.[123] Boardman sees them as a caesura between the cavalcade and the mortal procession;[124] they provide verticals and stillness that contrast with the horizontals and speed of the chariots. The excitement of sporting contest gives way to the solemnity of religious ceremony.

In front of the officials on the north side are musicians, four *kitharōdoi* (lyre-players) (N VII–VIII 24–27) and four pipers (N VI–VII 20–23), who are appropriate for the procession but also evoke the musical contests of the festival.[125] The former wear splendid robes: a *chitōn* with sleeves, a *peplos*, and on their backs a mantle.[126] Musicians were in great demand throughout the Greek world and the best of them, figures of considerable charisma, commanded high appearance fees.[127] It was necessary, therefore, to offer handsome rewards at the Panathenaia to secure an impressive field of contestants. The Odeion was rebuilt at great expense and opened *c.* 446; Perikles took a turn presiding over the musical contests in their new venue.[128] *IG* II² 2311, from the first half of the fourth century, indicates that the prize for lyre-playing was a silver crown worth 1000 drachmas plus 500 drachmas cash. These musicians in context, therefore, are more than mere functionaries or secondary figures. The sacrificial procession on the south side was badly damaged by Venetian bombardment in 1687, so it has gaps and is more difficult to reconstruct. Invaluable drawings made by the Flemish (possibly French) artist Jacques Carrey,[129] working for the Marquis de Nointel in 1674, show a group of men carrying rectangular objects in front of the officials (S XXXVII–XXXVIII 107–110). Brommer thinks they might have been carrying *pinakes* (writing-tablets).[130] Simon sees secretaries, whose job it was to ensure fair distribution of the meat from the sacrifice to the citizens of Athens.[131] Boardman sees *deltoi* (writing-boards) and thinks the men are state treasurers or accountants, supervisors of tribute.[132] It seems preferable to see the objects as musical instruments, as do Himmelmann and Jenkins, who identify the figures as lyre-players by analogy with those on the north frieze, though they are dressed differently.[133] In balance with the north, Jenkins restores pipers to the next part of the south frieze (which is completely lost).[134] He would seem to be on the right track with these figures, but in any case there is nothing in any of these reconstructions which in the present, imperfect state of our evidence rules out a contemporary celebration of the Great Panathenaia.

After the musicians, on the north side, come youths bearing *hydriai* (N VI 16–19), youths bearing trays (N V 13–15), and sacrificial victims together with their male attendants (N slabs I–IV). A fragment assigned to the south frieze seems to preserve a *skaphēphoros* or tray-bearer (S XL 120). These were metic males who wore purple *himatia* and carried bronze or silver trays (*skaphai*) on which were honeycombs and small cakes for placing on the altar in order to lure the sacrificial animals.[135] Jenkins plausibly restores hydria-bearers to the missing south frieze in parallel with the north (S XXXIX 115–118 conjectured).[136] Although wine is a possibility, the *hydriai* probably contain water, for water and music were needed in the ritual slaughtering of animals.[137]

The male *hydriaphoroi* have been seen as a major problem for the Stuart/Revett thesis because there is literary evidence (a fragment of Demetrios of Phaleron and later notices) that the daughters of metics carried *hydriai* and parasols (*skiadia*) for the wives of Athenian citizens in the Panathenaic procession.[138] If not part of the Panathenaia, thinks Connelly, they might be connected with the libations ordered by Athena in the wake of the sacrifice of Erechtheus' daughters.[139] Simon attempted to rescue the Panathenaic context by conjecturing that the *hydriaphoroi* were victors in the annual torch-races, for which the prize was a *hydria*. One of them, 'victor of the previous night, still exhausted, sets his vessel on the ground so that he can rest a little'.[140] Pollitt is unconvinced, arguing that they would be wearing victors' garlands if this were so.[141] Hurwit wonders whether there are coins, not water, in the jars.[142] Others have approached the problem from the point of view of gender associations and homoeroticism. Younger, mindful of the strained relationship between citizens and metics, feels that metic youths have been segregated at the east end of the north frieze where they are depicted in stigmatized and effeminizing occupations, bearing water jugs and trays.[143] This would mean, as Stewart argues too, that metic women have been banished from the frieze altogether, being replaced by the nude Eros (E VI 42), who holds a sunshade, as well as by the youths bearing water jars. Again, what is critical to bear in mind is that the frieze is not a realistic record. The complete absence of females on the west, north and south seems very deliberate, as though the east end is definitely the female end. Boardman thought that it may have seemed inappropriate to juxtapose any groups of women to the heroic cavalcade.[144] Stewart thinks that it is part and parcel of the emphasis placed upon awakening homoerotic desire.[145] Indeed, Younger and Stewart have much in common on this point, and together their findings permit a Panathenaic reading that is not apologetic about the males in this part of the frieze. On the other hand, there is probably a less dramatic answer to the problem of male *hydriaphoroi* on the frieze. Brommer simply assumed that the custom had changed in the period between the execution of the frieze and the much later date of the written sources.[146] Lefkowitz is noticeably careful in stating that metic women were afforded the honour of becoming *hydriaphoroi* 'by the middle of the [fourth] century', and Neils has found pottery evidence for males bearing *hydriai* in the fifth century.[147] There is a hydria by Phintias,[148] and a fragmentary pelike by the Pan Painter.[149] On the latter, the male hydria-bearer is preceded by a *kanēphoros* (basket-bearer), and their presence on the Panathenaic Way is perhaps indicated by the three herms on the other side of the vase, which might refer to the area of the herms at the north-west entrance to the Agora. The 'problem' of male *hydriaphoroi*, therefore, has probably been one of our own making, a matter of privileging one class of evidence over the other without fully appreciating the limitations of each.

Sacrificial beasts, their attendants and several marshals appear next (S XLI–XLVII 122–149, N I–IV 1–12). A point to note is that both ewes (N slab IV) and heifers (N slabs I–III) appear on the north side as prospective victims; a marshal (N V 12) divides them from the *skaphēphoroi*. Only heifers and their attendants appear on the south (S slabs XLI–XLVII). Could this indicate two different processions with separate groupings of victims? Simon points out that there are four heifers, four ewes, four *hydriaphoroi*, four pipers, and four lyre-players on the north side. She acknowledges that this might just refer to the quadrennial cycle of the Great Panathenaia, but is inclined to see a connection with the four Ionian tribes that preceded the ten tribes of Kleisthenes.[150] In her view the north procession was in honour of Athena Polias, the ewes being for Pandrosos, the daughter of Kekrops; the south procession was in honour of Athena Parthenos, the heifers being for Athena.[151] Harrison prefers to separate the processions in time, the north being pre-Kleisthenic, the south post-Kleisthenic.[152] As far as we know, however, there was no cult for Athena Parthenos in the Periklean age,[153] and it seems that there was only one relevant altar for both sacrifices, so the idea of two processions loses much of its point.[154] The gesture of the marshal (E VI 47) who turns his back on the northern procession to beckon to the southern one, suggests one sacrifice. Both heifers and ewes, moreover, are appropriate for the Panathenaia. Athens' allies sent heifers for sacrifice at the Panathenaia, though it is impossible to tell whether the beasts shown are from Attica or overseas,[155] and the occasion is overwhelmingly an Athenian one. More importantly, Erechtheus enjoyed an annual sacrifice of cattle and sheep which may have formed part of the Panathenaic celebrations.[156] The combination of ram and bull sacrifice on the Acropolis is attested as early as the *Iliad* (2.550). An old Attic law, which admittedly appears to refer to sacrifices by individuals rather than the state, prescribed a ewe for Pandrosos whenever Athena received a heifer.[157] The same combination of victims appears at an altar of Athena on a black-figure hydria by the Theseus Painter in Uppsala.[158]

On the east frieze (*Fig.* 8), at the front of the temple, the procession continues from either corner with a number of women, who shuffle forward in a stately, dignified manner (E II–III 2–17, VII 50–51, VII–IX 53–63). Movement now ceases. Before them stand a group of men, ten altogether (E III–IV 18–23, VI 43–46), who are generally taken to be the eponymous heroes of the ten tribes of post-Kleisthenic Athens. They are at ease, talking to each other, leaning on staves and awaiting the arrival of the main procession. Behind them are the twelve major Olympian gods, six at each side, with two attendant deities (E IV–V 24–30, V–VI 36–42). They also await the procession, seated on stools, with Zeus on a throne. They slightly overlap, with the figures of Zeus (E V 30) and Athena (E V 36)

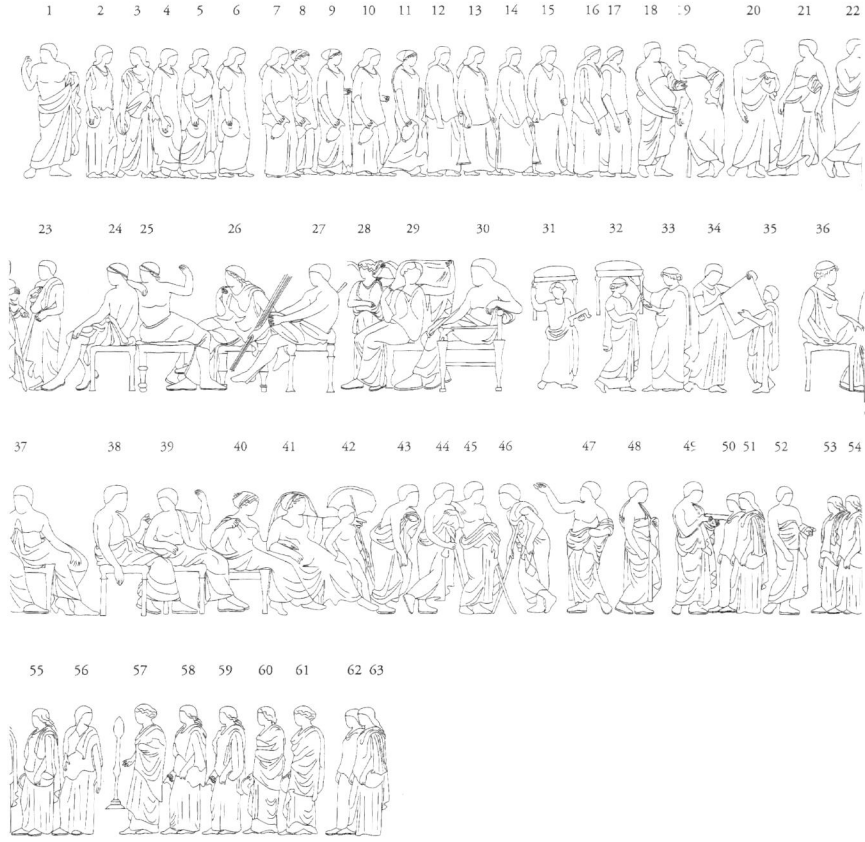

Fig. 8. The east frieze of the Parthenon (from J. Neils *The Parthenon Frieze*, Cambridge 2001, drawn by Rachel Rosenzweig). © Cambridge University Press.

257

being those nearest the centre of the frieze. The 'heroes', six on one side of the gods (E III–IV 18–23) and four on the other (E VI 43–6), are not appreciably taller than other males on this side, for instance the immediately adjacent marshals (E VI–VII 47–49, VII 52).

The first appearance of women on the east side is striking.[159] At least sixteen of them, distinguished by their long hair, are represented as unmarried women. Blundell reminds us that whether married or unmarried they relate to the (intense) femininity of Athena and to the importance of women and marriage in contemporary Athens.[160] Whatever their precise identity, the women are either nearing puberty or have just passed it, and they are closely associated with the art of wool-working, the prime task of the married woman.[161] The depiction of what they carry is entirely appropriate for a major Greek sacrifice. The first five at the southern end (E II 2–6) carry *phialai* (shallow bowls) and the next five (E III 7–11) carry jugs, the paraphernalia of libation.[162] Maidens at the northern end also carry *phialai* (E VII 55, E VIII 60–63) and jugs (E VIII 58–59). Others carry objects and furniture of cult, including two pairs at the southern end (E III 12–15) who hold peculiar trumpet-shaped objects that are generally interpreted as stands for burning incense, though Jenkins opts for stands for supporting the spit on which the meat was roasted.[163] Boardman thinks the objects might be legs of the loom on which the *peplos* was woven, and he is right to say that they are not shaped like the incense-burner (*thymiatērion*), a taller object with a flaring base, that is borne by another woman at the northern end (E VIII 57).[164] Some of the women are empty-handed (E III 16–17, E VII 53–54). Only the *peplos* comes to mind as a possible object for them to have borne, though we have seen apparently empty-handed men before now (the so-called *thallophoroi*). One man on the east (E VII 49) has a pair of women (E VII 50–51) standing in front of him. He is holding a shallow object, and they are empty-handed. Boardman expects two *kana* (baskets) if these are the *kanēphoroi* (basket-bearers), and the nearest maiden shows little sign of having just surrendered a single *kanoun* (basket).[165] He thinks the shallow object is a flat dish, since we might expect the *kanoun*, or several of them, in the hands of the girls who are known to have carried them, rather than in those of a man.[166] It might be, argues Boardman, a *phialē* from the women who prepared the wool for the *peplos*.[167] Simon, following Jochen Schelp, disagrees; the basket has been placed in the marshal's hands as a sign that the procession has just arrived at its goal, the Acropolis. The girl (E VII 51) would have her arms extended if she was about to receive it. In the barley was hidden the knife with which the animals were killed.[168] Harrison sees both *kanēphoroi* and *kanoun*, the type with low-slung handles.[169] Jenkins writes simply of an 'offering basket'.[170] Boardman's objections ought to have received greater attention, though the object does not look quite as flat as he makes out.

The next groups of men signal that the procession has come to its destination and also facilitate a smooth transition between the human and the divine.[171] The five bearded and five beardless figures are commonly identified as the eponymous heroes (E III–IV 18–23, E VI 43–46) – a reasonable idea, especially in light of Mattusch's study, which concludes that representations of the eponymous heroes were deliberately generic. Instead of being individualized, the point was to make them closely resemble one another.[172] The idea of no attributes for figures of such prominence in Athenian ideology seems remarkable at first, but it suits developments in democratic thought, and it is precisely this fact that has permitted a variety of identifications,[173] and rendered unconvincing previous attempts to identify and name the individual figures.[174] It is also worth noting that some of the tribal heroes actually had their sanctuaries on the Acropolis.[175] On the other hand, Ridgway's doubts are still cogent: the asymmetrical division of six (three groups of two in conversation) on the left and four (one group of four) on the right is a little odd; the uncertainty which surrounds attempts to make some of them marshals and vice versa shows that there is not a great deal of difference in height and physique between obvious marshals and the presumed heroes; their varied ages and costumes are paralleled elsewhere on the frieze; they seem unaware, like humans, of the presence of the gods; other figures, certainly mortal, turn their backs on their neighbours elsewhere on the frieze. She prefers to see them, noticing in particular their staves, as citizens who did not participate in the procession or who have already arrived and are chatting among themselves while waiting for their fellow participants.[176] They are in any case paternal figures among the citizens.[177] Jenkins notices that E III 18, who stands at the head of the procession coming from the south, and faces forward with it, is the only one of the ten to be depicted without a staff.[178] There is indeed a good chance that he should be separated from the other nine. In this event, the figures could be *athlothetai* (judges) or other officials or spectators – each would serve my argument, being equally applicable to the Periklean age.

It is not particularly problematic to have all the Olympians, plus Eros and Iris, at the Panathenaia (E IV–V 24–30, E V–VI 36–42). When Peisistratos occupied the Acropolis as his principal residence, he seems to have promoted the event in terms of Herakles' entry to Olympos.[179] More compellingly, the Olympians assemble on vases for the birth of Athena, an event at the heart of the Panathenaia and depicted in the pediment above this part of the frieze. They are present too for the return of Hephaistos and the entry of Herakles to Olympos.[180] An idealized procession, therefore, might well have warranted the attention of the gods.[181] Boardman insists that the Olympians on the frieze can only be present in order to receive the heroes of Marathon into their midst,[182] but this honour could have been deemed appropriate for ennobled Athenians in general. Also significant are parallels for inviting the gods to other festivals that ostensibly honour only one of their number. In Pindar's dithyramb for the Athenians on the occasion of the Great Dionysia (F 75 Snell), the Olympians are invited to take part in the festival in honour of Dionysos. Choral dances in the City Dionysia apparently took place at the Altar of the Twelve Gods in the Agora.[183] If the gods can celebrate the City Dionysia, they should be able to celebrate the Panathenaia too.[184] All the Olympians are present in the pediment and metopes of the east, witnessing Athena's birth and battling the giants, and they were woven into the *peplos* doing battle against the giants as well.[185] Athena's aegis (E V 36) lies in her lap, perhaps in readiness for her to receive the new *peplos*.[186]

All that remains now is the five-figure group involved with the *peplos* at the centre of the east side (E V 31–35) (*Fig.* 9). Most scholars readily accept its connection with the Panathenaia.[187] Connelly's thesis that the scene shows Erechtheus preparing to sacrifice his daughters is formidably put, but there are strong reasons not to see human sacrifice in this scene.

Fig. 9 . The *peplos* scene in the centre of the east frieze of the Parthenon (E V 31–35). © The British Museum.

There is no altar, no priest with a knife, and no hint of the standard iconography of such scenes, as in, for example, the numerous representations of sacrifices of Iphigeneia or Polyxena.[188] Moreover, the mood is not at all tragic. Connelly argues that the Olympians deliberately turn their backs on the sacrifice scene, having no wish to be tainted by pollution, considering it unseemly for gods to watch mortals die.[189] But they give every indication of being relaxed.[190] Their interest is in the ennobled mortals in the procession. The cattle and sheep, it may be added, are the real victims for the sacrifice, not any of the figures in the *peplos* scene.[191] In fairness, there are uncertainties surrounding both the figures and their actions, but these are not insurmountable for the present argument. The trump card, of course, is the *peplos*. There is no more famous piece of cloth in Athenian history than the Panathenaic *peplos*, and no other which so appropriately takes centre stage on the Acropolis at the head of an Athenian procession. It establishes very solidly the context I want. It must be the primary indicator in the scene; the figures largely derive their identities from it, not the other way around. Boardman sees no problem: it must be the *peplos*.[192] Is it the new or the old *peplos*?[193] Simon is sure we have the new *peplos*, which was not needed as a garment until the archaic statue (*xoanon*) of Athena Polias was dressed anew at the Plynteria festival, ten months later.[194] It is in any case hard to see the old rather than the new *peplos* taking the spotlight, so this looks to be the official rite of acceptance of the new *peplos* on behalf of Athena.[195] The most natural setting would seem to be in front of the temple.[196]

Most interpreters see the woman (E V 33) as the priestess of Athena Polias,[197] and the man wearing the long ungirt tunic of a priest as the archon basileus (E V 34).[198] The two young females at left (E V 31–32) are generally thought to be carrying cushioned stools,[199] though funeral shrouds, clothes, and trays and torches have been proposed too.[200] The most convincing view is still that these two young women are *diphrophoroi* (stool-bearers). For Osborne, the stools suggest that this is the place for the viewer to stop.[201] However, Simon thinks of *diphrophoroi* as minor characters, who would not have been important enough for the main scene of the whole frieze; thus the two figures must be *arrēphoroi* ('carriers of secret things', girls between the ages of seven and eleven dedicated for part of the year to serve Athena on the Acropolis).[202] Sourvinou-Inwood thinks that such young girls might have been depicted like this,[203] though to a modern eye they do look rather older than required.[204] For mine, Boardman decides the issue: they are *diphrophoroi* because they are dressed as adults, wearing *himatia* over a *chitōn*, they are too tall, and the *arrēphoroi* were known for carrying vessels in their rites, which were associated with neither the Panathenaia nor the Parthenon.[205] Parke believed the stools were for the gods, a thought which has induced others to contemplate the Theoxenia ritual, whereby gods were called upon and fêted.[206] But as the gods are already present and seated Boardman more plausibly thinks the stools were intended for the archon basileus and priestess.[207] Simon sees two chairs, one for Pandrosos, and one for Ge Kourotrophos.[208] This seems too obscure and there are no clinching attributes. One of the young females (E V 31) carries an object interpreted generally as a footstool in her left arm, the lion's paw of the left near leg just being visible.[209] Younger, thinking in terms of sexual pairings, sees this girl as a space-filler, a totally superfluous figure.[210] He is right that she is spatially a little apart from the other two pairs of figures in the scene (E V 32–33, E V 34–35), but not so much as to make her unconnected with them.[211] Boardman thinks the footstool she carries is for the priestess.[212] Connelly is sceptical that the priestess should get a footstool and the priest not. Her preference is for a pyxis, or jewellery-box, used in dressing rituals.[213] Simon argues for an incense box, whose contents would be burned in the *thymiatēria* shown elsewhere on the frieze.[214] While the examples illustrated by both scholars do good service to their arguments, Boardman is insistent. He illustrates in detail and draws the footstool, and seems right.[215]

Robertson saw the child on the right as a girl with Venus rings on her neck (E V 35),[216] and thus she had to be one of the *arrēphoroi*. Boardman, who argues that most of the women on the frieze show such rings, while very few of the males do, has since remained faithful to this line.[217] Others see a boy because similar rings appear, for example, on the tray-bearer in the south frieze (S XL 120).[218] Harrison believes the boy wears a draped *himation* with a triangular overfall in front; females never wear it without a *chitōn* underneath. This makes him the archetypal temple boy, like Ion in Euripides' play of that name.[219] Younger sees the 'Venus rings' as simple incisions, which are only apparent because of current display conditions, in which the light comes from above.[220] Hurwit sees a boy too, pointing to statues of boys with such rings. They are signs of well-fed plumpness not gender – and the garment is probably a *himation*, worn in this fashion (without an undergarment) exclusively by males.[221] Although a girl would not invalidate my argument, I am on balance inclined to see a boy, his nakedness not so different to that displayed by, for example, the boy helping the cavalryman dress at the start of the north frieze (N XLVII 136) (*Fig.* 10).[222] Both figures, it might be added, could be thought to be concerned with Neils' theme of dressing-up.[223] Connelly's thesis depends on having a girl here, one of the daughters of Erechtheus about to die, and she begins by pointing out that there is no literary evidence

Fig. 10. Scene from the west end of the north frieze of the Parthenon (N XLVII 133–136). © The British Museum.

for involvement by the archon basileus in the culminating ritual of the Panathenaia.[224] Yet our literary sources are marked by lack rather than detail. Then she argues that Athena would not have been served by a little boy; Greek cult practice would demand that she be served by girls and women; Euripides' Ion was serving Apollo.[225] This is compelling on the face of it, and would split the pairings of woman-with-girl (E V 32–33) and man-with-boy (E V 34–35) that Younger has recently invested with so much sexual and other significance.[226] I wonder, however, whether a boy could be thought to be helping the archon rather than Athena; there is so much of the fine detail about which we are unaware. In the context of a patriarchal society, moreover, it would not be surprising to see men, or at least the archon, taking so prominent a part here.[227] Finally, it has been argued that there were in fact two *peploi* at the Great Panathenaia, and that professional men made one of them – the huge one that acted like a sail for the ship-cart which may have featured in the procession from the period immediately following the battle of Salamis (480 BC). The *peplos* on the frieze is surely the smaller one meant for Athena Polias, made in the age-old, traditional way by women; a *peplos* of this kind was made annually, whereas the huge one was made only for the Great Pana-thenaia.[228] My point in calling the latter to attention is that it might also make the males-with-*peplos* idea more sustainable.

Of course, attempts at identification that are as precise as possible do not deny the symbolic or evocative power of this scene. The Panathenaia represented the first major festival at which the citizens could see the new archons together, soon after their assumption of office on the first day of Hekatombaion.[229] A number of scholars feel that the five figures might have stood in some minds as surrogates of the royal house, though this would mean that the (archon) basileus was conceived of as being accompanied by the basilinna rather than the priestess of Athena.[230] Some have wondered why we are shown the preparation for the dedication of the *peplos*, and not the dedication itself. Is the culminating act missing?[231] Do we have here a 'classical' moment, prefiguring and evoking the defining moment? Has the final act in fact been discovered, in traces of a sculptured scene over the cella doorway?[232] Osborne thinks that the statue of Athena Polias, which eventually found a home in the Erechtheion and was recipient of the *peplos*, is not here, but Athena herself is not missing – she can be glimpsed through the doors in the form of Pheidias' magnificent cult statue.[233] Simon's reminder is enough: the statue of Athena Polias was not draped until ten months later.[234] Neils asserts that it is the modern mindset which sees anticlimax in this handover scene. We do have the climax of the Panathenaia – 'the raison d'être of the procession as well as the high point of the festival'.[235]

The subject is fundamental for appreciating the style, setting and message of the frieze. The placing of contemporary mortals in such close proximity to the gods looks at first sight to be shameless self-aggrandizement. Yet the strident self-confidence is to some degree tempered. I have already referred to the monument's capacity for maintaining perpetual worship and perpetual benefits at the highest level. Athena is both praised and placated. Athenian power is both manifest and in need of support. Display and maintenance go together; this might be why the Parthenon was built before Athena Polias was given a new home in the Erechtheion. The mortal subject does much to explain the style: there is something fundamentally political in representing a *polis* of equals, a democracy where everyone is of the quality of aristocrats elsewhere, nourished in this belief by their myth of autochthony, an idealized group, both favouring Athena and favoured extraordinarily, a group moving to the plane of the gods, comprised of individuals towards whom one feels a passionate attachment. Subject and setting probably go together too. How immodest can you be on a monument that is displayed as the frieze is? It accompanies, maybe even induces, a procession, but it made no impression on Pausanias at least. Perhaps the mortal subject demanded the least conspicuous setting. At any rate, one's theory about the subject will have reverberations in these other areas, and vice versa. Self-assertiveness cannot be the entire story. For a start, there were more eye-catching ways to do it. Increasingly, the spectacle of the Panathenaic festival itself performed the function of communicating the greatness of Athens to its citizens and visitors.[236] There were also other ways to call the citizens to duty and destiny. Perikles' funeral oration shows that. I am not meaning to denigrate the power of the frieze to do these things, or to promote the image of a citizenry harmonious and superior. It is just that there are limits, which depend quite a lot on your idea of the subject of the frieze. It is not the evocative power of the frieze that is at issue, merely the base from which such evocations flow.

In contrast, then, to theories that see the Parthenon frieze commemorating the Panathenaic procession, or the idea of festival at Athens, or particular Panathenaic festivals or events from history or myth, this chapter favours the view that its subject is an idealized, contemporary celebration of the Great Panathenaia, whose depiction nonetheless permits the calling to mind of other festivals and ideas. In general and in detail this interpretation seems the most persuasive. Special mention ought to be made of how well the frieze alludes to the excitement of competition in several sporting events conducted over several days. Admittedly, given the present state of our knowledge, it is not possible to describe categorically what a celebration of the Great Panathenaia was like in the Periklean period. In one sense this is the point of the chapter. It does not seem right to proceed as though our literary and other sources, fragmentary and chronologically disparate as they are, provide a picture which can be used as a control against the frieze. In particular, differences between the frieze and the other sources do not justify the view that the frieze has problems or that it must not be representing a contemporary Panathenaia. Each class of evidence must be handled on its particular merits and the best that modern scholars can do is to exercise judgement. The frieze is limited physically and it employs representational conventions that are still far from perfectly understood. It transmits powerful subliminal messages and exploits fundamental attitudes and responses, especially among adult male citizens. It describes intimate, reciprocal and reinforcing links between sporting competition, religious ceremony, divine patronage and civic identity at Athens. Indeed, it takes for granted an articulation of power through these spheres that is not really comparable with modern conditions but is certainly suggestive. Modifications and omissions are part of the way all this was achieved, so that the Athenians could be praised and called upon, in Aristophanes' words, as 'men worthy of [their] land, and of [depiction on] the *peplos*'.[237]

Acknowledgments

This chapter was written during a period of research leave at Royal Holloway College, University of London, in the first half of 2000. I would like in particular to thank Professor Susanna Morton-Braund for her hospitality and encouragement. Unfortunately, it proved impossible to take into account Jenifer Neils' fine book, *The Parthenon Frieze* (Cambridge, 2001), which arrived when this chapter was in press. However, I recommend it warmly and welcome the many connections it makes between the frieze and the Panathenaia. Finally, thanks are due to Cambridge University Press for permission at a late stage to employ the line drawings of the frieze which accompany Neils' book (*Figs.* 4–7).

Notes

[1] Fundamental studies include: Robertson and Frantz 1975; Brommer 1977; Jenkins 1994; Berger and Gisler-Huwiler 1996. The numbering system of Jenkins is employed in this chapter.

[2] Boardman 1977, 39; Castriota 1992, 134–8.

[3] *IG* I³ 436, 449; Lewis 1992, 125.

[4] Schol. Ar. *Peace* 605.

[5] For the dates, see Ashmole 1972, 126; Pollitt 1972, 79. Jenkins 1994, 19 feels that the carving of the frieze could have gone on after 438. Korres 1994, 33 argues for a somewhat later date, believing that the frieze was added in response to changing ethical and political considerations.

[6] Lewis 1992, 125.

[7] Lewis 1992, 125, 139–40.

[8] Stewart 1997, 79.

[9] Note Osborne 1994, 143: 'I cannot prove that the sculptures of the Parthenon form a programme.'

[10] Jenkins 1995.

[11] Plans of the frieze: Ashmole 1972, 120; Boardman 1985, fig. 95; Boardman and Finn 1985, 238; Castriota 1992, 190, fig. 25; Jenkins 1994, 23, fig. 12b.

[12] Lawrence 1972, 139; Ashmole 1972, 118.

[13] Osborne 1987, 98–105.

[14] Korres 1988.

[15] Boardman 1999, 306–7. See Connelly 1996, 56, on art as *agalma*, 'pleasing gift for the gods'.

[16] Boardman 1999, 306.

[17] Ashmole 1972, 120; Pollitt 1972, figs. 29, 30; Jenkins 1994, 19. Blundell thinks that a spectator moving towards the east could have walked along either the north or the south side, though the northern route was 'the more likely, since this was on the shady side of the temple, and was followed by festival processions' (1998, 57, 69 n. 18).

[18] Ashmole 1972, 136 (the south may have been carved last as a result); Jenkins 1994, 22, cf. 18.

[19] Osborne 1987, 101 and n. 17; Connelly 1996, 70 n. 110.

[20] St Clair 1995, 5; Boardman 1984, 412 n. 38.

[21] For the date, see Kallisthenes *FGrHist* 124 F 52; Parke 1977, 33; Simon 1983, 55; Jenkins 1994, 24.

[22] Stuart and Revett 1787, vol. 2, 12.

[23] e.g. Ashmole 1972, 144–5; Pollitt 1972, 87–8; Robertson and Frantz 1975, 9; Boardman 1977, 42–3; Ridgway 1981, 77–8; Connelly 1996, 54; Blundell 1998, 59.

[24] Note the surprise of Brommer 1979, 40, that no spears are to be seen.

[25] This notation means north side, slab VI, figures 16–19, and south side, slab XXXIX, figures 115–118 (conjectured because missing). For discussion of the differences, mainly on the north and south sides, between the numbering system employed by Jenkins, and those pioneered by scholars like Michaelis 1871 and Smith 1910, see Jenkins 1994, 49–51; 1995. For drawings of the frieze following the figure but not slab numbers of Jenkins, see figures 4–7 above.

[26] Robertson and Frantz 1975, 8–12; Parke 1977, 37–50; Simon 1983, 55–72.

[27] Kardara 1961 (1964); Holloway 1966. Criticism of the theories of Kardara and Holloway in Boardman 1984, 210.

[28] Boardman 1977, 39–49; 1984, 210–15. For the Parthenon as a commemoration of the Persian Wars, see Plut. *Ant.* 34; Castriota 1992, 134–83. For criticism of Boardman's thesis, see Brommer 1977, 149 n. 15; Spence 1993, 268; Jenkins 1994, 26, 44; Harrison 1996, 200; Hurwit 1999, 224. For the Marathon dead portrayed as hoplites, see Harrison 1972, esp. 373–4; Bugh 1988, 77–8 n. 134. Pausanias 1.32.4 describes measures taken to heroize those who fell at Marathon.

[29] Simon 1983, 61, 68–9; Harrison 1984, 230–4; 1996, 198–214.

[30] Lawrence 1951; Root 1979; 1985; Castriota 1992, 184–229. One reply to Lawrence, Root and Castriota can be found in Shapiro 1996, 222.

[31] Younger 1997; Stewart 1997, 77–85.

[32] Osborne 1987, 98–105; 1994, 143–50. Veyne 1988 takes issue with Osborne's view that the subject is not really as important as the effect of the frieze.

[33] Connelly 1993, 309–10; 1996, 53–80. For the Euripidean fragments, see Austin 1968. Criticism of Connelly's thesis: Harrison 1996, 206; Spivey 1996, 146–7; Stewart 1997, 76; Hurwit 1999, 223–4.

[34] Jenkins 1994, 25 (intrinsic ambiguity); cf. 12 and 18 (a grandiose votive relief), 14 (a celebration of the city's current prestige), 21 (a procession), 25 (the epitome of both the Panathenaic procession and the Panathenaic festival), 32 (the idea of festival itself), 34 (the *peplos* is the main reason for seeing the Panathenaic procession), 39 (a general and universal idea of festival on the west, north and south sides, more specifically the Panathenaia on the east), 42 (an ideal procession, visual metaphor of the spirit of the Panathenaic festival). For criticism of Jenkins' equivocation, see Connelly 1996, 55 n. 16.

[35] Pollitt 1997, 51–65; Hurwit 1999, 227; Ridgway 1981, 78; Beschi 1984, 192; cf. Jenkins 1994, 32.

[36] Hurwit 1999, 228, 233. A gigantomachy was also woven into the *peplos*; see Eur. *Hec.* 466–74; Pl. *Euth.* 6b–c; Barber 1992, 103–17, esp. 112–17.

[37] Connelly 1996, 54, 76 n. 150; Neils 1992, 14; 1996, 182. The written sources are discussed most fully in Deubner 1932; Ziehen 1949; Parke 1977, 37–50; Simon 1983, 55–72. Neils 1992, 14, is good on the limitations of all types of relevant evidence, including inscriptions and pottery.

[38] Ashmole 1972, 145; Pollitt 1972, 88; Ridgway 1981, 77.

[39] On votive forerunners, see Kroll 1979; Simon 1983, 72; Jenkins 1994, 12, 18. Ridgway (1981, 79) and Boardman (1984, 210) are opposed to the idea.

[40] Castriota 1992, 215.

[41] Osborne 1994, 149.

[42] Payne and Mackworth Young 1950, 47.

[43] Brommer 1977, 152; Ridgway 1981, 77.

[44] Boardman 1978, 155, fig. 200.

[45] Castriota 1992, 306–7 n. 65.

[46] Ridgway 1981, 77, 79. Castriota 1992, 192, finds no precedent in temple sculpture for a religious event like that of the frieze.

[47] Neils 1996, 184, 194; cf. 1992, 26.

[48] Parker 1988, esp. 190.

[49] Paus. 1.15.1–3; Boedeker 1998, esp. 189 (on the Stoa Poikile), and 199 (on 'timeless' and 'historical' uses of the past, the former designed to suggest analogies). See Pl. *Menex.* 234c–235b, on public oratory for the war-dead.

[50] Cf. Hurwit 1999, 226: '…the frieze…is sculpture, not videotape'.

[51] See Parke 1977, 43; Ridgway 1981, 78 n. 11; Simon 1983, 58; Hurwit 1999, 226.

[52] Ridgway 1981, 83.

[53] Pollitt 1997, 63; Blundell 1998, 51; Boedeker 1998.

[54] Cf. Lewis 1992, 146. Note the number of writers who see varying degrees of apotheosis on the frieze: Pollitt 1972, 87; Boardman 1977, 46; Castriota 1992, 217; Neils 1992, 26; Hurwit 1999, 233.

[55] Cf. Boardman 1984, 211.

[56] See Parke 1977, 38, on omissions being unsurprising.

[57] Delivorrias 1994, 126 writes of 'deliberate polysemy'.

[58] Pollitt 1972, 81: 'The Greeks had a tendency to see the specific in…the generic.'

[59] Jenkins 1994, 32, cf. 34. Those who oppose this idea include Connelly 1996, 55 n. 16, Blundell 1998, 51 and Hurwit 1999, 227. Boardman 1984, 211 finds it 'hard to credit' that no specific festival is meant.

[60] Harrison 1996, 200. Boardman 1999, 329 and Spivey 2000, 255–6 express dissatisfaction with those who prefer open-ended, non-specific interpretations.

[61] Connelly 1996, 55 n. 16: 'the Parthenon's sculptural program presented images with unambiguous, primary meanings (Gigantomachy, Amazonomachy, Centauromachy, Birth of Athena, Contest of Poseidon and Athena), which could also be read on multiple, metaphorical levels (triumph of civilized order over barbaric chaos, birth of Athens and autochthonous nature of the Athenians,

victories of Athenians over exotic outsiders).'

[62] Noted by Ridgway 1981, 82.

[63] Osborne 1997, 519–20, cf. 523 (thus emasculating the beardless figures, signalling that they are not sexually active).

[64] Ridgway 1981, 83.

[65] Boardman 1977, 40; Boardman 1985, 107; Jenkins 1994, 30, 99; Pollitt 1997, 55; Boardman 1999, 328.

[66] There is still a tendency to call them mounted ephebes (e.g. Simon 1983, 59–60; Jenkins 1994, 33; Hurwit 1999, 233). Spence 1993, 269–70 demonstrates that they are not ephebes, who received no equestrian training in this period and whose very existence at this time is uncertain, but cavalrymen.

[67] Parke 1977, 43.

[68] Attic black-figure band cup, *c.* 550 BC, London, private collection: Simon 1983, 63, pls. 16.2, 17.2; Neils 1992, 54, fig. 33; 1996, 181–2, fig. 8.4; cf. 181.

[69] Castriota 1992, 202–26.

[70] Castriota 1992, 204; cf. Brommer 1977, 152; Vasic 1984.

[71] Cf. Castriota 1992, 218.

[72] Osborne 1994, 145, hinting at a relationship with the metopes and pediment.

[73] Brommer 1977, 151–3.

[74] Connelly 1996, 70 n.110 is both right and a little unfair in writing that 'though the cavalry dominates the frieze in terms of amount of space occupied, its location on the north, south, and west sides of the temple is secondary to the privileged position of the groups that occupy the east frieze'.

[75] Thuc. 2.13.8; [Arist.] *Ath. Pol.* 61.4–5; Bugh 1988, 39–52; Spence 1993, 9–10, 15–16; Worley 1994, 68–72.

[76] Bugh 1988, 77–8; Spence 1993, 191–202; Shapiro 1996, 219.

[77] Spence 1993, 211–12.

[78] Ar. *Frogs* 653; Xen. *Hipparchikos* 3.11. On prancing, see [Xen.] *Peri Hippikēs* 11.1, 8. For a good discussion of popular attitudes to horsemen in relation to other branches of the military in this period, see Pritchard 2000, 95–6, 110–15, 199–200, esp. 114–15.

[79] Boardman 1977, 40; Harrison 1984, 233; Boardman 1985, 107; Spence 1993, 267–71; Jenkins 1994, 55–63; Pollitt 1997, 55; Boardman 1999, 328.

[80] Worley 1994, 70, 195 n.61. Neither Bugh 1988 nor Spence 1993 believes in an intermediate phase of development between the old 300- and the new 1000-man force. Bugh 1988, 76 thinks the number was raised 'sometime between 445 and 431'. Spence 1993, 10 says 'some time between *c.* 445 and 438' (noting the division into ten sub-units on the Parthenon frieze).

[81] Spence 1993, 199–201, 268. For an argument that cavalrymen were predominantly in their 20s or 30s, see Bugh 1988, 64.

[82] Noted by Ridgway 1981, 79.

[83] Neils 1996, 189–94.

[84] Stewart 1997, 76. Note Osborne's arguments against nakedness alone being

taken as a pointer to heroization or idealization (1997, esp. 505).

[85] Kyle 1992, 91 refers to the nudity of the boy jockeys.

[86] See Kyle 1992, 89–94, for equestrian events at the Panathenaia. On p. 94, he notes that the javelin throw from horseback does not appear on Panathenaic prize amphorae until the very end of the fifth century.

[87] Pollitt 1997, 52–3. Spence (1993, xxxii–xxxiii, 77, 184, 187–8, 267–71) believes that they did participate in the Panathenaic procession.

[88] Xen. *Hipparchikos* 1.21–3; 3.1–2; cf. Dem. 4.26.

[89] Pollitt 1997, 55; cf. Neils 1992, 27.

[90] For the 'establishment loan' (*katastasis*) and 'grain allowance' (*sitos*), see Xen. *Hipparchikos* 1.2–3, 19; Bugh 1988, 56–7, 60; Spence 1993, 16; Worley 1994, 71.

[91] On cavalry dress, see Spence 1993, xxix–xxxiii, 60, 118.

[92] Yet I am sceptical of Harrison's attempt (1984, 232–3) to assign particular 'uniforms' on the south side to particular tribes via association with the figures on the frieze identified as the Eponymous Heroes. These figures have little in the way of attributes.

[93] *IG* II² 956.1.58–60; 957.1.36–41; 958.1.56–9; 960, ll. 22–4; 961, ll. 22–4; Bugh 1988, 92 n. 38.

[94] Boardman 1985, 107.

[95] Boardman 1985, 107, though Connelly 1996, 71 wonders whether the items of Thracian costume might have called to mind booty taken from Eumolpos' army by the heroic cavalry of Erechtheus' day.

[96] Osborne 1987, 103.

[97] Ridgway 1981, 82 n. 16.

[98] Xen. *Hipparchikos* 3.3, 5, 13; Pollitt 1997, 64 n. 19.

[99] Bugh 1988, 59–60; Kyle 1992, 94; cf. Neils 1994, 152 (end of the fifth century). Pollitt 1997, 57 accepts this as one of the performances at the Panathenaia.

[100] Harrison 1984, 234; 1996, 209.

[101] Ashmole 1972, 122–5.

[102] For the two bearded figures on the west, see Brommer 1977, pls. 13–14, 23–6. Simon 1983, 59 thinks one of them is the polemarch. The suggestion that they are hipparchs appears to go back to Robertson and Frantz 1975, 48 (an unnumbered page); cf. Spence 1993, 268–9; Pollitt 1997, 57.

[103] Spence 1993, 269; Stewart 1997, 76; cf. Jenkins 1994, 107, pl. II.

[104] For the processional route, see Neils 1992, 18, 19, fig. 3; cf. Lefkowitz 1996, 81.

[105] Cf. Pollitt 1972, 87. Brommer 1977, 149, 287 puts the cavalcade in the Attic plain. Boardman 1984, 212, puts the action of the entire frieze in the Agora.

[106] Pollitt 1997, 57.

[107] Ashmole 1972, 122.

[108] Beschi 1984 finds twelve on the north. For eleven and ten, see Harrison 1984, 230, 233; Gisler-Huwiler 1988, 15–18; Jenkins 1994, 30, 88–95 (north); 64–8, esp. 65 (south); Jenkins 1995, 446 n. 4; Berger and Gisler-Huwiler 1996, 51–66,

104–10; Boardman 1999, 328 n. 49.

[109] On the long saffron robe, see Brommer 1979, 40.

[110] Harrison 1984, 233. As with the cavalry, Boardman 1977, 40 sees more imagination in the less regular composition of the chariots on the north.

[111] Castriota 1992, 204.

[112] Connelly 1996, 69–70.

[113] Plutarch's *Life of Phocion* 20, and three Hellenistic inscriptions from the second century BC: *IG* II/III² 2314, ll. 36, 67–70; 2316, ll. 17–20, 40; 2317, l. 48 (where *apobatēs* is plausibly restored); cf. Pollitt 1997, 58 n. 22.

[114] Simon 1983, 62; Neils 1992, 15. Kyle 1992, 205 n. 69 shows that the matter is not beyond doubt.

[115] Boardman 1977, 45; 1984, 212, fig. 1; Neils 1992, 18, 20.

[116] Note Simon 1983, 61: '[The charioteers did not climb the Acropolis, but] they are included in the frieze to symbolize other parts of the procession and of the festival.'

[117] These features are strongly apparent in the two *apobatai* victory monuments which were included in the Sydney Olympics 2000 exhibition that is discussed in the last three chapters of this book. See Measham et al. 2000, cat. nos. 45, 46.

[118] Stewart 1997, 82.

[119] Rotroff 1977, 381.

[120] e.g. Ashmole 1972, 135; Boardman 1977, 40; Brommer 1979, 40; Neils 1994, 154. Parke 1977, 44 expresses doubts.

[121] Brommer 1977, 32–3, 217.

[122] Boardman 1999, 321–30, esp. 323, 329.

[123] Simon 1983, 62; Boardman 1984, 212; Jenkins 1994, 69; Pollitt 1997, 59.

[124] Boardman 1984, 212–13; 1999, 322.

[125] On which, see Shapiro 1992.

[126] Simon 1983, 63.

[127] Parke 1977, 35–6.

[128] Plut. *Per.* 13.11. Nagy 1992, 65–6, thinks that Perikles might even have re-instituted musical contests after an absence of a generation or so.

[129] Robertson and Frantz 1975, 15.

[130] See Brommer 1977, 220, pl. 113.

[131] Simon 1983, 62–3.

[132] Boardman 1984, 213, 412 n. 21.

[133] Himmelmann 1988; Jenkins 1994, 69–70. On p. 69, Jenkins observes that S XXXVII 107 holds what might be a plectrum in his right hand. Note also Jenkins 1995, 456.

[134] Jenkins 1994, 70–1.

[135] Parke 1977, 44; Jenkins 1994, 71.

[136] Cf. Jenkins 1995, 456.

[137] Brommer 1977, 30; Simon 1983, 65; Boardman 1984, 213; Jenkins 1994, 71.

[138] Demetrios of Phaleron 228 *FGrHist* F 5; Pollux III.55, s.v. *skiadophoros*; scholion Ar. *Birds* 1551; Ael. 6.1; cf. Boardman 1977, 40; Parke 1977, 44; Jenkins

1994, 70–1, 85–7.

[139] Connelly 1996, 69; cf. 54.

[140] Simon 1983, 64 (on N VI 19); cf. Castriota 1992, 305 n. 54.

[141] Pollitt 1997, 61.

[142] Hurwit 1999, 227.

[143] Younger 1997, 134–6, 150 n. 72.

[144] Boardman 1977, 45.

[145] Stewart 1997, 79.

[146] Brommer 1979, 42.

[147] Lefkowitz 1996, 80; Neils 1996, 183–4.

[148] London, British Museum E 159; *ARV*^{2} 24, 9.

[149] Paris, Louvre C 10793; *ARV*^{2} 555, 92; Neils 1996, 184, fig. 8.5.

[150] Simon 1983, 65; cf. Harrison 1984, 233. For ten heifers on the south, see Jenkins 1994, S XLI–XLVII; 1995, 456.

[151] Simon 1983, 61.

[152] Harrison 1984, 233–4.

[153] Jenkins 1994, 11, 29; Hurwit 1999, 225. Blundell (1998, 49, 68 n. 7) inclines to this view but with slight uncertainty.

[154] Boardman 1984, 210. On the *koinobōmia* shared by Pandrosos and Athena, see Simon 1983, 61; Connelly 1996, 76 n. 146.

[155] Parke 1977, 45.

[156] Jenkins 1994, 38.

[157] Philochoros *FGrHist* 328 F 10; Simon 1983, 61; Jenkins 1994, 29.

[158] Uppsala University 352; Neils 1996, 182, 195 n. 13.

[159] Ashmole 1972, 142; Connelly 1996, 80; Lefkowitz 1996, 79, 88. For the role of women of the Praxiergidai clan in bearing the *peplos* to the Acropolis, and later dressing the statue of Athena Polias, see Neils 1992, 17; Barber 1992, 113; Neils 1996, 185 – all refer to Mansfield 1985, 371–9 which I have not seen.

[160] Blundell 1998, 47–9, 53, 62–3.

[161] Blundell 1998, 63–4.

[162] Boardman 1977, 40.

[163] Jenkins 1994. 77.

[164] Boardman 1977, 40; 1984, 213; cf. Osborne 1994, 148–9 (loom stands).

[165] Boardman 1977, 41. Parke (1977, 43) can find no trace of the *kanēphoroi*, who carried on their heads baskets containing the barley that would be sprinkled over the victims' heads prior to the sacrifice.

[166] Boardman 1984, 213.

[167] Boardman 1984, 213.

[168] Simon 1983, 60.

[169] Harrison 1996, 210.

[170] Jenkins 1994, 81.

[171] Boardman 1977, 41, 46; 1984, 213; cf. Jenkins 1985, 125; Jenkins 1994, 81; Harrison 1996, 201–2.

[172] Mattusch 1994. Those who see the eponymous heroes include Robertson and Frantz (1975, pl. IV east), Boardman (1977, 41, 46; 1984, 213), Brommer (1977,

255–6, pls. 14, 19; 1979, 44), Osborne (1994, 149) and Harrison (1996, 200).

[173] *Agōnothetai* (games organizers) of the Great Panathenaia: Parke 1977, 42. Nine archons plus a marshal: Jenkins 1985, 121–7. Officials: Castriota 1992, 218. Spectators: DeVries 1992. *Athlothetai*: Nagy 1992. *Athlothetai* or *epōnymoi*: Jenkins 1994, 23, 77; Hurwit 1999, 227. Nagy 1992, 63, while emphasizing the role of the *athlothetai*, nevertheless admits that control of the Panathenaia was shared with other officials.

[174] Harrison 1979; Kron 1984. Boardman 1984, 213 n. 29 is against such attempts.

[175] Jones 1995, 506–11. I am grateful to David Pritchard for this reference.

[176] Ridgway 1981, 79 and n. 12.

[177] Harrison (1984, 234, with 1996, 202) thinks that the staves of the 'heroes' suggest their fatherhood. Connelly 1996, 68 favours generic elders, the male citizenry of Athens.

[178] Jenkins 1985, 124.

[179] Boardman 1972, 61–2; cf. Castriota 1992, 217.

[180] For the vases, see Shapiro 1989, 135–9.

[181] Numerous scholars (e.g. Osborne 1994, 149, and Connelly 1996, 67) have noted that the Olympians turn their backs on the *peplos* scene; their primary interest is in the procession by the people of Athens.

[182] Boardman 1977, 46.

[183] Pickard-Cambridge 1968, 62.

[184] Simon 1983, 71.

[185] Eur. *Hec.* 466–74; Pl. *Euth.* 6b–c; Simon 1983, 71; Barber 1992, esp. 112–17.

[186] Neils 1996, 189, 193; Hurwit 1999, 227. Blundell 1998, 67, noting that Hephaistos, a frustrated suitor, turns towards her, sees it lying 'defensively over her genitals'.

[187] Even Pollitt 1997, 61 is not against it. Nor is Hurwit 1999, 227.

[188] Stewart 1997, 76 and Hurwit 1999, 223–4 between them martial a long list of objections.

[189] Connelly 1996, 67.

[190] Harrison 1996, 206.

[191] Jenkins 1994, 29.

[192] Boardman 1977, 41; cf. Neils 1992, 26; Barber 1992, 209 n. 17.

[193] Old: Robertson and Frantz 1975, 11–12 (folded for storage). New: Parke 1977, 41; Barber 1992, 209 n. 17; Harrison 1996, 202.

[194] Simon 1983, 66.

[195] Cf. Harrison 1996, 203.

[196] Brommer 1979, 44 thinks we are meant to understand the group as being inside the temple.

[197] Ashmole 1972, 143; Parke 1977, 40; Boardman 1977, 41; Simon 1983, 66; Neils 1992, 26; Jenkins 1994, 79; Boardman 1999, 313–14; Hurwit 1999, 225 (or the basilinna, wife of the archon basileus).

[198] Ashmole 1972, 143; Boardman 1977, 41; 1984, 213; Simon 1983, 66;

Neils 1992, 26; Jenkins 1994, 79; Harrison 1996, 201; Boardman 1999, 313–14; Hurwit 1999, 225. Nagy 1992, 66–9 argues for Perikles, serving as one of the *athlothetai*.

[199] Ashmole 1972, 143; Boardman 1977, 41; Parke 1977, 40; Brommer 1979, 46; Boardman 1984, 213; Neils 1992, 26; Jenkins 1994, 35, 79; Harrison 1996, 205; Younger 1997, 121; Boardman 1999, 308–13.

[200] See Boardman 1999, 307 n. 5, for references. Hurwit 1999, 227 wonders whether they are the secret things of the *arrēphoroi*.

[201] Osborne 1987, 101.

[202] Simon 1983, 67; cf. Jenkins 1994, 35; Harrison 1996, 205.

[203] Sourvinou-Inwood 1988, 58–9.

[204] Cf. Hurwit 1999, 225.

[205] Boardman 1999, 313, 320.

[206] Parke 1977, 41. Ashmole 1972, 143 discounts the Theoxenia idea.

[207] Boardman 1977, 41; 1984, 214; 1999, 313.

[208] Simon 1983, 67–9.

[209] The interpretation goes back to Thompson 1956, 290; cf. Boardman 1977, 41; Jenkins 1994, 79; Boardman 1999, 307–9.

[210] Younger 1997, 137–8 (she is asexual, a space-filler).

[211] For the 'off-centre' arrangement of this scene, which might have something to do with a slight miscalculation brought on by the huge size of the central block, nearly fifteen feet long, see Ashmole 1972, 140, 143.

[212] Boardman 1984, 213.

[213] Connelly 1996, 58 n. 33, 64–5. See Neils 1996, 189–93, for the theme of dressing-up permeating the Panathenaia.

[214] Simon 1982, 141; Simon 1983, 67.

[215] Boardman 1999, 308–9.

[216] Robertson and Frantz 1975, on E 35.

[217] Boardman 1977, 41; 1984, 214; 1999, 314–21; cf. Neils 1992, 26. Stuart and Revett (1787, vol. 2, 2) saw a girl. Boardman 1991 replied strongly to Clairmont 1989 (arguing for a boy).

[218] Ashmole 1972, 143; Brommer 1977, pl. 152.2, 266–7; Simon 1983, 66 n. 50. Boardman 1999, 316–17 says that all such male figures have only a single line and none are in relaxed profile posture like all the women.

[219] Harrison 1996, 203; cf. Brommer 1979, 46; Jenkins 1994, 79. Boardman 1999, 318–19 answers Harrison.

[220] Younger 1997, 122–4.

[221] Hurwit 1999, 224.

[222] Younger 1997, 124–5 advances strong arguments for both figures being based on the same preliminary sketch of a boy (cf. W XII 24 and W III 6).

[223] Neils 1996, 189–93.

[224] Connelly 1996, 58.

[225] Connelly 1996, 59–60 and esp. n. 46; cf. Boardman 1984, 214.

[226] Younger 1997, 129–38.

[227] See also Goldhill 1994, esp. 354–7, for a discussion of the frieze as

a representation of Athens' democracy, introducing civic as well as religious concerns into the subject matter and affecting the ways that men and women might be related on it.

[228] More detailed argument in Neils 1992, 22; Barber 1992, 113, citing Mansfield 1985, 68–78, 295, 366–404.

[229] Jenkins 1985, 125; 1994, 38.

[230] Simon 1983, 67; Jenkins 1994, 36, 38; Hurwit 1999, 225.

[231] Boardman 1977, 42.

[232] Korres 1984, 52, fig. 5.

[233] Osborne 1987, 101. In fairness, one should note the view of Lewis 1992, 125 that changes to traditional rituals were probably made to incorporate the new statue in the Parthenon.

[234] Simon 1983, 66.

[235] Neils 1992, 26.

[236] Kyle 1992, 80.

[237] Ar. *Knights* 565–6. The translation is that of Nagy 1992, 68.

Bibliography

Ashmole, B.
  1972   *Architect and Sculptor in Classical Greece,* London.
Austin, C.
  1968   *Nova Fragmenta Euripidea in Papyris Reperta,* Berlin.
Barber, E.J.W.
  1992   'The *Peplos* of Athena', in Neils (ed.) *Goddess and Polis,* 103–17.
Berger, E. and Gisler-Huwiler, M.
  1996   *Der Parthenon in Basel: Dokumentation zum Fries,* Mainz.
Beschi, L.
  1984   'Il fregio del Partenone: una proposta di lettura', *Atti della Accademia Nazionale dei Lincei,* 173–95.
Blundell, S.
  1998   'Marriage and the maiden: narratives on the Parthenon', in S. Blundell and M. Williamson (eds.) *The Sacred and the Feminine in Ancient Greece,* London, 47–70.
Boardman, J.
  1972   'Herakles, Peisistratos, and Sons', *RA,* 60–4.
  1977   'The Parthenon Frieze – another view', in U. Höckmann and A. Krug (eds.) *Festschrift für Frank Brommer,* Mainz, 39–49.
  1978   *Greek Sculpture: The archaic period,* London.
  1984   'The Parthenon Frieze', in E. Berger (ed.) *Parthenon-Kongress Basel, Referate und Bericht 4. bis 8. April 1982,* Mainz, 210–15.
  1985   *Greek Sculpture: The classical period,* London.
  1991   'The naked truth', *OJA* 10, 119–21.
  1999   'The Parthenon Frieze, a closer look', *RA* 2, 305–30.

Boardman, J. and Finn, D.
1985   *The Parthenon and its Sculptures,* London.
Boedeker, D.
1998   'Presenting the past in fifth-century Athens', in D. Boedeker and K. Raaflaub (eds.) *Democracy, Empire and the Arts in Fifth-Century Athens,* Cambridge, Mass., 185–202, 387–92.
Brommer, F.
1977   *Der Parthenonfries,* Mainz.
1979   *The Sculptures of the Parthenon,* London.
Bugh, G.R.
1988   *The Horsemen of Athens,* Princeton.
Castriota, D.
1992   *Myth, Ethos, and Actuality: Official art in the fifth century* BC, Madison.
Clairmont, C.W.
1989   'Girl or boy? The Parthenon's East Frieze figure 35', *AA* 495–6.
Connelly, J.B.
1993   'The Parthenon Frieze and the sacrifice of the Erechtheids: reinterpreting the *Peplos* scene', *AJA* 97, 309–10 (abstract).
1996   'Parthenon and *Parthenoi*: a mythological interpretation of the Parthenon Frieze', *AJA* 100, 53–80.
Delivorrias, A.
1994   'The sculptures of the Parthenon: form and content', in P. Tournikiotis (ed.) *The Parthenon and its Impact in Modern Times,* Athens, 98–135.
Deubner, L.
1932   *Attische Feste,* Berlin.
DeVries, K.
1992   'The "Eponymous Heroes" on the Parthenon Frieze', *AJA* 96, 336.
Gisler-Huwiler, M.
1988   'À propos des apobates et de quelques cavaliers de la frieze nord du Parthénon', in M. Schmidt (ed.) *Kanon, Festschrift Ernst Berger,* Basel, 15–18.
Goldhill, S.
1994   'Representing Democracy: women at the Great Dionysia', in R. Osborne and S. Hornblower (eds.) *Ritual, Finance, Politics: Athenian democratic accounts presented to David Lewis,* Oxford, 347–69.
Harrison, E.B.
1972   'The south frieze of the Nike temple and the Marathon painting in the painted stoa', *AJA* 76, 353–78.
1979   'The iconography of the Eponymous Heroes on the Parthenon and in the Agora', in *Greek Numismatics and Archaeology: Essays in honour of Margaret Thompson,* Wetteren, 71–85.
1984   'Time in the Parthenon Frieze', in E. Berger (ed.) *Parthenon-Kongress Basel, Referate und Bericht 4. bis 8. April 1982,* Mainz, 230–4.
1996   'The web of history: a conservative reading of the Parthenon Frieze', in Neils (ed.) *Worshipping Athena,* Madison, 198–214.

Himmelmann, N.
1988   'Planung und Verdingung der Parthenon-Skulpturen', *Bathron: Beiträge zur Architektur und verwandten Künsten für Heinrich Drerup,* Saarbrücken, 213–24.

Holloway, R.
1966   'The archaic acropolis and the Parthenon Frieze', *Art Bulletin* 48, 223–7.

Hurwit, J.M.
1999   *The Athenian Acropolis: History, mythology, and archaeology from the neolithic era to the present,* Cambridge.

Jenkins, I.D.
1985   'The composition of the so-called Eponymous Heroes in the east frieze of the Parthenon', *AJA* 89, 121–7.
1994   *The Parthenon Frieze,* London.
1995   'The south frieze of the Parthenon: problems in arrangement', *AJA* 99, 445–56.

Jones, N.F.
1995   'The Athenian phylai as associations: disposition, function, and purpose', *Hesperia* 64, 503–42.

Kardara, C.
1961(1964)   'Glaukopis, the archaic *naos* and the theme of the Parthenon Frieze (in Greek)', *AEph,* 61–158.

Korres, M.
1984   'Der Pronaos und die Fenster des Parthenon', in E. Berger (ed.) *Parthenon-Kongress Basel, Referate und Bericht 4. bis 8. April 1982,* Mainz, 47–54.
1988   'Überzählige Werkstücke des Parthenonfrieses', in M. Schmidt (ed.) *Kanon, Festschrift Ernst Berger,* Basel, 19–27.
1994   'The sculptural adornment of the Parthenon', in R. Economakis (ed.) *Acropolis Restoration: The CCAM interventions,* London, 29–33.

Kroll, J.H.
1979   'The Parthenon Frieze as a votive relief', *AJA* 83, 348–52.

Kron, U.
1984   'Die Phylenheroen am Parthenonfries', in E. Berger (ed.) *Parthenon-Kongress Basel, Referate und Bericht 4. bis 8. April 1982,* Mainz, 235–44.

Kyle, D.G.
1992   'The Panathenaic games: sacred and civic athletics', in Neils (ed.) *Goddess and Polis,* 77–101.

Lagerlöf, M.R.
2000   *The Sculptures of the Parthenon: Aesthetics and interpretation,* Yale.

Lawrence, A.W.
1951   'The Acropolis and Persepolis', *JHS* 71, 111–19.
1972   *Greek and Roman Sculpture,* London.

Lefkowitz, M.R.
1996   'Women in the Panathenaic and other festivals', in Neils (ed.) *Worshipping Athena,* Madison, 78–91.

Lewis, D.M.
> 1992 'The Thirty Years' Peace', in *Cambridge Ancient History: Vol. 5: The Fifth Century BC*, 2nd edn, Cambridge, 121–46.

Mansfield, J.
> 1985 'The robe of Athena and the Panathenaic "peplos"', Ph.D. dissertation, Berkeley.

Mattusch, C.C.
> 1994 'The Eponymous Heroes: the idea of sculptural groups', in W.D.E. Coulson, O. Palagia, T.L. Shear, H.A. Shapiro, F.J. Frost (eds.) *The Archaeology of Athens and Attica under the Democracy*, Oxford, 73–81.

Measham, T., Spathari, E., Donnelly, P.
> 2000 *1000 Years of the Olympic Games: Treasures of ancient Greece*, exhibition catalogue, Sydney.

Michaelis, A.
> 1871 *Der Parthenon*, Leipzig.

Nagy, B.
> 1992 'Athenian officials on the Parthenon Frieze', *AJA* 96, 67–9.

Neils, J.
> 1992 'The Panathenaia: an introduction', in Neils (ed.) *Goddess and Polis*, 13–27.
> 1994 'The Panathenaia and Kleisthenic ideology', in W.D.E. Coulson, O. Palagia, T.L. Shear, H.A. Shapiro, F.J. Frost (eds.) *The Archaeology of Athens and Attica under the Democracy*, Oxford, 151–60.
> 1996 'Pride, pomp, and circumstance: the iconography of procession', in Neils (ed.) *Worshipping Athena*, 177–97.

Neils, J. (ed.)
> 1992 *Goddess and Polis: The Panathenaic Festival in ancient Athens*, Princeton.
> 1996 *Worshipping Athena: Panathenaia and Parthenon*, Madison.

Osborne, R.
> 1987 'The viewing and obscuring of the Parthenon Frieze', *JHS* 107, 98–105.
> 1994 'Democracy and imperialism in the Panathenaic Procession: the Parthenon Frieze in its context', in W.D.E. Coulson, O. Palagia, T.L. Shear, H.A. Shapiro, F.J. Frost (eds.) *The Archaeology of Athens and Attica under the Democracy*, Oxford, 143–50.
> 1997 'Men without clothes: heroic nakedness and Greek art', *Gender and History* 9.3, 504–28.

Parke, H.W.
> 1977 *Festivals of the Athenians*, London.

Payne, H. and Mackworth Young, G.
> 1950 *Archaic Marble Sculpture from the Acropolis*, 2nd edn, London.

Pickard-Cambridge, A.W.
> 1968 *The Dramatic Festivals of Athens*, 2nd edn, Oxford.

Pollitt, J.J.
> 1972 *Art and Experience in Classical Greece*, Cambridge.

1997 'The meaning of the Parthenon Frieze', in D. Buitron-Oliver (ed.) *The Interpretation of Architectural Sculpture in Greece and Rome,* Hanover and London, 51–65.

Pritchard, D.M.

2000 'The fractured imaginary: popular thinking on citizen soldiers and warfare in fifth century Athens', Ph.D. dissertation, Macquarie University.

Ridgway, B.

1981 *Fifth-Century Styles in Greek Sculpture,* Princeton.

Robertson, M. and Frantz, A.

1975 *The Parthenon Frieze,* London.

Root, M.C.

1979 *The King and Kingship in Achaemenid Art: Essays on the creation of an iconography of empire,* Leiden.

1985 'The Parthenon Frieze and the Apadana reliefs at Persepolis: reassessing a programmatic relationship', *AJA* 89, 103–20.

Rotroff, S.I.

1977 'The Parthenon Frieze and the sacrifice to Athena', *AJA* 81, 379–82.

St Clair, W.

1995 'Apocalypse Acropolis', *Times Literary Supplement,* 14 April, 4–5.

Shapiro, H.A.

1989 *Art and Cult under the Tyrants,* Mainz.

1992 'Mousikoi Agones: music and poetry at the Panathenaia', in Neils (ed.) *Goddess and Polis,* 53–75.

1996 'Democracy and imperialism: the Panathenaia in the age of Perikles', in Neils (ed.) *Worshipping Athena,* 215–25.

Simon, E.

1982 'Die Mittelszene im Ostfries des Parthenon', *MDAI(A)* 97, 127–44.

1983 *Festivals of Attica,* Madison.

Smith, A.H.

1910 *The Sculptures of the Parthenon,* London.

Sourvinou-Inwood, C.

1988 *Studies in Girls' Transitions,* Athens.

Spence, I.G.

1993 *The Cavalry of Classical Greece: A social and military history with particular reference to Athens,* Oxford.

Spivey, N.

1996 *Understanding Greek Sculpture: Ancient meanings, modern readings,* London.

2000 Review of Lagerlöf 2000, *G&R* 47, 253–4.

Stewart, A.

1997 *Art, Desire and the Body in Ancient Greece,* Cambridge.

Stuart, J. and Revett, N.

1787 *The Antiquities of Athens,* 2 vols., London.

Thompson, D.B.

1956 'The Persian spoils in Athens', in S. Weinberg (ed.) *The Aegean and the Near East: Studies presented to Hetty Goldman,* New York, 281–91.

Vasic, R.

1984   'The Parthenon Frieze and the Siphnian Frieze', in E. Berger (ed.) *Parthenon-Kongress Basel, Referate und Bericht 4. bis 8. April 1982,* Mainz, 307–11.

Veyne, P.

1988   'Conduct without belief and works of art without viewers', *Diogenes* 143, 1–22.

Worley, L.

1994   *Hippeis: The cavalry of ancient Greece,* Boulder, San Francisco and Oxford.

Younger, J.

1997   'Gender and sexuality in the Parthenon Frieze', in A.O. Koloski-Ostrow and C.L. Lyons (eds.) *Naked Truths: Women, sexuality and gender in classical art and archaeology,* London and New York, 120–53.

Ziehen, L.

1949   'Panathenaia', in *RE* 18.3, 457–89.

10

THE CURIOUS MATTER OF THE
LENAIA FESTIVAL OF 422 BC

Ian C. Storey

In a book commemorating a modern Olympic Games one may be forgiven for associating ancient games and competitions immediately with athletic events, but contests in the arts were as important in the ancient world as the competitions at the Academy Awards or the Cannes Film Festival are today. At the Pythian Games, musical competitions held pride of place; the athletic contests were in fact a later addition to that celebration. The Panathenaic Games were distinguished by contests for rhapsodes, and although Plutarch (*Perikles* 13.5–6) asserts that Perikles introduced these contests in the 430s, Shapiro (1992, 57) makes a compelling case that what Perikles did was re-organize the existing contests, which in his view go back well into the sixth century. Thus when drama became part of the public festivals at Athens in the late sixth and early fifth centuries, a competitive aspect was entirely natural.[1]

The ancients seem to have researched the records of the Athenian dramatic festivals as thoroughly as modern trivia adepts, who know who won what Oscar in what year. Aristotle wrote his lost *Didaskalia* ('Production Lists'), which must have supplied him with much of the raw material for *Poetics* and the Alexandrian scholars with the information for their hypotheses. We even have inscriptional evidence from the Roman period, listing the plays of individual comedians in terms of the place in which they finished (*IG* XIV 1097 [Kallias], 1098 [Anaxandrides]). Certain specific competitions also appear to have been memorable occasions; the tragic competition at the Dionysia of 468 BC, for example, where the young Sophokles on his first appearance defeated the veteran Aeschylus (Plut. *Kimon* 8.7–8); Euripides winning one of his rare victories at the Dionysia of 428 with (among other plays) an unparalleled revision of his earlier *Hippolytos*; and the comic competition at the Dionysia of 423 where Kratinos, responding to a jibe at his creative senility by Aristophanes (*Knights* 526–36), made himself the chief character of his own comedy

(*Pytine*), which finished first ahead of Aristophanes' *Clouds* (third place). Aristophanes would complain loudly about the indignity of this last result in his later comedies (*Clouds* 518–65; *Wasps* 54–66, 1043–7). Indeed such intense intertextuality, which is a standard feature of old comedy, is extremely useful to students of theatre, as it gives us information about non-extant plays, both comic and tragic, that would otherwise be lost to us. These combative intertextual exchanges, one of which will be the subject of this chapter, between Aristophanes and the other comedians also show how important victory was in the dramatic festivals.[2]

My starting-point is a vase in the Nicholson Museum in Sydney, an Apulian bell-krater by the Lecce Painter, from the first half of the fourth century (*Fig.* 1).[3] The obverse displays two characters in the familiar manner of comedy, both stage naked with grotesque masks, padded tights, and dangling phallos; both also wear head-gear, the character on the left a leafy wreath, that on the right a white head-band. The figure on the left is furtively moving (slinking?) away, holding a round white object in

Fig. 1. An Apulian bell-krater by the Lecce Painter (Nicolson Museum 88.02).

282

each hand and looking back over his shoulder at the second figure, who is advancing angrily and holds a club in one hand with an animal-skin draped over the other arm. At first sight the figure on the right would seem to be Herakles, chasing the man who has stolen two round-cakes (πλακοῦντες); these were presumably to have provided Herakles with a meal.[4] But Richard Green of Sydney points out in a personal communication that 'Herakles' is not wearing the Type J mask usual for him and regards the figure on the right as a 'pretend Herakles'. One thinks immediately of Dionysos as Herakles and the marvellous Herakleioxanthias in *Frogs*. For my reading of this vase it makes no real difference if the figure on the right is Herakles or a 'pretend Herakles'; in fact a 'pretend Herakles' would suggest more strongly that the source is comedy.

It used to be thought that these vases from South Italy were illustrating scenes from the local Italian comedy known as *phlyakes* (Ath. 611e), a genre attributed to Rhinthon of Syracuse (*AP* 7.414), a mixture of tragedy and comedy, also known as ἱλαροτραγῳδία. These *phlyakes* were usually seen as 'an old-fashioned folk-theatre appropriate to colonists distinct from the cultural mainstream'.[5] But the researches of Csapo (1986), Taplin (1987, 1993) and Green (1991) have established that the scenes on many of these vases reflect not local Italian comedy, but Athenian old comedy, which, contrary to the *opinio communis*, did travel and was exported to the Greek west. As early as Aeschylus, whose career spanned the years 498–456, Athenian culture was travelling to the west, and it appears that not only were Athenian potters and their red-figure vase techniques flourishing in the Greek west, but also Athenian plays which were being re-staged and formed the subject-matter for local artists and connoisseurs. Taplin anchored his study on the 'Würtzburg Telephos', which he argued cogently was a depiction of Aristophanes' *Thesmophoriazousai* (411 BC), and since then a strong case has been made for seeing other South Italian vases as renderings of originals of old comedy: the 'Phrynis/Pyronides vase' from Salerno (Eupolis' *Demoi*), the mysterious '*Choregoi*-vase', the two vases that depict the 'Goose play', and the 'Cheiron-vase'.[6] In fact Richard Green also suggests: 'I think there can be no doubt these days that the majority of 'phlyax' vases are based on local performances of Athenian comedy.'

Trendall sees the scene on the Apulian vase in Sydney as merely a 'comic version of the story of the robbing of Herakles and his subsequent pursuit of the thieves, who are normally shown as stealing various of his attributes (quiver, bow, club), while he is asleep after the feast' (1995, 126), and concludes that the 'scene depicted on our vase is, therefore, not so much an actual representation of Herakles in pursuit of a thief as a kind of parody of it' (1995, 128). But if the so-called '*phlyax*-vases' do depict scenes from transplanted old comedy, does this vase with Herakles (or pseudo-Herakles) and the round-cakes also represent an actual scene from an old comedy? It might be objected that Herakles and food was too common a mythological theme to allow this vase to refer to a specific scene from a specific comedy – he *was* the comic glutton par excellence.[7] But these vases do seem to fasten on brief but arresting moments in actual comedies, and I would proceed on the assumption that the scene on the vase in the Nicholson Museum does depict a scene from a lost work of old comedy.

In the prologue (line 60) of Aristophanes' *Wasps*, one of the slaves announces that in this comedy the audience will not be getting 'Herakles being cheated out of his dinner'. Here too some critics, citing the familiar portrayal of Herakles the glutton in comedy and satyr-play, regard the reference as generic and consider that no specific comedy is meant here.[8] But I shall argue in the remainder of this chapter that *Wasps* 60 does refer to an actual comedy, one that was presented with *Wasps* at the Lenaia of 422, and that this comedy might be the original of the one depicted on the vase by the Lecce Painter in the Nicholson Museum.

The comic productions at the Lenaia of 422 present an interesting problem for a number of reasons. It was Aristophanes' first production since the third-place finish of his *Clouds*, and the audience must have been wondering how the *Wunderkind* would react to his loss to Kratinos' brilliantly intertextual *Pytine*. There had also been a recent encounter between Aristophanes and Kleon, Aristophanes' target in his earlier comedies, in which the comedian seems to have promised not to make fun of Kleon (see *Wasps* 1284–91). Again the audience, and indeed Kleon, would have been eager to see how Aristophanes would behave at this festival.[9]

But there are other problems too with the comic productions at the Lenaia of 422. We may begin with the hypothesis to *Wasps*, which itself is confused and has puzzled critics since the nineteenth century. The following is a translation of MacDowell's text:

> It [*Wasps*] was produced in the archonship of Ameinias [423/2] through Philonides in the eighty-fourth Olympiad. It was second, at the Lenaia. Philonides won first prize with *Proagon*, Leukon was third with *Presbeis*.

The critic faces three immediate problems: firstly, Philonides seems to have produced two plays in his own name; secondly, dating by Olympiad is not usual in the comic hypotheses and the reading 'eighty-fourth' ($\pi\theta'$) is an emendation for the manuscript text 'in the city' ($\pi\acute{o}\lambda\epsilon\iota$); and thirdly, the mention of the second-place finish interrupts the normal order of presentation, that is, first, second and third. As Philonides is unlikely to have presented two comedies in his own name at this festival and since

Aristophanes makes much of the failure of his *Clouds* at the previous Dionysia (*Wasps* 64–6, 1043–7), I would agree with Merry (1898, vii) and MacDowell (1972, 43) that *Wasps* was presented in Aristophanes' own name, although MacDowell would leave the words 'through Philonides' in the text as an error of the ancient compiler. To deal with the other problems, a variety of emendations and re-writings have been proposed, van Leeuwen suggesting, for example, that only the reference to Philonides' *Proagon* belongs to the Lenaia of 422 and that *Wasps* in fact, with Leukon's *Presbeis*, was performed at the City Dionysia of 422.[10] For my purposes I shall assume that the three comedies at the Lenaia of 422 were *Wasps*, *Proagon*, and *Presbeis*.[11]

The final problem with Philonides' *Proagon* has been long recognized, that while Philonides is known as Aristophanes' producer on a number of occasions (427 [*Daitales*], 414-L(enaia) [*Amphiaraos*], 405-L [*Frogs*]) and as a comic poet in his own right (see Kassel-Austin 1989, 363–9),[12] when *Proagon* is cited by ancient sources, it is always attributed to Aristophanes.[13] 'So it appears that Aristophanes wrote two plays for the same festival; he himself presented one and Philonides the other'.[14]

During his opening monologue (*Wasps* 54–75), the slave Xanthias breaks down the fourth wall of the dramatic action and addresses the audience directly about the comedy that they are about to watch:

> φέρε νυν, κατείπω τοῖς θεαταῖς τὸν λόγον
> ὀλίγ᾽ ἄτθ᾽ ὑπειπὼν πρῶτον αὐτοῖσιν ταδί   55
> μηδὲν παρ᾽ ἡμῶν προσδοκᾶν λίαν μέγα,
> μηδ᾽ αὖ γέλωτα Μεγαρόθεν κεκλεμμένον.
> ἡμῖν γὰρ οὐκ ἔστ᾽ οὔτε κάρυ᾽ ἐκ φορμίδος
> δούλω διαρριπτοῦντε τοῖς θεωμένοις
> οὔθ᾽ Ἡρακλῆς τὸ δεῖπνον ἐξαπατώμενος   60
> οὐδ᾽ αὖθις ἀνασελγαινόμενος Εὐριπίδης·
> οὐδ᾽ εἰ Κλέων γ᾽ ἔλαμψε τῆς τύχης χάριν,
> αὖθις τὸν αὐτὸν ἄνδρα μυττωτεύσομεν
> ἀλλ᾽ ἔστιν ἡμῖν λογίδιον γμώμην ἔχον,
> ὑμῶν μὲν αὐτῶν οὐχὶ δεξιώτερον,   65
> κωμῳδίας δὲ φορτικῆς σοφώτερον

Well now, I shall explain the plot to the spectators, after giving them first these few words of introduction, not to expect anything too grand from us, no laughter stolen from Megara, for we won't have a pair of slaves tossing nuts from a basket to the audience, nor Herakles being cheated out of his dinner, nor Euripides being badly handled…again, nor even if Kleon has shone (thanks to luck!), will we make mincemeat of that same man…again. Ours is just a little theme with some intelligence, not too clever for you lot, but still better than vulgar comedy.

285

After two lines of initial comments to the audience, the slave's remarks fall into three parts which I will take separately. First, in lines 56–9 Xanthias eliminates the extremes of comedy, 'nothing too grand' and 'laughter stolen from Megara'. Megarian comedy is mentioned a number of times (Eupolis fr. 244; Ekphantides fr. 4; Aristotle *Poetics* 1448a31–2, *Eth. Nik.* 1123a24), always with the overtones of low and feeble humour. Some have thought that Aristophanes is deliberately eschewing vulgar comedy such as his own Megarian scene in *Acharnians* (729–836), but it would undercut the whole point of the praise of this new and ideal comedy, if he were to run down his own earlier comedy in this way.[15] The first production of *Clouds* 'failed', not because of its own demerits, but because of the shortcomings of the audience.

The next section is the crucial one for the thesis of this chapter that Aristophanes has the slave refer in the prologue to three specific comedies, the actual three plays being produced at the Lenaia of 422. To take the last first, with 'we will not make mincemeat of that same man [Kleon] again' Aristophanes is saying that the audience will not be getting *Knights* again (his victorious comedy of the Lenaia of 424, which was an attack from start to finish on Kleon). But *Wasps* is, like *Knights*, aimed squarely at Kleon, the principal differences being that the attack is covert until Aristophanes openly repudiates his truce with Kleon (*Wasps* 1284–91) and that it has more to do with Kleon's manipulation of the jury system than with his personal style.

The scholiast to line 61, 'nor Euripides being badly handled…again',[16] lists other appearances of Euripides in Aristophanes:

61a: αὐτοῦ γὰρ καθῆκε τὰς Θεσμοφοριαζούσας.
61c: οὐ μόνον δὲ ἐν τοῖς Δράμασιν [V – τούτῳ τῷ δράματι (Lh)] εἰσῆκται οὕτως Εὐριπίδης, ἀλλὰ καὶ ἐν τῷ Προαγῶνι καὶ ἐν τοῖς Ἀχαρνεῦσι.

61a: For he had launched his *Thesmophoriazousai* against him.
61c: Euripides is so brought on stage not only in his *Dramata*, but in both his *Proagon* and *Acharnians*.[17]

Starkie (1897, 118) dismissed the opinions of earlier critics who detected an allusion to *Proagon* here, on the grounds that Aristophanes could hardly be referring to a play at the same festival as his *Wasps*, but on my interpretation this is precisely what the comedian is doing.[18] Thus *Proagon* will have contained a humorous scene with Euripides or, like *Thesmophoriazousai*, was in large part directed against him. One ancient source (anonymous *peri komodias* = Koster Ia.iii 38–40) says that Kallistratos produced Aristophanes' political plays while Philonides produced those 'against Euripides and Sokrates'. *Proagon*, then, would have been an appropriate comedy to entrust to Philonides. None of the extant fragments has anything that might support Euripides' presence, although fr. 478 is a mock-tragic lament by a character who must be Thyestes.[19] On this reading *Wasps* 61 is a clever meta-theatrical joke, Aristophanes running down a rival who is in fact himself.[20]

If I am correct about this interpretation of *Wasps* 62–4, then 'Herakles being cheated out of his dinner' should refer to the third play of this Lenaia, the *Presbeis* (*Ambassadors*) by Leukon. The entry in Kassel-Austin (1986, 612) contains only a title and the date. Van Leeuwen (1893, xl) thought the comedy might have something to do with the embassy to Thessaly on which Amynias (see *Wasps* 1267–74) had served, but this is only a shot in the dark. How does one work a scene involving Herakles cheated out of his dinner into a comedy with the title *Ambassadors*? One thinks immediately of the penultimate scene in *Birds* (1565–1693), where Herakles and two other gods serve as ambassadors to Cloudcuckooland, but as the plural title should denote the chorus, Herakles (or pseudo-Herakles) may have appeared in a single episode, a character encountered along the way (see, for example, Herakles' appearance at *Frogs* 38–164) or an 'intruder' who was tricked by a crafty slave out of his food.

Since Leukon was producing again the next year at the Dionysia of 421 (with his *Phrateres*, against Aristophanes' *Peace* and Eupolis' *Kolakes*), I wonder if the sort of comedy rejected at *Peace* 741–4 is more than just a general reference. Here Aristophanes has his chorus claim that their poet:

τοὺς θ' Ἡρακλέας τοὺς μάττοντας καὶ τοὺς πεινῶντας ἐκείνους   741
ἐξήλασ' ἀτιμώσας πρῶτος, καὶ τοὺς δούλους παρέλυσεν   743
τοὺς φεύγοντας κἀξαπατῶντας καὶ τυπτομένους ἐπίτηδες,   742
οὓς ἐξῆγον κλάοντας ἀεί ...

> was the first to reject and drive off the stage those Herakleses kneading dough and very hungry, to get rid of those slaves running away, cheating and getting deservedly beaten, whom they brought on always wailing.[21]

I call attention to the 'hungry Herakleses' and the 'cheating and fleeing slaves' – the same verb ἐξαπατᾶν is used of Herakles at *Wasps* 60 and the slaves at *Peace* 742 – and if we take the two comic passages (*Wasps* 60, *Peace* 741–4) and the evidence from the vase in Sydney as referring to one comedy, Leukon's *Presbeis*, then we may reconstruct some of that comedy. At one point Herakles was forced to knead the dough for these round-cakes, which the slave snatched from him and then fled. The 'cheating' may refer to the irony of the great glutton having to make his own dinner, or to the manner in which the slave appropriated the cakes. If the figure on the vase is a 'pretend Herakles' and if the vase represents a scene from Leukon's *Presbeis*, then the comedy had someone pretending to be Herakles robbed of his meal. Would the real Herakles have appeared in the comedy? He does so in *Frogs*, and when Dionysos impersonates Paris in Kratinos' *Dionysalexandros*, the hypothesis tells us that the real Paris appeared later in the comedy. We might have a complicated sequence of disguise and deception, involving Herakles, a pretend Herakles, and a cunning slave. Whatever the original, this scene with the theft and the pursuit will have attracted the attention of the Lecce Painter or his patron.

Finally, this section of the prologue of *Wasps* closes with another intertextual reference (lines 64–6), this time to the poor showing of *Clouds* (third at the Dionysia of 423), 'ours is just a little theme with some intelligence, not too clever (δεξιός) for you lot, but still better (σοφός) than vulgar (φορτικός) comedy'. Twice in *Clouds* (521–2, 547–8) Aristophanes uses δεξιός and σοφός together in his complaint about the audience's lack of appreciation of his *Clouds*, and in the same passage (524) φορτικός describes those whose plays defeated his *Clouds*.

I would draw the following conclusions about the intertextual portion of the prologue. First, the poet begins and ends on the same note – the play's plot (*logos* [54], *logidion* [64]) is neither too grand (56) nor too clever for the audience (65), but still better than comedy from Megara (57) or the inferior stuff that defeated *Clouds* (66). Second, in lines 60–3 he gives details of three specific plays ('Herakles cheated out of his dinner', 'Euripides badly treated', and 'making mincemeat of Kleon'), which are actually the three plays produced at that very festival (Leukon's *Presbeis*, Philonides' or Aristophanes' *Proagon*, and Aristophanes' *Wasps*). Third, these plays may be listed in the order of production, although Aristophanes may just be reserving his own comedy to the end. In that case Aristophanes will have known what was in these plays partly because he had written *Proagon* himself (with Philonides?) and partly because they had already been performed.[22] These lines could have been added at the last minute. Aristophanes would have to instruct only one actor, and *Ekklesiazousai* 1154 ff. shows that lines could be added after the order of production was determined. Fourth, we may be able to infer about Leukon's *Presbeis* that it contained a scene with Herakles (or a 'pretend Herakles') preparing round-cakes for his dinner, being tricked out of that dinner by a slave, and angrily pursuing the culprit. Fifth and finally, if the bell-krater in Sydney does depict a scene from an old comedy, that comedy may be Leukon's *Presbeis*.

Acknowledgement

I would like to thank Karin Sowada of the Nicolson Museum for generously supplying the photograph of this vase and for giving permission for its publication here.

Notes

[1] For the introduction of the dithyrambic competitions into the Athenian festival of the City Dionysia in the late sixth century, see the chapter by Peter Wilson in this book.

[2] On intertextuality in old comedy, see Hubbard 1991 and Sommerstein 1992.

[3] Nicholson Museum inventory no. 88.02 and published formally at Trendall 1995.

[4] Trendall 1995, 129 n. 13 gives an excellent summary of the *plakountes*, including the observation that at *Frogs* 507 Xanthias, disguised as Herakles, is offered *plakountes* baked by Persephone herself.

[5] The standard treatments are those in Trendall 1967, 1989; see also Taplin 1993, 48–54. The quotation is from Taplin 1993, 48.

[6] Würzburg Telephos (Taplin 1993, 112, 11.4), Salerno vase (Taplin 1993, 114, 16.16), 'Choregoi-vase' (Taplin 1993, 111, 9.1), the 'Goose play' vases (Taplin 1993, 111, 10.2; Taplin 1993, 112, 11.3), 'Cheiron-vase' (Taplin 1993, 112, 12.6). Trendall (1995, 131), writing before the appearance of Taplin 1993, will admit one or two of Taplin's vases as old comic, but for him the influence of Old Comedy is much less than Taplin would allow. On the matter of the *phlyax*-vases, see also Green 1991; 1995, 143–6; Csapo 1986 which treated the Würzburg Telephos slightly earlier than Taplin 1987.

[7] In extant drama he appears in that guise in Aristophanes' *Birds* (1574–1693), *Frogs* (38–164), Alexis fr. 140 (where Herakles discovers a cookbook), and Euripides' *Alcestis*, a drama that takes the place of the expected satyr-play. Herakles the glutton and buffoon is a repeated motif in that dramatic genre (see Galinsky 1972, 81–100).

[8] MacDowell 1971, 137 f. is typical, 'there is no need to suppose that Ar. has a particular play in mind'. Van Leeuwen 1893, 13 and Starkie 1897, 114–8 think that Eupolis is meant throughout the passage here. Green 1868, 17 also allows that behind this line may lie 'some particular exhibition either by another comedian or by our poet himself in a former play', while Sommerstein (1985, 167 on *Peace* 741) also thinks that an actual comic scene is meant at that passage. Graves 1899, 86 allows for both possibilities: that Aristophanes is referring to his own comedies or (more likely) that he is satirizing the practice of his rivals.

[9] This is the starting-point for my study of *Wasps* (Storey 1995).

[10] Van Leeuwen 1893, xxxviii emended the text of the hypothesis to read Εὔπολις Πόλεσι δεύτερος ἦν, but later (van Leeuwen 1909) retracted this when *IG* II² 2318.115 showed that the victor's name for 422-D was ....]ος, where

Kantha]ros is generally restored. See Starkie 1897, 391 f.; Rogers 1915, v–xiii for earlier discussions.

[11] I am assuming that the number of comedies produced at the festivals had been cut from five to three during the Peloponnesian War. This is a hotly debated matter which I deal with in Storey 2002.

[12] For Philonides as producer of Aristophanes' first comedy (*Daitales*) see Welsh 1983 and MacDowell 1995, 34–41. One play of Philonides, *Kothornoi*, is attested in several ancient sources.

[13] *Proagon* appears on two lists of Aristophanes' comedies, and is assigned to Aristophanes on five occasions by Athenaios, twice by Photios, and once each by Pollux and the scholiasts to Lucian, Aristophanes, and Platon. The evidence and bibliography is collected at Kassel-Austin 1984, 253.

[14] MacDowell 1995, 34 n. 12. See also Marshall 2000, 19–21.

[15] Van Leeuwen 1893, 12 f. thinks that the words 'stolen from Megara' are a quotation from Eupolis commenting on the Megarian scene in *Acharnians*. See also Starkie 1897, 117 f.

[16] The participle could be middle, 'Euripides behaving badly'. See Marshall 2000, 19.

[17] Two problems in the scholion need comment. First in 61c I have translated the text of Σ^R 'in his *Dramata*', a lost comedy often dated to the Lenaia of 426. The text in Lh reads 'in the drama' (*Wasps*), but Euripides is not brought on stage in *Wasps*. Then the reference to *Thesmophoriazousai* has caused some problems, since the scholiast seems to be referring to productions before *Wasps* (422) and the extant comedy belongs to 411 (see Merry 1898, 8). Butrica 2001 argues a controversial thesis, that the other *Thesmophoriazousai*, which is universally dated after the extant comedy of 411, belongs to the Lenaia of 423.

[18] MacDowell 1971, 137 thinks that Aristophanes is referring to comedies by other poets; he suggests Kallias' *Pedetai* – but I date that play to the mid-410s (Storey 1988). Sommerstein 1983, 157 f. also recognizes that a comedy lies behind *Wasps* 61 and seeks a source other than Aristophanes. He suggests (but rejects) Kallias' *Pedetai*, and wonders about Telekleides frs. 39–40.

[19] Euripides' did write a *Thyestes*, which *Acharnians* 434 shows was earlier than 425.

[20] See Marshall 2000, 33 n. 6.

[21] Here the text of 741–4 is in dispute. Since the participles in 742 fit slaves better than they do Herakles, I would with Bergk transpose 742 and 743. See Sommerstein 1985, 167 f.; Olson 1998, 219.

[22] C.W. Marshall points out to me that if *Presbeis* had yet to be performed, Aristophanes, getting wind of the Herakles-scene, could be deflating its effect by insisting that it was just another stock scene involving the great glutton.

Bibliography

Butrica, J.
    2001   'The lost *Thesmophoriazusae* of Aristophanes', *Phoenix* 55, 44–76.

Csapo, E.
1986   'A note on the Würzburg bell-crater H5697 ("Telephus Travestitus")', *Phoenix* 40, 379–92.
Csapo, E. and Slater, W.J.
1995   *The Context of Ancient Drama*, Ann Arbor.
Galinsky, G.K.
1972   *The Herakles Theme*, Oxford.
Graves, C.E.
1899   *The Wasps of Aristophanes*, Cambridge.
Green, R.
1991   'Notes on phlyax vases', *NAC* 20, 49–56.
1995   'Theatre production 1897–1995', *Lustrum* 37, 7–202.
Green, W.C.
1868   *Aristophanes: The Wasps*, Cambridge.
Hubbard, T.
1991   *The Mask of Comedy: Aristophanes and the intertextual parabasis*, Ithaca.
Kassel, R. and Austin, C.
1984   *Poetae Comic Graeci*, vol. III.2, Berlin and New York.
1986   *Poetae Comici Graeci*, vol. V, Berlin and New York.
1989   *Poetae Comici Graeci*, vol. VII, Berlin and New York.
MacDowell, D.M.
1971   *Aristophanes Wasps*, Oxford.
1995   *Aristophanes and Athens*, Oxford.
Marshall, C.W.
2001   'What's so funny about ancient comedy?', *Social Identities* 7, 13–35.
Merry, W.W.
1899   *Aristophanes: The Wasps*, Oxford.
Olson, S.D.
1998   *Aristophanes'* Peace, Oxford.
Rogers, B.B.
1915   *The Wasps of Aristophanes*, London.
Shapiro, H.A.
1992   '*Mousikoi agones*: music and poetry at the Panathenaia', in J. Neils (ed.) *Goddess and Polis*, 53–75, Princeton.
Sommerstein, A.H.
1983   *The Comedies of Aristophanes, vol. 4, Wasps*, Warminster.
1985   *The Comedies of Aristophanes, vol.5, Peace*, Warminster.
1992   'Old comedians on old comedy', *Drama* 1, 14–33.
Starkie, W.J.M.
1897   *Aristophanes: The Wasps*, London.
Storey, I.C.
1988   'The date of Kallias' *Pedetai*', *Hermes* 116, 379–83.
1995   '*Wasps* 1284–91 and the portrait of Kleon in *Wasps*', *Scholia* 4, 3–23.
2002   'Cutting comedies', in J. Barsby (ed.) *Greek and Roman Drama: Translation and performance*, Drama 12, 146–76, Stuttgart.

Taplin, O.
    1987   'Phallology, *phlyakes*, iconography and Aristophanes', *PCPhS* 33, 92–104.
    1993   *Comic Angels*, Oxford.
Trendall, A.D.
    1967   *Phlyax Vases*, 2nd edn, BICS supplement 19, London.
    1989   *Red Figure Vases of South Italy and Sicily*, London.
    1995   'A phlyax bell-krater by the Lecce Painter', in A. Cambitoglou and E. Robinson (eds.) *Classical Art in the Nicholson Museum, Sydney*, Mainz, 125–31, pls. 39, 40.

11

ATHLETICS, EDUCATION AND PARTICIPATION IN CLASSICAL ATHENS

David Pritchard

The social background of ancient Greek athletes: the state of the question

For more than a century until the 1984 Olympic Games, participation in the athletic contests of ancient Greece remained an uncontroversial and settled issue. A long line of classicists, including Percy Gardner, E. Norman Gardiner and H.A. Harris, had elaborated how the golden age of Greek sport was the archaic period when athletes were drawn exclusively from the traditional landed elite and competed as amateurs for prizes of only symbolic value.[1] These scholars also argued that the supposed introduction by fifth-century Greek cities of valuable prizes at their own local sporting competitions and cash bonuses for those of their citizens victorious at the international games, like the Olympics, attracted members of the lower class into athletics and encouraged them to train and specialize. Within a few generations such non-elite specialists came to dominate the sporting scene and forced the elite, with its ethos of amateurism, to withdraw from athletics and to concentrate entirely on equestrian competition. Yet, in the year of the Los Angeles Olympics this hoary 'rise and fall' account of ancient Greek sport was directly attacked and effectively refuted with the publication of *The Olympic Myth of Greek Amateur Athletics* by David Young.[2]

What Young puts beyond doubt in the first half of his polemical book is that the traditional scholarly consensus about ancient Greek sport and the long-time amateur code of the modern Olympic Movement did not just parallel each other but developed symbiotically.[3] Playing sport on an amateur basis, that is, without monetary rewards, laboured preparation or an excessive interest in winning, was invented in the elite 'public' schools of nineteenth-century England as a way, amongst other things, to fortify boys in the normative values of the haute bourgeoisie.[4] From the 1860s onwards English and, to a lesser extent, American 'gentlemen' established amateur athletic clubs and associations. They did so, Young explains, in opposition to the well-developed popular sporting scene with its cash prizes and semi-professionals, and readily acknowledged that their insistence on the unblemished amateurism of their members aimed to keep out working-class athletes. It was this athletic credo and its most ardent Anglo-American spokesmen that Baron Pierre de Coubertin co-opted in the long campaign for his modern Olympic Movement. Young demonstrates that Gardner, Gardiner and Harris coined and perpetuated their 'rise and fall' version of ancient Greek sport in order for there to be a cautionary story from antiquity supporting the burgeoning amateur athletic and later Olympic movements. That these organizations and scholarly consensus did indeed develop hand in glove is confirmed by the explicit commitment of these English classicists to sporting amateurism and by the public use of their hallowed lesson by presidents of the International Olympic Committee (IOC), including de Coubertin and Avery Brundage, to justify the exclusion of athletes or even expulsion of medal winners who had been tainted by payment for their sporting pursuits.[5]

If the partisanship and elitism of these classical scholars were not concerning enough, Young goes on to show how their 'rise and fall' thesis rests on a marked falsification of the historical record. In the second part of his book Young substantiates a passing remark made several years earlier by Henri Pleket – one of the recognized founders of the disinterested study of ancient sport history – that long before the classical age there already were prizes of great value for athletic victory, which 'archaic nobles are not known to have rejected'.[6] Such prize-giving in fact predates the time when sporting contests were the exclusive preserve of the city and staged only as part of the religious festivals for its patron heroes and deities.[7] The poems of Homer and Hesiod evidence how the aristocrats of the eighth and seventh centuries competed for bullion, cauldrons and slave women at the funerals of fellow members of the upper class.[8] By the sixth century Greek communities were giving those of their citizens who had won at Olympia the proverbial keys to the city in the form of substantial gifts and rewards (e.g. Plutarch *Solon* 23.3; Xenophanes fr. 2 West).[9] They were also making available valuable prizes for the competitions at their own local festivals, such as the amphorae of precious olive oil at the Athenian festival of the Great Panathenaia.[10] It was, then, on the basis of good evidence that Pleket and Young concluded that the athletes of ancient Greece had *never* been amateurs. Nevertheless, that they did so around the same time as the IOC itself was debating and easing its insistence on Olympic amateurism points to an interesting ongoing relationship between historiography on ancient Greek sport and the modern Olympic Movement.[11]

Unwittingly, Young also demonstrates how the *philonikia* or contentiousness of the ancient Greeks lives on amongst contemporary ancient historians and classicists; for while he might acknowledge Pleket's pioneering work, Young lambasts him for refusing to repudiate the 'rise and fall' interpretation of ancient Greek sport in its entirety.[12] 'Even Pleket', Young writes, 'could not free himself from the nineteenth-century elitists' lingering grasp. He *almost* freed himself. But the ghosts of the Gard(i)ners march across many a page.'[13] Young charges Pleket with clinging unjustifiably to the traditional 'rise and fall' chronology that has non-elite athletes appearing only, and in significant numbers, towards the end of the fifth century. Certainly Young shows convincingly that the case mounted by Pleket for the late-fifth-century arrival of lower-class athletic competitors founders on an over-interpretation of a solitary piece of evidence (Isokrates 16.32–3).[14] He puts most of his efforts, however, into proving that the 'noble birth' of several of Pleket's archaic and early classical athletes 'evaporates under elementary analysis'.[15] To this end, he argues that Pleket uses special pleading to transform the first Olympic victor, Koroibos, who was reportedly a 'cook' (μάγειρος), into an upper-class priest (Athenaios 382b).[16] The ancient evidence, Young also suggests, for the late-sixth-century Olympic victor, Milon of Kroton, and the early classical Theogenes of Thasos does not justify Pleket's presentation of them as nobles, and even points to their having come from less well-heeled backgrounds.[17] Young also criticizes Pleket for passing over other better-documented cases of Olympic victors with non-elite beginnings. For example, he does not mention the late sixth-century Glaukos of Karystos who reputedly hammered opponents just like he punched metal blades back into ploughs with his bare hands when working on the family farm (Pausanias 6.10.1–3).[18] Nor does he note, Young complains, the early-sixth-century Polymestor of Miletos and the mid-fifth-century Amesinas of Barce whom Philostratos (*On Athletics* 13) and the Olympic victor list of Sextus Julius Africanus describe as a 'cowherd' and 'goatherd' respectively.[19] Finally, he mentions not at all the 'probably fifth-century' anonymous and one-time fish porter whose victory epigram is discussed by Aristotle (*Rhetoric* 1365a).[20]

By contrast Young believes that there were always good numbers of lower-class athletes in the classical *and* archaic periods, even though he thinks it impossible to establish at any juncture a 'reliable proportion of nobles to non-nobles'.[21] Nevertheless, while criticizing Pleket's allegiance to the chronology of the 'rise and fall' account of Greek sport, Young takes seriously his fellow scholar's judgment that it would have been very difficult for the poor of archaic and classical Greece to find the requisite money and leisure to train for, and travel to, international sporting competitions.[22] His taking pause here is understandable. The earliest evidence of a city providing financial support to cover the training and travel expenses of an athletically talented but indigent boy is an early Hellenistic inscription of 300 BC from Ephesos.[23] And the first attestation of a wealthy individual privately sponsoring the athletic training of a poor boy comes from Ptolemaic Egypt of the mid-third century.[24] In response, Young postulates that even before the Hellenistic period there was another way for a non-elite boy to circumvent the barriers to his participation in competitive athletics – the valuable prizes on offer at the so-called local contests beyond the *periodos* (circuit) of the Olympian, Pythian, Isthmian and Nemean Games.[25] Since natural ability, Young suggests, rather than training dictates sporting success during childhood, a poor boy could win at one of the sporting competitions in his neighborhood a reasonably valuable prize, which would allow him to travel to larger games, like the Great Panathenaia, that had more lucrative prizes. Victory at these contests would provide him with the necessary funds to hire a coach and so launch an athletic career, which could continue as long as he kept winning valuable prizes. Therefore, Young concludes, '…the athletic system itself removes the financial obstacle which Pleket sees in the path of the non-nobles who aspired to an athletic career'.[26]

The historians of ancient sport who have formally reviewed or systematically critiqued *The Olympic Myth of Greek Amateur Athletics* have been remarkably consistent in their assessment of Young's forcefully argued theses.[27] While most – including Pleket – remark upon his personal attacks and fiery language, all applaud and accept his explanation and refutation of the 'rise and fall' version of the history of ancient Greek sport. Nevertheless, with the same unanimity they also reject his case for significant numbers of non-elite athletes in the archaic and classical periods.

Every reviewer and critic of Young has serious doubts about the veracity of the evidence he provides for the non-elite backgrounds of athletic victors like Koroibos, Polymestor and Amesinas. Most of his ancient references, after all, come from authors of the late Roman period such as Pausanias, Philostratos and Sextus Julius Africanus and have an anecdotal or even fabulous character. Questions have also been raised about how Young interprets what sources there are for each of his supposed lower-class athletes. For example, while Aristotle does record the epigram of an Olympic victor of humble background (*Rhetoric* 1365a), Young omits that he does so as an example of someone who has performed 'beyond his ability, age and equals (παρὰ δύναμιν καὶ παρὰ ἡλικίαν καὶ παρὰ τοὺς ὁμοίους)' – a qualification suggesting this non-elite victor is the exception proving the rule.[28] The elite background of Theogenes appears also to be beyond doubt, as his relatives performed public duties which were the reserve of the upper-class citizens of the early classical city: his father was a priest of Herakles (Pausanias 6.11.2) and a brother served Thasos as a *theōros* (sacred ambassador).[29]

As noted above, Young infers the lower-class background of Glaukos from the report in a late source that his father decided to take him to the Olympic Games to be a boy boxer, when, one day on the family farm, he saw him beat a ploughshare back into the plough with his hands (Pausanias 6.10.1–3; cf. Philostratos *On Athletics* 20). Critically, the inference that father and son were impoverished smallholders is not the only one that can be drawn from this tale. As Michael Poliakoff writes, '…farming had far more status than other kinds of work in antiquity, to the extent that even a family with some social pretensions might still do some work on their own land'.[30] Further, this rather colourful story presupposes Glaukos and his father had the free time and spare funds not only to travel from Euboia to Olympia for the Games but also to spend the compulsory month of training for competitors at Elis before the Olympics proper.[31] In classical Athens at least such *skholē* (leisure) was considered one of the defining characteristics of the upper class.[32]

Finally, since military leadership was monopolized by the upper-class citizens of late archaic cities, the leading role Milon played in the war against Sybaris would seem to confirm his membership in the Krotoniate elite (Diodoros 12.9.5–6). Young argues of course that the wealth some athletic victors such as Milon enjoyed as mature men need not have been inherited and could well have come from winnings at local sporting contests. However, a source of the classical period, which Young overlooks, tends to suggest that this famous wrestler was born into well-heeled circumstances: once Demokedes of Kroton had grown rich on the medical fees he had earned from grateful cities and the Great King himself, he married the daughter of Milon so '…that he might seem to Darius a great man in his own country, too (Herodotos 3.130–7, especially 137)'.[33] Historically newly-rich characters like Demokedes improved their status by marrying, not fellow *nouveaux riches*, but into families that had long been part of a recognized elite.

Young does not gain much critical support either for the way he proposes an athletically gifted but poor boy could have launched a sporting career in archaic and classical Greece; for his critics judge the prizes on offer at local athletic competitions neither numerous nor large enough to cover the living and training expenses of any significant number of non-elite competitors. Certainly an early-fourth-century inscription shows the Athenians giving boy victors at the sporting contests of their festival of the Great Panathenaia quantities of olive oil worth several hundreds of drachmas (*IG* II^2 2311).[34] But these – the most prominent *agōnes* (competitions) after the four Panhellenic festivals – took place only every fifth year, and the prizes at other local games, where place-getters received no prizes, were far less generous. In the classical period such prizes ranged from ten obols for a victor in a 'heavy' event at an Attic contest (*IG* I³ 1386), ten drachmas as the largest prize at the Apollonia on Delos (*IG* II.2 203a.65–70), and a woollen cloak at the games of Pellene (Pindar *Olympian* 9.98) to a silver *phiale* (drinking cup), probably worth one or two mnai, for the victors in 'heavy' events at the games at Marathon (*Olympian* 9.90) and in equestrian competitions at Sicyon (9.98).[35] Moreover, Young seems to underestimate the intensity of competition even at these local *agōnes*. A poor boy would have had to compete not just with the well-trained elite athletes of his own community but also against the similarly prepared competitors from other cities whose victories at home had encouraged them to travel to games further afield. While coming from a period long after the city's heyday, six extant lists of victors from Great Panathenaias of the first half of the second century BC give an idea of the numbers of foreign competitors at local games (*IG* II² 2313–17).[36] 'Of the 200-odd victories listed…about half – including most boy victors – are not Athenian.'[37] Stiff competition like this would have made it very difficult for a poor but promising athlete to win and next to impossible for him to secure the constant stream of valuable prizes needed to launch and sustain a sporting career. In view of these poor odds, Young's reviewers and critics come to the same conclusion: while he establishes the *possibility* of a non-elite boy in archaic and classical Greece securing a sporting career by the prizes he had won, the *probability* is very low.[38]

This striking unanimity in the critical reception of *The Olympic Myth of Greek Amateur Athletics* has not guaranteed consensus in post-1984 scholarship on athletic participation. Indeed, since the publication of Young's book the whole question has become – especially in the last several years – increasingly disputed and controversial. Admittedly three of Young's reviewers and critics go against this trend by coming to an apparently common position on the issue in their own research. For example, Poliakoff concludes for the archaic and classical periods that the elite dominated the athletic scene and that the participation of good numbers of non-elite citizens in athletic competition is very improbable.[39] When it comes specifically to Athens, Donald Kyle judges it highly likely that an upper-class dominance of athletics remained constant across the archaic and classical periods and that lower-class citizens never participated in sporting competitions in any significant number.[40] Mark Golden comes to the same conclusion about fifth- and fourth-century Athens.[41] However, another critic of *The Olympic Myth of Greek Amateur Athletics* has long held a different view of the history of ancient Greek athletics, and used his very public critique of Young to restate – with surprisingly few nuances or changes – his original position.[42] In archaic times, Pleket suggests, the upper class dominated and possibly even monopolized athletics. But '…the rise of the *gymnasion* slowly facilitated the rise of middle-class hoplite-athletes'.[43] While this new group competed at first only with elite athletes in local competitions, a contemporary and *reliable* source proves that they had begun to participate in good numbers at Olympia by the end of the fifth century (Isokrates 16.32–3).

More recently a number of scholars have discounted or even ignored the unanimous reception of Young's book and gone on to employ his suggestions on non-elite athletic participation to bolster their own adventurous theses on the relationship between athletics and democracy. Nick Fisher for one argues that in classical Athens athletics, along with other one-time exclusively upper-class activities, '…became part of democratic expectations, at least for those roughly of hoplite status'.[44] In support of his case that athletic participation under the Athenian democracy was 'very extensive' and 'parallel indeed to participation in political life', Fisher deploys *The Olympic Myth of Greek Amateur Athletics* very carefully.[45] While he acknowledges 'strong counter-arguments' about how it would have been difficult for lower-class youths to find 'the time, support and training to compete' at Panhellenic events, this does not stop him rehearsing Young's case for just such non-elite participation and opining that whether or not athletics was an exclusively elite pastime 'even in the archaic period is disputable.'[46] Likewise, Fisher might note how one of Young's reviewers was concerned about the veracity of evidence for his supposedly non-elite athletes, but nonetheless writes that '…Young was able to point to a number of instances even in the archaic period of successful athletes who were originally poor and of non-noble birth'.[47] Fisher next argues that for classical Athens there are 'three texts' (Isokrates 16.33–4; Pseudo-Xenophon 1.13, 2.10; Euripides fr. 441 N[2]) suggesting '…a consciousness of increased non-elite athletic activity at least from the later fifth century'.[48]

Taking a leaf out of Young's book, Fisher also proposes two ways by which an athletically talented but poor boy of classical Athens could have secured the support needed to launch an athletic career. His first avenue concerns the local contests for tribal teams of youthful *lampadēphoroi* (torch racers) at the annual festivals of the Panathenaia, Hephaistia and Promethia.[49] The training of a tribal team for each torch race was financed and organized by a *gymnasiarkhos* or upper-class sponsor (e.g. Xenophon *Ways and Means* 4.51–2; *IG* II[2] 1250.3). Fisher suggests that such sponsors, eager as they were for their teams to win, would have recruited and trained any promising runner – regardless of class background. Thus a poor but gifted runner could have joined one of the torch-racing teams of his tribe and hence garnered the training he needed to be competitive in individual athletic events. A non-elite boy, Fisher continues, who showed athletic promise, for example, as a *lampadēphoros*, could also have received financial support – especially if he was comely and handsome – from a wealthy male suitor or lover.[50] Greek pederasty, then, provided a second way for a lower-class boy to launch an athletic career.[51]

Finally, Stephen Miller has recently argued that the ideological under-pinnings of democracy – *isonomia* (legal equality) and *isēgoria* (equality of speech), if not *dēmokratia* itself, 'developed out of athletics'.[52] Miller suggests that archaic Greeks first encountered equality in athletic competi-tions where winners were determined by reference, not to rank or class, but to 'absolute standards of distance and speed and strength'.[53] He explains: '...it is also possible to bring positive evidence to bear that shows that some competitors in the *gymnikos agon* were definitely of humble origin. This has already been done by David Young, and it is not necessary to rehearse the evidence here.'[54] Such participation by lower-class athletes, Miller maintains, not only helped to disseminate widely ideals of equality but developed democracy by breaking down class tensions and encouraging upper- and lower-class citizens to see each other as equals.

Such is the divided state of current scholarship on athletic participation in ancient Greece: a long-held and predominant interpretation of this important issue may have broken up, but no new consensus has emerged. Further investigation therefore seems justified, and the starting point for doing so in this chapter will be the training of athletes.

Athletic training in classical Athens: the point of departure

Authors of the classical period considered training indispensable for athletic victory and even for participation in athletic competitions. According to a range of sources, an athlete must devote large amounts of time to regular training if he wants to be competitive at the Olympics or any other Panhellenic games.[55] Any victory he might win at such a contest is due in large part to the lessons and expertise of his athletics trainer (e.g. Pindar *Olympian* 8.54–66; *Nemean* 4.93–6; 6.66–9; *Isthmian* 4.70–2). At the local level too it is only sustained training that turns boys and men into *athlētai* or athletic competitors (e.g. Isokrates 15.183–5; Plato *Statesman* 294d–e; cf. Aristophanes *Frogs* 1093–4), against whom the *idiōtai* or untrained have little chance (Plato *Republic* 422b–c; Xenophon *Hiero* 4.6). These passages help explain why athletic training can shed new light on the question of participation in athletics: sporting performance was highly dependent on adequate preparations. They suggest too that such a dependency was reasonably widely known – a realization that would by itself have discouraged those unable to train from entering athletic *agōnes* in the first place. Moreover, if an athletically inclined individual could not afford the time and money to do training that was widely considered indispensable, he would most probably have found it impossible to meet the other expenses of participating in athletic competition. An athlete also had to pay for the unusually hearty and meat-rich diet that was considered essential for enhancing strength and sporting performance, and to cover the fees of an *iatros* or doctor whose professional expertise included dietary matters.[56] And if he wanted to test his training at competitions outside his own community, there would also be traveling and living expenses to meet.

While athletic training appears to be a promising avenue for investigating athletic participation, working out who had access to it is a somewhat complex business; it requires a thorough consideration of what the demands and opportunity cost of athletic training in fact were, which social classes could have met these, and any explicit evidence about who exactly trained for, and took part in, athletic competitions. Unfortunately, the only Greek community of the archaic and classical periods for which much information on such social issues has survived is Athens in the fifth and especially fourth centuries BC. Nevertheless, as Athens was the most democratic and prosperous of classical cities and witnessed – as a result – social mobility amongst its free inhabitants, here we might well expect to find substantial non-elite involvement in athletics, if ever there was such participation in Greece before the Hellenistic and Roman periods.

Before investigating participation in athletic training, the terminology of social class used in this chapter and the model of classical Athenian society informing the analysis should be clarified and summarized.[57] Throughout this chapter terms such as 'elite' and 'non-elite', 'prosperous' and 'humble' and 'the upper class' and 'the lower class' are used strictly as synonyms for 'the wealthy' and 'the poor'. Although classical Athenians are known to have divided up the citizen body conceptually on the basis of military roles, occupation or place of residence, the distinction they used most often and thought 'cut at the social joints' best was between *hoi plousioi* (the wealthy) and *hoi penētes* (the poor).[58] According to the city's extant literature, the rich were marked out primarily by their *skholē* (leisure) and lack of the necessity to work, distinctive clothing and footwear, particular but not always highly esteemed attitudes and actions, and exclusive pastimes such as hunting, horsemanship, pederasty and mannered drinking parties. They also undertook expensive public services, paid the *eisphora* or extraordinary war tax and furnished the city's political and military leaders. In the late archaic and early classical periods, the recognition of a family as belonging to this social class had also depended on its having its wealth mainly in agricultural land and its membership of a *genos* or so-called aristocratic clan. Yet by the mid-fifth century, notwithstanding old comedy's barbs against the newly arrived, these traditional criteria no longer had to be met by an Athenian family in order to be recognized as part of the city's upper class. And by the next century they were very rarely cited as proof of elite membership. In both centuries the wealthy most probably numbered close to, but less than, five per cent of the citizen body.[59] Extraordinary as it is, fifth- and fourth-century Athenians classed the rest of the citizens, from the truly destitute to those sitting just below the elite, as 'the poor'. Classical sources suggest that what the varied members of this social class had in common was a need to work – and hence a lack of leisure – and a way of life that was frugal and moderate. This ancient and fundamental dichotomy between rich and poor serves as the main social classification in this chapter's investigation of athletic and educational participation in classical Athens.

The relationship between athletics and education

When turning to athletic preparations in classical Athens, thought needs to be given to what relationship, if any, existed between training for sporting competition and the time-honoured physical education of Athenian boys and youths. Of course a cursory reading of the late fifth-century comedy *Clouds* by Aristophanes might give the impression that young Athenians had abandoned the *palaistra* (wrestling school) and *gymnasion* (athletics field) for the 'new education' of the sophists with their lessons in *hoplo-makhia* (weapons training), oratory and philosophy (961–1054).[60] Nevertheless, while opportunities for male adolescents to learn 'new' disciplines did proliferate in the second half of the fifth century, physical education manifestly remained an established element of the normative and traditional *paideia* (education) of young Athenians throughout the classical period.[61] This branch of the so-called *arkhaia paideia* (old education) was taught by the *paidotribēs* (athletics teacher) who usually owned his own *palaistra* (wrestling school).[62] The lessons he gave were not one-on-one but for groups of students, and the verb often used to describe the attendance of boys at them – *phoitaō*, which literally means to go back and forth frequently – underscores how his lessons, like those of the other traditional teachers, were regular and ongoing.[63] It is an historical irony that while sophists at Athens in the late fifth and fourth centuries assimilated their newfangled lessons to traditional education or even argued for the superiority of what they were teaching, they were the first to describe the 'old education' systematically and to invent an abstract terminology to do so. Thus, in the classical period it is *only* in philosophical and medical literature that we find the convenient neologism *hē gymnastikē* (the athletic) being used to describe both the physical education of traditional *paideia* and the expertise of the *paidotribēs* himself.[64]

How this *gymnastikē* related to training for athletic competition, and what the circumstances of the latter were, have been largely overlooked by scholars currently working on ancient Greek sport who are usually content to write of 'training' or 'coaching' without providing any details.[65] An exception is Kyle who concludes, after considering such questions for several pages in his *Athletics in Ancient Athens*, that 'To a certain extent the activities of athletics and physical education overlapped but the degree of involvement and specialization differed.'[66] Taking his definitions from the late Roman period authors Galen and Philostratos (*On Athletics* especially 14), Kyle suggests that the *paidotribēs* was 'a wrestling school teacher with his own *palaestra* where he instructed boys in basic gymnastics and also where athletes trained'.[67] He was, in short, 'more of a preliminary physical trainer'. The so-called *gymnastēs*, by contrast, was a 'more specialized trainer, hired to prepare an athlete for competition, supervising his exercises and diet'. The *gymnastēs*, then, was 'the 'coach' or athletic expert' whose services were sought out by an individual in training for competition. 'The distinction between these two', Kyle writes, 'arose in practice in the fifth century and was established in terminology by the fourth.'[68] Unfortunately, while neat and logical, this proposed division of tasks is not borne out by the extant sources of classical Athens which suggest instead that regular attendance at the school classes of the *paidotribēs* was *the* means by which young Athenians prepared for athletic competition and that *gymnastēs* – far from describing a specialist athletics coach – was simply one of a few philosophical synonyms for *paidotribēs*.

The critical text for understanding the relationship between physical education and athletic competition in classical Athens is the *Antidosis* of Isokrates in which this Athenian intellectual compares lessons in *philosophia* to those of the *paidotribēs* (15.181–5). In the course of what is in reality a crafty justification of the new discipline of philosophy, Isokrates explains that athletics teachers (παιδοτρίβαι) teach (διδάσκουσιν) their pupils (μαθητάς, τοὺς φοιτῶντας) 'the moves that have been devised *for competition*' (τὰ σχήματα τὰ πρὸς τὴν ἀγωνίαν εὑρημένα – 15.183). Once they have made their students thoroughly familiar with 'the moves', the *paidotribai* train them in athletics (γυμνάζουσιν), accustom them to toil (πονεῖν) and compel them to combine each of the lessons they have learnt (184). This teaching and training by athletics teachers, according to Isokrates, turns pupils into competent athletic competitors (ἀθλητὰς...ἱκανοὺς) as long as they have sufficient natural talent (185). The picture drawn here of the *paidotribēs* teaching groups of students competitive athletics *and* overseeing their training in what they have learnt is confirmed by other classical Athenian texts. A few, for example, have pupils learning athletics under a *paidotribēs* (Aristophanes *Knights* 1238–9; Plato *Gorgias* 456c–e; cf. 460d), several have him supervising those in athletic training (γυμνάζομαι), and one, like Isokrates, puts the teaching (παιδεύω) and training (ἀσκέω) of an athlete into his hands (Plato *Lakhes* 184e).[69]

That the regular classes of the *paidotribēs* were indeed geared to turn students into *athlētai* (athletic competitors) is also borne out by the regular use of *agōnia* (competition) as a synonym for *gymnastikē* (physical education), and by the fact that the sporting events learnt and practised at school were nothing less than the standard athletic events of local and international games.[70] More often than not *paidotribai* are presented giving classes in wrestling (πάλη) or in the other 'heavy' events of boxing and the *pankration* – an unsurprising state of affairs in view of their typical ownership of wrestling schools and the fact that some of them had probably been victors in just such sports in their youth (e.g. Plato *Meno* 94c).[71] What is unexpected is that we also find classical Athenian *paidotribai* teaching and training their charges in other standard sports of ancient Greek athletics. In his *Statesmen*, for example, Plato outlines how there are in Athens, as in other cities, 'very many' supervised 'training sessions for groups' (ἀθρόων ἀνθρώπων ἀσκήσεις) where the instructions and toils (πόνους) are not just for wrestling but also 'for the sake of competition in the foot race or some other event' (εἴτε πρὸς δρόμον εἴτε πρὸς ἄλλο τι, φιλονικίας ἕνεκα – 294d–e). Elsewhere Plato writes of a *paidotribēs* receiving a wage (μισθός) for running lessons (*Gorgias* 520c–d), and Antiphon has a *paidotribēs* conducting a class in javelin throwing for a group of Athenian boys in the *gymnasion* (athletics field – 3.1.1; 3.2.3, 7; 3.3.6; 3.4.4, etc.).

Fourth-century works by intellectuals at Athens employ not only '*paidotribēs*' but also '*gymnastēs*' – along with a few other newly-invented words – to describe teachers or coaches of athletes. Critically, as these neologisms are often used for those performing duties traditionally associated with the *paidotribēs*, such as, for example, a *gymnastēs* or *tis gymnastikos* supervising athletes in training (Plato *Laws* 720e; *Statesman* 295c) or a *gymnastikos* with wrestling expertise (Aristotle *Eudemian Ethics* 1217b39–40), they appear to be synonyms for the more common and better-established word for athletics teacher.[72] This is put beyond doubt by the way in which Plato and Aristotle discuss the two crafts of *iaktrikē* (medicine) and *gymnastikē* (athletics).[73] Plato for his part repeatedly pairs the *iatros* (doctor) and the *paidotribēs* and presents them as the only two with expertise concerning care of the body (e.g. Plato *Kriton* 47b; *Protagoras* 313d; *Republic* 389c). Yet tellingly, in other passages, he, like Aristotle, gives this bodily expertise to the *iatros* and *gymnastēs*.[74] An excellent example of this exchange of *paidotribēs* for a synonym is to be found in the dialogue *Gorgias* in which Plato gives expertise with the body first to the *iatros* and *paidotribēs* (452a–b), next to the *iatros* and *tis gymnastikos* (464a) and soon after to *paidotribai te kai iatroi* (464d–e). Since *tis gymnastikos* and *gymnastēs* are found only in the so-called philosophical texts of classical Athens, they appear to be further examples of the linguistic inventiveness of the new intellectuals: once the sophists had come up with the useful abstract noun *gymnastikē* to describe the varied activities of traditional physical education, it was but a small step to derive cognates to describe those who teach and have expertise in athletics.

Nevertheless, we must admit that Kyle brings forward two *contemporary* passages, both from Aristotle's *Politics*, which do seem to suggest that *ho gymnastikos* did not remain a simple synonym for *paidotribēs* for all of the fourth century bc.[75] The first passage he cites is Aristotle's advice that, as the *paideia* (education) of the body must proceed that of the mind (1338b2–8), '…it is necessary to hand boys (τοὺς παῖδας) to *gymnastikē* and *paidotribikē* for one gives a certain quality to the condition of the body, and the other to its actions'. Although Aristotle certainly breaks here with the common practice of calling physical education *gymnastikē* alone, this reference to two athletic disciplines need not be taken automatically as evidence for two different sets of athletics teachers. A few decades earlier Isokrates also wrote of *paidotribikē* and *gymnastikē* – the latter being presented as a sub-discipline (μέρος) of the former (15.181) – but went on to make both of these the sole responsibility of the *paidotribēs* (183–4). However, the second passage cited by Kyle puts beyond doubt that Aristotle did in fact know of two different types of athletics teacher. He writes (*Politics* 1288b10–22):

> In all of the arts and sciences that are not merely sectional but that in relation to some one class of subject are complete, it is the function of a single art or science to study what is suited to each class, for instance what sort of exercise (ἄσκησις) is beneficial for what sort of bodily frame, and what is the best sort…, and also what one exercise taken by all is the best for the largest number (for this is also a question for athletic science (τῆς γυμναστικῆς)), and in addition, in case someone desires a habit of the body and a knowledge of competition (τὴν ἀγωνίαν) that are not the ones adapted to him, it is clearly the task of the *paidotribēs* and the *gymnastikos* to produce this capacity also just as much; and we notice this also happening similarly in regard to medicine, and ship-building, and the making of clothes, and every other craft.[76]

Here *ho gymnastikos* is no synonym for *paidotribēs* but denotes a new type of athletics instructor. Significantly however, although it is unclear from these two passages what each of these sports teachers did exactly, they absolutely do *not* bear out the division of labour Kyle proposes between his *gymnastēs* and *paidotribēs*: Aristotle does not present either of his athletics instructors as subordinate to, or less expert than, the other, and gives both complementary roles in the education of boys without making one take over from the other. If these two Aristotelian passages are accepted as evidence for Athens and combined, not with sources written half a millennium later, as done by Kyle, but with the other above-mentioned contemporary references, we can conclude that at the end of the classical period, when *Politics* was written (e.g. 1311b2), some differentiation in the teaching personnel of physical education was taking place: the teaching and training of young athletes, which had once been the sole responsibility of the *paidotribēs*, was being divided up somehow between himself and a new kind of athletics teacher.

To summarize briefly, in classical Athens the necessary preparations for athletic competition, either at home or abroad, were *part of* the traditional normative education of Athenian boys and youths. According to the extant contemporary evidence, technical instruction in the standard events of athletic *agōnes* was, for most of the classical period, given only in the regular group classes of the *paidotribēs*, which were also the only *attested* opportunity for practising these sports. This manifestly close relationship between physical education and athletic competition suggests that historians of ancient sport – with their almost exclusive focus on sporting *agōnes* – give a rather one-sided account of ancient Greek athletics. As Plato spells out in what appears to be a descriptive rather than prescriptive passage of his *Laws* (764c–d), *gymnastikē* (athletics) consists of two parts: *paideia* (education) and *agōnia* (competition). Further, in terms of time spent and the number of participants, athletics in classical Athens would have been more of an *educational* rather than a festival-based activity. Therefore, the question of athletic participation turns out to be a part of the much broader issue of participation in the traditional education of boys and youths in classical Athens.

The 'old education': organization, aims and socio-economic barriers to full participation

Athletics of course was only one of the three disciplines of the normative and traditional education of *paides* (boys and youths) in classical Athens. The two other were *mousikē* (music) and *grammata* (letters), to which some contemporaries added somewhat controversially choral lessons in singing and dancing dithyrambs (Aiskhines 1.9–11; Aristophanes *Frogs* 727–30) or even drawing (Aristotle *Politics* 1337b22–7).[77] While athletics was taught by the *paidotribēs*, school classes in *mousikē* were the preserve of the *kitharistēs* (lyre teacher) who instructed his charges in how to play the *kithara* and to sing lyric poems they had learnt by heart (e.g. Aristophanes *Clouds* 962–72; Plato *Protagoras* 326a–b).[78] The final widely-accepted discipline of the 'old education' was overseen by the so-called *grammatistēs* or letter teacher.[79] He not only taught his students literacy and numeracy but also made them memorize and recite edifying passages of epic poetry, principally that of Homer.[80] Significantly, although the word *grammatistēs* – like other terms concerning Greek education – appears to have been coined only in the early years of the fourth century, evidence for the presence of this specialist teacher in Athens throughout the fifth century is provided by comedy and finely-painted pottery.[81] Aristophanes brings on stage in *Peace* a boy whose effortless recitation of half a dozen or so lines of Homer and a few others from an epic poem no longer extant points towards the drills of the letter teacher (1265–99; cf. *Assembly Women* 677–80).[82] Still more suggestive is a fragment of one of Aristophanes' first comedies that shows just such a teacher at work quizzing a pupil on the meaning of Homeric vocabulary (fr. 233 Austin and Kassel). Ceramic evidence indicates that the letter teacher was already active in Athens several decades before the birth of Aristophanes. From the turn of the fifth century, painted pots begin to sport school scenes, frequently including a teacher supervising a youth who either reads from a scroll or gives a recitation without reference to the scroll included in the image.[83] Furthermore, when the pottery painters actually include legible letters on these book rolls, invariably they form lines from the two works of Homer or other, non-extant epic poems. Again we have only to remember that the instruction of the young in this genre of poetry was one of the chief functions of the *grammatistēs*.

Schooling in classical Athens – in contrast to how it is organized today – was a private affair largely beyond the purview of the state. Although laws were passed, probably in the mid-fourth century, to regulate school hours, class sizes and the minimum age of pupils (Aiskhines 1.9–11), the political institutions of classical Athens did not license the *didaskaloi* (teachers) of the 'old education', determine the curricula for their lessons, or pay or subsidize their salaries.[84] It was instead the fathers or guardians of Athenian boys and youths who paid the tuition fees and made the decisions about what their *paides* should study, who were the good teachers of each subject, and for how long they could afford to keep them at school. Another important organizational aspect of education was that students pursuing its three disciplines undertook classes for each component concurrently.[85]

As a consequence, groups of pupils travelled from one *didaskaleion* (school room) to another throughout the day (e.g. Aristophanes *Clouds* 963–4), and would probably have spent no more than a few hours at the establishment of each teacher.[86]

The one and only goal of education to be noted by the extant literature of classical Athens was not – surprising as it is to our own increasingly utilitarian sensibilities – the acquisition of valuable skills such as reading and writing, sporting know-how and *kithara*-playing, but the turning of *paides* into *agathoi andres* or virtuous men.[87] Precise ways in which each of the three disciplines of traditional Athenian education contributed to this moral end are postulated by the sophist Protagoras in the Platonic dialogue bearing his name (325a–326c). The physical education of the *paidotribēs*, he suggests, guarantees that bodily weakness will not be the cause of a young man playing the coward on the battlefield (326b–c; cf. Aristotle *Politics* 1337b26–7).[88] Interestingly, Protagoras isolates the source of moral fortification provided by the lessons in *mousikē*, not in the content of lyric poetry, but in the practising of scales and rhythms on the *kithara* that helps foster in young men a gentleness of character and an effectiveness in word and deed (326a–b).[89] Nevertheless, the sophist's musings reveal that Athenian boys received the lion's share of their instruction in morality sitting at the school benches of the letter teacher (325e–326a):

> …when the boys understand their letters and are on the point of compre-hending the written word…the teachers set before them on the benches poems of good poets to read, and they are compelled to learn by rote these works, which contain many admonitions, and numerous descriptions, eulogies and commendations of virtuous men of long ago (παλαιῶν ἀνδρῶν ἀγαθῶν), so that the boy out of a sense of jealousy imitates them and yearns to be this sort of man himself.

When using such a dialogue there is always some concern that Plato might be presenting, not Athenian realities, but distortions in aid of his own, at times novel, theses, or minority viewpoints of either his predomi-nantly upper-class readers or even the dialogue's named interlocutors. Fortunately, these comments by Protagoras on poetry and education – like the earlier Platonic references to athletics – correspond closely with other works written for an elite audience as well as with the so-called popular literature of classical Athens. Texts of this second class, which includes comedy, tragedy and oratory, were originally performed for and adjudi-cated by vocal and predominantly non-elite audiences and hence reflect a point of view which we might call 'popular thinking'.[90] Such a wealth of correspondences suggests that Protagoras here is doing no more than articulating conventional thoughts on the role of poems in Athenian education. A variety of authors agree, for example, that boys learnt poetry by heart, especially passages of Homer (e.g. Aristophanes *Frogs* 1038–9; Xenophon *Symposium* 3.5–6), for education in moral behaviour (e.g. Aiskhines 3.135; Isokrates 1.51, 2.3; Plato *Laws* 810e–811a).[91] And, like Protagoras, Aristophanes makes the didactic content of Homeric poetry its gallant and morally upstanding heroes, when he has the dead Aiskhylos claim in *Frogs* (1040–2; cf. Isokrates 2.13): 'In imitation of him, my purpose was to represent in poetry the many excellences (πολλὰς ἀρετὰς) of Patrokloses, lion-hearted Teukroses in order to induce the citizen to become a rival of these men whenever he heard the trumpet of war.' Fifth- and fourth-century Athenians believed, then, that the rote learning and recall of poetry – overwhelmingly that of Homer – was the chief method for instructing boys and youths in morality. Within the three traditional branches of Athenian education these instructive passages of epic poetry were encountered and studied only in the lessons of the *grammatistēs*.

Classical Athenian writers appreciate that the number of disciplines of the 'old education' that could be undertaken by an individual boy and the length of his schooling were dependent on the monetary resources of his family. This inequality of opportunity is again nicely articulated by Protagoras who notes that the three branches of the 'old education' were pursued by those '…who are most able; and the most able are the wealthiest (οἱ πλουσιώτατοι). Their sons begin school at the earliest stage, and are freed from it at the latest' (Plato *Protagoras* 326c; cf. *Apology* 23c).[92] Xenophon too acknowledges how sufficient monetary resources determine educational opportunities (*On Hunting* 2.1); Aristotle at times presents *paideia* as one of the exclusive attributes of the upper class (*Politics* 1291b28–30, 1317b38–41); Aristophanes makes out that education beyond the three disciplines of the 'old education' is the preserve of *kaloi te k'agathoi* or upper-class gentlemen (*Clouds* 101, 797–8); and Pseudo-Xenophon – admittedly not the most reliable of ancient writers – holds that poverty causes non-elite Athenians to be ignorant and uneducated (1.5; cf. Aristophanes *Wasps* 1174–5, 1183).[93] Schooling, most obviously, had to be paid for entirely by the families of students. The sophists teaching oratory, with their course fees of hundreds, even thousands of drachmas (e.g. Aristophanes *Clouds* 876), were absolutely the most expensive teachers of classical Athens.[94] Nonetheless, fees for traditional strands of education could also be prohibitively expensive. For example, towards the end of the fourth century the *paidotribēs* Hippomakhos appears to have charged pupils one hundred drachmas for a series of regular physical education classes (Athenaios 584c).[95]

Another way – largely overlooked by historians of classical Greek society – in which a family's resources determined educational opportunities was the requirement for students to be free of other significant demands during the day so that they could pursue the three strands of the 'old education' that were taught concurrently. Crucially, this necessary free time was only guaranteed for the young males of the upper class. Most poor citizens were unable to afford sufficient or even any household slaves, as Aristotle explains (*Politics* 1323a5–7; cf. Herodotos 6.137), and so needed their children and wives to help out with the daily operation of family farming or business concerns.[96] Athenians themselves recognized that this reliance of poor families on child labour restricted markedly the capacity of their sons to be fully educated. To begin with, since Xenophon treats his *Kyroupaideia* less as an objective history of a Persian king and more as a 'vehicle for developing and discussing his own cherished ideas and interests', his hybrid work can actually be a valuable source for Greek social history.[97] Of particular interest is the *symposion* (drinking party) – manifestly contrived to air again the author's views of wealth and poverty – in which the Persian courtier Pheraulas says of his impoverished childhood that (8.3.37–9) '…my father, while working himself and raising me, made sure with some difficulty that I received the standard education of boys (τὴν…τῶν παίδων παιδείαν). But when I became an adolescent (μειράκιον), since he could not support an idle offspring, he led me to the fields and ordered me to work'.[98] This passage, in addition to bearing out the claim of Protagoras that familial resources determine the length of a child's study (Plato *Protagoras* 326c), gives a clear example of a young man's education being cut short by the need to assist his father on the farm.

The approving account by Isokrates of how the unruly tendencies of the young were curbed in the glory days of Solon and Kleisthenes also assumes that young Athenians go to work in lieu of educational pursuits (7.43–5). He states that their forebears '…used to turn to farming and commerce those with inferior resources… But they compelled those in possession of sufficient funds to while away time with horsemanship, athletic exercises (τὰ γυμνάσια), hunting and philosophy' (7.45). Admittedly, this mid-fourth-century tract is notorious for the historical fabrications Isokrates uses in trying to convince the Athenians that a restriction of their democracy would be no more than a return to the beneficial regime of their ancestors. Nevertheless, the dichotomy it draws between the different educational opportunities of those with and without wealth is probably not due to partisan excess and is, at worst, anachronistic; for similar distinctions are made in the popular literature of classical Athens. For instance, an early-fourth-century litigant claims that as a wealthy young man his father attended classes in the city, while an age mate, because of the poverty of his family, was forced to be a shepherd boy (Lysias 20.11–12). And in a passage that continues to offend the egalitarian and liberal sensibilities of *some* ancient historians, Demosthenes takes up the same opposition when belittling his longstanding opponent Aiskhines (18.256–67).[99] He outlines the details of his extensive educational pursuits and involvement in civic events as a privileged young Athenian in order to draw a stark contrast with the straitened circumstances of his political enemy's childhood. Scornfully he exclaims that the poverty of his family forced the young Aiskhines to perform in his father's letter school the menial chores normally undertaken by slaves (18.258–9; cf. 19.249).

Letters

Taking into account the general statements of ancient authors on the dependency of education on private wealth, contemporary historians of education and class structure in ancient Greece have argued that poor families would have sent their sons to only one of the three disciplines of the 'old education'. They maintain that poor boys were not educated in *gymnastikē* and *mousikē*, but were definitely sent to the school classes of the *grammatistēs* that were 'more strictly useful' for participation in the politics and commerce of the city.[100] The weakness of this rosy assessment of non-elite participation in letter schools is that it is based on the assumption that almost all citizens of a democracy like classical Athens had to know how to read and write. However, since the whole issue of literacy in ancient Greece has become 'wildly controversial' in recent years, this premise is no longer secure.[101] Therefore, determining which social classes of Athenians took lessons in letters requires a reconsideration of the evidence and arguments for literary levels in classical Athens.[102]

A common argument brought forward for universal literacy amongst classical Athenians is that this competency one way or another was a basic prerequisite for involvement in the democracy. In this vein the standard English-language handbook on Greek education suggests that the institution of ostracism 'presupposes the widespread knowledge of writing among the citizen body and therefore the existence of schools for its introduction'.[103] This commonplace presupposition has several problems.[104] Firstly, although the capacity to scratch out the name of another person shows some writing capacity, it does not demonstrate the highly developed ability to read and write fluently. Secondly, Athenians who lacked even this limited writing ability could still take part in these institutional expulsions. An illiterate could always ask an educated fellow to incise a potsherd for him (e.g. Plutarch *Aristeides* 7.5–6). Furthermore, David Phillips has demonstrated that while their exact motivations are unclear, *literate* craftsmen in fifth-century Athens produced for ostracisms batches of sherds with the names of those prominent citizens who were potential targets for expulsion.[105] Unlettered Athenians presumably took advantage of this supply of prepared *ostraka*.

Other scholars have posed the necessity of literacy for political participation in far more general terms. Indicative of this are comments by Josh Ober: 'In order to function as a citizen, and certainly in order to carry out the responsibilities of many of the magistracies, the Athenian citizen needed a basic command of letters.'[106] Certainly two small groups involved in the administration of classical Athens did need very high levels of literacy and numeracy. Athenian politicians were expected to possess a confident grasp of public finances that could only have been acquired by analyzing closely the detailed accounts of the city's many different financial boards.[107] Moreover, although fifth-century political leaders were loth to be discovered writing up and circulating their speeches, out of a fear of being labelled sophists (e.g. Plato *Phaidros* 257d–258e; Plutarch *Perikles* 8.5), they would as young men have attended the public speaking lessons of these selfsame teachers which would have involved the study of rhetorical handbooks and the writing of compositional exercises.[108] Aspirants to leadership positions needed, then, to be highly literate and numerate. Consequently, upper-class parents, eager for their sons to be famous leaders one day, would have ensured their boys received schooling in these skills at the hands of the *grammatistēs*. The second small group manifestly able to read and write fluently were the non-elite functionaries of the democracy. These secretaries and heralds of individual magistrates, magisterial boards and the city's deliberative and legal organs were required to keep written records and accounts and to read aloud documents and proclamations (e.g. Demosthenes 19.249).[109]

Private lower-class Athenians would have perceived literacy and numeracy to be useful for taking part in the public affairs of the city. A hoplite or naval petty officer, for instance, would have found it more convenient to search himself for his name on a posted list of conscripts than to rely on another person's reading ability.[110] And a minor financial magistrate would have been far more relaxed and comfortable during his scrutiny at the end of his term of office if he was able to consult his financial accounts without the mediation of a secretary.[111] However, while these skills were undoubtedly seen by ordinary Athenians as attractive and useful for participating in civic life, they were in no way a precondition for participating in the major deliberative and judicial organs of the democracy.[112] These competencies were simply not necessary for passive participation in the law courts, the council of Five Hundred and the assembly. The debates of these institutions were conducted orally, and documents and testimonies relevant to them were read out by secretaries (e.g. *Ath. Pol.* 54.5; Isaios 5.2).

Importantly too, the existence of publicly-displayed inscriptions recording decisions taken at council and assembly meetings cannot be taken as evidence that the citizen masses demanded written records so that they could read them at their leisure. Taking as a guide the ways in which speakers of the first half of the fourth century used such records, inscriptions would appear to have been produced for very different reasons.[113] Citizens saw them, not as texts to be read, but as physical memorials commemorating a new law, treaty, or the granting of individual honours, and as concrete emblems of the democratic ideals of accountability, open government and legal equality. The existence of public inscriptions in classical Athens, then, does not in itself constitute evidence for widespread literacy. Finally, the decisions of the council and assembly, along with the instructions of the city's chief magistrates, were made known orally through the proclamations of heralds (e.g. *Ath. Pol.* 62.2).[114] Therefore, lower-class Athenians did not need to be literate and numerate to play various parts in the public affairs of the city. The operation of the Athenian democracy did not require universal literacy.

Support for the view that every Athenian was literate has also been sought in several classical texts said to demonstrate that the minimum level of educational attainment amongst the citizens of classical Athens was reading and writing.[115] The first of two ancient passages allowing such an interpretation comes from the *Laws* of Plato (689d).[116] In a statement on the necessity for people to harmonize their emotions and reasoning capacity, the Athenian interlocutor of this dialogue suggests that only those achieving this will be judged wise in his ideal state, '…even if, as the saying goes, they know neither letters nor how to swim (ἂν καὶ τὸ λεγόμενον μήτε γράμματα μήτε νεῖν ἐπίστωνται)'. Taking this as a popular saying about the profoundly ignorant, proponents of universal literacy believe it to show how not being able to read and write was considered very strange by the Athenians. A similar conclusion is also drawn from the opening scene of *Knights* by Aristophanes. In response to the unlikely suggestion that he is destined to be a political leader, the sausage seller objects (188–9): '…my good fellow I do not even know music, except letters, and these I actually do very badly (ἀλλ᾽, ὦγάθ᾽, οὐδὲ μουσικὴν ἐπίσταμαι πλὴν γραμμάτων, καὶ ταῦτα μέντοι κακὰ κακῶς).' Throughout this comedy Aristophanes characterizes the sausage seller, not as an average citizen, but as someone from an extremely deprived and criminal background.[117] Therefore, it is argued, if an impoverished and marginal character could read and write, the vast majority of Athenians, being as they were much better off, must have been able to do so as well.

A problem with the common way in which these two passages have

313

been interpreted is the assumption that *epistasthai grammata* (to know one's letters) denotes nothing less than the capacity to read and write with ease.[118] Such an assumption pays too scant regard to the fact that very different types of literacy exist.[119] Literacy covers a wide range of skills from the ability to sign one's own name and the sounding out of words syllable by syllable to the highly developed capacity to read and write without conscious effort.[120] At first glance it seems impossible to be sure where to locate the phrase *epistasthai grammata* along this spectrum of literacy levels. Fortunately, however, two other passages from the same authors prove to be valuable for delimiting what 'knowing letters' actually involves. Protagoras in the Platonic dialogue bearing his name succinctly outlines how *grammatistai* teach students to read (325e–326a; cf. *Statesman* 277e–278c): '...when the pupils understand letters and are on the point of comprehending the written word (ἐπειδὰν αὖ γράμματα μάθωσι καὶ μέλλωσι συνήσειν τὰ γεγραμμένα), just as when they are about to understand the spoken word, the teachers set before them on the benches poems of good poets to read (ἀναγιγνώσκειν)...'. What is striking here is the sharp distinction between learning and understanding the alphabet (μανθάνειν γράμματα) and the act of reading itself (συνιέναι τὰ γεγραμμένα, ἀναγιγνώσκειν). Crucially, since *manthanein* (to learn/understand) is very close, semantically speaking, to *epistasthai* (to know/understand), it follows that the phrase *epistasthai grammata*, like *manthanein grammata*, refers to a pre-reading familiarity with the alphabet. This inference seems to be backed up by a fuller consideration of the educational attainment of Aristophanes' sausage seller. Towards the end of *Knights* an exchange between Paphlagon and the sausage seller makes plain the latter's complete lack of schooling (1235–8):

> PAPHLAGON: When you were a boy the establishment of which teacher (εἰς τίνος διδασκάλου) did you attend?
> SAUSAGE SELLER: I was trained with knuckles in the swine singeing yards.
> PAPHLAGON: At the school of the athletics teacher (ἐν παιδοτρίβου) what wrestling technique did you learn?
> SAUSAGE SELLER: How to swear falsely and to steal while saying the opposite.

Since the generic term *didaskalos* can describe a lyre teacher just as easily as a letter teacher, these witty responses of the sausage seller suggest that he lacked schooling, not just in athletics, but in *mousikē* and *grammata* as well.[121] It is hard to imagine that any Athenian – not to mention an impoverished seller of small goods – could have acquired any competency in reading and writing without formal schooling.[122] Therefore, the earlier mention of 'knowing letters' by the sausage seller (188–9) cannot denote any reading ability, and indicates rather some sort of pre-reading knowledge of the alphabet. Therefore, in view of what the phrase *epistasthai grammata* most probably means, scholars appear to have been mistaken to present Plato *Laws* 689d and Aristophanes *Knights* 188–9 as good evidence for near universal literacy in classical Athens.

It is left to archaeology to provide the decisive evidence that literacy was not confined to upper-class Athenians. Small finds from the American excavation of the Athenian *agora* as well as finely-painted pots from Attic workshops suggest that many of the lower-class residents of Athens – in addition to the functionaries of the democracy – were reasonably literate and numerate. This in turn points to the classrooms of the letter teacher being filled also with the offspring of lower-class Athenians. The *agora* excavators have unearthed and inventoried over three thousand sherds of pottery with incised or painted texts, ranging in date from the early archaic period until the eighth century AD.[123] More than eight hundred of these pieces whose preserved texts are long enough to determine their original functions have been catalogued by Mabel Lang. Far and away the largest group in this selective catalogue are proprietary marks for pottery vessels.[124] Admittedly, sixty per cent of these marks do not demonstrate any significant level of literacy: they are no more than an abbreviated name or a complete name in the nominative case.[125] Nonetheless, over twenty per cent have names in the genitive or dative cases, and more than six per cent consist of short sentences.[126] Classical period examples of the latter consist of εἰμί (I am/belong to) plus the owner's name in the genitive case to which is often added the adverb δικαιῶς (rightly).[127] These simple sentences, and probably also the names in oblique cases, demonstrate a level of writing skill on the part of their composers that is higher than a simple knowledge of the alphabet or an ability to write one's own name. However, although the significant number of proprietary marks in itself points to a widespread capacity to write a personal name, the archaeological context of nearly every piece is too ambiguous or not sufficiently documented to determine the background of the individual who incised it. As a result, it is not possible to say in which section(s) of the Attic population this writing skill predominated. Nevertheless, enough is known of the taphonomy of two classical pots with proprietary marks to prove that name-signing literacy did exist amongst the city's craftsmen. A black glaze cup base of the second quarter of the fifth century, bearing the name Simon in the genitive case, most probably came from the workshop and home of a cobbler;[128] and the base of a fourth-century black glaze *kantharos* (drinking cup) found in the house of a family of marble workers was incised with the name Menon.[129]

In contrast to the situation with proprietary marks, the functions of several other types of marks in Lang's catalogue point to the socio-economic identity of those who made them. The largest group providing this valuable information are the records of capacity, tare, date, and contents originally placed on ceramic containers.[130] Of these it is perhaps the capacity marks which exemplify most clearly the variations possible in this class of 'commercial notations'.[131] Amongst capacity indications of the classical period, the simplest consists of tally marks alone.[132] More sophisticated texts display the first letter of the name of a standard measure followed by tally marks or numerals.[133] The most complex of capacity notations have complete words. For example, one fifth-century black glaze *olpē* has μηέτριο, which seems to be a misspelling of μέτριον that denotes a middle-sized measuring vessel, and a partially glazed juglet predictably bears the name χôς.[134] Other types of classical Athenian commercial notations also have full words and even phrases. Two amphorae, for instance, discovered in the Athenian marketplace record dates by means of the preposition ἐπί followed by the names in the genitive case of late–fourth-century eponymous archons of the city.[135] And a fifth-century wine amphora bears the painted label ὄχσος meaning ordinary wine.[136] Furthermore, several other pieces classified by Lang as 'numerical notations' are of a commercial nature as well.[137] Most notable amongst the pieces from the classical period is a tag recording the batch size of some ceramic product: it gives the word κεράμος and numerals.[138] Most of these commercial texts from the Athenian marketplace indicate reasonably high levels of literacy and numeracy on the part of those inscribing or painting them. Critically, as Athenian gentlemen abhorred direct contact with selling and the trades, these jottings were the work of non-elite craftsmen and retailers alone, and thus prove such levels of literacy and numeracy existed far below the city's upper class. Moreover, the obvious utility of these skills in the world of Attic business was no doubt a powerful motivation for those lower-class citizens who were businessmen to send their sons to the lessons of the letter teacher (Aristotle *Politics* 1338a15–19).

Other material evidence also points to the literacy of a good number of classical Athenian craftsmen. In the so-called house of Mikion and Menon there was discovered in a fifth-century floor level a bone stylus with the inscription ὁ Μικίον ἐποίεσε (Mikion made (me)).[139] Whether or not this tool was made by a marble worker living in this abode, its inscribed sentence points again to a reasonably high level of writing dexterity on the part of its maker. Certainly some painters of black- and red-figure pots of the archaic and classical periods possessed no more than a pre-reading knowledge of the alphabet as they could include only 'gibberish' words and phrases in their paintings.[140] Others though had more advanced writing skills. Many were literate enough to include the names of characters in mythological scenes, or to place an inscription that a particular boy is beautiful next to the image of a comely figure.[141] Other Attic vessels reveal still higher writing competencies on the part of their painters. Around one per cent of them have inscriptions recording that such and such a person painted the scene (ἔγραφσεν) and another manufactured (ἐποίεσεν) the pot.[142] More impressive are some of the letter school scenes on Greek red-figure pots with book scrolls bearing actual lines of Homer or other, non-extant, epic poetry.[143]

Material evidence from classical Athens confirms, then, that many lower-class citizens had quite high levels of literacy and numeracy and so must have as children attended the classes of the *grammatistēs*. In tune with this finding, it turns out on closer inspection that the participation of boys in the lessons of the letter teacher would not have been prohibitively expensive for poor parents, nor interfered terribly with their farming or business concerns. The tuition fees for each student at an Athenian letter school were probably set at the same very low level as they were in other Greek cities. References to such establishments outside Athens indicate that the daily wage of the letter teacher was no more than that of a skilled labourer (cf. Demosthenes 19.249) and that school classes were extremely large, including anything from sixty to one hundred and twenty boys (e.g. Herodotos 6.27; Pausanias 6.9.6).[144] In such circumstances, each pupil needed only to pay a small tuition fee (Theophrastos *Characters* 30.14). Moreover, the frequent absence of a son at a letter school would not necessarily have damaged the family's agrarian or business interests excessively; for, as classes in each discipline of the 'old education' lasted no more than a few hours, lower-class boys who only attended the classes of the *grammatistēs* had plenty of time out of school when they could help secure the livelihood of their families.[145]

It is striking that the complex poetry of Homer was introduced to Athenian boys very early in the course of their studies at the letter school. As we have already noted, the description of the 'old education' by Protagoras details how pupils received copies of epic poetry to read and memorize when they had just mastered the alphabet and were about to begin to read (Plato *Protagoras* 325e–326a). While it might seem extraordinary to modern educators that ancient Athenian teachers handed such complex texts to, at best, early readers, we need to bear in mind that these pupils were employing copies of Homer as a mnemonic device, and consequently only required a type of literacy that was far less advanced than fluent reading and writing. These tentative readers needed only the less advanced skill of 'phonetic literacy' which allowed them to 'decode texts syllable by syllable and pronounce them orally' in order to memorize passages of Homer.[146] Letter school students seem, then, not to have been made to complete the time-consuming tasks of learning to read and write fluently before being introduced to Homeric poetry. Consequently, even a pupil whose family's difficult economic circumstances prevented him completing his studies with the letter teacher would have been assured of encountering passages of Homer. This certainty of learning by heart stories of the heroes would have been another major motivation for Athenian fathers to send male offspring to the classes of the *grammatistēs*. Indeed, for those humble Athenians not associated with the trades, selling, or state administration it might be classified as the only motivation. After all, the solitary goal of education in the extant literature of classical Athens was the moral improvement of young males, and the chief means to achieve this was universally understood to be the memorization and recall of Homeric poetry. Therefore, their certain and extended introduction of boys to the poetry of Homer made the letter school appear to non-elite fathers, worried as they apparently were about the waywardness of contemporary youth, the surest and easiest of ways to guarantee the rectitude of their sons. We can say with some certainty, then, that the classes of the *grammatistēs* did contain good numbers of Athenian boys from upper- *and* lower-class backgrounds.

Athletics and music

The substantial participation of non-elite citizens in the lessons of the letter teacher means that education in this discipline of the 'old education' of classical Athens can be described as 'democratic'. Fisher of course makes a detailed case for the same level of lower-class involvement in the athletic competitions of classical Athens, while Young argues more generally for the existence of good numbers of lower-class athletes in ancient Greece. For classical Athens at least such an assessment presupposes that lower-class families also sent their sons to the classes of the athletics teacher which alone provided the technical training and practice required for satisfactory performance, not to mention victory, in athletic competitions. This supposed education of non-elite boys in athletics is very unlikely. In view of the recognized difficulties poor Athenians faced in educating their sons fully, it is doubtful that any number at all could have afforded to send their boys to the school classes of the letter teacher *and* the athletics teacher. Nor is it likely that they would have had their sons give up the practical and moral lessons of the *grammatistēs* for those of the *paidotribēs*. These doubts are confirmed by what literary evidence there is which suggests that schooling in *gymnastikē* and *mousikē*, participation in sports contests, and even knowledge of athletics and music were predominantly – or even exclusively – the preserve of upper-class Athenians.[147] Aristophanes, for example, makes physical education and *mousikē* a part of the normal education of well-born and upper-class Athenians in the famous *parabasis* of *Frogs* when he draws an analogy between the city's debasement of its coinage and its current embrace of scallywags as political leaders (718–37). In particular the chorus complain (727–33; cf. *Knights* 180–3):

> τῶν πολιτῶν θ᾽ οὓς μὲν ἴσμεν εὐγενεῖς καὶ σώφρονας
> ἄνδρας ὄντας καὶ δικαίους καὶ καλούς τε κἀγαθοὺς
> καὶ τραφέντας ἐν παλαίστραις καὶ χοροῖς καὶ μουσικῇ,
> προυσελοῦμεν, τοῖς δὲ χαλκοῖς καὶ ξένοις καὶ πυρρίαις
> καὶ πονηροῖς κἀκ πονηρῶν εἰς ἅπαντα χρώμεθα
> ὑστάτοις ἀφιγμένοισιν, οἷσιν ἡ πόλις πρὸ τοῦ
> οὐδὲ φαρμακοῖσιν εἰκῆ ῥᾳδίως ἐχρήσατ᾽ ἄν.

Of the citizens those we know to be well-born, moderate and just gentlemen who have been raised in wrestling schools, choruses and music we maltreat. We employ instead the copper coins that are foreigners, red-headed (Thracian slaves), wicked men sprung from men wicked in everything, whom the city formerly would not even have willingly used as scapegoats.

This complaint of course is quite baseless, as the Athenian masses believed consistently throughout the classical period that politicians had to be wealthy and well-educated if they were to advise and protect the city effectively (e.g. Aristophanes *Knights* 147–224; Lysias 16.20–1; Demosthenes 18.256–67).[148] The sort of unwarranted abuse and slander of the Athenian people we have in this *parabasis* seems to have been just what comic audiences expected and found very funny.[149] Despite appearances, these lines, then, evidence not political change but continuity in Athenian expectations about their political leaders and – by extension – the popular 'prejudice' or 'sentiment' that 'sport, like music, is the preserve of the upper classes'.[150] Strikingly, words almost identical to those of this comedy were used by Euripides, in a tragedy he wrote a decade earlier, to characterize athletics as a typically upper-class activity: the eponymous heroine of his *Elektra* describes a lock of her brother's hair as 'something raised in the wrestling school of the well-born man' (ὁ μὲν παλαίστραις ἀνδρὸς εὐγενοῦς τραφείς – 528).

Aristophanes couples music and especially athletics with the upper class much more tightly in one of the closing scenes of *Wasps* where a wealthy son, Bdelykleon, must struggle with his father, an unexpectedly poor man, to get him ready for an elite *symposion* (1122–264).[151] Bdelykleon at first battles with Philokleon to get him to exchange his *embades* (felt slippers) and *tribōn* (coarse cloak), which are the standard attire of lower-class citizens, for imported shoes and gown and to ape 'the walk of the wealthy' (1122–73).[152] Next he asks his old man whether he knows any 'posh stories' (λόγους σεμνοὺς) suitable for relating to 'well-educated and clever men' (ἀνδρῶν...πολυμαθῶν καὶ δεξιῶν – 1174–5). He learns very quickly that his father has no such anecdotes 'befitting a great man' (μεγαλοπρεπεῖς) and so suggests that he speak perhaps of an embassy in which he might have participated (1183–7). However, as only wealthy citizens with their overseas guest friends were able to be ambassadors (e.g. *Akharnians* 607–11; *Birds* 1570–1; Demosthenes 19.237–8), the best Philokleon can do is point to his rowing on an expedition to Paros (*Wasps* 1188–9). Instead of this, Bdelykleon encourages his father to talk about a famous 'heavy' athlete (1190–4; cf. Plato *Republic* 422b–c): '...you need to say for example that although he was grey and old, Ephoudion continued to fight well in the *pankration* with his very strong sides, hands and flank and his very fine trunk (θώρακ᾽ ἄριστον).' Philokleon, at this point, interrupts his son's extemporizing (1194–5): 'Stop! Stop! You're speaking nonsense. How could he fight in the *pankration* wearing a suit of armour (θώρακ᾽ ἔχων)?' The confusion here of two meanings of *thōrax* reveals Philokleon's unfamiliarity with what North Americans call 'jock talk' and points to his having spent no time as a boy with a *paidotribēs* or in athletic competition.[153]

Somehow undeterred, Bdelykleon instructs his father that he will need to relate 'a very manly exploit of his youth' (1197–9), and, in response to his father's inability even to do this (1200–1), suggests that he talk about '...how once you chased a wild boar or a hare, or you ran a torch race, after you have worked out your most dashing youthful exploit' (1202–5). Again his father's experience of such things seems unlikely. Hunting, for instance, was clearly an exclusively upper-class pursuit (e.g. Xenophon *On Hunting* 2.1; 12.1–13.18; Menander *Dyskolos* 39–44). It is a surprise, then, to find him relating what seems an anecdote about competitive athletics before, that is, we realize he is talking about something quite different (1205–7): '...well I certainly know the most impetuous and youthful deed of early years: while still a boy, the runner Phaullos I overtook (εἷλον), pursuing (διώκων) him for slander, by two votes'. The humour of this passage relies on another unusually innocent Aristophanic *double entendre*: *aireō* (aorist form, εἷλον) and *diōkō* can be employed in discussions of athletics and legal actions. Therefore, while Philokleon seems, with his talk of the runner Phaullos, to be relating a sporting exploit of his younger days, his last three words dash this impression: this long-time addict of the jury courts has been reminiscing about a legal prosecution all along. The old juror's lack of athletic nous receives another airing when, despite the demonstrations of his son, he makes a botch of reclining on a symposium couch *gymnastikōs* or athletically (1208–13). The final instructions of Bdelykleon also come to nought as his father founders badly in the singing of poetry that he will be called on to give as part of the evening's entertainment (1224–47). Since the singing of such drinking poems demanded a high level of musical and literary expertise that could only be acquired in the lessons of the lyre teacher, Philokleon's lack of dexterity here strongly suggests that he had not studied this discipline of the 'old education' either.[154]

What Aristophanes does in this scene is pair expertise in music and especially athletics with activities such as hunting and diplomatic service that we know to have been exclusively upper-class pursuits. Isokrates of course makes the same connection in his *Areopagiticus* when claiming that in the age of Solon and Kleisthenes well-off youths practised 'athletic exercises', hunting, horsemanship and – quite anachronistically – philosophy (7.45; cf. Menander *Men at Arbitration* 320–5).[155] But Aristophanes also goes further than Isokrates in that he explicitly denies experience and expertise in athletics to his 'Athenian Everyman' – Philokleon – and makes them instead the preserve of upper-class gentlemen.[156]

The fourth-century politician Aiskhines also couples athletics with exclusively upper-class activities and presents the undertaking of them by his relatives as proof of their elite credentials when he defends himself in court against the charge of treason brought by his political enemy Demosthenes.[157] In his prosecution speech Demosthenes had made a big issue out of the supposedly humble family background of Aiskhines by highlighting repeatedly how his father had been an impoverished *grammatistēs* (19.249) and how he and his brothers had worked as minor secretaries or even a painter of tambourines and boxes, before their elevation to positions of political and military leadership (19.237–8, 249, 287). Aiskhines responds directly to these comments, not just because he was 'sensitive to such slurs', but as they would have provided plausibility to the main charge against him that as an ambassador he had taken bribes from Philip of Macedon (e.g. Demosthenes 19.127, 248, 313, 343). Non-elite Athenians, from whose ranks jurors were predominantly drawn, believed that poor political leaders were especially susceptible to bribes and that newly rich politicians had most probably gained their social elevation by taking such tainted payments.[158] While never explicitly denying that he and his brothers were self-made, Aiskhines skilfully implies that his family is, and had been, upper class. His father, he explains, had actually been an athletic competitor (ἀθλεῖν τῷ σώματι), before the Peloponnesian War destroyed his property, and was linked with the *genos* or aristocratic clan of the Eteoboutadai (2.147). His eldest brother, Aiskhines continues, is not a man of 'ill-born pastimes' (ἀγεννεῖς διατριβάς), as Demosthenes slanderously suggests, but spends time at the athletics field (ἐν γυμνασίοις διατρίβων) and has been a general now for three years, whereas his youngest brother has been an ambassador to the king of Persia (2.149). Finally, Aiskhines reinforces his own claim to elite membership by dropping in here, just as in other speeches, athletic metaphors and details (e.g. 1.10, 26, 33; 2.183; 3.179–80, 206, 246). As Ober explains, 'Apparently he hoped to be perceived as the sort of man who spent a good deal of time in gymnasia and so naturally used athletic turns of phrase.'[159]

Contemporary sources, then, strongly suggest that athletics in classical Athens, both in school and at *agōnes*, was an upper-class activity on a par with, for example, hunting and horsemanship. In addition, as these sources are – with the exception of Isokrates – examples of popular literature, they attest both a reality of sporting participation and the popular beliefs that athletics was pursued exclusively by the wealthy and that experience and expertise in it were proof of membership of this class. Although historians of ancient sport have not done so, such widely-held perceptions really do need to be factored into any investigation of athletic participation. The need for this, when analyzing *modern* sporting choices, was well established by Pierre Bourdieu in his classic study of sport and class in 1970s France. What Bourdieu shows, with respect to 'the most distinctive sports, such as golf, riding, skiing or tennis', is that 'variations in economic and cultural capital or spare time' only ever provide a partial explanation why different classes or 'class fractions' take up or ignore different leisure pursuits.[160] For there are always 'hidden entry requirements, such as family tradition and early training, and also the obligatory clothing, bearing and techniques of sociability' that help to keep such sports closed to the working and middle classes. More important still for Bourdieu is that 'economic constraints' only ever determine 'the field of possibilities and impossibilities' for the members of different classes and not their 'positive orientation towards this or that practice'. Instead, inclinations and disinclinations towards this or that sport rest on how each class calculates the sport's 'immediate' and 'social' profits.[161]

For most of the non-elite families of classical Athens calculating the profits of physical education for their sons would have been entirely superfluous, since economics alone would have put athletics out of reach. However, there would have been undoubtedly a small percentage of families, sitting just below the elite, whose better financial circumstances could have allowed them to send their sons to the lessons of the *paidotribēs*. Never-theless, although this may have been a possibility, we should not assume automatically that such families had a positive orientation to having their sons be athletes. We must ask instead whether non-elite Athenians judged athletics to be something, on balance, which was profitable to pursue. This question – I believe – must be answered in the negative. Although lower-class Athenians did indeed think athletics helped turn youngsters into *agathoi andres* and – as we shall see – esteemed athletic victory highly, the popular perception of athletics as the preserve of gentlemen would have most probably made it a risky proposition for non-elite citizens.

Poor Athenians may have longed one day to be rich (e.g. Aristophanes *Birds* 592; *Wealth* 133–4; *Thesmophoriazousai* 289–90; *Wasps* 708–11) – and small numbers of them actually did become so year in, year out throughout the classical period – but they were aware too of the disadvantages of being wealthy in the democracy.[162] It was elite citizens, after all, who were obliged to undertake trierarchies (e.g. *Frogs* 1066–7) and other expensive public services (e.g. *Lysistrata* 652–4; Demosthenes 21.151, 208) and to pay the *eisphora* or extraordinary war tax (e.g. Aristophanes *Knights* 923–6; Lysias 22.13; 27.9–10).[163] Moreover, in popular thinking wealthy citizens were associated with a range of highly objectionable attitudes and actions. Non-elite Athenians considered them to be, for example, prone to commit *hybris*, that is, the violent or verbal assault of another citizen, and suspected them of hating the *dēmos*, plotting to overthrow the democracy, and conspiring with the city's external enemies.[164] Finally, wealthy individuals were frequently criticized for squandering their patrimonies on dissolute activities such as whoring, dicing, drinking and fish eating rather than using their wealth to perform vital public services.[165] Critically, 'Despite the importance of the contribution the rich made to the state, the state did very little to assess accurately or even record who owned what.'[166] Rather, being identified as rich, and hence liable for liturgies and war taxes, was a matter of perception: a citizen was a rich man as he and his family did the things the rich normally do.[167]

It was this subjective identification of elite citizens that would have most probably made athletics unattractive to an economically comfortable but non-elite family. Because it was considered proof of elite membership, for a non-elite father the danger of sending a son to a *paidotribēs* was that he would be marking himself out as an elite citizen, regardless of his actual financial resources or his own perception of his class position. As a result, he could be pressed into being a liturgist or payer of *eisphora* and would begin to be suspected of the stereotypical crimes and misdemeanours of the upper class by his lower-class relatives and (one-time) friends (e.g. Aristophanes *Wealth* 335–85). These negative implications would no doubt have dissuaded lower-class families from having their sons learn or compete in athletics and hence would have made athletics not a predominantly but an *exclusively* upper-class activity in classical Athens. Athletics, then, was not pursued by boys and youths on their way up to elite status, but was consciously taken up by those who wanted to show that they and their families had arrived at the top.

These inferences seem to be corroborated by Kyle's catalogue of the known athletes and equestrian victors in archaic and classical Athens, even though he himself holds that 'most' but 'not all' athletes 'came from well-off families'.[168] His catalogue of 78 Athenians provides no secure example of a non-elite sportsman: although the class position of 28 entries cannot be determined, because of inadequate biographical data, the remaining 50 are identifiable by one factor or another as upper-class residents of Athens.[169] Importantly though, Kyle also documents how members of the *nouveau riche* families of fifth- and fourth-century Athens quickly took up athletics or horsemanship and so concludes that athletics seems 'to follow rather than precede the social advancement of families'.[170]

My view of classical Athenian athletics as an exclusively upper-class pursuit is very much at odds with the recently published position of Fisher that participation in sports contests reached down to, and included, not just non-elite hoplites but even *thētes* or citizens of sub-hoplite status.[171] As Fisher crafts a detailed case for this extraordinary level of athletic participation and enjoys a deservedly high reputation as an ancient historian, it would be unsporting of me – and certainly undermining of my own argument – to pass over his interpretation without a few comments. I shall spell out what I see as the main problems with his three pieces of evidence and the two ways he proposes in which a poor but athletically talented boy could have launched a sporting career.

Fisher argues that two passages from Pseudo-Xenophon's *Constitution of the Athenians* are reliable evidence for 'widespread participation' in competitive athletics and 'a growth of new *gymnasia* and *palaistrai* aimed at a much wider clientele'.[172] Certainly Pseudo-Xenophon does make accurate comments from time to time on realities of imperial Athens. Frequently however, as many a commentator has remarked, his anti-democratic partisanship and class prejudice cause him to exaggerate and even misrepresent Athenian democracy and society.[173] The two passages Fisher cites are good examples of this falsifying modus operandi. Admittedly, what this author writes at 2.10 does appear, at first glance, to evidence a democratization of athletics: while the wealthy might have private 'athletics fields' (γυμνάσια), the people have built for their own enjoyment 'many wrestling schools'. But it finds no corroboration in other classical sources which consistently present the *gymnasion* as a public facility and the stand-alone *palaistra* as a venue – while open to the public – that was privately owned by individual athletics teachers.[174] Moreover, this suggestion directly contradicts what

Pseudo-Xenophon asserts at 1.13: 'Those practising athletics and music there (τοὺς δὲ γυμναζομένους αὐτόθι καὶ τὴν μουσικὴν ἐπιτηδεύοντας) the people have destroyed, as they do not believe this is a good thing and know themselves to be unable to practise these things.' This second passage also misrepresents what the Athenian *dēmos* thought about those of their fellow citizens who were sportsmen. From the 430s onwards they awarded *sitēsis* (free meals) and probably also *proedria* (front row seats in the theatre) *for life* to those citizens who had won at the Olympic, Pythian, Nemean or Isthmian games (*IG* I³ 131.12–18; Plato *Apology* 36d–e; Demosthenes 20.141).[175] Since these were amongst the democracy's most valuable public honours, their granting to athletic victors points, not to any negative assessment of athletes by the Athenian people, but to their extraordinarily high estimation of sportsmen and especially sporting victors. This positive popular assessment seems operative as well in old comedy where the city's athletes are the only group to escape almost entirely comic ridicule: thus while non-elite audiences revelled in the comedian's abuse and slander of the city's leaders, poets and otherwise prominent citizens, and even allowed comic mockery of their own political capacities, they did not encourage their comedians to mock athletes.[176] In view of these misrepresentations and contradictions Pseudo-Xenophon cannot be taken as a reliable source for classical Athenian athletics.

Another text Fisher presents as proof for substantial non-elite participation in the athletic competition of classical Athens is a fragment of the satyr play *First Autolykos*, quoted by Athenaios (413c–f; fr. 441 N²), in which Euripides launches a broadside against the 'race of athletes' (ἀθλητῶν γένους – 2). Fisher homes in on lines 3 to 7 of the fragment:

> In the first place, they are incapable of living, or of learning to live, properly. How can a man who is a slave to his jaws and a servant to his belly acquire more prosperity (ὄλβον) than his father? Moreover, they are not capable of working for a living and adapting themselves to their fortunes (οὐδ᾽ αὖ πένεσθαι καὶ ξυνηρετεῖν τύχαις οἷοί τε). Since they have not formed good habits, they face problems with difficulty.[177]

'Such a line of argument', Fisher suggests, 'seems to assume that some serious athletes went into the game expecting to get richer, and found it hard to cope with their winnings, or still harder to cope with relative failure.'[178] Thus the text assumes that '…Panhellenic athletics could be perceived as a major source of new wealth and social mobility'. There are two significant problems here. Firstly, it is hard to follow how the charge that athletes as a class are incapable of increasing family wealth, doing an honest day's work or coping with changed circumstances can be taken as evidence for the expectation of *some* athletes that sport brings wealth or the perception that the games of the *periodos* can do the same. These surely are assertions going beyond what the passage allows. These lines can also be understood quite differently. In classical Athens it was of course the wealthy that were thought to be free of the necessity to work and to be prone to whittling away their patrimonies on dissolute activites. Interestingly too, a rich man's volunteering to work could be a matter of praise (Menander *Dyskolos* 766–9) and taken as proof of his capacity to 'bear changes of fortune' (μεταβολὰς...τύχης).[179] In this passage, then, Euripides could simply be associating athletes with stereotypical misdemeanors of wealthy citizens.

Secondly, I am not as certain as Fisher that these lines reflect athletic realities or even perceptions of them in classical Athens. That Euripides presents criticisms of athletes, when the otherwise censorious poets of old comedy do not, alone should raise doubts about the fragment's value as evidence. These doubts are confirmed by the lines Fisher does not cite. Since classical Athenians esteemed athletics highly and lavished money and attention on their own sporting competitions (e.g. *Ath. Pol.* 60.1–3; Demosthenes 4.36; *IG* II² 2311), few in the theatre of Dionysos would have agreed with the fragment's opening complaint that 'Of the thousands of evils which exist in Greece there is no greater evil than the race of athletes' (1–2), or with its assessment of games as 'useless pleasures' which are only an excuse for a feast (13–15). Nor would the audience have accepted the next gripe about athletics: it does nothing to make men good warriors (16–23; cf. Tyrtaios fr. 12.1–2, 10–14 Edmonds). To the contrary, classical Athenians believed physical education gave young men the bodily strength they needed to be brave on the battlefield, and from the mid-330s onwards appointed two traditional athletics teachers to help train young citizens for military service (*Ath. Pol.* 42.3). In the last lines of this fragment Euripides gives the indignant advice, made first by the sixth-century philosopher Xenophanes (fr. 2 Diels; cf. Athenaios 413f) and often heard today amongst the chattering classes of sports-mad Australia, that intellectuals, because of their very critical contributions to the community, are much more deserving of the awards cities give sporting victors (23–8).[180] This too would have fallen on deaf ears. Sokrates after all gave similar advice at his trial (Plato *Apology* 36d–e). The Athenians neither took it up nor spared his life. While we know close to nothing about the dramatic context of this fragment, its sustained contrariness does point to a speech – like those regularly found in the tragedies of Euripides – in which a character presents material that appears to be deliberately contrived to confound popular thinking on a subject.[181]

The last of the texts Fisher presents as evidence of a 'consciousness of increased non-elite athletic activity' in classical Athens is the hotly debated passage of Isokrates 16 where the son of the late Alkibiades discusses his father's actions at the Olympic Games of 416 BC.[182] His entry of seven teams into the four-horse chariot race at these Games and his extraordinary winning of first, second and probably fourth places were unprecedented feats that greatly enhanced his reputation and political capital at home and abroad.[183] Yet in 397 BC, when his son was delivering this forensic speech, these victories were a significant liability; for even after two decades his lavish outlay at Olympia on the traditional sport of tyrants and kings continued to be taken by many as proof of his anti-democratic and tyrannical designs (Isokrates 16.2–3, 38; cf. Thucydides 6.15.4). Moreover, the charge against which Alkibiades the younger is arguing is that one of the chariot teams used by his father at the Olympics had been stolen from a fellow citizen. The hired speechwriter Isokrates deftly minimizes these negative associations by attributing to Alkibiades an unassailable, if somewhat predictable, motivation for his zeal and expenditure in 416 BC – patriotism. Alkibiades competed at Olympia because he realized that it was not just individuals who won renown there but also the cities of the victors (Isokrates 16.32). He understood too that while public services done at Athens gave prominence only to liturgists, those done at Olympia – a rather tendentious characterization of individual Olympic competition surely – made the city famous throughout Greece (32–3). Nevertheless, while a naturally talented sportsman and physically fit, Alkibiades saw that 'some of the athletes were ill-born, lived in small cities and were poorly educated' (εἰδὼς ἐνίους τῶν ἀθλητῶν καὶ κακῶς γεγονότας καὶ μικρὰς πόλεις οἰκοῦντας καὶ ταπεινῶς – 16.33). Thus, like the disillusioned aristocrats of Gardner, Gardiner and Harris, he passed over the athletic competitions for the equestrian events in which it was only possible for 'the wealthiest' to enter.

This text seems to me to shed very little new light on classical Athenian athletics. The supposed non-elite Olympians of these chapters do not come from Athens, and an Athenian gentleman refuses to compete with these athletes out of a concern for his own standing and that of his city. This scenario simply confirms what we know about athletics in classical Athens: it was the preserve of elite citizens. The text can also be interpreted as corroborating how athletics figured in popular thinking. In assembling his justification for why Alkibiades chose equestrian over athletic contest the logographer assumes lower-class jurors would agree that athletes should be of elite backgrounds and well-educated. Of course we have already noted that ordinary Athenians did indeed consider athletics a normative and probably exclusive pursuit of the upper class and believed that competition as an athlete – especially at the Olympics

– required much instruction. Finally, it seems legitimate to question the veracity of what is said here about Olympic athletes. 'Despite Isokrates, chariot racing was the obvious choice for Alcibiades, not something he was forced to pursue.'[184] In 416 BC this Athenian politician was probably in his mid-thirties and so at an age when many of the great Olympic victors had retired. Athletics, then, would have given him only a small chance for success.[185] By contrast, chariot racing was a much better bet for an older man, especially if pursued on a massive scale. And in view of the half-truths Isokrates peddles as part of his efforts to turn this controversial figure of Athenian history into an indefatigable democrat and patriot, a useful fib about some of the sportsmen of small towns being lower-class does not seem out of place.

I cannot accept either of the two ways Fisher proposes a poor but athletically-talented young Athenian could have gained the instruction and practice he needed to be a successful athletic competitor. Firstly, the training which tribal teams undertook for competition in one of the city's three annual torch races was far less appropriate for launching an athletic career and much less accessible to lower-class citizens than Fisher assumes.[186] Athenian *lampadēphoroi* were not boys, as Fisher states, but young adults. In the closing years of the classical period, after the reforms of the *ephēbeia* in 335 BC, those so-called *ephēboi* who joined this cadetship ran in the torch races as part of their first year of physical and military training.[187] Ephebes were eighteen and nineteen years old (*Ath. Pol.* 42.1–5). Before the reforms of 335 BC, it was again *ephēboi*, evidence for whom goes back to the 370s (Aiskhines 1.49; 2.167), who competed as *lampadēphoroi* (Xenophon *Ways and Means* 4.51–2).[188] And in the last decades of the fifth century, while there is no evidence of a formal set of normative exercises for eighteen- and nineteen-year-olds like the *ephēbeia* of the next century, participants in the torch races seem to have been of similar age, for Aristophanes characterizes running a torch race as one of the typical deeds done 'during youth' (ἐπὶ νεότητος – Aristophanes *Wasps* 1196–204). I am not convinced this training of young adults in running as part of a torch relay team would have helped launch athletic careers: eighteen seems too late to nurture athletic talent, and even if a lower-class citizen decided, after training under a tribal *gymnasiarkhos*, to enter individual athletic events, he would have had to compete against those who had done athletics and entered athletic competitions throughout their boyhoods.

For the fifth century and most of the fourth century, lower-class citizens do not appear to have joined the torch-racing teams of their tribes in any significant number. Instead, the high water mark for participation in these events was the last decade or so of the classical period, when the city was doing its level best to facilitate the involvement of as many eighteen- and nineteen-year-olds as possible in the cadetship, of which competing as a torch racer was a compulsory part. To this end, the city funded a new set of magistrates to supervise the day-to-day training of the cohorts of eighteen-year-olds the tribes got each year, and provided each new citizen who joined the cadetship with part of a hoplite's weaponry, daily maintenance and probably also accommodation (*Ath. Pol.* 42.2–4). Additionally, eighteen-year-olds in late-fourth-century Athens were most probably under strong social pressure to undertake the two years of military preparations the city was now generously backing. It was after all the solemn duty of every able-bodied citizen to fight and – if needs be – to die for Athens.[189] Moreover, in the aftermath of their crushing defeat at the hands of Philip of Macedon in 338 BC and the destruction of their ally Thebes by Alexander the Great three years later, the Athenians were no doubt very anxious about the preparedness and efficiency of their citizen soldiers. However, in spite of this likely social pressure to join the *ephēbeia* and the city's new support of those who did, participation appears to have been far from universal. From the honorary decrees of the 330s and 320s naming those who had completed their two-year stint in the *ephēbeia*, we can calculate that there were 50 nineteen-year-olds on average in each of the cadetship's tribally-based corps and hence 500 or so citizens graduating from the late classical *ephēbeia* each year.[190] Nevertheless, on the basis of the population figures and model life table that Mogens Hansen establishes, there were in the same period some 990 nineteen-year-old citizens each year.[191] Thus in the late classical period only one half or so of eighteen-year-old Athenians joined the reformed cadetship and hence trained for, and competed in, the tribal torch races.

In the mid-fourth century, before the reforms of 335 BC, no public funds were spent supporting the training of Athenian ephebes: those young men manning the guard posts or patrolling the countryside received no *trophē* or maintenance, whereas those assigned to practise for a tribal torch race received manifestly inadequate maintenance from their respective *gymnasiarkhos* (Xenophon *Ways and Means* 4.52). Notwithstanding this lack of proper support, torch racers were still required to train (4.52), as those of the late fifth century certainly had to do if they were to be competitive (Aristophanes *Frogs* 1087–98), and this training, like the lessons of the 'old education', consisted of regular classes (*IG* II² 1250.6).[192] In these circumstances, the participation of good numbers of non-elite Athenians in the torch races does not seem likely. That this was actually the case is suggested by a honorary tribal inscription, dating most probably to the 350s or 340s, that names a victorious gymnasiarch and his team of torch racers (*IG* II² 1250). In contrast to the ephebic teams of the late fourth century, this inscription gives the names of only thirteen or – what is more likely – ten victorious *lampadēphoroi*.[193] It is also quite improbable that the participation of poor citizens in the torch races of the fifth century would have been any more extensive; for we have no reason to believe that those training to run a torch race in this period received any more support than they did in the mid-fourth century.[194] What is more, Aristophanes actually characterizes torch racing as a normative upper-class activity in the *symposion* preparation scene of *Wasps*, when he couples it with exclusively elite pursuits like hunting, diplomatic service and – we can now say – athletics (1122–264, especially 1202–5).

Joining a torch-racing team of one's tribe was not the effective means Fisher would have us believe for a non-elite Athenian youth to launch a sporting career. As torch racers were not boys but young adults, the training offered by the *gymnasiarkhos* most probably came too late to develop natural sporting ability. And since the support *lampadēphoroi* received, until the reforms of 335 BC, was decidedly limited, young non-elite Athenians were not able to participate in torch races in any significant number.

Fisher proposes that pederasty provided another opportunity for an athletically talented boy of a lower-class background to launch a sporting career. He suggests that a poor adolescent working out in a *palaistra* or at a *gymnasion* could have been approached by a wealthy man offering to cover the cost of formal athletic training as part of his efforts to have the boy accept him as an *erastēs* or lover.[195] The older man would have maintained this sponsorship as long as the boy remained his *erōmenos* or beloved. Undeniably, wrestling schools and athletics fields were the most important venues for the creation and consummation of sexual relationships between boys and men. At these sporting facilities wealthy men came to admire the naked bodies of boys, to compete with each other to win the trust and affection of the most handsome, and, if they were accepted as lovers, to have sex with their beloveds (e.g. Aristophanes *Birds* 137–42; *Peace* 762–4; *Wasps* 1023–5).[196]

Nevertheless, although there was a profound link between athletics and pederasty in classical Athens, I do not understand how it could have provided any means for a poor boy to start a sporting career. Since the classes in athletics which the *paidotribēs* conducted at the wrestling school or at the athletics field were the exclusive preserve of upper-class boys, there would not have been, at these venues, any young athletes of a lower-class background whom Athenian gentlemen could ogle and fall in love. Moreover, even if a wealthy citizen had a chance to approach a good-looking boy somewhere else and to offer to pay for his training in athletics, it is very unlikely his generosity would have been accepted. The popular literature of classical Athens usually associates pederasty with the stereotypical misdemeanours of the wealthy and treats a person's pursuit of it as sure proof of his membership of this class.[197] Like athletics, then, pederasty was 'a strongly class-marked institution'.[198] Therefore, quite apart from their primarily negative view of pederasty, non-elite fathers or guardians most probably would have not allowed their boys to become *erōmenoi* for fear of having their families classed incorrectly as wealthy. No doubt they would also have been worried about how this acceptance of money from actual or would-be *erastai* would have been perceived by other citizens. After all, Aiskhines appears to have convinced an Athenian jury that admirers might pay for the dining and entertainment expenses of young male beauties in exchange for sexual favours (Aiskhines 1.75–6; cf. Demosthenes 19.284). And Aristophanes could even construe the traditional gifts of a lover to his beloved as equivalent to payment for the services of a male prostitute (*Wealth* 149–59). Thus the sponsorship of a poor boy's athletic education by a suitor or lover could quite easily have been interpreted as a form of male prostitution. Such a construction would have been a disaster for a boy and his family, for any citizen who had at any point prostituted himself was prohibited from participating in the democracy and, if caught taking part, could be sentenced to death (e.g. Aiskhines 1.20, 29–32; Demosthenes 22.30–1).[199] This risk of being accused of male prostitution would have been another reason why a poor father would have prevented his boy from accepting money offered by a would-be lover for his education in athletics.

Conclusion

Athletics for classical Athenians consisted of two closely-integrated activities – the traditional school classes of the athletics teacher and the athletic competitions at local and international festivals. Technical instruction in the standard events of ancient Greek games were given only in the school lessons of the athletics teacher, which doubled as the opportunity for boys to practise these sports. Since instruction and training in athletics were essential for ensuring that an athlete would be competitive and have a good chance of victory in his race or bout, participating in athletic competition was a function of educational participation. Yet wealthy and poor citizens, in classical Athens, did not enjoy equal access to education. This was mainly due to socio-economic barriers: poor families struggled to pay the fees teachers charged and needed to have their sons at home in order to keep farming or business interests going. As a result, most lower-class fathers could afford to send their sons to classes in only one of the three disciplines of traditional education. They judged the discipline of letters to be the most valuable for teaching morality and practical skills and so sent their boys to the classes of the letter teacher. It was only the sons of upper-class families who received instruction in each of the three disciplines of traditional education – athletics, music and letters. Therefore, without school-based training in athletics, which everyone recognized as necessary, poor boys would not have done well in sporting contests and would have been very much disinclined to compete in the first place. There also existed a cultural barrier to the participation of non-elite boys and youths in athletics. Since classical Athenians considered athletics to be the exclusive preserve of the city's elite, a person's pursuit of it was taken as evidence of his family's membership of the elite. They also understood that being wealthy in their democracy attracted expensive public duties and popular prejudice. Therefore, even if a small number of non-elite families could have afforded to send their sons to the classes of the athletics teacher, they would have decided against it for fear of being classified inappropriately as belonging to the elite. In classical Athens families took up athletics for the first time, not when they were getting close to elite status, but when they had arrived at the top and wanted to be publicly recognized for having done so. Thus, in the most prosperous and democratic of the cities of classical Greece, athletics remained an exclusive pursuit of the wealthy.

Acknowledgements

This chapter is a substantially modified and expanded version of the paper I delivered at the Sydney Olympics Conference and later in 2000 at the Powerhouse Museum. The paper's consideration of participation in the tribally-organized dithyrambic contests of classical Athens now appears elsewhere (Pritchard 2001, and forthcoming). A different version of the paper, focusing on participation in the 'old education' of classical Athens, was delivered in 2001 at a seminar of the Departments of Classics and Ancient History at the University of Sydney and, in 2002, at the 'Ancient History Teachers' Conference' at Macquarie University. I would like to thank the audiences of both versions of the paper for their useful comments. This chapter has also benefited from the valuable suggestions of Lesley Beaumont, Ben Brown, Margalit Finkelberg, Nick Fisher, Mark Golden, Nicole Mockler, Nigel Nicholson, David Phillips and Anton Powell. I am indebted to them all, but should single out Nick Fisher, who, in spite of his profound disagreement with my assessment of ancient Greek athletics, took the time to comment politely and helpfully on this chapter. I hope our published exchange will move the debate forward. Unless otherwise indicated, all translations of the Greek are my own.

Notes

[1] Gardner 1892; Gardiner 1910; 1930; Harris 1964; 1972.

[2] The first and second parts of Young 1984 are summarized by Young 1988 and 1983 respectively.

[3] Young 1984, 7–88; 1988.

[4] For additional analysis of the relationship between amateur schoolboy sport and the 'moral ideal' of the 'dominant fraction' of the 'dominant class' of nineteenth- and twentieth-century Europe, see Bourdieu 1978, 824–6; cf. Lucas 1988, 65.

[5] For detailed discussion of the restrictive amateurism of these presidents, see Lucas 1988, 66–7, 69–71.

[6] Quotation from Pleket 1975, 59.

[7] For the early history of Greek athletics and the transition from aristocratic funerary games to competitions as part of civic religious festivals, see the chapter by Ben Brown in this book.

[8] e.g. Homer *Iliad* 23.259–61, 557–62; Hesiod *Theogony* 435–8; *Works and Days* 654–7. Well discussed by Young 1984, 107–10 and now Kyle 1996, 108–11. For Homeric poetry as an admittedly imperfect reflection of early archaic Greek society, see Raaflaub 1997.

[9] Young 1984, 128–33. For a translation of this fragment of Xenophanes, see Miller 1991, no. 197.

[10] For a thorough consideration of the introduction of such prizes at the mid-sixth-century Panathenaia, see Kyle 1996, 116–23.

[11] For a good discussion of these reforms to eligibility rules, undertaken under the IOC presidencies of Lord Killanin and Juan Antonio Samaranch, see Lucas 1988, 71–9.

[12] Young 1984, 89–103, 107–10, 147–62; 1988, 72–3 critique Pleket 1974; 1975.

[13] Young 1984, 93.

[14] Pleket 1975, 73; Young 1984, 100–2. I consider the evidentiary value of this important Isokrates passage in the closing pages of this chapter.

[15] Quotation from Young 1984, 153.

[16] Pleket 1974, 60; Young 1984, 99, 115; Moretti 1957, no. 1 with references. For each Olympic victor in his catalogue Moretti lists the ancient evidence.

[17] For Milon, see Pleket 1974, 63; Young 1984, 153–4; Moretti 1957, no. 122. For Theogenes, see Pleket 1974, 63–7; 1975, 81; Young 1984, 150–3; Moretti 1957, no. 201.

[18] Young 1984, 155; Moretti 1957, no. 134.

[19] Young 1984, 155; Moretti 1957, nos. 79, 261.

[20] Quotation from Young 1984, 156. *Pace* Young 1984, 155–6, Biliński 1990 links this anonymous victor to the Olympics of 352 BC.

[21] Young so explains his position (1984, 163): '…I emphasize the case for non-noble participation in early Greek athletics; for others had badly overstated the argument for aristocratic exclusiveness. Lest I mislead, I hasten to reiterate the extensive participation of the nobility. No reliable proportion of nobles to non-

nobles can be established at present.'

[22] ibid., 158–62 explicitly responds to Pleket 1974, 76; 1975, 72.

[23] For the inscription and detailed analysis, see Robert 1967, 14–32.

[24] The particular Zenon papyrus attesting this dates to 257 BC and is translated and discussed at Miller 1991, no. 147.

[25] Young 1984, 159–60.

[26] Quotation from ibid., 159.

[27] Formal reviews of Young include: Instone 1986; Kyle 1985; cf. 1987, 123 n.53; 1997, 54–67; Poliakoff 1989 which repeats much of Poliakoff 1987, 117–33. The sustained critiques are Golden 1998, 141–5, 157–69; cf. 1990, 71–2; Pleket 1992.

[28] Kyle 1985, 141; Poliakoff 1987, 131.

[29] Pleket 1992, 149–51; Poliakoff 1987, 121–2, 183–4 n.10. The inscriptions evincing various public offices of his family are discussed by Pouilloux 1954, 62–105.

[30] Quotation from Poliakoff 1987, 124.

[31] For this compulsory training, see Stephen Miller's chapter in this book.

[32] e.g. Aristophanes *Wasps* 552–7; *Wealth* 281, 552–4; Aristotle *Politics* 1273a21–36, 1291b11–30; 1326b30–2; Menander *Dyskolos* 293–5. See Pritchard 1999, 2–3; Rosivach 2001, 127 – both with further references. Young details other evidence of the elite status of Glaukos but argues that he was only wealthy in adult life and as a result of his sporting triumphs (1984, 155 n.51, 162; 162 n.61).

[33] Translated by Grene. I am following the interpretation of this passage by Pleket 1992, 150; 1998, 318 *pace* Decker 1995, 131–3; Poliakoff 1989, 117–18, 182 n.2.

[34] For a photograph of the *stele* and a literal translation, see Neils 1992, 16. The drachma value of the prizes in this inscription are judiciously calculated by Young 1984, 115–17.

[35] Golden 1998, 76–7 with references. For the drachma value of silver drinking cups, see Vickers and Gill 1994, 40–1, 47–52.

[36] Three of these lists come from a recently published inscription; for its *editio princeps* and analysis, along with the other three lists, see Tracy and Habicht 1991 and Tracy 1991 respectively. Their significance for the ongoing debate on athletic participation is well appreciated by Golden (1998, 165–6; cf. 2000a, 172).

[37] Golden 1998, 166.

[38] Golden 1998, 144; Kyle 1985, 140; 1987, 153 n.23; Pleket 1992, 151; Poliakoff 1989, 169–70.

[39] Poliakoff 1987, 129–33.

[40] Kyle 1987, 123 n.53, 151, 153.

[41] Golden 1998, 160; 2000a, 171.

[42] The first publications of his position are Pleket 1974; 1975. He delivered this critique as a paper at the 1988 Athens symposium on the ancient Olympics (Pleket 1992). For his restatement of his position, see ibid., 148, 151–2; cf. 1998, 317.

[43] Quotation from Pleket 1992, 151 (my italics).

[44] Fisher 1998, 85. His case for substantial non-elite athletic participation has

already been criticized by Golden 2000a, 169–75. Elsewhere I critique his claim of a similar pattern of participation in the tribally organized dithyrambic competitions of classical Athens (Fisher 1998, 93; Pritchard 2001; forthcoming). In my opinion the case he makes for non-elite citizens of classical Athens increasingly enjoying forms of collective dining and drinking closely resembling the traditional *symposion* of the elite is much stronger (Fisher 2000).

[45] Fisher 1998, 89–90.

[46] ibid., 86–7.

[47] For his acknowledgment of Kyle's concern about the evidence Young brings forward, see Fisher 1998, 87 n. 12.

[48] Fisher goes on to discuss these three passages at some length (ibid., 87–9).

[49] ibid., 90–4.

[50] ibid., 94–104.

[51] The closing pages of this chapter give a detailed critique of Fisher's evidence and arguments for substantial non-elite participation in classical Athenian athletics.

[52] Quotation from Miller 2000, 278.

[53] ibid., 279.

[54] ibid., 282–3.

[55] e.g. Aiskhines 3.179–80; Aristotle *Politics* 1338b39–1339b4; Isokrates 16.32–3; Plato *Laws* 807c.

[56] For the special diets of the athletes of the classical period, see Golden 1998,157–8; Poliakoff 1987, 5–18 – both with ancient references. On the recognized dietary expertise of the doctor, note, for example, Plato *Alkibiades I* 108e; Aristotle *Eudemian Ethics* 1217b39–40. For his specific advice to athletes on dietary matters, see Plato *Kriton* 47b.

[57] What follows draws heavily on Davies 1981, 21–8; Markle 1985, 266–71; Pritchard 2000a, 51–63, 247; Rosivach 2001; and especially Vartsos 1978.

[58] The phrase in quotation marks is adapted from Vartsos 1978, 232.

[59] See Pritchard 2000a, 56–7; 2001, 11 with references.

[60] For the deceptive and contradictory picture that *Clouds* draws of the state of the so-called *arkhaia paideia* (961), and the complex relationship between the athletic component of the 'old education' and the new intellectuals, see the following chapter by Harold Tarrant.

[61] e.g. Aiskhines 1.10; Aristophanes *Clouds* 961, 973–80, 1002–9; *Frogs* 727–30; Aristotle *Politics* 1337b22–7; Plato *Alkibiades I* 118c–d; *Lakhes* 184e; *Laws* 743d–e, 764c–d; *Meno* 94b.

[62] For the *paidotribēs* as the physical education teacher, see Aristophanes *Clouds* 973; *Knights* 490–2, 1238–9; Plato *Alkibiades I* 118d; *Lakhes* 184e; and as the owner of a *palaistra*, see Aiskhines 1.10; Plato *Lysis* 204a, 207d; *Gorgias* 456c–e. On the *palaistra* in general, see Kyle 1987, 64–71; Poliakoff 1987, 12–14 – both with references.

[63] For the group lessons of the *paidotribēs*, see Aristotle *Politics* 1288b10–14; Isokrates 15.183–5; Plato *Statesman* 294c–d. For examples of *phoitaō* as the verb used to describe attendance at physical education classes, see Athenaios 584c;

Isokrates 15.183; Plato *Gorgias* 456d–e; cf. *Laws* 764c–d. For the use of this verb to describe school attendance in general, see Pritchard 2001, 8 with references.

[64] For examples of *gymnastikē* as physical education, see Aristotle *Politics* 1337b22–7; Isokrates 15.181; Plato *Alkibiades I* 118c–d; *Kriton* 50e. For some of the legion of examples of *gymnastikē* as the *tekhnē* (skill) or *epistēmē* (science) of the *paidotribēs*, see Aristotle *Politics* 1279a1–10; Plato *Alkibiades I* 108b; *Republic* 406a–b.

[65] e.g. Fisher 1998, 94, 96; Golden 1998, 143, 160; 2000a, 171; Poliakoff 1987, 17, 131; Young 1984, 159.

[66] Kyle 1987, 143.

[67] ibid., 141–2 with primary sources.

[68] Similarly Stefan Müller distinguishes contemporary 'Leistungssport' (high performance sport) and 'Schulsport' (school sport), which is rather relaxed and uncompetitive, and argues for the applicability of this distinction in the Graeco-Roman world (1995, 20–37).

[69] For the athletics teacher overseeing those in training, see Aristotle *Politics* 1279a1–10, 1287b1–2; Plato *Kriton* 47b; *Republic* 389c; *Theages* 123e; cf. *Statesman* 295c; *Laws* 720e.

[70] For examples of this use of *agōnia*, see Aristotle *Politics* 1288b17–18; Plato *Lakhes* 184e; *Laws* 765c; *Meno* 94b; cf. *Gorgias* 456c–e. The competitive focus of physical education is well appreciated at Pleket 1998, 316.

[71] For the examples of the athletics teacher giving lessons in these 'heavy events', see Aristophanes *Knights* 1238–9; Plato *Alkibiades I* 107e–108e; *Gorgias* 456d–e; cf. Aristotle *Eudemian Ethics* 1227b26–7. Kyle 1987, 143–4 gathers the testimonia for accomplished 'heavy' athletes who went on to train athletes; while none of these sources calls such a trainer a *paidotribēs*, I trust my discussion justifies the identification of them as such. For initial thoughts on the interesting but complex issue of the class position of athletics teachers, see Kyle 1987, 145; Poliakoff 1989, 169.

[72] For *ho gymnastēs* and *ho gymnastikos* as equivalents, see Plato *Statesman* 267e, 295c.

[73] In philosophical literature *iatrikē* and *gymnastikē* are frequently paired (e.g. Aristotle *Eudemnian Ethics* 1217b39–40; *Metaphysics* 1063b36–7; *Nicomachean Ethics* 1096a32–4, 1143b25–8; Plato *Republic* 406a–b; *Statesman* 289a; *Symposium* 187a).

[74] Plato *Laws* 684c; *Statesman* 267e; Aristotle *Nicomachean Ethics* 1180b12–16; *Topica* 137a4–6; cf. Xenophon *Memorabilia* 2.1.20.

[75] Kyle 1987, 141–3.

[76] Modified translation of Rackham.

[77] For athletics (γυμναστική), music and letters as the widely-agreed disciplines of the 'old education', see, for example, Plato *Alkibiades I* 118d; *Kleitophon* 407b–c; *Protagoras* 312b, 325e, 326c. While it is notoriously difficult to link terms for children and youths to actual ages, from the definitions of *pais* in the ancient Greek literature it seems to me that a 'boy' could be aged between 10 and 17 years. Similarly Wilson argues that a *pais* for the purposes of choral competition

was aged between *c.* 11 and 17 years (2000, 75) and Crowther finds evidence for those in the competitions for *paides* at the Olympic Games being aged between 12 and 17 years (1988). For a much more restrictive proposed age range for *paides*, see Stephen Miller's chapter in this collection. Elsewhere I argue that participation in the tribally organized dithyrambic choruses of classical Athens was a predominantly, or more often an exclusively, upper-class pursuit (Pritchard 2001; forthcoming). In my consideration of participation in the 'old education' of classical Athens I have found the following discussions especially useful: Beck 1964, 77–141; 1975; Golden 1990, 62–5; Kleijwegt 1991, 75–134; Marrou 1956; Morgan 1998, 9–21.

[78] For a discussion of the lessons of the lyre teacher, see Beck 1964, 126–9. For the possible authors of the lyric poems mentioned in these lines of Aristophanes, see Sommerstein 1982, 207.

[79] e.g. Demosthenes 19.281; Plato *Protagoras* 312b; Xenophon *Symposium* 4.27). The classes of the letter teacher are discussed in detail by Beck 1964, 111–26 with references.

[80] For the range of poetry encountered by the Athenian student and the predominance of Homer at the letter school, see Girard 1891, 139–60 with primary references.

[81] My discussion here draws partly on Robb 1994, 184–6 *pace* Morgan 1998, 10–12.

[82] The lines of poetry recited in this comedy are identified by Sommerstein 1985, 193.

[83] Images of scrolls on Attic pots are catalogued and analyzed by Immerwahr 1964; 1973.

[84] *Didaskalos* was a generic term that could be used to describe each of the three types of instructors of the 'old education' (e.g. Plato *Protagoras* 325d, 326c).

[85] Independent cases for the concurrent scheduling of classes are made by Beck 1964, 81–3; Golden 1990, 62–3; Marrou 1956, 148 – all with primary references.

[86] *Didaskaleion* seems to have been a generic word for premises used for education (e.g. Demosthenes 18.258; Theophrastos *Characters* 30.14; Thucydides 7.29.5; Xenophon *Kyroupaideia* 1.2.15).

[87] e.g. Euripides *Hekabe* 599–602; *Suppliant Women* 911–17; Hypereides *Funeral Oration* 8–9; Plato *Protagoras* 325d–e; *Meno* 94b; Xenophon *Memorabilia* 2.2.6–7.

[88] The benefit of physical education for hoplite battle is considered at Pritchard 2000a, 105.

[89] Protagoras is in no way the first to discuss the benefits of *mousikē* in such terms; Dickie gathers together the passages of Homer and Pindar where the phorminx is said to induce 'good cheer' as 'it promotes a peaceful and orderly state of mind' (1983, 255–6).

[90] For detailed discussions of the performance contexts of comedy, tragedy and oratory and my terms 'popular literature' and 'popular thinking', see Pritchard 1998, 38–44; 2000a, 2–74.

[91] The predominant place of Homer in the instruction of morality is also borne out by the claims that he had 'educated Greece' (e.g. Plato *Republic* 606e–607a), or was 'the greatest of the sages' (e.g. Xenophon *Symposium* 4.6).

[92] Translation by Lamb.

[93] Of the term *kalos k'agathos* Dover writes (1974, 45): 'Until persuaded otherwise by arguments which I have not yet encountered, I make the assumption that the poor Athenian was normally willing to apply the expression *kalos k' agathos* to any man who had what he himself would have liked to have (wealth, a great name, distinguished ancestors) and was what he himself would like to be (educated, cultured, well-dressed and well-groomed, with the physique and poise of a man trained in fighting, wrestling and dancing.' I consider the evidentiary value of Pseudo-Xenophon in some detail below.

[94] For further references to the fees of sophists, see Phillips 1981, 27; 1990, 139.

[95] This is how Beck 1964, 130 and Kyle 1987, 145 interpret this passage.

[96] For a discussion of Athenian child labour, see Golden 1990, 34–5. For the contribution of female labour to a family's livelihood, see Blundell 1995, 145; Hansen 1987, 149–50; Ober 1989, 134–6 – all with ancient references. For the extent of slave holding in classical Athens, see Garlan 1988, and especially Wood 1988, 173–84. Thus Young is mistaken to argue that non-elite boys did not need to work and so could train to be athletes (1984, 158).

[97] It is worth including more of the characterization of this work by Deborah Gera 1993, 2: 'The *Cyropaedia* is above all a didactic work, its author's vehicle for developing and discussing his own cherished ideas and interests. In this work Xenophon touches upon many areas covered in his other writings, and he uses a variety of literary forms which he has used elsewhere – philosophical dialogue, encomium, history, military memoirs, technical handbook – to present these favourite themes and topics. The narration of the life and deeds of Cyrus the Great is, in essence, a convenient framework, a peg upon which Xenophon hangs reflections and ideas of his own. Cyrus is not the real impetus for the *Cyropaedia* but is more akin to the tailor's dummy, a useful figure to be clothed as his author likes.'

[98] For analysis of the debate at this drinking party (8.3.35–50), see ibid., 173–83.

[99] This very snobbish passage is considered in more detail at Pritchard 2000a, 68.

[100] Quotation from Beck 1964, 83. This assumption is quite widely made (e.g. ibid., 79–80, 83, 94, 111; Donlan 1980, 156–7; Golden 1990, 63–4; Ober 1989, 157–8).

[101] Aptly described by Hedrick 1994, 162.

[102] I have found the following discussions of literacy in the overwhelmingly oral culture of classical Athens very helpful: Hedrick 1994; Phillips 1990, 133–40; Robb 1994; Thomas 1989, 15–94; 1992.

[103] Beck 1964, 77. For a detailed analysis of ostracism and the literary sources for it, see Phillips 1982.

[104] Its weakness is well recognized: Marrou 1956, 43; Phillips 1990, 137; Robb 1994, 135, 155 n. 23; Thomas 1989, 18.

[105] Phillips 1990, 134–7. Rhodes 1994, 94 is prepared to draw bolder conclusions about the motivations of these scribes.

[106] Ober 1989, 158.

[107] e.g. Aristotle *Rhetoric* 1.4.7–8; Thucydides 2.13; Xenophon *Memorabilia* 3.6.5–6. For further discussion of this requirement of political leadership, see Kallet-Marx 1994, 228–35.

[108] For the reluctance of fifth-century politicians to commit speeches to writing, see Loraux 1986, 178–9. On the dangers of being labelled an expert speaker and sophist, see Ober 1989, 170–7. Several rhetorical handbooks are discussed by Kennedy 1985, 473–4. Another work of this type is the *Tetralogies* by Antiphon. Rhodes argues that [Andokides] IV has a similar status (1994, 88–91).

[109] The status of this group and their duties are considered by Hansen 1991, 224–5 with primary references; Robb 1994, 137–8.

[110] For the conscription lists of hoplites and naval specialists, see Pritchard 2000a, 234–7; 2000b, 114.

[111] In contrast to actual treasurers, membership of minor financial boards was not restricted to the topmost Solonian property class (Kallet-Marx 1994, 229). For the range and duties of Athenian magistrates, see Hansen 1991, 225–44.

[112] A point well made by Phillips 1990, 139; Thomas 1989, 61–4 with references; 1992, 3.

[113] I am following the excellent discussion of this issue by Thomas 1989, 49–55, 64–94; 1992, 84–5, 144. Taking a different line of reasoning, Hedrick 1994, 165–74 arrives at conclusions similar to Thomas.

[114] Thomas 1989, 63–4.

[115] Modern historians interpreting one or more texts in this manner include Beck 1964, 83, Golden 1990, 64, and Thomas 1989, 30–1; 1992, 155.

[116] I have found indecisive other ancient passages often cited in debates over universal literacy in Athens (e.g. Aristophanes *Knights* 987–96; Athenaios 454b–c; Kratinos fr. 128 Kassel and Austin).

[117] See Pritchard 2000a, 68–9.

[118] Almost the same phrase appears in Kratinos fr. 128 Kassel and Austin, but the fragment's lack of context means it sheds no light on the meaning of 'knowing letters' or literacy levels in fifth-century Athens.

[119] Moreover, Aristophanes *Knights* 189 and Plato *Phaidros* 242c highlight that with each particular kind of literacy individuals were differently accomplished.

[120] On the existence of different kinds of literacy, see Phillips 1990, 137–8; Thomas 1989, 17; 1992, 8–9.

[121] The generic status of this term is noted above at note 84.

[122] Kleijwegt 1991, 78 with references.

[123] Lang 1976, 1.

[124] ibid., 23–51.

[125] ibid., 26.

[126] Although these percentages include many pieces dated later than the classical

period, specific examples used in the following discussion are from the fifth and fourth centuries BC.

¹²⁷ Classical examples of the basic sentence are Lang 1976, nos. F 58, F 107, and those with the extra adverb include F 131–2, F 139, F 154.

¹²⁸ In Lang's catalogue this piece is F 86. Its original inventory number is P 22,998. For reports on its archaeological context, see H.A. Thompson 1959, 51–4; D.B. Thompson 1960.

¹²⁹ In Lang 1976 this is F 164, while its inventory number is P 897. I re-analyse the archaeology and small finds of the so-called house of Mikion and Menon at Pritchard 1999, 14–21.

¹³⁰ Lang 1976, 55–81.

¹³¹ ibid., 55–64. This is Lang's designation.

¹³² e.g. ibid., nos. Ha 3–4.

¹³³ e.g. ibid., Ha 5–7, Ha 9–12.

¹³⁴ These two pieces are ibid., Ha 1 and Ha 8 respectively.

¹³⁵ ibid., Hc 1–2.

¹³⁶ ibid., Hd 1. For the meaning of this term see ibid., 72–5.

¹³⁷ ibid., 21–23.

¹³⁸ ibid., E 5.

¹³⁹ Its inventory number is BI 818. It is discussed at Pritchard 1999, 17.

¹⁴⁰ Quotation from Vickers and Gill 1994, 164. For the counting of painters and potters amongst the craftsmen of the ancient Greek city, see, for example, Arafat and Morgan 1989.

¹⁴¹ For 'kalos' inscriptions, see Vickers and Gill 1994, 163–4.

¹⁴² For examples of these inscriptions see ibid., 100, 154–171. Thomas also believes that these sentences demonstrate a fairly high level of literacy (1992, 10).

¹⁴³ Immerwahr 1973; 1974.

¹⁴⁴ The wages of letter teachers are recorded in Hellenistic inscriptions from Miletos and Teos (Beck 1964, 111–2; Marrou 1956, 204, 516 with primary references).

¹⁴⁵ This timetabling was discussed above.

¹⁴⁶ Thomas 1992, 9, 92. On the limited usage of reading in the letter schools to aid in the memorization of poetry, see Robb 1994, 188.

¹⁴⁷ Many of these references have been discussed by Dickie (1983, 248–9, 272–3 nn. 32–6) and Golden (1998, 157–8). Both are interested only in athletics but the passages they gather together shed light on physical education and music.

¹⁴⁸ For a detailed discussion of non-elite Athenian expectations about political leaders and their comic manipulation in this passage, see Pritchard 2000a, 67–70 with references.

¹⁴⁹ ibid., 71–4.

¹⁵⁰ As Poliakoff writes of these lines (1987, 130).

¹⁵¹ Sommerstein, for example, thinks the unexpected class difference between father and son in this play just as in *Clouds* is comic fantasy (1983, 162), whereas Fisher makes the plausible suggestion that the playwright might be portraying 'social mobility in a time of considerable change and generational conflict' (2000, 357).

[152] For these items as the standard attire of poor Athenians, see Aristophanes *Wasps* 33, 115–17; *Assembly Women* 633, 847–50, 882; *Wealth* 842–3; Isaios 5.11. Clothing, then, did mark out class differences in classical Athens (Davidson 2000, 147 *pace* Geddes 1987).

[153] e.g. Golden 1998, 160.

[154] The dependency is well appreciated by Beck 1964, 78; Kagan 1991, 21.

[155] For horsemanship as an upper-class activity, see Spence 1993, 191–3 with references.

[156] Philokleon is so described by Davidson 1997, 53.

[157] For intelligent discussions of this aspect of the speech, see Golden 1998, 158–9; 2000a 169–71; Ober 1989, 282–3.

[158] Quotation from Golden 2000a, 170. For this popular perception of lower-class politicians, see Ober 1989, 233–8 with references.

[159] Ober 1989, 283.

[160] Bourdieu 1978, 838.

[161] ibid., 835.

[162] For the popular but contradictory perceptions of wealth and poverty in classical Athens, see Pritchard 2000a, 51–63.

[163] The definition of the fourth-century Athenian elite is well established by Hansen 1991, 109–16.

[164] For *hybris* and the upper class, see, for example, Aristophanes *Wasps* 1251–67, 1299–303; *Wealth* 563–4; Demosthenes 21.98, 158; Lysias 24.16–17. For their hatred of the people and propensity to commit treason, see, for example, Aristophanes *Wasps* 464–70; *Wealth* 567–90; Demosthenes 21.203–4; Lysias 27.

[165] e.g. Aristophanes *Frogs* 431–3, 1065–8; Demosthenes 21.158–9; 36.39; Lysias 14.23–4; 19.9–11.

[166] Davidson 1997, 242–3.

[167] As is well appreciated by Vartsos (1978, 239).

[168] Kyle 1987, 123 n.53. For this catalogue and analysis of it, see ibid., 195–216 and 102–23 respectively. The view of archaic and classical Greek athletics as *predominantly* rather than exclusively upper-class is held by Golden and Poliakoff as well (see above).

[169] In Kyle's catalogue of certain Athenian sportsman (1987, 195–216) those individuals with an unclear class position have nos. 2, 7, 9, 10, 20, 22–3, 26–8, 32, 39, 41, 47, 50–4, 59, 60, 62, 67, 69, 72, 75–7. The elite position of 28 others is suggested by the fact that they belonged, according to J.K. Davies' *Athenian Propertied Families 600–300 BC*, to families who performed liturgies (3–6, 8, 11, 13–15, 30–1, 33–4, 38, 42–6, 55, 57, 61, 63, 65–6, 70–1, 73). Different factors confirm that the remainder were wealthy: 9 were equestrian victors and so owned horses (16, 19, 21, 35–6, 48–9, 56, 78); 8 could afford large works of sculpture to commemorate their sporting achievements (17–18, 24–5, 29, 37, 58, 74); 2 had the money to commission victory odes (1, 64); and 3 had positions of political or military leadership (12, 40, 68).

[170] See especially Kyle 1987, 113–21; 149–51. Quotation from ibid., 123.

[171] His case for this was canvassed above in the first several pages of this chapter.

341

[172] Fisher 1998, 89.

[173] Ceccarelli also questions the objectivity of this treatise on the grounds that it is 'un texte fortement connoté politiquement' and concludes that 'il faudra essayer de restituer la réalité historique à l'aide d'autres sources' (1993, 446). For comparable negative assessments of Pseudo-Xenophon, see, for example, Frisch 1942, 279; Kyle 1987, 143. His reliability decreases still further if we accept the recently made and not implausible argument of Hornblower that his treatise is '…a *fourth-century* work about the *fifth-century* Athenian democracy and empire, which the author pretends are still in existence; that it is in fact a clever (if clumsily written), ludic, work of imaginative fiction which perhaps belongs to the genre of literature associated with the *symposion* or ritualized drinking session…' (2000, 361). I cannot accept the new attempt by William Morison to explain away the apparent inaccuracies and contradictions of Pseudo-Xenophon 2.10, since the 'subtext' he proposes for his re-interpretation of the passage seems neither historically plausible nor germane to the Pseudo-Xenophon's theses (Morison 2000).

[174] See Kyle 1987, 64–71, especially 68, with references.

[175] I follow Kyle's thorough discussion of this inscription (ibid., 145–7). For a translation of the relevant lines, see Miller 1991, no. 161.

[176] Sommerstein 1996, especially 331. For the comic ridicule of the Athenian people and especially their political capacities, see Pritchard 2000a, 71–4.

[177] Modified translation of Miller. For a full translation of this fragment, see Miller 1991, no. 168.

[178] Fisher 1998, 88.

[179] With Dover 1974, 174–5 and Rosivach 2001, 132.

[180] For a translation of this fragment of Xenophanes, see Miller 1991, no. 167.

[181] For this technique of Euripidean tragedy, see Croally 1994, 15; Pritchard 2000a, 186 n. 18. In an excellent article Patrick O'Sullivan points out that such contrariness was most probably a genetic characteristic of the satyr play (2000, especially 355, 358–9).

[182] Fisher 1998, 87–8. Those scholars, in addition to Fisher, for whom Isokrates 16.32–3 is reliable evidence for the history of Greek sport include Pleket (1975, 73; 1992, 151; 1998, 317) and Young (1984, 156). Others judge it to be specious rhetoric (e.g. Dickie 1983, 273 n. 36; Golden 1998, 170; Kyle 1985, 141; 1987, 136–7).

[183] Ellis 1989, 50–2 with references.

[184] Quotation from Kyle 1987, 137.

[185] For his date of birth, see Ellis 1989, 1. For the retirement age of competitive athletes and the attractiveness of equestrian contests to older men, see Golden 1998, 117–23.

[186] For the dates when these contests were introduced and the festivals to which they were linked, see Davies 1967, 35–7. Sekunda 1990 should be used with caution: while its collection of the sources is useful, Nick Sekunda makes a number of egregious assumptions and inferences. For example, he assumes there was a formal *ephēbeia* in the fifth century, in which *all* young Athenians

participated (152–3, 155), and incorrectly infers from the texts he assembles that only the torch race at the Hephaistia was a relay race (154–6). The following paragraphs develop further my discussion of participation in these tribal contests at Pritchard 2000b, 110–1.

¹⁸⁷ For two inscriptions commemorating the victory of the ephebes of a tribe in a late classical torch race, see Reinmuth 1971, nos. 6 and 13. For ephebes most probably running torch races in the first of their two years of training, see Sekunda 1990, 152–3 with references.

¹⁸⁸ With Gauthier 1976, 193–4.

¹⁸⁹ See Pritchard 2000a, 80–6 with references.

¹⁹⁰ See Hansen 1985, 12, 47–50 with references.

¹⁹¹ The critical work here is Hansen 1985 which remains, as Golden 2000b shows, effectively unchallenged. Hansen's evaluation of the sources results in a figure of around 30,000 adult citizens *living in Attika* in the second half of the fourth century (1985, 67–8), and on the Coale-Demeny model life table he argues that nineteen-year-olds were 3.3 per cent of all males aged between 18 and 80+ years (9–13).

¹⁹² Although these lines from Aristophanes do evince the need for torch racers to train, it is quite unsound to infer from them, as Sekunda does (1990, 155; cf. Fisher 1998, 90–1; Golden 1998, 167–9), anything about the level of participation in this tribal event. After all they are part of an absurdist attack by the dead Aiskhylos against his dead rival Euripides. Thus if we take lines 1087–98 as largely descriptive, we must also accept the charges that Euripides has turned good citizens into villains (1010–11, 1013–17), encouraged the wealthy to dress as beggars to avoid trierarchies (1063–6) and so forth (1069–73).

¹⁹³ Ten comes from Sekunda's well justified restoration of the lines detailing the names of the gymnasiarch and his charges (1990, 162–3, 165–7).

¹⁹⁴ At 1.13 Pseudo-Xenophon suggests that while the *dēmos*, which he elsewhere characterizes as sub-hoplite (1.2), believe themselves unable to practise *mousikē* and athletics, they think it right nonetheless to take the 'money' offered by the rich for being a torch racer, dithyrambic chorister or sailor. We have already noted how this partisan author often misrepresents Athenian realities and there is no reason to believe this passage is an exception. There is surely a contradiction between a *dēmos* feeling unable to do athletics or music but happy to pursue just these things when they receive pay. It is worrying, too, that the other sources concerning what support *lampadēphoroi* received, write, not of a salary, but of *trophē* (*Ath. Pol.* 42.3; Xenophon *Ways and Means* 4.52).

¹⁹⁵ Fisher 1998, 94–103.

¹⁹⁶ See Dover 1989, 54–5; Fisher 1998, 94–6 – both with primary references.

¹⁹⁷ While these points are well established by Tom Hubbard in a valuable article (1998), he goes too far in discounting evidence implying that non-elite citizens sometimes did view pederasty positively (e.g. Aiskhines 1.135–57; Thucydides 2.43.1). Pederasty, like other aspects of the lifestyle of the Athenian upper class, was treated somewhat contradictorily in popular thinking. For the socio-economic barriers to the pursuit of pederasty by non-elite citizens, see Dover

1974, 150–1.
[198] Quotation from Hubbard 1998, 49.
[199] For this prohibition and the law concerning the breaking of it, see Dover 1989, 19–31; MacDowell 1978, 74, 126.

Bibliography

Arafat, K. and Morgan, C.
1989   'Pots and potters in Athens and Corinth', *OJA* 8, 311–46.
Beck, F.A.G.
1964   *Greek Education, 450–350 BC*, London.
1975   *Album of Greek Education: The Greeks at school and at play*, Sydney.
Biliński, B.
1990   'Un pescivendolo olimpionico (Aristoteles Rhet. 1.7 1365a – Ps. Simonides fr. 110 D)', *Nikephoros* 3, 157–75.
Blundell, S.
1995   *Women in Ancient Greece*, London.
Bourdieu, P.
1978   'Sport and social class', *Social Science Information* 17, 819–40.
Ceccarelli, P.
1993   'Sans thalassocratie, pas de démocratie? Le rapport entre thalassocratie et démocratie à Athènes dans la discussion du V et IV siècle av. J.-C.', *Historia* 42, 444–70.
Croally, N.
1994   *Euripidean Polemic: The Trojan Women and the function of tragedy*, Cambridge.
Crowther, N.B.
1988   'The age-category of boys at Olympia', *Phoenix* 42, 304–8.
Davidson, J.N.
1997   *Courtesans and Fishcakes: The consuming passions of classical Athens*, New York.
2000   'Private Life', in R. Osborne (ed.) *Classical Greece*, 139–69, Oxford.
Davies, J.K.
1967   'Demosthenes on liturgies: a note', *JHS* 87, 33–40.
1981   *Wealth and the Power of Wealth in Classical Athens*, New York.
Decker, W.
1995   *Griechischer Sport in der Antike: Von minoischen Wettkampf zu den olympischen Spielen*, Munich.
Dickie, M.
1983   'Phaeacian athletics', in F. Cairns (ed.) *Papers of the Liverpool Latin Seminar IV*, 237–76, Liverpool.
Donlan, W.
1980   *The Aristocratic Ideal in Ancient Greece: Attitudes of superiority from Homer to the end of the fifth century*, Lawrence.

Dover, K.J.
  1974 *Greek Popular Morality in the Time of Plato and Aristotle*, Oxford.
  1989 *Greek Homosexuality*, 2nd edn, New York.
Ellis, W.M.
  1989 *Alcibiades*, London and New York.
Fisher, N.
  1998 'Gymnasia and the democratic values of leisure', in P. Cartledge, P. Millett and S. von Reden (eds.) *Kosmos: Essays in order, conflict and community in classical Athens*, 84–104, Cambridge.
  2000 'Symposiasts, fish-eaters and flatterers: social mobility and moral concerns in Old Comedy', in D. Harvey and J. Wilkins (eds.) *The Rivals of Aristophanes: Studies in Athenian Old Comedy*, 355–96, Swansea and London.
Flensted-Jensen, P., Nielsen, T.H. and Rubinstein, L. (eds.)
  2000 *Polis and Politics: Studies in ancient Greek history: Presented to Mogens Herman Hansen on his sixtieth birthday, August 20, 2000*, Aarhus.
Frisch, H.
  1942 *The Constitution of the Athenians*, Copenhagen.
Gardiner, E.N.
  1910 *Greek Athletic Sports and Festivals*, London.
  1930 *Olympia: Its history and remains*, Oxford.
Gardner, P.
  1892 *New Chapters in Greek History*, London.
Garlan, Y.
  1988 *Slavery in Ancient Greece*, transl. J. Lloyd, revised and expanded edn, Ithaca and London.
Gauthier, P.
  1976 *Un commentaire historique des* Poroi *de Xénophon*, Paris.
Geddes, A.
  1987 'Rags and riches: the costume of Athenian men in the fifth century', *CQ* 37, 307–31.
Gera, D.L.
  1993 *Xenophon's* Cyropaedia*: Style, genre, and literary technique*, Oxford.
Girard, P.
  1891 *L'éducation athénienne au Ve et au IVe siècle avant J.-C.*, Paris.
Golden, M.
  1990 *Children and Childhood in Classical Athens*, Baltimore and London.
  1998 *Sport and Society in Ancient Greece*, Cambridge.
  2000a 'Demosthenes and the social historian', in I. Worthington (ed.) *Demosthenes*, 159–80, London and New York.
  2000b 'A decade of demography: recent trends in the study of Greek and Roman populations' in Flensted-Jensen et al. (eds.) *Polis and Politics*, 23–40.
Hansen, M.H.
  1985 *Demography and Democracy*, Herning.
  1987 *The Athenian Assembly in the Age of Demosthenes*, Oxford.
  1991 *The Athenian Democracy in the Age of Demosthenes: Structure, principles*

345

       and ideology, transl. J.A. Cook, Oxford and Cambridge, Mass.

Harris, H.A.
    1964   *Greek Athletes and Athletics*, London.
    1972   *Sport in Greece and Rome*, Ithaca.

Hedrick, C.W.
    1994   'Writing, reading, and democracy', in Osborne and Hornblower (eds.)
         Ritual, Finance, Politics, 157–74.

Hornblower, S.
    2000   '*The Old Oligarch* (Pseudo-Xenophon's *Athenaion Politeia*) and Thucy-
         dides: a fourth-century date for the *Old Oligarch*?', in Flensted-Jensen et
         al. (eds.) *Polis and Politics*, 363–84.

Hubbard, T.K.
    1998   'Popular perceptions of elite homosexuality in classical Athens', *Arion* 6,
         48–78.

Immerwahr, H.R.
    1964   'Book rolls on Attic vases', in C. Henderson (ed.) *Classical, Mediaeval,
         and Renaissance Studies in Honour of Berthold Louis Ullman*, Rome,
         17–48.
    1973   'More book rolls on Attic vases', *AK* 16, 143–7.

Instone, S.
    1986   Review of Young 1984, *JHS* 106, 238–9.

Kagan, D.
    1991   *Pericles of Athens and the Birth of Democracy*, New York.

Kallet-Marx, L.
    1994   'Money talks: rhetor, demos, and the resources of the Athenian Empire',
         in Osborne and Hornblower (eds.) *Ritual, Finance, Politics*, 229–37.

Kennedy, G.A.
    1985   'Sophists and physicians of the Greek enlightenment', in P.E. Easterling
         and B.M.W. Knox (eds.) *The Cambridge History of Classical Literature,
         Vol. I: Greek literature*, 472–7, Cambridge.

Kleijwegt, M.
    1991   *Ancient Youth: The ambiguity of youth and the absence of adolescence in
         Greco-Roman Society*, Amsterdam.

Kyle, D.G.
    1985   Review of Young 1984, *EMC* 29, 134–44.
    1987   *Athletics in Ancient Athens*, Leiden.
    1996   'Gifts and glory: Panathenaic and other Greek athletic prizes', in J. Neils
         (ed.) *Worshipping Athena: Panathenaia and Parthenon*, Madison, 106–
         36.
    1997   'The first hundred Olympiads: a process of decline or democratization?',
         Nikephoros 10, 53–75

Lang, M.
    1976   *Graffiti and Dipinti: The Athenian Agora Vol. X*, Princeton.

Loraux, N.
    1986   *The Invention of Athens: The funeral oration in the classical city*, transl.
         A. Sheridan, Cambridge, Mass.

Lucas, J.
   1988   'From Coubertin to Samaranch: the unsettling transformation of the Olympic ideology of athletic amateurism', *Stadion* 14, 65–84.
MacDowell, D.M.
   1978   *The Law in Classical Athens*, Ithaca.
Markle, M.M.
   1985   'Jury pay and assembly pay', in P. Cartledge and D. Harvey (eds.) *Crux: Essays presented to G.E.M. de Ste Croix on his seventy-fifth birthday*, 265–97, Exeter.
Marrou, H.
   1956   *A History of Education in Antiquity*, transl. G. Lamb, London.
Miller, S.G.
   1991   *Arete: Greek sports from ancient sources*, 2nd edn, Berkeley.
   2000   'Naked democracy', in Flensted-Jensen et al., *Polis and Politics*, 277–96.
Moretti, L.
   1957   *Olympionikai: i vincitori negli antichi agoni olimpici*, Rome.
Morgan, T.
   1998   *Literate Education in the Hellenistic and Roman World*, Cambridge.
Morison, W.S.
   2000   'Attic gymnasia and palaistrai: public or private?', *AncW* 31, 140–3.
Müller, S.
   1995   *Das Volk der Athleten: Untersuchungen zur Ideologie und Kritik des Sports in der griechisch-römishen Antike*, Trier.
Neils, J.
   1992   'The Panathenaia: an introduction', in J. Neils (ed.) *Goddess and Polis: The Panathenaic festival in ancient Athens*, 29–52, Princeton.
Ober, J.
   1989   *Mass and Elite in Democratic Athens: Rhetoric, ideology and the power of the people*, Princeton.
Osborne, R. and Hornblower, S. (eds.)
   1994   *Ritual, Finance, Politics: Athenian democratic accounts presented to David Lewis*, Oxford.
O'Sullivan, P.
   2000   'Satyr and image in Aeschylus' *Theoroi*', *CQ* 50, 353–66.
Phillips, D.J.
   1981   'Participation in Athenian democracy', *Ancient Society: Resources for Teachers* [now *AH*] 11, 5–48.
   1982   'Athenian ostracism', in G.H.R. Horsley (ed.) *Hellenika: Essays on Greek history and politics*, 21–44, Sydney.
   1990   'Observations on some ostraka from the Athenian agora', *ZPE* 83, 123–48.
Pleket, H.W.
   1974   'Zur Soziologie des antiken Sports', *MNIR* 36, 57–87.
   1975   'Games, prizes, athletes and ideology: some aspects of the history of sport in the Greco-Roman World', *Stadion* 1, 49–89.
   1992   'The participants in the ancient Olympic Games: social background

and mobility', in W. Coulson and H. Kyrieleis (eds.) *Proceedings of an International Symposium on the Olympic Games (5–9 September 1988)*, 147–52, Athens.

1998   'Sport and ideology in the Graeco-Roman world', *Klio* 80, 315–24.

Poliakoff, M.B.

1987   *Combat Sports in the Ancient World: Competition, violence and culture*, New Haven and London.

1989   Review of Young 1984, *AJPh* 110, 166–71.

Pouilloux, J.

1954   *Recherches sur l'histoire et les cultes de Thasos: De la fondation de la cité à 196 avant J.-C.*, Paris.

Pritchard, D.M.

1998   '"The fractured imaginary": popular thinking on military matters in fifth-century Athens', *AH* 28, 38–61.

1999   'Fool's gold and silver: reflections on the evidentiary status of finely painted Attic pottery', *Antichthon* 33, 1–27.

2000a   '"The fractured imaginary": popular thinking on citizen soldiers and warfare in fifth century Athens', Ph.D. dissertation, Macquarie University (Sydney).

2000b   'Tribal participation and solidarity in fifth-century Athens: a summary', *AH* 30, 104–18.

2001   'Dancing for Dionysos', *Classicum* 27, 6–13.

Forthcoming   'Participation in the tribally organized dithyrambic contests of late archaic and classical Athens.'

Raaflaub, K.A.

1997   'Homeric society', in I. Morris and B. Powell (eds.) *A New Companion to Homer*, 624–48, Leiden.

Reinmuth, O.W.

1971   *The Ephebic Inscriptions of the Fourth Century BC*, Leiden.

Rhodes, P.J.

1994   'The ostracism of Hyperbolus', in Osborne and Hornblower (eds.) *Ritual, Finance, Politics*, 85–98.

Robb, K.

1994   *Literacy and Paideia in Ancient Greece*, New York and Oxford.

Robert, L.

1967   'Sur des inscriptions d'Ephèse: fêtes, athlètes, empereurs, épigrammes', *RPh* 41, 7–84

Rosivach, V.J.

2001   'Class matters in the *Dyskolos* of Menander', *CQ* 51, 127–34.

Sekunda, N.

1990   '*IG* II² 1250: A decree concerning the *lampadephoroi* of the tribe Aiantis', *ZPE* 83, 149–82.

Sommerstein, A.H.

1982   *Aristophanes: Knights*, Warminster.

1983   *Aristophanes: Wasps*, Warminster.

1985   *Aristophanes: Peace*, Warminster.

1996   'How to avoid being a *komodoumenos*', *CQ* 46, 327–56.

Spence, I.G.

1993   *The Cavalry of Classical Greece: A social and military history with particular reference to Athens*, Oxford.

Thomas, R.

1989   *Oral Tradition and Written Record in Classical Athens*. Cambridge.

1992   *Literacy and Orality in Ancient Greece*, Cambridge.

Thompson, D.B.

1960   'The house of Simon the shoemaker', *Archaeology* 13, 234–40.

Thompson, H.A.

1959   'Excavations in the Athenian Agora: 1958', *Hesperia* 23, 31–67.

Tracy, S.V.

1991   'The Panathenaic festival and games: an epigraphic inquiry', *Nikephoros* 4, 133–53.

Tracy, S.V. and Habicht, C.

1991   'New and old Panathenaic victor lists', *Hesperia* 60, 187–236.

Vartsos, J.A.

1978   'Class division in fifth-century Athens', *Platon* 30, 226–44.

Vickers, M. and Gill, D.W.J.

1994   *Artful Crafts: Ancient Greek silverware and pottery*, Oxford.

Wilson, P.

2000   *The Athenian Institution of the* Khoregia: *The chorus, the city and the stage*, Cambridge.

Wood, E.M.

1988   *Peasant-Citizen and Slave*, London.

Young, D.C.

1983   'Professionalism in archaic and classical Greek athletics', *AncW* 7, 45–51.

1984   *The Olympic Myth of Greek Amateur Athletics*, Chicago.

1988   'How the amateurs won the Olympics', in W. Raschke (ed.) *The Archaeology of the Olympics: The Olympics and other festivals in antiquity*, 55–78, Madison.

12

ATHLETICS, COMPETITION
AND THE INTELLECTUAL

Harold Tarrant

Introduction: a mixed picture

If we were to take at face value the picture of philosophy students in Aristophanes' *Clouds* we should conclude that they failed to show even basic concern for their physique. In particular the new education is, in the eyes of its personified conservative opponent, associated with a shameful physical condition, including feeble chest and shoulders (1015–19). Its pupils are pale (103, 120, 1017, 1171b), like prisoners of war (186), and even semi-human (504). Their pale skin is no doubt connected with an unhealthy indoor existence, for philosophy functions behind closed doors. Furthermore, line 417 implies that they abstain from athletics, showing not only unhealthy symptoms but also an indifference to correcting them. Such indifference would be a serious charge against intellectual life, but abstention might be interpreted more favourably, like abstention from alcohol, as a logical step for avoiding situations that fostered folly; we may recall the erotic associations of places of physical exercise.[1] Further, physical hardships and privation are desired of the pupil (415–22), and actually associated with Socrates in particular,[2] as also in the *Connus* of Ameipsias.[3] Hence the final picture, in comedy as elsewhere,[4] is ambiguous, and it cannot be inferred that intellectuals promote physical unfitness.

There was in fact a strong tendency in the classical period for philosophy to commend and encourage both physical health and the exercise needed to maintain it, though naturally counting intellectual health an even greater blessing. Philosophers repeatedly emphasized the importance of their own pursuits through the analogy with care for the body, a tactic that would have had little point if care and exercise of the body were not assumed by all to be desirable. 'Is not the condition of bodies ruined by idleness and inertia, but preserved through exercising and motion?', asks Socrates in Plato's *Theaetetus* (153b) as he goes on to draw similar conclusions about the mind: 'Does not the condition of the mind get knowledge, improvement, and salvation through learning and application, which are

351

motions, while it learns nothing and fails to remember what it's learned through idleness, i.e. lack of application and study?' Hence, while the picture of the unmanly philosopher whispering with young men away from places of action endured, and even Plato can present a less than healthy picture of his rivals,[5] health, strength, and beauty remained qualities to be admired by the philosopher and his audience alike.[6]

Physical culture, then, was not forgotten with the rise of the intellectual. But sport is also about competition. Competitiveness was central to philosophy at an early stage.[7] Philosophy was often in danger of undermining its own credibility by the φιλοτιμία, or competitiveness, that its rival contenders demonstrated in public. The image of bickering philosophers surfaces in the agon of Aristophanes' *Clouds*, where figures personifying Right and Wrong Argument emerge to do battle from the recesses of Socrates' thinking-house. It is a plausible conjecture from ancient evidence that the original combatants might even have been depicted as fighting cocks.[8] The image continues in the fourth century with Isocrates' *Against the Sophists* and Plato's *Euthydemus*, is utilized by the Sceptic philosophers for whom the disagreement (διαφωνία) of their rivals constituted a splendid argument for the suspension of judgement, and reaches its peak in the second century AD in the works of Lucian.[9] Verbs for contention, such as ἀγωνίζομαι and ἐρίζω, were pressed into service by sophists and philosophers for debating practices of disputed legitimacy.[10]

As for *physical* competitive activity, though its value was challenged in the late sixth or early fifth century by Xenophanes and certainly remained open to debate,[11] it remains a part of the Platonic state's festivals at *Laws* 828c, and of its *daily* preparations for war (830d). However, 832e makes it quite clear that athletic contests are only to be pursued where they have a use for war, so it seems improbable that Plato, or those from Sparta and Crete who join his 'Athenian Stranger' in this discussion, would have approved of the idea that sport can be for its own sake.[12] These reservations do not stop Plato from sanctioning official participation in the festivals and sports of Delphi, Olympia, Nemea, and the Isthmus, or from seeing international reputation as a goal in such participation (950e). In the late fifth century the sophist Hippias had regularly graced the Olympics with the grandeur of his presence,[13] delivered competitive epideictic displays on requested topics in the temple there,[14] made his own clothes, shoes, and jewellery for the purpose, and played a part in establishing a list of Olympic victors.[15]

Sophistic competition

Hippias' activities at Olympia stem from his own competitive desire to win the highest reputation in a variety of areas of wisdom, and Plato shows how he transfers the competitive ideal into the intellectual arena when he complains to 'Socrates': 'You do not engage competitively with the argument as a whole.'[16] This shows how the heroic ideals, in which Hippias is interested,[17] can be adapted to suit an educator and polymath like himself. He and his fellow sophists were forced, by the nature of what they claimed to do, to sponsor a rethinking of competitive ideals. As is well known, competition had been central to the image of the noble individual (ἀγαθός) in Homer, so that it was embedded in early concepts of excellence (ἀρετή). The sophists, at least according to narrower definitions of the practice,[18] claimed to be able to teach ἀρετή, that is, to impart ἀρετή directly through teaching. Homeric ἀρετή, displayed primarily on the battlefield and in other physical endeavours, was clearly not the ἀρετή possessed and communicated by sophists. Such ἀρετή had to reveal itself intellectually rather than physically, and to equip one for leadership challenges of the classical rather than the heroic age. Happily the Homeric hero had also been able to reveal his might in debate, and the controversial figure of Odysseus, the vehicle for the remoulding of the heroic ideal in Sophocles' *Aias*, possessed a mental dexterity that could justify a clever and more civilized kind of ἀρετή – still involving a competitive element.[19]

Plato depicts the first of the sophists, Protagoras, declining to see the excellence that he taught as new. He insisted that his newly-named profession had a long and honourable pedigree.[20] While he did not see human ἀρετή as an ideal, for it admitted many degrees, his teaching was intended to help people to excel rather than to satisfy criteria.[21] Those who sought his services would themselves be aiming at a *competitive advantage* in the city rather than the basic qualifications for participation. A central plank of the new education was the teaching of public speaking: how to argue one's case most plausibly in order to achieve one's goals. Within a democracy speaking skills would give an individual a competitive advantage in the law-courts and in the assembly (now the most important arenas for 'helping friends and hurting enemies' and for acquisition of power respectively).[22] Consequently, what Protagoras had to do was to shift the pre-existing competitive ethic away from physical towards verbal competition. It is said, therefore, that he instituted competitions in speech-making (ἀγῶνες λόγων).[23] It might be said that the fact that his best known work, *Truth*, had the secondary title *Down-Throwers* was a remarkable reminder of how directly he utilized the physical language of wrestling for his central intellectual activities.[24]

The fragmentary remains of Protagoras' works testify to his having claimed there are always two (contrasting) arguments on every subject.[25] It is this commitment to the existence of pairs of arguments that has driven the plot of Aristophanes' *Clouds*, in which the arguments are personified, characterized as just and unjust, and regarded as 'superior' and 'inferior'.[26] Presumably it was the object of budding civic competitors to be able to further their own interests and influence by 'making the weaker argument appear stronger'.[27] Though the terms ἥττων and κρείττων in this phrase do not suggest physical strength, to judge from Plato Protagoras saw physical strength (ἰσχύς) as somehow analogous to courage, which is treated as *mental* strength.[28] Since courage was part of excellence, this means that the strength of the Homeric ἀγαθός also has its counterpart in the new ἀγαθός of the fifth-century polis.

Protagoras seems to have systematically employed counter-argument or 'antilogic' (ἀντιλογία), for at least one of his works was given a title suggesting this.[29] Pairs of arguments were regularly used during the ensuing period, in the *Tetralogies* of Antiphon, in the anonymous sophistic work *Dissoi Logoi*, in the contrasting speeches of Ajax and Achilles by Antisthenes, and so on. Such works as were designed to give a demonstration of the possibilities, whether for the purpose of display or instruction, were obviously not aimed at the truth, and this divorce of the practice of antilogic from considerations of truth sometimes made it attractive to charge one's opponent of it *with the general implication that truth was being disregarded*. Needless to say, the practitioners of antilogic had their answers prepared. Protagoras, Prodicus, the sophist brothers of Plato's *Euthydemus*, and Antisthenes were all prepared to argue, apparently on slightly different grounds, that antilogic was impossible.[30] The story goes that it was after Plato had asked Antisthenes about his project, been told it was on the impossibility of contradiction, and found this an absurd and self-contradictory subject for him to espouse, that Antisthenes decided to name his dialogue *Sathon* – an obscene perversion of Plato's own name.[31]

The close association of physical competition and intellectual competitiveness is illustrated by the career of the sophist brothers Euthydemus and Dionysodorus in the *Euthydemus*. Insofar as these two operate as a pair, they personify the opposing arguments that Protagoras was said to have postulated, and they are regularly referred to using the dual. Since Dionysodorus is not independently attested, he may be the product of Plato's imagination, designed to give an almost Aristophanic pair of faces to the two sides of the argument. The two are described as 'pancratiasts' (271c, cf. 272a5), a word intended to show their keenness to compete in virtually any arena. They are supposed to have begun their career as instructors in hoplite combat (271d, 273e) and military strategy (273c), then to have moved on to become best at competing in 'the battle in the law-courts', and to teaching others how to write and deliver law-court speeches (272a). Finally, in their old age they have taken up question-and-answer combat: they have become invincible in argument and refutation (272a8). Further, this invincibility in argument (cf. 303a9) is equated by them with 'excellence' (273d, 274e). From being teachers of physical competitive excellence, they have moved on to teach the excellence associated with public success, and finally to teaching (by their own invincible example) what superficially resembled Socratic debate. The difference is that only winning is valued, while truth is forgotten (272b1). This intellectual sport was subject to no moral restraints!

Close to the sophists was the senior follower of Socrates, Antisthenes. His fragments (in Giannantoni 1990), together with his portrait in Xenophon's *Symposium*, reveal an argumentative figure competing in sophistic controversies such as the one concerning contradiction. It is clear from Diogenes Laertius 6.4 (= fr. 3) that being a wrestling-sort (παλαιστικός) was of some pride to him. It appears from fr. 163 that he regarded education (παίδευσις) for the soul as the equivalent of athletics for the body, and from fr. 162 that the 'crown [deriving] from education' was the greatest, that is, superior to victors' crowns in the games. Education, then, was seen again as a competition, and excellence itself was regarded as the mental equivalent of military advantages (fr. 134). It was a 'shield that cannot be taken away' (ἀναφαίρετον ὅπλον, Diogenes Laertius 6.12), and its intellectual component, φρόνησις, together with its associated calculations, was 'the safest wall of all' (Diogenes Laertius 6.13). This shows how military thinking had shaped the competitive ideal in Antisthenes as elsewhere, and it may also have led to an admiration for Sparta and distaste for Athenian ways (frs. 68, 71, 72).

The world of Plato's Socrates

Given Protagoras' pivotal role in redirecting the competitive spirit, it is not surprising that in Plato's dialogue *Protagoras* 'Socrates' is most obviously *in competition with* his interlocutor,[32] trying to trip up his wary competitor, and sharing too readily his opponent's lack of commitment to investigating the truth.[33] 'Protagoras' also competes here with rival sophists, Prodicus and Hippias.[34] However, the *Protagoras* is not one of the dialogues of Plato in which 'Socrates' is at work in the gymnasia and palaestrae,[35] for it is when 'Socrates' supplies intellectual exercise *for a young man* that such settings are favoured. They suggest Plato's conviction that physical training is important for the young, and his acceptance that intellectual training will involve the same desire for competition and victory as was found in the palaestra.

The importance for Socrates and Plato of athletics is demonstrated by the *Gorgias*, important for its distinction between false arts and true. Usually they accept the old-fashioned arts (τέχναι) as genuine, while treating novelties with scepticism. This dialogue sees false arts as knacks of flattery aimed at pleasure rather than the good (463a–466a, 503d–504a, 517c–520d). True arts aim at the good, two at the good of the body, those of the παιδοτρίβης and doctor. These correspond to two arts of the soul, temperance (σωφροσύνη) and justice (δικαιοσύνη) for its training and correction respectively. The corresponding flatteries are fancy cookery and cosmetics for the body, and sophistry and rhetoric for a *seemingly* excellent soul. It is taken for granted here that the art of the παιδοτρίβης, generally referred to as γυμναστική,[36] is true and worthwhile – the physical counterpart of σωφροσύνη, which involves properly controlled routines in the soul. The endorsement of athletics is powerful, subject only to the proviso that body is less important than soul. However, the praise of athletics is not here related to the competitive ideal, but rather to the pupil's physical well-being consequent upon correct exercise routines.

The place of physical training in the basic educational programme of Plato's *Republic* (403c–412b) is a central one.[37] However, the competitive aspect of athletics, within the *polis* at least, is secondary to its educational function in the development of individuals who are well rounded and equipped to serve the city. Even when it is a matter of including sexual privileges among the prizes for those who are successful in war and other arenas (460b), Plato is thinking less of victory-prizes, and more of rewards for the attainment of a certain standard. This accords with the idea that the victory-loving part of the soul is inferior to the rational part whose rule Plato favours;[38] to make victory the overriding goal of athletic competition would endorse the goal of the second-best part of a human-being. A further aim of physical education is the need for Plato's *polis* to defend itself in war,[39] which is made most obvious in the *Timaeus*, where 'Socrates' expresses his longing as follows:

> I should be glad to hear somebody outlining in words the contests (ἄθλοι) that the city competed in (ἀθλεῖν), contending (ἀγωνίζεσθαι) itself in these [contests] against other cities, approaching war in an appropriate way, and giving a dutiful display of its education and upbringing both in the execution of deeds and in its verbal representations to each of the cities. (19c)

This is seen as being the manner in which one might praise such a city (19d). Metaphors from the games are prominent, and *inter-state* competitiveness, including the warfare between Athens and Atlantis, is idealized – showing how difficult it was for Plato to break free of ingrained competitive ideals. Individuals have to some extent been released from the obligation to compete *personally*, and the foreshadowed Atlantis-story will not highlight the deeds of individual heroes; rather, those ideals are present in inter-state behaviour. Consequently education must continue to prepare the youth for confrontation on and off the battlefield.

Plato's 'Socrates' must therefore have concern for 'arts' that promote the right action in warfare as elsewhere. The *Laches* is the dialogue that raises this issue, in response to a new course in hoplite combat. What effects will this physical competitive activity have on individuals and on Athens? Plato is here just as critical of the wrong kind of sporting activity as of misguided intellectual sports. The initial focus is on two fathers and their concern for the upbringing of their sons. Stesilaus' education in hoplite combat has been recommended to them (179e), and they ask what benefits it may have. They are anxious that their sons should not be 'without repute' (ἀκλεεῖς), and search for a discipline to make them as excellent as possible (ὅτι ἄριστοι).

The fathers intend to give their sons a competitive advantage. It is not for the city that they desire this excellence, but for their sons as individuals. The hoplite teacher's own qualities are those of a private entrepreneur. He is mocked by Laches for his distinctly personal contribution to a naval battle, where his novel weapon becomes entangled in an enemy ship's rigging.[40] Learning such an art commits one either to overshadowing others in excellence or to being a laughing-stock.[41]

The dialogue now moves between individual and co-operative ideals of excellence, as also between physical and intellectual manners of realizing them. There is a contrast between the individual excellence required for the sons and the co-operative behaviour demanded from mature advisors.[42] Stesilaus and the two fathers had assumed that excellence was something demanding that individuals excel, and that the right kind of training in deeds would promote such excellence. As 'Socrates' takes control of this inquiry he projects a co-operative image, in contrast to the two generals who are his principal interlocutors and who spar with each other. Though Laches remains a man of deeds rather than words, his practical views involve a co-operative view of courage that shuns individualism. His paradigmatic case of courage is remaining in the battle-line, playing one's designated role alongside others (190e). He praises the deeds of Socrates in the retreat from Delium (181b) 'with me', not because it brought glory to the individual, but because it showed qualities that might have secured the city's safety. Hence he mocks the self-aggrandising idiosyncrasies of Stesilaus. The glory seeker was a misfit in Laches' battle-line.

Nicias, in taking an intellectualist line derived from Socrates (194c–d), reverts to a position that requires a rare personal excellence. Courage in his view is a science of what one should be afraid of and what one should be cheered by (194e–195a), which Laches sees as a prophet's privilege (195e), or even a god's (196a). It is explicitly denied to fierce animals and children (197a), and while Nicias has no wish to deny this wisdom to Laches and other brave Athenians, he is shown by 'Socrates' that such bravery would entail knowledge of good and evil, and hence total excellence (199d). In the end everybody appears to agree that education with 'Socrates' is what the lads and others need in order to make the desired progress. 'Socrates' prescribes a path that is both intellectual and co-operative: all must search *together* for the most excellent *teacher* (201a). Physical studies such as hoplite combat are forgotten. The emphasis will fall on debate.[43]

Plato has moved beyond the sophists in adapting the ideals of old. They had intellectualized the competitive ethic to suit the specialized teaching that they offered. Socrates and Plato, with a new emphasis on the importance – even for individual happiness – of promoting good qualities within the community, were also responding to the needs of democracy to develop a co-operative excellence.[44] So just as sport was no longer about winning, so the struggles of philosophy were not about glory nor about maximizing the individual's private happiness without regard for that of others. Plato's 'Socrates', though maximally happy (*Phaedo* 58e), died inglorious, but committed to bringing his recipe for happiness to others (*Apology* 29c–31b).

Coda

The competitive ideal was vividly captured for the Greeks in the figure of Homer's Achilles. The model of an Achilles is not easily forgotten, but Plato comes to see the heroic age as characteristic of a type of constitution, timarchy (or the rule of an honour-motivated elite), that has allowed individual honour to become an obsession.[45] He must therefore adopt a more questioning attitude to competition, as a result of which he progresses further than those who preceded him in shaking off the Achilles complex that so haunted the Greek male. By this move the value of the competitive life, not only in physical competition, but also in intellectual competition, is diminished. The value of sport for training and fitness, and the part of competitive behaviour within an education that relies heavily on sport, continues to be accepted without question. But as with mental exercise, it is not winning that is of importance. Only between communities, and perhaps only in warfare, does winning one's physical contests actually matter, for even Plato found it difficult to envisage a co-operative ethic that extended far beyond the confines of the polis. There would always be an enemy without.

Notes

1 See Dover 1968, 154, for the notion that folly here has strong sexual overtones; *palaistrai* are more likely erotic venues than *gymnasia*, as shown by the introductions to Pl. *Lysis* and *Chrm.*

2 Line 363 only; however, there is a good chance that lines 412–19 were in the original version of the play addressed *to Socrates himself* in a form implying that wisdom and hardihood had already been attained. See Diogenes Laertius 2.27 and Tarrant 1991, 166–73.

3 Diogenes Laertius 2.28.

4 Plato's 'Callicles', in criticizing the unmanliness of philosophers (*Gorgias* 485d), stops short of claiming that pupils become *physically* feeble.

5 Pl. *Grg.* 485d–e spoken by Callicles; *Prt.* 315d with 316a1 (of Prodicus).

6 See particularly Pl. *Laws* 631c, where they are 'goods', albeit subservient to the virtues.

7 'All ancient Greek culture was essentially performative and competitive…', Cartledge, 2000, 21. Cartledge continues 'and Greek intellectuals reflected the competitiveness of politics in both the manner and the matter of their own internal disputes'. Political competitiveness should not be seen in isolation from physical competitions, or from competitions in recital, dance, and drama.

8 See Dover 1968; Taplin 1987; Fowler 1989; Tarrant 1991. We should in any case be reminded that the Greeks saw the model for the struggle to excel in the animal world, where it is unmitigated by the presence of codes of conduct, a world entered into by their mythical super-man Heracles.

9 I think above all of Lucian's *Symposium or Lapiths* whose humour depends largely on the incompatibility of the intellectual group gathered at a wedding; the group includes Stoics, and one each of the other major schools. The letter from the uninvited Stoic neighbour Hermodorus provides also for the worst of rivalry between members of the Stoic school. Compare his *Eunuch*, in which two peripatetics contend for an official Chair in Peripatetic Philosophy at Athens.

10 An ancient division of the Platonic corpus by the χαρακτήρ ('stamp') of their approaches lists five works under the competitive species (ἀγωνιστικός), and four under the contentious (ἐριστικός) subspecies. That reflects vocabulary that can be traced back to Plato's own works, while *Theaetetus* (167e–8a) has provided much of the rationale for the terminology (Tarrant 1993, 46–57).

11 Xenophanes fr. 2; see Kyle 1987, 127; Marcovich 1978.

12 Aristotle takes it for granted that Spartan laws and education were all aimed at war and domination (*Politics* 1333b5–14, cf. 1338b9–14). The latter passage implies that physical development for war is at odds with physical development for athletic competition.

13 Plato *Hp. Mi.* 363c–d (= Hippias A8DK), cf. 368b–d (= A12DK); grandeur seems to have been his greatest love to judge from Plato's *Hippias Major*, even from its first line at 281a1.

14 *Hp. Mi.* 364a: Hippias is said to enter the intellectual competition there more confidently than any of the physical athletes, and both 'Socrates' and 'Hippias' use the verb ἀγωνίζεσθαι.

[15] For dress, *Hp. Mi.* 368b–c; for victory lists, Plut. *Num.* 1 (=Hippias B3DK); Hippias is also connected with Olympia by the story at Pausanias 5.25.4 (= B1DK).

[16] *Hp. Mi.* 369c1: οὐχ ὅλῳ ἀγωνίζῃ τῷ λόγῳ; this brief dialogue contains three out of the thirty two uses of the verb ἀγωνίζεσθαι in the corpus. His competitiveness seems evident also at *Prt.* 337c–338b.

[17] Such may be inferred from *Hp. Mi.* 363c and often thereafter, but is perhaps more explicit in the speech of 'Hippias' at *Hp. Ma.* 286a3–c2.

[18] Clearly Gorgias' rhetorical teaching and Socrates' incessant questioning were the product of the same intellectual climate that supported the sophists, and some would number these two among them; but their rejection of the claim to teach excellence is often seen as putting them in different classes of intellectual. Certainly Plato, in identifying the sophists as the one group who profess to teach excellence, seems to be of this belief, *Meno* 95b–c, cf. 91b. For our present purposes the earliest and most influential sophist, Protagoras, is of great importance, and his claims to teach excellence are discussed extensively in Plato's *Protagoras*, particularly 318d–320b, 324e–328c.

[19] For Protagoras' view that the human race was making genuine progress, see his great speech in Plato's *Protagoras*, particularly 321d–323a.

[20] See *Prt.* 316d–317c.

[21] Degrees of excellence: ibid. 325c–326c, 327a–e; Protagoras' aim as a teacher: 328b, particularly διαφερόντως ἂν τῶν ἄλλων ἀνθρώπων ὀνῆσαί τινα πρὸς τὸ καλὸν καὶ ἀγαθὸν γενέσθαι, and above all 318e–319a: 'The lesson is good counsel concerning households about how one might manage his own household best (ἄριστα), and concerning one's city about how one might be the ablest (δυνατώτατος) at conducting and debating public affairs.

[22] For the continued importance of the belief that friends should be helped and enemies harmed, see Blundel 1989; Lycos 1987 83–92.

[23] Diogenes Laertius 9.52 (= A1DK); his introduction of such competitions is followed in Diogenes by the words 'and he introduced clever devices for those conducting business' (καὶ σοφίσματα τοῖς πραγματολογοῦσι προσήγαγε). This suggests that clever devices were being taught to those involved in certain verbal practices, whether in law-courts, business, or study: possibly the competitive πραγματεῖαι just mentioned.

[24] On the wrestling metaphor, see Hawtrey 1981, 70.

[25] Diogenes Laertius 9.51 (= A1DK); cf. Arist. *Met.* 1007b20–23 (= A19), also A20, A21, B5.

[26] 113–14, 883–4, 894, 990, 1038, 1337, 1444, 1451; see Dover 1968, lvii–lviii; cf. Arist. *Rhet.* 1402b23–29 (= Protagoras A21).

[27] See Pl. *Ap.* 18b–c, 19b–c, 23d; Ar. *Clouds* 114–15. In *Clouds* we are left in no doubt that Strepsiades has the ambition to ensure that he or his son acquire precisely this ability. If there is any social critique at all in this play, then it seems clear that there was a threat of unscrupulous use of new argumentative techniques by pupils. As a result of his instruction in argument, Pheidippes emerges with the appearance of a 'contradictionist' (ἀντιλογικός – 1173).

28 *Prt.* 350c–351b, and in particular 351a3–4 and b1–2, where physical strength comes from the nature and nurture of bodies while courage comes from the nature and nurture of minds.

29 Diogenes Laertius twice speaks of Ἀντιλογικά (3.37, 3.57 = B5DK), but the only similar title in his list (9.55 = A1DK) is the two books entitled Ἀντιλογιῶν. On antilogic, see Kerferd 1981, 61–7.

30 Pl. *Euthd.* 285d–286c; Prodicus in Didymus the Blind *Comm. in Eccl.* I 8b = *CPF* I 1, 87.3T pp. 656–62; Antisthenes fr. 148 (= Diogenes Laertius 3.35); cf. frs. 154–6 *SSR*, Protagoras A19. Note also Isocrates *Helen* 1.

31 Diogenes Laertius 3.35 = Antisthenes fr. 148 *SSR*. The fact that Antisthenes had a title περὶ τοῦ διαλέγεσθαι ἀντιλογικός (*Antilogical Work on Dialectic?*, Diogenes Laertius 6.16 = *SSR* VA41) suggests that he could never credibly maintain such a thesis.

32 The competitive spirit does of course surface in Socrates' other encounters with sophists, but less on the sophists' own terms. In the *Euthydemus* 'Socrates' cannot allow himself to be overtaken by the brothers' obsession with victory at all costs. In the 'Hippias' dialogues he is able to control his opponent better, and to conceal from him the fact that he is involved in a contest. In the *Gorgias* the orator can be shamed and flattered into compliance.

33 In the literary digression, 342a–347a, 'Socrates' seems indifferent both to the plausibility and the truth of what he is saying. Artistically, the long monologue of the literary digression balances Protagoras' earlier great speech, in which self-justification is again more of a concern that actual truth.

34 See particularly *Prt.* 317c–d, 336e–338b, 339e–341d.

35 As are *Lysis* (204a), *Charmides* (153a), *Euthydemus* (271a); other references imply that Socrates' conversations regularly took place at such locations (*Lysis* 203a; *Laches* 180c; *Euthyphro* 2a). The discussion described in *Protagoras* takes place in the house of Callias.

36 464b6, b7, c2; 465b2, b6, c1; 517e4; 518a4, c3; 520b3. For further discussion of παιδοτρίβης and γυμναστική, see the chapter by David Pritchard in this book.

37 Aristotle (*Politics* 1338b38–9a10) is able to speak as if a moderate programme of athletics until about three years after puberty is already uncontroversial; heavier programmes for the young are criticized for their interference with both bodily and mental development. He illustrates his reservations with the observation that those who succeed in the Olympics as boys rarely do so as men.

38 The victory-loving part of the soul is the θυμοειδής (550b6); it is this in particular that is awakened by physical exercise (410b).

39 See in particular Craig 1994, especially 14–15, which notes (6–7): 'The philosopher expressly reserves judgment as to whether war works bad or good (373e), but observes that their city must now be made "still greater" by the addition of "a whole army, which will go out and do battle with invaders for all the wealth and other things".'

40 183c–184a. The fact that Stesilaus is not one of a team is highlighted at 183d: ἐμάχετο ἔχων δορυδρέπανον, διαφέρον δὴ ὅπλον ἅτε καὶ αὐτὸς τῶν ἄλλων

διαφέρων ('he fought with a spear-scythe, an outstanding weapon because he was a man who stood out from the rest himself').

⁴¹ εἰ μή τι θαυμαστὸν ὅσον διαφέρει τῇ ἀρετῇ τῶν ἄλλων ('unless he stands out from the rest in excellence to an amazing degree'), 184c.

⁴² 179e–180a, 181c, 200d; the need for such co-operation in the pursuit of self-improvement is strongly felt at the end of the investigation too (200e–201c).

⁴³ It is not totally clear from this dialogue that 'Socrates' has a co-operative and intellectualist view of what courage is, though clear from the wider corpus. In the *Republic* it is seen as a kind of 'preservative' of right opinion about what should and should not be feared, not just within the individual (442b–c) but also at the important community level (429b–d). There are major differences from Nicias' view here, even though bravery still depends on the mind rather than the body. No longer is the brave soldier required to have any unusual knowledge, for he can depend on the knowledge handed down by others. It is the strength of his commitment to this advice, in battle and under other pressures, that provides the explanation of the courageous behaviour that he displays. In these circumstances a whole army can theoretically be brave.

⁴⁴ It might be claimed that Protagoras had already anticipated Plato's co-operative virtues, for Plato's 'Protagoras' (*Prt.* 322c–328a) did promote the virtues as something that whole cities needed to share in. At Athens this helped to reconcile his teaching with democratic values. His own superiority as a teacher of excellence, while claimed (318a), was not much emphasized (328b). However, even where he stresses the need for co-operative excellence (326a), the heroic model for individual excellence remained in evidence.

⁴⁵ After noting how important the example of Achilles had been at *Republic* 379d–391d, Hobbs 2000, 199, remarks: 'I suggest that by the time of the *Republic* and its more sophisticated psychology, Plato has come to see Achilles as the archetypal exemplar of the *thumos* gone awry…'

Bibliography

Blundell, M.W.
   1989   *Helping Friends and Harming Enemies: A study in Sophocles and Greek ethics*, Cambridge
Cartledge, P.
   2000   'Greek political thought: the historical context', in C.J. Rowe and M. Schofield (eds.) *The Cambridge History of Greek and Roman Political Thought*, Cambridge, 11–22.
Craig, L.H.
   1994   *The War Lover: A study of Plato's* Republic, Toronto.
Dover, K.J. (ed.)
   1968   *Aristophanes* Clouds, Oxford.
Fowler, D.
   1989   'Taplin on cocks', *CQ* 39, 257–9.

Giannantoni G. (ed.)
  1990   *Socratis et Socraticorum Reliquiae*, 4 vols., Naples.
Golden, M.
  1998   *Sport and Society in Ancient Greece*, Cambridge
Hawtrey, R.S.W.
  1981   *Commentary on Plato's Euthydemus*, Philadelphia
Hobbs, A.
  2000   *Plato and the Hero: Courage, manliness, and the impersonal good*, Cambridge.
Kerferd, G.B.
  1981   *The Sophistic Movement*, Cambridge.
Kyle, D.
  1987   *Athletics in Ancient Athens*, Leiden.
Lloyd, G.E.R.
  1979   *Magic, Reason, and Experience*, Cambridge.
Lycos, K.
  1987   *Plato on Justice and Power*, Basingstoke.
Marcovich, M.
  1978   'Xenophanes on drinking parties and the Olympic Games', *ICS* 3, 1–26.
Schmid, W.T.
  1992   *On Manly Courage: A study of Plato's* Laches, Carbondale.
Taplin, O.
  1987   'Phallocracy, *phlyakes*, iconography and Aristophanes', *PCPhS* 33, 92–104.
Tarrant, H.
  1991   'Clouds I: steps towards reconstruction', *Arctos* 25, 157–81.
  1993   *Thrasyllan Platonism*, Ithaca.

1000 YEARS OF THE OLYMPIC GAMES:
TREASURES OF ANCIENT GREECE:
THE POWERHOUSE MUSEUM EXHIBITION

Paul Donnelly and Kevin Fewster

Talk to any Sydneysider who remained in the city during its much-anticipated Olympic Games, and almost without fail their reminiscences will be positive. Inspiring competition, superb weather, universal neighbourliness, no transport problems, no flies... Epictetus, the ancient philosopher who complained bitterly about the bad conditions for spectators at the ancient Olympics, would have been impressed (1.6.23–8).[1] For the culture buffs Sydney staged activities to please any taste, and one of the most pertinent was the exhibition *1000 Years of the Olympic Games: Treasures of Ancient Greece* held at the Powerhouse Museum.[2] The exhibition was the most significant collection of ancient material from Greece ever to come to Australia.[3] Previous Olympic host cities had developed exhibitions of Greek antiquities from their local collections, but borrowing original antiquities from the home of the Olympics itself was a singular achievement. This chapter will detail the events which led to the Powerhouse Museum obtaining the material and outline the design and curatorial decisions involved in presenting these ancient objects in a museum otherwise reputed for its innovative exhibitions of technology, science and design.

Plans for an exhibition began with the First Greek-Australian Museum Foundation, an organization dedicated to exhibiting Greek material culture in New South Wales. As its name suggests, the Foundation's initial scheme was the establishment of a Hellenic Museum in Sydney. In the mid 1990s, discussions with the Premier of New South Wales, Bob Carr, led instead to the lobbying of the Greek government for an Olympics-focused exhibition of antiquities from Greece. Armed with the knowledge that both Barcelona and Atlanta had tried to source similar exhibitions and failed, the likelihood of success at the outset seemed small. Sydney's eventual victory involved tenacious campaigning, and six separate delegations to Greece between 1996 and 2000.

The first approach was made to the Greek Ministry of Culture by the Foundation's chairman, Professor Manuel Aroney, who returned from Athens in late 1996 encouraged by the initial Greek response. At the suggestion of the Premier the Museum and the Foundation joined forces and in May 1997 sent a joint delegation which included Evan Williams, Secretary of the New South Wales Ministry for the Arts and a leading cultural bureaucrat in the state government.[4] Although the delegation was warmly received there was stiff opposition to the idea of an exhibition from some quarters.[5] For nations like Greece, whose material culture has been exploited by foreign powers for centuries, the lending of archaeological artefacts overseas is seen by some as potentially undermining major cultural issues such as the restitution of the Parthenon marbles.[6] The September 1997 signing of an exhibition agreement between Premier Carr and the Greek Minister for Culture, Professor Evangelos Venizelos, demonstrates the outstanding generosity of the Hellenic Republic in spite of political dissension.

A key factor which contributed to goodwill during the discussions was Australia's sizeable Greek-Australian population. The negotiations for the exhibition were conducted on the basis of promoting Greek culture in Australia, as well as providing a vicarious spiritual 'homecoming' for Greek-Australians. Greek is second only to Italian as the most frequently spoken foreign language in Australia, with speakers numbering almost 260,000.[7] Also significant is that after indigenous languages, Greek has the highest proportion of Australian-born speakers (46.7%), reflecting a greater rate of maintenance of the language among the second and even later generations. This impressive statistic demonstrates an emotional and cultural continuity which is valued by the Greek government, and which played a significant role in securing the exhibition. As Professor Aroney remarked, 'The reason...that they agreed in the end to allow these [antiquities] to come to Australia was, of course, partly the Olympic Games but, in large measure, the close ties that exist – emotional ties between the Greek-Australians and the Greeks of Greece.'[8]

In November 1999, two years after the signing of the exhibition agreement, a delegation came to the Museum from the Hellenic Ministry of Culture with the confirmed details of the loan.[9] During those two years changes in the Ministry and their senior officials, as well as the devastating Athens earthquake in September 1999, had combined to delay confirmation of the object list, and ultimately to reduce the number of objects to be loaned. Although only eight months remained until opening day, significant decisions about the structure of the exhibition had already been made. Its location had been set in the Museum's most prestigious space under the barrel-vaulted ceiling of the 'Grand Foyer'. Given the still outstanding quality of the loan material there was also consensus in favour of focusing on the ancient Olympics without reference to the modern; this story, it was felt, was complex and engaging in itself.

The final selection of objects travelled to Sydney on two separate Olympic Airways-sponsored flights and totalled fifty-four – a reduction of twenty-eight from the original list of objects.[10] Amongst those culled the most lamented were sculptures, specifically the 'Mourning Athena' (Acropolis Museum inventory no. 695), a *kouros* (NAM 12) from the Ptoon, and a *kore* (Acropolis Museum 672) from the Athenian Acropolis. However the bulk of the cutback was from the ceramics, several items of which had been damaged in the Athens earthquake (which had necessitated the closure of the ceramic sections in the National Archaeological Museum). The final object list included material from museums all over Greece, with about half from Athens, and included renowned carved reliefs, ceramic figures, examples of sporting equipment, and sculptures of bronze and marble. The sculptural reliefs were without doubt the stars of the show.[11] In addition to sublime Attic grave reliefs depicting athletes in their prime, were the famous archaic Discus Holder (Powerhouse catalogue no. 30 = NAM 38), the Kerameikos Boxer from the same period (cat. no. 43 = P 1054), and the base of a *kouros* sculpture carved in relief with *palaistra* scenes (cat. no. 24 = NAM 3476). The bronzes included several renowned sixth-century BC sculptural figures from Dodona such as the rare statuette of a running girl (cat. no. 28 = NAM Kar. 24), and the statuette of a horse and rider who is probably one of the *Dioskouroi* (cat. no. 50 = NAM Kar. 27 + X16547), as well as the third-century AD engraved votive discus from Olympia dedicated by Publius Asklepiades (cat. no. 10 = Olympia M891). Amongst the pottery were examples of Mycenaean, geometric, and black and red figure – the latter supplemented from the Powerhouse Museum's own collection, and all of it chosen for its figural and thematic representations of sport.

In terms of the exhibition's design, the intention was to achieve a balance between the Museum's desire for dramatic display and the more traditional 'gallery style' presentations seen in the museums of Greece. In keeping with its exhibition philosophy of presenting objects within a scholarly yet accessible framework, museum staff collaborated to create an inviting, stimulating and aesthetically appealing exhibition environment, with appropriate use of interactive modules to engage, inform and entertain the visitors.[12] Two major exhibition themes were elucidated throughout the display: the origins and rapid growth of the ancient Greek fascination with sport, and the remarkable longevity of the ancient Olympic Games which, with minimal interruptions, lasted a thousand years.[13]

In order to create a striking envelope for this collection of internationally renowned objects, four theatre designers were invited by the Museum to submit exhibition design proposals. The winner was Stephen Curtis, a designer who had worked extensively in stage and film, and who responded to the challenge of a museum display with a creative vigour inspired by the architecture of ancient Greece. The entrance to the exhibition was an immense stylized temple front flanked by large-scale photographic murals taken that year at Olympia.[14] A ramp beckoned visitors up to the structure, where they entered a six-metre high aperture cut in the shape of a shadow thrown by a single column: a replica from the temple of Hera at Olympia (*Fig.* 1). A short corridor led visitors to a dark antechamber displaying

Fig. 1. The dramatic entrance to the exhibition was a twelve-metre high, stylized temple façade. Photograph: Marinco Kojdanovski. Reproduced courtesy of the Powerhouse Museum, Sydney, © 2000.

objects of mythological and religious importance to Olympia, and introducing Zeus and Herakles as the divine patrons of the Olympic Games and athletics respectively. Visitors then emerged into a light-filled central colonnade from which all the other rooms branched off. The colonnade and other display rooms were open at the top to capture the natural light filtering through the glass walls of the seventeen-metre high 'Grand Foyer'. Within the thousand square metre floor-space, this configuration of smaller rooms radiating from a central axis provided intimate spaces of an appropriate scale to the objects.

The broad central colonnade was designed to evoke the peristyle between the columns of a temple and the exterior wall of the *cella* (*Fig.* 2). Niches suggested the spaces between temple columns, the effect aided by painted shadows and shielded lights or 'gobos' angled to a false focal

Fig. 2. View down the central colonnade looking towards the icon of the exhibition, the Sounion Youth. The colonnade's exaggerated perspective was achieved through niches, painted shadows and lighting. Photograph: Marinco Kojdanovski. Reproduced courtesy of the Powerhouse Museum, Sydney, © 2000.

point to give an exaggerated perspective. The sense of light and serenity in the colonnade conjured by these effects was consistently commented on by visitors.[15] At the far end of the colonnade could be seen, immortalised in his self-congratulation, the renowned Sounion Youth (*Fig.* 3). Described as being 'among the finest specimens of ancient Greece', this superb early classical relief sculpture, whose age-old symbolism seemed to reflect Sydney's own Olympic success, was the icon of the exhibition (cat. no. 56 = NAM 3344).[16]

Every effort was made to enhance the visitor's experience of the material through carefully considered room arrangement, lighting and other details that maximised the presentation of the objects. Larger-scale sculpture was arranged so as to be visible from different parts of the exhibition, providing 'sightlines' throughout the display as well as navigation points. Walls and case interiors were prepared in weathered, stone-textured paint by stage artists, and some of the rooms featured murals from details of black and red figure vessels. Depicting athletes or scenes from mythology,

Fig. 3. View of 'Victory' section at the end of the central colonnade. Photograph: Marinco Kojdanovski. Reproduced courtesy of the Powerhouse Museum, Sydney, © 2000.

Fig. 4. The first room presented the mythological origins for the Olympic Games. The mural depicts the treachery of Hippodameia and Pelops. Photograph: Marinco Kojdanovski. Reproduced courtesy of the Powerhouse Museum, Sydney, © 2000.

these adhesive prints were enlarged to human size, as if bringing to life the figures on the pottery (*Fig.* 4)

In a practical sense the central colonnade performed the task of dividing up the 'real' and the 'virtual' components of the exhibition, with the antiquities housed in rooms to the left of the colonnade, and the two virtual reality rooms and theatre space to the right. The rooms presenting the objects were arranged thematically, starting with the bronze age antecedents for sporting activity in Greece and Crete, including a geometric pyxis surmounted by four horses (cat. no. 7 = NAM 17604) and a Mycenaean chariot model (cat. no. 4 = NAM 2262). The next room focused on the *palaistra* and gymnasium, with a statuette of Herakles standing as patron in the centre (cat. no. 18 = NAM 253). Two following rooms considered the footraces and pentathlon, and the visitor then entered interlinked rooms beginning with combat sports. At the entrance to the first of these was placed the wonderful Kerameikos Boxer fragment (cat. no. 43 = P 1054), presented within a life-size vertical recess in the shape of an archaic period funerary stele (*Fig.* 5).

A room on equestrian events incorporated the objects and a video presentation dealing with the other Panhellenic and Panathenaic games.

Fig. 5. The Kerameikos Boxer displayed in a recess imitating a funerary stele surmounted by a sphinx. Photograph: Marinco Kojdanovski. Reproduced courtesy of the Powerhouse Museum, Sydney, © 2000.

This allowed an exploration of musical and dramatic contests that were not included in the Olympic Games, but which were part of the competition programs of other festivals. At the end of the central colonnade the Powerhouse Museum antiquities case was located, and the final theme of the exhibition, 'Victory', was expounded, with the icon 'Sounion Youth' as its crowning central feature.

While the objects depicting athletes overwhelmingly presented a male iconography, women's limited participation in ancient Greek sport was represented through a single object displayed in a specially dedicated recess in the colonnade. Along with an explanatory video, this famous bronze figure of a young female runner wearing a short chiton, the hem of which she raises with her left hand, represented the role of women in ancient Greek society through rare sporting representations (cat. no. 28 = NAM Kar. 24).

Thought to be the product of a Laconian workshop originally from the rim or shoulder of a large vessel, the bronze female runner played an important part in redressing the general gender imbalance of the exhibition.

Textual and contextual information in the exhibition was presented using the Museum's customary label hierarchy of introduction, theme, and object. Each room had a freestanding introductory label with an illustration, a timeline and a map of Greece highlighting the sites from which objects in that room originated. An interactive coin map spanning from Italy to the Levant with thirty-seven examples of the Powerhouse Museum's ancient coins supplemented information about chronology and geography. A computer touch screen allowed the visitor to choose any coin and view a magnified image whilst hearing about the relevant region and its sporting achievements. Labels were also supplemented by a digital audio guide (included in the ticket price), which presented information on the social and political history of Greek sport, and provided a choice of child or adult level. The detailed and often humorous commentary proved extremely popular and greatly enhanced the accessibility of the material. A full-colour catalogue of all the objects in the exhibition was also published by the Powerhouse Museum and available for purchase.

The Powerhouse Museum's reputation for innovative interactive presentations was further enhanced in this exhibition by the groundbreaking contributions presented in the rooms to the right of the central colonnade. Short-listed for a British Film and Television Award, the virtual reconstruction of Olympia model (VROOM) was a 3D digital presentation recreating the ancient site with a choice of navigation routes and an information-packed narration.[17] In addition, a 3D model of the legendary Zeus of Artemision was digitally captured in Athens and presented in the exhibition in its own virtual reality room. The real Zeus, displayed at the 1936 Olympics in Berlin along with the charioteer from Delphi, is unlikely ever to leave Greece again.[18] Both these virtual reality components were presented on the award-winning web site, together with a tour of the exhibition. The web tour enabled the viewer to 'wander' from room to room by panning around a series of panoramic photographs. 'Hotspots' gave access to close-ups of selected objects, which had been cleared for copyright, and detailed interpretative essays on the site of Olympia were also available.

Almost a hundred thousand visitors mounted the ramp to the sanctuary housing this unique display during its four-month stay in Australia. Among them were International Olympic Committee President, Juan Antonio Samaranch, members of European royalty, politicians, ambassadors, government officials and a good number of the world's media. In an important cultural sense the ancient material echoed the modern sporting activities being held in Sydney at that time, and created a temporal bridge that provided a comforting reminder of how little we have changed as spectators and participants. People still enjoy a spectacle, admire achievement and relish victory. During the Olympic Games Sydney was the centre of the world, and *1000 Years of the Olympic Games: Treasures of Ancient Greece* ensured Olympia shared in the glory.

Acknowledgments

Many thanks to Tiffany Donnelly for editorial comment.

Notes

[1] For a translation of these complaints of Epictetus, see Miller 1991, no. 94.

[2] The Powerhouse Museum and the Sydney Observatory together constitute the Museum of Applied Arts and Sciences. The Collection dates back to 1879 with the opening of the Sydney International Exhibition, and is Sydney's largest museum with a staff of over three hundred and fifty.

[3] The exhibition was open from 19 July to 19 November 2000 with significant overlap before and after the Olympic Games (15 September to 1 October) and the Paralympic Games (18 to 29 October) to ensure maximum visitation from both international and local audiences.

[4] Other members of the delegation included the Foundation's Professor Manuel Aroney, Dr Nicholas Pappas, Nicholas Malaxos, and the Museum's Terence Measham and Brad Baker.

[5] One official was quoted as saying at the time: 'If I have anything to do with it this exhibition will not happen.' Quoted in Dennis 2000.

[6] During the period of the exhibition, the Powerhouse Museum hosted a travelling display about the Parthenon marbles debate. On 26 August 2000 in association with the 'International Organising Committee – Australia – for the Restitution of the Parthenon Marbles' (now known as 'Australians for the Return of the Parthenon Marbles'), the Museum held a day-long forum on the issue with speakers including ex-Prime Minister, the Hon. Gough Whitlam AC QC, David Hill (Committee Director of International Affairs), George Vardas (Committee Secretary), and Powerhouse Museum Trustee, Kylie Winkworth. The publication of the forum proceedings is available online at www.phm.gov.au, and will be available there at least until 2005.

[7] Australian Bureau of Statistics 2001, 165. The top five are Italian, Greek, Cantonese, Arabic, and Vietnamese.

[8] Professor Manuel James Aroney, AM, OBE, interviewed on the *7.30 Report*, Australian Broadcasting Commission, 18 July 2000.

[9] The Hellenic Ministry of Culture representatives were: Dr Lina Mendoni (Secretary General), Dr Liana Palarma (Director of Prehistoric and Classical Antiquities), Mrs Nikoletta Valikou (Head of Museums Division), and

Ms Smaragda Boutopoulou (Curator of Antiquities).

[10] See Tzachou-Alexandri 1989. The original list of objects was selected from the material presented in this exhibition.

[11] See the catalogue for the exhibition: Measham, Spathari and Donnelly 2000. Catalogue numbers in the text are from this publication.

[12] The Museum's credentials are supported by many awards including the prestigious International Society for the History of Technology Dibner Award for Excellence in Museum Exhibits awarded in 2000. This was for the exhibition *Universal Machine: Computers and Connections* (re-named *Cyberworlds*).

[13] The uniqueness of the time span particularly impressed the Museum's then director Terence Measham AM, who coined the title: *1000 Years of the Olympic Games: Treasures of Ancient Greece.*

[14] With a selection of objects confirmed, teams from the Powerhouse travelled to Greece to prepare for travel and installation. The Museum appreciates the assistance and encouragement of the Australian Archaeological Institute at Athens.

[15] For a discussion of the Powerhouse Museum's research on the audience reactions to the exhibition, see the chapter by Carol Scott in this book.

[16] As described by Professor J.R. Green of the University of Sydney in Dennis 2000.

[17] For further discussion of this model, see the next chapter in the collection by Kate da Costa et al.

[18] For the Zeus of Artemision (NAM Br. 15161) and the Delphic charioteer (Delphi 3485), see Blümel 1936, cat. nos. 2 and 1 respectively.

Bibliography

Australian Bureau of Statistics
   2001   *Year Book Australia 2001*, no. 83, Canberra.
Blümel, C.
   1936   *Sport der Hellenen*, Berlin. Catalogue of the exhibition at the 1936 Berlin Olympic Games.
Dennis, A.
   2000   'God's gifts', *The Sydney Morning Herald*, 17 June.
Measham, T., Spathari, E., and Donnelly, P.
   2000   *1000 Years of the Olympic Games: Treasures of ancient Greece*, Sydney.
Miller, S.G.
   1991   *Arete: Greek sports from ancient sources*, 2nd edn, Berkeley.
Tzachou-Alexandri, O. (ed.)
   1989   *Mind and Body: Athletic contests in Ancient Greece*, Athens.

14

VROOM
(Virtual Reconstruction Of Olympia Model):
THE CREATION OF A VIRTUAL TOUR
FROM A DIGITAL MODEL

Kate da Costa, Sarah Kenderdine, Cliff Ogleby and John Ristevski

From July to November 2000 the Powerhouse Museum hosted the exhibition *1000 Years of the Olympic Games: Treasures of Ancient Greece* in association with the Sydney 2000 Olympic Games.[1] The Powerhouse Museum, along with the Sydney Observatory, form the Museum of Applied Arts and Sciences, and as such constitute the premier institution in New South Wales for displaying and using new technologies. The Museum wanted to use a variety of new delivery methods to extend the available contextual material for the artefact section of the exhibition. Indeed the exhibition was an opportunity to supplement the traditional experience of a museum visitor with virtual reality components. The viewing of the exhibition's fifty-four antiquities, most of which had travelled from Greece for the first time, was enhanced using a large scale interactive digital tour of a reconstruction of ancient Olympia and a three-dimensional model of the statue of Zeus from Artemision (a national treasure on permanent display at the National Archaeological Museum in Athens). The exhibition was further supplemented by a website that took advantage of the latest delivery technologies to present both three-dimensional images and high resolution 'zoomable' images in a complex of historical, architectural, archaeological, cultural and contemporary data about the site of Olympia.

This chapter discusses only the Virtual Reconstruction of Olympia Model (VROOM) and the animated three-dimensional tour derived from VROOM and shown in the exhibition.[2] *Fig.* 1 is a bird's-eye view of the main section of the site in VROOM which served as the introduction to the tour. The linked panorama tour on the website is also taken from VROOM.[3] It is important to stress at the outset that the model was not a product of an academic research design, but was commissioned by the Museum for a primary use in an exhibition and on a website. However,

Fig. 1. Bird's-eye view of the Virtual Reconstruction of Olympia Model (VROOM). Produced courtesy of the Powerhouse Museum, Sydney, © 2000.

secondary uses can be made of the data and the model can support teaching and research.

Academic and technical decision-making for the model and tour

The digital project was conceived quite late in the preparation period for the exhibition, due to the development of a sponsorship arrangement with Intel Corporation that had not been originally envisaged. This meant that the project had under six months to plan, develop, produce and deliver both a complex website and a virtual tour based on a virtual model. Quite obviously, such a time frame restricted the complexity of the model and its derivatives. Nonetheless, there was a commitment to create the most academically rigorous depiction of the site possible in the time available. Before the building of the model could commence several general decisions had to be made which determined the final appearance of both the VROOM and the tour.

Allowing for the fact that we cannot actually determine the condition of individual buildings in a particular year from the archaeological or literary record, the nominal date chosen for depiction was 200 BC. This date, chosen to be just before the Roman takeover of the Greek world, allowed us to include the maximum number of Greek period buildings in the model. The virtual site thus would more closely correspond to the current state of the actual site, which was especially important for visitors on the virtual tour who were familiar with Olympia. The 145th Olympiad was held in 200 BC, and the year had a nice resonance with 2000 AD, neither fact, strictly speaking, having any academic purpose, but certainly suiting the aesthetic of the exhibition. Since the inclusion of people into digital models is fraught with difficulty (discussed below), which is overcome generally speaking only by an extremely large budget, it was decided to depict the site as it would have been in springtime. This meant that at least the Olympic crowds would have been justifiably absent, and foliage at the virtual site would look similar to photographs taken in March 2000 at Olympia for the website and exhibition tour. Since humans – or indeed any independent scale – would also be missing, a 'walk-through' rather than 'fly-over' format for the tour was chosen. This gives a more or less 65 degrees perspective from 1.8 m above the ground, that is, a slightly wider view than that of a person of a slightly above average height. This perspective can be observed in *Fig.* 2.

In order to remain within the total time limit set on the tour by the available animating time, the pace set for the 'walk-through' was a minimum of around 8 km per hour. This is more than an extremely brisk natural walking pace, though the nature of a virtual experience tends to disguise it. The time of day was fixed at mid-afternoon, as moving the

Fig. 2. View of the stadium *dromos*, the Zanes and some of the treasuries, from VROOM. Produced courtesy of the Powerhouse Museum, Sydney, © 2000.

Fig. 3. View to the interior courtyard of the *palaistra*, from VROOM. Produced courtesy of the Powerhouse Museum, Sydney, © 2000.

sun and shadows to correspond with the fairly short time spent at the virtual site by the visitor would have added unnecessarily to the complexity of the computer rendering of the tour. Thus the shadows in the *palaistra* (*Fig.* 3), for example, remain in the same place regardless of whether tour participants take a short or long tour of the site.

Virtual reconstructions of sites are no longer rare, difficult or achievable by only a few highly specialized technicians. Such limitations in early years resulted in many reconstructions with strange perspectives and alarming textures, resembling the type of thing found in children's comic books. Photorealism in textures is now relatively simple, requiring, rather than technical skills, a co-operative approach between the technical and archaeological members of a reconstruction team. The only restrictions now are animating and delivery times. Thus, allowing for the fact that no one knows the maintenance schedule at ancient Olympia, the selection of textures for the buildings and grounds was based on the decision that the major temples would have been in reasonable condition in an Olympic year, but the subsidiary buildings probably would have been looking a little scruffy. The smaller treasury buildings (*Fig.* 4), for example, have mouldy or damaged plaster on their side walls, and the paint work is slightly faded.

For the virtual tour there were constraints in both production and delivery stages. We were limited to a total animation length, if all tour

Fig. 4. Treasury of Megara, from VROOM. Produced courtesy of the Powerhouse Museum, Sydney, © 2000.

options are included, of twenty minutes due to the time it would take to render each of the frames in three dimensions for the tour. The computer used in the exhibition to deliver the tour sequences was not powerful enough to cope, at the level of resolution we required, with potential changes of view and path at any second, as in a computer game. This quickly led to the decision to restrict the interactivity of the tour to a minimum and to force the tour participants to follow a largely preset path. This meant that the tour audience could not go to, or into, buildings we knew too little about to include with confidence in the reconstruction. This included the hippodrome, the baths and the interiors of almost all buildings. The only exception was the interior of the temple of Zeus, which was included in the tour, and there at least – or at most – we had Pausanias' description of around 170 AD (5.11.1–12.5).

At this point it is perhaps useful to summarize the animation process in order to show why decisions to reduce complexity had to be made. Each individual object in the model, whether it be a building, statue, pathway or tree, had to be computer-generated in three dimensions and then have appropriate surface textures applied. Each object then had to be placed into three-dimensional space within the virtual precinct of Olympia. A lighting design was implemented, which generated the correct shadows to be 'pasted' onto each object and the ground 'behind' it. The virtual camera was then 'positioned' within this virtual space and its direction, aperture, height and focus programmed in. The computer then regenerated every object, with its surfaces and shadows, from the perspective that the programmed camera would observe. This regeneration could literally take hours depending on how many three-dimensional objects were in view. Once completed, this regeneration is equal to a single frame in a video or film. One second of video or film normally has 25 frames. For a tour with 20 minutes of animating, this equates to 30,000 frames. As it can easily take an hour to produce a single reasonably complex frame, the rendering of 30,000 could potentially have taken 1,250 days or over three years of non-stop computer time.

To speed up the process it is common to use multiple computer processors simultaneously and to reduce the complexity and number of objects. The ways in which computers were employed simultaneously and the complexity of objects reduced are detailed in the technical specifications section below. Reducing the number of objects was a difficult subjective decision, but our limits gave precedence to architecture over sculpture, known over unknown, and stationary over moving. This meant that we focused on including as many buildings as possible, incorporated only a handful of sculptures and one major altar, and were unable to include moving or still human figures, either computer-generated or video imposed real actors. By these means the animation was completed in two weeks.

Data collection

Data collection for VROOM was a two-part process. A survey of the site of Olympia was made by those members of the team from the University of Melbourne in order to generate a digital map of the modern terrain. At the Powerhouse Museum data for each building was collected and divided into floor plan, elevation, materials, colour and relative position.

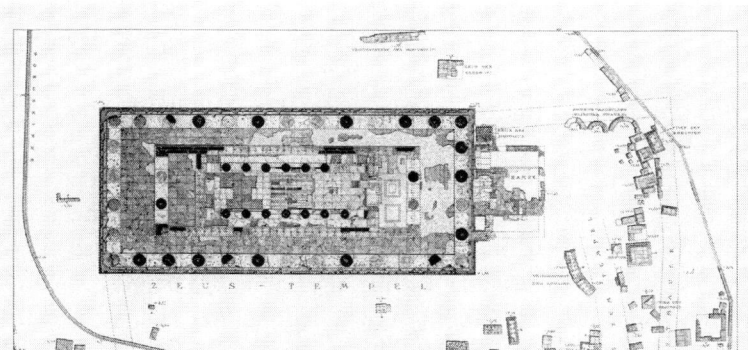

Fig. 5. Plan of the temple of Zeus, from Adler et al. 1897, Plan VIE. © Springer Verlag.

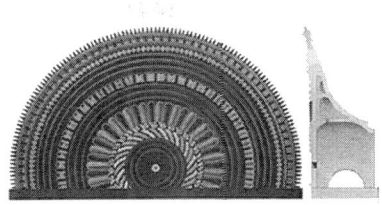

Fig. 6. Various *simae*, Adler et al. 1892, Plate CXXI. © Springer Verlag.

Fig. 7. Terracotta *akroterion* from the temple of Hera, reconstruction from Adler et al. 1892, Plate CXV. © Springer Verlag.

This information was obtained from publications of the site and especially from the five volumes detailing its first extensive excavation in the late nineteenth century by the Germans.[4] The detailed ground plans of these volumes, such as the one of the temple of Zeus and the altar bases found *in situ* to its east (*Fig.* 5), coupled with equally detailed elevations of structures, made the task of modelling each building relatively straightforward. Architectural decorations, like *simae* patterns (*Fig.* 6) and terracottas (*Fig.* 7), were scanned in and pasted as surface textures. Subsequent publications, usually focusing on single buildings, were also used.[5] As for all researchers who have worked on ancient Olympia, the descriptions of Pausanias, especially of the structures for which no physical trace remains, were essential.

Differing standards of certainty for the data for each building were apparent at the initial collection stages, though problems with fine detail occurred throughout the model building phase. Some information was certain, such as the floor plans and elevations of most buildings, the *simae* decorations based on surviving terracottas and some sculptural details. Other elements of the buildings, such as the colour of the triglyphs, could be reconstructed reasonably well. Especially useful here was the publication by Graef of the detailed evidence for the colour on buildings that were excavated by the Germans.[6]

The temple of Zeus reconstruction is a good example of our methods. The plans and elevations of the temple were taken directly from the Curtius and Adler volumes. As the VROOM team modelled the building in units, like entire columns, and not in individual blocks, the most detailed data from the original publications, along with the updated discussion of the *geison* blocks by Grunauer (1971), did not need to be incorporated. Time also prevented us making use of the data from the study on the spouts by Willemsen (1959) to place individual fifth- and fourth-century lion heads correctly. Placing the palmettes along the ridge line, rather than above the gutter, was based on an article by Grunauer (1972, 74–5). Elsewhere Grunauer also discusses the significance of a series of column drums with slots for screens, some of which were found in the Echo Stoa and the South-East Building and others of which had been re-cut and reused in the east façade of the temple of Zeus (1981, 277–9). He also considers the large dump of fifth-century architectural fragments that Mallwitz excavated in 1978 (1981, n. 129a). These two groups of architectural material lead Grunauer to the conclusion that the entire east front of the temple of Zeus and most of its west end, including the pedimental sculptures, had fallen down in the Helike earthquake of 374 BC and were subsequently rebuilt, repaired and reinserted into the structure (1981, 279). He also clearly shows that the columns which remained *in situ* had the screen-slots plastered over (1981, 280). While these are important findings, it had little practical effect on our modelling, in view of our chosen date of 200 BC for depicting the site. It did allow us, though, to confidently leave out the inter-column screening.

Grunauer's speculation about whether the pediments Pausanias saw followed the original arrangement (Grunauer 1981, 280) was also irrelevant to our model: even if it were different to what had been there in the mid-fifth century BC, the pedimental arrangement in 200 BC must have been the same as the one Pausanias observed. Of course, what that arrangement was, even in Pausanias' time, has been the subject of much discussion. The examination of the east pediment statues by Kyrieleis (1997) is a recent, excellent summary of the state of opinion. While agreeing with him that the figures of Pelops and Oinomaos faced away from Zeus on the east pediment, we were committed in the model to following the arrangement of the sculptures in the Olympia Museum. Since the model was to be used on the website as well as in the tour, and panoramic photographs taken in the Olympia Museum in 2000 were to be linked to the virtual temple, it was considered too confusing – and possibly unacceptable to the Hellenic Ministry of Culture which was authorizing the model and tour – that the virtual pediment be different to the reconstructed one. On the website, at least, we were able to incorporate into the essay section a sketch of our preferred arrangement.

Considerable artistic licence was taken by the VROOM team in the colouring of the pedimental sculptures, although such evidence as does survive was followed exactly. The locations of the surviving traces of the paint – all red in colour – on the pediments are recorded by Treu (1895, 23): a protected section of Apollo's cape, the tail of the relief horse for the northern team, the lips of the sage on the east pediment and the belt and dress of the elderly woman B on the west pediment. On the basis of other colours painted on the metopes of the temple and by analogy with other painted marble sculpture, Treu suggests colours and patterns for other figures and clothing (1895, 27–33). Although we remained within Treu's palette and his suggestions of hair, hide and clothing colours, we deliberately made the colours strong and lively in order to correct the mistaken impression of most visitors to virtual Olympia that Greek temples and statues were pristine, white and virginally Victorian.

The interior of the temple of Zeus does not follow as closely as we would have liked the extremely detailed description by Pausanias (5.11.1–12.5). While this was partly due to uncertainty over what would have been inside in 200 BC (and this uncertainty applies to much of Pausanias' descriptions of undated objects), our timetable was the major limiting factor.

Information about other structures at Olympia – especially the great altar of Zeus, the *prytaneion* and the hippodrome – is much more uncertain. As no trace survives of the great altar of Zeus, our only indication is from Pausanias, who describes steps and the mound made by generations of animal sacrifices there (5.13.8–11; *Fig.* 8). The *prytaneion*, despite three excavations, still has no generally accepted ground plan or dating.[7] Despite the convincing critique of Dörpfeld's original dating by Miller and his conviction that no central shrine to Hestia existed (1971, 92–3), we again felt it prudent to follow convention and so modelled three wings as in Dörpfeld's original. No one has yet made sense of Pausanias' description of the hippodrome (6.20.10–15). Generally speaking, we followed

Fig. 8. Great altar of Zeus, from VROOM. Produced courtesy of the Powerhouse Museum, Sydney, © 2000.

the reconstructions of the original German excavators at the site which were based on parallels from other sites and what little can be made from Pausanias' description (Adler et al. 1892, pls. CXXIX–CXXXII).

How to accommodate these different levels of certainty into virtual reconstructions is currently at the forefront of debate. There are several problems involved and different methods for dealing with them. Some of these solutions were included in the model and tour. Probably the major problem, which increases as photorealistic textures, lighting and animation standards all improve, is the seductiveness of a virtual reconstruction. Because objects, buildings or sites seem so 'real', the guesswork is more easily overlooked than in the reconstructions of early generations of artists or in technical drawings.

There is a general '6 foot/6 inch' rule for object conservation. This holds that at a distance of 6 feet (2 m) a viewer enjoys the overall effect of an object or building, but at 6 inches (15 cm) those sections rebuilt or filled in with plaster or some other material can be discerned. This allows the viewer to calculate what is original and what is not, while maintaining the aesthetic values of the original shape. The rule can be incorporated into static model building, and quite complex proposals for its application have been made.[8] Since computer aided design (CAD) packages are set up specifically to show different layers in a building or object, such layers can be used to convey different categories of information about the reconstructed object or building. In our case, for example, we could have had one layer with the certain ground plan and elevations of buildings in plain rendering, another layer with the reasonably certain colour schemes and another with the conjectured colours, damage, mould and weeds. These could have been seen individually or all together, as the viewer chose. While extra information on buildings and features in a *static* computer model can also be provided by attaching 'hotspots' which are linked to text documents, the technology does not appear to exist at present to use this feature in *dynamic* models like the virtual tour of Olympia derived from VROOM.[9] As it turned out, the question of how layers could be used remained hypothetical as the production timetable ruled out any layering at the model building stage.

The method we developed to show the tour participants the difference between the actual remains and the reconstructed buildings was to incorporate points at which they could choose to see 360 degree photographic panoramas of the site taken in March 2000.[10] When the tour got to such a point an icon appeared on the screen. By pressing the corresponding button on the console in the tour room the participants could suspend the tour and have a photograph appear in the centre of the screen. Left and right buttons on the console allowed them to turn full circle. This was intended to indicate the differences between the actual and virtual remains, but was somewhat unsatisfactory, since information such as the entablatures of most buildings which is certain but no longer *in situ* appears to be conjectural.

A final restriction on the model caused by the timetable constraints concerned the portrayal of the animate and inanimate population of the Altis. Pausanias describes some four hundred statues (5.21.1–27.12; 6.1–18.7) and makes clear that he is only discussing those with some claim to distinction (5.21.1; 5.25.1). He also mentions sixty-six altars scattered about the Altis or inside temples (5.14.4–15.10). It was simply impossible, again due to the lack of available time in the modelling and rendering stages, to incorporate more than a tiny number of statues. Those we did include were mainly the cluster around the east end of the temple of Zeus, the statues in front of the Echo Stoa and the famous Zanes (*Fig.* 2). This meant that the atmosphere of a forest of monuments, which cannot be created at any ancient site today, also eludes the visitor to virtual Olympia. Equally, the false impression that the site was unused between Olympic festivals is unlikely to be overturned by our virtual tour, because of the difficulties of incorporating people. The restrictions of computer rendering and delivery power meant that not even birds, stray dogs or cats could be incorporated, let alone Eleans sacrificing honey and wheat cakes. Pausanias, for example, is certain that these old-fashioned offerings, along with olive branches and wine, were made at every altar on his long list, once a month by a large procession led by a priest appointed for that month (5.15.10).[11] Since he also writes of a constant fire on a hearth near the altar of Pan in the *bouleutērion* (5.15.9), there must have been permanent attendants at Olympia for this too.[12] A longer production schedule would have permitted the incorporation of more of these elements, though convincing human inhabitants may always have been beyond the scope of the project.

Technical specifications

All of the model elements such as buildings, trees and terrain were created in 3d Studio Max™. The statues were modelled originally in Poser™ version 4, and modified in 3d Studio Max™. All of the animations were created using 3d Studio Max™ version 3. Consideration was given to using a variety of other packages, however the render-farm facility of 3d Studio Max™ offered substantial (indeed essential) time savings. The render-farm finally consisted of approximately eighty machines, ranging from very fast Pentium III™ to Pentium I™ computers, spread across the campus of the University of Melbourne.

Once the high resolution model of the entire precinct had been completed, element by element, proxy buildings were developed for all of the structures to facilitate rendering scenes where background buildings were not required in high three-dimensional detail. The texture maps for the proxy buildings were derived from renders of the high-resolution models.

The normal production sequence of several drafts of storyboard, roughed in animations and several script drafts, with audio recording being left until near the end of the production process, was not followed in this project, again due to timetable constraints. An additional factor was the requirement of the Hellenic Ministry of Culture that it was to have the final approval over the script; this meant that the script had to be finished very early in the process.

The delivery of the virtual reality reconstruction in the exhibition itself posed many challenges. A rear-projection polarized projection system with inexpensive plastic glasses was developed so that there was no need for a museum attendant to be present in the virtual reality room. A custom built console was designed to facilitate user interaction at the decision points, and mounted on a stand approximately one metre from the screen.

Two JVC DLA-C15 rear projection-capable projectors were used to overlap the left and right channel images onto a four-metre-wide screen

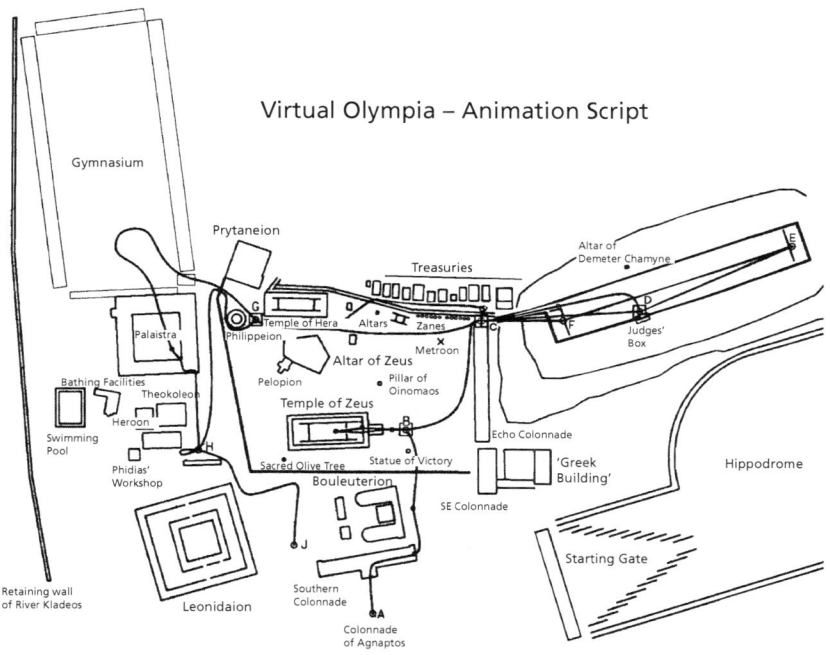

Fig. 9. Animation path, showing decision points and alternative paths for visitors. Produced courtesy of the Powerhouse Museum, Sydney, © 2000.

in a five-metre-square room. The three-dimensional experience offered to visitors was developed in Macromedia Director™ using a stage that was 1600 by 600 pixels. Two 800 by 600 animation sequences were placed side by side in the movie ensuring very close synchronization between the left and right eye channels. The projectors were located in an air-conditioned alcove behind the virtual reality room, and mounted so that the two images exactly overlapped on the rear projection screen. The audio was delivered using a Soundblaster Live™ audio card with two front speakers with a subwoofer all mounted behind the screen.

The computer used to deliver the movies was a twin 800 MHz Pentium III™ machine, with 500 megabyte of RAM, fast disk access and a Matrox G400™ graphics card. This card had a twin screen output of 800 by 600 resolution which was used to drive the two projectors.

Finally, a requirement of the Museum was that the tour be interactive. It was decided that an affordable solution was that visitors would be able to decide at certain points which direction the tour should take (*Fig.* 9). At these decision points, at which a visitor made a selection using a console button, the relevant sequence would be loaded from disk and played through the projectors. Use was made of still frames to allow the large animation sequences to be read off disk and played without the appearance of delay.

Potential academic uses of the model

The three-dimensional tour of Olympia in *1000 Years of the Olympic Games: Treasures of Ancient Greece* represents only one of several possible uses of the underlying model. Several other potential uses can be identified. At the most basic level, opportunities for the refinement of the model exist, both for individual buildings or areas of the site. Examples include the pedimental sculpture of the *mētrōon* and the treasuries, which were not included, or experimentation with the various proposed versions of the hippodrome. This level of research is probably best suited to senior undergraduates.

The model in its entirety or individual buildings from it might be used to investigate more theoretical research problems. One immediately springing to mind is an investigation of the earthquake of 374 BC. In view of the data available on this event (Grunauer 1981), research could show how other buildings at Olympia besides the temple of Zeus might have been affected or even the magnitude of the quake itself. Because many buildings were originally made in Bentley System's MicroStation CAD™, architectural studies of building structures could easily be undertaken. It might, for instance, be interesting to investigate fully the engineering implications of marble roof tiling on the temple of Zeus (*Fig.* 10).

389

Fig. 10. Temple of Zeus, view from east, from VROOM. Produced courtesy of the Powerhouse Museum, Sydney, © 2000.

Spatial analysis of the site is a potentially rewarding area of further research, particularly if the lack of statuary and altars could be remedied. Koenigs (1984) theorized, on the basis of the irrefutably late date of the roof terracottas, that the Echo Stoa was not roofed until the Augustan period. Whether or not his argument is sound on archaeological grounds, regenerating the Altis with the Echo Stoa as a tribune rather than a building would lead to interesting speculation on the relationship of the Altis to the stadium. Precise sightlines could be established. Studies of religious practice, enhanced by the experience of buildings at realistic scales, might be undertaken. Two of the authors are currently using the model to study the alignment of the temple of Zeus in relation to the sun's path, and other archaeoastronomical studies could profitably be undertaken.[13]

Conclusion

The development of a multi-purpose virtual model to high scholarly standards involved unexpected challenges, but many of these were overcome during the production process. A pleasing and very important success was the development of a team with complementary skills, and importantly, overlapping vocabularies. As well, creative solutions to issues of 'transparency' in delivering images of the ancient world were developed. It is clear that the model and tour provided accurate information to an interested lay audience and, at the same time, has created a valuable resource for academic research into one of the most important of ancient cult sites.[14]

Acknowledgements

This chapter has benefited from the reports of its two anonymous referees and David Pritchard. Also valuable were comments from the audience when the chapter was delivered by Kate da Costa as a paper at the Sydney Olympics Conference and later at a seminar of the Department of Classical Archaeology at the University of Sydney. The authors thank all those who made constructive suggestions.

Notes

[1] For a general discussion of the exhibition, see the previous chapter by Paul Donnelly and Kevin Fewster.

[2] The project management, design and creative production of the VROOM was undertaken by Sarah Kenderdine (Powerhouse Museum). The three-dimensional development and animation of the tour was carried out by Cliff Ogleby and John Ristevski (University of Melbourne). The classical archaeological research was undertaken by Kate da Costa. The final stages of three-dimensional modelling, rendering and transferring to video was provided by Asher Graham, Vu Nguyen (Osmosis Solutions) and Cliff Ogleby.

[3] The still current access point for a two dimensional version of the tour and for examining individual buildings is http://www.phm.gov.au/ancient_greek_olympics .

[4] Curtius and Adler 1890–1897. Each of the five volumes of the nineteenth-century excavations was differently authored and has a separate listing in the bibliography. For the data collection for VROOM the 1966 reprints of these volumes by Verlag Adolf M. Hakkert (Amsterdam) were used. For a discussion of this and subsequent phases of the German excavations at Olympia, see the chapter by Helmut Kyrieleis in this book.

[5] e.g. Treu 1895; Ashmole, Yalouris and Frantz 1967; Grunauer 1971 and 1981; Miller 1971; Mallwitz 1972; Herrmann 1972; Fellmann and Scheyhing 1972; Koenigs 1984.

[6] For a detailed discussion of this evidence for colour and the challenges in using the descriptions and colour plates of Graef, see the article 'The archaeological basis for the digital reconstruction of Olympia project' by Kate da Costa on the Powerhouse Museum's official website for the Olympics exhibition (http://203.10.106.20/greek/4/pdf/archaeological_basis.pdf).

[7] It was excavated by the original German team (see Dörpfeld in Adler et al. 1892, 58–60, table 44), then Stephen Miller in 1969 (Miller 1971) and finally in the last few years as part of the site restoration project of the DAI in Athens (Kienast, personal correspondence).

[8] See especially the article 'CSA layer naming convention: A proposal for archaeological layering convention for use with CAD systems and archaeological or architectural history projects' by H. Eiteljorg II on the website of the Center for Studies in Architecture and Archaeology at Bryn Mawr College (http://csanet.org/inftech/csalnc.html).

[9] Note, for example, the linked HTML files within the *Nuovo Museo Elettronico della Città di Bologna* (Bonfigli and Guidazzoli 2000, 144). Although the many projects presented at the Twenty-Sixth Computer Applications and Quantitative Methods in Archaeology Conference, convened in Barcelona in 1998 (see Barceló et al. 2000), ranged from single object reconstructions accessible in a museum (Brogni et al. 2000, 129–34) to immersion multi-actor collaborative virtual environments (CVEs) (Mitchell and Economou 2000, 152–4), only those operated by a single user or visitor seemed able to support linked documents. CVEs with avatars may be solutions when the application allows real time navigation, but a good script seems the most economical solution for a pre-recorded sequence virtual tour.

[10] The photographs were taken and prepared by Peter Murphy using a custom-built medium format camera with a specially commissioned 185 degree fish-eye lens mounted on a 6-metre pole. The images at each panorama point were scanned, stitched together and then viewed in the tour and on the website using LivePicture™ (now MGI™) software.

[11] For further evidence of permanent religious personnel at Olympia *between* Olympic Games, see Stephen Miller's chapter in this book.

[12] For the importance of Olympia as the civic and religious centre for the Eleans and for the activities unrelated to the Games that they conducted there, see the chapter by Nigel Crowther in this book.

[13] The two are Kate da Costa and John Ristevski.

[14] The project has attracted a number of awards since completion. A presentation of it was judged the 'Best Virtual World Heritage Paper' at the 6th International Virtual Systems and Multimedia Conference, 4–6 October 2000, Gifu (Japan). The project as a whole was a short-listed finalist for the 'Factual' category in the BAFTA Interactive Entertainment Awards for 2000. In the 7th Annual Australian Interactive Multimedia Industry Association Awards in 2000 the website was a finalist in the 'Best Arts and Cultural' category and it won the 'Best of the Best Website' category and its designer, Gary Broadbent (Massive Designs), won the 'Interface Designer of the Year' category. The virtual tour from VROOM has been purchased by the International Olympic Committee (IOC) for installation in the Olympics Museum in Lausanne.

Bibliography

Adler, F., Borrmann, R., Dörpfeld, W., Graeber, F. and Graef, P.

   1892   *Olympia II: Die Baudenkmäler von Olympia*, Berlin.

Adler, F., Curtius, E., Dörpfeld, W., Graef, P., Partsch, J. and Weil, R.

   1897   *Olympia I: Topographie und Geschichte*, Berlin.

Ashmole, B., Yalouris, N. and Frantz, A.

   1967   *Olympia: The sculptures of the temple of Zeus*, London.

Barceló, J.A., Forte, M. and Sanders, D.H. (eds.)

   2000   *Virtual Reality in Archaeology (Festival of Virtual Reality in Archaeology,* accompanying the 26th Computer Applications and Quantitative Methods in Archaeology Conference, 25–28 March 1998, Barcelona), BAR International Series 843, Oxford.

Bonfigli, M.E. and Guidazzoli, A.
1. 2000 'A WWW virtual museum for improving the knowledge of the history of a city', in Barceló et al. (eds.) *Virtual Reality in Archaeology*, 143–8.

Brogni, A., Bresciani, E., Bergamasco, M. and Silvano, F.
2000 'An interactive system for the presentation of a virtual Egyptian flute in a real museum', in Barceló et al. (eds.) *Virtual Reality in Archaeology*, 129–34.

Curtius, E. and Adler, F. (eds.)
1890–1897 *Olympia: Die Ergebnisse der vom Deutschen Reich veranstalteten Ausgrabungen*, vols. 1–5, Berlin.

Dittenberger, W. and Purgold, K.
1896 *Olympia V: Die Inschriften von Olympia*, Berlin.

Fellmann, B and Scheyhing, H. (eds.)
1972 *100 Jahre deutsche Ausgrabung in Olympia: Ausstellung 1.7–1.10.1972, Deutschen Museum*, Munich.

Furtwängler, A.
1897 *Olympia IV: Die Bronzen und die übrigen kleineren Funde von Olympia*, Berlin.

Grunauer, P.
1971 'Der Zeustempel in Olympia: Neue Aspekte', *BJ* 171, 114–31.
1972 'Der Zeustempel', in Fellmann and Scheyhing (eds.) *100 Jahre deutsche Ausgrabung in Olympia*, 69–76.
1981 'Zur Ostansicht des Zeus Tempels', in *Olympische Bericht X*, 256–301.

Herrmann, H.-V.
1972 *Olympia: Heiligtum und Wettkampfstätte*, Munich.

Koenigs, W.
1984 *Die Echohalle*, Olympische Forschungen XIV, Berlin.

Kyrieleis, H.
1997 'Zeus and Pelops in the east pediment of the Temple of Zeus at Olympia', in D. Buitron-Olivier (ed.) *The Interpretation of Architectual Sculpture in Greece and Rome*, National Gallery of Art Studies in the History of Art 49, Centre for Advanced Study in the Visual Arts Symposium Papers XXIX, 13–27, Hanover (New Hampshire) and Washington.

Mallwitz, A.
1972 *Olympia und seine Bauten*, Munich.

Miller, S.G.
1971 'The prytaneion at Olympia', *MDAI(A)* 86, 79–107.

Mitchell, W.L. and Economou, D.
2000 'The internet and virtual environments in heritage education: more than just a technical problem', in Barceló et al. (eds.) *Virtual Reality in Archaeology*, 149–54.

Treu, G.
1895 'Die technische Herstellung und Bemalung der Giebelgruppen am

olympischen Zeustempel, *Jahrbuch des kaiserlich Deutschen Archäologischen Instituts* 10, 1–35.

1897   *Olympia III: Die Bildwerke in Stein und Thon*, Berlin.

Willemsen, F.

1959   *Die Löwenkopf-Wasserspeier vom Dach des Zeustempels*, Olympische Forschungen IV, Berlin.

1000 YEARS OF THE OLYMPIC GAMES: TREASURES OF ANCIENT GREECE: A STUDY OF AUDIENCES AND IMPACT

Carol Scott

The relationship between museums and their audiences is at the core of the role of museums in society. In the writings of the museology pioneers Pitt Rivers (1891) and Jevons (1883) the focus was on the educative and civilizing role of museums in relation to the general public (Bennett 1989). The current focus on audiences is of a different nature, and the emergence of evaluation and audience research as a field of practice within the new museology is the result of two recent major developments. The first is the impact of economic reform and the culture of accountability that has required public sector institutions to report regularly their use of public monies against quantitative indicators (Douglas 1991). To address these requirements, public institutions, including museums, have implemented a range of measures to demonstrate the use of programs and services. Reporting the number of people who come to museums, the nature of their participation and their levels of satisfaction has been made possible through the use of audience data and the establishment of systems to collect it. Secondly, the relationship between museums and their publics has undergone significant change in the last two decades. Less respect for subject expertise and authority and the development of a consumer culture have resulted in demands for not just fiscal but also public accountability (Weil 1994; 1996; 1997). Museums have become more 'audience oriented' as a consequence.

A further aspect of this change can be seen in the recognition that the visitor plays a significant role in the 'making of meaning' (Silverman 1995; Falk and Dierking 2000). Increasingly, museums acknowledge that visitors bring to the museum highly personalized expectations, preconceptions, attitudes, knowledge and life experience which influence the meanings that they take from the objects and the stories they encounter in the museum setting. Exploring the perspectives and expectations that audiences bring to exhibition subjects is an important aspect of exhibition evaluation and a major indication that cultural institutions take seriously the roles of the audience as a partner in the making of meaning and as a consumer.

The Powerhouse Museum in Sydney was the first museum in Australia and New Zealand to establish a full-time position to co-ordinate, manage and develop this field of practice. The appointment in 1991 of the first permanent evaluation and audience research co-ordinator signalled a more visitor-centred approach to museum planning and exhibition development. In the ensuing eleven years, similar positions have been established in museums throughout Australasia, a professional reference group under the umbrella of Museums Australia has been established, universities have included subjects on evaluation and audience research in museum studies courses, and the literature on Australian museum audiences has grown exponentially.

Methodologies

Definitional distinctions assist us when discussing audience evaluation and research in the museum context. 'Audience research' identifies and monitors trends, patterns and changes in our audiences over time. 'Audience evaluation' is used to judge the merit or worth of a museum service or product from the user's point of view. Though the processes have different aims, both use similar methods to collect data. Quantitative and qualitative methods including questionnaires, focus groups, in-depth interviews, tracking, systematic observational studies and cognitive mapping are all employed.

One of the great advantages of integrating evaluation and audience research into the exhibition development process is the wealth of data that is produced from many diverse audience studies over time. Evaluation of exhibitions is conducted at any one of four stages. Front-end evaluations are implemented at an early stage when a brief for the exhibition is in the process of being developed. The purpose of this kind of study is to determine what knowledge, preconceptions and attitudes the audience will bring to the subject so that planning can take account of these perspectives in the development of the exhibition. At the formative stage, the proposed design of the exhibition is evaluated. Remedial evaluation assesses visitor use of the exhibition once it has opened to the public to identify problem areas and correct them early in the life of the exhibition. The summative or final stage of evaluation explores visitor reactions to the exhibition (Screven 1990).

In the ten years since exhibition evaluation was first implemented at the Powerhouse Museum, front-end evaluation studies for nine exhibitions have been undertaken, as well as eight formative, four remedial and eighteen summative evaluations.

One of the important uses of this accumulated data on audiences and their responses to exhibitions is as a source for meta-evaluation. Meta-evaluation is the analysis of a body of studies in order to identify trends and patterns that have emerged over time. When we recently undertook a meta-evaluation of the front-end and summative exhibition evaluations done since 1991 at the Powerhouse Museum, we explored a diverse range of audiences including teachers and students from primary, secondary and tertiary education, children from 7 to 17 years of age, parents, young people between 18 and 24 years of age, culturally active adults between 25 to 55 years of age, seniors, subject specialists, industry professionals, critics, artists, Museum members and other constituencies of interest. Many of the findings from this meta-evaluation are useful in understanding the visitor study of *1000 Years of the Olympic Games: Treasures of Ancient Greece* (Scott 2000).

Audiences and objects

One of the findings from the meta-evaluation concerned the perspectives that audiences bring to objects. In an age of virtual realities, it is interesting that museum audiences do not believe that a simulated experience is a meaningful substitute for the 'real thing'. Presenting authentic material is considered the key role of museums. Moreover, audiences across all the front-end evaluation studies wanted museums to present objects that were a contrast to the everyday and the familiar. Their interest was in objects that were unusual, bizarre, symbolic, exciting and which were set apart by some significant element associated with their history or beauty.

When we conducted a survey of 302 visitors to *1000 Years of the Olympic Games: Treasures of Ancient Greece*, this finding was confirmed. The objects displayed in this exhibition had considerable power in themselves. The majority of those surveyed identified the objects as the outstanding feature of the exhibition. The authenticity, the beauty and the quality of the objects on display were all features that made an impact. For example, one visitor noted that 'The quality of the pieces was excellent so it's hard to isolate three, but seeing the bronze and stone discuses was terrific and some of the earlier stone sculpture was quite amazing.' Another indicated as outstanding 'the beauty of the ancient sculptured form and the information that can be gathered from a simple sculpture'. And a third highlighted the 'beautiful crafted statues and vessel building' and their 'surprise at the fine casting of the bronze statues'.

Audiences and history

When we undertook the meta-evaluation, generational differences with respect to an interest in history emerged. Attitudes to history are often a factor of age. As people grow older and acquire their own 'personal past', the ability to relate to a collective past is augmented and exhibitions with an historical focus become more relevant and meaningful (Silverman 1991). When we explored the attitudes of young people to history across the many studies included in the meta-evaluation, we discovered the predominance of a strong future focus: any information that reveals the world into which they are emerging as young adults is eagerly explored, but 'history' appears irrelevant in this context. As one teacher put it, 'It is very hard to get children interested in history because it seems so far away.'

The meta-evaluation revealed one exception to this strong future focus amongst young people. If it can be demonstrated that history is somehow *connected* to the present and the future, it assumes relevance for young people. *1000 Years of the Olympic Games: Treasures of Ancient Greece,* though an exhibition about the history of the ancient Olympics, was opened during the Sydney 2000 Olympic Games and was related to a current event. Perhaps this accounts for the finding that 24 per cent of the visitors surveyed were between the ages of 16 and 24 years and that the exhibition was popular amongst them.

Audiences and interactivity

Engaging visitors through interactive experiences is now a feature of most contemporary exhibitions. It has developed because of a belief that people learn by doing and as a result of the availability of increasingly user-friendly technology. At the Powerhouse Museum 'hands on' exhibition experiences are a key aspect of the 'house style' and are expected.

Interactive experiences enable visitors to have a 'role' in the exhibition: they extend the insights of visitors, engage the senses and enable them to approach objects from different perspectives. In the case of *1000 Years of the Olympic Games: Treasures of Ancient Greece* the range of interactive experiences was, according to the visitor feedback, a particularly welcome feature of the exhibition. The virtual 'walk through' of the simulated Olympic site was a highlight and the free audio guide extended visitors' understanding of the subject. When asked to describe their main preferences for exhibition features, visitors made the following kinds of remarks:

> The virtual reconstruction – Olympia. The full explanations accompanying the artefacts. The atmospheric backdrops.

> Audio tour idea was great. I loved the virtual reality production. The ancient history details were just detailed enough without being boring.

The audio certainly made the exhibit more interesting. The 3D displays were great.

[I liked] the interactive elements, such as the 3D tour of Olympia, and the commentary on the headphones.

The free audio was well spoken and very informative with accurate accent inflections for the Greek names.

The 3D walkthrough tour of the Olympic Games site was fascinating.

The theatrical setting and presentation of the exhibition were also identified as enhancing the overall experience. But it was the *combination* of all these elements that worked for visitors. On the basis of the comments, it appears that the richness of the objects combined with the diversity of the presentation style enabled visitors to engage with the subject on many levels. For example, one surveyed visitor suggested: 'The layout and lighting was outstanding, the artefacts were extremely informative, and the commentary was of a high standard.' Another thought 'it was beautifully lit, very tasteful'. While one other explained: 'The way it was so clearly set out and easy to follow. The amount of things on display. The 3D exhibits.'

Learning in museums

Other research undertaken at the Powerhouse Museum reveals that museums are strongly associated with learning (Boomerang! Marketing and Advertising Pty Ltd 1998). 'Educational', 'intellectual' and 'absorbing places' are some of the terms used to describe museums. Visitors expect that they will learn in museums and often choose museums over other leisure options because they want to spend their leisure time doing something 'worthwhile' (Hood 1995).

However, the *nature* of the learning that occurs in museums is the subject of current debate and discussion. We know that it is voluntary and self-selective and occurs in what Falk and Dierking (2000) call 'a free choice environment'. The fact that learning acquired in museums can be recalled long after the museum visit has been documented by Falk and Dierking (1995) and McManus (1993). Ferguson (1997) suggests that learning through objects is particularly effective in stimulating visual memory. The visual memory of the object serves as a trigger to stimulate associated learning to a degree that a purely semantic memory based on concepts and facts does not. The special evocative power of objects is captured by Weil (1997, 265):

...the response to a real, three dimensional object, be it a moon rock, George Washington's false teeth or an original painting by Rembrandt, is entirely different from our response to a photograph, video image or verbal description of that same object…authentic objects in a museum type setting can trigger powerful cognitive and affective responses.

The theory of 'constructivist learning' has added to the discourse by suggesting that knowledge in museums is both personally and environmentally constructed (Hein 1991). Environmental construction refers to the necessary selection of objects, subject approach and narrative. Personal construction occurs when the individual visitor, influenced by prior knowledge and experience, encounters the object and the narrative. Constructivists assert that an appropriate museum environment can be 'constructed' to stimulate this personal learning.

What can we conclude about learning in museums? On the one hand, the learning that occurs in museums is affected by the prior knowledge and life experience of the individual, mediated by others and self-directed. At the same time, people expect to learn in museums and we know that learning can be facilitated through carefully constructed exhibition environments that have the unique power of objects to produce an impact that lasts long after the visit has ended (Csikzentmihalyi 1995).

1000 Years of the Olympic Games: Treasures of Ancient Greece stimulated considerable learning. Many of the visitors surveyed went to some length to give detailed accounts of learning associated with the history and traditions of the Olympics (35%), the specific sports and competitions (17%), Greek civilisation (9%), the role of the Olympics in Greek society and culture (8%), and the role of women in the Olympics (8%).

One of the additional findings was the number of surveyed visitors who went into some detail to emphasize the fact that they had learnt something *new*. Such reports of new learning included the following:

> Didn't know about Zeus as patron, etc of the Games at Olympia. Did not know games were held in various cities. Didn't know women didn't participate except in Sparta, etc.

> I was surprised to hear about the involvement of many Hellenic groups (outside Athens) in the early history of the games.

> I didn't know that much about ancient boxing and wrestling and I always thought that all (including poorer) people could compete.

> I did not know that people who rode horses were faced with death each time they got upon the horses!! (Very informative).

> Didn't realise games began as worship to the gods. Naked, bloodthirsty. Limited role for women probably enlightened for the day.

> Had no idea there was a separate Olympics for women, [about] the weights used in long jumping, [or about how] victors experienced considerable rewards (indirectly).

This finding about learning contradicts a widely held view that no new learning occurs in museums and that, in fact, '...the primary impact of visiting a museum exhibition is to confirm, reinforce and extend the visitors' existing beliefs' (Doering in Weil 1997, 265). While the sample of this study may be too small for generalization, it does raise interesting questions for further research on the potential for museums to stimulate new learning.

Conclusion

Overall, the findings of the audience evaluation reveal that the exhibition was an overwhelmingly positive experience for visitors, with 83 per cent giving it a good/very good rating and 82 per cent saying that it met their expectations; 77 per cent stated that they had learned something. This follows a pattern of high learning scores associated with topics which introduce the visitor to unfamiliar subjects, such as medieval warfare in the Powerhouse Museum exhibition *Knights of Imperial Austria* (80%) and Aboriginal music and dance in *Ngaramang Bayumi* (81%). Of the visitors surveyed 94% stated that they would recommend *1000 Years of the Olympic Games: Treasures of Ancient Greece* to others. Just as importantly, the outcomes of this study raise interesting questions about the potential for museums to stimulate new learning and offer possibilities for future research in this compelling field of visitor experience in museums.

Bibliography

Bennett, T.
  1989   'Museums, and public culture: history, theory and politics', *Media Information Australia* 53, 57–65.
Boomerang! Marketing and Advertising Pty Ltd.
  1998   *Powerhouse Museum Brand Audit and Positioning Options,* internal report prepared for the Powerhouse Museum, Sydney.
Cronin, V.
  2000   *1000 Years of the Olympic Games: Treasures of Ancient Greece: Evaluation Report,* internal report prepared for the Powerhouse Museum, Sydney.
Csikzentmihalyi, M.
  1995   'Intrinsic motivation in museums: what makes visitors want to learn?', *Museum News* (U.S.A.) 74.3, 36–8.
Douglas, L.
  1991   'The politics of performance: measuring the value of museums', paper submitted for the graduate diploma in arts management at the University of Technology, Sydney.
Falk, J.H. and Dierking, L.D.
  1995   'Recalling the museum experience', *Journal of Museum Education* Spring/ Summer, 10–13.

2000   *Learning from Museums: Visitor experience and the making of meaning*, Walnut Creek (California).

Ferguson, L.
1997   'Evaluating learning', *Museums National* 5.4, 15–16.

Hein, G.
1991   'Constructivist learning theory', paper presented at 'The Museum and the Needs of the People Conference' of the International Congress of Museums (ICOM), Jerusalem.

Hood, M.
1995   'Audience research tells us why visitors come to museums – and why they don't', in C. Scott (ed.) *Evaluation and Visitor Research in Museums: Towards 2000: Conference papers: Powerhouse Museum, Sydney Australia, 16–19 March 1995*, 3–10, Sydney.

Jevons, W.S.
1883   *Methods of Social Reform*, New York.

McManus, P.
1993   'Memories as indicators of the impact of museum visits', *Museum Management and Curatorship* 12, 367–80.

Pitt Rivers, H.
1891   'Typological museums, as exemplified by the Pitt-Rivers Museum at Oxford, and his Provincial Museum at Farnham', *Journal of the Society of the Arts* 40.

Scott, C.A.
2000   'Evaluation and audience research: what we've learned from the first ten years', internal presentation to Powerhouse Museum management and staff, Sydney.

Screven, C.
1990   'The uses of evaluation before, during and after exhibit design', *ILVS Review: A Journal of Visitor Behaviour* 1/2, 33–66.

Silverman, L.
1991   'Tearing down walls', *Museum News* November/December, 62–4.
1995   'Visitor meaning-making in museums for a new age', *Curator* 38.3, 161–70.

Weil, S.E.
1994   'Creampuffs and hardball: are you really worth what you cost?', *Museum News* (U.S.A.) 73.5, 42–3, 60, 62–3.
1996   'The distinctive numerator', *Museum News* March/April, 64–5.
1997   'The museum and the public', *Museum Management and Curatorship* 16.3, 257–71.

INDEX AND GLOSSARY

Greek names and words are given in their transliterated form except where they only occur in the text in their Latinized form.